WHITAKER'S SCOTTISH ALMANACK 2000

Whitaker's Scottish Almanack

2000

LONDON
THE STATIONERY OFFICE

© The Stationery Office Ltd 1999

The Stationery Office Ltd
51 Nine Elms Lane, London SW8 5DR

First published 1999

ISBN 0 11 702251 9

A CIP catalogue record for this book is
available from the British Library

Published by The Stationery Office and
available from:

The Publications Centre
(mail, telephone and fax orders only)
PO Box 276, London SW8 5DT
General enquiries 0207 873 0011
Telephone orders 0207 873 9090
Fax orders 0207 873 8200

The Stationery Office Bookshops
123 Kingsway, London WC2B 6PQ
0207 242 6393 Fax 0207 242 6394
68–69 Bull Street, Birmingham B4 6AD
0121 236 9696 Fax 0121 236 9699
33 Wine Street, Bristol BS1 2BQ
0117 9264306 Fax 0117 9294515
9–21 Princess Street, Manchester M60 8AS
0161 834 7201 Fax 0161 833 0634
16 Arthur Street, Belfast BT1 4GD
02890 238451 Fax 02890 235401
The Stationery Office Oriel Bookshop
18–19 High Street, Cardiff CF1 2BZ
02920 395548 Fax 02920 384347
71 Lothian Road, Edinburgh EH3 9AZ
0131 228 4181 Fax 0131 622 7017

The Stationery Office's Accredited Agents
(see Yellow Pages)

and through good booksellers

Editorial Staff

Editors, Hilary Marsden, Mandy Macdonald
Editorial Assistant, Dan Carroll
Researchers, Dan Carroll, Mandy Macdonald,
Bridie Macmahon, Neil Mackay
Database Co-ordinator, Arlene Zuccolo

Contributors

Astronomical data, Gordon Taylor
Economy, Prof. Peter McGregor, Department
of Economics, University of Strathclyde
Education, Diana Clayton
Government of Scotland, Alan Boyd, McGrigor
Donald
Legal Notes, Robson McLean WS

Text designed by Jennifer Hannaford
Jacket designed by Compendium
Jacket photographs © PA News Ltd; Telegraph
Colour Library
Line illustrations by Yvonne Halton
Maps by Oxford Cartographers
Typeset by Eclipse Design, Norwich
Printed and bound in Great Britain by Bell &
Bain Ltd, Glasgow

FOREWORD

by the Rt. Hon. Sir David Steel, KBE

The year 1999 has been momentous for Scotland and its people; on 6 May the nation went to the polls to elect the new Scottish Parliament. The last Scottish Parliament was dissolved by the Act of Union 1707 and the people of Scotland, through this new parliament, will determine both how they shall be governed and how they shall live to a degree that has not been possible for nearly three hundred years.

Devolution is both symbolically and literally the reinstatement of Scotland as a nation in its own right and is the culmination of over 20 years of consistent hard work and determination. So many people have planned and striven for constitutional power to be restored in Scotland and devolution can be said to have sealed Scotland's identity at last.

It is sometimes hard to distinguish where one stops considering devolution politically and starts thinking of it personally, as a Scot. The long path to devolution is deeply embedded in Scotland's psyche and evokes strong feelings of power and an awareness of national, personal and cultural identity. Scotland now has a unique opportunity to work together with England, Wales and Northern Ireland in a United Kingdom.

The State opening of Parliament was a proud event for Scotland. The mix of tradition and modernity engendered feelings not only of deep pride and solemnity but of sheer joy and happiness for the future. My office was, and still is, inundated with correspondence expressing these feelings. The euphoria at the reinstatement of Scotland's Parliament has settled into a keen anticipation of the accountability and relevance that the Parliament will offer to the Scottish people.

As Presiding Officer my role is, and must be, strictly apolitical. My principal duty is to ensure that the momentum associated with the establishment of the Parliament does not dwindle. It must be maintained in order to foster openness and interaction with every person, group and denomination of Scotland, with the United Kingdom and the rest of the world.

Over its 130-year lifespan, *Whitaker's Almanack* has recorded and published the essential facts about the major institutions of the United Kingdom, becoming, in the process, a staple of any well-stocked reference shelf and library, whose name carries a guarantee of authority and reliability. It gives me great pleasure to welcome this first edition of *Whitaker's Scottish Almanack*, the very existence of which recognizes the status of a self-governing Scotland.

The first edition of *Whitaker's Almanack* was a mere 360 pages but the book grew over time to its present 1,280 pages as the contents developed to reflect the changing world and the information requirements of its readers. *Whitaker's Scottish Almanack* also starts small but, I trust, will grow as Scotland grows, developing new institutions and a new role in the wider world.

PREFACE

by Lauren Hill, Editor, Whitaker's Almanack

As Editor of *Whitaker's Almanack*, the most comprehensive of general reference books, I am proud to introduce the first edition of a sister publication, *Whitaker's Scottish Almanack*.

Since the first edition of *Whitaker's Almanack* in 1868, both the publication and the information requirements of its readers have grown and the idea of *Whitaker's Scottish Almanack* was born from a desire to provide information for a changing world.

For the first time in nearly 300 years, we are witnessing self-government in Scotland. I hope that the following pages provide not only a helpful account of recent constitutional and political events, but also useful and interesting information on the people and institutions of Scotland.

Like *Whitaker's Almanack* 131 years ago, *Whitaker's Scottish Almanack* has simple beginnings. However, it is anticipated that the publication will develop and grow as the society and institutions it encompasses develop and grow within a more independent Scotland.

Whitaker's Scottish Almanack complements the other publications bearing the *Whitaker's Almanack* name, and, like all *Whitaker's Almanack* titles, its content is determined by what the reader needs. In the light of this, readers' comments and suggestions of additional information that they would find useful are always welcome and should be sent to me at the address below.

Whitaker's Almanack
51 Nine Elms Lane
London SW8 5DR
Fax: 0171-873 8723
E-mail: whitakers.almanack@theso.co.uk

CONTENTS

KEY DATES IN 2000

PUBLIC HOLIDAYS

STATUTORY PUBLIC HOLIDAYS

New Year	3, *4 January
Good Friday	21 April
May Day	1 May
Spring	*29 May
Summer	7 August
Christmas	25, *26 December

* Subject to proclamation

LOCAL AND FAIR HOLIDAYS

In most parts of Scotland there are local and fair holidays; dates vary according to the locality. Dates can usually be obtained from the local authority; the only central source is Glasgow Chamber of Commerce (tel: 0141-204 2121) which publishes each January a diary of holiday dates for the year.

LEGAL CALENDAR

LAW TERMS

The terms of the Court of Session for the legal year 1999–2000 are:

Winter	21 September to 17 December 1999
Spring	6 January to 31 March 2000
Summer	25 April to 14 July 2000

No Division, Lord Ordinary or Vacation Judge may sit on 1 and 22 May 2000.

TERM DAYS

Candlemas	28 February
Whitsunday	28 May
Lammas	28 August
Martinmas	28 November
Removal Terms	28 May, 28 November

RELIGIOUS CALENDARS

CHRISTIAN

Epiphany	6 January
Ash Wednesday	8 March
Maundy Thursday	20 April
Good Friday	21 April
Easter Day (western churches)	23 April
Easter Day (Eastern Orthodox)	30 April
Ascension Day	1 June
Pentecost (Whit Sunday)	11 June
Trinity Sunday	18 June
Corpus Christi	22 June
All Saints' Day	1 November
Advent Sunday	3 December
Christmas Day	25 December

HINDU

Makara Sankranti	15 January
Vasant Panchami (Sarasvati-puja)	10 February
Mahashivaratri	4 March
Holi	19 March
Chaitra (Hindu new year)	5 April
Ramanavami	12 April
Raksha-bandhan	15 August
Janmashtami	22 August
Ganesh Chaturthi, first day	1 September
Ganesh festival, last day	12 September
Durga-puja	28 September
Navaratri festival, first day	28 September
Sarasvati-puja	5 October
Dasara	7 October
Diwali, first day	24 October
Diwali, last day	29 October

JEWISH

Passover, first day	20 April
Feast of Weeks, first day	9 June
Jewish new year (AM 5761)	30 September
Yom Kippur (Day of Atonement)	9 October
Feast of Tabernacles, first day	14 October
Chanucah, first day	22 December

MUSLIM

Muslim new year (AH 1421)	6 April
Ramadan, first day	28 November

SIKH

Birthday of Guru Gobind Singh Ji	14 January
Baisakhi Mela (Sikh new year)	13 April
Martyrdom of Guru Arjan Dev Ji	5 June
Birthday of Guru Nanak Dev Ji	11 November
Martyrdom of Guru Tegh Bahadur Ji	1 December

OTHER SIGNIFICANT DATES

Burns Night	25 January
Chinese year of the Dragon	5 February
Commonwealth Day	13 March
Europe Day	9 May
Remembrance Sunday	12 November
St Andrew's Day	30 November
Hogmanay	31 December

EVENTS

March 1–5	Bright Ideas: Home Interior Design Show Scottish Exhibition and Conference Centre, Glasgow
April 5–8	Celtic Film and Television Festival Aberystwyth
April 7	Donald Macleod Memorial Piping Competition Seaforth Hotel, Stornoway
May 6–7*	Highlands and Islands Music and Dance Festival
May 19–20*	Royal Scottish National Proms Dundee
May 25–26*	Royal Scottish National Proms Aberdeen
May 26–June 10	Highland Festival
June 1–3*	Royal Scottish National Proms Edinburgh
June 2–4	National Gardening Show Strathclyde Country Park, nr Glasgow
June 10–25	West End Festival Glasgow
June 15–July 1*	Royal Scottish National Proms Glasgow
June 22–25	Royal Highland Show Royal Highland Centre, Newbridge, Midlothian
July 5–9*	Glasgow International Jazz Festival The Old Fruitmarket, Glasgow
July 8–9*	Hebridean Celtic Festival
July 11–21	Feis An Eilein Sàbhal Mor Ostaig, Skye
July 28–end October	Pitlochry Festival Theatre season Pitlochry
August 2–12	Aberdeen International Youth Festival
August 4–26	Edinburgh Military Tattoo Edinburgh Castle
August 12	World Pipe Band Championship Glasgow Green
August 12–28	Edinburgh International Book Festival Charlotte Square Gardens, Edinburgh
August 13–27	Edinburgh International Film Festival
August 13–September 2	Edinburgh International Festival
September 2	Braemar Royal Highland Gathering Princess Royal and Duke of Fife Memorial Park, Braemar
September 2	Scottish Pipe Band Championship Balloch
September 16	Leuchars International Air Show RAF Leuchars
October 13–20	Royal National Mod Dunoon
October–November	Scottish International Story-telling Festival

SPORTS EVENTS

February 5	Rugby Union: Italy v. Scotland Rome
February 15–20	Curling: Scottish Championship finals Braehead
February 19	Rugby Union: Ireland v. Scotland Dublin
March 4	Rugby Union: Scotland v. France Murrayfield, Edinburgh
March 18/19*	Rugby Union: Wales v. Scotland Cardiff
March 28–April 9	Snooker: Regal Scottish International Open Aberdeen Exhibition and Conference Centre
April 2	Rugby Union: Scotland v. England Murrayfield, Edinburgh
April 8	Rugby Union: Melrose Sevens Melrose
April 15	Horse-racing: Scottish Grand National Ayr

April 22	Rugby Union: Scottish Club Championship final Murrayfield, Edinburgh
May 27	Football: Scottish FA Cup final
June 3	Shinty: Camanachd Cup Fort William*
July 20–23	Golf: The Open The Old Course, St Andrews
July 31–August 5	Golf: Scottish Amateur Golf Championship Royal Dornoch
August 5–8	Golf: WPGA Tournament Gleneagles
October 7–10	Golf: Alfred Dunhill Cup The Old Course, St Andrews

* provisional

GAMES AND GATHERINGS

There are about 100 Gatherings each year, mostly in towns and districts in the Highlands but also in other parts of Scotland. Details can be obtained from the Scottish Games Association (tel: 01738-627782) and the Scottish Tourist Board (tel: 0131-332 2433 and 01463-716996).

RIDINGS

Ridings of the Marches and Common Ridings are held in the Borders between June and August. Of some antiquity, the ridings symbolize the patrolling of the disputed border areas, or Marches, between Scotland and England, and the laying of claim to common lands. Details can obtained from local authorities and the Scottish Tourist Board.

THE GOVERNMENT OF SCOTLAND

On 6 May 1999 the people of Scotland elected the first Parliament to sit in Scotland since the Act of Union 1707. The newly elected Members of the Scottish Parliament (MSPs) met for the first time on 12 May 1999. The Scottish Parliament was officially opened by the Queen on 1 July 1999, from which date devolution became effective, the Scottish Parliament and Scottish Ministers assuming their full powers under the Scotland Act 1998.

PRE-DEVOLUTION GOVERNMENT

Scotland's parliament and administration developed in medieval times and were established by 1603, when James VI of Scotland acceded to the English throne following the death of Elizabeth I of England. Despite the union of the crowns, the independence of the two countries' parliamentary systems was unaffected until 1707, when the Act of Union transferred the government of Scotland to Westminster.

From the late 19th century the office of Secretary of State for Scotland (formerly the Secretary for Scotland) increased in importance, and became a Cabinet post in 1926. Over that period the Scottish Office also grew in size and importance. It provided the government departments in Scotland for education, health, local government, housing, economic development, agriculture and fisheries, home affairs, and law and order. Although required to operate within overall levels of funding set down by Westminster, the Scottish Office under the Secretary of State for Scotland and the Scottish Office ministers enjoyed a freedom of operation and flexibility of budget far greater than the departments of state in Whitehall. The 'Scottish Block' comprised a total allocation of money to Scotland with the Secretary of State being able to set his own spending priorities within the overall budget.

Movement Towards Devolution

However, the concept of Scottish home rule did not die with the Union. Following the general election in October 1974 which saw the Scottish National Party return 11 MPs to Westminster, the Scottish home rule movement gained fresh momentum. Legislation was put in place to establish a Scottish assembly (the Scotland Act 1978) but the required qualified majority did not materialize at the referendum held in March 1979. During the 1980s, support for a measure of home rule continued and a Scottish Constitutional Convention was established in 1989. The Convention, which included representatives from many political parties and other bodies representative of Scottish public life, produced a blueprint for a Scottish Parliament. The Labour government returned at the general election in May 1997 promised constitutional reform as one of its legislative priorities and an early referendum on the establishment of a Scottish Parliament.

The new Labour government published a White Paper, Scotland's Parliament, in July 1997. This document set out in detail the Government's proposals to devolve to a Scottish Parliament the power to legislate in respect of all matters not specifically reserved to Westminster. It further proposed limited tax-raising powers, a single-chamber Parliament with powerful committees, and also considered the Scottish Parliament's relationship with Westminster and the European Union. It proposed a measure of proportional representation for the first time in a British parliamentary election.

In a referendum on 11 September 1997, almost 75 per cent of those voting agreed 'that there should be a Scottish Parliament'. On the question 'that the Scottish Parliament should have tax-varying powers', almost two-thirds voted for the proposition. The Scotland Bill was introduced to the House of Commons on 17 December 1997. The Bill completed its Commons stages on 20 May 1998 after 32 days of debate and was subjected to 17 days of line-by-line scrutiny in the House of Lords before receiving royal assent on 19 November 1998. The Government itself tabled 670 amendments to the Bill.

In November 1997 the Government announced the establishment of an all-party Consultative Steering Group to take forward consideration of how the Scottish Parliament might operate in practice and to develop proposals for rules of procedure and standing orders; the Group reported to the Secretary of State in January 1999. The report enshrined four main principles: sharing the power; accountability; accessibility and participation; and equal opportunities. It proposed a modern, accessible Parliament which would operate in a different manner from Westminster.

POST-DEVOLUTION GOVERNMENT

The Scottish Parliament is a subordinate legislature and can only legislate in respect of matters devolved to it. Westminster is sovereign and could, in theory, repeal the Scotland Act and do away with the Scottish Parliament, although all political parties have stated their commitment to ensure that the new Parliament works effectively. The role of the monarch is unchanged and Acts of the Scottish Parliament will require royal assent before becoming law.

Devolved powers

The Scottish Parliament is empowered to pass primary legislation (known as Acts of the Scottish Parliament) and Scottish Ministers can also make secondary legislation in respect of devolved matters. The principal devolved matters are: health, education, local government, social work and housing, planning, economic development, tourism, some aspects of transport, most aspects of criminal and civil law, the criminal justice and prosecution system, police and fire services, environment, natural and built heritage, agriculture and fisheries, food standards, forestry, sport, and the arts. The Scottish Parliament is also responsible for implementing European Community legislation in respect of matters devolved to it (*see* below). It is an absolute requirement that all laws of the Scottish Parliament, whether in the form of primary or secondary legislation, must comply with the European Convention on Human Rights, which has been given effect by the Human Rights Act, as well as being consistent with EU law.

Reserved powers

Despite the extent of devolved powers, a substantial range of matters are reserved to Westminster, including the constitution, foreign affairs, defence, the civil service, financial and economic matters, transport regulation, social security, employment and equal opportunities. If the Scottish Parliament attempts to legislate in respect of these reserved areas, the Secretary of State and the law officers may challenge in the courts the right of the Parliament to make a law. Such challenges will ultimately be dealt with by the Judicial Committee of the Privy Council, which assumes a new role as Scotland's principal constitutional court and will be the final arbiter in disputes between Westminster and Edinburgh regarding legislative competence.

THE SCOTTISH EXECUTIVE

The Scottish Executive is the government in Scotland in respect of all devolved matters. The Scottish Executive comprises the First Minister, the law officers (the Lord Advocate and the Solicitor-General for Scotland) and other ministers appointed by the First Minister. The members of the Scottish Executive are referred to collectively as the Scottish Ministers. The Scottish Ministers assumed their full powers on 1 July 1999, the day on which were transferred to them powers and duties and other functions relating to devolved matters which were previously exercised by the then UK Ministers in Scotland.

The Lord Advocate and Solicitor-General for Scotland are entitled to participate, but not vote, in the proceedings of the Parliament even if they are not MSPs. In addition to being the senior law officer in Scotland, the Lord Advocate continues to be the independent head of the systems of criminal prosecution and investigation of deaths in Scotland and this independence is entrenched in the Scotland Act 1998.

The Secretary of State for Scotland continues to be appointed as a member of the UK Government and is not a member of Scottish Executive. The Scotland Act recognizes that the UK Government will continue to need advice on Scots law, whether relating to reserved or devolved matters. To that end, a new law officer post in the UK Government, the Advocate-General for Scotland, is created; the first holder of this post is Lynda Clark, QC.

The Scottish Ministers are supported by staff largely drawn from the staff of the Scottish Office and its agencies. On 1 July 1999 the departments of the Scottish Office transferred to the Scottish Executive. This new name reflects the fact that the departments of the Scottish Office now work to the First Minister and his ministerial team. Some changes were made to the structure and titles of the departments that make up the Scottish Executive, reflecting the new ministerial portfolios (for details, *see* Scottish Executive section).

All officials of the Executive hold office under the Crown on terms and conditions of service determined in accordance with the provisions of the Civil Service Management Code and remain members of the Home Civil Service. Established arrangements for interchange with other government departments also remain in place.

THE LEGISLATURE

The Scottish Parliament is a single-chamber legislature with 129 members. Of these, 73 represent constituencies and are elected on a first-past-the-post system. These constituencies are the same as for elections to Westminster with the exception of Orkney and Shetland, which comprise separate constituencies in the Scottish Parliament. In addition, 56 regional members (seven members for each of the eight former Scottish constituencies in the European Parliament) are elected on a proportional basis; this is intended to ensure that the overall composition of the Scottish Parliament reflects closely the total number of votes cast for each of the political parties. Each elector casts two votes, one for a constituency member and one for the party of their choice.

The Scottish Parliament has a fixed term of four years; governments will not be able to hold snap general elections. Elections will normally be held on the first Thursday in May, although there is a limited measure of flexibility should this date prove unsuitable. Extraordinary general elections can be held in exceptional circumstances, such as failure of the Parliament to nominate a First Minister within 28 days or if the Parliament itself resolves that it should be dissolved with the support of at least two-thirds of the members.

The Parliament is responsible for agreeing its own methods of operation; however, it has always been envisaged that it will operate in an open, accessible and transparent manner. The transitional standing orders make specific reference to public access to meetings of the Parliament and most of the committees. They also propose hours of operation which are 'family friendly' and take into account traditional periods of school holidays in Scotland.

The Legislative Process

There are three stages to the legislative process: pre-parliamentary procedure, parliamentary procedure, and procedure leading up to royal assent.

Under the pre-parliamentary procedure, before a Bill may be introduced to the Parliament, a member of the Scottish Executive must make a written statement to the effect that the Bill is within the legislative competence of the Scottish Parliament. Furthermore, the Presiding Officer must also decide whether the provisions of the Bill would be within the legislative competence of the Parliament.

All Bills on introduction must be accompanied by a Financial Memorandum setting out the best estimates of the administrative, compliance and other costs to which the provisions of the Bill give rise, best estimates of time-scales over which such costs are expected to arise, and an indication of the margins of uncertainty in such estimates. Furthermore, government Bills must be accompanied by explanatory notes summarizing the provisions of the Bill, and a Policy Memorandum which sets out the policy objectives of the Bill, what alternative ways of meeting these objectives were considered, summary of any consultation undertaken on the objectives of the Bill, and an assessment of the effects of the Bill on equal opportunities, human rights, island communities, local government, sustainable development and any other matter which the Scottish Ministers consider relevant.

The parliamentary procedure has three stages: a general debate on the principle of the Bill with an opportunity to vote (analogous to the second reading debate in the House of Commons); detailed consideration of the Bill with the opportunity to move amendments (analogous to the Committee stage); and a final stage at which the Bill can be passed or rejected (analogous to the third reading).

After a Bill completes its parliamentary procedure, the Presiding Officer submits it for royal assent. There is an in-built delay of four weeks before royal assent is granted to allow one of the law officers or the Secretary of State to challenge the competency of the Parliament to pass the Act.

Committees

As the Scottish Parliament is a single chamber, there is no body such as the House of Lords to undertake detailed scrutiny of legislation. Instead, the Scottish Parliament has powerful all-purpose committees to undertake substantial pre-legislative scrutiny (for details, see pages 22–3). These committees combine the role of Westminster standing and select committees and:
– consider and report on policy and administration of the Scottish Administration
– have the power to conduct enquiries
– scrutinize primary, secondary and proposed EU legislation
– initiate legislation
– scrutinize financial proposals of the Scottish Executive (including taxation, estimates, appropriation and audit)
– scrutinize procedures relating to the Parliament and its members
Ministers are required to inform committees of

the Government's legislative intentions in its area, including discussions about which relevant bodies should be involved in the pre-legislative consultation process.

Management of Parliament

The management of the business of the Parliament is undertaken by the Parliamentary Bureau (for members, *see* page 22). This meets in private and its main functions are:
– to prepare the programme of business of the Parliament
– to timetable the daily order of business for the plenary session
– to timetable the progress of legislation in committees
– to propose the remit, membership, duration and budget of parliamentary committees
The Parliamentary Bureau gives priority on certain days to business of the committees, to business chosen by political parties which are not represented in the Scottish Executive, and to private members' business.

The management of the business of Parliament as a corporate entity is the responsibility of the Scottish Parliamentary Corporate Body (for members, *see* page 22). This has legal powers to hold property, make contracts and handle money and also to bring or defend legal proceedings by or against the Scottish Parliament. It also employs staff engaged in the running of the Parliament who are not civil servants.

BUDGET AND RUNNING COSTS

The annual budget of the Parliament will initially be £14–£15 billion and the UK Government has agreed to the continuing application of the Barnett Formula to allow for uprating of the Parliament's budget in line with increases for corresponding matters for the rest of the UK. In addition, the Parliament has limited powers to vary the basic rate of income tax by a maximum of 3 pence. The only other financial powers held by the Scottish Parliament relate to the manner in which local authorities raise revenue, presently by way of council tax and business rates.

The Scottish Parliament will be permanently housed in a custom-built building under construction at Holyrood, Edinburgh. The building, due to be completed in 2001, was designed by the Spanish architect Enriq Miralles and the cost is estimated at present to be in excess of £100 million. Until the new Parliament building is completed, the Scottish Parliament is occupying the Church of Scotland General Assembly buildings at The Mound, Edinburgh.

The total additional running costs of the Parliament, including salaries and allowances for MSPs, staff costs and accommodation costs, are estimated to be between £20 million and £30 million per annum. These costs will be met from the budget assigned to the Scottish Parliament and represent around £5 per head of the Scottish population.

Salaries and allowances

The initial salaries of MSPs were set at Westminster (for current salaries, *see* page 22), but in future the setting of salaries will be a matter for the Scottish Parliament. Enhanced salaries are payable to the Scottish Ministers and there is a system of allowances to cover MSPs' expenses in carrying out constituency and parliamentary work.

THE JUDICIARY

The role of the judiciary is specifically acknowledged in the Scotland Act and there are detailed proposals for the appointment and removal of judges. Judges are likely to be increasingly involved in matters of political significance, including legal challenges to legislation made by the Scottish Parliament and issues arising out of the European Convention on Human Rights.

Because of their increasing involvement in matters of political sensitivity, the procedures for removing judges have been made more rigorous. Judges can only be removed from office by the Queen on the recommendation of the First Minister following a resolution of the Parliament. Parliament may only pass such a motion following a written report by an independent tribunal concluding that the person in question is unfit for office by reason of inability, neglect of duty or misbehaviour.

RELATIONSHIP WITH THE UK GOVERNMENT

The devolution settlement has resulted in changes to the UK constitutional framework. The role of the Secretary of State for Scotland is diminished to the extent that he or she will only represent Scotland's interests with regard to reserved matters; there is no guarantee that the Secretary of State will continue to have a place in the Cabinet.

A system of concordats is being put in place to ensure that the business of government in Scotland and at the UK level is conducted smoothly. The concordats will be non-statutory agreements, and will cover a range of administrative procedures relating to devolution. They are intended to ensure that good working relationships and communications continue between the Scottish administration and UK government departments. As a rule, concordats will be bilateral, between the Scottish Executive and the UK Government. They will generally set out the principles on which working relationships will be based rather than prescribe the details of what those relationships should be. Concordats are intended to ensure that consultation takes place in relation to proposals for legislative and executive action, including advance notification.

There are likely to be further changes in future, for example, the number of Scottish MPs at Westminster is expected to be reduced following the next review of electoral areas carried out by the Boundary Commission for Scotland. As the legislation stands, this would also have the consequence of reducing the number of MSPs. Exact numbers will only be known after the Boundary Commission completes its work, but estimates suggest that the number of MSPs could drop from 129 to around 110.

RELATIONSHIP WITH THE EUROPEAN UNION

Relations with the EU remain a reserved matter. While the Scottish Parliament will have the responsibility of scrutinizing European legislation affecting Scotland, and the Scottish Executive the responsibility for applying that legislation in Scotland, it will be the UK Government that represents Scottish interests in the Council of Ministers; this includes areas such as farming and fishing, where Scottish Office ministers may previously have led UK delegations. The Government has indicated that Scottish Ministers might be able to participate, on behalf of the UK, in EU meetings. It has indicated that it sees UK and Scottish Ministers agreeing a common line prior to negotiating with other EU member states.

One of the concerns expressed about the proposed relationship between the Scottish Executive and the EU institutions is accountability. Scottish Ministers are not members of the UK Parliament and will therefore not be accountable to Westminster. As Scotland is not a member state of the EU, the responsibility for ensuring compliance with EU legislation rests with the UK Government. There is potential for conflict between the Scottish Parliament and Westminster with regard to the implementation of European legislation. In that event the proposed concordats between the Scottish Parliament and Westminster will be tested.

Any financial penalties imposed by the EU for non-observance of an EU measure, even in respect of devolved matters, will be met by the UK. Where the fault is due to the failure of the Scottish Executive to implement EU legislation in respect of devolved matters, the financial consequences will be met out of the Scottish Block.

THE HEAD OF STATE

ELIZABETH II, by the Grace of God, of the United Kingdom of Great Britain and Northern Ireland and of her other Realms and Territories Queen, Head of the Commonwealth, Defender of the Faith

Her Majesty Elizabeth Alexandra Mary of Windsor, elder daughter of King George VI and of HM Queen Elizabeth the Queen Mother

Born 21 April 1926, at 17 Bruton Street, London W1

Ascended the throne 6 February 1952

Crowned 2 June 1953, at Westminster Abbey

Married 20 November 1947, in Westminster Abbey, HRH The Prince Philip, Duke of Edinburgh, KG, KT, OM, GBE, AC, QSO, PC (*born* 10 June 1921, son of Prince and Princess Andrew of Greece and Denmark, naturalized a British subject 1947, created Duke of Edinburgh, Earl of Merioneth and Baron Greenwich 1947)

Official residences: Buckingham Palace, London SW1A 1AA; Palace of Holyroodhouse, Edinburgh; Windsor Castle, Berks

Private residences: Balmoral Castle, Aberdeenshire; Sandringham, Norfolk

THE HEIR TO THE THRONE

HRH THE PRINCE CHARLES, DUKE OF ROTHESAY (Prince Charles Philip Arthur George), KG, KT, GCB and Great Master of the Order of the Bath, AK, QSO, PC, ADC(P)

Born 14 November 1948, created Prince of Wales and Earl of Chester 1958, succeeded as Duke of Cornwall, Duke of Rothesay, Earl of Carrick and Baron Renfrew, Lord of the Isles and Prince and Great Steward of Scotland 1952

Married 29 July 1981 Lady Diana Frances Spencer (Diana, Princess of Wales (1961–97), youngest daughter of the 8th Earl Spencer and the Hon. Mrs Shand Kydd), marriage dissolved 1996

Issue:

HRH Prince William of Wales (Prince William Arthur Philip Louis), *born* 21 June 1982

HRH Prince Henry of Wales (Prince Henry Charles Albert David), *born* 15 September 1984

Residences: St James's Palace, London SW1A 1BS; Highgrove, Doughton, Tetbury, Glos GL8 8TN

Office: St James's Palace, London SW1A 1BS. Tel: 0171-930 4832

ORDER OF SUCCESSION TO THE THRONE

1 HRH The Prince Charles, Duke of Rothesay
2 HRH Prince William of Wales
3 HRH Prince Henry of Wales
4 HRH The Duke of York
5 HRH Princess Beatrice of York
6 HRH Princess Eugenie of York
7 HRH The Earl of Wessex
8 HRH The Princess Royal
9 Peter Phillips
10 Zara Phillips
11 HRH The Princess Margaret, Countess of Snowdon
12 Viscount Linley
13 Hon. Charles Linley
14 Lady Sarah Chatto
15 Samuel Chatto
16 Arthur Chatto
17 HRH The Duke of Gloucester
18 Earl of Ulster
19 Lady Davina Windsor
20 Lady Rose Windsor
21 HRH The Duke of Kent
22 Baron Downpatrick
23 Lady Marina Charlotte Windsor
24 Lady Amelia Windsor
25 Lord Nicholas Windsor
26 Lady Helen Taylor
27 Columbus Taylor
28 Cassius Taylor
29 Lord Frederick Windsor
30 Lady Gabriella Windsor
31 HRH Princess Alexandra, the Hon. Lady Ogilvy
32 James Ogilvy
33 Alexander Ogilvy
34 Flora Ogilvy
35 Marina, Mrs Paul Mowatt
36 Christian Mowatt
37 Zenouska Mowatt
38 The Earl of Harewood

The Earl of St Andrews and HRH Prince Michael of Kent lost the right of succession to the throne through marriage to a Roman Catholic. Their children remain in succession provided that they are in communion with the Church of England.

THE ROYAL ARMS

SHIELD

1st and 4th quarters (representing Scotland) –
Or, a lion rampant within a double tressure
flory counterflory Gules

2nd quarter (representing England) – Gules,
three lions passant guardant in pale Or

3rd quarter (representing Ireland) – Azure, a
harp Or, stringed Argent

The whole shield is encircled with the Thistle

SUPPORTERS

Dexter (right) – a unicorn Argent, armed,
crined, imperially crowned and unguled
Or, gorged with a coronet composed of
crosses patées and fleurs-de-lis, a chain
affixed, passing between the forelegs, and
reflexed over the back

Sinister (left) – a lion rampant guardant Or,
imperially crowned

CREST

Upon an imperial crown Proper a lion sejant
affrontée Gules imperially crowned Or,
holding in the dexter paw a sword and in the
sinister a sceptre erect, also Proper

BADGE

A thistle, slipped and leaved proper

Flags bearing an earlier version of the royal
arms of Scotland – Or, a lion rampant Gules,
armed and langued Azure, within a double
tressure flory counter-flory of fleur-de-lis of
the second – are often flourished by supporters
of the Scottish team at football and rugby
matches.

THE SCOTTISH EXECUTIVE

The Scottish Executive is the government of Scotland in respect of all devolved matters. The Scottish Executive consists of the First Minister, the law officers (the Lord Advocate and the Solicitor-General for Scotland), and the other Scottish Ministers appointed by the First Minister. The First Minister is also able to appoint junior ministers to assist the Scottish Ministers.

The Secretary of State for Scotland continues to be appointed as a member of the UK Government and is not a member of the Scottish Executive.

Certain UK Ministers continue to have a degree of responsibility for reserved matters.

THE SCOTTISH MINISTERS

First Minister, The Rt. Hon. Donald Dewar, MP, MSP (*Lab.*)
Deputy First Minister and Minister for Justice, Jim Wallace, QC, MP, MSP (*LD*)
Finance Minister, Jack McConnell, MSP (*Lab.*)
Minister for Health and Community Care, Susan Deacon, MSP (*Lab.*)
Minister for Communities, Wendy Alexander, MSP (*Lab.*)
Minister for Transport and the Environment, Sarah Boyack, MSP (*Lab.*)
Minister for Enterprise and Lifelong Learning, Henry McLeish, MP, MSP (*Lab.*)
Minister for Rural Affairs, Ross Finnie, MSP (*LD*)
Minister for Education and Children, Sam Galbraith, MP, MSP (*Lab.*)
Minister for Parliament and Chief Whip, Tom McCabe, MSP (*Lab.*)
Lord Advocate, The Lord Hardie, QC (*Lab.*)

JUNIOR MINISTERS*

COMMUNITIES
Deputy Minister for Local Government, Frank McAveety, MSP
Deputy Minister for Social Inclusion, Equality and the Voluntary Sector, Jackie Baillie, MSP

EDUCATION AND CHILDREN
Deputy Minister for Culture and Sport, Rhona Brankin, MSP
Deputy Minister for Children and Education, Peter Peacock, MSP

ENTERPRISE AND LIFELONG LEARNING
Deputy Minister for Enterprise and Lifelong Learning, Nicol Stephen, MSP

Deputy Minister for Highlands and Islands and Gaelic, Alasdair Morrison, MSP

HEALTH AND COMMUNITY CARE
Deputy Minister for Community Care, Iain Gray, MSP

JUSTICE
Deputy Minister for Justice, Angus Mackay, MSP

PARLIAMENT
Deputy Minister for Parliament and Whip, Iain Smith, MSP

RURAL AFFAIRS
Deputy Minister for Fisheries, John Home Robertson, MSP

LORD ADVOCATE
Solicitor-General for Scotland, Colin Boyd, QC

*Not members of the Scottish Executive

THE SCOTTISH PARLIAMENT

Edinburgh Assembly Hall, Edinburgh
EH99 1SP
Tel: 0131-348 5000 (switchboard)
0845-278 1999 (general enquiries)
E-mail:
sp.info@scottish.parliament.uk (public
information)
sp.media@scottish.parliament.uk (media
enquiries)
education.service@scottish.parliament.uk
(schools and colleges)
chamber.office@scottish.parliament.uk
(business in the debating chamber)
committee.office@scottish.parliament.uk
(business in committees)
petitions@scottish.parliament.uk (petitions)
presiding.officer@scottish.parliament.uk
(office of the Presiding Officer)
webmaster@scottish.parliament.uk (web site)
Web: http://www.scottish.parliament.uk

Elected: 6 May 1999; turnout was 59 per cent
of the electorate
First session: 12 May 1999
Official opening: 1 July 1999 at Edinburgh
Assembly Hall
Budget: £14–£15 billion
Devolved responsibilities: education, health, law,
environment, economic development,
local government, housing, police, fire
services, planning, financial assistance to
industry, tourism, some transport,
heritage and the arts, sport, agriculture,
forestry, fisheries, food standards
Powers: can introduce primary legislation; can
raise or lower income tax by up to three
pence in the pound
Number of members: 129

STATE OF THE PARTIES
as at end May 1999

	Constit-uency MSPs	Regional MSPs	Total
Labour	53	3	56
SNP	7	28	35
Conservative	0	18	18
Liberal Democrats	12	4*	16*
Green	0	1	1
Socialist	0	1	1
Independent	1	0	1
Presiding Officer	0	1	1
Total	73	56	129

* Excludes the Presiding Officer, who has no party
allegiance while in post

SALARIES
from 1 April 1999

MSPs and officers are paid by the Scottish
Parliamentary Corporate Body; ministers are
paid out of the Scottish Consolidated Fund.

First Minister	£64,308*
Ministers	£33,360*
Lord Advocate	£43,585
Solicitor-General for Scotland	£31,515
Junior Ministers	£17,305*
MSPs	£40,092†
Presiding Officer	£33,360*
Deputy Presiding Officers	£17,305*

* In addition to salary as an MSP
† Reduced by two-thirds (to £13,364) if the member
is already an MP or an MEP

OFFICERS

The Presiding Officer, The Rt. Hon. Sir David
Steel, KBE, MSP, QC
Deputy Presiding Officers, George Reid, MSP
(SNP); Patricia Ferguson, MSP *(Lab.)*

THE PARLIAMENTARY BUREAU
The Presiding Officer
Tom McCabe, MSP *(Lab.)*
Mike Russell, MSP *(SNP)*
The Rt. Hon. Lord James Douglas Hamilton,
MSP, QC *(C.)*
Iain Smith, MSP *(LD)*

SCOTTISH PARLIAMENTARY CORPORATE BODY
The Presiding Officer
Robert Brown, MSP *(LD)*
Des McNulty, MSP *(Lab.)*
Andrew Welsh, MSP *(SNP)*
John Young, MSP *(C.)*

THE COMMITTEES
The committees of the Scottish Parliament
are:

MANDATORY COMMITTEES

PROCEDURES
Convenor, Murray Tosh, MSP
Committee Clerk, John Patterson

STANDARDS
Convenor, Mike Rumbles, MSP
Committee Clerk, Vanessa Glynn

FINANCE
Convenor, Mike Watson, MSP
Committee Clerk, Sarah Davidson

LOCAL GOVERNMENT
Convenor, Patricia Godman, MSP
Committee Clerks, Craig Harper; Lynn Tullis

AUDIT
Convenor, Andrew Welsh, MP, MSP
Committee Clerk, Gillian Baxendine

EUROPEAN
Convenor, Hugh Henry, MSP
Committee Clerk, Stephen Imrie

EQUAL OPPORTUNITIES
Convenor, Kate MacLean, MSP
Committee Clerk, Martin Verity

PUBLIC PETITIONS
Convenor, John McAllion, MP, MSP
Committee Clerk, Steve Farrell

SUBORDINATE LEGISLATION
Convenor, Kenny MacAskill, MSP
Committee Clerk, Alasdair Rankin

SUBJECT COMMITTEES

JUSTICE AND HOME AFFAIRS
Convenor, Roseanna Cunningham, MP, MSP
Committee Clerk, Andrew Mylne

EDUCATION, CULTURE AND SPORT
Convenor, Mary Mulligan, MSP
Committee Clerk, Gillian Baxendine

SOCIAL INCLUSION, HOUSING AND
VOLUNTARY SECTOR
Convenor, Margaret Curran, MSP
Committee Clerk, Martin Verity

ENTERPRISE AND LIFELONG LEARNING
Convenor, John Swinney, MP, MSP
Committee Clerk, Simon Watkins

HEALTH AND COMMUNITY CARE
Convenor, Margaret Smith, MSP
Committee Clerk, Jennifer Stuart

TRANSPORT AND THE ENVIRONMENT
Convenor, Andy Kerr, MSP
Committee Clerk, Lynn Tullis

RURAL AFFAIRS
Convenor, Alex Johnstone, MSP
Committee Clerk, Richard Davies

MEMBERS OF THE SCOTTISH PARLIAMENT

Adam, Brian, *SNP, Scotland North East region*

Aitken, William, *C., Glasgow region*

Alexander, Ms Wendy, *Lab., Paisley North,* maj. 4,616

Baillie, Ms Jackie, *Lab., Dumbarton,* maj. 4,758

Barrie, Scott, *Lab., Dunfermline West,* maj. 5,021

Boyack, Ms Sarah, *Lab., Edinburgh Central,* maj. 4,626

Brankin, Ms Rhona, *Lab. Co-op., Midlothian,* maj. 5,525

Brown, Robert, *LD, Glasgow region*

Campbell, Colin, *SNP, Scotland West region*

Canavan, Dennis A., *MP, Lab., Falkirk West,* maj. 12,192

Chisholm, Malcolm G. R., *MP, Lab., Edinburgh North and Leith,* maj. 7,736

Craigie, Ms Cathy, *Lab., Cumbernauld and Kilsyth,* maj. 4,259

Crawford, Bruce, *SNP, Scotland Mid and Fife region*

Creech, Ms Christine, *SNP, Scotland South region*

Cunningham, Ms Roseanna, *MP, SNP, Perth,* maj. 2,027

Curran, Ms Margaret, *Lab., Glasgow Baillieston,* maj. 3,072

Davidson, David, *C., Scotland North East region*

Deacon, Ms Susan, *Lab., Edinburgh East and Musselburgh,* maj. 6,714

Dewar, Rt. Hon. Donald C., *MP, Lab., Glasgow Anniesland,* maj. 10,993

Douglas Hamilton, Rt. Hon. Lord James (The Lord Selkirk of Douglas), *QC, C., Lothians region*

Eadie, Ms Helen, *Lab. Co-op., Dunfermline East,* maj. 8,699

Elder, Ms Dorothy, *SNP, Glasgow region*

Ewing, Fergus, *SNP, Inverness East, Nairn and Lochaber,* maj. 441

Ewing, Mrs Margaret A., *MP, SNP, Moray,* maj. 4,129

Ewing, Mrs Winnifred, *SNP, Highlands and Islands region*

Fabiani, Ms Linda, *SNP, Scotland Central region*

Farquhar-Munro, John, *LD, Ross, Skye and Inverness West,* maj. 1,539

Ferguson, Ms Patricia, *Lab., Glasgow Maryhill,* maj. 4,326

Fergusson, Alex, *C., Scotland South region*

Finnie, Ross, *LD, Scotland West region*

Galbraith, Samuel L., *MP, Lab., Strathkelvin and Bearsden,* maj. 12,121

Gallie, Phil, *C., Scotland South region*

Gibson, Kenneth, *SNP, Glasgow region*

Godman, Ms Patricia, *Lab., Renfrewshire West,* maj. 2,893

Goldie, Miss Annabel, *C., Scotland West region*

Gorrie, Donald C. E., *MP, LD, Scotland Central region*

Grant, Ms Rhoda, *Lab., Highlands and Islands region*

Gray, Iain, *Lab., Edinburgh Pentlands,* maj. 2,885

Hamilton, Duncan, *SNP, Highlands and Islands region*

Harding, Keith, *C., Scotland Mid and Fife region*

Harper, Robin, *Green, Lothians region*

Henry, Hugh, *Lab., Paisley South,* maj. 4,495

Home Robertson, John D., *MP, Lab., East Lothian,* maj. 10,946

Hughes, Ms Janice, *Lab., Glasgow Rutherglen,* maj. 7,287

Hyslop, Ms Fiona, *SNP, Lothians region*

Ingram, Adam, *SNP, Scotland South region*

Jackson, Gordon, *Lab., Glasgow Govan,* maj. 1,756

Jackson, Ms Sylvia, *Lab., Stirling,* maj. 3,981

Jamieson, Ms Cathy, *Lab. Co-op., Carrick, Cumnock and Doon Valley,* maj. 8,803

Jamieson, Ms Margaret, *Lab., Kilmarnock and Loudoun,* maj. 2,760

Jenkins, Ian, *LD, Tweeddale, Ettrick and Lauderdale,* maj. 4,478

Johnston, Nicholas, *C., Scotland Mid and Fife region*

Johnstone, Alex, *C., Scotland North East region*

Kerr, Andy, *Lab., East Kilbride,* maj. 6,499

Lamont, Johann, *Lab. Co-op., Glasgow Pollock,* maj. 4,642

Livingstone, Ms Marilyn, *Lab. Co-op., Kirkcaldy,* maj. 4,475

Lochhead, Richard, *SNP, Scotland North East region*

Lyon, George, *LD, Argyll and Bute,* maj. 2,057

McAllion, John, *MP, Lab., Dundee East,* maj. 2,854

MacAskill, Kenny, *SNP, Lothians region*

McAveety, Frank, *Lab. Co-op., Glasgow Shettleston,* maj. 5,467

McCabe, Tom, *Lab., Hamilton South,* maj. 7,176

McConnell, Jack, *Lab., Motherwell and Wishaw,* maj. 5,076

Macdonald, Lewis, *Lab., Aberdeen Central,* maj. 2,696

MacDonald, Ms Margo, *SNP, Lothians region*

MacGrigor, Jamie, *C., Highlands and Islands region*

McGugan, Ms Irene, *SNP, Scotland North East region*

Macintosh, Ken, *Lab., Eastwood,* maj. 2,125

McIntosh, Mrs Lindsay, *C., Scotland Central region*

MacKay, Angus, *Lab., Edinburgh South,* maj. 5,424

MacLean, Ms Kate, *Lab., Dundee West,* maj. 121

McLeish, Henry B., MP, *Lab.*, *Fife Central*, maj. 8,675

McLeod, Ms Fiona, *SNP, Scotland West region*

McLetchie, David, *C.*, *Lothians region*

McMahon, Michael, *Lab.*, *Hamilton North and Bellshill*, maj. 5,606

MacMillan, Ms Maureen, *Lab.*, *Highlands and Islands region*

McNeil, Duncan, *Lab.*, *Greenock and Inverclyde*, maj. 4,313

McNeill, Ms Pauline, *Lab.*, *Glasgow Kelvin*, maj. 4,408

McNulty, Des, *Lab.*, *Clydebank and Milngavie*, maj. 4,710

Martin, Paul, Lab., *Glasgow Springburn*, maj. 7,893

Marwick, Ms Tricia, *SNP, Scotland Mid and Fife region*

Matheson, Michael, *SNP, Scotland Central region*

Monteith, Brian, *C.*, *Scotland Mid and Fife region*

Morgan, Alasdair N., MP, *SNP, Galloway and Upper Nithsdale*, maj. 3,201

Morrison, Alasdair, *Lab.*, *Western Isles*, maj. 2,093

Muldoon, Bristow, *Lab.*, *Livingston*, maj. 3,904

Mulligan, Ms Mary, *Lab.*, *Linlithgow*, maj. 2,928

Mundell, David, *C.*, *Scotland South region*

Murray, Ms Elaine, *Lab.*, *Dumfries*, maj. 3,654

Neil, Alex, *SNP, Scotland Central region*

Oldfather, Ms Irene, *Lab.*, *Cunninghame South*, maj. 6,541

Paterson, Gil, *SNP, Scotland Central region*

Peacock, Peter, *Lab.*, *Highlands and Islands region*

Peattie, Ms Cathy, *Lab.*, *Falkirk East*, maj. 4,139

Quinan, Lloyd, *SNP, Scotland West region*

Radcliffe, Ms Nora, *LD, Gordon*, maj. 4,195

Raffan, Keith, *LD, Scotland Mid and Fife region*

Reid, George, *SNP, Scotland Mid and Fife region*

Robison, Ms Shona, *SNP, Scotland North East region*

Robson, Euan, *LD, Roxburgh and Berwickshire*, maj. 3,585

Rumbles, Mike, *LD, Aberdeenshire West and Kincardine*, maj. 2,289

Russell, Michael, *SNP, Scotland South region*

Salmond, Alex E. A., MP, *SNP, Banff and Buchan*, maj. 11,292

Scanlon, Mrs Mary, *C.*, *Highlands and Islands region*

Scott, Tavish, *LD, Shetland*, maj. 3,194

Sheridan, Tommy, *SSP, Glasgow region*

Simpson, Richard, *Lab.*, *Ochil*, maj. 1,303

Smith, Ms Elaine, *Lab.*, *Coatbridge and Chryston*, maj. 10,404

Smith, Iain, *LD, Fife North East*, maj. 5,064

Smith, Ms Margaret, *LD, Edinburgh West*, maj. 4,583

Steel, Rt. Hon. Sir David (The Lord Steel of Aikwood), KBE, QC, *LD, Lothians region*

Stephen, Nicol, *LD, Aberdeen South*, maj. 1,760

Stone, Jamie, *LD, Caithness, Sutherland and Easter Ross*, maj. 4,391

Sturgeon, Ms Nicola, *SNP, Glasgow region*

Swinney, John R., MP, *SNP, Tayside North*, maj. 4,192

Thomson, Ms Elaine, *Lab.*, *Aberdeen North*, maj. 398

Tosh, Murray, *C.*, *Scotland South region*

Turnbull, Ms Karen, *Lab.*, *Clydesdale*, maj. 3,880

Ullrich, Ms Kay, *SNP, Scotland West region*

Wallace, Ben, *C.*, *Scotland North East region*

Wallace, James R., MP, *LD, Orkney*, maj. 4,619

Watson, Mike (The Lord Watson of Invergowrie), *Lab.*, *Glasgow Cathcart*, maj. 5,374

Welsh, Andrew P., MP, *SNP, Angus*, maj. 8,901

Welsh, Ian, *Lab.*, *Ayr*, maj. 25

White, Ms Sandra, *SNP, Glasgow region*

Whitefield, Ms Karen, *Lab.*, *Airdrie and Shotts*, maj. 8,985

Wilson, Allan, *Lab.*, *Cunninghame North*, maj. 4,796

Wilson, Andrew, *SNP, Scotland Central region*

Young, John, *C.*, *Scotland West region*

SCOTTISH PARLIAMENT CONSTITUENCIES AND REGIONS

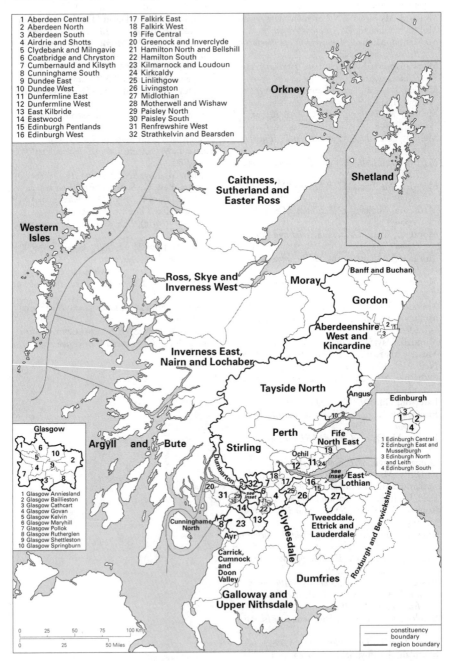

1 Aberdeen Central
2 Aberdeen North
3 Aberdeen South
4 Airdrie and Shotts
5 Clydebank and Milngavie
6 Coatbridge and Chryston
7 Cumbernauld and Kilsyth
8 Cunninghame South
9 Dundee East
10 Dundee West
11 Dunfermline East
12 Dunfermline West
13 East Kilbride
14 Eastwood
15 Edinburgh Pentlands
16 Edinburgh West

17 Falkirk East
18 Falkirk West
19 Fife Central
20 Greenock and Inverclyde
21 Hamilton North and Bellshill
22 Hamilton South
23 Kilmarnock and Loudoun
24 Kirkcaldy
25 Linlithgow
26 Livingston
27 Midlothian
28 Motherwell and Wishaw
29 Paisley North
30 Paisley South
31 Renfrewshire West
32 Strathkelvin and Bearsden

Orkney

Caithness,
Sutherland and
Easter Ross

Shetland

Western
Isles

Ross, Skye and
Inverness West

Moray

Banff and Buchan

Gordon

Aberdeenshire
West and
Kincardine

Inverness East,
Nairn and Lochaber

Tayside North

Angus

Edinburgh

1 Edinburgh Central
2 Edinburgh East and
  Musselburgh
3 Edinburgh North
  and Leith
4 Edinburgh South

Glasgow

1 Glasgow Anniesland
2 Glasgow Baillieston
3 Glasgow Cathcart
4 Glasgow Govan
5 Glasgow Kelvin
6 Glasgow Maryhill
7 Glasgow Pollok
8 Glasgow Rutherglen
9 Glasgow Shettleston
10 Glasgow Springburn

Argyll and Bute

Perth

Fife
North East

Stirling

Ochil

East
Lothian

Cunninghame
North

Tweeddale,
Ettrick and
Lauderdale

Ayr

Carrick,
Cumnock
and
Doon
Valley

Clydesdale

Dumfries

Roxburgh and Berwickshire

Galloway and
Upper Nithsdale

| 0 | 25 | 50 | 75 | 100 Km |
| 0 | 25 | 50 Miles |

constituency
boundary
region boundary

SCOTTISH PARLIAMENT ELECTIONS
on 6 May 1999

CONSTITUENCIES

ABERDEEN CENTRAL
(Scotland North East region)
E. 52,715   *T.* 50.26%

L. Macdonald, *Lab.*	10,305
R. Lochhead, *SNP*	7,609
Ms E. Anderson, *LD*	4,403
T. Mason, *C.*	3,655
A. Cumbers, *SSP*	523

Lab. majority 2,696

ABERDEEN NORTH
(Scotland North East region)
E. 54,553   *T.* 51.00%

Ms E. Thomson, *Lab.*	10,340
B. Adam, *SNP*	9,942
J. Donaldson, *LD*	4,767
I. Haughie, *C.*	2,772

Lab. majority 398

ABERDEEN SOUTH
(Scotland North East region)
E. 60,579   *T.* 57.26%

N. Stephen, *LD*	11,300
M. Elrick, *Lab.*	9,540
Ms N. Milne, *C.*	6,993
Ms I. McGugan, *SNP*	6,651
S. Sutherland, *SWP*	206

LD majority 1,760

ABERDEENSHIRE WEST AND KINCARDINE
(Scotland North East region)
E. 60,702   *T.* 58.87%

M. Rumbles, *LD*	12,838
B. Wallace, *C.*	10,549
Ms M. Watt, *SNP*	7,699
G. Guthrie, *Lab.*	4,650

LD majority 2,289

AIRDRIE AND SHOTTS
(Scotland Central region)
E. 58,481   *T.* 56.79%

Ms K. Whitefield, *Lab.*	18,338
G. Paterson, *SNP*	9,353
P. Ross-Taylor, *C.*	3,177
D. Miller, *LD*	2,345

Lab. majority 8,985

ANGUS
(Scotland North East region)
E. 59,891   *T.* 57.66%

A. Welsh, *SNP*	16,055
R. Harris, *C.*	7,154
I. McFatridge, *Lab.*	6,914
R. Speirs, *LD*	4,413

SNP majority 8,901

ARGYLL AND BUTE
(Highlands and Islands region)
E. 49,609   *T.* 64.86%

G. Lyon, *LD*	11,226
D. Hamilton, *SNP*	9,169
H. Raven, *Lab.*	6,470
D. Petrie, *C.*	5,312

LD majority 2,057

AYR
(Scotland South region)
E. 56,338   *T.* 66.48%

I. Welsh, *Lab.*	14,263
P. Gallie, *C.*	14,238
R. Mullin, *SNP*	7,291
Ms E. Morris, *LD*	1,662

Lab. majority 25

BANFF AND BUCHAN
(Scotland North East region)
E. 57,639   *T.* 55.06%

A. Salmond, *SNP*	16,695
D. Davidson, *C.*	5,403
M. Mackie, *LD*	5,315
Ms M. Harris, *Lab.*	4,321

SNP majority 11,292

CAITHNESS, SUTHERLAND AND EASTER ROSS
(Highlands and Islands region)
E. 41,581   *T.* 62.60%

J. Stone, *LD*	10,691
J. Hendry, *Lab.*	6,300
Ms J. Urquhart, *SNP*	6,035
R. Jenkins, *C.*	2,167
J. Campbell, *Ind.*	554
E. Stewart, *Ind.*	282

LD majority 4,391

CARRICK, CUMNOCK AND DOON VALLEY
(Scotland South region)
E. 65,580   *T.* 62.66%

Ms C. Jamieson, *Lab. Co-op.*	19,667
A. Ingram, *SNP*	10,864
J. Scott, *C.*	8,123
D, Hannay, *LD*	2,441

Lab. Co-op. majority 8,803

CLYDEBANK AND MILNGAVIE
(Scotland West region)
E. 52,461   *T.* 63.55%

D. McNulty, *Lab.*	15,105
J. Yuill, *SNP*	10,395
R. Ackland, *LD*	4,149
Ms D. Luckhurst, *C.*	3,688

Lab. majority 4,710

CLYDESDALE
(Scotland South region)
E. 64,262   T. 60.61%

Ms K. Turnbull, *Lab.*	16,755
Ms A. Winning, *SNP*	12,875
C. Cormack, *C.*	5,814
Ms S. Grieve, *LD*	3,503
Lab. majority 3,880	

COATBRIDGE AND CHRYSTON
(Scotland Central region)
E. 52,178   T. 57.87%

Ms E. Smith, *Lab.*	17,923
P. Kearney, *SNP*	7,519
G. Lind, *C.*	2,867
Ms J. Hook, *LD*	1,889
Lab. majority 10,404	

CUMBERNAULD AND KILSYTH
(Scotland Central region)
E. 49,395   T. 61.97%

Ms C. Craigie, *Lab.*	15,182
A. Wilson, *SNP*	10,923
H. O'Donnell, *LD*	2,029
R. Slack, *C.*	1,362
K. McEwan, *SSP*	1,116
Lab. majority 4,259	

CUNNINGHAME NORTH
(Scotland West region)
E. 55,867   T. 59.95%

A. Wilson, *Lab.*	14,369
Ms K. Ullrich, *SNP*	9,573
M. Johnston, *C.*	6,649
C. Irving, *LD*	2,900
Lab. majority 4,796	

CUNNINGHAME SOUTH
(Scotland South region)
E. 50,443   T. 56.06%

Ms I. Oldfather, *Lab.*	14,936
M. Russell, *SNP*	8,395
M. Tosh, *C.*	3,229
S. Ritchie, *LD*	1,717
Lab. majority 6,541	

DUMBARTON
(Scotland West region)
E. 56,090   T. 61.86%

Ms J. Baillie, *Lab.*	15,181
L. Quinan, *SNP*	10,423
D. Reece, *C.*	5,060
P. Coleshill, *LD*	4,035
Lab. majority 4,758	

DUMFRIES
(Scotland South region)
E. 63,162   T. 60.93%

Ms E. Murray, *Lab.*	14,101

D. Mundell, *C.*	10,447
S.Norris, *SNP*	7,625
N. Wallace, *LD*	6,309
Lab. majority 3,654	

DUNDEE EAST
(Scotland North East region)
E. 57,222   T. 55.33%

J. McAllion, *Lab.*	13,703
Ms S. Robison, *SNP*	10,849
I. Mitchell, *C.*	4,428
R. Lawrie, *LD*	2,153
H. Duke, *SSP*	530
Lab. majority 2,854	

DUNDEE WEST
(Scotland North East region)
E. 55,725   T. 52.19%

Ms K. MacLean, *Lab.*	10,925
C. Cashley, *SNP*	10,804
G. Buchan, *C.*	3,345
Ms E. Dick, *LD*	2,998
J. McFarlane, *SSP*	1,010
Lab. majority 121	

DUNFERMLINE EAST
(Scotland Mid and Fife region)
E. 52,087   T. 56.94%

Ms H. Eadie, *Lab. Co-op.*	16,576
D. McCarthy, *SNP*	7,877
Ms C. Ruxton, *C.*	2,931
F. Lawson, *LD*	2,275
Lab. Co-op. majority 8,699	

DUNFERMLINE WEST
(Scotland Mid and Fife region)
E. 53,112   T. 57.75%

S. Barrie, *Lab.*	13,560
D. Chapman, *SNP*	8,539
Ms E. Harris, *LD*	5,591
J. Mackie, *C.*	2,981
Lab. majority 5,021	

EAST KILBRIDE
(Scotland Central region)
E. 66,111   T. 62.49%

A. Kerr, *Lab.*	19,987
Ms L. Fabiani, *SNP*	13,488
C. Stevenson, *C.*	4,465
E. Hawthorn, *LD*	3,373
Lab. majority 6,499	

EAST LOTHIAN
(Scotland South region)
E. 58,579   T. 64.16%

J. Home Robertson, *Lab.*	19,220
C. Miller, *SNP*	8,274
Ms C. Richard, *C.*	5,941
Ms J. Hayman, *LD*	4,147
Lab. majority 10,946	

EASTWOOD
(Scotland West region)
E. 67,248   *T.* 67.51%

K. Macintosh, *Lab.*	16,970
J. Young, *C.*	14,845
Ms R. Findlay, *SNP*	8,760
Ms A. McCurley, *LD*	4,472
M. Tayan, *Ind.*	349
Lab. majority 2,125	

EDINBURGH CENTRAL
(Lothians region)
E. 65,945   *T.* 56.73%

Ms S. Boyack, *Lab.*	14,224
I. McKee, *SNP*	9,598
A. Myles, *LD*	6,187
Ms J. Low, *C.*	6,018
K. Williamson, *SSP*	830
B. Allingham, *Ind. Dem.*	364
W. Wallace, *Braveheart*	191
Lab. majority 4,626	

EDINBURGH EAST AND MUSSELBURGH
(Lothians region)
E. 60,167   *T.* 61.48%

Ms S. Deacon, *Lab.*	17,086
K. MacAskill, *SNP*	10,372
J. Balfour, *C.*	4,600
Ms M. Thomas, *LD*	4,100
D. White, *SSP*	697
M. Heavey, *Ind. You*	134
Lab. majority 6,714	

EDINBURGH NORTH AND LEITH
(Lothians region)
E. 62,976   *T.* 58.19%

M. Chisholm, *Lab.*	17,203
Ms A. Dana, *SNP*	9,467
J. Sempill, *C.*	5,030
S. Tombs, *LD*	4,039
R. Brown, *SSP*	907
Lab. majority 7,736	

EDINBURGH PENTLANDS
(Lothians region)
E. 60,029   *T.* 65.97%

I. Gray, *Lab.*	14,343
D. McLetchie, *C.*	11,458
S. Gibb, *SNP*	8,770
I. Gibson, *LD*	5,029
Lab. majority 2,885	

EDINBURGH SOUTH
(Lothians region)
E. 64,100   *T.* 62.61%

A. MacKay, *Lab.*	14,869
Ms M. MacDonald, *SNP*	9,445
M. Pringle, *LD*	8,961
I. Whyte, *C.*	6,378
W. Black, *SWP*	482
Lab. majority 5,424	

EDINBURGH WEST
(Lothians region)
E. 61,747   *T.* 67.34%

Ms M. Smith, *LD*	15,161
Lord J. Douglas-Hamilton, *C.*	10,578
Ms C. Fox, *Lab.*	8,860
G. Sutherland, *SNP*	6,984
LD majority 4,583	

FALKIRK EAST
(Scotland Central region)
E. 57,345   *T.* 61.40%

Ms C. Peattie, *Lab.*	15,721
K. Brown, *SNP*	11,582
A. Orr, *C.*	3,399
G. McDonald, *LD*	2,509
R. Stead, *Soc. Lab.*	1,643
V. MacGrain, *SFPP*	358
Lab. majority 4,139	

FALKIRK WEST
(Scotland Central region)
E. 53,404   *T.* 63.04%

D. Canavan, *Falkirk W.*	18,511
R. Martin, *Lab.*	6,319
M. Matheson, *SNP*	5,986
G. Miller, *C.*	1,897
A. Smith, *LD*	954
Falkirk W. majority 12,192	

FIFE CENTRAL
(Scotland Mid and Fife region)
E. 58,850   *T.* 55.82%

H. McLeish, *Lab.*	18,828
Ms P. Marwick, *SNP*	10,153
Ms J. A. Liston, *LD*	1,953
K. Harding, *C.*	1,918
Lab. majority 8,675	

FIFE NORTH EAST
(Scotland Mid and Fife region)
E. 60,886   *T.* 59.03%

I. Smith, *LD*	13,590
E. Brocklebank, *C.*	8,526
C. Welsh, *SNP*	6,373
C. Milne, *Lab.*	5,175
D. Macgregor, *Ind.*	1,540
R. Beveridge, *Ind.*	737
LD majority 5,064	

GALLOWAY AND UPPER NITHSDALE
(Scotland South region)
E. 53,057   *T.* 66.56%

A. Morgan, *SNP*	13,873
A. Fergusson, *C.*	10,672
J. Stevens, *Lab.*	7,209
Ms J. Mitchell, *LD*	3,562
SNP majority 3,201	

GLASGOW ANNIESLAND
(Glasgow region)
E. 54,378 T. 52.37%

D. Dewar, *Lab.*	16,749
K. Stewart, *SNP*	5,756
W. Aitken, *C.*	3,032
I. Brown, *LD*	1,804
Ms A. Lynch, *SSP*	1,000
E. Boyd, *Soc. Lab.*	139

Lab. majority 10,993

GLASGOW BAILLIESTON
(Glasgow region)
E. 49,068 T. 48.32%

Ms M. Curran, *Lab.*	11,289
Ms D. Elder, *SNP*	8,217
J. McVicar, *SSP*	1,864
Ms K. Pickering, *C.*	1,526
Ms J. Fryer, *LD*	813

Lab. majority 3,072

GLASGOW CATHCART
(Glasgow region)
E. 51,338 T. 52.55%

M. Watson, *Lab.*	12,966
Ms M. Whitehead, *SNP*	7,592
Ms M. Leishman, *C.*	3,311
C. Dick, *LD*	2,187
R. Slorach, *SWP*	920

Lab. majority 5,374

GLASGOW GOVAN
(Glasgow region)
E. 53,257 T. 49.52%

G. Jackson, *Lab.*	11,421
Ms N. Sturgeon, *SNP*	9,665
Ms T. Ahmed-Sheikh, *C.*	2,343
M. Aslam Khan, *LD*	1,479
C. McCarthy, *SSP*	1,275
J. Foster, *Comm. Brit.*	190

Lab. majority 1,756

GLASGOW KELVIN
(Glasgow region)
E. 61,207 T. 46.34%

Ms P. McNeill, *Lab.*	12,711
Ms S. White, *SNP*	8,303
Ms M. Craig, *LD*	3,720
A. Rasul, *C.*	2,253
Ms H. Ritchie, *SSP*	1,375

Lab. majority 4,408

GLASGOW MARYHILL
(Glasgow region)
E. 56,469 T. 40.75%

Ms P. Ferguson, *Lab.*	11,455
W. Wilson, *SNP*	7,129
Ms C. Hamblen, *LD*	1,793
G. Scott, *SSP*	1,439
M. Fry, *C.*	1,194

Lab. majority 4,326

GLASGOW POLLOCK
(Glasgow region)
E. 47,970 T. 54.37%

J. Lamont, *Lab. Co-op.*	11,405
K. Gibson, *SNP*	6,763
T. Sheridan, *SSP*	5,611
R. O'Brien, *C.*	1,370
J. King, *LD*	931

Lab. Co-op. majority 4,642

GLASGOW RUTHERGLEN
(Glasgow region)
E. 51,012 T. 56.89%

Ms J. Hughes, *Lab.*	13,442
T. Chalmers, *SNP*	6,155
R. Brown, *LD*	5,798
I. Stewart, *C.*	2,315
W. Bonnar, *SSP*	832
J. Nisbet, *Soc. Lab.*	481

Lab. majority 7,287

GLASGOW SHETTLESTON
(Glasgow region)
E. 50,592 T. 40.58%

F. McAveety, *Lab. Co-op.*	11,078
J. Byrne, *SNP*	5,611
Ms R. Kane, *SSP*	1,640
C. Bain, *C.*	1,260
L. Clarke, *LD*	943

Lab. Co-op. majority 5,467

GLASGOW SPRINGBURN
(Glasgow region)
E. 55,670 T. 43.77%

P. Martin, *Lab.*	14,268
J. Brady, *SNP*	6,375
M. Roxburgh, *C.*	1,293
M. Dunnigan, *LD*	1,288
J. Friel, *SSP*	1,141

Lab. majority 7,893

GORDON
(Scotland North East region)
E. 59,497 T. 56.51%

Ms N. Radcliffe, *LD*	12,353
A. Stronach, *SNP*	8,158
A. Johnstone, *C.*	6,602
Ms G. Carlin-Kulwicki, *Lab.*	3,950
H. Watt, *Ind.*	2,559

LD majority 4,195

GREENOCK AND INVERCLYDE
(Scotland West region)
E. 48,584 T. 58.95%

D. McNeil, *Lab.*	11,817
R. Finnie, *LD*	7,504
I. Hamilton, *SNP*	6,762
R. Wilkinson, *C.*	1,699
D. Landels, *SSP*	857

Lab. majority 4,313

HAMILTON NORTH AND BELLSHILL
(Scotland Central region)
E. 53,992 T. 57.82%

M. McMahon, *Lab.*	15,227
Ms K. McAlorum, *SNP*	9,621
S. Thomson, *C.*	3,199
Ms J. Struthers, *LD*	2,105
Ms K. McGavigan, *Soc. Lab.*	1,064

Lab. majority 5,606

HAMILTON SOUTH
(Scotland Central region)
E. 46,765 T. 55.43%

T. McCabe, *Lab.*	14,098
A. Ardrey, *SNP*	6,922
Ms M. Mitchell, *C.*	2,918
J. Oswald, *LD*	1,982

Lab. majority 7,176

INVERNESS EAST, NAIRN AND LOCHABER
(Highlands and Islands region)
E. 66,285 T. 63.10%

F. Ewing, *SNP*	13,825
Ms J. Aitken, *Lab.*	13,384
D. Fraser, *LD*	8,508
Ms M. Scanlon, *C.*	6,107

SNP majority 441

KILMARNOCK AND LOUDOUN
(Scotland Central region)
E. 61,454 T. 64.03%

Ms M. Jamieson, *Lab.*	17,345
A. Neil, *SNP*	14,585
L. McIntosh, *C.*	4,589
J. Stewart, *LD*	2,830

Lab. majority 2,760

KIRKCALDY
(Scotland Mid and Fife region)
E. 51,640 T. 54.88%

Ms M. Livingstone, *Lab. Co-op.*	13,645
S. Hosie, *SNP*	9,170
M. Scott-Hayward, *C.*	2,907
J. Mainland, *LD*	2,620

Lab. Co-op. majority 4,475

LINLITHGOW
(Lothians region)
E. 54,262 T. 62.26%

Ms M. Mulligan, *Lab.*	15,247
S. Stevenson, *SNP*	12,319
G. Lindhurst, *C.*	3,158
J. Barrett, *LD*	2,643
Ms I. Ovenstone, *Ind.*	415

Lab. majority 2,928

LIVINGSTON
(Lothians region)
E. 62,060 T. 58.93%

B. Muldoon, *Lab.*	17,313
G. McCarra, *SNP*	13,409
D. Younger, *C.*	3,014
M. Oliver, *LD*	2,834

Lab. majority 3,904

MIDLOTHIAN
(Lothians region)
E. 48,374 T. 61.51%

Ms R. Brankin, *Lab. Co-op.*	14,467
A. Robertson, *SNP*	8,942
J. Elder, *LD*	3,184
G. Turnbull, *C.*	2,544
D. Pryde, *Ind.*	618

Lab. Co-op. majority 5,525

MORAY
(Highlands and Islands region)
E. 58,388 T. 57.50%

Mrs M. Ewing, *SNP*	13,027
A. Farquharson, *Lab.*	8,898
A. Findlay, *C.*	8,595
Ms P. Kenton, *LD*	3,056

SNP majority 4,129

MOTHERWELL AND WISHAW
(Scotland Central region)
E. 52,613 T. 57.71%

J. McConnell, *Lab.*	13,955
J. McGuigan, *SNP*	8,879
W. Gibson, *C.*	3,694
J. Milligan, *Soc. Lab.*	1,941
R. Spillane, *LD*	1,895

Lab. majority 5,076

OCHIL
(Scotland Mid and Fife region)
E. 57,083 T. 64.58%

R. Simpson, *Lab.*	15,385
G. Reid, *SNP*	14,082
N. Johnston, *C.*	4,151
Earl of Mar and Kellie, *LD*	3,249

Lab. majority 1,303

ORKNEY
(Highlands and Islands region)
E. 15,658 T. 56.95%

J. Wallace, *LD*	6,010
C. Zawadzki, *C.*	1,391
J. Mowat, *SNP*	917
A. Macleod, *Lab.*	600

LD majority 4,619

PAISLEY NORTH
(Scotland West region)
E. 49,020   T. 56.61%

Ms W. Alexander, *Lab.*	13,492
I. Mackay, *SNP*	8,876
P. Ramsay, *C.*	2,242
Ms T. Mayberry, *LD*	2,133
Ms F. Macdonald, *SSP*	1,007

Lab. majority 4,616

PAISLEY SOUTH
(Scotland West region)
E. 53,637   T. 57.15%

H. Henry, *Lab.*	13,899
W. Martin, *SNP*	9,404
S. Callison, *LD*	2,974
Ms S. Laidlaw, *C.*	2,433
P. Mack, *Ind.*	1,273
Ms J. Forrest, *SWP*	673

Lab. majority 4,495

PERTH
(Scotland Mid and Fife region)
E. 61,034   T. 61.27%

Ms R. Cunningham, *SNP*	13,570
I. Stevenson, *C.*	11,543
Ms J. Richards, *Lab.*	8,725
C. Brodie, *LD*	3,558

SNP majority 2,027

RENFREWSHIRE WEST
(Scotland West region)
E. 52,452   T. 64.89%

Ms P. Godman, *Lab.*	12,708
C. Campbell, *SNP*	9,815
Ms A. Goldie, *C.*	7,243
N. Ascherson, *LD*	2,659
A. McGraw, *Ind.*	1,136
P. Clark, *SWP*	476

Lab. majority 2,893

ROSS, SKYE AND INVERNESS WEST
(Highlands and Islands region)
E. 55,845   T. 63.42%

J. Farquhar-Munro, *LD*	11,652
D. Munro, *Lab.*	10,113
J. Mather, *SNP*	7,997
J. Scott, *C.*	3,351
D. Briggs, *Ind.*	2,302

LD majority 1,539

ROXBURGH AND BERWICKSHIRE
(Scotland South region)
E. 47,639   T. 58.52%

E. Robson, *LD*	11,320
A. Hutton, *C.*	7,735
S. Crawford, *SNP*	4,719
Ms S. McLeod, *Lab.*	4,102

LD majority 3,585

SHETLAND
(Highlands and Islands region)
E. 16,978   T. 58.77%

T. Scott, *LD*	5,435
J. Wills, *Lab.*	2,241
W. Ross, *SNP*	1,430
G. Robinson, *C.*	872

LD majority 3,194

STIRLING
(Scotland Mid and Fife region)
E. 52,904   T. 67.68%

Ms S. Jackson, *Lab.*	13,533
Ms A. Ewing, *SNP*	9,552
B. Monteith, *C.*	9,158
I. Macfarlane, *LD*	3,407
S. Kilgour, *Ind.*	155

Lab. majority 3,981

STRATHKELVIN AND BEARSDEN
(Scotland West region)
E. 63,111   T. 67.17%

S. Galbraith, *Lab.*	21,505
Ms F. McLeod, *SNP*	9,384
C. Ferguson, *C.*	6,934
Ms A. Howarth, *LD*	4,144
Ms M. Richards, *Anti-Drug*	423

Lab. majority 12,121

TAYSIDE NORTH
(Scotland Mid and Fife region)
E. 61,795   T. 61.58%

J. Swinney, *SNP*	16,786
M. Fraser, *C.*	12,594
Ms M. Dingwall, *Lab.*	5,727
P. Regent, *LD*	2,948

SNP majority 4,192

TWEEDDALE, ETTRICK AND LAUDERDALE
(Scotland South region)
E. 51,577   T. 65.37%

I. Jenkins, *LD*	12,078
Ms C. Creech, *SNP*	7,600
G. McGregor, *Lab.*	7,546
J. Campbell, *C.*	6,491

LD majority 4,478

WESTERN ISLES
(Highlands and Islands region)
E. 22,412   T. 62.26%

A. Morrison, *Lab.*	7,248
A. Nicholson, *SNP*	5,155
J. MacGrigor, *C.*	1,095
J. Horne, *LD*	456

Lab. majority 2,093

REGIONS

GLASGOW
E. 531,956   *T.* 48.19%

Lab.	112,588 (43.92%)
SNP	65,360 (25.50%)
C.	20,239 (7.90%)
SSP	18,581 (7.25%)
LD	18,473 (7.21%)
Green	10,159 (3.96%)
Soc. Lab.	4,391 (1.71%)
ProLife	2,357 (0.92%)
SUP	2,283 (0.89%)
Comm. Brit.	521 (0.20%)
Humanist	447 (0.17%)
NLP	419 (0.16%)
SPGB	309 (0.12%)
Choice	221 (0.09%)

Lab. majority 47,228
(May 1997, Lab. maj. 166,061)

ADDITIONAL MEMBERS
W. Aitken, *C.*
R. Brown, *LD*
Ms D. Elder, *SNP*
Ms S. White, *SNP*
Ms N. Sturgeon, *SNP*
K. Gibson, *SNP*
T. Sheridan, *SSP*

HIGHLANDS AND ISLANDS
E. 326,553   *T.* 61.76%

SNP	55,933 (27.73%)
Lab.	51,371 (25.47%)
LD	43,226 (21.43%)
C.	30,122 (14.94%)
Green	7,560 (3.75%)
Ind. Noble	3,522 (1.75%)
Soc. Lab.	2,808 (1.39%)
Highlands	2,607 (1.29%)
SSP	1,770 (0.88%)
Mission	1,151 (0.57%)
Int. Ind.	712 (0.35%)
NLP	536 (0.27%)
Ind. R.	354 (0.18%)

SNP majority 4,562
(May 1997, LD maj. 1,388)

ADDITIONAL MEMBERS
J. MacGrigor, *C.*
Mrs M. Scanlon, *C.*
Ms M. MacMillan, *Lab.*
P. Peacock, *Lab.*
Ms R. Grant, *Lab.*
Mrs W. Ewing, *SNP*
D. Hamilton, *SNP*

LOTHIANS
E. 539,656   *T.* 61.25%

Lab.	99,908 (30.23%)
SNP	85,085 (25.74%)
C.	52,067 (15.75%)
LD	47,565 (14.39%)
Green	22,848 (6.91%)
Soc. Lab.	10,895 (3.30%)
SSP	5,237 (1.58%)
Lib.	2,056 (0.62%)
Witchery	1,184 (0.36%)
ProLife	898 (0.27%)
Rights	806 (0.24%)
NLP	564 (0.17%)
Braveheart	557 (0.17%)
SPGB	388 (0.12%)
Ind. Voice	256 (0.08%)
Ind. Ind.	145 (0.04%)
Anti-Corr.	54 (0.02%)

Lab. majority 14,823
(May 1997, Lab. maj. 101,991)

ADDITIONAL MEMBERS
Rt. Hon. Lord James Douglas Hamilton, *C.*
D. McLetchie, *C.*
Rt. Hon. Sir David Steel, *LD*
K. MacAskill, *SNP*
Ms M. MacDonald, *SNP*
Ms F. Hyslop, *SNP*
R. Harper, *Green*

SCOTLAND CENTRAL
E. 551,733   *T.* 59.90%

Lab.	129,822 (39.28%)
SNP	91,802 (27.78%)
C.	30,243 (9.15%)
Falkirk W.	27,700 (8.38%)
LD	20,505 (6.20%)
Soc. Lab.	10,956 (3.32%)
Green	5,926 (1.79%)
SSP	5,739 (1.74%)
SUP	2,886 (0.87%)
ProLife	2,567 (0.78%)
SFPP	1,373 (0.42%)
NLP	719 (0.22%)
Ind. *Prog.*	248 (0.08%)

Lab. majority 38,020
(May 1997, Lab. maj. 143,376)

ADDITIONAL MEMBERS
Mrs L. McIntosh, *C.*
D. Gorrie, *LD*
A. Neil, *SNP*
M. Matheson, *SNP*
Ms L. Fabiani, *SNP*
A. Wilson, *SNP*
G. Paterson, *SNP*

SCOTLAND MID AND FIFE
E. 509,387   T. 60.01%

Lab.	101,964 (33.36%)
SNP	87,659 (28.68%)
C.	56,719 (18.56%)
LD	38,896 (12.73%)
Green	11,821 (3.87%)
Soc. Lab.	4,266 (1.40%)
SSP	3,044 (1.00%)
ProLife	735 (0.24%)
NLP	558 (0.18%)

Lab. majority 14,305
(May 1997, Lab. maj. 54,087)

ADDITIONAL MEMBERS
N. Johnston, C.
B. Monteith, C.
K. Harding, C.
K. Raffan, LD
B. Crawford, SNP
G. Reid, SNP
Ms P. Marwick, SNP

SCOTLAND NORTH EAST
E. 518,521   T. 55.05%

SNP	92,329 (32.35%)
Lab.	72,666 (25.46%)
C.	52,149 (18.27%)
LD	49,843 (17.46%)
Green	8,067 (2.83%)
Soc. Lab.	3,557 (1.25%)
SSP	3,016 (1.06%)
Ind. Watt.	2,303 (0.81%)
Ind. SB	770 (0.27%)
NLP	746 (0.26%)

SNP majority 19,663
(May 1997, Lab. maj. 17,518)

ADDITIONAL MEMBERS
D. Davidson, C.
A. Johnstone, C.
B. Wallace, C.
R. Lochhead, SNP
Ms S. Robison, SNP
B. Adam, SNP
Ms I. McGugan, SNP

SCOTLAND SOUTH
E. 510,634   T. 62.35%

Lab.	98,836 (31.04%)
SNP	80,059 (25.15%)
C.	68,904 (21.64%)
LD	38,157 (11.99%)
Soc. Lab.	13,887 (4.36%)
Green	9,468 (2.97%)
Lib.	3,478 (1.09%)
SSP	3,304 (1.04%)
UK Ind.	1,502 (0.47%)
NLP	775 (0.24%)

Lab. majority 18,777
(May 1997, Lab. maj. 79,585)

ADDITIONAL MEMBERS
P. Gallie, C.
D. Mundell, C.
M. Tosh, C.
A. Fergusson, C.
M. Russell, SNP
A. Ingram, SNP
Ms C. Creech, SNP

SCOTLAND WEST
E. 498,466   T. 62.27%

Lab.	119,663 (38.55%)
SNP	80,417 (25.91%)
C.	48,666 (15.68%)
LD	34,095 (10.98%)
Green	8,175 (2.63%)
SSP	5,944 (1.91%)
Soc. Lab.	4,472 (1.44%)
ProLife	3,227 (1.04%)
Individual	2,761 (0.89%)
SUP	1,840 (0.59%)
NLP	589 (0.19%)
Ind. Water	565 (0.18%)

Lab. majority 39,246
(May 1997, Lab. maj. 115,995)

ADDITIONAL MEMBERS
Miss A. Goldie, C.
J. Young, C.
R. Finnie, LD
L. Quinan, SNP
Ms F. McLeod, SNP
Ms K. Ullrich, SNP
C. Campbell, SNP

ABBREVIATIONS OF PARTY NAMES

Anti-Corr.	Anti-Corruption, Mobile Home Scandal, Roads
Anti-Drug	Independent Anti-Drug Party
AS	Anti-sleaze
BNP	British National Party
C.	Conservative
Ch. U.	Christian Nationalist
Comm. Brit.	Communist Party of Britain
D. Nat.	Democratic Nationalist
Falkirk W.	MP for Falkirk West
Green	Green Party
Highlands	Highlands and Islands Alliance
Ind.	Independent
Ind. Dem.	Independent Democrat
Ind. Ind.	Independent Independent
Ind. Prog.	Independent Progressive
Ind. R.	Independent Robertson
Ind. SB	Independent Sleaze-Buster
Ind. Voice	Independent Voice for Scottish Parliament
Ind. Water	Independent Labour Keep Scottish Water Public
Ind. Watt.	Independent Watt

Individual	Independent Individual
Ind. You	Independent of London: Independent for You
Lab.	Labour
Lab. Co-op.	Labour Co-operative
LD	Liberal Democrat
Mission	Scottish People's Mission
NLP	Natural Law Party
ProLife	ProLife Alliance
Ref.	Referendum Party
SCU	Scottish Conservative Unofficial
SFPP	Scottish Families and Pensioners Party
SLI	Scottish Labour Independent
SLU	Scottish Labour Unofficial
Soc. Lab.	Socialist Labour Party
SPGB	Socialist Party of Great Britain
SSA	Scottish Socialist Alliance
SNP	Scottish National Party
SSP	Scottish Socialist Party
SUP	Scottish Unionist Party
SWP	Socialist Workers Party
UK Ind.	UK Independence Party
Witchery	Witchery Tour Party
WRP	Workers' Revolutionary Party

THE UK PARLIAMENT

MEMBERS FOR SCOTTISH SEATS

*Member of last Parliament
†Former Member of Parliament

*Adams, Mrs K. Irene (b. 1948), *Lab.*, *Paisley North*, majority 12,814

†Alexander, Douglas G. (b. 1967), *Lab.*, *Paisley South*, majority 2,731

Begg, Ms Anne (b. 1955), *Lab.*, *Aberdeen South*, majority 3,365

*Brown, Rt. Hon. J. Gordon, PH.D. (b. 1951), *Lab.*, *Dunfermline East*, majority 18,751

Brown, Russell L. (b. 1951), *Lab.*, *Dumfries*, majority 9,643

Browne, Desmond (b. 1952), *Lab.*, *Kilmarnock and Loudoun*, majority 7,256

*Bruce, Malcolm G. (b. 1944), *LD*, *Gordon*, majority 6,997

*Campbell, Rt. Hon. W. Menzies, CBE, QC (b. 1941), *LD*, *Fife North East*, majority 10,356

*Canavan, Dennis A. (b. 1942), *Lab.*, *Falkirk West*, majority 13,783

*Chisholm, Malcolm G. R. (b. 1949), *Lab.*, *Edinburgh North and Leith*, majority 10,978

Clark, Ms Lynda M. (b. 1949), *Lab.*, *Edinburgh Pentlands*, majority 4,862

*Clarke, Eric L. (b. 1933), *Lab.*, *Midlothian*, majority 9,870

*Clarke, Rt. Hon. Thomas, CBE (b. 1941), *Lab.*, *Coatbridge and Chryston*, majority 19,295

*Connarty, Michael (b. 1947), *Lab.*, *Falkirk East*, majority 13,385

*Cook, Rt. Hon. R. F. (Robin) (b. 1946), *Lab.*, *Livingston*, majority 11,747

*Cunningham, Ms Roseanna (b. 1951), *SNP*, *Perth*, majority 3,141

*Dalyell, Tam (Sir Thomas Dalyell of the Binns, Bt.) (b. 1932), *Lab.*, *Linlithgow*, majority 10,838

*Darling, Rt. Hon. Alistair M. (b. 1953), *Lab.*, *Edinburgh Central*, majority 11,070

*Davidson, Ian G. (b. 1950), *Lab. Co-op.*, *Glasgow Pollok*, majority 13,791

*Dewar, Rt. Hon. Donald C. (b. 1937), *Lab.*, *Glasgow Anniesland*, majority 15,154

*Donohoe, Brian H. (b. 1948), *Lab.*, *Cunninghame South*, majority 14,869

Doran, Frank (b. 1949), *Lab.*, *Aberdeen Central*, majority 10,801

*Ewing, Mrs Margaret A. (b. 1945), *SNP*, *Moray*, majority 5,566

*Foulkes, George (b. 1942), *Lab. Co-op.*, *Carrick, Cumnock and Doon Valley*, majority 21,062

*Fyfe, Ms Maria (b. 1938), *Lab.*, *Glasgow Maryhill*, majority 14,264

*Galbraith, Samuel L. (b. 1945), *Lab.*, *Strathkelvin and Bearsden*, majority 16,292

*Galloway, George (b. 1954), *Lab.*, *Glasgow Kelvin*, majority 9,665

*Godman, Norman A., PH.D. (b. 1938), *Lab.*, *Greenock and Inverclyde*, majority 13,040

Gorrie, Donald C. E. (b. 1933), *LD*, *Edinburgh West*, majority 7,253

*Graham, Thomas (b. 1944), *SLI*, *Renfrewshire West*, majority 7,979

*Griffiths, Nigel (b. 1955), *Lab.*, *Edinburgh South*, majority 11,452

*Home Robertson, John D. (b. 1948), *Lab.*, *East Lothian*, majority 14,221

*Hood, James (b. 1948), *Lab.*, *Clydesdale*, majority 13,809

*Ingram, Rt. Hon. Adam P. (b. 1947), *Lab.*, *East Kilbride*, majority 17,384

*Kennedy, Charles P. (b. 1959), *LD*, *Ross, Skye and Inverness West*, majority 4,019

*Kirkwood, Archibald J. (b. 1946), *LD*, *Roxburgh and Berwickshire*, majority 7,906

*Liddell, Rt. Hon. Helen (b. 1950), *Lab.*, *Airdrie and Shotts*, majority 15,412

*McAllion, John (b. 1948), *Lab.*, *Dundee East*, majority 9,961

*McAvoy, Thomas M. (b. 1943), *Lab. Co-op.*, *Glasgow Rutherglen*, majority 15,007

*Macdonald, Calum A., PH.D. (b. 1956), *Lab.*, *Western Isles*, majority 3,576

*McFall, John (b. 1944), *Lab. Co-op.*, *Dumbarton*, majority 10,883

McGuire, Mrs Anne (b. 1949), *Lab.*, *Stirling*, majority 6,411

McKenna, Ms Rosemary (b. 1941), *Lab.*, *Cumbernauld and Kilsyth*, majority 11,128

*McLeish, Henry B. (b. 1948), *Lab.*, *Fife Central*, majority 13,713

*Maclennan, Rt. Hon. Robert A. R. (b. 1936), *LD*, *Caithness, Sutherland and Easter Ross*, majority 2,259

*Marshall, David, PH.D. (b. 1941), *Lab.*, *Glasgow Shettleston*, majority 15,868

*Martin, Michael J. (b. 1945), *Lab.*, *Glasgow Springburn*, majority 17,326

*Maxton, John A. (b. 1936), *Lab.*, *Glasgow Cathcart*, majority 12,245

*Michie, Mrs J. Ray (b. 1934), *LD*, *Argyll and Bute*, majority 6,081

*Moonie, Dr Lewis G. (b. 1947), *Lab. Co-op.*, *Kirkcaldy*, majority 10,710

Moore, Michael K. (b. 1965), *LD*, *Tweeddale, Ettrick and Lauderdale*, majority 1,489

Morgan, Alastair N. (b. 1945), *SNP*, *Galloway and Upper Nithsdale*, majority 5,624

Murphy, James (b. 1967), *Lab.*, *Eastwood*, majority 3,236

*O'Neill, Martin J. (b. 1945), *Lab.*, *Ochil*,
    majority 4,652
Osborne, Mrs Sandra C. (b. 1956), *Lab.*, *Ayr*,
    majority 6,543
*Reid, Rt. Hon. John, Ph.D. (b. 1947), *Lab.*,
    Hamilton North and Bellshill, majority
    17,067
*Robertson, Rt. Hon. George I. M. (b. 1946),
    Lab., *Hamilton South*, majority 15,878
*Ross, Ernest (b. 1942), *Lab.*, *Dundee West*,
    majority 11,859
Roy, Frank (b. 1958), *Lab.*, *Motherwell and
    Wishaw*, majority 12,791
*Salmond, Alexander E. A. (b. 1954), *SNP*,
    Banff and Buchan, majority 12,845
Sarwar, Mohammad (b. 1952), *Lab.*, *Glasgow
    Govan*, majority 2,914
Savidge, Malcolm K. (b. 1946), *Lab.*, *Aberdeen
    North*, majority 10,010
Smith, Sir Robert, Bt. (b. 1958), *LD*,
    Aberdeenshire West and Kincardine, majority
    2,662
*Squire, Ms Rachel A. (b. 1954), *Lab.*,
    Dunfermline West, majority 12,354
Stewart, David J. (b. 1956), *Lab.*, *Inverness East,
    Nairn and Lochaber*, majority 2,339
*Strang, Rt. Hon. Gavin S., Ph.D. (b. 1943),
    Lab., *Edinburgh East and Musselburgh*,
    majority 14,530
Swinney, John R. (b. 1964), *SNP*, *Tayside North*,
    majority 4,160
*Wallace, James R. (b. 1954), *LD*, *Orkney and
    Shetland*, majority 6,968
*Welsh, Andrew P. (b. 1944), *SNP*, *Angus*,
    majority 10,189
*Wilson, Brian D. H. (b. 1948), *Lab.*,
    Cunninghame North, majority 11,039
*Worthington, Anthony (b. 1941), *Lab.*,
    Clydebank and Milngavie, majority 13,320
*Wray, James (b. 1938), *Lab.*, *Glasgow
    Baillieston*, majority 14,840

SCOTTISH CONSTITUENCIES IN UK PARLIAMENT

1 Aberdeen Central
2 Aberdeen North
3 Aberdeen South
4 Airdrie and Shotts
5 Clydebank and Milngavie
6 Coatbridge and Chryston
7 Cumbernauld and Kilsyth
8 Cunninghame South
9 Dundee East
10 Dundee West
11 Dunfermline East
12 Dunfermline West
13 East Kilbride
14 Eastwood
15 Edinburgh Pentlands
16 Edinburgh West

17 Falkirk East
18 Falkirk West
19 Fife Central
20 Greenock and Inverclyde
21 Hamilton North and Bellshill
22 Hamilton South
23 Kilmarnock and Loudoun
24 Kirkcaldy
25 Linlithgow
26 Livingston
27 Midlothian
28 Motherwell and Wishaw
29 Paisley North
30 Paisley South
31 Renfrewshire West
32 Strathkelvin and Bearsden

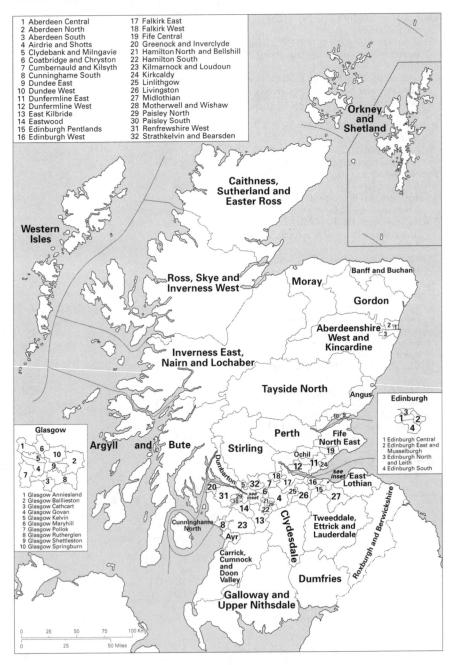

Glasgow

1 Glasgow Anniesland
2 Glasgow Baillieston
3 Glasgow Cathcart
4 Glasgow Govan
5 Glasgow Kelvin
6 Glasgow Maryhill
7 Glasgow Pollok
8 Glasgow Rutherglen
9 Glasgow Shettleston
10 Glasgow Springburn

Edinburgh

1 Edinburgh Central
2 Edinburgh East and Musselburgh
3 Edinburgh North and Leith
4 Edinburgh South

Orkney and Shetland

Caithness, Sutherland and Easter Ross

Western Isles

Ross, Skye and Inverness West

Moray

Banff and Buchan

Gordon

Aberdeenshire West and Kincardine

Inverness East, Nairn and Lochaber

Tayside North

Angus

Argyll and Bute

Perth

Fife North East

Stirling

Ochil

Cunninghame North

Ayr

Carrick, Cumnock and Doon Valley

East Lothian

Tweeddale, Ettrick and Lauderdale

Clydesdale

Roxburgh and Berwickshire

Dumfries

Galloway and Upper Nithsdale

0   25   50   75   100 Km

0   25   50 Miles

UK PARLIAMENT ELECTIONS
as at 1 May 1997

SCOTTISH CONSTITUENCIES

* Member of the last Parliament in unchanged constituency

† Member of the last Parliament in different constituency or one affected by boundry changes

For abbreviations, *see* pages 34–5

ABERDEEN CENTRAL
*E.*54,257   *T.*65.64%

F. Doran, *Lab.*	17,745
Mrs J. Wisely, *C.*	6,944
B. Topping, *SNP*	5,767
J. Brown, *LD*	4,714
J. Farquharson, *Ref.*	446

Lab. majority 10,801
(Boundary change: notional Lab.)

ABERDEEN NORTH
*E.*54,302   *T.*70.74%

M. Savidge, *Lab.*	18,389
B. Adam, *SNP*	8,379
J. Gifford, *C.*	5,763
M. Rumbles, *LD*	5,421
A. Mackenzie, *Ref.*	463

Lab. majority 10,010
(Boundary change: notional Lab.)

ABERDEEN SOUTH
*E.*60,490   *T.*72.84%

Ms A. Begg, *Lab.*	15,541
N. Stephen, *LD*	12,176
† R. Robertson, *C.*	11,621
J. Towers, *SNP*	4,299
R. Wharton, *Ref.*	425

Lab. majority 3,365
(Boundary change: notional C.)

ABERDEENSHIRE WEST AND KINCARDINE
*E.*59,123   *T.*73.05%

Sir R. Smith, *LD*	17,742
† G. Kynoch, *C.*	15,080
Ms J. Mowatt, *SNP*	5,639
Ms Q. Khan, *Lab.*	3,923
S. Ball, *Ref.*	805

LD majority 2,662
(Boundary change: notional C.)

AIRDRIE AND SHOTTS
*E.*57,673   *T.*71.40%

† Mrs H. Liddell, *Lab.*	25,460
K. Robertson, *SNP*	10,048
Dr N. Brook, *C.*	3,660
R. Wolseley, *LD*	1,719
C. Semple, *Ref.*	294

Lab. majority 15,412
(Boundary change: notional Lab.)

ANGUS
*E.*59,708   *T.*72.14%

† A. Welsh, *SNP*	20,792
S. Leslie, *C.*	10,603
Ms C. Taylor, *Lab.*	6,733
Dr R. Speirs, *LD*	4,065
B. Taylor, *Ref.*	883

SNP majority 10,189
(Boundary change: notional SNP)

ARGYLL AND BUTE
*E.*49,451   *T.*72.23%

* Mrs R. Michie, *LD*	14,359
Prof. N. MacCormick, *SNP*	8,278
R. Leishman, *C.*	6,774
A. Syed, *Lab.*	5,596
M. Stewart, *Ref.*	713

LD majority 6,081
(April 1992, LD maj. 2,622)

AYR
*E.*55,829   *T.*80.17%

Mrs S. Osborne, *Lab.*	21,679
† P. Gallie, *C.*	15,136
I. Blackford, *SNP*	5,625
Miss C. Hamblen, *LD*	2,116
J. Enos, *Ref.*	200

Lab. majority 6,543
(Boundary change: notional Lab.)

BANFF AND BUCHAN
*E.*58,493   *T.*68.69%

† A. Salmond, *SNP*	22,409
W. Frain-Bell, *C.*	9,564
Ms M. Harris, *Lab.*	4,747
N. Fletcher, *LD*	2,398
A. Buchan, *Ref.*	1,060

SNP majority 12,845
(Boundary change: notional SNP)

CAITHNESS, SUTHERLAND AND EASTER ROSS
*E.*41,566   *T.*70.18%

† R. Maclennan, *LD*	10,381
J. Hendry, *Lab.*	8,122
E. Harper, *SNP*	6,710
T. Miers, *C.*	3,148
Ms C. Ryder, *Ref.*	369
J. Martin, *Green*	230
M. Carr, *UK Ind.*	212

LD majority 2,259
(Boundary change: notional LD)

CARRICK, CUMNOCK AND DOON VALLEY
*E.*65,593   *T.*74.96%

† G. Foulkes, *Lab. Co-op.*	29,398
A. Marshall, *C.*	8,336
Mrs C. Hutchison, *SNP*	8,190
D. Young, *LD*	2,613
J. Higgins, *Ref.*	634

Lab. Co-op. majority 21,062
(Boundary change: notional Lab. Co-op.)

CLYDEBANK AND MILNGAVIE
E.52,092   T.75.03%
† A. Worthington, *Lab.*   21,583
J. Yuill, *SNP*   8,263
Ms N. Morgan, *C.*   4,885
K. Moody, *LD*   4,086
I. Sanderson, *Ref.*   269
Lab. majority 13,320
(Boundary change: notional Lab.)

CLYDESDALE
E.63,428 T.71.60%
* J. Hood, *Lab.*   23,859
A. Doig, *SNP*   10,050
M. Izatt, *C.*   7,396
Mrs S. Grieve, *LD*   3,796
K. Smith, *BNP*   311
Lab. majority 13,809
(April 1992, Lab. maj. 10,187)

COATBRIDGE AND CHRYSTON
E.52,024 T.72.30%
† T. Clarke, *Lab.*   25,697
B. Nugent, *SNP*   6,402
A. Wauchope, *C.*   3,216
Mrs M. Daly, *LD*   2,048
B. Bowsley, *Ref.*   249
Lab. majority 19,295
(Boundary change: notional Lab.)

CUMBERNAULD AND KILSYTH
E.48,032 T.75.00%
Ms R. McKenna, *Lab.*   21,141
C. Barrie, *SNP*   10,013
I. Sewell, *C.*   2,441
J. Biggam, *LD*   1,368
Ms J Kara, *ProLife*   609
K. McEwan, *SSA*   345
Ms P. Cook, *Ref.*   107
Lab. majority 11,128
(April 1992, Lab. maj. 9,215)

CUNNINGHAME NORTH
E.55,526 T.74.07%
* B. Wilson, *Lab.*   20,686
Mrs M. Mitchell, *C.*   9,647
Ms K. Nicoll, *SNP*   7,584
Ms K. Freel, *LD*   2,271
Ms L. McDaid, *Soc. Lab.*   501
I. Winton, *Ref.*   440
Lab. majority 11,039
(April 1992, Lab. maj. 2,939)

CUNNINGHAME SOUTH
E.49,543 T.71.54%
* B. Donohoe, *Lab.*   22,233
Mrs M. Burgess, *SNP*   7,364
Mrs P. Paterson, *C.*   3,571
E. Watson, *LD*   1,604

K. Edwin, *Soc. Lab.*   494
A. Martlew, *Ref.*   178
Lab. majority 14,869
(April 1992, Lab. maj. 10,680)

DUMBARTON
E.56,229   T.73.39%
* J. McFall, *Lab. Co-op.*   20,470
W. Mackechnie, *SNP*   9,587
P. Ramsay, *C.*   7,283
A. Reid, *LD*   3,144
L. Robertson, *SSA*   283
G. Dempster, *Ref.*   255
D. Lancaster, *UK Ind.*   242
Lab. Co-op. majority 10,883
(April 1992, Lab. maj. 6,129)

DUMFRIES
E.62,759   T.78.92%
R. Brown, *Lab.*   23,528
S. Stevenson, *C.*   13,885
R. Higgins, *SNP*   5,977
N. Wallace, *LD*   5,487
D. Parker, *Ref.*   533
Ms E. Hunter, *NLP*   117
Lab. majority 9,643
(Boundary change: notional C.)

DUNDEE EAST
E.58,388   T.69.41%
† J. McAllion, *Lab.*   20,718
Ms S. Robison, *SNP*   10,757
B. Mackie, *C.*   6,397
Dr G. Saluja, *LD*   1,677
E. Galloway, *Ref.*   601
H. Duke, *SSA*   232
Ms E. MacKenzie, *NLP*   146
Lab. majority 9,961
(Boundary change: notional Lab.)

DUNDEE WEST
E.57,346   T.67.67%
† E. Ross, *Lab.*   20,875
J. Dorward, *SNP*   9,016
N. Powrie, *C.*   5,105
Dr E. Dick, *LD*   2,972
Ms M. Ward, *SSA*   428
J. MacMillan, *Ref.*   411
Lab. majority 11,859
(Boundary change: notional Lab.)

DUNFERMLINE EAST
E.52,072   T.70.25%
† Rt. Hon. G. Brown, *Lab.*   24,441
J. Ramage, *SNP*   5,690
I. Mitchell, *C.*   3,656
J. Tolson, *LD*   2,164
T. Dunsmore, *Ref.*   632
Lab. majority 18,751
(Boundary change: notional Lab.)

DUNFERMLINE WEST
E.52,467   T.69.44%

† Ms R. Squire, *Lab.*	19,338
J. Lloyd, *SNP*	6,984
Mrs E. Harris, *LD*	4,963
K. Newton, *C.*	4,606
J. Bain, *Ref.*	543

Lab. majority 12,354
(Boundary change: notional Lab.)

EAST KILBRIDE
E.65,229   T.74.81%

† A. Ingram, *Lab.*	27,584
G. Gebbie, *SNP*	10,200
C. Herbertson, *C.*	5,863
Mrs K. Philbrick, *LD*	3,527
J. Deighan, *ProLife*	1,170
Ms J. Gray, *Ref.*	306
E. Gilmour, *NLP*	146

Lab. majority 17,384
(Boundary change: notional Lab.)

EAST LOTHIAN
E.57,441   T.75.61%

† J. Home Robertson, *Lab.*	22,881
M. Fraser, *C.*	8,660
D. McCarthy, *SNP*	6,825
Ms A. MacAskill, *LD*	4,575
N. Nash, *Ref.*	491

Lab. majority 14,221
(Boundary change: notional Lab.)

EASTWOOD
E.66,697   T.78.32%

J. Murphy, *Lab.*	20,766
P. Cullen, *C.*	17,530
D. Yates, *SNP*	6,826
Dr C. Mason, *LD*	6,110
D. Miller, *Ref.*	497
Dr M. Tayan, *ProLife*	393
D. McPherson, *UK Ind.*	113

Lab. majority 3,236
(Boundary change: notional C.)

EDINBURGH CENTRAL
E.63,695   T.67.09%

† A. Darling, *Lab.*	20,125
M. Scott-Hayward, *C.*	9,055
Ms F. Hyslop, *SNP*	6,750
Ms K. Utting, *LD*	5,605
Ms L. Hendry, *Green*	607
A. Skinner, *Ref.*	495
M. Benson, *Ind. Dem.*	98

Lab. majority 11,070
(Boundary change: notional Lab.)

EDINBURGH EAST AND MUSSELBURGH
E.59,648   T.70.61%

† Dr G. Strang, *Lab.*	22,564
D. White, *SNP*	8,034
K. Ward, *C.*	6,483
Dr C. MacKellar, *LD*	4,511
J. Sibbet, *Ref.*	526

Lab. majority 14,530
(Boundary change: notional Lab.)

EDINBURGH NORTH AND LEITH
E.61,617   T.66.45%

† M. Chisholm, *Lab.*	19,209
Ms A. Dana, *SNP*	8,231
E. Stewart, *C.*	7,312
Ms H. Campbell, *LD*	5,335
A. Graham, *Ref.*	441
G. Brown, *SSA*	320
P. Douglas-Reid, *NLP*	97

Lab. majority 10,978
(Boundary change: notional Lab.)

EDINBURGH PENTLANDS
E.59,635   T.76.70%

Ms L. Clark, *Lab.*	19,675
† Rt. Hon. M. Rifkind, *C.*	14,813
S. Gibb, *SNP*	5,952
Dr J. Dawe, *LD*	4,575
M. McDonald, *Ref.*	422
R. Harper, *Green*	224
A. McConnachie, *UK Ind.*	81

Lab. majority 4,862
(Boundary change: notional C.)

EDINBURGH SOUTH
E.62,467   T.71.78%

† N. Griffiths, *Lab.*	20,993
Miss E. Smith, *C.*	9,541
M. Pringle, *LD*	7,911
Dr J. Hargreaves, *SNP*	5,791
I. McLean, *Ref.*	504
B. Dunn, *NLP*	98

Lab. majority 11,452
(Boundary change: notional Lab.)

EDINBURGH WEST
E.61,133   T.77.91%

D. Gorrie, *LD*	20,578
† Rt. Hon. Lord J. Douglas-Hamilton, *C.*	13,325
Ms L. Hinds, *Lab.*	8,948
G. Sutherland, *SNP*	4,210
Dr S. Elphick, *Ref.*	277
P. Coombes, *Lib.*	263
A. Jack, *AS*	30

LD majority 7,253
(Boundary change: notional C.)

FALKIRK EAST
E.56,792   T.73.24%
† M. Connarty, *Lab.* — 23,344
K. Brown, *SNP* — 9,959
M. Nicol, *C.* — 5,813
R. Spillane, *LD* — 2,153
S. Mowbray, *Ref.* — 326
Lab. majority 13,385
(Boundary change: notional Lab.)

FALKIRK WEST
E.52,850   T.72.60%
† D. Canavan, *Lab.* — 22,772
D. Alexander, *SNP* — 8,989
Mrs C. Buchanan, *C.* — 4,639
D. Houston, *LD* — 1,970
Lab. majority 13,783
(Boundary change: notional Lab.)

FIFE CENTRAL
E.58,315   T.69.90%
† &kern; H. McLeish, *Lab.* — 23,912
Mrs P. Marwick, *SNP* — 10,199
J. Rees-Mogg, *C.* — 3,669
R. Laird, *LD* — 2,610
J. Scrymgeour-Wedderburn, *Ref.* — 375
Lab. majority 13,713
(Boundary change: notional Lab.)

FIFE NORTH EAST
E.58,794   T.71.16%
* M. Campbell, *LD* — 21,432
A. Bruce, *C.* — 11,076
C. Welsh, *SNP* — 4,545
C. Milne, *Lab.* — 4,301
W. Stewart, *Ref.* — 485
LD majority 10,356
(Boundary change: notional LD)

GALLOWAY AND UPPER NITHSDALE
E.52,751   T.79.65%
A. Morgan, *SNP* — 18,449
† Rt. Hon. I. Lang, *C.* — 12,825
Ms K. Clark, *Lab.* — 6,861
J. McKerchar, *LD* — 2,700
R. Wood, *Ind.* — 566
A. Kennedy, *Ref.* — 428
J. Smith, *UK Ind.* — 189
SNP majority 5,624
(Boundary change: notional C.)

GLASGOW ANNIESLAND
E.52,955   T.63.98%
† Rt. Hon. D. Dewar, *Lab.* — 20,951
Dr W. Wilson, *SNP* — 5,797
A. Brocklehurst, *C.* — 3,881
C. McGinty, *LD* — 2,453
A. Majid, *ProLife* — 374
W. Bonnar, *SSA* — 229

A. Milligan, *UK Ind.* — 86
Ms G. McKay, *Ref.* — 84
T. Pringle, *NLP* — 24
Lab. majority 15,154
(Boundary change: notional Lab.)

GLASGOW BAILLIESTON
E.51,152   T.62.27%
† J. Wray, *Lab.* — 20,925
Mrs P. Thomson, *SNP* — 6,085
M. Kelly, *C.* — 2,468
Ms S. Rainger, *LD* — 1,217
J. McVicar, *SSA* — 970
J. McClafferty, *Ref.* — 188
Lab. majority 14,840
(Boundary change: notional Lab.)

GLASGOW CATHCART
E.49,312   T.69.17%
† J. Maxton, *Lab.* — 19,158
Ms M. Whitehead, *SNP* — 6,913
A. Muir, *C.* — 4,248
C. Dick, *LD* — 2,302
Ms Z. Indyk, *ProLife* — 687
R. Stevenson, *SSA* — 458
S. Haldane, *Ref.* — 344
Lab. majority 12,245
(Boundary change: notional Lab.)

GLASGOW GOVAN
E.49,836   T.64.70%
M. Sarwar, *Lab.* — 14,216
Ms N. Sturgeon, *SNP* — 11,302
W. Thomas, *C.* — 2,839
R. Stewart, *LD* — 1,915
A. McCombes, *SSA* — 755
P. Paton, *SLU* — 325
I. Badar, *SLI* — 319
Z. J. Abbasi, *SCU* — 221
K. MacDonald, *Ref.* — 201
J. White, *BNP* — 149
Lab. majority 2,914
(Boundary change: notional Lab.)

GLASGOW KELVIN
E.57,438   T.56.85%
† G. Galloway, *Lab.* — 16,643
Ms S. White, *SNP* — 6,978
Ms E. Buchanan, *LD* — 4,629
D. McPhie, *C.* — 3,539
A. Green, *SSA* — 386
R. Grigor, *Ref.* — 282
V. Vanni, *SPGB* — 102
G. Stidolph, *NLP* — 95
Lab. majority 9,665
(Boundary change: notional Lab.)

GLASGOW MARYHILL
E.52,523   T.56.59%

† Ms M. Fyfe, *Lab.*	19,301
J. Wailes, *SNP*	5,037
Ms E. Attwooll, *LD*	2,119
S. Baldwin, *C.*	1,747
Ms L. Blair, *NLP*	651
Ms A. Baker, *SSA*	409
J. Hanif, *ProLife*	344
R. Paterson, *Ref.*	77
S. Johnstone, *SEP*	36

Lab. majority 14,264
(Boundary change: notional Lab.)

GLASGOW POLLOK
E.49,284   T.66.56%

† I. Davidson, *Lab. Co-op.*	19,653
D. Logan, *SNP*	5,862
T. Sheridan, *SSA*	3,639
E. Hamilton, *C.*	1,979
D. Jago, *LD*	1,137
Ms M. Gott, *ProLife*	380
D. Haldane, *Ref.*	152

Lab. Co-op. majority 13,791
(Boundary change: notional Lab. Co-op.)

GLASGOW RUTHERGLEN
E.50,646   T.70.14%

† T. McAvoy, *Lab. Co-op.*	20,430
I. Gray, *SNP*	5,423
R. Brown, *LD*	5,167
D. Campbell Bannerman, *C.*	3,288
G. Easton, *Ind. Lab.*	812
Ms R. Kane, *SSA*	251
Ms J. Kerr, *Ref.*	150

Lab. Co-op. majority 15,007
(Boundary change: notional Lab. Co-op.)

GLASGOW SHETTLESTON
E.47,990   T.55.87%

† D. Marshall, *Lab.*	19,616
H. Hanif, *SNP*	3,748
C. Simpson, *C.*	1,484
Ms K. Hiles, *LD*	1,061
Ms C. McVicar, *SSA*	482
R. Currie, *BNP*	191
T. Montguire, *Ref.*	151
J. Graham, *WRP*	80

Lab. majority 15,868
(Boundary change: notional Lab.)

GLASGOW SPRINGBURN
E.53,473   T.59.05%

† M. Martin, *Lab.*	22,534
J. Brady, *SNP*	5,208
M.Holdsworth, *C.*	1,893
J. Alexander, *LD*	1,349
J. Lawson, *SSA*	407
A. Keating, *Ref.*	186

Lab. majority 17,326
(Boundary change: notional Lab.)

GORDON
E.58,767   T.71.89%

† M. Bruce, *LD*	17,999
J. Porter, *C.*	11,002
R. Lochhead, *SNP*	8,435
Ms L. Kirkhill, *Lab.*	4,350
F. Pidcock, *Ref.*	459

LD majority 6,997
(Boundary change: notional C.)

GREENOCK AND INVERCLYDE
E.48,818   T.71.05%

† Dr N. Godman, *Lab.*	19,480
B. Goodall, *SNP*	6,440
R. Ackland, *LD*	4,791
H. Swire, *C.*	3,976

Lab. majority 13,040
(Boundary change: notional Lab.)

HAMILTON NORTH AND BELLSHILL
E.53,607   T.70.88%

† Dr J. Reid, *Lab.*	24,322
M. Matheson, *SNP*	7,255
G. McIntosh, *C.*	3,944
K. Legg, *LD*	1,924
R. Conn, *Ref.*	554

Lab. majority 17,067
(Boundary change: notional Lab.)

HAMILTON SOUTH
E.46,562   T.71.07%

† G. Robertson, *Lab.*	21,709
I. Black, *SNP*	5,831
R. Kilgour, *C.*	2,858
R. Pitts, *LD*	1,693
C. Gunn, *ProLife*	684
S. Brown, *Ref.*	316

Lab. majority 15,878
(Boundary change: notional Lab.)
See also page 45

INVERNESS EAST, NAIRN AND LOCHABER
E.65,701   T.72.71%

D. Stewart, *Lab.*	16,187
F. Ewing, *SNP*	13,848
S. Gallagher, *LD*	8,364
Mrs M. Scanlon, *C.*	8,355
Ms W. Wall, *Ref.*	436
M. Falconer, *Green*	354
D. Hart, *Ch. U.*	224

Lab. majority 2,339
(Boundary change: notional LD)

KILMARNOCK AND LOUDOUN
E.61,376   T.77.24%

D. Browne, *Lab.*	23,621
A. Neil, *SNP*	16,365
D. Taylor, *C.*	5,125
J. Stewart, *LD*	1,891
W. Sneddon, *Ref.*	284

W. Gilmour, *NLP* 123
Lab. majority 7,256
(April 1992, Lab. maj. 6,979)

KIRKCALDY
*E.*52,186 *T.*67.02%
† L. Moonie, *Lab. Co-op.* 18,730
S. Hosie, *SNP* 8,020
Miss C. Black, *C.* 4,779
J. Mainland, *LD* 3,031
V. Baxter, *Ref.* 413
Lab. Co-op. majority 10,710
(Boundary change: notional Lab. Co-op.)

LINLITHGOW
*E.*53,706 *T.*73.84%
† T. Dalyell, *Lab.* 21,469
K. MacAskill, *SNP* 10,631
T. Kerr, *C.* 4,964
A. Duncan, *LD* 2,331
K. Plomer, *Ref.* 259
Lab. majority 10,838
(Boundary change: notional Lab.)

LIVINGSTON
*E.*60,296 *T.*71.04%
† Rt. Hon. R. Cook, *Lab.* 23,510
P. Johnston, *SNP* 11,763
H. Craigie Halkett, *C.* 4,028
E. Hawthorn, *LD* 2,876
Ms H. Campbell, *Ref.* 444
M. Culbert, *SPGB* 213
Lab. majority 11,747
(Boundary change: notional Lab.)

MIDLOTHIAN
*E.*47,552 *T.*74.13%
† E. Clarke, *Lab.* 18,861
L. Millar, *SNP* 8,991
Miss A. Harper, *C.* 3,842
R. Pinnock, *LD* 3,235
K. Docking, *Ref.* 320
Lab. majority 9,870
(Boundary change: notional Lab.)

MORAY
*E.*58,302 *T.*68.21%
† Mrs M. Ewing, *SNP* 16,529
A. Findlay, *C.* 10,963
L. Macdonald, *Lab.* 7,886
Ms D. Storr, *LD* 3,548
P. Mieklejohn, *Ref.* 840
SNP majority 5,566
(Boundary change: notional SNP)

MOTHERWELL AND WISHAW
*E.*52,252 *T.*70.08%
F. Roy, *Lab.* 21,020
J. McGuigan, *SNP* 8,229

S. Dickson, *C.* 4,024
A. Mackie, *LD* 2,331
C. Herriot, *Soc. Lab.* 797
T. Russell, *Ref.* 218
Lab. majority 12,791
(Boundary change: notional Lab.)

OCHIL
*E.*56,572 *T.*77.40%
† M. O'Neill, *Lab.* 19,707
G. Reid, *SNP* 15,055
A. Hogarth, *C.* 6,383
Mrs A. Watters, *LD* 2,262
D. White, *Ref.* 210
I. McDonald, *D. Nat.* 104
M. Sullivan, *NLP* 65
Lab. majority 4,652
(Boundary change: notional Lab.)

ORKNEY AND SHETLAND
*E.*32,291 *T.*64.00%
* J. Wallace, *LD* 10,743
J. Paton, *Lab.* 3,775
W. Ross, *SNP* 2,624
H. Vere Anderson, *C.* 2,527
F. Adamson, *Ref.* 820
Ms C. Wharton, *NLP* 116
A. Robertson, *Ind.* 60
LD majority 6,968
(April 1992, LD maj. 5,033)

PAISLEY NORTH
*E.*49,725 *T.*68.65%
† Mrs I. Adams, *Lab.* 20,295
I. Mackay, *SNP* 7,481
K. Brookes, *C.* 3,267
A. Jelfs, *LD* 2,365
R. Graham, *ProLife* 531
E. Mathew, *Ref.* 196
Lab. majority 12,814
(Boundary change: notional Lab.)

PAISLEY SOUTH
*E.*54,040 *T.*69.12%
† G. McMaster, *Lab. Co-op.* 21,482
W. Martin, *SNP* 8,732
Ms E. McCartin, *LD* 3,500
R. Reid, *C.* 3,237
J. Lardner, *Ref.* 254
S. Clerkin, *SSA* 146
Lab. Co-op. majority 12,750
(Boundary change: notional Lab. Co-op.)
See also page 45

PERTH
*E.*60,313 *T.*73.87%
† Ms R. Cunningham, *SNP* 16,209
J. Godfrey, *C.* 13,068
D. Alexander, *Lab.* 11,036

C. Brodie, *LD*	3,583
R. MacAuley, *Ref.*	366
M. Henderson, *UK Ind.*	289

SNP majority 3,141
(Boundary change: notional C.)

RENFREWSHIRE WEST
*E.*52,348   *T.*76.00%

† T. Graham, *Lab.*	18,525
C. Campbell, *SNP*	10,546
C. Cormack, *C.*	7,387
B. MacPherson, *LD*	3,045
S. Lindsay, *Ref.*	283

Lab. majority 7,979
(Boundary change: notional Lab.)

ROSS, SKYE AND INVERNESS WEST
*E.*55,639   *T.*71.81%

† C. Kennedy, *LD*	15,472
D. Munro, *Lab.*	11,453
Mrs M. Paterson, *SNP*	7,821
Miss M. Macleod, *C.*	4,368
L. Durance, *Ref.*	535
A. Hopkins, *Green*	306

LD majority 4,019
(Boundary change: notional LD)

ROXBURGH AND BERWICKSHIRE
*E.*47,259   *T.*73.91%

† A. Kirkwood, *LD*	16,243
D. Younger, *C.*	8,337
Ms H. Eadie, *Lab.*	5,226
M. Balfour, *SNP*	3,959
J. Curtis, *Ref.*	922
P. Neilson, *UK Ind.*	202
D. Lucas, *NLP*	42

LD majority 7,906
(Boundary change: notional LD)

STIRLING
*E.*52,491   *T.*81.84%

Mrs A. McGuire, *Lab.*	20,382
† Rt. Hon. M. Forsyth, *C.*	13,971
E. Dow, *SNP*	5,752
A. Tough, *LD*	2,675
W. McMurdo, *UK Ind.*	154
Ms E. Olsen, *Value Party*	24

Lab. majority 6,411
(Boundary change: notional C.)

STRATHKELVIN AND BEARSDEN
*E.*62,974   *T.*78.94%

† S. Galbraith, *Lab.*	26,278
D. Sharpe, *C.*	9,986
G. McCormick, *SNP*	8,111
J. Morrison, *LD*	4,843
D. Wilson, *Ref.*	339
Ms J. Fisher, *NLP*	155

Lab. majority 16,292
(Boundary change: notional Lab.)

TAYSIDE NORTH
*E.*61,398   *T.*74.25%

J. Swinney, *SNP*	20,447
† W. Walker, *C.*	16,287
I. McFatridge, *Lab.*	5,141
P. Regent, *LD*	3,716

SNP majority 4,160
(Boundary change: notional C.)

TWEEDDALE, ETTRICK AND LAUDERDALE
*E.*50,891   *T.*76.64%

M. Moore, *LD*	12,178
K. Geddes, *Lab.*	10,689
A. Jack, *C.*	8,623
I. Goldie, *SNP*	6,671
C. Mowbray, *Ref.*	406
J. Hein, *Lib.*	387
D. Paterson, *NLP*	47

LD majority 1,489
(Boundary change: notional LD)

WESTERN ISLES
*E.*22,983   *T.*70.08%

* C. Macdonald, *Lab.*	8,955
Dr A. Lorne Gillies, *SNP*	5,379
J. McGrigor, *C.*	1,071
N. Mitchison, *LD*	495
R. Lionel, *Ref.*	206

Lab. majority 3,576
(April 1992, Lab. maj. 1,703)

BY-ELECTION
since general election

PAISLEY SOUTH
(6 November 1997)
*E.*54,040   *T.*42%

D. Alexander, *Lab.*	10,346
I. Blackford, *SNP*	7,615
Ms E. McCartin, *LD*	2,582
Ms S. Laidlaw, *C.*	1,643
J. Deighan, *ProLife*	578
F. Curran, *Soc. All. Fighting Corruption*	306
C. McLauchlan, *Scottish Ind. Lab.*	155
C. Herriot, *Soc. Lab.*	153
K. Blair, *NLP*	57

Lab. majority 2,731

HAMILTON SOUTH
A by-election will be held in autumn 1999 as the seat becomes vacant when George Robertson takes up his appointment as Secretary-General of NATO in October.

THE EUROPEAN PARLIAMENT

European Parliament elections take place at five-yearly intervals; the first direct elections to the Parliament were held in 1979. In mainland Britain MEPs were elected in all constituencies on a first-past-the-post basis until the elections of 10 June 1999, when a 'closed-list' regional system of proportional representation was used for the first time. Scotland constitutes a region.

Parties submitted a list of candidates for each region in their own order of preference. Voters voted for a party or an independent candidate, and the first seat in each region was allocated to the party or candidate with the highest number of votes. The rest of the seats in each region were then allocated broadly in proportion to each party's share of the vote. The Scotland region returned eight members.

British subjects and citizens of the Irish Republic are eligible for election to the European Parliament provided they are 21 or over and not subject to disqualification. Since 1994, nationals of member states of the European Union have had the right to vote in elections to the European Parliament in the UK as long as they are entered on the electoral register.

MEPs currently receive a salary from the parliaments or governments of their respective member states, set at the level of the national parliamentary salary and subject to national taxation rules (the salary of British MEPs is £47,008). A proposal that all MEPs should be paid the same rate of salary out of the EU budget, and subject to the EC tax rate, was under negotiation between the European Parliament and the Council of Ministers at the time of going to press.

SCOTTISH MEMBERS

Attwooll, Ms Elspeth M.-A. (b. 1943), LD, Scotland
* Hudghton, Ian (b. 1951), SNP, Scotland
MacCormick, Prof. D. Neil, FBA (b. 1941), SNP, Scotland
* Martin, David W. (b. 1954), Lab., Scotland
* Miller, William (b. 1954), Lab., Scotland
Purvis, John R., CBE (b. 1938), C., Scotland
Stevenson, Struan (b. 1948), C., Scotland
Taylor, Ms Catherine D. (b. 1973), Lab., Scotland

* Member of the last European Parliament
For party abbreviations, see pages 34–5

BY-ELECTION 1998–9

SCOTLAND NORTH EAST
(26 November 1998)
E. 584,061   T. 20.53%

I. Hudghton, SNP	57,445
S. Stevenson, C.	23,744
Mrs K. Walker Shaw, Lab.	22,086
K. Raffar, LD	11,753
H. Duke, SSP	2,510
R. Harper, Green	2,067

SNP majority 33,701

SCOTLAND REGION
at election on 10 June 1999
E. 3,979,845   T. 24.83%

Lab.	283,490 (28.68%)
SNP	268,528 (27.17%)
C.	195,296 (19.76%)
LD	96,971 (9.81%)
Green	57,142 (5.78%)
SSP	39,720 (4.02%)
Pro Euro C.	17,781 (1.80%)
UK Ind.	12,549 (1.27%)
Soc. Lab.	9,385 (0.95%)
BNP	3,729 (0.38%)
NLP	2,087 (0.21%)
Lower Tax	1,632 (0.17%)

Lab. majority 14,962
(June 1994, Lab. maj. 148,718)

POLITICAL PARTIES

Financial support for opposition parties has been set at £5,000 per MSP until 31 March 2000 in a draft SI laid at Westminster. The Scottish Parliament has no statutory power to overturn this level, although some MSPs are pressing for it to be reviewed by the Neill Committee as opposition parties at Westminster get £10,000 per MP. From 1 April 2000, the Scottish Parliament will set the level of financial support.

Although there are Liberal Democrat MSPs in the Executive, the party is deemed an opposition party because its members make up less than 20 per cent of the total number of ministers (four out of 22).

SCOTTISH CONSERVATIVE AND UNIONIST CENTRAL OFFICE
Suite 1/1, 14 Links Place, Leith, Edinburgh EH6 7EZ
Tel 0131-555 2900; fax 0131-555 2869
E-mail: SCUCO@Scottish.tory.org.uk
Web: http://www.conservative-party.org.uk/scottish

Chairman, R. Robertson
Deputy Chairman, Mrs K. Donald
Hon. Treasurer, D. Mitchell, CBE
Head of Campaigns and Operations, D. Canzini

SCOTTISH GREEN PARTY
14 Albany Street, Edinburgh EH1 3QB
Tel 0131-478 7896; fax 0131-478 7890
E-mail: info@scottishgreens.org.uk
Web: http://www.scottishgreens.org.uk

Party Leaders, Ms M. Coyne; Robin Harper, MSP
Convenor, G. Corbett
Treasurer, G. Farmer

SCOTTISH LABOUR PARTY
Delta House, 50 West Nile Street, Glasgow G1 2NA
Tel 0141-572 6900; fax 0141-572 2566
E-mail: general@scottish-labour.org
Web: http://www.scottish.labour.co.uk

Party Leader, Rt. Hon. Donald Dewar, MP MSP
Chair, N. Wilson
Treasurer, R. Thomson
General Secretary, A. Rowley

SCOTTISH LIBERAL DEMOCRATS
4 Clifton Terrace, Edinburgh EH12 5DR
Tel 0131-337 2314; fax 0131-337 3566
E-mail: scotlibdem@cix.co.uk
Web: http://www.scotlibdems.org.uk

Party President, R. Thomson
Party Leader, Jim Wallace, MP, MSP
Convener, I. Yuill
Treasurer, D. R. Sullivan
Chief Executive, W. Rennie

SCOTTISH NATIONAL PARTY
6 North Charlotte Street, Edinburgh EH2 4JH
Tel 0131-226 3661; fax 0131-225 9597
E-mail: snp.administration@snp.org.uk
Web: http://www.snp.org.uk

Parliamentary Party Leader, Alex Salmond, MP, MSP
Chief Whip, Bruce Crawford, MSP
National Convener, Alex Salmond, MP, MSP
Senior Vice-Convener, John Swinney, MP, MSP
National Treasurer, I. Blackford
National Secretary, Colin Campbell, MSP

SCOTTISH SOCIALIST PARTY
73 Robertson Street, Glasgow G2 8QD
Tel: 0141-221 7714; fax: 0141-221 7715
Web: http://www.scotsocialistparty.org

Convener, T. Sheridan
Treasurer, K. Baldasara
General Secretary, A. Green

DEPARTMENTS OF THE SCOTTISH EXECUTIVE

St Andrew's House, Regent Road, Edinburgh EH1 3DG
Tel: 0131-556 8400; enquiry line: 0345-741741
Fax: 0131-244 8240
E-mail: ceu@scotland.gov.uk
Web: http://www.scotland.gov.uk

The Scottish Ministers are supported by staff largely drawn from the staff of the Scottish Office, as constituted before devolution, and its agencies. On 1 July 1999 the departments of the Scottish Office transferred to the Scottish Executive and now work to the First Minister and his team. All officials of the Executive hold office under the Crown on terms and conditions of service determined in accordance with the provisions of the Civil Service Management Code and remain members of the Home Civil Service.

On 1 July 1999 the Scottish Office changed its name to the Scottish Executive and its departments were renamed; some reassignment of responsibilities also took place.

Scottish Executive Development Department – Development Department responsibilities for social inclusion, housing, local government, transport, planning and building control, European structural funds

Scottish Executive Education Department – primary and secondary education functions of Education and Industry Department; children's services functions of Social Work Services Group (to form part of the Children and Young People Group); culture (including the arts, cultural and built heritage, architectural policy); Gaelic; sports

Scottish Executive Enterprise and Lifelong Learning Department – further and higher education, lifelong learning, and business and industry functions of Education and Industry Department; the New Deal

Scottish Executive Health Department – Health Department; community care functions of the Social Work Services Group

Scottish Executive Justice Department – Home Department; Scottish Courts Administration; criminal justice social work functions of the Social Work Services Group

Scottish Executive Rural Affairs Department – Agriculture, Environment and Fisheries Department

Scottish Executive Finance – replaces Finance Division

Scottish Executive Corporate Services – central support functions, including human resources, equal opportunities, the Modernizing Government agenda

Scottish Executive Secretariat – parliamentary liaison; co-ordination of relations with UK Government; support to Scottish Ministers

The information given below reflects the situation at the time of going to press a few weeks after the Scottish Parliament and Scottish Executive had assumed their responsibilities. It is possible that some further reorganization of the Scottish Executive departments may take place. The most recent information can be obtained from the contact points at the main Scottish Executive offices at St Andrew's House.

The following includes details of the departments of the Scottish Executive; details of the executive agencies of the Scottish Executive departments can be found in the Other Government Departments and Public Bodies section.

SCOTTISH EXECUTIVE CORPORATE SERVICES

16 Waterloo Place, Edinburgh EH1 3DN
Tel: 0131-556 8400

Principal Establishment Officer,
  C. C. MacDonald, CB
Head of Personnel, D. F. Middleton

DIRECTORATE OF ADMINISTRATIVE SERVICES
Saughton House, Broomhouse Drive, Edinburgh EH11 3DX
Tel: 0131-556 8400

Director of Administrative Services,
  A. M. Brown
Chief Estates Officer, J. A. Andrew
Head of Information Technology,
  Ms M. McGinn
Director of Telecommunications,
  K. Henderson, OBE
Chief Quantity Surveyor, A. J. Wyllie

James Craig Walk, Edinburgh EH1 3BA
Head of Purchasing and Supplies, N. Bowd

SCOTTISH EXECUTIVE FINANCE

Victoria Quay, Edinburgh EH6 6QQ
Tel: 0131-556 8400

Principal Finance Officer, Dr P. S. Collings
Assistant Secretaries, M. T. S. Batho;
J. G. Henderson; D. G. N. Reid; W. T. Tait
Head of Accountancy Services Unit, I. M. Smith
Assistant Director of Finance Strategy,
I. A. McLeod

SCOTTISH EXECUTIVE SECRETARIAT

St Andrew's House, Regent Road, Edinburgh
EH1 3DG
Tel: 0131-556 8400

Head of Secretariat, R. S. B. Gordon
Constitutional Policy, J. A. Ewing
Scotland Act Implementation, W. G. Burgess
Functions and Whitehall Negotiations,
I. N. Walford
Legal Adviser, J. L. Jamieson, CBE

MANAGEMENT GROUP SUPPORT STAFF UNIT
Head of Unit, P. J. Rycroft

SCOTTISH EXECUTIVE INFORMATION
DIRECTORATE
For the Scottish Executive and certain UK
services in Scotland.

Head of Information Directorate, R. Williams

SOLICITOR'S OFFICE
Solicitor, R. M. Henderson
Deputy Solicitor, J. S. G. Maclean
Divisional Solicitors, R. Bland *(seconded to Scottish
Law Commission);* G. C. Duke;
I. H. Harvie; H. F. Macdiarmid;
J. G. S. Maclean; N. Raven;
Mrs L. A. Towers

SCOTTISH EXECUTIVE DEVELOPMENT DEPARTMENT

Victoria Quay, Edinburgh EH6 6QQ
Tel: 0131-556 8400

Secretary, K. MacKenzie
Under-Secretaries, D. J. Belfall; J. S. B. Martin
Assistant Secretaries, M. T. Affolter;
A. M. Burnside; E. C. Davidson;
J. D. Gallacher; R. A. Grant;
D. S. Henderson; Mrs D. Mellon;
W. J. R. McQueen; R. Tait
Senior Economic Adviser, C. L. Wood

PROFESSIONAL STAFF
Chief Planner, A. Mackenzie, CBE
Deputy Chief Architect, Dr J. P. Cornish
Chief Statistician, C. R. MacLean

INQUIRY REPORTERS
Robert Stevenson House, 2 Greenside Lane,
Edinburgh EH1 3AG
Tel: 0131-244 5680

Chief Reporter, R. M. Hickman
Deputy Chief Reporter, J. M. McCulloch

NATIONAL ROADS DIRECTORATE
Victoria Quay, Edinburgh EH6 6QQ
Tel: 0131-556 8400

Deputy Chief Engineers, J. A. Howison *(Roads);*
N. B. MacKenzie *(Bridges)*

SCOTTISH EXECUTIVE EDUCATION DEPARTMENT

Victoria Quay, Edinburgh EH6 6QQ
Tel: 0131-556 8400

Secretary, J. Elvidge
Under-Secretaries, D. J. Crawley;
Mrs G. Stewart
Assistant Secretaries, R. N. Irvine;
J. W. L. Lonie; S. Y. MacDonald;
A. K. MacLeod; G. McHugh;
Mrs R. Menlowe; Ms J. Morgan;
Chief Statistician, C. R. MacLean
Chief Architect, J. E. Gibbons, Ph.D., FSA Scot.
Chief Inspector of Social Work Services,
A. Skinner
Assistant Chief Inspectors, Mrs G. Ottley; D. Pia;
I. C. Robertson

HM INSPECTORS OF SCHOOLS
Senior Chief Inspector, D. A. Osler
Depute Senior Chief Inspectors, F. Crawford;
G. H. C. Donaldson
Chief Inspectors, P. Banks; J. Boyes;
Miss K. M. Fairweather; D. E. Kelso;
J. J. McDonald; A. S. McGlynn;
H. M. Stalker
There are 79 Grade 6 Inspectors.

EXECUTIVE AGENCIES
HISTORIC SCOTLAND
— *see page 59*

SCOTTISH PUBLIC PENSIONS AGENCY
— *see page 71*

SCOTTISH EXECUTIVE ENTERPRISE AND LIFELONG LEARNING DEPARTMENT

Victoria Quay, Edinburgh EH6 6QQ
Tel: 0131-556 8400

Secretary, E. Frizzell
Under-Secretaries, E. J. Weeple; M. B. Foulis
Assistant Secretaries, C. Smith; J. A. Brown;
I. McGhee; D. A. Stewart;
G. F. Dickson; C. M. Reeves

INDUSTRIAL EXPANSION
Meridian Court, 5 Cadogan Street, Glasgow
G2 6AT
Tel: 0141-248 2855

Under-Secretary, G. Robson
Industrial Adviser, D. Blair
Scientific Adviser, Prof. D. J. Tedford
Assistant Secretaries, W. Malone; J. K. Mason;
  Dr J. Rigg

LOCATE IN SCOTLAND
120 Bothwell Street, Glasgow G2 7JP
Tel: 0141-248 2700

Director, M. Togneri

SCOTTISH TRADE INTERNATIONAL
120 Bothwell Street, Glasgow G2 7JP
Tel: 0141-248 2700

Director, D. Taylor

EXECUTIVE AGENCY

STUDENT AWARDS AGENCY FOR SCOTLAND
— *see* page 72

SCOTTISH EXECUTIVE HEALTH DEPARTMENT

St Andrew's House, Regent Road, Edinburgh
EH1 3DG
Tel: 0131-556 8400

NATIONAL HEALTH SERVICE IN SCOTLAND
MANAGEMENT EXECUTIVE
Chief Executive, G. R. Scaife, CB
Director of Purchasing, Dr K. J. Woods
Director of Primary Care, Mrs A. Robson
Director of Finance, J. Aldridge
Director of Human Resources, G. Marr
Director of Nursing, Miss A. Jarvie
Director of Community Care, Ms E. Lewis
Medical Director, Dr A. Fraser
Director of Trusts, P. Wilson
Director of Information Services, NHS,
  C. B. Knox
Director of Estates, H. R. McCallum
Chief Pharmacist, W. Scott
Chief Scientist, Prof. G. R. D. Catto
Chief Dental Officer, T. R. Watkins

PUBLIC HEALTH POLICY UNIT
Head of Unit and Chief Medical Officer,
  Prof. Sir David Carter, FRCSE., FRCSGlas.,
  FRCPE
Deputy Chief Medical Officer, Dr A. Fraser
Head of Group, Mrs N. Munro
Assistant Secretary, J. T. Brown
Principal Medical Officers, Dr J. B. Louden
  (*part-time*); Dr A. MacDonald (*part-time*);
  Dr R. Skinner; Dr E. Sowler
Senior Medical Officers, Dr A. Anderson;
  Dr E. Bashford; Dr K. G. Brotherston;

Dr D. Campbell; Dr J. Cumming;
Dr B. Davis; Dr D. J. Ewing;
Dr D. Findlay; Dr G. R. Foster;
Dr A. Keel; Dr P. Madden;
Dr H. Whyte; Dr D. Will

STATE HOSPITAL
Carstairs Junction, Lanark ML11 8RP
Tel: 01555-840293; fax: 01555-840024
E-mail: info@tsh.org.uk

The State Hospital provides high security
mental health services to patients from
Scotland and Northern Ireland.
Chairman, D. N. James
General Manager, R. Manson

COMMON SERVICES AGENCY
Trinity Park House, South Trinity Road,
Edinburgh EH5 3SE
Tel: 0131-552 6255

Chairman, G. R. Scaife, CB
General Manager, Dr F. Gibb

HEALTH BOARDS
— *see* page 134

SCOTTISH EXECUTIVE JUSTICE DEPARTMENT

Saughton House, Broomhouse Drive,
Edinburgh EH11 3XD
Tel: 0131-556 8400

Secretary, J. Hamill, CB
Under-Secretaries, C. Baxter; N. G. Campbell
Assistant Secretaries, Mrs M. H. Brannan;
  Mrs M. B. Gunn; R. S. T. MacEwen
Chief Research Officer, Dr C. P. A. Levein
Senior Principal Research Officer, Mrs A. Millar

SOCIAL WORK SERVICES GROUP
James Craig Walk, Edinburgh EH1 3BA
Tel: 0131-556 8400

Under-Secretary, N. G. Campbell
Assistant Secretaries, G. A. Anderson;
  Dr J. M. Francis; Mrs V. M. Macniven

HM INSPECTORATE OF CONSTABULARY
2 Greenside Lane, Edinburgh EH1 3AH
Tel: 0131-244 5614
HM Chief Inspector of Constabulary, W. Taylor,
  QPM

SCOTTISH POLICE COLLEGE
Tullialan Castle, Kincardine, Alloa FK10 4BE
Tel: 01259-732000
Commandant, H. I. Watson, OBE, QPM

HM INSPECTORATE OF FIRE SERVICES
Saughton House, Broomhouse Drive,
Edinburgh EH11 3XD
Tel: 0131-244 2342
HM Chief Inspector of Fire Services, D. Davis,
  QFSM

SCOTTISH FIRE SERVICE TRAINING SCHOOL
Main Street, Gullane, East Lothian EH31 2HG
Tel: 01620-842236
Commandant, D. Grant, QFSM

HM CHIEF INSPECTOR OF PRISONS FOR
SCOTLAND
Saughton House, Broomhouse Drive,
Edinburgh EH11 3XD
Tel: 0131-244 8481; fax: 0131-244 8446
HM Chief Inspector of Prisons, C. Fairweather,
OBE

OFFICE OF THE SCOTTISH PARLIAMENTARY
COUNSEL
Victoria Quay, Edinburgh EH6 6QQ
Tel: 0131-556 8400

First Scottish Parliamentary Counsel,
J. C. McCluskie, CB, QC
Scottish Parliamentary Counsel, G. M. Clark;
C. A. M. Wilson
Depute Scottish Parliamentary Counsel,
J. D. Harkness; Miss M. Mackenzie
Assistant Scottish Parliamentary Counsel,
A. C. Gordon

PRIVATE LEGISLATION OFFICE UNDER THE
PRIVATE LEGISLATION PROCEDURE (SCOTLAND)
ACT 1936
50 Frederick Street, Edinburgh EH2 1EN
Tel: 0131-226 6499

Senior Counsel, G. S. Douglas, QC
Junior Counsel, N. M. P. Morrison

EXECUTIVE AGENCIES

NATIONAL ARCHIVES OF SCOTLAND
— see pages 61–2

REGISTERS OF SCOTLAND
— see page 66

SCOTTISH COURT SERVICE
— see pages 75–6

SCOTTISH PRISON SERVICE
— see pages 84–5

SCOTTISH EXECUTIVE RURAL AFFAIRS DEPARTMENT

Pentland House, 47 Robb's Loan, Edinburgh
EH14 1TY
Tel: 0131-556 8400

Secretary, J. S. Graham
Under-Secretaries, T. A. Cameron *(Agriculture);*
S. F. Hampson *(Environment)*
Fisheries Secretary, Dr P. Brady
Assistant Secretaries, I. R. Anderson;
D. R. Dickson; D. Feeley; Ms I. M. Low;
Ms J. Polley; A. J. Rushworth;

Dr P. Rycroft; G. M. D. Thomson;
J. R. Wildgoose
Chief Agricultural Officer, A. J. Robertson
Assistant Chief Agricultural Officers,
W. A. Aitken; J. Henderson; A. Robb
Chief Agricultural Economist, D. J. Greig
Chief Food and Dairy Officer, S. D. Rooke
Senior Principal Scientific Officers,
Mrs L. A. D. Turl; Dr R. Waterhouse

ENVIRONMENTAL AFFAIRS GROUP
Under-Secretary, S. F. Hampson
Assistant Secretaries, A. G. Dickson;
Ms B. Campbell
Chief Water Engineer, P. Wright
Ecological Adviser, Dr J. Miles

STRATEGY AND CO-ORDINATION UNIT
Head of Unit, A. J. Cameron

EXECUTIVE AGENCIES

FISHERIES RESEARCH SERVICES
— see page 57

INTERVENTION BOARD
— see page 60

SCOTTISH AGRICULTURAL SCIENCE AGENCY
— see page 67

SCOTTISH FISHERIES PROTECTION AGENCY
— see page 69

GENERAL REGISTER OFFICE FOR SCOTLAND
New Register House, Edinburgh EH1 3YT
Tel: 0131-334 0380; fax: 0131-314 4400
E-mail: records@gro-scotland.gov.uk
Web: http://www.open.gov.uk/gros/
groshome.htm

The General Register Office for Scotland is a department forming part of the Scottish Executive. It is the office of the Registrar-General for Scotland, who has responsibility for civil registration and the taking of censuses in Scotland and has in his custody the following records: the statutory registers of births, deaths, still births, adoptions, marriages and divorces; the old parish registers (recording births, deaths and marriages, etc., before civil registration began in 1855); and records of censuses of the population in Scotland.

Hours of public access: Monday–Friday 9–4.30. Internet access: http://www.origins.net
Registrar-General, J. N. Randall
Deputy Registrar-General, B. V. Philp
Census Manager, D. A. Orr
Heads of Branch, D. B. L. Brownlee;
R. C. Lawson; F. D. Garvie;
G. Compton; G. W. L. Jackson;
F. G. Thomas

OTHER GOVERNMENT DEPARTMENTS AND PUBLIC OFFICES

This section covers executive agencies of the Scottish Executive, regulatory bodies, tribunals and other statutory independent organizations and non-governmental public bodies. UK Civil Service departments and public bodies are included where their remit continues to extend to Scotland.

The information given below reflects the situation at the time of going to press a few weeks after the Scottish Parliament and Scottish Executive had assumed their responsibilities. It is possible that some further reorganization of the Scottish Executive departments may take place. The most recent information can be obtained from the contact points at the main Scottish Executive offices at St Andrew's House (*see* page 48).

ACCOUNTS COMMISSION FOR SCOTLAND

18 George Street, Edinburgh EH2 2QU
Tel: 0131-477 1234; fax: 0131-477 4567

The Commission was set up in 1975. It is responsible for securing the audit of the accounts of local authorities and certain joint boards and joint committees, and for value-for-money audits of authorities. In 1995 it assumed responsibility for securing the audit of National Health Service bodies in Scotland. The Commission is required to deal with reports made by the Controller of Audit on items of account contrary to law; on incorrect accounting; and on losses due to misconduct, negligence and failure to carry out statutory duties.

Members are appointed by the First Minister.
Chairman, Prof. J. P. Percy, CBE
Controller of Audit, R. W. Black
Secretary, W. F. Magee

ADJUDICATOR'S OFFICE

Haymarket House, 28 Haymarket, London SW1Y 4SP
Tel: 0171-930 2292; fax: 0171-930 2298
E-mail: adjudicators@gtnet.gov.uk
Web: http://www.open.gov.uk/adjolt/acctemo1.htm

The Adjudicator's Office investigates complaints about the way the Inland Revenue (including the Valuation Office Agency) and Customs and Excise have handled an individual's affairs.
The Adjudicator, Dame Barbara Mills, DBE, QC
Head of Office, M. Savage

ADVISORY COMMITTEE ON SCOTLAND'S TRAVELLING PEOPLE

Room 1-F, Victoria Quay, Edinburgh EH6 6QQ
Tel: 0131-244 5577; fax: 0131-244 5596

The Committee advises on issues relating to travelling people.
Chairman, R. Ashton
Secretary, vacant

ADVISORY COMMITTEE ON SITES OF SPECIAL SCIENTIFIC INTEREST

c/o Scottish Natural Heritage, 2 Anderson Place, Edinburgh EH6 5NP
Tel: 0131-446 2436; fax: 0131-446 2405

The Committee advises Scottish Natural Heritage in cases where there are sustained objections to the notification of Sites of Special Scientific Interest.
Chairman, Prof. W. Ritchie
Secretary, D. Howell

ADVISORY, CONCILIATION AND ARBITRATION SERVICE

Regional Office
Franborough House, 123–157 Bothwell Street, Glasgow G2 7JR
Tel: 0141-248 1400; fax: 0141-221 4697
Web: http://www.acas.org.uk

The Advisory, Conciliation and Arbitration Service (ACAS) promotes the improvement of industrial relations in general, provides facilities for conciliation, mediation and arbitration as means of avoiding and resolving industrial disputes, and provides advisory and information services on industrial relations matters to employers, employees and their representatives.
Director, Scotland, F. Blair

ANCIENT MONUMENTS BOARD FOR SCOTLAND

Longmore House, Salisbury Place, Edinburgh EH9 1SH
Tel: 0131-668 8764; fax: 0131-668 8765

The Ancient Monuments Board for Scotland advises the Scottish Ministers on the exercise of their functions, under the Ancient Monuments and Archaeological Areas Act 1979, of providing protection for monuments of national importance.
Chairman, Prof. M. Lynch, PH.D., FRSE, FSA Scot.

Members, M. Baughan; Ms J. Cannizzo, ph.D.;
P. Clarke, FSA; Mrs K. Dalyell, FSA Scot.;
Ms J. Harden, FSA Scot.; J. Higgitt, FSA;
R. J. Mercer, FRSE, FSA, FSA Scot.;
Prof. C. D. Morris, FRSE, FSA, FSA Scot.;
S. Peake, ph.D.; Ms A. Ritchie, OBE,
ph.D., FSA, FSA Scot.; Ms C.Swanson,
ph.D., FSA Scot.; M. Taylor; Miss L. M.
Thoms, FSA Scot.; A. Wright, FRS
Secretary, R. A. J. Dalziel
Assessor, D. J. Breeze, ph.D., FRSE, FSA, FSA Scot.

THE APPEALS SERVICE

Whittington House, 19–30 Alfred Place,
London WC1E 7LW
Tel 0171-814 6520

The Service (formerly the Independent
Tribunal Service) is responsible for the
functioning of tribunals hearing appeals
concerning child support assessments, social
security benefits and vaccine damage
payments. Judicial authority for the Service
rests with the President, while administrative
responsibility is exercised by the Appeals
Service Agency, which is an executive agency
of the Department of Social Security.
President, His Hon. Judge Michael Harris
Chief Executive, Appeals Service Agency, N. Ward

THE BANK OF ENGLAND

Threadneedle Street, London EC2R 8AH
Tel: 0171-601 4444; fax: 0171-601 4771
Web: http://www.bankofengland.co.uk

The Bank of England is the banker of the UK
Government and manages the note issue. Since
1997 its new Monetary Policy Committee has
had responsibility for setting short-term
interest rates to meet the Government's
inflation target. As the central reserve bank of
the country, the Bank keeps the accounts of
British banks, who maintain with it a
proportion of their cash resources, and of most
overseas central banks.
Governor, The Rt. Hon. E. A. J. George
Monetary Policy Committee, The Governor; the
   Deputy Governors; Prof. W. Buiter;
   Prof. C. Goodhart; Dr D. Julius;
   I. Plenderleith; J. Vickers;
   Dr S. Wadhwani
*Chief Cashier and Deputy Director, Banking and
   Market Services*, Ms M. V. Lowther

SCOTLAND AGENCY
19 St Vincent Place, Glasgow G1 2DT
Tel: 0171-601 4444; fax: 0171-601 4771
Scotland Agent, Ms J. Bulloch

BENEFITS AGENCY

Quarry House, Quarry Hill, Leeds LS2 7UA
Tel: 0113-232 4000

The Agency is an agency of the Department of
Social Security. It administers claims for and
payments of social security benefits.
Chief Executive, P. Mathison
Directors, J. Codling *(Finance)*;
   M. Fisher *(Personnel and Communications)*;
   S. Heminsley *(Strategic and Planning)*;
   A. Cleveland *(Operations Support)*;
   N. Haighton *(Projects)*

MEDICAL POLICY
Principal Medical Officers, Dr M. Aylward;
   Dr P. Dewis; Dr P. Sawney;
   Dr A. Braidwood; Dr P. Stidolph

BOUNDARY COMMISSION FOR SCOTLAND

3 Drumsheugh Gardens, Edinburgh EH3 7QJ
Tel: 0131-538 7200; fax: 0131-538 7240

The Commission is required by law to keep
the parliamentary constituencies in Scotland
under review. The latest review was completed
in 1995 and its proposals took effect at the
1997 general election. The next review is due
to be completed between 2002 and 2006.

Chairman (ex officio), The Speaker of the
   House of Commons
Deputy Chairman, The Hon. Lady Cosgrove
Secretary, R. Smith

BRITISH BROADCASTING CORPORATION

Broadcasting House, Portland Place, London
W1A 1AA
Tel: 0171-580 4468; fax: 0171-637 1630

The BBC is the UK's public broadcasting
organization. It is financed by revenue from
receiving licences for the home services and by
grant-in-aid from Parliament for the World
Service (radio). For services, *see* Media section.

BBC SCOTLAND
BBC Broadcasting House, Queen Margaret
Drive, Glasgow G12 8DG
Tel: 0141-339 8844

National Governor for Scotland, N. Drummond
Director, National and Regional Broadcasting,
   M. Thompson
Controller, BBC Scotland, J. McCormick

BRITISH WATERWAYS

Willow Grange, Church Road, Watford, Herts
WD1 3QA
Tel: 01923-226422; fax: 01923-201400
E-mail: info@canalshq.demon.co.uk
Web: http://www.britishwaterways.co.uk

British Waterways conserves and manages over 2,000 miles/3,250 km of canals and rivers in Great Britain. Its responsibilities include maintaining the waterways and structures on and around them; looking after wildlife and the waterway environment; and ensuring that canals and rivers are safe and enjoyable places to visit.
Chairman (part-time), B. Henderson, CBE
Chief Executive, D. Fletcher

SCOTTISH OFFICE
Canal House, Applecross Street, Glasgow G4 9SP
Tel: 0141-332 6936; fax: 0141-331 1688

BUILDING STANDARDS ADVISORY COMMITTEE
Construction and Building Control Group, 2-H Victoria Quay, Edinburgh EH6 6QQ
Tel: 0131-244 7440; fax: 0131-244 7454

The Committee advises the Scottish Ministers on questions relating to their functions under Part II of the Building (Scotland) Act 1959.
Chairman, Ms M. Marshall
Secretary, J. Carter

CENTRAL ADVISORY COMMITTEE ON JUSTICES OF THE PEACE (SCOTLAND)
Spur W1(E), Saughton House, Broomhouse Drive, Edinburgh EH11 3XD
Tel: 0131-244 2691; fax: 0131-244 2623

The Committee advises and makes recommendations as to problems arising in relation to the appointment and distribution of justices of the peace and the work of JPs in general and of the district court in particular.
Chairman, The Rt. Hon. Lord Cullen
Secretary, Ms J. Richardson

CERTIFICATION OFFICE FOR TRADE UNIONS AND EMPLOYERS' ASSOCIATIONS
180 Borough High Street, London SE1 1LW
Tel: 0171-210 3734/5; fax: 0171-210 3612

The Certification Office is an independent statutory authority responsible for receiving and scrutinizing annual returns from trade unions and employers' associations; for investigating allegations of financial irregularities in the affairs of a trade union or employers' association; for dealing with complaints concerning trade union elections; for ensuring observance of statutory requirements governing political funds and trade union mergers; and for certifying the independence of trade unions.
Certification Officer, E. G. Whybrew

SCOTTISH OFFICE
58 Frederick Street, Edinburgh EH2 1LN
Tel: 0131-226 3224; fax: 0131-200 1300
Assistant Certification Officer for Scotland, J. L. J. Craig

CHILD SUPPORT AGENCY
DSS Long Benton, Benton Park Road, Newcastle upon Tyne NE98 1YX
Tel: 0191-213 5000

The Agency is an agency of the Department of Social Security. It is responsible for the administration of the Child Support Act and for the assessment, collection and enforcement of maintenance payments for all new cases. From June 1999 the Chief Executive took over the responsibilities of the Chief Child Support Officer when that office was abolished.
Chief Executive, Ms F. Boardman
Directors, M. Davison; C. Peters; M. Isaacs; T. Read

CIVIL AVIATION AUTHORITY
— *see* Scottish Oceanic Area Control Centre

CIVIL SERVICE COLLEGE
Branch Offices
Suite 19, 1 St Colme Street, Edinburgh EH3 6AA
Tel: 0131-220 8267; fax: 0131-220 8367
199 Cathedral Street, Glasgow G4 0QU
Tel: 0141-553 6021; fax: 0141-553 6171

The College provides training in management and professional skills for the public and private sectors.

COMMISSION FOR RACIAL EQUALITY
Regional Office
Hanover House, 45–51 Hanover Street, Edinburgh EH2 2PJ
Tel: 0131-226 5186; fax: 0131-226 5243

The Commission was established in 1977, under the Race Relations Act 1976, to work towards the elimination of discrimination and promote equality of opportunity and good relations between different racial groups. It is funded by the Home Office.
Director, Scottish and North-East Region, E. Seward

COMMISSIONER FOR LOCAL ADMINISTRATION IN SCOTLAND

23 Walker Street, Edinburgh EH3 7HX
Tel: 0131-225 5300; fax: 0131-225 9495

The Local Commissioner for Scotland is the local government ombudsman for Scotland, responsible for investigating complaints from members of the public against local authorities and certain other authorities. The Commissioner is appointed by the Crown on the recommendation of the First Minister.
Local Commissioner, F. C. Marks, OBE
Deputy Commissioner and Secretary,
  Ms J. H. Renton

COMPANIES HOUSE (SCOTLAND)

37 Castle Terrace, Edinburgh EH1 2EB
Tel: 0131-535 5800; fax: 0131-535 5820
Web: http://www.companieshouse.gov.uk

Companies House is an executive agency of the Department of Trade and Industry. It incorporates companies, registers company documents and provides company information.
Registrar for Scotland, J. Henderson

EDINBURGH SEARCH ROOM
Tel: 0131-535 5868; fax: 0131-535 5820

GLASGOW SATELLITE OFFICE
7 West George Street, Glasgow G2 1BQ
Tel: 0141-221 5513

COPYRIGHT TRIBUNAL

Harmsworth House, 13–15 Bouverie Street, London EC4Y 8DP
Tel: 0171-596 6510; fax: 0171-596 6526

The Copyright Tribunal resolves disputes over copyright licences, principally where there is collective licensing.
  The chairman and two deputy chairmen are appointed by the Lord Chancellor. Up to eight ordinary members are appointed by the Secretary of State for Trade and Industry.
Chairman, C. P. Tootal
Secretary, Miss J. E. M. Durdin

COURT OF THE LORD LYON

HM New Register House, Edinburgh EH1 3YT
Tel: 0131-556 7255; fax: 0131-557 2148

The Court of the Lord Lyon is the Scottish Court of Chivalry (including the genealogical jurisdiction of the Ri-Sennachie of Scotland's Celtic Kings). The Lord Lyon King of Arms has jurisdiction, subject to appeal to the Court of Session and the House of Lords, in questions of heraldry and the right to bear arms. The Court also administers the Scottish Public Register of All Arms and Bearings and the Public Register of All Genealogies. Pedigrees are established by decrees of Lyon Court and by letters patent. As Royal Commissioner in Armory, the Lord Lyon grants patents of arms (which constitute the grantee and heirs noble in the Noblesse of Scotland) to 'virtuous and well-deserving' Scots and to petitioners (personal or corporate) in the Queen's overseas realms of Scottish connection, and issues birthbrieves.
Lord Lyon King of Arms, Sir Malcolm Innes of Edingight, KCVO, WS

HERALDS
Albany, J. A. Spens, MVO, RD, WS
Rothesay, Sir Crispin Agnew of Lochnaw, Bt., QC
Ross, C. J. Burnett, FSA Scot.

PURSUIVANTS
Kintyre, J. C. G. George, FSA Scot.
Unicorn, Alastair Campbell of Airds, FSA Scot.
Carrick, Mrs C. G. W. Roads, MVO, FSA Scot.

Lyon Clerk and Keeper of Records,
  Mrs C. G. W. Roads, MVO, FSA Scot.
Procurator-Fiscal, D. F. Murby, WS
Herald Painter, Mrs J. Phillips
Macer, A. M. Clark

CRIMINAL INJURIES COMPENSATION AUTHORITY AND BOARD

Tay House, 300 Bath Street, Glasgow G2 4JR
Tel: 0141-331 2726; fax: 0141-331 2287

All applications for compensation for personal injury arising from crimes of violence in Scotland are dealt with by the Board (applications received up to 31 March 1996) or the Authority (applications received since 1 April 1996). Applications received on or after 1 April 1996 are assessed under a tariff-based scheme by the Criminal Injuries Compensation Authority (CICA); there is a separate avenue of appeal to the Criminal Injuries Compensation Appeals Panel (CICAP).
Chairman of the Criminal Injuries Compensation Board (part-time), The Lord Carlisle of Bucklow, PC, QC
Director of the Board and Chief Executive of the Criminal Injuries Compensation Authority, H. Webber
Chairman of the Criminal Injuries Compensation Appeals Panel, M. Lewer, QC
Secretary to the Panel, Miss V. Jenson

CROFTERS COMMISSION

4–6 Castle Wynd, Inverness IV2 3EQ
Tel: 01463-663450; fax: 01463-711820
E-mail: crofters_commission@cali.co.uk

The Crofters Commission is a non-departmental public body established in 1955. It advises the Scottish Ministers on all matters relating to crofting, and works with other organizations and with communities to develop and promote thriving crofting communities and simplify legislation. It administers the Crofting Counties Agricultural Grants Scheme, Croft Entrant Scheme, and livestock improvement schemes.
Chairman, I. MacAskill
Secretary, M. Grantham

CROWN ESTATE COMMISSIONERS

Scottish Estates
10 Charlotte Square, Edinburgh EH2 4BR
Tel: 0131-226 7241; fax: 0131-220 1366
Web: http://www.crownestate.co.uk

The land revenues of the Crown in Scotland were transferred to the predecessors of the Crown Estate Commissioners in 1833. The Scottish office manages a variety of agricultural, forest and marine resources.
Crown Estate Receiver for Scotland and Head of Scottish Estates, M. Cunliffe

CUSTOMS AND EXCISE

Scottish Collection
44 York Place, Edinburgh EH1 3JW
Tel: 0131-469 2000; fax: 0131-469 7340
Web: http://www.hmce.gov.uk *and*
http://www.open.gov.uk/customs/c&ehome.htm

HM Customs and Excise is responsible for collecting and administering customs and excise duties and VAT, and advises the Chancellor of the Exchequer on any matters connected with them. The Department is also responsible for preventing and detecting the evasion of revenue laws and for enforcing a range of prohibitions and restrictions on the importation of certain classes of goods. In addition, the Department undertakes certain agency work on behalf of other departments, including the compilation of UK overseas trade statistics from customs import and export documents.
Collector of HM Customs and Excise for Scotland, I. Mackay

DATA PROTECTION TRIBUNAL

c/o The Home Office, Queen Anne's Gate, London SW1H 9AT
Tel 0171-273 3755

The Data Protection Tribunal determines appeals against decisions of the Data Protection Registrar (*see* Office of the Data Protection Registrar, below). The chairman and deputy chairman are appointed by the Lord Chancellor and must be legally qualified. Lay members are appointed by the Home Secretary to represent the interests of data users or data subjects.

A tribunal consists of a legally-qualified chairman sitting with equal numbers of the lay members appointed to represent the interests of data users and data subjects.
Chairman, J. A. C. Spokes, QC
Secretary, R. Hartley

DEER COMMISSION FOR SCOTLAND

Knowsley, 82 Fairfield Road, Inverness IV3 5LH
Tel: 01463-231751; fax: 01463-712931
E-mail: deercom@aol.com

The Deer Commission for Scotland has the general functions of furthering the conservation, control and sustainable management of deer in Scotland. It has the statutory duty, with powers, to prevent damage to agriculture, forestry and the habitat by deer. It is funded by the Scottish Executive.
Chairman (part-time), A. Raven
Members, G. Campbell; R. Callander;
    R. Cooke; R. Dennis; J. Duncan-Millar;
    S. Gibbs; G. Lewis; Dr J. Milne;
    J. MacKintosh; Dr P. Ratcliffe
Director, A. Rinning
Technical Director, R. W. Youngson

DRIVER AND VEHICLE LICENSING AGENCY

Longview Road, Morriston, Swansea SA6 7JL
Tel: 01792-772151 *(drivers)*; 01792-772134 *(vehicles)*

The Agency is an executive agency of the Department of the Environment, Transport and the Regions. It issues driving licences, registers and licenses vehicles, and collects excise duty.
Chief Executive, Dr S. J. Ford

EDINBURGH VEHICLE REGISTRATION OFFICE
Saughton House, Broomhouse Drive, Edinburgh EH11 3XE
Tel: 0131-455 7919; fax: 0131-443 2478
Scottish Area Manager, D. Drury

DRIVING STANDARDS AGENCY

Stanley House, Talbot Street, Nottingham NG1 5GU
Tel: 0115-901 2500; fax: 0115-955 7334

The Agency is an executive agency of the Department of the Environment, Transport and the Regions. Its role is to carry out driving tests and approve driving instructors.
Chief Executive, vacant

EMPLOYMENT APPEAL TRIBUNAL
Divisional Office
52 Melville Street, Edinburgh EH3 7HF
Tel: 0131-225 3963

The Employment Appeal Tribunal hears appeals on a question of law arising from any decision of an employment tribunal. A tribunal consists of a high court judge and two lay members, one from each side of industry.
Scottish Chairman, The Hon. Lord Johnston
Registrar, Miss V. J. Selio

THE EMPLOYMENT SERVICE
Argyll House, 3 Lady Lawson Street,
Edinburgh EH3 9SD
Tel: 0131-229 9191; fax: 0131-221 4004
Web: http://www.employmentservice.gov.uk

The Employment Service is an executive agency of the Department for Education and Employment. Its aims are to contribute to high levels of employment and growth by helping all people without a job to find work and by helping employers to fill their vacancies, and to help individuals lead rewarding working lives.
Director for Scotland, A. R. Brown

EMPLOYMENT TRIBUNALS
Central Office (Scotland)
Eagle Building, 215 Bothwell Street, Glasgow
G2 7TS
Tel: 0141-204 0730

Employment tribunals deal with matters of employment law, redundancy, dismissal, contract disputes, sexual, racial and disability discrimination, and related areas of dispute which may arise in the workplace. A central registration unit records all applications and maintains a public register at Southgate Street, Bury St Edmunds, Suffolk IP33 2AQ.
  Chairmen are appointed by the Lord President of the Court of Session and lay members by the Secretary of State for Trade and Industry.
President, Mrs D. Littlejohn, CBE

EQUAL OPPORTUNITIES COMMISSION
Scottish Office
Stock Exchange House, 7 Nelson Mandela Place, Glasgow G2 1QW
Tel: 0141-248 5833; fax: 0141-248 5834
E-mail: info@eoc.org.uk
Web: http://www.eoc.org.uk

The Commission works towards the elimination of discrimination on the grounds of sex or marital status and to promote equality of opportunity between men and women generally. It is responsible to the Department for Education and Employment.
Director, Scotland, Ms M. Alexander

EXTRA PARLIAMENTARY PANEL
The Scotland Office, Dover House,
Whitehall, London SW1A 2AU
Tel: 0171-270 6758; fax: 0171-270 6730

The Panel hears evidence for and against draft provision orders in private legislation procedure at an inquiry, and makes recommendations as to whether an order should proceed, be amended or be refused. This is a reserved function and the secretariat for the panel is based at the Scotland Office.

THE FISHERIES COMMITTEE
Pentland House, Robb's Loan, Edinburgh
EH14 1TY
Tel: 0131-244 6229

The Committee advises and assists the Scottish Ministers and any person engaging in, or proposing to engage in, the generation of hydro-electric power on any question relating to the effect of hydro-electric works on fisheries or stocks of fish.
Chairman, R. McGillivray
Secretary, Miss J. Dunn

FISHERIES RESEARCH SERVICES
Marine Laboratory, PO Box 101, Victoria Road, Aberdeen AB11 9DB
Tel: 01224-876544; fax: 01224-295511

The Agency provides scientific information and advice on marine and freshwater fisheries, aquaculture and the protection of the aquatic environment and its wildlife.
Director, Dr A. D. Hawkins, FRSE
Deputy Director, Dr J. M. Davies

FRESHWATER FISHERIES LABORATORY
Faskally, Pitlochry, Perthshire PH6 5LB
Tel: 01796-472060

Senior Principal Scientific Officers,
  Dr R. M. Cook; Dr J. M. Davies;
  Dr A. E. Ellis; R. G. J. Shelton;
  Dr R. Stagg; Dr P. A. Stewart;
  Dr C. S. Wardle
Inspector of Salmon and Freshwater Fisheries for Scotland, D. A. Dunkley

FORESTRY COMMISSION

231 Corstorphine Road, Edinburgh EH12 7AT
Tel: 0131-334 0303; fax: 0131-334 3047

The Forestry Commission is the government department responsible for forestry policy in Great Britain. It reports directly to forestry ministers to whom it is responsible for advice on forestry policy and for the implementation of that policy. The Scottish Ministers have responsibility for forestry in Scotland, the Minister of Agriculture, Fisheries and Food for forestry in England, and the National Assembly for Wales for forestry in Wales. For matters affecting forestry in Britain as a whole, all three ministers have equal responsibility but the Minister of Agriculture, Fisheries and Food takes the lead.

The Commission's principal objectives are to protect Britain's forests and woodlands; expand Britain's forest area; enhance the economic value of the forest resources; conserve and improve the biodiversity, landscape and cultural heritage of forests and woodlands; develop opportunities for woodland recreation; and increase public understanding of and community participation in forestry.
Chairman (part-time), Sir Peter Hutchison, Bt.,
　CBE
Director-General, D. J. Bills
Secretary to the Commissioners, F. Strang

Forestry Commission National Office for Scotland

231 Corstorphine Road, Edinburgh EH12 7AT
Tel: 0131-334 0303; fax: 0131-314 6152
Chief Conservator, D. Henderson-Howat

FOREST ENTERPRISE
231 Corstorphine Road, Edinburgh EH12 7AT
Tel: 0131-334 0303

Forest Enterprise, a trading body operating as an executive agency of the Commission, manages its forestry estate on a multi-use basis.
Chief Executive, Dr B. McIntosh

Forest Enterprise Scotland

North – 21 Church Street, Inverness IV1 1EL.
　Tel: 01463-232811; fax: 01463-243846
South – 55–57 Moffat Road, Dumfries DG1 1NP.
　Tel: 01387-2724400; fax: 01387-251491

FOREST RESEARCH
Alice Holt Lodge, Wrecclesham, Farnham, Surrey GU10 4LU
Tel: 01420-22255

Forest Research provides research, development and advice to the forestry industry in support of the development and implementation of forestry policy.
Chief Executive, J. Dewar

Northern Research Station

Roslin, Midlothian EH25 9SY
Tel: 0131-445 2176

HEALTH AND SAFETY EXECUTIVE

Scotland Office
Belford House, 59 Belford Road, Edinburgh EH4 3UE
Tel: 0131-247 2000; fax: 0131-247 2121

The Health and Safety Executive enforces health and safety law in the majority of industrial premises. The Executive advises the Health and Safety Commission in its major task of laying down safety standards through regulations and practical guidance for many industrial processes. The Executive is also the licensing authority for nuclear installations and the reporting officer on the severity of nuclear incidents in Britain.

HM INSPECTORATE OF MINES
Daniel House, Trinity Road, Bootle L20 7HE
Tel: 0151-951 4000; fax: 0151-951 3758
HM Chief Inspector of Mines, B. Langdon

NUCLEAR SAFETY DIRECTORATE
Rose Court, 2 Southwark Bridge, London SE1 9HS
Tel: 0171-717 6000; fax: 0171-717 6717
HM Chief Inspector of Nuclear Installations,
　Dr L. G. Williams

RAILWAY INSPECTORATE
Rose Court, 2 Southwark Bridge, London SE1 9HS
Tel: 0171-717 6000; fax: 0171-717 6717
HM Chief Inspecting Officer of Railways, V. Coleman

HEALTH APPOINTMENTS ADVISORY COMMITTEE

Room 181, St Andrews House, Edinburgh EH1 3DG
Tel: 0131-244 2579

The Committee advises on non-executive appointments to health boards, NHS Trusts and health non-departmental public bodies.
Chairman, N. Irons, CBE
Secretary, Mrs E. Gray

HERITAGE LOTTERY FUND (SCOTLAND)

28 Thistle Street, Edinburgh EH2 1EN
Tel: 0131-225 9450; fax: 0131-225 9454
Web: http://www.hlf.org.uk

The Heritage Lottery Fund is the designated distributor of the heritage share of proceeds

from the National Lottery. The Scottish office receives and assesses all applications for projects based in Scotland. A Committee for Scotland makes decisions on grant requests up to £1 million; the main board of trustees in London is responsible for decisions on larger applications, with input from the Committee for Scotland.
Chairman, Committee for Scotland, Sir Angus Grossart, CBE
Manager, Scotland, C. McLean

HIGHLANDS AND ISLANDS ENTERPRISE

Bridge House, 20 Bridge Street, Inverness IV1 1QR
Tel: 01463-234171; fax: 01463-244241
E-mail: hie.General@hient.co.uk
Web: http://www.hie.co.uk

Highlands and Islands Enterprise (HIE) was set up under the Enterprise and New Towns (Scotland) Act 1991. Its role is to design, direct and deliver enterprise development, training, environmental and social projects and services. HIE is made up of a strategic core body and ten local enterprise companies (*see* pages 193–4) to which many of its individual functions are delegated.
Chairman, Dr J. Hunter
Chief Executive, I. A. Robertson, CBE

HILL FARMING ADVISORY COMMITTEE FOR SCOTLAND

c/o Room 239, Pentland House, Robb's Loan, Edinburgh EH14 1TW
Tel: 0131-244 6417; fax: 0131-244 6006

The Committee advises the First Minister on the exercise of his powers under the Hill Farming Act.
Chairman, T. A. Cameron
Secretary, Mrs A. Quirie

HISTORIC BUILDINGS COUNCIL FOR SCOTLAND

Longmore House, Salisbury Place, Edinburgh EH9 1SH
Tel: 0131-668 8600; fax: 0131-668 8788
Web: http://www.historic-scotland.go.uk

The Historic Buildings Council for Scotland is the advisory body to the Scottish Ministers on matters related to buildings of special architectural or historical interest and in particular to proposals for awards by them of grants for the repair of buildings of outstanding architectural or historical interest or lying within outstanding conservation areas.
Chairman, Sir Raymond Johnstone, CBE
Members, R. Cairns; Mrs P. Chalmers;

Mrs A. Dundas-Bekker; Dr J. Frew; D. Gauci; J. Hunter Blair; E. Jamieson; K. Martin; Revd C. Robertson; Mrs P. Robertson; Ms F. Sinclair
Secretary, Ms S. Adams

HISTORIC SCOTLAND

Longmore House, Salisbury Place, Edinburgh EH9 1SH
Tel: 0131-668 8600; fax: 0131-668 8699
Web: http://www.historic-scotland.gov.uk

Historic Scotland is an executive agency of the Scottish Executive Education Department. The agency's role is to protect Scotland's historic monuments, buildings and lands, and to promote public understanding and enjoyment of them.
Chief Executive, G. N. Munro
Directors, F. J. Lawrie; I. Maxwell; B. Naylor; B. O'Neil; L. Wilson
Chief Inspector of Ancient Monuments, Dr D. J. Breeze
Chief Inspector, Historic Buildings, R. Emerson, FSA, FSA Scot.

IMMIGRATION APPELLATE AUTHORITIES

Taylor House, 88 Rosebery Avenue, London EC1R 4QU
Tel: 0171-862 4200

The Immigration Appeal Adjudicators hear appeals from immigration decisions concerning the need for, and refusal of, leave to enter or remain in the UK, refusals to grant asylum, decisions to make deportation orders and directions to remove persons subject to immigration control from the UK. The Immigration Appeal Tribunal hears appeals direct from decisions to make deportation orders in matters concerning conduct contrary to the public good, and from refusals to grant asylum. Its principal jurisdiction is, however, the hearing of appeals from adjudicators by the party who is aggrieved by the decision. Appeals are subject to leave being granted by the tribunal.
An adjudicator sits alone. The tribunal sits in divisions of three, normally a legally qualified member and two lay members.

Immigration Appeal Tribunal
President, The Hon. Mr Justice Collins
Vice-Presidents, Mrs J. Chatwani; A. F. Hatt; M. Rapinet; A. O'Brien-Quinn

Immigration Appeal Adjudicators
Chief Adjudicator, His Hon. Judge Dunn, QC
Deputy Chief Adjudicator, J. Latter

INDEPENDENT REVIEW SERVICE FOR THE SOCIAL FUND

4th Floor, Centre City Podium, 5 Hill Street, Birmingham B5 4UB
Tel: 0121-606 2100; fax: 0121-606 2180

The Social Fund Commissioner is appointed by the Secretary of State for Social Security. The Commissioner appoints Social Fund Inspectors, who provide an independent review of decisions made by Social Fund Officers in the Benefits Agency of the Department of Social Security.
Social Fund Commissioner, J. Scampion

INDEPENDENT TELEVISION COMMISSION (SCOTLAND)

123 Blythswood Street, Glasgow G2 2AN
Tel: 0141-226 4436; fax: 0141-226 4682
Web: http://www.itc.org.uk

The Independent Television Commission is responsible for licensing and regulating all commercially funded television services broadcast from the UK. Members are appointed by the Secretary of State for Culture, Media and Sport.
Head of ITC (Scotland) and Controller, Regions, B. Marjoribanks

INLAND REVENUE (SCOTLAND)

The Board of Inland Revenue administers and collects direct taxes and advises the Chancellor of the Exchequer on policy questions involving them. The Department's Valuation Office is an executive agency responsible for valuing property for tax purposes.

REGIONAL EXECUTIVE OFFICE (INCOME TAXES)
Clarendon House, 114–116 George Street, Edinburgh EH2 4LH
Tel: 0131-473 4000
Director, I. S. Gerrie

CAPITAL TAXES OFFICE (SCOTLAND)
Mulberry House, 16 Picardy Place, Edinburgh EH1 3NF
Tel: 0131-556 8511; fax: 0131-556 9894
Registrar, Mrs J. Templeton

EDINBURGH STAMP OFFICE
16 Picardy Place, Edinburgh EH1 3NF
Tel: 0131-556 8998

FINANCIAL INTERMEDIARIES AND CLAIMS OFFICE (SCOTLAND)
Trinity Park House, South Trinity Road, Edinburgh EH5 3SD
Tel: 0131-551 8127
Assistant Director, Ms L. Clayton

SOLICITOR'S OFFICE (SCOTLAND)
Clarendon House, 114–116 George Street, Edinburgh EH2 4LH
Tel: 0131-473 4053; fax: 0131-473 4143
Solicitor, I. K. Laing

VALUATION OFFICE AGENCY
50 Frederick Street, Edinburgh EH2 1NG
Tel: 0131-465 0700; fax: 0131-465 0799
Chief Valuer, Scotland, A. Ainslie

INTERVENTION BOARD

PO Box 69, Reading RG1 3YD
Tel: 0118-958 3626; fax: 0118-953 1370

The Intervention Board is an executive agency of the four agriculture ministries in the UK; in Scotland it is an agency of the Scottish Executive Rural Affairs Department. It is responsible for the implementation of European Union regulations covering the market support arrangements of the Common Agricultural Policy. Members are appointed by and are responsible to the four agriculture ministers.
Chairman, I. Kent
Chief Executive, G. Trevelyan

REGIONAL VERIFICATION OFFICE
Room E1/5, Saughton House, Broomhouse Drive, Edinburgh EH11 3XA
Tel: 0131-244 8382; fax: 0131-244 8117
Regional Verification Officer, P. R. Drummond

JUDICIAL COMMITTEE OF THE PRIVY COUNCIL

Downing Street, London SW1A 2AJ
Tel: 0171-270 0483

Following devolution, the Judicial Committee of the Privy Council assumes a new role as Scotland's principal constitutional court and will be the final arbiter in disputes between the UK and Scottish Parliaments regarding legislative competence.

The members of the Judicial Committee include the Lord Chancellor, the Lords of Appeal in Ordinary, other Privy Counsellors who hold or have held high judicial office and certain judges from the Commonwealth.
Registrar of the Privy Council, J. A. C. Watherston
Chief Clerk, F. G. Hart

JUSTICES OF THE PEACE ADVISORY COMMITTEES

c/o Spur W1(E), Saughton House, Broomhouse Drive, Edinburgh EH11 3XD
Tel: 0131-244 2222; fax: 0131-244 2623

The committees, of which there are 32, keep under review the strength of the Commissions of the Peace in Scotland and advise on the appointment of new justices of the peace. Each committee has its own chairman and secretary. The Scottish Executive provides central services to the committees.

LANDS TRIBUNAL FOR SCOTLAND

1 Grosvenor Crescent, Edinburgh EH12 5ER
Tel: 0131-225 7996

The Lands Tribunal for Scotland determines questions relating to the valuation of land, rating appeals from valuation tribunals, the discharge or modification of restrictive covenants, compulsory purchase orders, and questions relating to tenants' rights. The president is appointed by the Lord President of the Court of Session.
President, The Hon. Lord McGhie, QC
Members, J. Devine, FRICS; A. R. MacLeary, FRICS
Members (part-time), Sheriff A. C. Henry; R. A. Edwards, CBE, WS
Clerk, N. M. Tainsh

LOCAL GOVERNMENT BOUNDARY COMMISSION FOR SCOTLAND

3 Drumsheugh Gardens, Edinburgh EH3 7QJ
Tel: 0131-538 7510; fax: 0131-538 7511

The Commission keeps under review the boundaries of local government administrative and electoral areas.
Chairman, The Hon. Lord Osborne
Secretary, R. Smith

LORD ADVOCATE'S OFFICE

Crown Office, 25 Chambers Street, Edinburgh EH1 1LA
Tel: 0131-226 2626; fax: 0131-226 6910

Lord Advocate, The Lord Hardie, QC
  Private Secretary, J. Gibbons
Solicitor-General for Scotland, Colin Boyd, QC
  Private Secretary, J. Gibbons
Legal Secretary to the Law Officers,
  P. J. Layden, TD

MARITIME AND COASTGUARD AGENCY

Spring Place, 105 Commercial Road, Southampton SO15 1EG
Tel: 01703-329100

The Agency is an executive agency of the Department of the Environment, Transport and the Regions, formed in 1998 by the merger of the Coastguard Agency and the Marine Safety Agency. Its role is to develop, promote and enforce high standards of marine safety; to minimize loss of life amongst seafarers and coastal users; and to minimize pollution from ships of the sea and coastline.
Chief Executive, M. Storey
Chief Coastguard, J. Astbury

HM COASTGUARD

North and East Scotland Search and Rescue Region

HM Coastguard, Marine House, Blaikies Quay, Aberdeen AB11 5PB
Tel: 01224-592275; fax: 01224-584716
Regional Inspector, R. Crowther

West of Scotland and Northern Ireland Search and Rescue Region

HM Coastguard, Navy Buildings, Eldon Street, Greenock PA16 7QY
Tel: 01475-784621; fax: 01475-724006
Regional Inspector, B. Cunningham

MENTAL WELFARE COMMISSION FOR SCOTLAND

K Floor, Argyle House, 3 Lady Lawson Street, Edinburgh EH3 9SH
Tel: 0131-222 6111

The Commission protects the mentally disordered by the investigation of irregularities and by visiting patients in hospitals and in the community, and reports as appropriate to the relevant authorities.
Chairman, Sir William Reid, KCB
Vice-Chairman, Mrs N. Bennie
Commissioners (part-time), C. Campbell, QC;
  Mrs F. Cotter; W. Gent; Dr P. Jauhar;
  Dr S. Jiwa; Dr E. McCall-Smith;
  D. J. Macdonald; Dr J. Morrow;
  M. D. Murray; Dr L. Pollock; A. Robb;
  Mrs M. Ross; Dr M. Thomas;
  Dr M. Whoriskey
Director, Dr J. A. T. Dyer

NATIONAL ARCHIVES OF SCOTLAND

HM General Register House, Edinburgh EH1 3YY
Tel: 0131-535 1314; fax: 0131-535 1360
E-mail: research@nas.gov.uk

The history of the national archives of Scotland can be traced back to the 13th century. The National Archives of Scotland (formerly the Scottish Record Office) is an executive agency of the Scottish Executive Justice Department. It keeps the administrative records of pre-Union Scotland, the registers of central and local courts of law, the public registers of property rights and legal documents, and many collections of local and church records and private archives. Certain groups of records, mainly the modern records of government departments in Scotland, the Scottish railway records, the plans collection, and private archives of an industrial or commercial nature, are preserved in the branch repository at the West Register House in Charlotte Square. The National Register of Archives (Scotland) is based in the West Register House.

The search rooms in both buildings are open Monday–Friday, 9–4.45. A permanent exhibition at the West Register House and changing exhibitions at the General Register House are open to the public on weekdays, 10–4.

Keeper of the Records of Scotland, P. M. Cadell
Deputy Keeper, Dr P. D. Anderson

NATIONAL AUDIT OFFICE

22 Melville Street, Edinburgh EH3 7NS
Tel: 0131-244 2739; fax: 0131-244 2721
E-mail: edin.nao@gtnet.gov.uk
Web: http://www.open.gov.uk/nao.home.htm

The National Audit Office provides independent information, advice and assurance to Parliament and the public about all aspects of the financial operations of government departments and many other bodies receiving public funds. It does this by examining and certifying the accounts of these organizations and by regularly publishing reports to Parliament on the results of its value-for-money investigations of the economy, efficiency and effectiveness with which public resources have been used. The National Audit Office is also the auditor by agreement of the accounts of certain international and other organizations. In addition, the Office authorizes the issue of public funds to government departments.

Director, Value-for-Money Audit, A. Roberts
Director, Financial Audit, R. Frith

NATIONAL GALLERIES OF SCOTLAND

The Mound, Edinburgh EH2 2EL
Tel: 0131-624 6200; fax: 0131-343 3250
E-mail: pressinfo@natgalscot.ac.uk
Web: http://www.natgalscot.ac.uk

The National Galleries of Scotland comprise the National Gallery of Scotland, the Scottish National Portrait Gallery, the Scottish National Gallery of Modern Art and the Dean Gallery. There are also outstations at Paxton House, Berwickshire, and Duff House, Banffshire. Total government grant-in-aid for 1999–2000 is £10.197 million.

Trustees

Chairman, The Countess of Airlie, CVO
Trustees, Ms V. Atkinson; J. H. Blair;
G. Gemmell, CBE; Lord Gordon of Strathblane, CBE; A. Leitch; Prof. C. Lodder; Dr I. McKenzie Smith, OBE; Dr M. Shea; G. Weaver; Prof. I. Whyte

Officers

Director, T. Clifford
Keeper of Conservation, M. Gallagher
Head of Press and Information, Mrs A. M. Wagener
Keeper of Education, M. Cassin
Registrar, Miss A. Buddle
Secretary, Ms S. Edwards
Buildings, R. Galbraith
Keeper, National Gallery of Scotland, M. Clarke
Keeper, Scottish National Portrait Gallery, J. Holloway
Curator of Photography, Miss S. F. Stevenson
Keeper, Scottish National Gallery of Modern Art and of Dean Gallery, R. Calvocoressi

NATIONAL HEALTH SERVICE TRIBUNAL (SCOTLAND)

66 Queen Street, Edinburgh EH2 4NE
Tel: 0131-226 4771

The tribunal considers representations that the continued inclusion of a doctor, dentist, optometrist or pharmacist on a health board's list would be prejudicial to the efficiency of the service concerned. The tribunal sits when required and is composed of a chairman, one lay member, and one practitioner member drawn from a representative professional panel. The chairman is appointed by the Lord President of the Court of Session, and the lay member and the members of the professional panel are appointed by the First Minister.

Chairman, M. G. Thomson, QC
Lay member, J. D. M. Robertson
Clerk, D. G. Brash, WS

NATIONAL LIBRARY OF SCOTLAND

George IV Bridge, Edinburgh EH1 1EW
Tel: 0131-226 4531; fax: 0131-622 4803
E-mail: enquiries@nls.uk
Web: http://www.nls.uk

The Library, which was founded as the Advocates' Library in 1682, became the National Library of Scotland in 1925. It is funded by the Scottish Executive. It contains about six million books and pamphlets, 18,000 current periodicals, 230 newspaper titles and 100,000 manuscripts. It has an unrivalled Scottish collection.

The Reading Room is for reference and research which cannot conveniently be pursued elsewhere. Admission is by ticket issued to an approved applicant.

Opening hours

Reading Room, weekdays, 9.30–8.30 (Wednesday, 10–8.30); Saturday 9.30–1
Map Library, weekdays, 9.30–5 (Wednesday, 10–5); Saturday 9.30–1
Exhibition, weekdays, 10–5; Saturday 10–5; Sunday 2–5
Scottish Science Library, weekdays, 9.30–5 (Wednesday, 10–8.30)

Chairman of the Trustees, The Earl of Crawford and Balcarres, PC
Librarian and Secretary to the Trustees, I. D. McGowan
Secretary of the Library, M. C. Graham
Keeper of Printed Books, Ms A. Matheson, OBE, Ph.D.
Keeper of Manuscripts, I. C. Cunningham
Director of Public Services, A. M. Marchbank, Ph.D.

NATIONAL LOTTERY CHARITIES BOARD (SCOTLAND)

Norloch House, 36 King's Stables Road, Edinburgh EH1 2EJ
Tel: 0131-221 7100; fax: 0131-221 7120

The Board is the independent body set up under the National Lottery Act 1993 to distribute funds from the Lottery to support charitable, benevolent and philanthropic organizations. The Board's main aim is to help meet the needs of those at greatest disadvantage in society and to improve the quality of life in the community through grants programmes in the UK and an international grants programme for UK-based agencies working abroad.
Director for Scotland, vacant

NATIONAL MUSEUMS OF SCOTLAND

Chambers Street, Edinburgh EH1 1JF
Tel: 0131-225 7534; fax: 0131-220 4819
E-mail: Feedback@nms.ac.uk
Web: http://www.nms.ac.uk

The National Museums of Scotland comprise the Royal Museum of Scotland, the Scottish United Services Museum, the Scottish Agricultural Museum, the Museum of Flight, Shambellie House Museum of Costume and the Museum of Scotland. Total funding from the Scottish Executive for 1999–2000 is £19.9 million.

Board of Trustees

Chairman, R. Smith, FSA Scot.
Members, Prof. T. Devine; Dr L. Glasser, MBE, FRSE; S. G. Gordon, CBE; Dr V. van Heyingen, FRSF; G. Johnston, OBE, TD; Prof. P. H. Jones; Ms C. Macaulay; N. McIntosh, CBE; Prof. A. Manning, OBE; Prof. J. Murray; Sir William Purves, CBE, DSO; Dr A. Ritchie, OBE; The Countess of Rosebery; I. Smith; Sir John Thomson; Lord Wilson of Tillyorn, GCMG

Officers

Director, M. Jones, FSA, FSA Scot., FRSA
Depute Director (Resources) and Project Director, Museum of Scotland, I. Hooper, FSA Scot.
Depute Director (Collections) and Keeper of History and Applied Art, Miss D. Idiens, FRSA, FSA Scot.
Development Director, C. McCallum
Keeper of Archaeology, D. V. Clarke, Ph.D., FSA, FSA Scot.
Keeper of Geology and Zoology, M. Shaw, D.Phil.
Keeper of Social and Technological History, G. Sprott
Head of Public Affairs, Ms M. Bryden
Head of Museum Services, S. R. Elson, FSA Scot.
Head of Administration, A. G. Young
Keeper, Scottish United Services Museum, S. C. Wood
Curator, Scottish Agricultural Museum, G. Sprott
Curator, Museum of Flight, A. Smith
Keeper, Shambellie House Museum of Costume, Miss N. Tarrant

NORTHERN LIGHTHOUSE BOARD

84 George Street, Edinburgh EH2 3DA
Tel: 0131-473 3100; fax: 0131-220 2093
E-mail: NLB@dial.pipex.com

The Lighthouse Board is the general lighthouse authority for Scotland and the Isle of Man. The present board owes its origin to an Act of Parliament passed in 1786. At present the Commissioners operate under the Merchant Shipping Act 1894 and are 19 in number.

The Commissioners control 84 major automatic lighthouses, 116 minor lights and many lighted and unlighted buoys. They have a fleet of two motor vessels.

Commissioners

The Lord Advocate
The Solicitor-General for Scotland
The Lord Provosts of Edinburgh, Glasgow and Aberdeen
The Provost of Inverness
The Convener of Argyll and Bute Council
The Sheriffs-Principal of North Strathclyde,

Tayside, Central and Fife, Grampian, Highlands and Islands, South Strathclyde, Dumfries and Galloway, Lothians and Borders, and Glasgow and Strathkelvin
A. J. Struthers
W. F. Hay, CBE
Capt. D. M. Cowell
Adm. Sir Michael Livesay, KCB
The Lord Maclay

Officers

Chief Executive, Capt. J. B. Taylor, RN
Director of Finance, D. Gorman
Director of Engineering, W. Paterson
Director of Operations and Navigational Requirements, P. J. Christmas

OFFICE OF THE ACCOUNTANT IN BANKRUPTCY

George House, 126 George Street, Edinburgh EH2 4HH
Tel: 0131-473 4600; helpline 0345-626171
Fax: 0131-473 4737

The Office is responsible for the administration of personal bankruptcies in Scotland.
Accountant in Bankruptcy, G. Leslie-Kerr

OFFICE OF THE DATA PROTECTION REGISTRAR

Wycliffe House, Water Lane, Wilmslow, Cheshire SK9 5AF
Tel: 01625-545745; fax: 01625-524510

The Data Protection Registrar compiles and maintains the register of data users and computer bureaux and provides facilities for members of the public to examine the register; promotes observance of data protection principles; considers complaints made by data subjects; disseminates information about the Data Protection Act; encourages the production of codes of practice by trade associations and other bodies; guides data users in complying with data protection principles; and co-operates with other parties to the Council of Europe Convention and acts as the UK authority for the purposes of Article 13 of the Convention.

The Data Protection Act 1998, which comes into effect in March 2000, implements the EU Data Protection Directive in the UK; on 1 March 2000 the Registrar will be renamed the Data Protection Commissioner.
Registrar, Mrs E. France

OFFICE OF GAS AND ELECTRICITY MARKETS (SCOTLAND)

Regent Court, 70 West Regent Street, Glasgow G2 2QZ
Tel: 0141-331 2678; fax: 0141-331 2777

The Office of Gas and Electricity Markets (Ofgem) is the independent regulatory body for the gas and electricity supply industries following the merger of the Office of Gas Supply and the Office of Electricity Regulation in 1999. Its functions are to promote competition and to protect customers' interests in relation to prices, security of supply and quality of services.
Director-General for Electricity and Gas Supply, C. McCarthy
Deputy Director-General for Scotland, D. Wilson

OFFICE OF THE SOCIAL SECURITY AND CHILD SUPPORT COMMISSIONERS

23 Melville Street, Edinburgh EH3 7PW
Tel: 0131-225 2201

The Social Security Commissioners are the final statutory authority to decide appeals relating to entitlement to social security benefits. The Child Support Commissioners are the final statutory authority to decide appeals relating to child support. Appeals may be made in relation to both matters only on a point of law.
Chief Social Security Commissioner and Chief Child Support Commissioner, His Hon. Judge Machin, QC
Secretary (Edinburgh), Mrs M. Watts

OFFICE OF TELECOMMUNICATIONS

50 Ludgate Hill, London EC4M 7JJ
Tel: 0171-634 8700; fax: 0171- 634 8943

The Office of Telecommunications (Oftel) is responsible for supervising telecommunications activities and broadcast transmission in the UK. Its principal functions are to ensure that holders of telecommunications licences comply with their licence conditions; to maintain and promote effective competition in telecommunications; and to promote the interests of purchasers and other users of telecommunication services and apparatus in respect of prices, quality and variety.

The Director-General has powers to deal with anti-competitive practices and monopolies. He also has a duty to consider all reasonable complaints and representations about telecommunication apparatus and services.
Director-General, D. Edmonds

PARLIAMENTARY COMMISSIONER FOR ADMINISTRATION AND HEALTH SERVICE COMMISSIONER

The Parliamentary Commissioner for Administration (the Parliamentary Ombudsman) is independent of Government and is an officer of Parliament. He is responsible for investigating complaints referred to him by MPs from members of the public who claim to have sustained injustice in consequence of maladministration by or on behalf of UK government departments and certain non-departmental public bodies. The Parliamentary Commissioner also investigates complaints, referred by MPs, about wrongful refusal of access to official information.

The Health Service Commissioner (the Health Service Ombudsman) for Scotland is responsible for investigating complaints against National Health Service authorities and trusts that are not dealt with by those authorities to the satisfaction of the complainant. The Ombudsman's jurisdiction now covers complaints about family doctors, dentists, pharmacists and opticians, and complaints about actions resulting from clinical judgment. The Health Service Ombudsman is also responsible for investigating complaints that information has been wrongly refused under the Code of Practice on Openness in the National Health Service 1995. The office is presently held by the Parliamentary Commissioner (*see also* Scottish Parliamentary Commissioner for Administration).

PARLIAMENTARY COMMISSIONER'S OFFICE
Millbank Tower, Millbank, London SW1P 4QP
Tel: 0845-015 4033; fax: 0171-217 4000
Web: http://www.ombudsman.org.uk

Parliamentary Commissioner and Health Service Commissioner, M. S. Buckley
Deputy Parliamentary Commissioner,
  J. E. Avery, CB
Directors of Investigations, Ms J. Binstead;
  N. Cleary; Mrs S. P. Maunsell;
  G. Monk; A. Watson

HEALTH SERVICE COMMISSIONERS' OFFICE
Millbank Tower, Millbank, London SW1P 4QP
Tel: 0845-015 4033; fax: 0171-217 4000
28 Thistle Street, Edinburgh EH2 1EN
Tel: 0845-601 0456; fax: 0131-226 4447
Web: http://www.ombudsman.org.uk

Health Service Commissioner, M. S. Buckley
Deputy Health Service Commissioner,
  Ms H. Scott
Director of Investigations for Scotland,
  N. J. Jordan

PAROLE BOARD FOR SCOTLAND

Saughton House, Broomhouse Drive,
Edinburgh EH11 3XD
Tel: 0131-244 8755; fax: 0131-244 6974

The Board is an independent body which directs and advises the First Minister on the release of prisoners on licence, and related matters.
Chairman, I. McNee
Vice-Chairmen, Sheriff G. Shiach; Ms J.
  Freeman
Secretary, H. P. Boyle

PATENT OFFICE

Cardiff Road, Newport NP9 1RH
Tel: 0645-500505 (enquiries); fax: 01633-814444
E-mail: enquiries@patent.gov.uk
Web: http://www.patent.gov.uk

The Patent Office is an executive agency of the Department of Trade and Industry. The duties of the Patent Office are to administer the Patent Acts, the Registered Designs Act and the Trade Marks Act, and to deal with questions relating to the Copyright, Designs and Patents Act 1988. The Search and Advisory Service carries out commercial searches through patent information.

The Patent Office has two information points in Scotland where patent searches can be conducted:

BUSINESS AND TECHNICAL DEPARTMENT
Central Library, Rosemount Viaduct,
Aberdeen AB25 1GW
Tel: 01224-652500

BUSINESS USERS' SERVICE
Mitchell Library, North Street, Glasgow G3 7DN
Tel: 0141-287 2905

PENSIONS APPEAL TRIBUNALS FOR SCOTLAND

20 Walker Street, Edinburgh EH3 7HS
Tel 0131-220 1404

The Pensions Appeal Tribunals are responsible for hearing appeals from ex-servicemen or women and widows who have had their claims for a war pension rejected by the Secretary of State for Social Security. The Entitlement Appeal Tribunals hear appeals in cases where the Secretary of State has refused to grant a war pension. The Assessment Appeal Tribunals hear appeals against the Secretary of State's assessment of the degree of disablement caused by an accepted condition. The tribunal members are appointed by the Lord Chancellor.
President, C. N. McEachran, QC

POST-QUALIFICATION EDUCATION BOARD FOR HEALTH SERVICE PHARMACISTS IN SCOTLAND

c/o Scottish Centre for Post-Qualification Pharmaceutical Education, Room 163, SIBS Todd Wing, 27 Taylor Street, University of Strathclyde, Glasgow G4 0NR
Tel: 0141-548 4273; fax: 0141-553 4102
E-mail: scppe@strath.ac.uk

The Board advises on the post-qualification educational requirements of all registered pharmacists working in the NHS in Scotland.
Chairman, Dr G. Jefferson
Secretary, Ms R. M. Parr

REGISTERS OF SCOTLAND

Meadowbank House, 153 London Road, Edinburgh EH8 7AU
Tel: 0131-659 6111; fax: 0131-479 3688
E-mail: keeper@ros.gov.uk
Web: http://www.ros.gov.uk

Registers of Scotland is an executive agency of the Scottish Executive Justice Department. It is responsible for framing and maintaining records relating to property and further legal documents. Information from these public registers can be obtained through personal visits, by post or telecommunications, or via the Internet.

The agency holds 15 registers; two property registers (General Register of Sasines and Land Register of Scotland), which form the chief security in Scotland of the rights of land and other heritable (or real) property; and the remaining 13 grouped under the collective name of the Chancery and Judicial Registers (Register of Deeds in the Books of Council and Session; Register of Protests; Register of Judgments; Register of Service of Heirs; Register of the Great Seal; Register of the Quarter Seal; Register of the Prince's Seal; Register of Crown Grants; Register of Sheriffs' Commissions; Register of the Cachet Seal; Register of Inhibitions and Adjudications; Register of Entails; Register of Hornings).
Keeper of the Registers, A. W. Ramage
Deputy Keeper, A. G. Rennie
Managing Director, F. Manson

REGISTRY OF FRIENDLY SOCIETIES (SCOTLAND)

58 Frederick Street, Edinburgh EH2 1NB
Tel: 0131-226 3224

The Registry of Friendly Societies is a non-ministerial government department comprising the Central Office of the Registry of Friendly Societies, together with the Assistant Registrar of Friendly Societies for Scotland.

The Central Office of the Registry of Friendly Societies provides a public registry for mutual organizations registered under the Building Societies Act 1986, Friendly Societies Acts 1974 and 1992, and the Industrial and Provident Societies Act 1965.

The Registry will be subsumed into the Financial Services Authority at a date to be fixed following the enactment of the Financial Services and Markets Bill.
Assistant Registrar for Scotland, J. L. J. Craig, WS

ROYAL BOTANIC GARDEN EDINBURGH

20A Inverleith Row, Edinburgh EH3 5LR
Tel: 0131-552 7171; fax: 0131-248 2901
E-mail: press@rbge.org.uk
Web: http://www.rbge.org.uk

The Royal Botanic Garden Edinburgh (RBGE) originated as the Physic Garden, established in 1670 beside the Palace of Holyroodhouse. The Garden moved to its present 28-hectare site at Inverleith, Edinburgh, in 1821. There are also three specialist gardens: Younger Botanic Garden Benmore, near Dunoon, Argyllshire; Logan Botanic Garden, near Stranraer, Wigtownshire; and Dawyck Botanic Garden, near Stobo, Peeblesshire. Since 1986, RBGE has been administered by a board of trustees established under the National Heritage (Scotland) Act 1985. It receives an annual grant from the Scottish Executive Rural Affairs Department.

RBGE is an international centre for scientific research on plant diversity and for horticulture education and conservation. It has an extensive library and a herbarium with over two million dried plant specimens.

Public opening hours

Edinburgh site – daily (except Christmas Day and New Year's Day) November–January 9.30–4; February and October 9.30–5; March and September 9.30–6; April–August 9.30–7; admission free
Specialist gardens – 1 March–31 October 9.30–6; admission charge

Chairman of the Board of Trustees, Dr P. Nicholson
Regius Keeper, Prof. S. Blackmore

ROYAL COMMISSION ON THE ANCIENT AND HISTORICAL MONUMENTS OF SCOTLAND

John Sinclair House, 16 Bernard Terrace, Edinburgh EH8 9NX
Tel: 0131-662 1456; fax: 0131-662 1477
E-mail: postmaster@rcahms.gov.uk
Web: http://www.rcahms.gov.uk

The Royal Commission was established in 1908 and is appointed to provide for the survey and recording of ancient and historical monuments connected with the culture, civilization and conditions of life of people in Scotland from the earliest times. It is funded by the Scottish Executive.

The Commission compiles and maintains the National Monuments Record of Scotland as the national record of the archaeological and historical environment. The National Monuments Record is open for reference Monday–Thursday 9.30–4.30, Friday 9.30–4.
Chairman, Sir William Fraser, GCB, FRSE
Commissioners, Prof. J. M Coles, Ph.D., FBA;
    Prof. R. Cramp, GCB, FSA; Dr B. Crawford,
    FSA, FSA Scot.; Dr D. Howard, FSA; Prof.
    M. Mackay, Ph.D.; R. A. Paxton, FRSE;
    Miss A. Riches; J. Simpson, FSA Scot.;
    Prof. T. C. Smout, CBE, FRESE, FBA
Secretary, R. J. Mercer, FSA, FRSE

ROYAL FINE ART COMMISSION FOR SCOTLAND

Bakehouse Close, 146 Canongate, Edinburgh EH8 8DD
Tel: 0131-556 6699; fax: 0131-556 6633
E-mail: rfacscot@gtnet.gov.uk

The Commission was established in 1927 and advises ministers and local authorities on the visual impact and quality of design of construction projects. It is an independent body and gives its opinions impartially.
Chairman, The Lord Cameron of Lochbroom, PC, FRSE
Commissioners, Prof. G. Benson; W. A. Cadell;
    Mrs K. Dalyell; Ms J. Malvenan;
    R. G. Maund; M. Murray; D. Page;
    B. Rae; R. Russell; M. Turnbull; A. Wright
Secretary, C. Prosser

SCOTLAND OFFICE

Dover House, Whitehall, London, SW1A 2AU
Tel: 0171-270 3000; fax: 0171-270 6730

The Scotland Office is the Office of the Secretary of State for Scotland, who represents Scottish interests in the Cabinet on matters reserved to the UK Parliament, i.e. national financial and economic matters, social security, defence and international relations, and employment. *See also* Scottish Executive.
Secretary of State for Scotland, The Rt. Hon. Dr John Reid, MP
    Private Secretary, Ms J. Coulquhoun
Minister of State, Brian Wilson, MP
    Private Secretary, D. Ferguson
Advocate-General for Scotland, Lynda Clark, MP
Head of Office, I. Gordon

SCOTTISH ADVISORY COMMITTEE ON DRUG MISUSE

Public Health Policy Unit, Department of Health, St Andrews House, Edinburgh EH1 3DG
Tel: 0131-244 2496; fax: 0131-244 2689

The Committee advises and reports on policy, priorities and strategic planning in relation to drug misuse in Scotland.
Chairman, The Scottish Health Minister
Secretary, Mrs M. Robertson

SCOTTISH ADVISORY COMMITTEE ON THE MEDICAL WORKFORCE

Room 62, St Andrews House, Edinburgh EH1 3DG
Tel: 0131-244 2486

The Committee advises on all matters relating to medical workforce planning in Scotland, other than matters concerning terms and conditions of service. (The Committee's status as a non-departmental public body is under review.)
Chairman, Dr D. Ewing
Secretary, Ms A. Roberts

SCOTTISH AGRICULTURAL SCIENCE AGENCY

East Craig, Edinburgh EH12 8NJ
Tel: 0131-244 8890; fax: 0131-244 8988

The Agency is an executive agency of the Scottish Executive Rural Affairs Department. It provides scientific information and advice on agricultural and horticultural crops and the environment, and has various statutory and regulatory functions.
Director, Dr R. K. M. Hay
Deputy Director, S. R. Cooper
Senior Principal Scientific Officer, W. J. Rennie

SCOTTISH AGRICULTURAL WAGES BOARD

Pentland House, 47 Robb's Loan, Edinburgh EH14 1TY
Tel: 0131-244 6392

The Board fixes minimum wage rates, holiday entitlements and other conditions for agricultural workers in Scotland.
Chairman, Mrs C. Davis, CBE
Secretary, Miss F. Anderson

SCOTTISH ARTS COUNCIL

12 Manor Place, Edinburgh EH3 7DD
Tel: 0131-226 6051; fax: 0131-225 9833
E-mail: help.desk.SAC@artsfb.org.uk
Web: http://www.sac.org.uk

The Scottish Arts Council funds arts organizations and artists in Scotland and

receives funding directly from the Scottish Executive and the National Lottery Fund. The Scottish Executive grant for 1999–2000 is £28.097 million; National Lottery funding is approximately £20 million.
Chairman, M. Linklater
Members, Ms S. Ainsley; H. Buchanan; Ms E. Cameron; R. Chester; W. English; J. Faulds; Ms D. Idiens; Ms M. Marshall; Dr A. Matheson; Ms J. Richardson; J. Scott Moncrieff; W. Speirs; Ms J. Urquart
Director, Ms T. Jackson

SCOTTISH CHARITIES OFFICE

Crown Office, 25 Chambers Street, Edinburgh EH1 1LA
Tel: 0131-226 2626; fax: 0131-226 6912

The Scottish Charities Office is responsible for the supervision and regulation of charities in Scotland with the aim of enhancing the integrity and effectiveness of charities.
Director, B. M. Logan

SCOTTISH CHILDREN'S REPORTER ADMINISTRATION

Ochil House, Springkerse Business Park, Stirling FK7 7XE
Tel: 01786-459500; fax: 01786-495933

The Scottish Children's Reporter Administration supports the Principal Reporter in his statutory functions in relation to children who may be in need of care, and provides suitable accommodation and facilities for children's hearings.
Chairman, Ms S. Kuenssberg

SCOTTISH COMMITTEE OF THE COUNCIL ON TRIBUNALS

44 Palmerston Place, Edinburgh EH12 5BJ
Tel: 0131-220 1236; fax: 0131-225 4271

The Council on Tribunals is an independent body that advises on and keeps under review the constitution and working of administrative tribunals, and considers and reports on administrative procedures relating to statutory inquiries. Some 70 tribunals are currently under the Council's supervision. It is consulted by and advises government departments on a wide range of subjects relating to adjudicative procedures. The Scottish Committee of the Council generally considers Scottish tribunals and matters relating only to Scotland.
Chairman, R. J. Elliot, WS
Members, The Parliamentary Commissioner for Administration (*ex officio*); Mrs P. Y. Berry, MBE; Mrs B. Bruce;

I. J. Irvine; Mrs A. Middleton; I. D. Penman, CB; Mrs H. Sheerin, OBE
Secretary, Mrs E. M. MacRae

SCOTTISH COURTS ADMINISTRATION

— *see* pages 75–6

SCOTTISH CRIMINAL CASES REVIEW COMMISSION

5th Floor, Portland House, 17 Renfield Street, Glasgow G2 5AH
Tel: 0141-730 7030; fax: 0141-730 7040
E-mail: info@SCCRC.co.uk

The Commission is a non-departmental public body which started operating on 1 April 1999. It took over from the Secretary of State for Scotland powers to consider alleged miscarriages of justice in Scotland and refer cases meeting the relevant criteria to the Appeal Court for review. Members are appointed by the First Minister; senior executive staff are appointed by the Commission.
Chairperson, Prof. S. McLean
Members, A. Bonnington; Prof. P. Duff; Very Revd G. Forbes; A. Gallen; Sheriff G. Gordon, CBE, QC; W. Taylor, QC
Chief Executive, R. Eadie

SCOTTISH ENTERPRISE

120 Bothwell Street, Glasgow G2 7JP
Tel 0141-248 2700; fax 0141-221 3217
E-mail: scotent.co.uk
Web: http://www.scotent.co.uk

Scottish Enterprise was established in 1991 and its purpose is to create jobs and prosperity for the people of Scotland. It is funded largely by the Scottish Executive and is responsible to the Scottish Minister for Enterprise and Lifelong Learning. Working in partnership with the private and public sectors, Scottish Enterprise aims to further the development of Scotland's economy, to enhance the skills of the Scottish workforce and to promote Scotland's international competitiveness. Through Locate in Scotland (*see* page 50), Scottish Enterprise is concerned with attracting firms to Scotland, and through Scottish Trade International (*see* page 50) is helps Scottish companies to compete in world export markets. Scottish Enterprise has a network of 13 local enterprise companies (*see* pages 193–4) that deliver economic development services at local level.
Chairman, Sir Ian Wood, CBE
Chief Executive, C. Beveridge, CBE

SCOTTISH ENVIRONMENT PROTECTION AGENCY

Erskine Court, The Castle Business Park, Stirling FK9 4TR
Tel: 01786-457700; fax: 01786-446885
E-mail: publicaffairs@sepa.org.uk
Web: http://www.sepa.org.uk

The Scottish Environment Protection Agency is Scotland's environmental regulator, responsible for preventing and controlling pollution to land, air and water. Its main aim is to provide an efficient and integrated environmental protection system for Scotland which will improve the environment and contribute to the Government's goal of sustainable development. It has regional offices in East Kilbride, Riccarton and Dingwall, and 18 offices throughout Scotland. It receives funding from the Scottish Executive.

The Board

Chairman, K. Collins
Members (until October 1999), A. Buchan; G. Gordon, OBE; D. Hughes Hallett, FRICS; A. Hewat, OBE; Mrs D. Hutton; Prof. C. Johnston; N. Kuenssberg; C. McChord; Ms A. Magee; A. Paton; Ms J. Shaw

The Executive

Chief Executive, A. Paton
Director of Finance, J. Ford
Director of Environmental Strategy, Ms P. Henton
Director, North Region, Prof. D. Mackay
Director, East Region, W. Halcrow
Director, West Region, J. Beveridge

SCOTTISH FISHERIES PROTECTION AGENCY

Pentland House, 47 Robb's Loan, Edinburgh EH14 1TY
Tel: 0131-556 8400; fax: 0131-244 6086

The Agency is an executive agency of the Scottish Executive Rural Affairs Department. It enforces fisheries law and regulations in Scottish waters and ports.
Chief Executive, Capt. P. Du Vivier, RN
Director of Corporate Strategy and Resources, J. B. Roddin
Director of Operational Enforcement, R. J. Walker
Marine Superintendent, Capt. W. A. Brown

SCOTTISH HOMES

Thistle House, 91 Haymarket Terrace, Edinburgh EH12 5HE
Tel: 0131-313 0044; fax: 0131-313 2680

Scottish Homes, the national housing agency for Scotland, aims to improve the quality and variety of housing available in Scotland by working in partnership with the public and private sectors. The agency is a major funder of new and improved housing provided by housing associations and private developers. It is currently transferring its own rented houses to alternative landlords. It is also involved in housing research. Board members are appointed by the First Minister.
Chairman, J. Ward, CBE
Chief Executive, P. McKinlay, CBE

SCOTTISH HOSPITAL ENDOWMENTS RESEARCH TRUST

Saltire Court, 20 Castle Terrace, Edinburgh EH1 2EF
Tel: 0131-473 7516; fax: 0131-228 8118
E-mail: sshert4578@aol.com
Web: http://www.shert.com/www.shert.org.uk

The Trusts holds endowments, donations and bequests and makes grants from these funds to improve health standards by funding research into the cause, diagnosis, treatment and prevention of all forms of illness and genetic disorders and into the advancement of medical technology. It also engages in fundraising activities.
Chairman, The Lord Kilpatrick of Kincraig, CBE
Secretary, T. Connell, WS

SCOTTISH INDUSTRIAL DEVELOPMENT ADVISORY BOARD

Meridian Court, 5 Cadogan Street, Glasgow G2 6AT
Tel: 0141-242 5674

The Board advises the Scottish Ministers on the exercise of their powers under Section 7 of the Industrial Development Act 1982.
Chairman, I. Good
Secretary, Ms M. Hildebrand

SCOTTISH LAW COMMISSION

140 Causewayside, Edinburgh EH9 1PR
Tel: 0131-668 2131; fax: 0131-662 4900
E-mail: info@scotlawcom.gov.uk

The Commission keeps the law in Scotland under review and makes proposals for its development and reform. It is responsible to the Scottish Courts Administration (*see* pages 75–6).
Chairman (part-time), The Hon. Lord Gill
Commissioners (full-time), Dr E. M. Clive; N. R. Whitty;
(part-time) Prof. K. G. C. Reid; P. S. Hodge, QC
Secretary, N. Raven

SCOTTISH LEGAL AID BOARD

44 Drumsheugh Gardens, Edinburgh EH3 7SW
Tel: 0131-226 7061; fax: 0131-220 4878
E-mail: general@slab.org.uk
Web: http://www.scotlegalaid.gov.uk/
www.slab.org.uk

The Scottish Legal Aid Board was set up under the Legal Aid (Scotland) Act 1986. It is responsible for ensuring that advice and assistance and representation are available in accordance with the Act. The Board is a non-departmental public body whose members are appointed by the First Minister.
Chairman, Mrs J. Couper
Members, B. C. Adair; Mrs K. Blair;
  Prof. P. H. Grinyer; Sheriff A. Jessop;
  N. Kuenssberg; D. O'Carroll;
  Mrs Y. Osman; Ms M. Scanlan;
  M. C. Thomson, QC; A. F. Wylie, QC
Chief Executive, L. Montgomery

SCOTTISH LEGAL SERVICES OMBUDSMAN

Mulberry House, 16-22 Picardy Place,
Edinburgh EH1 3JT
Tel: 0131-556 5574; fax: 0131-556 1519
E-mail: complaints@scot-legal-ombud.org.uk
Web: http://www.scot-legal-ombud.org.uk

The Legal Services Ombudsman oversees the handling of complaints against solicitors, advocates, licensed conveyancers and legal executives by their professional bodies. A complainant must first complain to the relevant professional body before raising the matter with the Ombudsman. The Ombudsman is independent of the legal profession and his services are free of charge.
Scottish Legal Services Ombudsman,
  G. S. Watson

SCOTTISH MEDICAL PRACTICES COMMITTEE

Scottish Health Service Centre, Crewe Road South, Edinburgh EH4 2LF
Tel: 0131-623 2532

The Committee ensures that there is an adequate number of GPs providing general medical services in Scotland.
Chairman, Dr G. McIntosh, MBE
Secretary, Mrs K. McGeary

SCOTTISH NATURAL HERITAGE

12 Hope Terrace, Edinburgh EH9 2AS
Tel: 0131-447 4784; fax: 0131-446 2277
Web: http://www.snh.org.uk

Scottish Natural Heritage was established in 1992 under the Natural Heritage (Scotland) Act 1991. It provides advice on nature conservation to all those whose activities affect wildlife, landforms and features of geological interest in Scotland, and seeks to develop and improve facilities for the enjoyment and understanding of the Scottish countryside. It is funded by the Scottish Executive.
Chairman, Dr J. Markland, CBE
Chief Executive, R. Crofts
Chief Scientific Adviser, M. B. Usher
Directors of Operations, J. Thomson (*West*);
  I. Jardine (*East*); J. Watson (*North*)
Director of Corporate Services, vacant

SCOTTISH OCEANIC AREA CONTROL CENTRE

Atlantic House, Sherwood Road, Prestwick KA9 2NR
Tel: 01292-479800; fax: 01292-692733

The Centre is the Scottish division of the Civil Aviation Authority, which is responsible for the economic regulation of UK airlines, for the safety regulation of UK civil aviation, and (through its subsidiary company National Air Traffic Services Ltd) provides air traffic control and telecommunications services.

SCOTTISH OFFICE (FORMER)

— *see* Scotland Office

SCOTTISH PARLIAMENTARY COMMISSIONER FOR ADMINISTRATION

28 Thistle Street, Edinburgh EH2 1EN
Tel: 0845-601 0456; fax: 0131-226 4447
Web: http://www.ombudsman.org.uk

The Scottish Parliamentary Commissioner for Administration (the Scottish Commissioner) is responsible for investigating complaints referred to him by Members of the Scottish Parliament on behalf of members of the public who have suffered an injustice through maladministration by the Scottish Executive, the Parliamentary Corporation and a wide range of public bodies involved in devolved Scottish affairs. The Scottish Commissioner also investigates complaints, referred by MSPs, about wrongful refusal of access to official information.
Scottish Parliamentary Commissioner,
  M. S. Buckley
Head of Scottish Office, G. Keil

SCOTTISH POST OFFICE BOARD

102 West Port, Edinburgh EH3 9HS
Tel: 0131-228 7300; fax: 0131-228 7218
Web: http://www.ukpo.com

The Post Office is a public authority responsible for running the postal services. In December 1998 the Government announced plans to give the Post Office greater commercial freedom and to set up an

independent regulator to protect consumer interests.
Chairman, J. Ward, CBE
Secretary to the Scottish Post Office Board, M. Cummins

SCOTTISH PRISONS COMPLAINTS COMMISSION

Government Buildings, Broomhouse Drive, Edinburgh EH11 3XD
Tel: 0131-244 8423; fax: 0131-244 8430

The Commission was established in 1994. It is an independent body to which prisoners in Scottish prisons can make application in relation to any matter where they have failed to obtain satisfaction from the Prison Service's internal grievance procedures. Clinical judgments made by medical officers, matters which are the subject of legal proceedings and matters relating to sentence, conviction and parole decision-making are excluded from the Commission's jurisdiction. The Commissioner is appointed by the First Minister.
Commissioner, Dr J. McManus

SCOTTISH PRISON SERVICE

— see pages 84–5

SCOTTISH PUBLIC PENSIONS AGENCY

St Margaret's House, 151 London Road, Edinburgh EH8 7TG
Tel: 0131-556 8400; fax: 0131-244 3334

The Agency is an executive agency of the Scottish Executive Education Department. It is responsible for the pension arrangements of some 300,000 people, mainly NHS and teaching services employees and pensioners.
Chief Executive, R. Garden
Directors, G. Mowat *(Policy)*; A. M. Small *(Operations)*; M. J. McDermott *(Resources and Customer Services)*

SCOTTISH RECORDS ADVISORY COUNCIL

HM General Register House, Edinburgh EH1 3YY
Tel: 0131-535 1314; fax: 0131-535 1360
E-mail: research@nas.gov.uk
The Council was established under the Public Records (Scotland) Act 1937. Its members are appointed by the First Minister and it may submit proposals or make representations to the First Minister, the Lord Justice-General or the Lord President of the Court of Session on questions relating to the public records of Scotland.
Chairman, Prof. A. Crowther
Secretary, Dr A. Rosie

SCOTTISH SCREEN

249 West George Street, Glasgow G2 4RB
Tel: 0141-302 1700; fax: 0141-302 1711
E-mail: info@scottishscreen.com
Web: http://www.scottishscreen.com

Scottish Screen is the national body for promoting film culture and the film, television and convergent media industries in Scotland.
Chairman, J. Lee
Chief Executive, J. Archer

SCOTTISH SOLICITORS' DISCIPLINE TRIBUNAL

22 Rutland Square, Edinburgh EH1 2BB
Tel: 0131-229 5860

The Scottish Solicitors' Discipline Tribunal is an independent statutory body with a panel of 18 members, ten of whom are solicitors; members are appointed by the Lord President of the Court of Session. Its principal function is to consider complaints of misconduct against solicitors in Scotland.
Chairman, J. W. Laughland
Clerk, J. M. Barton, WS

SCOTTISH SPORTS COUNCIL

— see Sportscotland

SCOTTISH TOURIST BOARD

23 Ravelston Terrace, Edinburgh EH4 3EU
Tel: 0131-332 2433; fax: 0131-343 1513
Thistle House, Beechwood Park North, Inverness IV2 3ED
Tel: 01463-716996; fax: 01463-717233
Web: http://www.holiday.scotland.net

The Scottish Tourist Board is responsible for developing and marketing the tourist industry in Scotland. The Board's main objectives are to promote holidays and to encourage the provision and improvement of tourist amenities.
Chief Executive, T. Buncle

SCOTTISH VALUATION AND RATING COUNCIL

c/o LG3A-Area 3-J, Victoria Quay, Edinburgh EH6 6QQ
Tel: 0131-244 7003; fax: 0131-244 7058

The Council advises on any matter pertaining to valuation and rating, including evaluation of representations and recommendations made to the First Minister, the identification of issues requiring consideration, and advice in the preparation of legislation.
Chairman, Prof. G. Milne
Secretary, P. A. Hancock

SEA FISH INDUSTRY AUTHORITY

18 Logie Mill, Logie Green Road, Edinburgh EH7 4HG

Tel: 0131-558 3331; fax: 0131-558 1442

E-mail: seafish@seafish.demon.uk

Established under the Fisheries Act 1981, the Authority is required to promote the efficiency of the sea fish industry. It carries out research relating to the industry and gives advice on related matters. It provides training, promotes the marketing, consumption and export of sea fish and sea fish products, and may provide financial assistance for the improvement of fishing vessels in respect of essential safety equipment. It is responsible to the Ministry of Agriculture, Fisheries and Food.

Chairman, E. Davey

Chief Executive, A. C. Fairbairn

SECRETARY OF COMMISSIONS FOR SCOTLAND

Spur W1 (E), Saughton House, Broomhouse Drive, Edinburgh EH11 3XD

Tel: 0131-244 2691; fax: 0131-244 2623

The Secretary of Commissions deals with the appointment of justices of the peace and of general commissioners of income tax, and with lord lieutenancy business.

Secretary of Commissions for Scotland, Mrs J. Richardson

SECRETARY OF STATE FOR SCOTLAND'S ADVISORY PANEL OF ECONOMIC CONSULTANTS

3rd Floor, Meridian Court, 5 Cadogan Street, Glasgow G2 6AT

Tel: 0141-242 5452; fax: 0141-242 5579

The Panel, which provides advice on the Scottish economy, has not met since 1998. Responsibility for it has passed to the Scottish Parliament; its future was under review at the time of going to press.

Chairman, The First Minister

Secretary, G. Storie

SPECIAL COMMISSIONERS OF INCOME TAX

15–19 Bedford Avenue, London WC1B 3AS

Tel: 0171-631 4242

The Special Commissioners are an independent body appointed by the Lord Chancellor to hear complex appeals against decisions of the Board of Inland Revenue and its officials. In addition to the Presiding Special Commissioner there are two full-time and 13 deputy special commissioners; all are legally qualified.

Presiding Special Commissioner, His Hon. Stephen Oliver, QC

Special Commissioners, T. H. K. Everett; one vacancy

Clerk, R. P. Lester

SPORTSCOTLAND

Caledonia House, South Gyle, Edinburgh EH12 9DQ

Tel: 0131-317 7200; fax: 0131-317 7202

Sportscotland (formerly the Scottish Sports Council) is responsible for the development of sport and physical recreation in Scotland. It aims to increase participation in sport among young people and to provide the highest level of coaching and support for aspiring top performers. It advises the Scottish Parliament on sports matters, and it administers the Lottery Sports Fund in Scotland.

Chairman, A. Dempster

Chief Executive, F. A. L. Alstead, CBE

STUDENT AWARDS AGENCY FOR SCOTLAND

Gyleview House, 3 Redheughs Rigg, Edinburgh EH12 9HH

Tel: 0131-476 8212; fax: 0131-244 5887

The Agency is an executive agency of the Scottish Executive Enterprise and Lifelong Learning Department. It awards grants to Scottish students undertaking full-time or sandwich course courses.

Chief Executive, K. MacRae

TRAFFIC COMMISSIONER (SCOTLAND)

Argyll House, J Floor, 3 Lady Lawson Street, Edinburgh EH3 9SE

Tel: 0131-529 8500; fax: 0131-529 8501

The Traffic Commissioners are responsible for licensing operators of heavy goods and public service vehicles. They also have responsibility for appeals relating to the licensing of operators and for disciplinary cases involving the conduct of drivers of these vehicles. Each Traffic Commissioner constitutes a tribunal for the purposes of the Tribunals and Inquiries Act 1971.

Scottish Traffic Commissioner, M. W. Betts, CBE

TRANSPORT TRIBUNAL

48–49 Chancery Lane, London WC2A 1JR

Tel: 0171-936 7493

The Transport Tribunal hears appeals against decisions of Traffic Commissioners/licensing authorities on passenger or goods vehicle operator licensing applications. The tribunal consists of a legally-qualified president, two

legal members who may sit as chairmen, and five lay members. The president and legal members are appointed by the Lord Chancellor and the lay members by the Secretary of State for the Environment, Transport and the Regions.
President (part-time), H. B. H. Carlisle, QC
Legal member (part-time), His Hon. Judge Brodrick
Lay members, L. Milliken; P. Rogers;
Ms P. Steel; J. W. Whitworth;
D. Yeomans
Secretary, P. J. Fisher

UK PASSPORT AGENCY

Regional Office
3 Northgate, 96 Milton Street, Cowcaddens,
Glasgow G4 0BB
Tel: 0990-210410
Central telephone number: 0870-521 0410
Central fax number: 0171-271 8581
Web site: http://www.open.gov.ukpass/ukpass.htm

The UK Passport Agency is an executive agency of the Home Office. It is responsible for the issue of British passports. The passport offices are open Monday–Friday 9–4.30. Telephone calls are normally routed automatically to the nearest office unless all lines are busy, when the call will be rerouted to other offices in the UK. Recorded messages to deal with routine enquiries operate 24 hours a day.
Head of Glasgow Regional Office, R. D. Wilson

VALUATION APPEAL PANELS

c/o Convention of Scottish Local Authorities,
Rosebery House, Haymarket Terrace,
Edinburgh EH12 5XZ
Tel: 0131-474 9200; fax: 0131-474 9292

The valuation panels and valuation appeal panels drawn from them hear and determine council tax and non-domestic rating appeals. Members of the local valuation panels are appointed by the Sheriff Principal for the area and are required to live or work in the area covered by the panel. A central secretariat service to the valuation appeal panels is provided by COSLA.
COSLA contact, Ms D. Burrows

VAT AND DUTIES TRIBUNALS

44 Palmerston Place, Edinburgh EH12 5BJ
Tel: 0131-226 3551

VAT and Duties Tribunals are administered by the First Minister in Scotland. They are independent, and decide disputes between

taxpayers and Customs and Excise. Chairmen in Scotland are appointed by the Lord President of the Court of Session.
President, His Hon. Stephen Oliver, QC
Vice-President, Scotland, T. G. Coutts, QC
Registrar, R. P. Lester

WAR PENSIONS AGENCY

Norcross, Blackpool, Lancs FY5 3WP
Tel: 01253-856123

The Agency is an executive agency of the Department of Social Security. It administers the payment of war disablement and war widows' pensions and provides welfare services and support to war disablement pensioners, war widows and their dependants and carers.
Chief Executive, G. Hextall

Central Advisory Committee on War Pensions

6th Floor, The Adelphi, 1–11 John Adam Street, London WC2 N6HT
Tel: 0171-962 8062
Secretary, C. Pike

THE SCOTTISH JUDICATURE

Scotland has a legal system separate from and differing greatly from the English legal system in enacted law, judicial procedure and the structure of courts.

The system of public prosecution is headed by the Lord Advocate and is independent of the police, who have no say in the decision to prosecute. The Lord Advocate, discharging his functions through the Crown Office in Edinburgh, is responsible for prosecutions in the High Court, sheriff courts and district courts. Prosecutions in the High Court are prepared by the Crown Office and conducted in court by one of the law officers, by an advocate-depute, or by a solicitor advocate. In the inferior courts the decision to prosecute is made and prosecution is preferred by procurators fiscal, who are lawyers and full-time civil servants subject to the directions of the Crown Office. A permanent, legally qualified civil servant known as the Crown Agent is responsible for the running of the Crown Office and the organization of the Procurator Fiscal Service, of which he is the head.

Scotland is divided into six sheriffdoms, each with a full-time sheriff principal. The sheriffdoms are further divided into sheriff court districts, each of which has a legally qualified resident sheriff or sheriffs, who are the judges of the court.

Criminal Courts

In criminal cases sheriffs principal and sheriffs have the same powers; sitting with a jury of 15 members, they may try more serious cases on indictment, or, sitting alone, may try lesser cases under summary procedure. Minor summary offences are dealt with in district courts, which are administered by the local government authorities of the districts and the islands and presided over by lay justices of the peace (of whom there are about 4,000) and, in Glasgow only, by stipendiary magistrates. Juvenile offenders (children under 16) may be brought before an informal children's hearing comprising three local lay people.

The superior criminal court is the High Court of Justiciary, which is both a trial and an appeal court. Cases on indictment are tried by a High Court judge, sitting with a jury of 15, in Edinburgh and on circuit in other towns. Appeals from the lower courts against conviction or sentence are heard also by the High Court, which sits as an appeal court only

in Edinburgh. There is no further appeal to the House of Lords in criminal cases.

Civil Courts

In civil cases the jurisdiction of the sheriff court extends to most kinds of action. Appeal against decisions of the sheriff may be made to the sheriff principal and thence to the Court of Session, or direct to the Court of Session, which sits only in Edinburgh. The Court of Session is divided into the Inner and the Outer House. The Outer House is a court of first instance in which cases are heard by judges sitting singly, sometimes with a jury of 12. The Inner House, itself subdivided into two divisions of equal status, is mainly an appeal court. Appeals may be made to the Inner House from the Outer House as well as from the sheriff court. An appeal may be made from the Inner House to the House of Lords.

Court of Session Judges

The judges of the Court of Session are the same as those of the High Court of Justiciary, the Lord President of the Court of Session also holding the office of Lord Justice-General in the High Court. Senators of the College of Justice are Lords Commissioners of Justiciary as well as judges of the Court of Session. On appointment, a Senator takes a judicial title, which is retained for life. Although styled 'The Hon./Rt. Hon. Lord —', the Senator is not a peer.

Sudden Deaths

The office of coroner does not exist in Scotland. The local procurator fiscal inquires privately into sudden or suspicious deaths and may report findings to the Crown Agent. In some cases a fatal accident inquiry may be held before the sheriff.

COURT OF SESSION AND HIGH COURT OF JUSTICIARY

The Lord President and Lord Justice-General (£147,214)
　　The Rt. Hon. the Lord Rodger of Earlsferry, *born* 1944, *apptd* 1996
　　Secretary, A. Maxwell

INNER HOUSE

Lords of Session (each £139,931)

FIRST DIVISION

The Lord President

Hon. Lord Sutherland (Ranald Sutherland), *born* 1932, *apptd* 1985

Hon. Lord Prosser (William Prosser), *born* 1934, *apptd* 1986

Hon. Lord Caplan (Philip Caplan), *born* 1929, *apptd* 1989

SECOND DIVISION

Lord Justice Clerk (£139,931), The Rt. Hon. Lord Cullen (William Cullen), *born* 1935, *apptd* 1997

Rt. Hon. the Lord McCluskey, *born* 1929, *apptd* 1984

Hon. Lord Kirkwood (Ian Kirkwood), *born* 1932, *apptd* 1987

Hon. Lord Coulsfield (John Cameron), *born* 1934, *apptd* 1987

OUTER HOUSE

Lords of Session (each £123,787)

Hon. Lord Milligan (James Milligan), *born* 1934, *apptd* 1988

Rt. Hon. the Lord Cameron of Lochbroom, *born* 1931, *apptd* 1989

Hon. Lord Marnoch (Michael Bruce), *born* 1938, *apptd* 1990

Hon. Lord MacLean (Ranald MacLean), *born* 1938, *apptd* 1990

Hon. Lord Penrose (George Penrose), *born* 1938, *apptd* 1990

Hon. Lord Osborne (Kenneth Osborne), *born* 1937, *apptd* 1990

Hon. Lord Abernethy (Alistair Cameron), *born* 1938, *apptd* 1992

Hon. Lord Johnston (Alan Johnston), *born* 1942, *apptd* 1994

Hon. Lord Gill (Brian Gill), *born* 1942, *apptd* 1994

Hon. Lord Hamilton (Arthur Hamilton), *born* 1942, *apptd* 1995

Hon. Lord Dawson (Thomas Dawson), *born* 1948, *apptd* 1995

Hon. Lord Macfadyen (Donald Macfadyen), *born* 1945, *apptd* 1995

Hon. Lady Cosgrove (Hazel Aronson), *born* 1946, *apptd* 1996

Hon. Lord Nimmo Smith (William Nimmo Smith), *born* 1942, *apptd* 1996

Hon. Lord Philip (Alexander Philip), *born* 1942, *apptd* 1996

Hon. Lord Kingarth (Derek Emslie), *born* 1949, *apptd* 1997

Hon. Lord Bonomy (Iain Bonomy), *born* 1946, *apptd* 1997

Hon. Lord Eassie (Ronald Mackay), *born* 1945, *apptd* 1997

Hon. Lord Reed (Robert Reed), *born* 1956, *apptd* 1998

COURT OF SESSION AND HIGH COURT OF JUSTICIARY

Parliament House, Parliament Square, Edinburgh EH1 1RQ

Tel: 0131-225 2595

Principal Clerk of Session and Justiciary (£32,293–£53,879), J. L. Anderson

Deputy Principal Clerk of Justiciary and Administration (£28,314–£43,873), T. Fyffe

Deputy Principal Clerk of Session and Principal Extractor (£28,314–£43,873), G. McKeand

Deputy Principal Clerk (Keeper of the Rolls) (£28,314–£43,873), T. Thomson

Depute Clerks of Session and Justiciary (£21,613–£28,414), N. J. Dowie; I. F. Smith; T. Higgins; T. B. Cruickshank; Q. A. Oliver; F. Shannly; A. S. Moffat; G. G. Ellis; W. Dunn; A. M. Finlayson; C. C. Armstrong; R. Jenkins; J. O. McLean; M. Weir; R. M. Sinclair; E. G. Appelbe; B. Watson; D. W. Cullen; D. J. Cullum; I. D. Martin; N. McGinley; J. Lynn; E. Dickson; K. O. Carter; F. Petrie

SCOTTISH COURTS ADMINISTRATION

Hayweight House, 23 Lauriston Street, Edinburgh EH3 9DQ

Tel: 0131-229 9200

The Scottish Courts Administration is responsible to the Scottish Ministers for the performance of the Scottish Court Service and central administration pertaining to the judiciary in the Supreme and Sheriff Courts; and for policy in relation to civil court procedures, the law of diligence, evidence, arbitration and dispute resolution, private international law jurisdiction, law reform and other matters.

Director, J. Hamill, CB

Deputy Director (Legal Policy), P. M. Beaton

Deputy Director (Resources and Liaison), D. Stewart

SCOTTISH COURT SERVICE

Hayweight House, 23 Lauriston Street, Edinburgh EH3 9DQ

Tel: 0131-229 9200

The Scottish Court Service became an executive agency within the Scottish Courts Administration in 1995. It is responsible to the Scottish Ministers for the provision of staff, court houses and associated services for the Supreme and Sheriff Courts.

Chief Executive, M. Ewart

SHERIFF COURT OF CHANCERY

27 Chambers Street, Edinburgh EH1 1LB
Tel: 0131-225 2525
The Court deals with service of heirs and completion of title in relation to heritable property.
Sheriff of Chancery, C. G. B. Nicholson, QC

HM COMMISSARY OFFICE

27 Chambers Street, Edinburgh EH1 1LB
Tel: 0131-225 2525
The Office is responsible for issuing confirmation, a legal document entitling a person to execute a deceased person's will, and other related matters.
Commissary Clerk, J. Moyes

SCOTTISH LAND COURT

1 Grosvenor Crescent, Edinburgh EH12 5ER
Tel: 0131-225 3595
The court deals with disputes relating to agricultural and crofting land in Scotland.
Chairman (£96,214), The Hon. Lord McGhie (James McGhie), QC
Members, D. J. Houston; D. M. Macdonald; J. Kinloch *(part-time)*
Principal Clerk, K. H. R. Graham, WS

SHERIFFDOMS

SALARIES

Sheriff Principal	£100,209
Sheriff	£92,810
Regional Sheriff Clerk/	
Area Director	£32,293–£63,490
Sheriff Clerk	£12,719–£43,873

*Floating Sheriff

GRAMPIAN, HIGHLANDS AND ISLANDS

Sheriff Court House, Castle Street, Aberdeen AB10 1WP
Tel: 01224-648316
Sheriff Principal, D. J. Risk, QC
Area Director North, J. Robertson

SHERIFFS AND SHERIFF CLERKS
Aberdeen and Stonehaven, D. Kelbie; L. A. S. Jessop; A. Pollock; Mrs A. M. Cowan; C. J. Harris, QC; I. H. L. Miller; *G. K. Buchanan; *Sheriff Clerks*, Mrs E. Laing *(Aberdeen)*; B. J. McBride *(Stonehaven)*
Peterhead and Banff, K. A. McLernan; *Sheriff Clerk*, A. Hempseed *(Peterhead)*; *Sheriff Clerk Depute*, Mrs F. L. MacPherson *(Banff)*
Elgin, N. McPartlin; *Sheriff Clerk*, M. McBey
Inverness, Lochmaddy, Portree, Stornoway, Dingwall, Tain, Wick and Dornoch, W. J. Fulton; D. Booker-Milburn; J. O. A. Fraser; I. A. Cameron; *Sheriff Clerks*, J. Robertson *(Inverness)*; W. Cochrane *(Dingwall)*; *Sheriff Clerks Depute*, Miss M. Campbell *(Lochmaddy and Portree)*; Miss A. B. Armstrong *(Stornoway)*; L. MacLachlan *(Tain)*; Mrs J. McEwan *(Wick)*; K. Kerr *(Dornoch)*
Kirkwall and Lerwick, C. S. Mackenzie; *Sheriff Clerks Depute*, vacant *(Kirkwall)*; M. Flanagan *(Lerwick)*
Fort William, C. G. McKay (also *Oban*); *Sheriff Clerk Depute*, D. Hood

TAYSIDE, CENTRAL AND FIFE

Sheriff Court House, Tay Street, Perth PH2 8NL
Tel: 01738-620546
Sheriff Principal, J. F. Wheatley, QC
Area Director East, M. Bonar

SHERIFFS AND SHERIFF CLERKS
Arbroath and Forfar, K. A. Veal; *C. N. R. Stein; *Sheriff Clerks*, M. Herbertson *(Arbroath)*; S. Munro *(Forfar)*
Dundee, R. A. Davidson; A. L. Stewart, QC; *J. P. Scott; G. J. Evans (also *Cupar*); *Sheriff Clerk*, D. Nicoll

Perth, J. C. McInnes, QC; Mrs F. L. Reith, QC; *Sheriff Clerk*, J. Murphy
Falkirk, A. V. Sheehan; A. J. Murphy; *Sheriff Clerk*, R. McMillan
Stirling, The Hon. R. E. G. Younger; *Sheriff Clerk*, J. Clark
Alloa, W. M. Reid; *Sheriff Clerk*, R. G. McKeand
Cupar, G. J. Evans (also *Dundee*); *Sheriff Clerk*, R. Hughes
Dunfermline, J. S. Forbes; C. W. Palmer; *Sheriff Clerk*, W. McCulloch
Kirkcaldy, F. J. Keane; Mrs L. G. Patrick; *I. D. Dunbar; *B. G. Donald; *Sheriff Clerk*, W. Jones

LOTHIAN AND BORDERS

Sheriff Court House, 27 Chambers Street, Edinburgh EH1 1LB
Tel: 0131-225 2525
Sheriff Principal, C. G. B. Nicholson, QC
Area Director East, M. Bonar

SHERIFFS AND SHERIFF CLERKS

Edinburgh, R. G. Craik, QC (also *Peebles*); R. J. D. Scott (also *Peebles*); Miss I. A. Poole; A. M. Bell; J. M. S. Horsburgh, QC; G. W. S. Presslie (also *Haddington*); J. A. Farrell; *A. Lothian; I. D. Macphail, QC; C. N. Stoddart; A. B. Wilkinson, QC; Mrs D. J. B. Robertson; N. M. P. Morrison, QC; *Miss M. M. Stephen; Mrs M. L. E. Jarvie, QC; *Sheriff Clerk*, J. Ross
Peebles, R. G. Craik, QC (also *Edinburgh*); R. J. D. Scott (also *Edinburgh*); *Sheriff Clerk Depute*, M. L. Kubeczka
Linlithgow, H. R. MacLean; G. R. Fleming; *K. A. Ross; *Sheriff Clerk*, R. D. Sinclair
Haddington, G. W. S. Presslie (also *Edinburgh*); *Sheriff Clerk*, J. O'Donnell
Jedburgh and Duns, J. V. Paterson; *Sheriff Clerk*, I. W. Williamson
Selkirk, J. V. Paterson; *Sheriff Clerk Depute*, L. McFarlane

NORTH STRATHCLYDE

Sheriff Court House, St James's Street, Paisley PA3 2AW
Tel: 0141-887 5291
Sheriff Principal, B. A. Kerr, QC
Area Director West, I. Scott

SHERIFFS AND SHERIFF CLERKS
Oban, C. G. McKay (also *Fort William*); *Sheriff Clerk Depute*, J. G. Whitelaw
Dumbarton, J. T. Fitzsimons; T. Scott; S. W. H. Fraser; *Sheriff Clerk*, P. Corcoran
Paisley, J. Spy; C. K. Higgins; N. Douglas;

D. J. Pender; *W. Dunlop; G. C. Kavanagh (also *Campbeltown*); *Sheriff Clerk*, Miss S. Hinder
Greenock, J. Herald (also *Rothesay*); Sir Stephen Young; *Sheriff Clerk*, J. Tannahill
Kilmarnock, T. M. Croan; D. B. Smith; T. F. Russell; *Sheriff Clerk*, G. Waddell
Dunoon, Mrs C. M. A. F. Gimblett; *Sheriff Clerk Depute*, Mrs C. Carson
Campbeltown, *W. Dunlop (also *Paisley*); *Sheriff Clerk Depute*, P. G. Hay
Rothesay, J. Herald (also *Greenock*); *Sheriff Clerk Depute*, Mrs C. K. McCormick

GLASGOW AND STRATHKELVIN

Sheriff Court House, PO Box 23, 1 Carlton Place, Glasgow G5 9DA
Tel: 0141-429 8888
Sheriff Principal, E. F. Bowen, QC
Area Director West, I. Scott

SHERIFFS AND SHERIFF CLERKS
Glasgow, B. Kearney; G. H. Gordon, CBE, Ph.D., QC; B. A. Lockhart; Mrs A. L. A. Duncan; A. C. Henry; J. K. Mitchell; A. G. Johnston; J. P. Murphy; Miss S. A. O. Raeburn, QC; D. Convery; J. McGowan; I. A. S. Peebles, QC; C. W. McFarlane, QC; K. M. Maciver; H. Matthews, QC; J. A. Baird; Miss R. E. A. Rae, QC; T. A. K. Drummond, QC; Mrs P. M. M. Bowman; A. W. Noble; *J. D. Friel; *Mrs D. M. MacNeill, QC; J. A. Taylor; G. A. L. Scott; *Sheriff Clerk*, R. Cockburn

SOUTH STRATHCLYDE, DUMFRIES AND GALLOWAY

Sheriff Court House, Graham Street, Airdrie ML6 6EE
Tel: 01236-751121
Sheriff Principal, G. L. Cox, QC
Area Director West, I. Scott

SHERIFFS AND SHERIFF CLERKS
Hamilton, L. Cameron; D. C. Russell; V. J. Canavan (also *Airdrie*); W. E. Gibson; J. H. Stewart; H. S. Neilson; S. C. Pender; *Sheriff Clerk*, P. Feeney
Lanark, J. D. Allan; *Sheriff Clerk*, A. Whyte
Ayr, N. Gow, QC; R. G. McEwan, QC; *C. B. Miller; *Sheriff Clerk*, Miss C. D. Cockburn
Stranraer and Kirkcudbright, J. R. Smith (also *Dumfries*); *Sheriff Clerks*, W. McIntosh (*Stranraer*); B. Lindsay (*Kirkcudbright*)
Dumfries, K. G. Barr; M. J. Fletcher; J. R. Smith (also *Stranraer and Kirkcudbright*); *Sheriff Clerk*, P. McGonigle

Airdrie, V. J. Canavan (also *Hamilton*);
R. H. Dickson; I. C. Simpson; J. C.
Morris, QC; Sheriff Clerk, D. Forester

STIPENDIARY MAGISTRATES

GLASGOW
R. Hamilton, *apptd* 1984; J. B. C. Nisbet,
apptd 1984; R. B. Christie, *apptd* 1985;
Mrs J. A. M. MacLean, *apptd* 1990

PROCURATOR FISCAL SERVICE

CROWN OFFICE
25 Chambers Street, Edinburgh EH1 1LA
Tel 0131-226 2626

Crown Agent (£80,020–£116,860), A. C.
   Normand
Deputy Crown Agent (£55,750–£92,930), F. R.
Crowe

PROCURATORS FISCAL

SALARIES
Regional Procurator Fiscal
Grade 3   £61,110–£98,400
Grade 4   £55,750–£92,930
Procurator Fiscal
Upper level   £41,550–£65,270
Lower level   £36,000–£43,822

**GRAMPIAN, HIGHLANDS AND ISLANDS
REGION**
Regional Procurator Fiscal, L. A. Higson
   (Aberdeen)
Procurators Fiscal, E. K. Barbour (Stonehaven);
   A. J. M. Colley (Banff); A. N. Perry
   (Peterhead); D. J. Dickson (Elgin);
   J. Bamber (Portree, Lochmaddy);
   F. Redman (Stornoway); G. Napier
   (Inverness); R. W. Urquhart (Kirkwall,
   Lerwick); D. J. Buchanan (Fort William);
   A. N. MacDonald (Dingwall, Tain)

TAYSIDE, CENTRAL AND FIFE REGION
Regional Procurator Fiscal, B. K. Heywood
   (Dundee)
Procurators Fiscal, J. I. Craigen (Forfar);
   I. A. McLeod (Perth); W. J. Gallacher
   (Falkirk); C. Ritchie (Stirling and Alloa);
   E. B. Russell (Cupar); R. G. Stott
   (Dunfermline); Miss H. M. Clack
   (Kirkcaldy)

LOTHIAN AND BORDERS REGION
Regional Procurator Fiscal, N. McFadyen
   (Edinburgh)
Procurators Fiscal, Miss L. M. Ruxton
   (Linlithgow); A. J. P. Reith (Haddington);
   A. R. G. Fraser (Duns, Jedburgh);
   D. MacNeill (Selkirk)

NORTH STRATHCLYDE REGION
Regional Procurator Fiscal, W. A. Gilchrist
   (Paisley)
Procurators Fiscal, I. Henderson
   (Campbeltown); C. C. Donnelly
   (Dumbarton); W. S. Carnegie

(Greenock); D. L. Webster (Dunoon);
J. G. MacGlennan (Kilmarnock);
B. R. Maguire (Oban)

GLASGOW AND STRATHKELVIN REGION
Regional Procurator Fiscal, A. D. Vannet
(Glasgow)

SOUTH STRATHCLYDE, DUMFRIES AND GALLOWAY REGION
Regional Procurator Fiscal, D. A. Grown
(Hamilton)
Procurators Fiscal, S. R. Houston (Lanark); J.
T. O'Donnell (Ayr); F. R. Crowe
(Stranraer); D. J. Howdle (Dumfries);
A. S. Kennedy (Stranraer, Kirkcudbright);
D. Spiers (Airdrie)

THE POLICE SERVICE

The Scottish Executive is responsible for the organization, administration and operation of the police service. The Scottish Executive Justice Department works in partnership with chief constables and local police to implement this responsibility, which includes the making of regulations covering matters such as police ranks, discipline, hours of duty, and pay and allowances.

Police authorities are responsible for maintaining an effective and efficient police force in their areas. There are six joint police boards made up of local councillors; the other two police authorities are councils.

A review of the structure of police forces began in April 1998.

Police authorities are financed by central and local government grants and a precept on the council tax. They are responsible for setting a budget, providing the resources necessary to police the area adequately, appointing officers of the rank of Assistant Chief Constable and above, and determining the number of officers and civilian staff in the force.

All police forces in the UK are subject to inspection by HM Inspectors of Constabulary, who report to the Scottish Ministers.

Complaints

Chief constables are obliged to investigate a complaint against one of their officers; if there is a suggestion of criminal activity, the complaint is investigated by an independent public prosecutor.

The Special Constabulary

Each police force has its own special constabulary, made up of volunteers who work in their spare time. Special Constables have full police powers within their force and adjoining force areas, and assist regular officers with routine policing duties.

Police Strengths

As at March 1998, there were:

Officers	14,988
men	12,762
women	2,226
Special constables	1,723
Support staff	4,670

Pay

Basic rates of pay since 1 September 1998 have been:

Chief Constable*	
No fixed term	£71,058–£101,613
Fixed term appointment	£74,616–£106,569
Chief Constable, Strathclyde	
No fixed term	£93,297–£105,291
Fixed term appointment	£97,848–£110,430
Assistant Chief Constable	
No fixed term	£59,292–£68,064
Fixed term appointment	£62,259–£71,466
Designated deputies/	The higher of 80%
Assistant Chief Constable	of their Chief
designate	Constable's basic
	salary, or
No fixed term	£68,064
Fixed term appointment	£71,466
Superintendent	£43,143–£53,556
Chief Inspector	£35,454–£38,307
Inspector	£31,719–£36,918
Sergeant	£24,525–£28,605
Constable	£16,056–£25,410

*Depending on the population of the police force area
Source: Home Office

Scottish Crime Squad

The Scottish Crime Squad investigates organized and serious crime occurring across police force boundaries and abroad. It also supports police forces investigating serious crime.

HQ, Osprey House, Inchinnan Road, Paisley PA3 2RE
Tel: 0141-302 1000
Commander, DCS Johnstone

JOINT POLICE BOARDS

The Dumfries and Galloway council area and the Fife council area do not have joint boards as a single authority covers the whole of the police area. The chairman of the authority for these two forces is given with the force's details.

CENTRAL SCOTLAND JOINT POLICE BOARD
Covers Clackmannanshire, Falkirk and Stirling areas
Municipal Buildings, Falkirk FK1 5RS
Tel: 01324-506070; fax 01324-506071
Convener, I. Miller
Clerk to the Board, Ms E. Morton

GRAMPIAN JOINT POLICE BOARD
Covers Aberdeen City, Aberdeenshire and
Moray areas
Town House, Aberdeen AB10 1AQ
Tel: 01224-523010; fax 01224-522965
Convenor, Ms M. Stewart
Clerk to the Board, C. Langley

LOTHIAN AND BORDERS POLICE BOARD
Covers City of Edinburgh, East Lothian,
Midlothian, Scottish Borders and West
Lothian areas
City Chambers, High Street, Edinburgh
EH1 1YG
Tel: 0131-529 4955; fax 0131-529 4764
Convenor, Ms L. Hinds
Clerk to the Board, T. Aitchison

NORTHERN JOINT POLICE BOARD
Covers Highland, Orkney Islands, Shetland
Islands and Western Isles areas
Glenurquhart Road, Inverness IV3 5NX
Tel: 01463-702845; fax 01463-702182
Convenor, Ms J. Home
Clerk to the Board, J. Black

STRATHCLYDE JOINT POLICE BOARD
Covers Argyll and Bute, East Ayrshire, East
Dunbartonshire, East Renfrewshire, Glasgow
City, Inverclyde, North Ayrshire, North
Lanarkshire, Renfrewshire, South Ayrshire,
South Lanarkshire and West Dunbartonshire
areas
City Chambers, George Square, Glasgow
G2 1DU
Tel: 0141-287 5894; fax 0141-287 4173
Chair, B. Maan
Clerk to the Board, J. Andrews

TAYSIDE JOINT POLICE BOARD
Covers Angus, Dundee City, and Perth and
Kinross areas
St James House, St James Road, Forfar
DD8 2ZE
Tel: 01307-461460; fax 01307-464834
Chair, J. Corrigan
Clerk to the Board, Ms C. Coull

POLICE FORCES

Strength: actual strength of force as at mid
1999

CENTRAL SCOTLAND POLICE
HQ, Randolphfield, Stirling FK8 2HD
Tel: 01786-456000; fax 01786-451177
Web: http://www.centralscotland.police.uk
Strength, 713
Chief Constable, W. J. M. Wilson, QPM

DUMFRIES AND GALLOWAY
CONSTABULARY
HQ, Cornwall Mount, Dumfries DG1 1PZ
Tel: 01387-252112; fax 01387-260501
Web: http://www.dumfriesandgalloway.
   police.uk
Strength, 439
Chief Constable, W. Rae, QPM
Chair, B. Conchie

FIFE CONSTABULARY
HQ, Detroit Road, Glenrothes, Fife KY6 2RJ
Tel: 01592-418888; fax 01592-418444
Web: http://www.fife.police.uk
Strength, 840
Chief Constable, J. P. Hamilton, QPM
Chair, A. Keddie

GRAMPIAN POLICE
HQ, Queen Street, Aberdeen AB10 1ZA
Tel: 01224-386000; fax 01224-643366
Web: http://www.grampian.police.uk
Strength, 1,220
Chief Constable, A. G. Brown, QPM

LOTHIAN AND BORDERS POLICE
HQ, Fettes Avenue, Edinburgh EH4 1RB
Tel: 0131-311 3131; fax 0131-332 0115
Web: http://www.lbp.police.uk
Strength, 2,615
Chief Constable, R. Cameron, QPM

NORTHERN CONSTABULARY
HQ, Old Perth Road, Inverness IV2 3SY
Tel: 01463-715555; fax 01463-720373
Web: http://www.northern.police.uk
Strength, 659
Chief Constable, W. A. Robertson, QPM

STRATHCLYDE POLICE
HQ, 173 Pitt Street, Glasgow G2 4JS
Tel: 0141-532 2000; fax 0141-532 2618
Web: http://www.strathclyde.police.uk
Strength, 7,008
Chief Constable, J. Orr, OBE, QPM

TAYSIDE POLICE
HQ, PO Box 59, West Bell Street, Dundee
DD1 9JU
Tel: 01382-223200; fax: 01382-200449
Strength, 1,150
Chief Constable, W. A. Spence, QPM

OTHER POLICE FORCES

BRITISH TRANSPORT POLICE
Scottish HQ: 90 Cowcaddens Road, Glasgow
G4 0LU
Tel: 0141-332 3649
UK strength (March 1999), 2,106
Assistant Chief Constable, Scotland, S. Manion

MINISTRY OF DEFENCE POLICE
Operational Command Unit HQ Scotland:
HMNB Clyde, Helensburgh, Dunbartonshire
G84 8HL
Tel: 01436-674321
UK strength (March 1999), 3,577
Operational Commander, Scotland, Supt. S. R.
Mason

UK ATOMIC ENERGY AUTHORITY
CONSTABULARY
UK HQ: Building E6, Culham Science
Centre, Abingdon, Oxon OX14 3DB
Tel: 01235-463760
UK strength (June 1999), 498
Chief Constable, W. F. Pryke

STAFF ASSOCIATIONS

Police officers are not permitted to join a trade
union or to take strike action. All ranks have
their own staff associations.

ASSOCIATION OF CHIEF POLICE OFFICERS
IN SCOTLAND
Represents the Chief Constables, Deputy and
Assistant Chief Constables of the Scottish
police forces
Police Headquarters, Fettes Avenue,
Edinburgh EH4 1RB
Tel: 0131-311 3051
Hon. Secretary, H. R. Cameron, QPM

THE ASSOCIATION OF SCOTTISH POLICE
SUPERINTENDENTS
Represents officers of the rank of
Superintendent
Secretariat, 173 Pitt Street, Glasgow G2 4JS
Tel: 0141-221 5796
President, Chief Supt. S. Davidson

THE SCOTTISH POLICE FEDERATION
Represents officers up to and including the
rank of Chief Inspector
5 Woodside Place, Glasgow G3 7QF
Tel: 0141-332 5234
General Secretary, D. J. Keil, QPM

THE PRISON SERVICE

The prison service is the responsibility of the Scottish Executive Justice Department. The chief executive of the Scottish Prison Service is responsible for the day-to-day running of the system.

There are 23 prison establishments in Scotland. Convicted prisoners are classified according to their perceived security risk and are housed in establishments appropriate to that level of security. Female prisoners are housed in women's establishments or in separate wings of mixed prisons. Remand prisoners are, where possible, housed separately from convicted prisoners. Offenders under the age of 21 are usually detained in a young offenders' institution, which may be a separate establishment or part of a prison.

One prison, Kilmarnock, was built, financed and is being run by private contractors.

The prison inspectorate (*see* page 51) is independent and reports annually to the Scottish Executive Justice Department on prison conditions and the treatment of prisoners. Every prison establishment also has an independent board of visitors or visiting committee made up of local volunteers appointed by the Justice Minister. Any prisoner whose complaint is not satisfied by the internal complaints procedures may complain to the Scottish Prisons Complaints Commission (*see* page 71).

Women make up only 3 per cent of the Scottish prison population. Custody is less frequently used as a sanction against female offenders; in 1996, for example, only 4 per cent of women convicted of offences received a custodial sentence, whereas 11.1 per cent of all offenders received such a sentence.

AVERAGE DAILY POPULATION IN
SCOTTISH PENAL ESTABLISHMENTS
1993-8

1993–4	5,588
1994–5	5,630
1995–6	5,632
1996–7	5,992
1997–8	6,059

Source: Scottish Prison Service, *Annual Report and Accounts 1997–8*

AVERAGE DAILY PRISON POPULATION 1997
(BY TYPE OF CUSTODY AND SEX)

	Total	Male	Female
Remand: total	947	901	46
untried	850	816	34
convicted awaiting sentence	98	86	12
Under sentence: total	5,134	4,996	138
young offenders	787	768	19
adult prisoners	4,281	4,163	118
persons recalled from supervision/ licence	46	45	1
others	19	19	—
Sentenced by court martial	1	1	—
Civil prisoners	1	1	—
Total	6,083	5,899	184

Source: Scottish Office Statistical Bulletin, December 1998

AVERAGE DAILY SENTENCED
POPULATION BY LENGTH OF SENTENCE
1997-8

	Adults	Young Offenders
Less than 4 years	2,141	574
4 years or over (including life)	2,218	200
Total	4,359	774

Source: Scottish Prison Service, *Annual Report and Accounts 1997–8*

RECEPTIONS TO PENAL ESTABLISHMENTS
BY TYPE OF CUSTODY 1997-8

Remand: total	14,723
untried	11,711
convicted awaiting sentence	3,012
Under sentence: total	21,352
young offenders	4,433
adult prisoners	16,906
persons recalled from supervision/licence	13
Persons sentenced by court martial	6
Civil prisoners	21

Total receptions cannot be calculated by adding together receptions in each category because persons received first on remand and then under sentence in relation to the same set of charges are counted in both categories

Source: Scottish Prison Service, *Annual Report and Accounts 1997–8*

MAIN CRIMES AND OFFENCES OF
SENTENCED PRISONERS IN CUSTODY ON
30 JUNE 1997

Main crime/offence	Total	Male	Female
Non-sexual crimes			
of violence: total	2,188	2,146	42
homicide	644	631	13
robbery	699	697	2
Crimes of			
indecency: total	354	351	3
sexual assault	161	161	—
Crimes of			
dishonesty	1,062	1,018	44
Fire-raising,			
vandalism, etc.	69	68	1
Other crimes: total	788	757	31
drugs offences	702	674	28
Total crimes	4,461	4,340	121
Miscellaneous			
offences	450	435	15
Motor vehicle			
offences	231	229	2
Total offences	681	664	17
Unknown charge	8	8	—
Other jurisdiction			
charge	27	27	—
Total crimes			
and offences	5,177	5,039	138

Source: Scottish Office Statistical Bulletin, December
1998

PRISON SUICIDES 1997–8

	1996	1997	1998
Male	13	13	12
Female	3	1	1
Total	16	14	13

Source: Scottish Prison Service

OPERATING COSTS OF THE SCOTTISH
PRISON SERVICE 1997–8

	£
Total income	1,598,000
Total expenditure	172,071,000
Staff costs	110,874,000
Running costs	47,675,000
Other current expenditure	13,522,000
Operating deficit	(170,473,000)
Interest on capital	(23,199,000)
Interest payable and	
similar charges	(15,000)
Interest receivable	145,000
Deficit for financial year	(193,542,000)
Average annual cost per	
prisoner per place	26,170

Source: Scottish Prison Service, *Annual Report and
Accounts 1997–8*

SCOTTISH PRISON SERVICE

Calton House, 5 Redheughs Rigg, Edinburgh
EH12 9HW
Tel: 0131-556 8400

SALARIES
The following pay bands have applied since 1
October 1998:

I	£36,000–£55,600
H	£30,000–£46,350
G	£25,100–£38,150
F	£19,150–£29,450/£32,700
E	£15,300–£24,050/£27,250
D	£12,250–£19,150/£22,900
C	£10,000–£15,300/£17,500
B	£7,900–£12,250
A	£6,600–£10,300

Bands C to F have a normal maximum and an
operational maximum rate

STAFF NUMBERS
The number of Scottish Prison Service staff
(full-time and part-time) in post at 31 March
1998 was 4,856, of whom 4,069 were male and
787 female.

Chief Executive of Scottish Prison Service,
   E. W. Frizzell
Director of Custody, J. Durno, OBE
Director, Human Resources, P. Russell
Director, Finance and Information Systems,
   W. Pretswell
Director, Strategy and Corporate Affairs,
   Ms J. Hutchison
Deputy Director, Regime Services and Supplies,
   J. McNeill
Deputy Director, Estates and Buildings,
   B. Paterson
Area Director, South and West, M. Duffy
Area Director, North and East, P. Withers
Head of Training, Scottish Prison Service College,
   J. Matthews
Head of Communications, M. Mulford

PRISON ESTABLISHMENTS

The figures given here refer to the average
number of prisoners/young offenders in
1998–9.

* ABERDEEN
Craiginches, Aberdeen AB9 2HN
Prisoners, 181
Governor, I. Gunn

BARLINNIE
Barlinnie, Glasgow G33 2QX
Prisoners, 1,124
Governor, R. L. Houchin

CASTLE HUNTLY
Castle Huntly, Longforgan, nr Dundee DD2
5HL
Prisoners, 106
Governor, K. Rennie

*‡ CORNTON VALE
Cornton Road, Stirling FK9 5NY
Prisoners and Young Offenders, 180
Governor, Mrs K. Donegan

*‡ DUMFRIES
Terregles Street, Dumfries DG2 9AX
Young Offenders, 137
Governor, G. Taylor

DUNGAVEL
Dungavel House, Strathaven, Lanarkshire
ML10 6RF
Prisoners, 113
Governor, T. Pitt

EDINBURGH
33 Stenhouse Road, Edinburgh EH1 3LN
Prisoners, 731
Governor, A. Spencer

FRIARTON
Friarton, Perth PH2 8DW
Prisoners, 77
Governor, Mrs A. Mooney

‡ GLENOCHIL
King O'Muir Road, Tullibody,
Clackmannanshire FK10 3AD
Prisoners and Young Offenders, 573
Governor, L. McBain, OBE

GREENOCK
Gateside, Greenock PA16 9AH
Prisoners, 236
Governor, R. MacCowan

* INVERNESS
Porterfield, Inverness IV2 3HH
Prisoners, 122
Governor, H. Ross

KILMARNOCK
Bowhouse, Mauchline Road, Kilmarnock
KA1 5JH
Prisoners, 500
Director, J. Bywalec

LONGRIGGEND
Longriggend, nr Airdrie, Lanarkshire
ML6 7TL
Prisoners, 158
Governor, Ms R. Kite

LOW MOSS
Low Moss, Bishopbriggs, Glasgow G64 2QB
Prisoners, 362
Governor, E. Murch

NATIONAL INDUCTION UNIT
Shotts ML7 4LE
Prisoners, 48
Governor, J. Gerrie

NORANSIDE
Noranside, Fern, by Forfar, Angus DD8 3QY
Prisoners, 102
Governor, A. MacDonald

PENNINGHAME
Penninghame, Newton Stewart DG8 6RG
Prisoners, 89
Governor, S. Swan

PERTH
3 Edinburgh Road, Perth PH2 8AT
Prisoners, 477
Governor, W. Millar

PETERHEAD
Salthouse Head, Peterhead, Aberdeenshire
AB4 6YY
Prisoners, 297
Governor, W. Rattray
Governor, Peterhead Unit, B. McConnell

‡ POLMONT
Brightons, Falkirk, Stirlingshire FK2 0AB
Young Offenders, 443
Governor, D. Gunn

SHOTTS
Shotts ML7 4LF
Prisoners, 467
Governor, W. McKinlay
Governor, Shotts Unit, G. Storer

* Women's establishments or establishments with units
for women
‡ Young Offender Institution or establishment with
units for young offenders

THE FIRE SERVICE

The Scottish Executive Justice Department has overall responsibility for fire services, including the provision of training at the Scottish Fire Service Training School.

Each local council in Scotland is the fire authority for its area. There are six joint fire boards, comprising groups of council areas which have delegated their fire authority responsibilities to the boards. The remaining two councils, Dumfries and Galloway and Fife, each act as the fire authority for their whole council area. Membership of the joint boards comprises elected members of each of the constituent councils. The fire authorities are responsible for setting a budget, making an establishment scheme (which details fire brigade, fire stations and equipment), a 'mutual assistance' scheme for handling major incidents, and hearing disciplinary cases or appeals. Subject to the approval of the Scottish Ministers, fire authorities appoint a firemaster, who is responsible for the operation of the fire brigade, and other senior fire brigade officials.

Fire brigades are financed by local government, with the exception of some central services (e.g. the Scottish Fire Service Training School) which are financed by the Scottish Executive. Joint fire boards set their budgets and requisition the necessary finance from their constituent councils. The two councils that directly administer their fire brigades set budgets as for their other services. The Scottish Executive pays an annual civil defence grant to each joint board for its role in emergency planning.

HM Inspectorate of Fire Services for Scotland (see page 50) carries out inspections of fire brigades in order to improve the efficiency, effectiveness and standards of the fire service. HM Chief Inspector of Fire Services publishes an annual report. The interests of fire authorities and members of the fire brigades are considered by the Scottish Central Fire Brigades Advisory Council.

JOINT FIRE BOARDS

The Dumfries and Galloway council area and the Fife council area do not have joint boards as a single authority covers the whole of the fire brigade area. The chairman/convenor of the authority for these two brigades is given with the brigade's details.

CENTRAL SCOTLAND FIRE BOARD
Covers Clackmannanshire, Falkirk and Stirling areas

Municipal Buildings, Falkirk FK1 5RS
Tel: 01324-506070; fax 01324-506071
Convenor, T. Coll
Clerk to the Board, Ms E. Morton

GRAMPIAN FIRE BOARD
Covers Aberdeen City, Aberdeenshire and Moray areas
Woodhill House, Westburn Road, Aberdeen AB16 5GB
Tel: 01224-665430; fax 01224-664888
Chairman, R. Stroud
Clerk to the Board, N. McDowall

HIGHLAND AND ISLANDS FIRE BOARD
Covers Highland, Orkney Islands, Shetland Islands and Western Isles areas
Glenurquhart Road, Inverness IV3 5NX
Tel: 01463-702854; fax 01463-702182
Chairman, A. R. Macfarlane Slack
Clerk to the Board, M. Notman

LOTHIAN AND BORDERS FIRE BOARD
Covers City of Edinburgh, East Lothian, Midlothian, Scottish Borders and West Lothian areas
City Chambers, High Street, Edinburgh EH1 1YG
Tel: 0131-469 3002; fax 0131-529 4764
Convenor, K. Harrold
Clerk to the Board, T. Aitchison

STRATHCLYDE JOINT FIRE BOARD
Covers Argyll and Bute, East Ayrshire, East Dunbartonshire, East Renfrewshire, Glasgow City, Inverclyde, North Ayrshire, North Lanarkshire, Renfrewshire, South Ayrshire, South Lanarkshire and West Dunbartonshire areas
Council Offices, Almada Street, Hamilton ML3 0AA
Tel: 01698-454872
Clerk to the Board, A. MacNish

TAYSIDE FIRE BOARD
Covers Angus, Dundee City and Perth and Kinross areas
2 High Street, Perth PH1 5PH
Tel: 01738-475101
Clerk to the Board, R. Jackson

FIRE BRIGADES

CENTRAL SCOTLAND FIRE BRIGADE
HQ, Main Street, Maddiston, Falkirk FK2 0LG
Tel: 01324-716996; fax 01324-715353
Firemaster, I. Adam, OBE, QFSM

DUMFRIES AND GALLOWAY FIRE BRIGADE
HQ, Brooms Road, Dumfries DG1 2DZ
Tel: 01387-252222; fax 01387-260995
Chairman, B. Conchie
Firemaster, L. Ibbotson

FIFE FIRE AND RESCUE SERVICE
HQ, Strathore Road, Thornton, Kirkcaldy
KY1 4DF
Tel: 01592-774451; fax 01592-630105
Chairman, A. Keddie
Firemaster, N. Campion

GRAMPIAN FIRE BRIGADE
HQ, 19 North Anderson Drive, Aberdeen
AB15 6DW
Tel: 01224-696666; fax 01224-692224
Firemaster, J. Williams

HIGHLAND AND ISLANDS FIRE BRIGADE
HQ, 16 Harbour Road, Longman West,
Inverness IV1 1TB
Tel: 01463-227000; fax 01463-236979
Firemaster, B. Murray

LOTHIAN AND BORDERS FIRE BRIGADE
HQ, Lauriston Place, Edinburgh EH3 9DE
Tel: 0131-228 2401; fax 0131-228 6662
Firemaster, C. Cranston

STRATHCLYDE FIRE BRIGADE
HQ, Bothwell Road, Hamilton ML3 0EA
Tel: 01698-300999; fax 01698-338444
Firemaster, J. Jameson, CBE, QFSM

TAYSIDE FIRE BRIGADE
HQ, Blackness Road, Dundee DD1 5PA
Tel: 01382-322222; fax 01382-200791
Firemaster, D. Marr, QFSM

STAFF ASSOCIATIONS

THE CHIEF AND ASSISTANT CHIEF FIRE
OFFICERS' ASSOCIATION
10-11 Pebble Close, Amington, Tamworth
B77 4RD
Tel: 01827-61516; fax 01827-61530
General Manager, K. Rose, MBE

THE FIRE BRIGADES UNION
4th Floor, 52 St Enoch Square, Glasgow
G1 4AA
Tel: 0141-221 2309
Scottish Regional Secretary, T. Tierney

SCOTTISH CENTRAL FIRE BRIGADES
ADVISORY COUNCIL
Scottish Executive Justice Department, Room
F1-8, Saughton House, Edinburgh EH11 3XD
Tel: 0131-244 2166
Chairman, J. Hamill
Secretary, R. Knowles

EMERGENCY PLANNING

Emergency planning grew out of arrangements under the Civil Defence Grant Regulations 1956. After the Cold War, it was decided that emergency planning should continue to be dealt with under these regulations. The term 'civil defence' has now fallen into disuse, as the system deals solely with emergency planning.

The Scottish Executive Justice Department is responsible for promoting emergency planning for both peacetime and wartime by central government and local authorities, and co-ordinating preparation for civil emergencies by the Scottish Executive departments.

Each local council, police force and fire authority receives an annual grant from the Scottish Executive for emergency planning and has at least one emergency planning officer. At the end of the financial year, each body reports to the Scottish Executive. In addition, each local council is required to keep a contingency fund for emergencies, calculated according to a formula based on the number of council tax payers in the area. If this fund is exceeded in spending on an emergency, there is a scheme whereby the council can be reimbursed by the Scottish Executive for 85 per cent of the uninsured balance.

Emergency Management

The basis of emergency planning and response is 'integrated emergency management', which requires close co-ordination and co-operation between all the emergency services and agencies involved. The approach aims to dovetail the capabilities of the emergency services closely with those of local authorities and other agencies while retaining flexibility in response to suit local circumstances. Emergencies are dealt with locally, in liaison with the relevant 'lead' Scottish or UK department. If an emergency occurs off the coast, the Coastguard has overall responsibility. The lead department co-ordinates the activities of central government departments in response to the emergency, co-ordinates the gathering of information on the emergency, and informs both ministers and Parliament and the public.

During an emergency, response management is divided into three levels of command and control:
- operational, involving immediate on-site actions (e.g. controlling cordons, putting out fires, evacuating casualties)
- tactical, taking decisions about priorities and resource allocation, assigning expertise
- strategic, activity at police headquarters (e.g. taking an overview establishing a policy framework to support incident officers working at the tactical level)

The police co-ordinate during the initial phase at the scene of the emergency (known as the 'blue light phase'), with the assistance of the fire brigade if necessary. After this phase the police formally hand over control to the chief executive of the local council, who co-ordinates the subsequent stages.

Because civil defence grant is now spent solely on emergency planning, which is in any case a function of local government, it is probable that in the next two years there will be a proposal to abolish the civil defence grant paid to local authorities, police and fire authorities, and subsume the amount into overall revenue support grant. This would be subject to the decision of the Scottish Parliament.

LOCAL GOVERNMENT

The Local Government etc. (Scotland) Act 1994 abolished the two-tier structure of nine regional and 53 district councils which had existed since 1975 and replaced it, from 1 April 1996, with a single-tier structure consisting of 29 unitary authorities on the mainland; the three islands councils remain. Each unitary authority has inherited all the functions of the regional and district councils, except water and sewerage (now provided by public bodies whose members are appointed by the Scottish Ministers) and reporters panels (now a national agency).

On taking office, the Scottish Parliament assumed responsibility for legislation on local government. The Commission on Local Government, established to make recommendations on the relationship between local authorities and the Scottish Parliament and on increasing local authorities' accountability, reports to the First Minister.

Elections

The unitary authorities consist of directly elected councillors. Elections take place every three years, normally on the first Thursday in May. The 1999 local government elections were held on 6 May, simultaneously with the elections for the Scottish Parliament.

Generally, all British subjects and citizens of the Republic of Ireland who are 18 years or over and resident on the qualifying date in the area for which the election is being held, are entitled to vote at them. A register of electors is prepared and published annually by local electoral registration officers. Candidates, who are subject to various statutory qualifications and disqualifications designed to ensure that they are suitable persons to hold office, must be nominated by electors for the electoral area concerned. The electoral roll that came into effect on 16 February 1999 showed 4,027,433 people registered to vote in the Scottish Parliament and local government elections.

The Local Government Boundary Commission (see page 61) for Scotland is responsible for carrying out periodic reviews of electoral arrangements and making proposals to the Scottish Ministers for any changes found necessary.

Internal Organization and Functions

The council as a whole is the final decision-making body within any authority. Councils are free to a great extent to make their own internal organizational arrangements. Normally, questions of policy are settled by the full council, while the administration of the various services is the responsibility of committees of councillors. Day-to-day decisions are delegated to the council's officers, who act within the policies laid down by the councillors.

The functions of the councils and islands councils are: education; social work; strategic planning; the provision of infrastructure such as roads; consumer protection; flood prevention; coast protection; valuation and rating; the police and fire services; emergency planning; electoral registration; public transport; registration of births, deaths and marriages; housing; leisure and recreation; development control and building control; environmental health; licensing; allotments; public conveniences; and the administration of district courts.

The chairman of a local council in Scotland may be known as a convenor; a provost is the equivalent of a mayor. The chairman of the council in the cities of Aberdeen, Dundee, Edinburgh and Glasgow are Lord Provosts.

Lord-Lieutenants

The Lord-Lieutenant of a county is the permanent local representative of the Crown in that county. They are appointed by the Sovereign on the recommendation of the Prime Minister. The retirement age is 75.

The office of Lord-Lieutenant dates from 1557, and its holder was originally responsible for the maintenance of order and for local defence in the county. The duties of the post include attending on royalty during official visits to the county, performing certain duties in connection with armed forces of the Crown (and in particular the reserve forces), and making presentations of honours and awards on behalf of the Crown.

LORD-LIEUTENANTS

Title	Name
Aberdeenshire	A. D. M. Farquharson
Angus	The Earl of Airlie, KT, GCVO, PC
Argyll and Bute	The Duke of Argyll
Ayrshire and Arran	Maj. R. Y. Henderson, TD
Banffshire	J. A. S. McPherson, CBE

Berwickshire	Maj.-Gen. Sir John Swinton, KCVO, OBE
Caithness	Maj. G. T. Dunnett TD
Clackmannan	Lt.-Col. R. C. Stewart, CBE, TD
Dumfries	Capt. R. C. Cunningham-Jardine
Dunbartonshire	Brig. D. D. G. Hardie, TD
East Lothian	Sir Hew Hamilton-Dalrymple, Bt., KCVO
Eilean Siar/ Western Isles	The Viscount Dunrossil, CMG
Fife	Mrs C. M. Dean
Inverness	The Lord Gray of Contin, PC
Kincardineshire	The Viscount of Arbuthnott, KT, CBE, DSC, FRSE
Lanarkshire	H. B. Sneddon, CBE
Midlothian	Capt. G. W. Burnet, LVO
Moray	Air Vice-Marshal G. A. Chesworth, CB, OBE, DFC
Nairn	vacant
Orkney	G. R. Marwick
Perth and Kinross	Sir David Montgomery, Bt.
Renfrewshire	C. H. Parker, OBE
Ross and Cromarty	Capt. R. W. K. Stirling of Fairburn, TD
Roxburgh, Ettrick and Lauderdale	Dr June Paterson-Brown
Shetland	J. H. Scott
Stirling and Falkirk	Lt.-Col. J. Stirling of Garden, CBE, TD, FRICS
Sutherland	Maj.-Gen. D. Houston, CBE
The Stewartry of Kirkcudbright	Lt.-Gen. Sir Norman Arthur, KCB
Tweeddale	Capt. J. D. B. Younger
West Lothian	The Earl of Morton
Wigtown	Maj. E. S. Orr-Ewing

The Lord Provosts of the four city districts of Aberdeen, Dundee, Edinburgh and Glasgow are Lord-Lieutenants for those districts ex officio.

Community Councils

Unlike the parish councils and community councils in England and Wales, Scottish community councils are not local authorities. Their purpose as defined in statute is to ascertain and express the views of the communities which they represent, and to take in the interests of their communities such action as appears to be expedient or practicable. Over 1,000 community councils have been established under schemes drawn up by district and islands councils in Scotland.

Since 1996 community councils have had an enhanced role, becoming statutory consultees on local planning issues and on the decentralization schemes which the new councils have to draw up for delivery of services.

FINANCE

Local government is financed from four sources: the council tax, non-domestic rates, government grants, and income from fees and charges for services.

Council Tax

Under the Local Government Finance Act 1992, from 1 April 1993 the council tax replaced the community charge, which had been introduced in April 1989 in place of domestic rates. The council tax is a local tax levied by each local council. Liability for the council tax bill usually falls on the owner-occupier or tenant of a dwelling which is their sole or main residence.

Each island council and unitary authority sets its own rate of council tax. The tax relates to the value of the dwelling. Each dwelling is placed in one of eight valuation bands, ranging from A to H, based on the property's estimated market value as at 1 April 1991.

The valuation bands and ranges of values in Scotland are:

A	Up to £27,000
B	£27,001–£35,000
C	£35,001–£45,000
D	£45,001–£58,000
E	£58,001–£80,000
F	£80,001–£106,000
G	£106,001–£212,000
H	Over £212,000

The council tax within a local area varies between the different bands according to proportions laid down by law. The charge attributable to each band as a proportion of the Band D charge set by the council is approximately:

A	67%
B	78%
C	89%
D	100%
E	122%

F   144%
G   167%
H   200%

The Band D rate for each council is given on pages 93–109. There may be variations from the given figure within each district council area because of different community precepts being levied.

Non-Domestic Rates

Non-domestic (business) rates are collected by the billing authorities, which in Scotland are the local authorities. Rates are levied in accordance with the Local Government (Scotland) Act 1975. From 1995–6, the Secretary of State for Scotland prescribed a single non-domestic rates poundage to apply throughout the country at the same level as the uniform business rate (UBR) in England. The UBR for 1998–9 was 48p for property up to a rateable value of £10,000 and 48.9p for property over a rateable value of £10,000. Rate income is pooled and redistributed to local authorities on a per capita basis.

Rateable values for the current rating lists came into force on 1 April 1995. They are derived from the rental value of property as at 1 April 1993 and determined on certain statutory assumptions by Regional Assessors. New property which is added to the list, and significant changes to existing property, necessitate amendments to the rateable value on the same basis. Valuation rolls remain in force until the next general revaluation. Such revaluations take place every five years. New ratings lists come into force on 1 April 2000, based on rental levels as at 1 April 1998.

Certain types of property, such as places of public religious worship and agricultural land and buildings, are exempt from rates. Charities, other non-profit-making organizations, sole village shops and post offices, and certain other businesses may receive full or partial relief. Empty property is liable to pay rates at 50 per cent, except for certain specified classes which are entirely exempt.

In 1998–9, total receipts were £1,441 million (provisional) from non-domestic rates and £1,046 million from the council tax. The amount of council tax budgeted to be collected in 1999–2000 is £1,470.1 million.

Government Grants

In addition to specific grants in support of revenue expenditure on particular services, central government pays revenue support grant to local authorities. This grant is paid to each local authority so that if each authority budgeted at the level of its standard spending assessment, all authorities in the same class can set broadly the same council tax.

Expenditure

Local authority current budgeted expenditure, supported by aggregate external finance (AEF), for 1999–2000 was:

Service	£m
Tourism	8
Roads and transport	355
Housing	4
Other environmental services	749
Law, order and protective services	914
Education	2,875
Arts and libraries	115
Social work services	1,172
Housing benefit administration	30
Sheltered employment	10
Consumer protection	19
Total	6,251
Total excluding housing benefits, sheltered employment and consumer protection	6,192

COMPLAINTS

Commissioners for Local Administration (*see* page 54) are responsible for investigating complaints from members of the public who claim to have suffered injustice as a consequence of maladministration in local government or in certain local bodies.

Complaints are made to the relevant local authority in the first instance and are referred to the Commissioners if the complainant is not satisfied.

LOCAL AUTHORITY AREAS

1 Aberdeen City	9 Glasgow City
2 City of Edinburgh	10 Inverclyde
3 Clackmannanshire	11 Midlothian
4 Dundee City	12 North Ayrshire
5 East Ayrshire	13 North Lanarkshire
6 East Dunbartonshire	14 Renfrewshire
7 East Renfrewshire	15 West Dunbartonshire
8 Falkirk	16 West Lothian

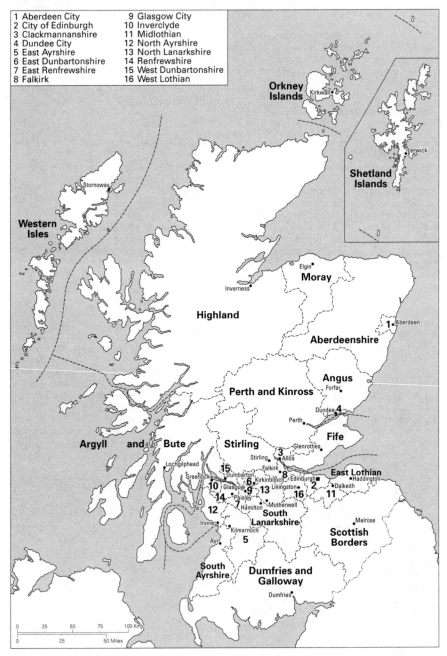

COUNCIL DIRECTORY

ABERDEEN CITY COUNCIL
Town House
Broad Street
Aberdeen
AB10 1FY
Tel: 01224-522000; fax: 01224-627213
Web: http://www.aberdeen.net.uk

Statistical profile
Area (1998): 186 sq. km
Population (1998 estimate): 213,070
population density (1998): 1,147 persons per sq. km
projected population in 2006 (1996-based): 213,247
number of households (1996): 96,800

Council tax (average Band D per two-person household), as at 1 April 1999: £1,033.25
Non-domestic rateable value (1997–8): £263,037,000

Education (pupils on register, 1997–8):
primary: 15,824
secondary: 10,577
special: 468
entitled to free meals: 13.3%

The Council
Total number of seats: 43
Political composition (as at end May 1999):
Lab. 22, LD 12, C. 6, SNP 3

Lord Provost: Rt. Hon. M. Smith
Leader of the Council: L. Ironside

Chief Officers:
Chief Executive, D. Paterson
Director of Community Services, J. Tomlinson
Director of Contracting Services, D. Gordon
Director of Education, J. Stodter
Director of Environmental Health, G. Duffus
Director of Finance, G. Edwards
Director of Housing, M. Scott
Director of Information Technology, A. Lawtie
Director of Legal Services, C. Langley
Director of Personnel, L. Common
Director of Planning, P. Cockhead
Director of Social Services, P. Cassidy
Local Agenda 21 contact, G. Robertson

Lord Lieutenancy: The Lord Provost is also, ex officio, Lord Lieutenant of Aberdeen
(for current holder of post, *see* above)
Scottish Parliament constituencies: Aberdeen Central; Aberdeen North; Aberdeen South*
UK Parliament constituencies: Aberdeen Central; Aberdeen North; Aberdeen South†

ABERDEENSHIRE COUNCIL
Woodhill House, Westburn Road,
Aberdeen AB16 5GB
Tel: 01467-620981; fax: 01224-665444
Web: http://www.aberdeenshire.gov.uk

Statistical profile
Area (1998): 6,318 sq. km
Population (1998 estimate): 226,260
population density (1998): 36 persons per sq. km
projected population in 2006 (1996-based): 238,034
number of households (1996): 87,100

Council tax (average Band D per two-person household), as at 1 April 1999: £719.00
Non-domestic rateable value (1997–8): £117,582,000

Education (pupils on register, 1997–8):
primary: 21,290
secondary: 14,717
special: 367
entitled to free meals: 5.6%

The Council
Total number of seats: 68
Political composition (as at end May 1999):
LD 28, SNP 23, Ind. 10, Com. 7

Convenor: R. Bisset
Leader of the Council: Ms A. M. Findlay

Chief Officers:
Chief Executive, A. G. Campbell
Director of Education and Recreation, M. White
Director of Environmental Health and Consumer Protection, E. Melrose
Director of Finance, A. McLean
Director of Law and Administration, N. McDowall
Director of Personnel and Information Technology, P. Hay
Director of Planning and Development, A. G. Garvie *(acting)*
Director of Social Work and Housing, Mrs M. Wells
Local Agenda 21 Officer, Ms D. Burroughs

Lord Lieutenancy areas: Aberdeenshire; Banffshire; Kincardineshire
(for current holder of posts, *see* pages 89,90)
Scottish Parliament constituencies: Aberdeenshire West and Kincardine; Banff and Buchan; Gordon*
UK Parliament constituencies: Aberdeenshire West and Kincardine; Banff and Buchan; Gordon†

ANGUS COUNCIL

The Cross
Forfar, Angus DD8 1BX
Tel: 01307-461460; fax: 01307-461874
Web: http://www.angus.gov.uk

Statistical profile

Area (1998): 2,181 sq. km
Population (1998 estimate): 110,070
population density (1998): 50 persons per sq.
km
projected population in 2006 (1996-based):
110,130
number of households (1996): 46,200

Council tax (average Band D per two-person
household), as at 1 April 1999: £938.60
Non-domestic rateable value (1997–8):
£51,395,000

Education (pupils on register, 1997–8):
primary: 9,373
secondary: 7,069
special: —
entitled to free meals: 10.4%

The Council

Total number of seats: 29
Political composition (as at end May 1999):
SNP 21, Ind. 3, C. 2, LD 2, Lab.1

Provost: Mrs F. E. Duncan
Leader of the Council: R. Murray

Chief Officers:
Chief Executive, A. B. Watson
Director of Contract Services, M. Graham
Director of Cultural Services, G. Drummond
Director of Education, J. Anderson
Director of Environmental and Consumer
Protection, S. Heggie
Director of Finance, D. Sawers
Director of Housing, R. Ashton
Director of Information Technology,
A. Greenhill
Director of Law and Administration,
Ms C. Coull
Director of Personnel, Ms J. Torbet
Director of Planning and Transport,
A. Anderson
Director of Property Services, M. Lunny
Director of Recreation Services, J. Zimny
Director of Roads, R. McLellan
Director of Social Work, W. Robertson
Local Agenda 21 Officer, Ms P. Coutts

Lord Lieutenancy area: Angus
(for current holder of post, see page 89)
Scottish Parliament constituencies: Angus;
Tayside North*
UK Parliament constituencies: Angus; Tayside
North†

ARGYLL AND BUTE COUNCIL

Kilmory
Lochgilphead
Argyll
PA31 8RT
Tel: 01546-602127; fax: 01546-604138
Web: http://www.argyll-bute.gov.uk

Statistical profile

Area (1998): 6,930 sq. km
Population (1998 estimate): 89,980
population density (1998): 13 persons per sq.
km
projected population in 2006 (1996-based):
89,461
number of households (1996): 37,700

Council tax (average Band D per two-person
household), as at 1 April 1999: £1,070.10
Non-domestic rateable value (1997–8):
£65,985,000

Education (pupils on register, 1997–8):
primary: 7,747
secondary: 5,390
special: 54
entitled to free meals: 13.4%

The Council

Total number of seats: 36
Political composition (as at end May 1999):
Ind. 19, LD 6, SNP 5, C. 4, Lab. 1, NP 1

Convenor: D. C. Currie
Leader of the Council: Ms A. Hay

Chief Officers:
Chief Executive, J. A. McLellan
Director of Corporate and Legal Services,
N. Stewart
Director of Development and Environment
Services, G. Harper
Director of Education, A. Morton
Director of Finance, S. MacGregor
Director of Housing and Social Work,
D. Hendry
Director of Information Technology,
G. Williamson
Local Agenda 21 Officer, vacant

Lord Lieutenancy area: Argyll and Bute
(for current holder of post, see page 89)
Scottish Parliament constituencies: Argyll and
Bute; Dumbarton*
UK Parliament constituencies: Argyll and Bute;
Dumbarton†

---

* For election results and MSPs, see pages 24–35
† For election results and MPs, see pages 36–45

CITY OF EDINBURGH COUNCIL

Wellington Court
10 Waterloo Place
Edinburgh EH1 3EG
Tel: 0131-200 2000; fax: 0131-529 7477
Web: http://www.edinburgh.gov.uk

Statistical profile

Area (1998): 262 sq. km
Population (1998 estimate): 450,180
  population density (1998): 1,716 persons per
  sq. km
  projected population in 2006 (1996-based):
  455,608
  number of households (1996): 198,200

*Council tax (average Band D per two-person
household), as at 1 April 1999:* £889.00
Non-domestic rateable value (1997–8):
£520,273,000

Education (pupils on register, 1997–8):
  primary: 30,256
  secondary: 17,952
  special: 792
  entitled to free meals: 24.6%

The Council

Total number of seats: 58
Political composition (as at end May 1999):
  Lab. 31, C. 13, LD 13, SNP 1

Lord Provost: Rt. Hon. E. Milligan
Leader of the Council: D. Anderson

Chief Officers:
  Chief Executive, T. N. Aitchison
  Director of City Development, vacant
  Director of Corporate Services, D. Hume
  Director of Education, R. Jobson
  *Director of Environmental and Consumer
  Services,* M. Drewry
  Director of Finance and Information Technology,
  D. McGougan
  Director of Housing, M. Turley
  Director of Recreation, H. Coutts *(acting)*
  Director of Social Work, L. McEwan
  Local Agenda 21 Officer, D. Hume

Lord Lieutenancy: The Lord Provost is also, ex
  officio, Lord Lieutenant of Edinburgh
  (for current holder of post, *see* above)
Scottish Parliament constituencies: Edinburgh
  Central; Edinburgh East and Musselburgh;
  Edinburgh North and Leith; Edinburgh
  Pentlands; Edinburgh South; Edinburgh
  West*
UK Parliament constituencies: Edinburgh
  Central; Edinburgh East and Musselburgh;
  Edinburgh North and Leith; Edinburgh
  Pentlands; Edinburgh South; Edinburgh
  West†

CLACKMANNANSHIRE COUNCIL

Greenfield
Alloa
Clackmannanshire
FK10 2AD
Tel: 01259-450000; fax: 01259-452230

Statistical profile

Area (1998): 157 sq. km
Population (1998 estimate): 48,560
  population density (1998): 310 persons per
  sq. km
  projected population in 2006 (1996-based):
  49,272
  number of households (1996): 20,000

*Council tax (average Band D per two-person
household), as at 1 April 1999:* £753.00
Non-domestic rateable value (1997–8):
£27,897,000

Education (pupils on register, 1997–8):
  primary: 4,542
  secondary: 2,960
  special: 66
  entitled to free meals: 20.0%

The Council

Total number of seats: 18
Political composition (as at end May 1999):
  SNP 9, Lab. 8, Com.1

Provost: W. McAdam
Leader of the Council: K. Brown

Chief Officers:
  Chief Executive, R. Allan
  Executive Director of Corporate Services,
  R. Dunbar
  Executive Director of Development Services,
  G. Dallas
  *Executive Director of Education and Community
  Services,* K. Bloomer
  *Executive Director of Environmental and
  Contract Services,* W. Cunningham
  Executive Director of Social Services,
  Ms B. Dickie
  Head of Housing and Advice Services,
  C. J. Thirkettle
  Head of Information Technology, Ms A. Easton
  Head of Legal Services, Mrs J. McGuire
  Head of Personnel, B. Hutchison
  Local Agenda 21 contacts, N. Deasley; A. Shaw

Lord Lieutenancy area: Clackmannan
  (for current holder of post, *see* page 90)
Scottish Parliament constituency: Ochil*
UK Parliament constituency: Ochil†

DUMFRIES AND GALLOWAY COUNCIL

Council Offices
English Street
Dumfries
DG1 2DD
Tel: 01387-260000; fax: 01387-260034
Web: http://www.dumgal.gov.uk

Statistical profile

Area (1998): 6,439 sq. km
Population (1998 estimate): 147,300
 population density (1998): 23 persons per sq.
 km
 projected population in 2006 (1996-based):
 146,469
 number of households (1996): 62,300

*Council tax (average Band D per two-person
 household), as at 1 April 1999:* £766.00
Non-domestic rateable value (1997–8):
£82,164,000

Education (pupils on register, 1997–8):
 primary: 12,958
 secondary: 9,362
 special: 32
 entitled to free meals: 12.0%

The Council

Total number of seats: 47
Political composition (as at end May 1999):
 Ind. 15, Lab. 13, C. 8, LD 6, SNP 5

Convenor: A. Campbell
Leader of the Council: J. Forteath

Chief Officers:
 Chief Executive, P. N. Jones
 Director of Community Services, L. Jardine
 Director of Contracting Services, R. Blackburn
 Director of Education, F. Sanderson *(acting)*
 Director of Environment and Infrastructure,
 Dr R. Guy
 Director of Environmental Health, D. A. Grant
 Director of Finance, J. Cowie
 Director of Housing, Ms Y. MacQuarrie
 Director of Information Services, Dr J. Pearson
 Director of Legal Services, B. Kearney
 Director of Personnel, D. Archibald
 Director of Social Services, K. Makin
 Local Agenda 21 Officer, Ms J. Gray

Lord Lieutenancy areas: Dumfries; Stewartry of
 Kirkcudbright; Wigtown
 (for current holder of posts, *see* page 90)
Scottish Parliament constituencies: Dumfries;
 Galloway and Upper Nithsdale*
UK Parliament constituencies: Dumfries;
 Galloway and Upper Nithsdale†

DUNDEE CITY COUNCIL

21 City Square
Dundee DD1 3BY
Tel: 01382-434000; fax: 01382-434666
Web: http://www.dundeecity.gov.uk

Statistical profile

Area (1998): 65 sq. km
Population (1998 estimate): 146,690
 population density (1998): 2,252 persons per
 sq. km
 projected population in 2006 (1996-based):
 141,965
 number of households (1996): 67,500

*Council tax (average Band D per two-person
 household), as at 1 April 1999:* £1,238.60
Non-domestic rateable value (1997–8):
£123,422,000

Education (pupils on register, 1997–8):
 primary: 12,287
 secondary: 8,556
 special: 185
 entitled to free meals: 21.5%

The Council

Total number of seats: 29
Political composition (as at end May 1999):
 Lab. 14, SNP 10, C. 4, Ind. Lab. 1

Lord Provost: Rt. Hon. H. W. Wright
Leader of the Council: Ms J. Sturrock

Chief Officers:
 Chief Executive, A. Stephen
 Chief Neighbourhood Resources Officer,
 F. Patrick
 Director of Contract Services, R. Jackson
 Director of Education, Ms A. Wilson
 *Director of Environmental and Consumer
 Protection,* R. Gabriel
 Director of Finance, D. Dorward
 Director of Housing, Mrs E. Zwirlein
 Director of Information Technology, A. Allan
 Director of Personnel and Management Services,
 J. Petrie
 Director of Planning and Transportation,
 M. Galloway
 Director of Social Work, Ms J. Roberts
 Director of Support Services, Ms P. McIlquham
 Local Agenda 21 Officer, Ms A. Anderson

Lord Lieutenancy: The Lord Provost is also, ex
 officio, Lord Lieutenant of Dundee
 (for current holder of post, *see* above)
Scottish Parliament constituencies: Dundee East;
 Dundee West*
UK Parliament constituencies: Dundee East;
 Dundee West†

EAST AYRSHIRE COUNCIL

Council Headquarters
London Road
Kilmarnock
Ayrshire
KA3 7BU
Tel: 01563-576000; fax: 01563-576500
Web: http://www.east-ayrshire.gov.uk

Statistical profile

Area (1998): 1,252 sq. km
Population (1998 estimate): 121,300
  population density (1998): 97 persons per sq. km
  projected population in 2006 (1996-based): 115,597
  number of households (1996): 50,100

Council tax (average Band D per two-person household), as at 1 April 1999: £1,037.80
Non-domestic rateable value (1997–8): £55,385,000

Education (pupils on register, 1997–8):
  primary: 11,414
  secondary: 7,611
  special: 187
  entitled to free meals: 20.5%

The Council

Total number of seats: 32
Political composition (as at end May 1999):
  Lab. 17, SNP 14, C. 1

Provost: J. Boyd
Leader of the Council: A. McIntyre

Chief Officers:
  Chief Executive, D. Montgomery
  Director of Community Services, W. Stafford
  Director of Education, J. Mulgrew
  Director of Finance, A. McPhee
  Director of Housing and Technical Services, J. Lavery
  Director of Social Work, D. Bulloch
  Head of Information Technology, M. Roulston
  Head of Legal Services, Ms K. McVey
  Head of Personnel, G. Hough
  Head of Planning, A. Neish
  Head of Protective Services, J. Crawford
  Local Agenda 21 Officer, M. Buchanan

Lord Lieutenancy area: Ayrshire and Arran
  (for current holder of post, *see* page 89)
Scottish Parliament constituencies:, Carrick, Cumnock and Doon Valley; Kilmarnock and Loudoun*
UK Parliament constituencies: Carrick, Cumnock and Doon Valley; Kilmarnock and Loudoun†

EAST DUNBARTONSHIRE COUNCIL

Tom Johnston House
Civic Way
Kirkintilloch
Glasgow
G66 4TJ
Tel: 0141-578 8000; fax: 0141-777 8576

Statistical profile

Area (1998): 172 sq. km
Population (1998 estimate): 109,570
  population density (1998): 638 persons per sq. km
  projected population in 2006 (1996-based): 109,761
  number of households (1996): 41,300

Council tax (average Band D per two-person household), as at 1 April 1999: £830.00
Non-domestic rateable value (1997–8): £41,320,000

Education (pupils on register, 1997–8):
  primary: 10,614
  secondary: 8,412
  special: 143
  entitled to free meals: 10.0%

The Council

Total number of seats: 24
Political composition (as at end May 1999):
  Lab. 11, LD 10, C. 3

Provost: R. McSkimming
Leader of the Council: C. Kennedy

Chief Officers:
  Chief Executive, Dr V. Nash
  Director of Connect Services, J. Mundell
  Director of Corporate Services, M. Cocozza
  Director of Education, I. Mills
  Director of Social Services, B. Fearon
  Head of Environmental Health, A. McNicol
  Head of Finance, I. Fergus
  Head of Housing, A. McKnight
  Head of Human Resources, Ms A. Macpherson
  Head of Information Technology, K. Atkinson
  Head of Legal Services, J. Crawford Gordon
  Head of Planning, D. Jamie
  Local Agenda 21 Officer, A. McNicol

Lord Lieutenancy area: Dunbartonshire
  (for current holder of post, *see* page 90)
Scottish Parliament constituencies: Clydebank and Milngavie; Coatbridge and Chryston; Strathkelvin and Bearsden*
UK Parliament constituencies: Clydebank and Milngavie; Coatbridge and Chryston; Strathkelvin and Bearsden†

EAST LOTHIAN COUNCIL

Council Buildings
25 Court Street
Haddington
East Lothian
EH41 3HA
Tel: 01620-827827; fax: 01620-827888
Web: http://www.eastlothian.gov.uk

Statistical profile

Area (1998): 678 sq. km
Population (1998 estimate): 89,570
 population density (1998): 132 persons per
 sq. km
 projected population in 2006 (1996-based):
 91,649
 number of households (1996): 36,300

*Council tax (average Band D per two-person
household), as at 1 April 1999:* £789.00
Non-domestic rateable value (1997–8):
£61,920,000

Education (pupils on register, 1997–8):
 primary: 7,961
 secondary: 4,640
 special: —
 entitled to free meals: 13.3%

The Council

Total number of seats: 23
Political composition (as at end May 1999):
 Lab. 17, C. 5, SNP 1

Convenor: P. O'Brien
Leader of the Council: N. Murray

Chief Officers:
 Chief Executive, J. Lindsay
 Director of Community Services, T. Shearer
 Director of Contracting Services, R. Hannah
 Director of Education, A. Blackie
 Director of Environmental Health, D. Evans
 Director of Finance, A. McCrome
 Director of Housing, B. Walker
 Director of Information Technology, R. Dowie
 Director of Legal Services, vacant
 Director of Personnel, G. Britain
 Director of Planning, P. Collins
 Director of Social Work, M. Cairns
 Local Agenda 21 Officer, Ms L. Wason

Lord Lieutenancy area: East Lothian
 (for current holder of post, *see* page 90)
Scottish Parliament constituency: East
 Lothian*
UK Parliament constituency: East Lothian†

EAST RENFREWSHIRE COUNCIL

Council Offices
Eastwood Park
Rouken Glen Road
Giffnock
G46 6UG
Tel: 0141-577 3000; fax: 0141-620 0884
Web: http://www.eastrenfrewshire.gov.uk

Statistical profile

Area (1998): 173 sq. km
Population (1998 estimate): 87,980
 population density (1998): 509 persons per
 sq. km
 projected population in 2006 (1996-based):
 90,854
 number of households (1996): 33,100

*Council tax (average Band D per two-person
household), as at 1 April 1999:* £765.00
Non-domestic rateable value (1997–8):
£27,166,000

Education (pupils on register, 1997–8):
 primary: 8,609
 secondary: 6,612
 special: 45
 entitled to free meals: 10.2%

The Council

Total number of seats: 20
Political composition (as at end May 1999):
 Lab. 9, C. 8, LD 2, RA 1

Provost: A. Steele
Leader of the Council: O. Taylor

Chief Officers:
 Chief Executive, P. Daniels
 Assistant Chief Executive, A. Cahill
 Director of Central Services, J. Hawkins
 Director of Commercial Operations,
  R. A. Russell
 Director of Community and Leisure,
  Mrs A. Saunders
 Director of Education, Mrs E. Currie
 Director of Environment, D. M. Porch
 Director of Finance, D. Dippie
 Director of Social Work, Dr S. Ross
 Local Agenda 21 Officer, M. Valenti

Lord Lieutenancy area: Renfrewshire
 (for current holder of post, *see* page 90)
Scottish Parliament constituency: Eastwood*
UK Parliament constituency: Eastwood†

EILEAN SIAR/WESTERN ISLES COUNCIL

Council Offices
Sandwick Road
Stornoway
Isle of Lewis
HS1 2BW
Tel: 01851-703773; fax: 01851-705349
Web: http://www.w-isles.gov.uk

Statistical profile

Area (1998): 3,134 sq. km
Population (1998 estimate): 27,940
  population density (1998): 9 persons per sq. km
  projected population in 2006 (1996-based): 27,554
  number of households (1996): 11,600
Council tax (average Band D per two-person household), as at 1 April 1999: £898.95
Non-domestic rateable value (1997–8): £12,563,000
Education (pupils on register, 1997–8):
  primary: 2,535
  secondary: 2,002
  special: —
  entitled to free meals: 12.5%

The Council

Total number of seats: 31
Political composition (as at end May 1999):
  NP 22, Lab. 6, SNP 3
Convenor: A. A. Macdonald
Chief Officers:
  Chief Executive, N. Galbraith *(acting)*
  Director of Corporate Services, D. O'Loan
  Director of Education, M. Macleod *(acting)*
  Director of Environmental Health, M. Gold *(acting)*
  Director of Finance, R. Bennie
  Director of Housing, A. Lamont
  Director of Social Services, M. Smith
  Director of Technical Services, M. Murray
  Local Agenda 21 Officer, D. McKim
Lord Lieutenancy area: Eilean Siar/Western Isles
  (for current holder of post, *see* page 90)
Scottish Parliament constituency: Western Isles*
UK Parliament constituency: Western Isles†

---

* For election results and MSPs, *see* pages 24–35
† For election results and MPs, *see* pages 36–45

FALKIRK COUNCIL

Municipal Buildings
West Bridge Street
Falkirk
FK1 5RS
Tel: 01324-506070; fax: 01324-506071

Statistical profile

Area (1998): 299 sq. km
Population (1998 estimate): 144,110
  population density (1998): 482 persons per sq. km
  projected population in 2006 (1996-based): 142,109
  number of households (1996): 59,100
Council tax (average Band D per two-person household), as at 1 April 1999: £892.00
Non-domestic rateable value (1997–8): £115,964,000
Education (pupils on register, 1997–8):
  primary: 12,316
  secondary: 8,551
  special: 297
  entitled to free meals: 18.1%

The Council

Total number of seats: 32
Political composition (as at end May 1999):
  Lab. 15, SNP 9, Ind. 5, C. 2, Ind. Lab. 1
Provost: D. Goldie
Leader of the Council: J. Connolly
Chief Officers:
  Chief Executive, Ms M. Pitcaithly
  Director of Community and Environmental Services, S. Dunlop
  Director of Contract Services, vacant
  Director of Corporate Services, S. Ritchie
  Director of Education, Dr G. Young
  Director of Finance, A. Jannetta
  Director of Housing, I. Walker
  Director of Law and Administration, Ms E. S. Morton
  Director of Social Work Services, Ms C. Wilkinson
  Director of Strategic Services, G. Peart
  Local Agenda 21 contact, D. Gorman
Lord Lieutenancy area: Stirling and Falkirk
  (for current holder of post, *see* page 90)
Scottish Parliament constituencies: Falkirk East; Falkirk West*
UK Parliament constituencies: Falkirk East; Falkirk West†

FIFE COUNCIL

Fife House
North Street
Glenrothes
Fife
KY7 5LT
Tel: 01592-414141; fax: 01592-414142
Web: http://www.fife.gov.uk

Statistical profile

Area (1998): 1,323 sq. km
Population (1998 estimate): 348,900
  population density (1998): 264 persons per
  sq. km
  projected population in 2006 (1996-based):
  349,020
  number of households (1996): 145,600

*Council tax (average Band D per two-person
household), as at 1 April 1999:* £986.50
Non-domestic rateable value (1997–8):
£258,076,000

Education (pupils on register, 1997–8):
  primary: 30,848
  secondary: 21,958
  special: 253
  entitled to free meals: 17.4%

The Council

Total number of seats: 78
Political composition (as at end May 1999):
  Lab. 43, LD 21, SNP 9, Ind. 2, C. 1, Comm.
  1, Dem. Left 1

Convenor: J. MacDougall
Leader of the Council: Ms C. May

Chief Officers:
  Chief Executive, D. Sinclair
  Head of Community Services, D. Somerville
  Head of Corporate Procurement, J. McHugh
  Head of Education, A. McKay
  Head of Environmental Health, J. Stark
  Head of Finance, P. Ritchie
  Head of Housing, A. Davidson
  Head of Information Technology, E. Brewster
  Head of Law and Administration, S. Allan
  Head of Personnel, M. Burnell
  Head of Planning, D. Rae
  Head of Social Work, M. Sawyer
  Local Agenda 21 Co-ordinator, Ms S. Keast

Lord Lieutenancy area: Fife
  (for current holder of post, *see* page 90)
Scottish Parliament constituencies: Dunfermline
  East; Dunfermline West; Fife Central; Fife
  North East; Kirkcaldy*
UK Parliament constituencies: Dunfermline East;
  Dunfermline West; Fife Central; Fife North
  East; Kirkcaldy†

GLASGOW CITY COUNCIL

City Chambers
George Square
Glasgow
G2 1DU
Tel: 0141-287 2000; fax: 0141-287 5666
Web: http://www.glasgow.gov.uk

Statistical profile

Area (1998): 175 sq. km
Population (1998 estimate): 619,680
  population density (1998): 3,540 persons per
  sq. km
  projected population in 2006 (1996-based):
  578,866
  number of households (1996): 271,900

*Council tax (average Band D per two-person
household), as at 1 April 1999:* £1,263.10
Non-domestic rateable value (1997–8):
£625,824,000

Education (pupils on register, 1997–8):
  primary: 48,876
  secondary: 27,832
  special: 2,054
  entitled to free meals: 41.4%

The Council

Total number of seats: 79
Political composition (as at end May 1999):
  Lab. 74, SNP 2, C. 1, LD 1, SSP 1

Lord Provost: Rt. Hon. A. Mosson
Leader of the Council: C. Gordon

Chief Officers:
  Chief Executive, J. Andrews
  Director of Building Services, D. Angus
  Director of Cultural and Leisure Services,
  Ms B. McConnell
  *Director of Development and Regeneration
  Services,* R. McConnell
  Director of Direct and Care Services,
  F. Chambers
  Director of Education Services, K. Corsar
  Director of Financial Services, G. Black
  Director of Housing Services, D. Comley
  Director of Land Services, A. Young
  Director of Personnel and Administration,
  H. Burke
  Director of Protective Services, B. Kelly
  *Director of Social Work and Chief Social Work
  Officer,* I. Gilmour *(acting)*
  Local Agenda 21 Officer, Ms A. Beyer

Lord Lieutenancy area: The Lord Provost is
  also, ex officio, Lord Lieutenant of Glasgow
  (for current holder of post, *see* above)
Scottish Parliament constituencies: Glasgow
  Anniesland; Glasgow Baillieston; Glasgow

Cathcart; Glasgow Govan; Glasgow Kelvin;
Glasgow Maryhill; Glasgow Pollok;
Glasgow Rutherglen; Glasgow Shettleston;
Glasgow Springburn*
UK Parliament constituencies: Glasgow
Anniesland; Glasgow Baillieston; Glasgow
Cathcart; Glasgow Govan; Glasgow Kelvin;
Glasgow Maryhill; Glasgow Pollok;
Glasgow Rutherglen; Glasgow Shettleston;
Glasgow Springburn†

HIGHLAND COUNCIL

Glenurquhart Road
Inverness IV3 5NX
Tel: 01463-702000; fax: 01463-702111
Web: http://www.highland.gov.uk

Statistical profile

Area (1998): 25,784 sq. km
Population (1998 estimate): 208,300
  population density (1998): 8 persons per sq. km
  projected population in 2006 (1996-based):
  214,031
  number of households (1996): 85,800

*Council tax (average Band D per two-person
household), as at 1 April 1999:* £799.00
Non-domestic rateable value (1997–8):
  £136,932,000

Education (pupils on register, 1997–8):
  primary: 18,982
  secondary: 14,440
  special: 150
  entitled to free meals: 12.9%

The Council

Total number of seats: 80
Political composition (as at end May 1999):
  Ind. 50, LD 12, Lab. 10, SNP 8

Convenor: D. Green
Leader of the Council: D. Green

Chief Officers:
  Chief Executive, A. D. McCourt
  Director of Commercial Operations,
    C. Mackenzie
  Director of Corporate Services, A. Dodds
  Director of Culture and Leisure, A. Jones
  Director of Education, B. Robertson
  Director of Finance, A. Geddes
  Director of Housing, G. Fisher
  Director of Information Systems, R. Metcalfe
  Director of Planning and Development,
    J. Rennilson
  Director of Property and Architectural Services,
    Dr A. Coutts
  Director of Protective Services, D. Thompson
  Director of Roads and Transport, P. Shimin
    (acting)
  Director of Social Services, P. Bates
  Local Agenda 21 contact, A. Dorin

Lord Lieutenancy areas: Caithness; Inverness;
  Nairn; Ross and Cromarty; Sutherland
  (for current holder of posts, *see* page 90)
Scottish Parliament constituencies: Caithness,
  Sutherland and Easter Ross; Inverness East,
  Nairn and Lochaber; Ross, Skye and
  Inverness West*
UK Parliament constituencies: Caithness,
  Sutherland and Easter Ross; Inverness East,
  Nairn and Lochaber; Ross, Skye and
  Inverness West†

---

*   For election results and MSPs, *see* pages 24–35
†   For election results and MPs, *see* pages 36–45

INVERCLYDE COUNCIL

Municipal Buildings
Clyde Square
Greenock
Renfrewshire
PA15 1LY
Tel: 01475-717171; fax: 01475-712010

Statistical profile

Area (1998): 162 sq. km
Population (1998 estimate): 85,400
   population density (1998): 528 persons per
   sq. km
   projected population in 2006 (1996-based):
   77,840
   number of households (1996): 38,000

*Council tax (average Band D per two-person
household), as at 1 April 1999:* £863.00
Non-domestic rateable value (1997–8):
£47,829,000

Education (pupils on register, 1997–8):
   primary: 7,791
   secondary: 5,583
   special: 145
   entitled to free meals: 23.9%

The Council

Total number of seats: 20
Political composition (as at end May 1999):
   Lab. 11, LD 8, C. 1

Provost: D. Roach
Leader of the Council: R. Jackson

Chief Officers:
   Chief Executive, R. Cleary
   *Executive Director of Community Services and
      Protective Services,* N. Graham
   *Executive Director of Economic Development
      Services,* G. Malone
   Executive Director of Education Services, B.
      McLeary
   *Executive Director of Legal, Information and
      Support Services,* Ms E. Paterson
   Executive Director of Resource Services,
      Ms M. McCrossan
   *Executive Director of Social Work and Housing
      Services,* T. Keenan
   Local Agenda 21 Officer, Ms J. Stitt

Lord Lieutenancy area: Renfrewshire
   (for current holder of post, *see* page 90)
Scottish Parliament constituencies: Greenock and
   Inverclyde; Renfrewshire West*
UK Parliament constituencies: Greenock and
   Inverclyde; Renfrewshire West†

MIDLOTHIAN COUNCIL

Midlothian House
40-46 Buccleuch Street
Dalkeith
Midlothian
EH22 1DJ
Tel: 0131-271 7500; fax: 0131-271 3050
Web: http://www.midlothian.gov.uk

Statistical profile

Area (1998): 356 sq. km
Population (1998 estimate): 80,860
   population density (1998): 227 persons per
   sq. km
   projected population in 2006 (1996-based):
   80,152
   number of households (1996): 30,800

*Council tax (average Band D per two-person
household), as at 1 April 1999:* £936.00
Non-domestic rateable value (1997–8):
£34,974,000

Education (pupils on register, 1997–8):
   primary: 7,479
   secondary: 5,053
   special: 192
   entitled to free meals: 16.5%

The Council

Total number of seats: 18
Political composition (as at end May 1999):
   Lab. 17, LD 1

Provost: S. Campbell
Leader of the Council: G. Purcell

Chief Officers:
   Chief Executive, T. Muir
   Director of Community Services, G. Marwick
   Director of Contract Services, B. Page
   Director of Corporate Services, J. Webster
   Director of Education, D. MacKay
   Director of Social Services, S. Adams
   Director of Strategic Services, J. Allan
   Local Agenda 21 Officer, Ms J. Faucett

Lord Lieutenancy area: Midlothian
   (for current holder of post, *see* page 90)
Scottish Parliament constituencies: Midlothian;
   Tweeddale, Ettrick and Lauderdale*
UK Parliament constituencies: Midlothian;
   Tweeddale, Ettrick and Lauderdale†

---

* For election results and MSPs, *see* pages 24–35
† For election results and MPs, *see* pages 36–45

MORAY COUNCIL

Council Office
High Street
Elgin
Morayshire
IV30 1BX
Tel: 01343-543451; fax: 01343-540183
Web: http://www.moray.gov.uk

Statistical profile

Area (1998): 2,238 sq. km
Population (1998 estimate): 85,870
    population density (1998): 38 persons per sq. km
    projected population in 2006 (1996-based): 87,213
    number of households (1996): 34,900

Council tax (average Band D per two-person household), as at 1 April 1999: £724.00
Non-domestic rateable value (1997–8): £48,791,000

Education (pupils on register, 1997–8):
    primary: 8,048
    secondary: 5,542
    special: 22
    entitled to free meals: 9.4%

The Council

Total number of seats: 26
Political composition (as at end May 1999):
    Ind. 13, Lab. 6, LD 2, SNP 2, Scottish Ind. 2, C. 1

Convenor: E. Aldridge
Leader of the Council: E. Aldridge

Chief Officers:
    Chief Executive, B. Stewart
    Director of Community Services, M. Martin
    Director of Corporate Services, Ms K. Williams
    Director of Education, K. Gavin
    Director of Finance and Information Technology, A. Keddie
    Director of Planning and Economic Development, R. Stewart
    Director of Technical and Leisure Services, vacant
    Local Agenda 21 Officer, N. Brown

Lord Lieutenancy areas: Banffshire; Morayshire
    (for current holder of posts, *see* pages 89,90)
Scottish Parliament constituencies: Gordon; Moray*
UK Parliament constituencies: Gordon; Moray†

NORTH AYRSHIRE COUNCIL

Cunninghame House
Irvine
Ayrshire
KA12 8EE
Tel: 01294-324100; fax: 01294-324144

Statistical profile

Area (1998): 884 sq. km
Population (1998 estimate): 139,660
    population density (1998): 158 persons per sq. km
    projected population in 2006 (1996-based): 139,718
    number of households (1996): 57,700

Council tax (average Band D per two-person household), as at 1 April 1999: £977.10
Non-domestic rateable value (1997–8): £92,021,000

Education (pupils on register, 1997–8):
    primary: 12,593
    secondary: 8,746
    special: 201
    entitled to free meals: 25.4%

The Council

Total number of seats: 30
Political composition (as at end May 1999):
    Lab. 25, C. 2, SNP 2, Ind. 1

Convenor: S. Taylor
Leader of the Council: D. O'Neill

Chief Officers:
    Chief Executive, B. Devine
    Assistant Chief Executive, Development and Promotion, B. MacDonald
    Assistant Chief Executive, Finance, A. Herbert
    Assistant Chief Executive, Information Technology, J. Barrett
    Assistant Chief Executive, Legal and Regulatory, I. Mackay
    Assistant Chief Executive, Personnel, J. M. MacFarlane
    Corporate Director, Educational Services, J. Travers
    Corporate Director, Property Services, T. Orr
    Corporate Director, Social Services, G. Irving
    Local Agenda 21 Officer, Ms S. King

Lord Lieutenancy area: Ayrshire and Arran
    (for current holder of post, *see* page 89)
Scottish Parliament constituencies: Cunninghame North; Cunninghame South*
UK Parliament constituencies: Cunninghame North; Cunninghame South †

NORTH LANARKSHIRE COUNCIL

PO Box 14
Civic Centre
Motherwell
Lanarkshire ML1 1TW
Tel: 01698-302222; fax: 01698-275125
Web: http://www.northlan.gov.uk

Statistical profile

Area (1998): 474 sq. km
Population (1998 estimate): 326,720
  population density (1998): 690 persons per
  sq. km
  projected population in 2006 (1996-based):
  317,922
  number of households (1996): 128,500

*Council tax (average Band D per two-person
household), as at 1 April 1999:* £844.00
Non-domestic rateable value (1997–8):
£181,228,000

Education (pupils on register, 1997–8):
  primary: 29,843
  secondary: 22,383
  special: 692
  entitled to free meals: 24.7%

The Council

Total number of seats: 70
Political composition (as at end May 1999):
  Lab. 56, SNP 12, Ind. 2

Provost: B. McCulloch
Leader of the Council: J. McCabe

Chief Officers:
  Chief Executive, A. Cowe
  Director of Administration, J. O'Hagan
  Director of Community Services, P. Jukes
  Director of Education, M. O'Neill
  Director of Finance, R. Hinds
  Director of Housing and Property Services,
  G. Whitefield
  Director of Planning and Environment,
  D. Porch
  Director of Social Work, J. Dickie
  General Manager of Contracting Services,
  R. Ellerby
  Local Agenda 21 Officer, A. Hendry

Lord Lieutenancy area: Lanarkshire
  (for current holder of post, *see* page 90)
Scottish Parliament constituencies: Airdrie and
  Shotts; Coatbridge and Chryston;
  Cumbernauld and Kilsyth; Hamilton North
  and Bellshill; Motherwell and Wishaw*
UK Parliament constituencies: Airdrie and
  Shotts; Coatbridge and Chryston;
  Cumbernauld and Kilsyth; Hamilton North
  and Bellshill; Motherwell and Wishaw†

ORKNEY ISLANDS COUNCIL

Council Offices
School Place
Kirkwall
Orkney
KW15 1NY
Tel: 01856-873535; fax: 01856-874615

Statistical profile

Area (1998): 992 sq. km
Population (1998 estimate): 19,550
  population density (1998): 20 persons per sq.
  km
  projected population in 2006 (1996-based):
  20,037
  number of households (1996): 8,100

*Council tax (average Band D per two-person
household), as at 1 April 1999:* £624.00
Non-domestic rateable value (1997–8):
£14,651,000

Education (pupils on register, 1997–8):
  primary: 1,819
  secondary: 1,421
  special: 17
  entitled to free meals: 8.4%

The Council

Total number of seats: 21
Political composition (as at end May 1999):
  Ind. 20, vacant 1

Convenor: H. Halcro-Johnston
Leader of the Council: H. Halcro-Johnston

Chief Officers:
  Chief Executive, A. Buchan
  Chief Environmental Services Officer,
  D. Tonge
  Chief Legal Officer, D. Fairnie
  Director of Community Social Services,
  H. Garland
  Director of Development and Planning,
  J. Baster
  Director of Education, L. Manson
  Director of Finance and Housing, D. Robertson
  Director of Technical Services, J. Panton
  Local Agenda 21 Officer, J. Baster
  Personnel Officer, B. Evans

Lord Lieutenancy area: Orkney
  (for current holder of post, *see* page 90)
Scottish Parliament constituency: Orkney*
UK Parliament constituency: Orkney and
  Shetland†

---

* For election results and MSPs, *see* pages 24–35
† For election results and MPs, *see* pages 36–45

PERTH AND KINROSS COUNCIL

PO Box 77, 2 High Street
Perth PH1 5PH
Tel: 01738-475000; fax: 01738-475710
Web: http://www.pkc.gov.uk

Statistical profile

Area (1998): 5,311 sq. km
Population (1998 estimate): 133,040
    population density (1998): 25 persons per sq. km
    projected population in 2006 (1996-based): 137,089
    number of households (1996): 55,000

Council tax (average Band D per two-person household), as at 1 April 1999: £758.00
Non-domestic rateable value (1997–8): £94,345,000

Education (pupils on register, 1997–8):
    primary: 10,142
    secondary: 7,282
    special: 53
    entitled to free meals: 8.1%

The Council

Total number of seats: 41
Political composition (as at end May 1999):
    SNP 16, C. 11, Lab. 6, LD 6, Ind. 2

Provost: M. O'Malley
Leader of the Council: J. Doig

Chief Officers:
    Chief Executive, H. Robertson
    Director of Education, R. McKay
    Director of Environmental and Consumer Services, J. Milne
    Director of Finance, A. R. McArthur
    Director of Housing and Building Services, G. Black
    Director of Human Resources, G. Farquhar
    Director of Information Systems and Technology, A. J. Nairn
    Director of Legal, Administrative and Property Services, R. Jackson
    Director of Leisure and Cultural Services, J. Blair
    Director of Planning and Development Services, D. Munro
    Director of Roads, Transport and Architectural Services, J. Irons
    Director of Social Work Services, Mrs B. Bridgeford
    Local Agenda 21 Officer, Ms J. Muse

Lord Lieutenancy area: Perth and Kinross
    (for current holder of post, *see* page 90)
Scottish Parliament constituencies: Angus; Ochil; Perth; Tayside North*
UK Parliament constituencies: Angus; Ochil; Perth; Tayside North†

RENFREWSHIRE COUNCIL

Council Headquarters
North Building
Cotton Street
Paisley
PA1 1BU
Tel: 0141-842 5000; fax: 0141-840 3335
Web: http://www.renfrewshire.gov.uk

Statistical profile

Area (1998): 261 sq. km
Population (1998 estimate): 177,830
    population density (1998): 680 persons per sq. km
    projected population in 2006 (1996-based): 175,632
    number of households (1996): 75,100

Council tax (average Band D per two-person household), as at 1 April 1999: £972.10
Non-domestic rateable value (1997–8): £135,294,000

Education (pupils on register, 1997–8):
    primary: 15,783
    secondary: 11,235
    special: 302
    entitled to free meals: 21.6%

The Council

Total number of seats: 40
Political composition (as at end May 1999):
    Lab. 21, SNP 15, LD 3, C. 1

Provost: J. McDowell
Leader of the Council: J. Harkins

Chief Officers:
    Chief Executive, T. Scholes
    Director of Corporate Services, Ms M. Quinn
    Director of Education and Leisure Services, Ms S. Rae
    Director of Environmental Services, B. Forteath
    Director of Finance and Information Technology, W. Hughes
    Director of Housing and Property Services, M Bailey
    Director of Planning and Transport, I. Snodgrass
    Director of Social Work, Ms S. Duncan
    Head of Legal Services, D. Sillars
    Head of Personnel Services, Ms C. Proudfoot
    Local Agenda 21 Officer, Ms J. Brooke

Lord Lieutenancy area: Renfrewshire
    (for current holder of post, *see* page 90)
Scottish Parliament constituencies: Paisley North; Paisley South; Renfrewshire West*
UK Parliament constituencies: Paisley North; Paisley South; Renfrewshire West†

SCOTTISH BORDERS COUNCIL

Council Headquarters
Newtown St Boswells
Melrose
Roxburghshire
TD6 0SA
Tel: 01835-824000; fax: 01835-825001

Statistical profile

Area (1998): 4,734 sq. km
Population (1998 estimate): 106,300
  population density (1998): 22 persons per sq.
  km
  projected population in 2006 (1996-based):
  107,477
  number of households (1996): 44,900

Council tax (average Band D per two-person
household), as at 1 April 1999: £639.00
Non-domestic rateable value (1997–8):
£50,069,000

Education (pupils on register, 1997–8):
  primary: 8,920
  secondary: 6,284
  special: —
  entitled to free meals: 6.6%

The Council

Total number of seats: 34
Political composition (as at end May 1999):
  Ind. 14, LD 14, SNP 4, Lab. 1, C. 1

Convenor: A. L. Tulley
Leader of the Council: A. L. Tulley

Chief Officers:
  Chief Executive, A. M. Croall
  Director of Central Services, W. R. Millan
  Director of Education, J. Christie
  Director of Finance, J. Campbell
  Director of Housing, H. Blacklaws
  Director of Leisure and Recreation, I. Yates
  Director of Planning, P. Gregory
  Director of Protective Services, W. Lillico
  Director of Social Services, C. Johnson
  Director of Technical Services, I. Brown
  Head of Information Technology,
    Ms G. Hanham
  Head of Personnel, D. Hunter
  Local Agenda 21 Officer, Ms P. Biberbach

Lord Lieutenancy areas: Berwickshire;
  Roxburgh, Ettrick and Lauderdale;
  Tweeddale (for current holder of posts,
  see page 90)
Scottish Parliament constituencies: Roxburgh and
  Berwickshire; Tweeddale, Ettrick and
  Lauderdale*
UK Parliament constituencies: Roxburgh and
  Berwickshire; Tweeddale, Ettrick and
  Lauderdale†

SHETLAND ISLANDS COUNCIL

Town Hall
Hillhead
Lerwick
Shetland
ZE1 0HB
Tel: 01595-693535; fax: 01595-744509
Web: http://www.shetland.gov.uk

Statistical profile

Area (1998): 1,438 sq. km
Population (1998 estimate): 22,910
  population density (1998): 16 persons per sq.
  km
  projected population in 2006 (1996-based):
  22,383
  number of households (1996): 8,900

Council tax (average Band D per two-person
household), as at 1 April 1999: £830.75
Non-domestic rateable value (1997–8):
£37,429,000

Education (pupils on register, 1997–8):
  primary: 2,316
  secondary: 1,571
  special: —
  entitled to free meals: 7.7%

The Council

Total number of seats: 22
Political composition (as at end May 1999):
  Ind. 13, LD 8, Ind. LD 1

Convenor: T. Stove

Chief Officers:
  Chief Executive, B. Bennett
  Director of Education and Community Services,
    J. Halcrow
  Director of Environment and Transportation,
    G. Spall
  Director of Finance and Housing, A. Matthews
  Director of Social Services, Ms B. Fullerton
    (acting)
  Local Agenda 21 Officer, A. Hamilton
  Manager of Information Technology, J. Smith

Lord Lieutenancy area: Shetland
  (for current holder of post, see page 90)
Scottish Parliament constituency: Shetland*
  UK Parliament constituency: Orkney and
  Shetland†

---

* For election results and MSPs, see pages 24–35
† For election results and MPs, see pages 36–45

SOUTH AYRSHIRE COUNCIL

County Buildings
Wellington Square
Ayr
KA7 1DR
Tel: 01292-612000; fax: 01292-612143
Web: http://www.south-ayrshire.gov.uk

Statistical profile

Area (1998): 1,202 sq. km
Population (1998 estimate): 114,440
population density (1998): 95 persons per sq.
km
projected population in 2006 (1996-based):
113,577
number of households (1996): 47,600

Council tax (average Band D per two-person
household), as at 1 April 1999: £792.00
Non-domestic rateable value (1997–8):
£71,833,000

Education (pupils on register, 1997–8):
primary: 9,458
secondary: 7,622
special: 102
entitled to free meals: 15.5%

The Council

Total number of seats: 30
Political composition (as at end May 1999):
Lab. 17, C. 13

Provost: Ms E. Foulkes
Leader of the Council: J. Baillie

Chief Officers:
Chief Executive, G. W. F. Thorley
Director of Community Services, Ms E. Noad
Director of Contracting Services, R. Sheed
Director of Education, M. McCabe
Director of Environmental Health, J. Millar
Director of Finance, T. Cairns
Director of Planning, A. Harkness
Head of Housing, P. Whyte
Head of Information Technology,
Ms I. Gillespie
Head of Legal Services, D. Russell
Head of Personnel, A. Stewart
Head of Social Services, Ms J. Thompson
Local Agenda 21 Officer, K. Gibb

Lord Lieutenancy area: Ayrshire and Arran
(for current holder of post, see page 89)
Scottish Parliament constituencies: Ayr; Carrick,
Cumnock and Doon Valley*
UK Parliament constituencies: Ayr; Carrick,
Cumnock and Doon Valley†

SOUTH LANARKSHIRE COUNCIL

Council Offices, Almada Street, Hamilton
Lanarkshire ML3 0AA
Tel: 01698-454904; fax: 01698-454949
Web: http://www.southlanarkshire.gov.uk

Statistical profile

Area (1998): 1,771 sq. km
Population (1998 estimate): 306,860
population density (1998): 173 persons per
sq. km
projected population in 2006 (1996-based):
303,554
number of households (1996): 122,300

Council tax (average Band D per two-person
household), as at 1 April 1999: £880.00
Non-domestic rateable value (1997–8):
£175,979,000

Education (pupils on register, 1997–8):
primary: 26,810
secondary: 19,821
special: 490
entitled to free meals: 20.4%

The Council

Total number of seats: 67
Political composition (as at end May 1999):
Lab. 54, SNP 10, C. 2, LD 1

Provost: A. Dick
Leader of the Council: E. McAvoy

Chief Officers:
Chief Executive, vacant
Executive Director of Community Resources,
Ms G. Pain
Executive Director of Corporate Resources,
A. Cuthbertson
Executive Director of Education Resources,
Ms M. Allan
Executive Director of Enterprise Resources,
M. Docherty
Executive Director of Finance and Information
Technology Resources, W. Kirk
Executive Director of Housing and Technical
Resources, S. Gilchrist
Executive Director of Social Work, S. Cameron
Head of Enforcement, R. Howe
Head of Information Technology, Ms K. Brown
Head of Legal Services, Ms S. Dickinson
Local Agenda 21 Officer, K. Boag

Lord Lieutenancy area: Lanarkshire
(for current holder of post, see page 90)
Scottish Parliament constituencies: Clydesdale;
East Kilbride; Glasgow Rutherglen;
Hamilton North and Bellshill; Hamilton
South*
UK Parliament constituencies: Clydesdale; East
Kilbride; Glasgow Rutherglen; Hamilton
North and Bellshill; Hamilton South†

STIRLING COUNCIL

Viewforth
Stirling
FK8 2ET
Tel: 01786-443322; fax: 01786-443078
Web: http://www.stirling.gov.uk

Statistical profile

Area (1998): 2,196 sq. km
Population (1998 estimate): 83,130
  population density (1998): 38 persons per sq.
  km
  projected population in 2006 (1996-based):
  86,120
  number of households (1996): 33,100

*Council tax (average Band D per two-person
  household), as at 1 April 1999:* £819.00
Non-domestic rateable value (1997–8):
£66,907,000

Education (pupils on register, 1997–8):
  primary: 6,817
  secondary: 5,446
  special: 58
  entitled to free meals: 16.0%

The Council

Total number of seats: 22
Political composition (as at end May 1999):
  Lab. 11, C. 9, SNP 2

Provost: T. Brookes
Leader of the Council: C. McChord

Chief Officers:
  Chief Executive, K. Yates
  Director of Civic Services, R. Jack
  Director of Community Services, Ms H. Munro
  Director of Education Services, G. Jeyes
  Director of Environmental Services, D. Martin
  Director of Finance and Information Services,
    W. Dickson
  Director of Housing and Social Services, vacant
  Director of Technical and Commercial Services,
    A. Nicholls
  Head of Personnel, Ms J. Jones
  Local Agenda 21 Officer, A. Speedie

Lord Lieutenancy area: Stirling and Falkirk
  (for current holder of post, *see* page 90)
  Scottish Parliament constituencies: Ochil;
  Stirling*
UK Parliament constituencies: Ochil; Stirling†

WEST DUNBARTONSHIRE COUNCIL

Garshake Road
Dumbarton
G82 3PU
Tel: 01389-737000; fax: 01389-737582
Web: http://www.west-dunbarton.gov.uk

Statistical profile

Area (1998): 162 sq. km
Population (1998 estimate): 94,880
  population density (1998): 585 persons per
  sq. km
  projected population in 2006 (1996-based):
  90,596
  number of households (1996): 40,400

*Council tax (average Band D per two-person
  household), as at 1 April 1999:* £1,170.10
Non-domestic rateable value (1997–8):
£58,056,000

Education (pupils on register, 1997–8):
  primary: 8,844
  secondary: 6,681
  special: 195
  entitled to free meals: 28.8%

The Council

Total number of seats: 22
Political composition (as at end May 1999):
  Lab. 14, SNP 7, Ind. 1

Provost: A. Macdonald
Leader of the Council: A. White

Chief Officers:
  Chief Executive, T. Huntingford *(acting)*
  *Deputy Chief Executive and Solicitor to the
    Council,* I. Leitch
  Director of Contract Services, A. Findlay
  *Director of Economic, Planning and
    Environmental Services,* vacant
  Director of Education and Leisure Services,
    I. McMurdo
  Director of Finance, E. Walker
  Director of Roads and Technical Services,
    P. Cleary
  Director of Social Work and Housing,
    T. Huntingford
  Head of Corporate Policy and Public Relations,
    Ms M. Cullen
  Head of Information Services, Ms A. Clements
  Head of Personnel and Training, vacant
  Local Agenda 21 Officer, T. Moan

Lord Lieutenancy area: Dunbartonshire
  (for current holder of post, *see* page 90)
Scottish Parliament constituencies: Clydebank and
  Milngavie; Dumbarton*
UK Parliament constituencies: Clydebank and
  Milngavie; Dumbarton†

WEST LOTHIAN COUNCIL

West Lothian House
Almondvale Boulevard
Livingston
West Lothian
EH54 6QC
Tel: 01506-777000; fax: 01506-777102
Web: http://www.westlothian.gov.uk

Lord Lieutenancy area: West Lothian
(for current holder of post, *see* page 90)
Scottish Parliament constituencies: Linlithgow;
Livingston*
UK Parliament constituencies: Linlithgow;
Livingston†

Statistical profile

Area (1998): 425 sq. km
Population (1998 estimate): 153,090
   population density (1998): 360 persons per
   sq. km
   projected population in 2006 (1996-based):
   160,620
   number of households (1996): 60,300

*Council tax (average Band D per two-person
household), as at 1 April 1999:* £858.00
Non-domestic rateable value (1997–8):
   £108,235,000

Education (pupils on register, 1997–8):
   primary: 14,987
   secondary: 9,510
   special: 152
   entitled to free meals: 18.5%

The Council

Total number of seats: 32
Political composition (as at end May 1999):
   Lab. 20, SNP 11, C. 1

Provost: J. Thomas
Leader of the Council: G. Morrice

Chief Officers:
   Chief Executive, A. M. Linkston
   Corporate Manager, Community Services,
      D. Kelly
   Corporate Manager, Education Services,
      R. Stewart
   *Corporate Manager, Environmental and
      Protective Services,* G. McNeill
   Corporate Manager, Strategic Services,
      J. Dickson
   Corporate Manager, West Lothian Contracts,
      B. Dixon
   Head, Housing Services, J. Ritchie
   Head, Social Work, G. Blair
   Local Agenda 21 Officer, Ms C. Braithwaite
   Manager, Administration and Legal, G. Blair
   Manager, Development and Building Control,
      R. Hartland
   *Manager, Environmental Health and Trading
      Standards,* A. Campbell
   Manager, Finance, A. Logan
   Manager, Human Resources, J. Nowak
   Manager, Information Technology, Ms S. Aird

---

* For election results and MSPs, *see* pages 24–35
† For election results and MPs, *see* pages 36–45

EDUCATION

Overall responsibility for all aspects of education in Scotland lies with the Scottish Ministers acting through the Scottish Executive Education Department and the Enterprise and Lifelong Learning Department (formerly the Scottish Office Education and Industry Department (SOEID); references to SOEID occur below where data, e.g. statistics, refer to the period before 1 July 1999).

The main concerns of the Scottish Executive Education Department are the formulation of policies for education and the maintenance of consistency in educational standards in Scotland. It is responsible for the broad allocation of resources for education, the rate and distribution of educational building and the supply, training and superannuation of teachers.

Expenditure

Expenditure on education by SOEID, in real terms, was £1,309 million in 1998–9, with a planned expenditure of £1,450 million for 1999–2000.

The major elements of central government expenditure are: support for higher and further education in universities and colleges, grant-aided special schools, student awards and bursaries (through the Student Award Agency for Scotland), curriculum development, special educational needs and community education.

Significant expenditure is incurred by local authorities, which make their own expenditure decisions according to their local situations and needs. Planned net expenditure on education by local education authorities for 1999–2000 was £2,605 million.

Local Education Administration

The education service at present is a national service in which the provision of most school education is locally administered.

The duty of providing education locally in Scotland rests with the education authorities. They are responsible for the construction of buildings, the employment of teachers and other staff, and the provision of equipment and materials. Devolved School Management (DSM) is in place for all primary, secondary and special schools.

Education authorities are required to establish school boards consisting of parents and teachers as well as co-opted members. These are responsible, among other things, for the appointment of staff.

The Inspectorate

HM Inspectors of Schools in Scotland inspect schools and publish reports on further education institutions and community education, and are involved in assessing the quality of teacher education. HMIs work in teams alongside lay people and associate assessors, who are practising teachers seconded for the inspection. The inspection of higher education is the responsibility of inspectors appointed to the Scottish Higher Education Funding Council.

In 1998–9 there were 83 HMIs and eight Chief Inspectors in Scotland.

SCHOOLS AND PUPILS

Schooling is compulsory for all children between five and 16 years of age. Provision is being increased for children under five and many pupils remain at school after the minimum leaving age. No fees are charged in any publicly maintained school in Scotland.

Throughout the UK, parents have a right to express a preference for a particular school and to appeal if dissatisfied. The policy, known as more open enrolment, requires schools to admit children up to the limit of their capacity if there is a demand for places, and to publish their criteria for selection if they are over-subscribed, in which case parents have a right of appeal.

The 'Parents' Charter', available free from education departments, is a booklet which tells parents about the education system. Schools are now required to make available information about themselves, their public examination results, truancy rates, and destination of leavers. Corporal punishment is no longer legal in publicly maintained schools in the UK.

The number of schools by sector in 1997–8 was:

Publicly maintained schools:

Nursery	1,010
Primary	2,300
Secondary	401
Special	158
Independent schools	114
Total	3,983

Education authority schools (known as public schools) are financed by local government, partly through revenue support grants from central government and partly from local taxation. There is a small number of grant-aided schools, mainly in the special sector, which are conducted by boards of managers and receive grants direct from the Scottish Executive Education Department. Independent schools receive no direct grant and charge fees, but are subject to inspection and registration. An additional category exists of self-governing schools which opt to be managed entirely by a board of management. These schools remain in the public sector and are funded by direct government grant set to match the resources the school would receive under education authority management. Two such schools were established, but it is planned to return them to the education authority framework.

THE STATE SYSTEM

Nursery Education

Nursery education is for children from two to five years and is not compulsory. It takes place in nursery schools or nursery classes in primary schools.

Many children also attend pre-school playgroups organized by parents and voluntary bodies. The nursery voucher scheme, whereby every parent of a four-year-old received a voucher worth £1,100 exchangeable for up to three terms of pre-school education, was introduced in April 1997 and remained in place until June 1998; thereafter local authorities undertook the funding and management of services. All providers of pre-school education are subject to inspection.

NURSERY SCHOOLS 1997–8

No. of schools	1,010
No. of pupils	53,260
No. of teachers (full-time equivalent)	1,175
Pupil-teacher ratio	23.1

Primary Education

Primary education begins at five years and is almost always co-educational. The primary school course lasts for seven years and pupils transfer to secondary courses at about the age of 12.

Primary schools consist mainly of infants' schools for children aged five to seven, junior schools for those aged seven to 12, and combined junior and infant schools for both age groups. Many primary schools provide nursery classes for children under five (see above).

PRIMARY SCHOOLS 1997–8

No. of schools	2,300
No. of pupils	440,594
No. of teachers (full-time equivalent)	22,187
Pupil-teacher ratio	19.9

Secondary Education

Secondary schools are for children aged 11 to 16 and for those who choose to stay on to 18. Most secondary schools in Scotland are co-educational. All pupils in Scottish education authority secondary schools attend schools with a comprehensive intake. Most of these schools provide a full range of courses appropriate to all levels of ability from first to sixth year.

SECONDARY SCHOOLS 1997–8

No. of schools	401
No. of pupils	314,916
No. of teachers (full-time equivalent)	23,875
Pupil-teacher ratio	13.2

Special Education

Special education is provided for children with special educational needs, usually because they have a disability which either prevents or hinders them from making use of educational facilities of a kind generally provided for children of their age in schools within the area of the local authority concerned.

It is intended that pupils with special education needs should have access to as much of the national curriculum as possible, but there is provision for them to be exempt from it or for it to be modified to suit their capabilities. The number of full-time pupils with statements of special needs in January 1997 was:

In special schools	6,400
In public sector primary and secondary schools	8,200

The school placing of children with special needs is a matter of agreement between education authorities and parents. Parents have the right to say which school they want their child to attend, and a right of appeal where their wishes are not being met. Whenever possible, children with special needs are integrated into ordinary schools. However, for those who require a different environment or specialized facilities, there are special schools, both grant-aided by central government and independent, and special classes within ordinary schools. Education authorities are required to respond to reasonable requests for independent special schools and to send children with special needs to schools outside Scotland if appropriate provision is not available within the country.

SPECIAL SCHOOLS 1997–8

No. of schools	158
No. of pupils	8,056
No. of teachers (full-time equivalent)	1,699
Pupil-teacher ratio	4.7

Alternative Provision

There is no legal obligation on parents anywhere in the UK to educate their children at school, provided that the local education authority is satisfied that the child is receiving full-time education suited to its age, abilities and aptitudes. The education authority need not be informed that a child is being educated at home unless the child is already registered at a state school, in which case the parents must arrange for the child's name to be removed from the school's register before education at home can begin. Neither are parents educating their children at home required to be in possession of a teaching qualification.

Information and support on all aspects of home education can be obtained from Education Otherwise (see page 120).

INDEPENDENT SCHOOLS

Independent schools receive no grants from public funds. They charge fees, and are owned and managed under special trusts, with profits being used for the benefit of the schools concerned. There is a wide variety of provision, from kindergartens to large day and boarding schools, and from experimental schools to traditional institutions. A number of independent schools have been instituted by religious and ethnic minorities.

Most independent schools offer a similar range of courses to state schools and enter pupils for the same public examinations. Those in Scotland tend to follow the English examination system, i.e. GCSE followed by A-levels, although some take the Scottish Education Certificate at Standard Grade followed by Highers or Advanced Highers.

Most Scottish independent schools in membership of the Headmasters' and Headmistresses' Conference, the Governing Bodies Association or the Governing Bodies of Girls' Schools Association are single-sex, but there are some mixed schools, and an increasing number of schools have mixed sixth forms.

INDEPENDENT SCHOOLS 1997–8

No. of schools	114
No. of pupils	32,782
No. of teachers (full-time equivalent)	3,225
Pupil-teacher ratio	9.9

Assisted Places Scheme

The Assisted Places Scheme enables children to attend independent secondary schools which their parents could not otherwise afford, by providing help with tuition fees and other expenses, except boarding costs, on a sliding scale depending on the family's income. The scheme is administered and funded in Scotland by the Scottish Executive Education Department. In the 1998–9 academic year, about 2,800 pupils participated in the scheme in 50 schools in Scotland.

However, the Assisted Places Scheme started to be phased out after the September 1997 entry. Pupils in secondary education holding their places at the beginning of the 1997–8 school year will keep them until they have completed their education at their current school. Those at the primary stage will hold them until they have completed that phase of their education, although some may exceptionally be allowed to hold their places until they have completed their secondary education.

Further information can be obtained from the Independent Schools Information Service (see page 120).

THE CURRICULUM

The content and management of the curriculum in Scotland are not prescribed by statute but are the responsibility of education authorities and individual headteachers. Advice and guidance are provided by the Scottish Executive Education Department and the Scottish Consultative Council on the Curriculum, which also has a developmental role. The Scottish Executive Education Department has produced guidelines on the structure and balance of the curriculum for the five to 14 age group, as well as for each of the curriculum areas for this age group, although they are currently under review. There are also guidelines on assessment across the whole curriculum, on reporting to parents, and on standardized national tests for English language and mathematics at five levels.

The curriculum for 14- to 16-year-olds includes study within each of eight modes: language and communication; mathematical studies; science; technology; social studies; creative activities; physical education; and religious and moral education. There is a recommended percentage of class time to be devoted to each area over the two years. Provision is made for teaching in Gaelic in Gaelic-speaking areas. Testing is carried out on a voluntary basis when the teacher deems it appropriate; most pupils are expected to move from one level to the next at roughly two-year intervals. National testing is largely in place in most primary schools but secondary school participation rates are lower.

For 16- to 18-year-olds, there is available a modular system of vocational courses, certificated by the Scottish Qualifications Authority (SQA), in addition to academic courses. A new unified framework of courses and awards, known as 'Higher Still', which brings together both academic and vocational courses, was introduced in 1999 (see below). The SQA will award the new certificates.

THE PUBLIC EXAMINATION SYSTEM

Scotland has its own system of public examinations, separate from that in England, Wales and Northern Ireland. At the end of the fourth year of secondary education, at about the age of 16, pupils take the Standard Grade of the Scottish Certificate of Education. Standard Grade courses and examinations have been designed to suit every level of ability, with assessment against nationally determined standards of performance.

For most courses there are three separate examination papers at the end of the two-year Standard Grade course. They are set at Credit (leading to awards at grade 1 or 2), General (leading to awards at grade 3 or 4) and Foundation (leading to awards at grade 5 or 6) levels. Grade 7 is available to those who, although they have completed the course, have not attained any of these levels. Normally pupils will take examinations covering two pairs of grades, either grades 1–4 or grades 3–6. Most candidates take seven or eight Standard Grade examinations.

Above Standard Grade, Higher Grade will be available after a one-year course in the fifth or sixth year of secondary school until 2000–1. The one-year Certificate of Sixth Year Studies (CSYS) will be available until 2001–2.

A new system of courses and qualifications is being phased in under the 'Higher Still' reforms, bringing together academic and vocational qualifications. It will replace Highers, CSYS and National Certificate modules, for everyone studying beyond Standard Grade in Scottish schools, and for non-advanced students in further education colleges. Qualifications will be available at five

levels: Access, Intermediate 1, Intermediate 2, Higher and Advanced Higher; the latter will not be available until 2000–1. Courses will be made up of internally assessed units, with external assessment of the full course determining the grade (A to C). The core skills of communication, numeracy, problem-solving, information technology and working with others are embedded in the 'Higher Still' qualifications, although the skills and levels covered vary between subjects; there are also separate core skill units.

All of these qualifications are awarded by the Scottish Qualifications Authority (SQA), which in 1997 assumed the functions of the Scottish Examinations Board and the Scottish Vocational Education Council.

At the end of the 1996–7 academic year, 65,988 pupils left school. Their achievement, by highest Scottish Certificate of Education qualification held, was:

Higher grades A–C	
1 or 2	9,041 (13.7%)
3 or 4	8,428 (12.8%)
5 or over	11,572 (17.5%)
Standard grades 1–3	
1 or 2	9,650 (14.6%)
3 or 4	6,529 (9.9%)
5 or over	7,997 (12.1%)
Standard grades 4–7	8,457 (12.8%)
None	4,314 (6.5%)

The International Baccalaureate

The International Baccalaureate is an internationally recognized two-year pre-university course and examination designed to facilitate the mobility of students and to promote international understanding. Candidates must offer one subject from each of six subject groups, at least three at higher level and the remainder at subsidiary level. Single subjects can be offered, for which a certificate is received. The International Baccalaureate diploma is offered by 33 schools and colleges in the UK, of which one school, the International School of Aberdeen, is in Scotland.

Records of Achievement

The National Record of Achievement (NRA) has been reviewed and will be replaced from 1999–2000 by the Scottish Qualification Certificate, which will be issued by the Scottish Qualifications Authority and will record all qualifications achieved at all levels. In Scotland the school report card gives parents information on their child's progress.

TEACHERS

All teachers in publicly maintained schools must be registered with the General Teaching Council for Scotland. They are registered provisionally for a two-year probationary period, which can be extended if necessary. Only graduates are accepted as entrants to the profession; primary school teachers undertake either a four-year vocational degree course or a one-year postgraduate course, while teachers of academic subjects in secondary schools undertake the latter. Most initial teacher training is classroom-based. Colleges of education provide both in-service and pre-service training for teachers which is subject to inspection by HM Inspectors. The colleges are funded by the Scottish Higher Education Funding Council.

The General Teaching Council advises the Scottish Executive Education Department on the professional suitability of all training courses in colleges of education.

TEACHERS IN PUBLICLY MAINTAINED
SCHOOLS 1997–8
(full-time equivalent)

	Total	Male	Female
Primary			
Headteacher	2,277	566	1,711
Deputy headteacher	936	103	833
Assistant headteacher	597	65	532
Senior teacher*	3,201	247	2,954
Unpromoted teacher	15,177	946	14,231
Secondary			
Headteacher	393	356	37
Deputy headteacher	389	318	71
Assistant headteacher	1,021	703	318
Principal teacher	7,089	4,367	2,722
Assistant principal teacher	3,018	1,337	1,681
Senior teacher*	1,773	721	1,052
Unpromoted teacher	10,192	3,705	6,487

* Includes other promoted posts

Salaries

Teachers in Scotland are paid on a ten-point scale. The entry point depends on type of qualification, and additional allowances are payable under certain circumstances.

SALARIES
from 1 April 1998
<LEAD4>
Head	£27,846–£51,582
Deputy head	£27,846–£38,589
Teacher	£13,206–£28,893

FURTHER EDUCATION

Further education is defined as all provision outside schools to people aged over 16 of education up to and including A-level and its equivalent. It comprises non-advanced courses up to SCE Higher Grade, GCE A-level and GSVQ work-based awards. The Scottish Executive Enterprise and Lifelong Learning Department, through the Scottish Further Education Funding Council, has the duty to secure provision of adequate facilities for further education in Scotland. Courses are taught mainly at colleges of further education, but may also be provided in schools, in higher education institutions and in the work place.

There are 47 further education colleges, funded by the Scottish Further Education Funding Council. The responsibility for 43 of these (incorporated colleges) has been transferred to individual boards of management, which run the colleges and employ staff. The boards include the principal, staff and student representatives among their ten to 16 members; at least half the members must have experience of commerce, industry or the practice of a profession. Two colleges, in Orkney and Shetland, are under Islands Council control, and two other colleges, Sàbhal Mor Ostaig (the Gaelic college on Skye) and Newbattle Abbey College, are managed by trustees.

The Scottish Qualifications Authority (SQA) awards qualifications for most occupations. It awards at non-advanced level the National Certificate, which is available in over 4,000 individual modules and covers the whole range of non-advanced further education provision in Scotland. Students may study for the National Certificate on a full-time, part-time, open learning or work-based learning basis. National Certificate modules can be taken in further education colleges, secondary schools and other centres, normally from the age of 16 onwards. New unified qualifications for non-advanced post-16 education began to be phased in from August 1999 under the 'Higher Still' reforms, which bring together academic and vocational qualifications. 'Higher Still' courses will be available at five levels (Access, Intermediate 1, Intermediate 2, Higher and Advanced Higher), and will replace SCE Higher Grades, CSYS, General Scottish Vocational Qualifications (GSVQ) and National Certificate modules, but not Standard Grade or Scottish Vocational Qualifications (SVQ). SQA also offers modular advanced-level HNC/HND qualifications, which are available in further education colleges and higher education institutions. SQA accredits and awards Scottish Vocational

Qualifications (SVQs), which have mutual recognition with the NVQs available in the rest of the UK. SVQs are assessed in the work-place, but can also be taken in further education colleges and other centres where work-place conditions can be simulated.

SQA will issue the Scottish Qualification Certificate (formerly the National Record of Achievement, *see* above) from 1999–2000.

In the academic year 1997–8 there were 35,750 full-time and sandwich-course students and 249,215 part-time students on non-advanced vocational courses of further education in further education colleges (excluding Newbattle Abbey College). In the same year there were 5,000 full-time teaching staff at the 43 incorporated colleges on a full-time basis and 7,687 on a part-time basis.

Course Information

Applications for further education courses are generally made directly to the colleges concerned. Information on further education courses in the UK and addresses of colleges can be found in the *Directory of Further Education* published annually by the Careers Research and Advisory Centre (*see* page 121).

HIGHER EDUCATION

The term 'higher education' is used to describe education above A-level, Higher and Advanced Higher grade and their equivalent, which is provided in universities, colleges of higher education and some further education colleges.

The Further and Higher Education (Scotland) Act 1992 removed the distinction between higher education provided by the universities and that provided by the former central institutions and other institutions, allowing all higher education institutions which satisfy the necessary criteria to award their own taught course and research degrees and to adopt the title of university. All the polytechnics, art colleges and some colleges of higher education have since adopted the title of university. The change of name does not affect the legal constitution of the institutions. All are funded by the Scottish Higher Education Funding Council.

The number of students in higher education in Scotland in 1996–7 was:

Full-time	156,997
postgraduate	17,506
first degree	102,567
other HE	36,924
Part-time	82,308
postgraduate	24,192
first degree	8,407
other HE	49,709

Undergraduates	139,491
overseas	9,351
Postgraduates	17,506
overseas	5,684

In the 1996–7 academic year, there were 33,182 full-time first degree entrants to higher education; 15,683 were male and 17,499 female. The number of mature entrants (those aged 21 and over when starting a first degree course) was 9,074.

The most heavily subscribed first degree subjects among male students entering full-time higher education courses in 1996–7 were: engineering and technology (2,977), business administration (2,328), multi-disciplinary studies (1,934), maths and computing (1,316), social studies (1,063), architecture (1,060), and physical sciences (1,003). Among female students entering full-time higher education in 1996–7, the most heavily subscribed first degree subjects were: business administration (3,414), multi-disciplinary studies (2,426), subjects allied to medicine (2,011), social studies (1,750), and biological sciences (1,596).

Universities and Colleges

The Scottish Higher Education Funding Council (SHEFC) funds 21 institutions of higher education, including 13 universities. Responsibility for universities in Scotland rests with the Scottish Ministers. Advice to the Government on matters relating to the universities is provided by the SHEFC. The SHEFC receives a block grant from central government which it allocates to the universities and colleges.

The universities each have their own system of internal government, but most are run by two main bodies: the senate, which deals primarily with academic issues and consists of members elected from within the university; and the council, which is the supreme body and is responsible for all appointments and promotions, and bidding for and allocation of financial resources. At least half the members of the council are drawn from outside the university. Joint committees of senate and council are becoming increasingly common.

The institutions of higher education other than universities are managed by independent governing bodies which include represen-tatives of industrial, commercial, professional and educational interests.

Each body appoints its own academic staff on its own conditions. The salary structure in the universities is in line with that of the rest of the UK. The salary scales for staff in the 'post-1992' universities and colleges of higher education in Scotland are determined at individual college level.

SALARIES FOR NON-CLINICAL ACADEMIC STAFF IN UNIVERSITIES 1998-9

Professor	from £35,120
Senior lecturer	£30,498–£34,464
Lecturer grade B	£22,726–£29,048
Lecturer grade A	£15,735–£21,815

Although universities and colleges are expected to look to a wider range of funding sources than before, and to generate additional revenue in collaboration with industry, they are still largely financed, directly or indirectly, from government resources.

Courses

In the UK all universities, including the Open University, and some colleges award their own degrees and other qualifications and can act as awarding and validating bodies for neighbouring colleges which are not yet accredited.

Higher education courses last full-time for at least four weeks or, if part-time, involve more than 60 hours of instruction. Facilities exist for full-time and part-time study, day release, sandwich or block release. Most of the courses outside the universities have a vocational orientation and a substantial number are sandwich courses.

Higher education courses comprise:
- first degree and postgraduate (including research)
- Diploma in Higher Education (Dip.HE), a two-year diploma usually intended to serve as a stepping-stone to a degree course or other further study
- Higher National Diploma (HND), awarded after two years of full-time or three years of sandwich-course or part-time study
- Higher National Certificate (HNC), awarded after two years part-time study
- preparation for professional examinations
- in-service training of teachers

In some Scottish universities the title of Master is sometimes used for a first degree in arts subjects; otherwise undergraduate courses lead to the title of Bachelor. Most undergraduate courses at universities and colleges of higher education run for four years. Professional courses in subjects such as medicine, dentistry and veterinary science take longer. Post-experience short courses are also forming an increasing part of higher education provision.

Details of courses on offer and of predicted entry requirements for the following year's intake are provided in *University and College Entrance: Official Guide*, published annually by the Universities and Colleges Admissions Service (UCAS) and available from bookshops. It includes degree, Dip.HE and HND courses at all universities (excluding the Open University) and most colleges of higher education.

Postgraduate studies vary in length, with taught courses which lead to certificates, diplomas or master's degrees usually taking less time than research degrees. Details of taught postgraduate courses and research degree opportunities can be found in the *Directory of Graduate Studies*, published annually for the Careers Research and Advisory Centre (CRAC) by Hobsons Publishing PLC.

Admissions

For admission to a degree, Dip.HE or HND, potential students apply through a central clearing house. All universities and most colleges providing higher education courses in the UK (except the Open University, which conducts its own admissions) are members of the Universities and Colleges Admission Service (UCAS).

Most applications for admission as a postgraduate student are made to individual institutions but there are two clearing houses of relevance. Applications for postgraduate teacher training courses may be made direct to the institution or through the Graduate Teacher Training Registry. For social work the Social Work Admissions System operates.

Details of initial teacher training courses in Scotland can be obtained from colleges of education and those universities offering such courses, and from the Committee of Scottish Higher Education Principals (COSHEP).

For contact details of the admissions bodies, etc., *see* page 121.

FEES

Tuition fees for existing students with mandatory awards (*see* below) are paid by the grant-awarding body. Since September 1998, new entrants to undergraduate courses have paid the institution an annual contribution to their fees (up to £1,025 in 1999–2000), depending on their own level of income and that of their spouse or parents. Scottish and EU students in the fourth year of a four-year degree course at a Scottish institution are among the classes of students exempt from this payment.

For postgraduate students, the maximum tuition fee to be reimbursed through the awards system in 1999–2000 was £2,675.

STUDENT SUPPORT

Student Grants

Students who started a full-time or sandwich undergraduate course of higher education from the academic year commencing September 1998 are no longer eligible for a grant. Grants for such students have been replaced entirely by loans which are partly income-contingent. Students who started designated courses prior to that date continue to be eligible for means-tested maintenance grants from which a parental contribution is deductible on a sliding scale dependent on income or, for married students, from a spouse's income. However, a parental contribution is not deducted from the grant to students over 25 years of age who have been self-supporting for at least three years. The main rates of mandatory grant have been frozen since 1991–2 while the amount available as a loan has increased in compensation. Some categories of student, including single parents and those with dependants, are entitled to a means-tested grant for help in meeting certain living costs. Disabled students are eligible for non-means tested disabled students allowances.

In Scotland grants are made by the Scottish Executive through the Student Awards Agency. Applications should not be made earlier than the January preceding the start of the course. The local education authority should be consulted for advice about eligibility for a grant and designated courses.

A means-tested maintenance grant, usually paid once a term, covers periods of attendance during term as well as the Christmas and Easter vacations, but not the summer vacation. The basic grant rates for 1998–9 for Scottish students are:

Living in	Existing students
College/lodgings in London area	£2,200
College/lodgings outside London area	£1,780
Parental home	£1,360

Additional allowances are available if, for example, the course requires a period of study abroad. Expenditure on student fees and maintenance in 1997–8 was £298 million; about 115,100 mandatory awards were made.

Access funds are allocated by education departments to the appropriate funding council and administered by further and higher education institutions. They are available to students whose access to education might otherwise be inhibited by financial considerations or where real financial difficulties are faced. For the academic year

1999–2000, provision in Scotland is £8.7 million.

Student Loans

In the academic year 1999–2000, students will be eligible to apply for interest-free but indexed loans of up to £4,480 through the Student Awards Agency. Loans are available to students on designated courses, which are those full-time courses leading to a degree, Dip.HE, HND, initial teacher-training qualification, or other qualification specifically designated as being comparable to a first degree. Certain residency conditions also apply. From autumn 2000 loans of up to £500 will be available to part-time students on low incomes.

Postgraduate Awards

Postgraduate students, with the exception of students on loan-bearing diploma courses such as teacher training, are not eligible to apply for student loans, but can apply for grants for postgraduate study. These are of two types, both discretionary: 30-week bursaries, which are means-tested and apply to certain vocational and diploma courses; and studentship awards, which are dependent on the class of first degree, especially for research degrees, are not means-tested, and cover students undertaking research degrees or taught master's degrees.

Postgraduate funding is provided by the Scottish Executive education departments through the Student Awards Agency for Scotland, the Scottish Executive Rural Affairs Department, and government research councils. An increasing number of scholarships is also available from research charities, endowments, and particular industries or companies.

The Scottish rates for 30-week bursaries for professional and vocational training in 1999–2000 are:

Living in	
College/lodgings in London area	£3,749
College/lodgings outside London area	£2,958
Parental home	£2,235

Studentship awards are payable at between £5,455 and £7,060 a year (1999–2000).

ADULT AND CONTINUING EDUCATION

The term 'adult education' covers a broad spectrum of educational activities ranging from non-vocational courses of general interest, through the acquiring of special vocational skills needed in industry or commerce, to degree-level study at the Open University. The Scottish Executive Enterprise and Lifelong Learning Department funds adult education, including that provided by the universities and the Workers' Educational Association, at vocational further education colleges (47 in 1998) and evening centres. In addition, it provides grants to a number of voluntary organizations.

Courses are provided by the education authorities, further and higher education colleges, universities, residential colleges, the BBC, independent television and local radio stations, and several voluntary bodies.

Although the lengths of courses vary, most courses are part-time. Newbattle Abbey College (*see* page 124), the only long-term residential adult education college in Scotland, offers one-year full-time diploma courses in European studies and Scottish studies which normally provide a university entrance qualification. Some colleges and centres offer short-term residential courses, lasting from a few days to a few weeks, in a wide range of subjects. Local education authorities sponsor many of the colleges, while others are sponsored by universities or voluntary organizations.

Adult education bursaries for students at the long-term residential colleges of adult education are the responsibility of the colleges themselves. In Scotland the awards are funded by central government and administered by the education authorities. Information is available from the Scottish Executive Enterprise and Lifelong Learning Department.

The involvement of universities in adult education and continuing education has diversified considerably and is supported by a variety of administrative structures ranging from dedicated departments to a devolved approach. Membership of the Universities Association for Continuing Education (*see* page 121) is open to any university or university college in the UK. It promotes university continuing education, facilitates the interchange of information, and supports research and development work in continuing education.

Of the voluntary bodies, the biggest is the Workers' Educational Association (WEA), which operates throughout the UK, reaching about 150,000 adult students annually. As well as the Scottish Executive, LEAs make grants towards provision of adult education by WEA Scotland.

Advice on adult and community education, and promotion thereof, is provided by Community Learning Scotland (see page 121).

PARTICIPATION IN COMMUNITY EDUCATION 1996–7

Children	
pre-school age	37,974
primary school age	83,875
Youth	
in groups	127,247
one to one	5,001
Adult	
in groups	240,362
one to one	15,429
Total	509,886

Sources: SOEID; Whitaker's Almanack 1999

DIRECTORY OF EDUCATION ORGANIZATIONS

LOCAL EDUCATION AUTHORITIES

ABERDEEN
Summerhill Education Centre, Stronsay
Drive, Aberdeen AB15 6JA
Tel: 01224-346060
Director of Education, J. Stodter

ABERDEENSHIRE
Woodhill House, Westburn Road, Aberdeen
AB16 5GB
Tel: 01224-665420
Director of Education and Recreation, M. White

ANGUS
County Buildings, Market Street, Forfar DD8
3WE
Tel: 01307-461460
Director of Education, J. Anderson

ARGYLL AND BUTE
Argyll House, Alexandra Parade, Dunoon
PA23 8AG
Tel: 01369-704000
Director of Education, A. Morton

CITY OF EDINBURGH
Wellington Court, 10 Waterloo Place,
Edinburgh EH1 3EG
Tel: 0131-469 3000
Director of Education, R. Jobson

CLACKMANNANSHIRE
Lime Tree House, Alloa FK10 1EX
Tel: 01259-452431
*Executive Director of Education and Community
Services*, K. Bloomer

DUMFRIES AND GALLOWAY
30 Edinburgh Road, Dumfries DG1 1JG
Tel: 01387-260000
Director of Education, F. Sanderson *(acting)*

DUNDEE
8th Floor, Tayside House, Crichton Street,
Dundee DD1 3RJ
Tel: 01382-434000
Director of Education, Ms A. Wilson

EAST AYRSHIRE
Council Headquarters, London Road,
Kilmarnock KA3 7BU
Tel: 01563-576017
Director of Education, J. Mulgrew

EAST DUNBARTONSHIRE
Boclair House, 100 Milngavie Road,
Bearsden, Glasgow G61 2TQ
Tel: 0141-578 8000
Director of Education, I. Mills

EAST LOTHIAN
John Muir House, Haddington EH41 3HA
Tel: 01620-827562
Director of Education, A. Blackie

EAST RENFREWSHIRE
Council Offices, Eastwood Park, Rouken
Glen Road, Giffnock G46 6UG
Tel: 0141-577 3431
Director of Education, Mrs E. J. Currie

EILEAN SIAR/WESTERN ISLES
Council Offices, Sandwick Road, Stornoway,
Isle of Lewis HS1 2BW
Tel: 01851-703773
Director of Education, M. Macleod *(acting)*

FALKIRK
McLaren House, Marchmont Avenue,
Polmont, Falkirk FK2 0NZ
Tel: 01324-506600
Director of Education, Dr G. Young

FIFE
Rothesay House, North Street, Glenrothes
KY7 5PN
Tel: 01592-413656
Director of Education, A. McKay

GLASGOW
Nye Bevan House, 20 India Street, Glasgow
G2 4PF
Tel: 0141-287 6898
Director of Education Services, K. Corsar

HIGHLAND
Council Buildings, Glenurquhart Road,
Inverness IV3 5NX
Tel: 01463-702802
Director of Education, B. Robertson

INVERCLYDE
105 Dalrymple Street, Greenock PA15 1HT
Tel: 01475-712824
Executive Director of Education Services,
B. McLeary

MIDLOTHIAN
Fairfield House, 8 Lothian Road, Dalkeith
EH22 3ZJ
Tel: 0131-270 7500
Director of Education, D. MacKay

MORAY
Council Offices, High Street, Elgin IV30 1BX
Tel: 01343-563170
Director of Education, K. Gavin

NORTH AYRSHIRE
Cunninghame House, Irvine KA12 8EE
Tel: 01294-324400
Corporate Director, Educational Services,
J. Travers

NORTH LANARKSHIRE
Municipal Buildings, Kildonan Street,
Coatbridge ML5 3BT
Tel: 01236-812222
Director of Education, M. O'Neill

ORKNEY
Council Offices, School Place, Kirkwall,
Orkney KW15 1NY
Tel: 01856-873535
Director of Education, L. Manson

PERTH AND KINROSS
Blackfriars, Perth PH1 5LU
Tel: 01738-476200
Director of Education, R. McKay

RENFREWSHIRE
Council Headquarters, South Building,
Cotton Street, Paisley PA1 1LE
Tel: 0141-842 5601
Director of Education and Leisure Services,
Ms S. Rae

SCOTTISH BORDERS
Council Headquarters, Newtown St Boswells,
Melrose, Roxburghshire TD6 0SA
Tel: 01835-824000
Director of Education, J. Christie

SHETLAND
Hayfield House, Hayfield Lane, Lerwick,
Shetland ZE1 0QD
Tel: 01595-744000
Director of Education and Community Services,
J. Halcrow

SOUTH AYRSHIRE
County Buildings, Wellington Square, Ayr
KA7 1DR
Tel: 01292-612000
Director of Education, M. McCabe

SOUTH LANARKSHIRE
Council Headquarters, Almada Street,
Hamilton ML3 0AA
Tel: 01698-454545
Executive Director of Education Resources,
Ms M. Allan

STIRLING
Viewforth, Stirling FK8 2ET
Tel: 01786-442678
Director of Education Services, G. Jeyes

WEST DUNBARTONSHIRE
Garshake Road, Dumbarton G82 3PU
Tel: 01389-737301
Director of Education and Leisure Services,
I. McMurdo

WEST LOTHIAN
Lindsay House, South Bridge Street, Bathgate
EH48 1TS
Tel: 01506-776000
Corporate Manager, Education Services,
R. Stewart

ADVISORY BODIES

EDUCATION OTHERWISE
PO Box 7420, London N9 9SG
Helpline: 0870-730 0074

INDEPENDENT SCHOOLS INFORMATION
SERVICE
21 Melville Street, Edinburgh EH3 7PE
Tel: 0131-220 2106
Administrator, Mrs F. Valpy

INTERNATIONAL BACCALAUREATE
ORGANIZATION
Peterson House, Fortran Road, St Mellons,
Cardiff CF3 0LT
Tel: 01222-774000
Director of Academic Affairs, Dr H. Drennan

SCOTTISH COUNCIL FOR EDUCATIONAL
TECHNOLOGY
74 Victoria Crescent Road, Glasgow G12 9JN
Tel: 0141-337 5000
Chief Executive, R. Pietrasik

SCOTTISH COUNCIL OF INDEPENDENT
SCHOOLS
21 Melville Street, Edinburgh EH3 7PE
Tel: 0131-220 2106
Director, Mrs J. Sischy

SCOTTISH STUDENTSHIP SELECTION
COMMITTEE
c/o Student Awards Agency for Scotland
Gyleview House, 3 Redheughs Rigg,
Edinburgh EH12 9HH
Tel: 0131-244 5846
Chairman, Prof. D. Harding

CURRICULUM COUNCIL

SCOTTISH CONSULTATIVE COUNCIL ON
THE CURRICULUM
Gardyne Road, Broughty Ferry,
Dundee DD5 1NY
Tel: 01382-455053
Chief Executive, M. Baughan

EXAMINING BODY

SCOTTISH QUALIFICATIONS AUTHORITY
Hanover House, 24 Douglas Street,
Glasgow G2 7NQ
Tel: 0141-248 7900
Chief Executive, R. Tuck

FUNDING BODIES

SCOTTISH FURTHER EDUCATION
FUNDING COUNCIL
Donaldson House, 97 Haymarket Terrace,
Edinburgh EH12 5HD
Tel: 0131-313 6590
Chief Executive, Prof. J. Sizer, CBE

SCOTTISH HIGHER EDUCATION FUNDING
COUNCIL
Donaldson House, 97 Haymarket Terrace,
Edinburgh EH12 5HD
Tel: 0131-313 6500
Chief Executive, Prof. J. Sizer, CBE

STUDENT AWARDS AGENCY FOR
SCOTLAND
Gyleview House, 3 Redheughs Rigg,
Edinburgh EH12 9HH
Tel: 0131-244 5868
Chief Executive, K. MacRae

STUDENT LOANS COMPANY LTD
100 Bothwell Street, Glasgow G2 7JD
Tel: 0141-306 2000
Chief Executive, C. Ward

ADMISSIONS AND COURSE INFORMATION

CAREERS RESEARCH AND ADVISORY
CENTRE
Sheraton House, Castle Park, Cambridge CB3
0AX
Tel: 01223-460277
Publishers, Hobson Publishing PLC
159-173 St John Street, London EC1V 4DR
Tel: 0171-336 6633

COMMITTEE OF SCOTTISH HIGHER
EDUCATION PRINCIPALS (COSHEP)
53 Hanover Street, Edinburgh EH2 2PJ
Tel: 0131-226 1111
Secretary, Dr R. L. Crawford

GENERAL TEACHING COUNCIL FOR
SCOTLAND
Clerwood House, 96 Clermiston Road,
Edinburgh EH12 6UT
Tel: 0131-314 6000
Registrar, D. I. M. Sutherland

GRADUATE TEACHER TRAINING
REGISTRY
Rosehill, New Barn Lane, Cheltenham, Glos
GL52 3LZ
Tel: 01242-544788
Registrar, Mrs M. Griffiths

SOCIAL WORK ADMISSIONS SYSTEM
Rosehill, New Barn Lane, Cheltenham, Glos
GL52 3LZ
Tel: 01242-544600
Admissions Officer, Mrs M. Griffiths

UNIVERSITIES AND COLLEGES
ADMISSIONS SERVICE
Rosehill, New Barn Lane, Cheltenham, Glos
GL52 3LZ
Tel: 01242-222444
Chief Executive, M. A. Higgins, Ph.D.

ADULT AND CONTINUING EDUCATION

COMMUNITY LEARNING SCOTLAND
Rosebery House, 9 Haymarket Terrace,
Edinburgh EH12 5EZ
Tel: 0131-313 2488
Chief Executive, C. McConnell

THE OPEN UNIVERSITY
Walton Hall, Milton Keynes MK7 6AA
Tel: 01908-274066

UNIVERSITIES ASSOCIATION FOR
CONTINUING EDUCATION
University of Cambridge Board for
Continuing Education, Madingley Hall,
Madingley, Cambridge CB3 8AQ
Tel: 01954-280279
Administrator, Ms S. Irwin

WEA SCOTLAND (WORKERS'
EDUCATIONAL ASSOCIATION)
Riddle's Court, 322 Lawnmarket, Edinburgh
EH1 2PG
Tel: 0131-226 3456
Scottish Secretary, Ms J. Connon

UNIVERSITIES

THE UNIVERSITY OF ABERDEEN (1495)
Regent Walk, Aberdeen AB24 3FX
Tel: 01224-272000
Web: http://www.abdn.ac.uk
Full-time students (1998–9), 11,036
Chancellor, The Lord Wilson of Tillyorn,
   GCMG (1997)
Vice-Chancellor and Principal, Prof. C. D. Rice
Registrar, Dr P. J. Murray
Secretary, S. Cannon
Rector, Miss C. Dickson Wright

THE UNIVERSITY OF ABERTAY DUNDEE
(1994)
Bell Street, Dundee DD1 1HG
Tel: 01382-308000
Web: http://www.abertay-dundee.ac.uk
Full-time students (1998–9), 3,957
Chancellor, The Earl of Airlie, KT, GCVO, PC
   (1994)
Vice-Chancellor and Principal, Prof. B. King
Registrar, Dr D. Button
Secretary, D. Hogarth

THE UNIVERSITY OF DUNDEE (1967)
Dundee DD1 4HN
Tel: 01382-344000
Web: http://www.dundee.ac.uk
Full-time students (1998–9), 8,355
Chancellor, Sir James Black, FRCP, FRS (1992)
Vice-Chancellor and Principal, Dr I. J. Graham-
   Bryce
Secretary, R. Seaton
Rector, T. Slattery (1998–2001)

THE UNIVERSITY OF EDINBURGH (1583)
7-11 Nicholson Street, Edinburgh EH8 9BE
Tel: 0131-650 1000
Web: http://www.ed.ac.uk
Full-time students (1998–9), 17,842
Chancellor, HRH The Prince Philip, Duke of
   Edinburgh, KG, KT, OM, GBE, PC, FRS
   (1952)
Vice-Chancellor and Principal, Prof. Sir Stewart
   Sutherland, FBA, FRSE
Secretary, M. J. B. Lowe, Ph.D.
Rector, J. Colquhoun (1997–2000)

THE UNIVERSITY OF GLASGOW (1451)
University Avenue, Glasgow G12 8QQ
Tel: 0141-339 8855
Web: http://www.gla.ac.uk
Full-time students (1998–9), 19,900
Chancellor, Sir William Fraser, GCB, FRSE
Vice-Chancellor, Prof. Sir Graeme Davies,
   FREng, FRSE
Secretary, D. Mackie, FRSA
Rector, R. Kemp (1999–2002)

GLASGOW CALEDONIAN UNIVERSITY
(1993)
Cowcaddens Road, Glasgow G4 0BA
Tel: 0141-331 3000
Web: http://www.gcal.ac.uk
Full-time students (1998–9), 8,500
Chancellor, The Lord Nickson, KBE (1993)
Vice-Chancellor and Principal, Dr I. A. Johnston
Head of Academic Administration,
   E. B. Ferguson
Secretary, B. M. Murphy

HERIOT-WATT UNIVERSITY (1966)
Riccarton Campus, Edinburgh EH14 4AS
Tel: 0131-449 5111
Web: http://www.hw.ac.uk
Full-time students (1998–9), 5,800, plus 9,000
   full-time distance learning students
Chancellor, The Lord Mackay of Clashfern,
   PC, QC, FRSE (1979)
Vice-Chancellor and Principal, Prof.
   J. S. Archer, FREng
Secretary, P. L. Wilson

NAPIER UNIVERSITY (1992)
219 Colinton Road, Edinburgh EH14 1DJ
Tel: 0131-444 2266
Web: http://www.napier.ac.uk
Full-time students (1998–9), 11,412
Chancellor, The Viscount Younger of Leckie,
   KT, KCVO, TD, PC, FRSE (1993)
Vice-Chancellor and Principal, Prof. J. Mavor
Secretary and Registrar, I. J. Miller

UNIVERSITY OF PAISLEY (1992)
Paisley PA1 2BE
Tel: 0141-848 3000
Web: http://www.paisley.ac.uk
Full-time students (1998–9), 8,500
Chancellor, Sir Robert Easton, CBE (1993)
Vice-Chancellor, Prof. R. W. Shaw, CBE
Registrar, D. Rigg
Secretary, J. Fraser

THE ROBERT GORDON UNIVERSITY (1992)
Schoolhill, Aberdeen AB10 1FR
Tel: 01224-262000
Web: http://www.rgu.ac.uk
Full-time students (1998–9), 7,582
Chancellor, Sir Bob Reid (1993)
Vice-Chancellor and Principal, Prof. W. Stevely
Secretary, D. Caldwell

THE UNIVERSITY OF ST ANDREWS (1411)
College Gate, St Andrews, Fife KY16 9AJ
Tel: 01334-476161
Web: http://www.st-and.ac.uk
Full-time students (1998–9), 5,843
Chancellor, Sir Kenneth Dover, DLitt., FRSE,
   FBA (1981)
Vice-Chancellor and Principal, Prof. S. Arnott,
   CBE, FRS, FRSE
Secretary and Registrar, D. J. Corner
Rector, D. R. Findlay, QC, FRSA (1996–9)

THE UNIVERSITY OF STIRLING (1967)
Stirling FK9 4LA
Tel: 01786-473171
Web: http://www.stir.ac.uk
Full-time students (1998–9), 5,887
Chancellor, Dame Diana Rigg, DBE
Vice-Chancellor, Prof. A. Miller, CBE, FRSE
Academic Registrar, D. G. Wood
Secretary, K. J. Clarke

THE UNIVERSITY OF STRATHCLYDE (1964)
John Anderson Campus, Glasgow G1 1XQ
Tel: 0141-552 4400
Web:http://www.strath.ac.uk/campus/info.html
Full-time students (1998–9), 16,528
Chancellor, The Lord Hope of Craighead, PC
   (1998)
Vice-Chancellor and Principal, Prof. Sir John
   Arbuthnott, FRSE, FRCPath
Registrar, Dr S. Mellows
Secretary, P. W. A. West

HIGHER EDUCATION COLLEGES

It is not possible to include all the colleges
offering courses of higher or further education.
This list includes institutions providing at least
one full-time course leading to a first degree
granted by an accredited validating body.
(Colleges forming part of a university are
excluded.)

BELL COLLEGE OF TECHNOLOGY
Almada Street, Hamilton, Lanarkshire ML3
0JB
Tel: 01698-283100
Principal, Dr K. MacCallum

DUMFRIES AND GALLOWAY COLLEGE
Heathhall, Dumfries DG1 3QZ
Tel: 01387-261261
Principal, J. Neil

FIFE COLLEGE OF FURTHER AND HIGHER
EDUCATION
St Brycedale Avenue, Kirkcaldy, Fife KY1 1EX
Tel: 01592-268591
Principal, Mrs J. S. R. Johnston

GLASGOW SCHOOL OF ART
167 Renfrew Street, Glasgow G3 6RQ
Tel: 0141-353 4500
Director, Ms S. Reid

INVERNESS COLLEGE
Longman Road, Inverness IV1 1SA
Tel: 01463-236681
Principal, Dr G. Clark

LEWS CASTLE COLLEGE
Stornoway, Isle of Lewis HS2 0XR
Tel: 01851-703311
Principal, D. Green

MORAY COLLEGE
Moray Street, Elgin, Moray IV30 1JJ
Tel: 01343-554321
Principal, Dr R. J. Chalmers

NORTHERN COLLEGE
Hilton Place, Aberdeen AB24 4FA
Tel: 01224-283500
Dundee Campus: Gardyne Road, Dundee
   DD5 1NY. Tel: 01382-464000
Principal, D. Adams

ORKNEY COLLEGE
Kirkwall, Orkney KW15 1LX
Tel: 01856-872839
Principal, P. Scott

QUEEN MARGARET UNIVERSITY COLLEGE
Duke Street, Edinburgh EH6 8HF
Tel: 0131-317 3000
Campuses: Clerwood Terrace, Edinburgh
   EH12 8TS (Corstorphine campus); 41 Elm
   Row, Edinburgh EH7 4AH (Scottish
   International Drama Centre)
Principal, Dr J. Stringer

ROYAL SCOTTISH ACADEMY OF MUSIC
AND DRAMA
100 Renfrew Street, Glasgow G2 3DB
Tel: 0141-332 4101
Principal, Sir Philip Ledger, CBE, FRSE

SÀBHAL MOR OSTAIG
Sleat, Isle of Skye IV44 8RQ
Tel: 01471-844373
Director, N. N. Gillies

SAC (SCOTTISH AGRICULTURAL COLLEGE)
Central Office: West Mains Road, Edinburgh
EH9 3JG
Tel: 0131-535 4000
Campuses: Aberdeen, Auchincruive,
Edinburgh
Principal, K. Linklater

THURSO COLLEGE
Ormlie Road, Thurso, Caithness KW14 7EE
Tel: 01847-896161
Principal, R. Murray

**LONG-TERM RESIDENTIAL COLLEGE FOR
ADULT EDUCATION**

NEWBATTLE ABBEY COLLEGE
Dalkeith, Midlothian EH22 3LL
Tel: 0131-663 1921
Principal, W. M. Conboy

SCOTLAND'S HEALTH

Public health policy is a devolved power and is now the responsibility of the Scottish Executive.

Health education in Scotland is the responsibility of the Health Education Board for Scotland (*see* page 135). The role of the Board is to provide health information and advice to the public, health professionals, and other organizations, and to advise the Government on health education needs and strategies.

SELECTED CAUSES OF DEATH, BY SEX 1997

	Males	Females
Intestinal infectious disease	7	12
Tuberculosis	38	27
Other infectious and parasitic diseases	167	180
Malignant neoplasms	7,538	7,351
Benign neoplasms	11	18
Other and unspecified neoplasms	61	75
Endocrine and metabolic diseases, immunity disorders	354	366
Nutritional deficiencies	1	6
Diseases of the blood and blood-forming organs	96	104
Mental disorders	657	954
Diseases of the nervous system and sense organs	431	469
Rheumatic fever and rheumatic heart disease	47	138
Hypertensive disease	127	167
Ischaemic heart disease	7,355	6,658
Other heart disease	1,124	1,776
Cerebrovascular disease	2,609	4,350
Other diseases of the circulatory system	757	803
Diseases of the respiratory system	3,528	4,363
Diseases of the digestive system	1,158	1,270
Diseases of the genito-urinary system	371	533
Complications of pregnancy, childbirth and puerperium	—	4
Diseases of the skin, musculo-skeletal system and connective tissue	79	276
Congenital anomalies	95	87
Certain conditions originating in the perinatal period	82	58
Signs, symptoms and ill-defined conditions	148	235
Accidents and adverse effects	739	674
Suicide and self-inflicted injury	451	148
Homicide and other violence	274	87
All causes	28,305	31,189

Source: The Stationery Office, *Scottish Abstract of Statistics 1998* (Crown copyright)

MOST FREQUENTLY DIAGNOSED CANCERS 1995
By sex, and percentage change in age-standardized incidence rates 1986 to 1995

	Incidence 1995	Change 1986–95 %
Males		%
Lung	2,754	23.2	−15.6
Prostate	1,703	14.3	+48.8
Colon and rectum	1,604	13.5	+23.2
Bladder	929	7.8	+5.1
Stomach	595	5.0	−25.3
Oesophagus	443	3.7	+49.0
Non-Hodgkin's lymphoma	396	3.3	+25.4
Kidney	315	2.7	+23.2
Leukaemia	268	2.3	+9.2
Pancreas	251	2.1	−19.0
All malignant neoplasms*	11,878	100.0	+7.4
Females			
Breast	3,168	25.2	+27.4
Lung	1,822	14.5	+18.1
Colon and rectum	1,647	13.1	+4.8
Ovary	509	4.1	−6.1
Bladder	454	3.6	+12.5
Stomach	417	3.3	−26.7
Corpus uteri	400	3.2	+14.2
Malignant melanoma of skin	393	3.1	+36.2
Non-Hodgkin's lymphoma	367	2.9	+31.9
Oesophagus	339	2.7	+47.7
All malignant neoplasms*	12,553	100.0	+12.9

* Excluding non-melanoma skin cancer

Source: Scottish Office, *Health in Scotland 1997* (Crown copyright)

NOTIFICATIONS OF SELECTED INFECTIOUS DISEASES

	1996	1997
All diseases	39,642	42,421
Of which:		
Bacillary dysentery	176	124
Chickenpox	28,509	33,413
Cholera	3	1
Diphtheria	2	1
Food poisoning*	10,234	10,144

Legionellosis	17	21
Malaria	70	57
Measles	1,055	762
Meningococcal infection	201	271
Mumps	368	282
Rubella	2,449	818
Scarlet fever	750	645
Tuberculosis (respiratory)	406	335
Tuberculosis (non-respiratory)	103	98
Viral hepatitis	360	359
Whooping cough	186	545

* Including *E.coli* 157:H7 outbreak, November 1996
Source: Scottish Office, *Health in Scotland 1997*
(Crown copyright)

AIDS CASES REGISTERED IN SCOTLAND 1981–97

	Male	Female	Total
Cumulative total to			
30 September 1997	715	175	890
Transmission categories			
Intravenous drug user	228	96	324
Sexual intercourse			
between men*	356	—	356
Sexual intercourse			
between men			
and women	74	64	138
Haemophiliac	35	—	35
Recipient of blood or			
blood product	9	6	15
Mother to child	4	8	12
Other/undetermined	9	1	10

* Figures include several males who are also injecting drug users
Source: The Stationery Office, *Scottish Abstract of Statistics 1998* (Crown copyright)

AIDS DEATHS REGISTERED IN SCOTLAND 1981–97

	Male	Female	Total
Cumulative total to			
30 September 1997	562	122	684
Transmission categories			
Intravenous drug user	186	75	261
Sexual intercourse			
between men*	275	—	275
Sexual intercourse			
between men			
and women	53	35	88
Haemophiliac	32	—	32
Recipient of blood or			
blood product	7	6	13
Mother to child	4	5	9
Other/undetermined	5	1	6

* Figures include several males who are also injecting drug users
Source: The Stationery Office, *Scottish Abstract of Statistics 1998* (Crown copyright)

HIV-INFECTED PERSONS 1981–97

	Male	Female	Total
Cumulative total to			
30 September 1997	2,032	644	2,676
Transmission categories			
Intravenous drug user	786	355	1,141
Sexual intercourse			
between men*	868	—	868
Sexual intercourse between			
men and women	212	244	456
Haemophiliac	84	—	84
Recipient of blood			
or blood product	17	15	32
Mother to child	12	14	26
Other/undetermined	53	16	69

* Figures include several males who are also injecting drug users
Source: The Stationery Office, *Scottish Abstract of Statistics 1998* (Crown copyright)

SEXUALLY TRANSMITTED INFECTIONS*

	1995–6	1996–7
Males	9,303	9,455
Females	8,688	8,918

* New cases of syphilis, gonorrhea, chlamydia, genital herpes, genital warts, trichomoniasis, bacterial vaginosis, non-specific genital infections and other sexually transmitted infections seen at genito-urinary clinics
Source: The Stationery Office, *Scottish Abstract of Statistics 1998* (Crown copyright)

ADMISSIONS TO MENTAL ILLNESS HOSPITALS AND PSYCHIATRIC UNITS, BY SEX 1996*

	Male		Female	
	No.	Rate†	No.	Rate†
Senile and presenile organic psychotic conditions	2,295	92.3	3,438	130.1
Alcohol psychosis, alcohol dependence syndrome	2,251	90.6	968	36.6
Drug abuse	849	34.2	408	15.4
Schizophrenic psychoses	2,317	93.2	1,268	48.0
Affective psychoses	1,320	53.1	2,179	82.5
Other psychoses	1,241	49.9	1,362	51.5
Disorders of childhood	20	0.8	15	0.6
Neurotic disorders	294	11.8	428	16.2
Depressions (non-psychotic)	2,045	82.3	3,691	139.7
Personality disorders	293	11.8	379	14.3
Mental handicap	30	1.2	29	1.1
Other conditions	1,048	42.2	1,335	50.5
All diagnoses	14,003	563.3	15,500	567.7

*Figures for year ending 31 March 1996; figures are provisional
†Rate per 100,000
Source: Scottish Office, *Scottish Abstract of Statistics 1998* (Crown copyright)

PEOPLE WHO HAVE EVER TAKEN DRUGS 1996
By type of drug, sex and age (percentage)

	Males						Females						All ages
	16-19	20-24	25-29	30-39	40-59	Total	16-19	20-24	25-29	30-39	40-59	Total	16-59
Any drug	40.1	49.5	42.3	32.4	11.6	26.7	38.2	42.5	27.6	14.2	10.6	19.1	22.5
Cannabis	38.6	45.0	38.3	28.1	8.8	23.3	35.7	38.5	23.9	11.8	5.7	15.3	19.0
Amphetamines	14.2	23.0	20.0	11.4	1.6	9.4	16.3	21.4	9.3	2.4	0.6	5.5	7.3
LSD	15.9	22.8	14.2	7.3	1.7	8.0	11.5	12.2	4.3	1.3	0.7	3.4	5.5
Psilocybin	15.0	25.7	13.3	8.4	0.6	7.9	7.7	5.8	6.5	2.0	0.2	2.6	5.1
Ecstasy	12.7	22.7	7.5	2.9	0.2	5.3	8.8	11.9	3.8	1.1	0.1	2.7	4.0
Temazepam	8.5	16.6	4.5	3.8	1.3	4.6	7.6	9.9	3.2	1.5	1.0	2.9	3.7
Valium	2.9	11.6	3.3	3.5	3.6	4.4	4.2	7.1	3.2	1.5	1.0	4.1	4.2
Solvents	6.6	8.2	6.1	2.7	0.1	2.8	3.2	4.8	3.1	0.7	0.2	1.4	2.1
Cocaine	2.2	12.1	4.4	5.3	0.8	3.7	6.4	5.3	2.5	1.1	0.1	1.7	2.6
Crack	0.0	1.6	2.0	0.8	0.2	0.7	3.4	1.2	0.5	0.8	0.0	0.7	0.7
Heroin	0.0	3.5	2.5	1.7	0.2	1.2	3.4	0.3	0.6	0.7	0.0	0.5	0.8
Methadone	1.0	4.0	2.4	1.5	0.3	1.3	3.6	1.3	0.6	0.7	0.0	0.7	0.9

Source: The Stationery Office, Scottish Crime Survey 1996 (Crown copyright)

PREVALENCE OF CIGARETTE SMOKING (SELF-REPORTED) AMONG ADULTS (1995 BASED)
Percentages among adults aged 16–64, by sex

Men: number supplying data	3,902
Current smoker*	34%
Former regular smoker	21%
Never regular smoker/never smoked	45%
Women: number supplying data	3,992
Current smoker*	36%
Former regular smoker	16%
Never regular smoker/never smoked	49%

* Includes those who smoked less than one cigarette per day on average
Source: Scottish Office, Scottish Health Survey 1995 (Crown copyright)

CONSUMPTION OF SELECTED FOODS 1995
Men

Butter or hard margarine	24%
Soft margarine	24%
Reduced fat spread	16%
Low fat spread	31%
No spread used	5%
Whole milk	36%
Semi-skimmed milk	57%
Skimmed milk	6%
Other milk	0%
Wholemeal bread	16%
Brown, granary, wheatmeal bread	15%
White or softgrain bread	69%
Eats cereal	68%
Does not eat cereal	32%

Women

Butter or hard margarine	22%
Soft margarine	20%
Reduced fat spread	15%
Low fat spread	35%
No spread used	8%
Whole milk	29%
Semi-skimmed milk	59%
Skimmed milk	11%
Other milk	1%
Wholemeal bread	23%
Brown, granary, wheatmeal bread	19%
White or softgrain bread	58%
Eats cereal	71%
Does not eat cereal	29%

Source: Scottish Office, Scottish Health Survey 1995 (Crown copyright)

FREQUENCY OF CONSUMPTION OF SELECTED FOODS 1995
Men

Eats meat daily	6%
Eats fruit daily	39%
Eats cooked green vegetables daily	26%
Eats chips daily	5%

Women

Eats meat daily	3%
Eats fruit daily	52%
Eats cooked green vegetables daily	30%
Eats chips daily	2%

Source: Scottish Office, Scottish Health Survey 1995 (Crown copyright)

HEALTH TARGETS FOR SCOTLAND

A White Paper on public health in Scotland, *Towards a Healthier Scotland*, was published in February 1999. This announced initiatives to improve the health of people in Scotland, including prevention and early detection of cancer and coronary heart disease and redressing inequalities in health between richer and poorer communities in Scotland,

and set targets to measure the impact of these measures by 2010. In certain fields, targets for 2000 already existed. Targets set for 2010 include:
– reducing by 20 per cent the death rate from all cancers of Scots under 75
– reducing by 50 per cent adult deaths from heart disease
– reducing by 50 per cent the death rate from cerebrovascular disease in Scots under 75
– eliminating dental disease in 60 per cent of five-year-olds
– reducing incidence of smoking by pregnant women from 29 to 20 per cent, and by young people by 20 per cent
– reducing the pregnancy rate among 13–15 year olds by 20 per cent
– reducing alcohol consumption exceeding recommended weekly limits from 33 to 29 per cent for men and from 13 to 11 per cent for women
– increasing the proportion of people taking 30 minutes of moderate exercise five or more times a week to 60 per cent of men and 50 per cent of women

Four 'demonstration projects' announced in the White Paper will concentrate on child health, sexual health, cancer and coronary heart disease.

A network of Healthy Living Centres promoting best practice in public health was announced in 1998, with £34.5 million funding over three years from the National Lottery's New Opportunities Fund.

Diet

Government plans to improve the Scottish diet were first outlined in 1991. The *Report on the Scottish Diet* (the James Report) was published in 1993 and, after further consultation, led to the announcement of the Scottish Diet Action Plan. This set targets for healthier eating among people in Scotland by 2005. These targets have now been incorporated into the *Towards a Healthier Scotland* programme, and include:
– increasing average daily intake of non-sugar carbohydrates by 25 per cent through increased consumption of fruit, vegetables, bread (especially wholemeal and brown breads), breakfast cereals, rice, pasta and potato
– reducing average daily intake of fats to no more than 35 per cent, and of saturated fatty acids to no more than 11 per cent, of food energy
– reducing average daily sodium intake (from common salt and other sodium salts such as sodium glutamate) to 100 mmol

– reducing children's average daily intake of NME sugars by half to less than 10 per cent of total food energy
– doubling average weekly consumption of oil-rich fish
– increasing to over 50 per cent the proportion of mothers breastfeeding their babies for the first six weeks

THE NATIONAL HEALTH SERVICE

The National Health Service (NHS) came into being on 5 July 1948. Its function is to provide a comprehensive health service designed to secure improvement in the physical and mental health of the population and to prevent, diagnose and treat illness. It was founded on the principle that treatment should be provided according to clinical need rather than ability to pay, and should be free at the point of delivery. However, prescription charges and charges for some dental and ophthalmic treatment have been introduced over the years.

The NHS covers a comprehensive range of hospital, specialist, family practitioner (medical, dental, ophthalmic and pharmaceutical), artificial limb and appliance, ambulance, and community health services. Everyone normally resident in the UK is entitled to use any of these services.

Structure

The structure of the NHS underwent a series of reorganizations in the 1970s and, especially, the 1990s. The National Health Service and Community Care Act 1990 introduced the concept of an 'internal market' in health care provision, whereby care was provided through NHS contracts, with health authorities or boards and GP fundholders (the purchasers) being responsible for buying health care from hospitals, non-fundholding GPs, community services and ambulance services (the providers). The Act provided for the establishment of NHS Trusts. These operate as self-governing health care providers independent of health authority control and responsible to the Minister for Health. They derive their income principally from contracts to provide services to health authorities and fund-holding GPs. The community care reforms, introduced in 1993, govern the way care is administered for elderly people, the mentally ill, the physically handicapped and people with learning disabilities.

The Scottish Executive Health Department is responsible for health policy and the administration of the NHS in Scotland. The NHS in Scotland is currently administered by 15 health boards, which are responsible for health services in their areas and also for assessing the health care needs of the local population and developing integrated strategies for meeting these needs in partnership with GPs and in consultation with the public, hospitals and others. The health boards are overseen by the Management Executive at the Scottish Executive Health Department. There are also local health councils, whose role is to represent the interests of the public to health authorities and boards.

Proposed Reforms

In July 1999, responsibility for administering the NHS in Scotland was devolved from the Secretary of State for Scotland to the Scottish Executive. The White Paper *Designed to Care*, presented to Parliament by the then Secretary of State for Scotland, Donald Dewar, in 1997, lays the foundations for the work of the Scottish Parliament in developing Scotland's devolved health care service provision. The White Paper proposed several reforms, including the establishment of primary care trusts and the replacement of GP fundholding by networks of GPs organized in local health care co-operatives.

The primary health trusts will be responsible for the planning and provision of all primary health care, including mental health services and community hospitals. Their role will include support to general practice in delivering integrated primary health care services, strategic planning and policy development, and promoting improvements in the quality and standards of clinical care. The organization of GPs into local health care co-operatives emphasizes collective health care provision on a community basis. The co-operatives will have the option of holding budgets for providing primary and community services, and the present fundholding management allowance will be redirected towards their development.

Other reforms proposed in the White Paper include:
- a review of acute services, reduction and restructuring of the number of acute hospital trusts
- a single stream of funds to cover both hospital services and drugs
- development of health improvement programmes
- one-stop clinics that will provide tests, results and diagnosis on the same day
- use of new technology to support services, e.g. electronic links between all GP surgeries
- establishment of a Scottish health technology assessment centre
- establishment of a process of quality assurance for clinical services

Finance

The NHS is still funded mainly (81.5 per cent) through general taxation, although in recent years greater reliance has been placed on the NHS element of National Insurance contributions, patient charges and other sources of income. Total UK expenditure on the NHS in 1997–8 was £44,719 million, of which £42,787 million derived from public monies and £1,932 million from patient charges and other receipts. NHS expenditure represented 5.7 per cent of GDP.

The Government announced in July 1998 that an additional £21,000 million would be spent on the NHS between 1999 and 2002.

NET COSTS OF THE NATIONAL HEALTH
SERVICE IN SCOTLAND 1996–7

Central administration	£8,378,000
Total NHS cost	4,377,923,000
NHS contributions	468,770,000
Net costs to Exchequer	3,909,153,000
Health Board administration	89,282,000
Hospital and community health services	3,108,575,000
Family practitioner services	986,616,000
Central health services	120,586,000
State Hospital*	22,400,000
Training	3,326,000
Research	10,517,000
Disabled services	2,331,000
Welfare foods	13,835,000
Miscellaneous health services	20,455,000
Total	4,386,301,000

* Under the direct responsibility of the Scottish Executive Health Department
Source: Scottish Office, Scottish Abstract of Statistics 1998 (Crown copyright)

NET EXPENDITURE 1996–7[1]

	Revenue expenditure[2]		Capital expenditure[3]	
	Total £'000	Per capita £	Total £'000	Per capita £
Argyll and Clyde	353,509	789	9,355	21
Ayrshire and Arran	292,473	769	11,316	30
Borders	92,403	804	2,293	20
Dumfries and Galloway	128,779	796	2,575	16
Fife	260,858	776	5,968	18
Forth Valley	210,368	794	5,597	21
Grampian	401,386	822	16,123	33
Greater Glasgow	822,428	837	43,778	45
Highland	179,339	817	10,070	46
Lanarkshire	408,409	773	11,962	23
Lothian	599,003	829	18,409	25
Orkney	19,589	970	685	34
Shetland	21,022	862	304	12
Tayside	359,157	859	29,518	71
Western Isles	33,535	909	1,106	30
State Hospital	17,386		5,014	
Central Services Agency	106,380		2,852	
Scottish Ambulance Service	75,756		6,874	
Total	4,381,780	813	183,799	33

1. Data taken from the unaudited accounts of health boards

2. Includes health care purchases and the costs of purchasing and administration

3. Includes expenditure incurred by NHS Trusts in health board areas

Source: Scottish Office, Scottish Abstract of Statistics 1998 (Crown copyright)

Employees

NHS EMPLOYEES IN SCOTLAND
Full-time equivalent[1] as at 30 September 1997

Medical[2]	11,214.7
Hospital[3]	7,079.5
General practitioners[4]	3,767.0
Community	368.3
Dental[2]	2,398.6
Hospital[3]	215.7
General practitioners[5]	1,941.0
Community	241.9
Nursing and midwifery[6]	51,468.4
Scientific and professional	1,559.1
Clinical psychologists	463.2
Clinical scientists	487.6
Optometrists[7]	20.3
Pharmacists[7]	588.0
Professions allied to medicine	6,406.7
Technical	5,313.9
Ambulance	2,327.3
Works	358.6
Senior management	2,360.0
Administrative and clerical	16,467.0
Ancillary	10,767.7
Trades	1,610.6
Total staff and practitioners[6]	112,252.7

1. Figures include data for the State Hospital, Carstairs

2. Those holding maximum part-time contracts are counted as one full-time equivalent

3. Includes general medical/dental practitioners employed part-time in hospitals; they may also be counted in general practitioners

4. As at 1 October. Comprises principals, assistants, trainees and associates. Consists of full-time equivalent for unrestricted principals and numbers for all other practitioners

5. Number; comprises principals, assistants and trainees

6. The number of staff employed by the NHS in Scotland is affected by the phased transfer of basic nurse training to the higher education sector. Nurse teachers and nurses in training who are still

employed by the NHS are excluded from these totals

7. Excludes high-street pharmacists and optometrists

Source: Scottish Office, Scottish Abstract of Statistics 1998 (Crown copyright)

Salaries

General practitioners (GPs), dentists, optometrists and pharmacists are self-employed, and work for the NHS under contract. Average salaries as at 1 December 1998 were:

Consultant	£45,740–£59,040
Specialist Registrar	£22,510–£32,830
Registrar	£22,510–£27,310
Senior House Officer	£20,135–£26,910
House Officer	£16,145–£18,225
GP	*£49,030
Nursing Grades G–I (Senior Ward Sister)	£19,240–£26,965
Nursing Grade F (Ward Sister)	£16,310–£19,985
Nursing Grade E (Senior Staff Nurse)	£14,705–£17,030
Nursing Grades C–D (Staff/Enrolled Nurse)	£11,210–£14,705
Nursing Grades A–B (Nursing Auxiliary)	£8,315–£11,210

* Average intended net remuneration

HEALTH SERVICES

PRIMARY AND COMMUNITY HEALTH CARE SERVICES

Primary and community health care services comprise the family health services (i.e. the general medical, personal medical, pharmaceutical, dental, and ophthalmic services) and community services (including family planning and preventive activities such as cytology, vaccination, immunization and fluoridation) commissioned by health boards and provided by NHS Trusts, health centres and clinics.

The primary and community nursing services include practice nurses based in general practice, district nurses and health visitors, community psychiatric nursing for mentally ill people living outside hospital, and ante- and post-natal care. Pre-school services at GP surgeries or child health clinics monitor children's physical, mental and emotional health and development, and provide advice to parents on their children's health and welfare.

The School Health Service provides for the health monitoring of schoolchildren of all ages, with a focus on prevention. The service includes medical and dental examination and advice to the local education authority, the school, the parents and the pupil of any health factors which may require special consideration during the pupil's school life.

Family Doctor Service

Any doctor may take part in the Family Doctor Service (provided the area in which he/she wishes to practise has not already an adequate number of doctors). GPs may also have private fee-paying patients.

GENERAL PRACTITIONER SERVICES 1997

Number of doctors	3,650
Average list size*	1,468
Percentage of patients with doctors in:	
single-handed practice	5.1
partnership	94.9

* Excludes doctors with restricted lists, e.g. residents in homes, schools or other institutions.

Source: Scottish Office, Scottish Abstract of Statistics 1998 (Crown copyright)

Pharmaceutical Service

Patients may obtain medicines, appliances and oral contraceptives prescribed under the NHS from any pharmacy whose owner has entered into arrangements to provide this service, and from specialist suppliers of medical appliances. In rural areas, where access to a pharmacy may be difficult, patients may be able to obtain medicines and other prescribed health care products from their doctor.

Except for contraceptives (for which there is no charge), a charge of £5.90 is payable for each item supplied unless the patient is exempt and a declaration of exemption on the prescription form is completed; booklet HC11, available from main post offices and local social security offices, shows which categories of people are exempt.

GENERAL PHARMACEUTICAL SERVICES 1996–7

Pharmacies open	1,142
Prescriptions dispensed	54,990,000
Average prescriptions per person	10.24
Gross cost of prescriptions	£551,220,000
Average cost per person	£102.70

Source: Scottish Office, Scottish Abstract of Statistics 1998 (Crown copyright)

Dental Service

Dentists, like doctors, may take part in the NHS and also have private patients. They are responsible to the health boards in whose areas they provide services.

Patients may go to any dentist who is taking part in the NHS and is willing to accept them. Patients are required to pay 80 per cent of the cost of NHS dental treatment. Since 1 April 1998 the maximum charge for a course of treatment has been £340. As with pharmaceutical services, certain people are exempt from dental charges or have charges remitted; full details are given in booklet HC11.

GENERAL DENTAL SERVICES 1997

Number of dentists	1,798
Number of patients registered	
Adults	2,035,000
Children	710,000
Number of courses of treatment	4,246,000
Cost	
Gross	£154,879,000
Patient charge	£71,617,000
Average per course	£36

Source: Scottish Office, *Scottish Abstract of Statistics 1998* (Crown copyright)

General Ophthalmic Services

General ophthalmic services are administered by health boards. Testing of sight may be carried out by any ophthalmic medical practitioner or ophthalmic optician (optometrist). The optician must give the prescription to the patient, who can take this to any supplier of glasses to have them dispensed. Only registered opticians can supply glasses to children and to people registered as blind or partially sighted.

Those on a low income may qualify for help with the cost of NHS sight testing. Certain categories of people qualify for sight testing free of charge or are automatically entitled to help with the purchase of glasses under an NHS voucher scheme; booklet HC11 gives details.

Diagnosis and specialist treatment of eye conditions, and the provision of special glasses, are available through the Hospital Eye Service.

GENERAL OPHTHALMIC SERVICES 1997

Ophthalmic medical practitioners	98
Ophthalmic opticians	1,117
NHS sight tests undertaken	656,000
Voucher claims paid for	
by health boards	488,000
Total gross costs	£29,588,000

Source: Scottish Office, *Scottish Abstract of Statistics 1998* (Crown copyright)

HOSPITALS AND OTHER SERVICES

Hospital, medical, dental, nursing, ophthalmic and ambulance services are provided by the NHS to meet all reasonable requirements. Facilities for the care of expectant and nursing mothers and young children, and other services required for the diagnosis and treatment of illness, are also provided. Rehabilitation services (occupational therapy, physiotherapy and speech therapy) may also be provided, and surgical and medical appliances are supplied where appropriate.

Specialists and consultants who work in NHS hospitals can also engage in private practice, including the treatment of their private patients in NHS hospitals.

Charges

Certain hospitals have accommodation in single rooms or small wards which, if not required for patients who need privacy for medical reasons, may be made available to other patients for a small charge. These patients are still NHS patients and are treated as such.

In a number of hospitals, accommodation is available for the treatment of private in-patients who undertake to pay the full commercial-rate costs of hospital accommodation and services and (usually) separate medical fees to a specialist as well.

NHS HOSPITAL ACTIVITY 1997–8[1]
Year ending 31 March

	1997	1998p
Bed complement	41,736	40,783
Average available staffed beds	38,427	36,619
In-patient discharges[2]	964,791	973,325
Mean stay (days)	11.7	11.0
Occupancy (% of beds)	80.3	80.2
In-patient true waiting list[3]	47,717	47,081
Day-case discharges	384,260	419,277
New out-patients[4]	2,675,025	2,708,811
Out-patient attendances	6,271,570	6,327,395

p provisional

1. Excludes NHS activity in joint-user and contractual hospitals

2. Comprises discharges, deaths, transfers out of hospitals and transfers between specialties within same hospital

3. Excludes day-case waiting lists and repeat and deferred waiting lists

4. At consultant clinics, including accident and emergency and genito-urinary medicine

Source: Scottish Office, *Scottish Abstract of Statistics 1998* (Crown copyright)

Ambulance Service

The NHS provides emergency ambulance services free of charge via the 999 emergency telephone service. The Scottish Ambulance Service is responsible for all ambulance provision, including the air ambulance service. It controls a fleet of dedicated emergency air ambulance helicopters and two non-dedicated fixed-wing aircraft. In 1997–8, 2,412 missions were flown (917 emergency, 652 very urgent, 354 urgent, 489 pre-planned), compared to 2,156 missions in 1996–7.

The Patient's Charter in Scotland requires emergency ambulances to respond to 95 per cent of calls within 14 minutes in areas with a high population density (over 3 persons per acre), 18 minutes in areas of medium density (0.5–3 persons per acre), and 21 minutes in areas of low density (fewer than 0.5 persons per acre). In the year ending 31 March 1997, 104,075 responses were made in high-density areas, 105,955 in medium-density areas and 34,386 in low-density areas. The percentages of calls answered within the target times were 91, 96 and 92 per cent respectively.

Hospices

Hospice or palliative care for patients with life-threatening illnesses may be provided at the patient's home, in a voluntary or NHS hospice, or in hospital; it is intended to ensure the best possible quality of life for patients during their illness, and to provide help and support to both patients and their families. The Scottish Partnership Agency for Palliative and Cancer Care co-ordinates NHS and voluntary hospice services.

PATIENT'S CHARTERS

The Patient's Charter sets out the rights of patients in relation to the NHS (i.e. the standards of service which all patients will receive at all times) and patients' reasonable expectations (i.e. the standards of service that the NHS aims to provide, even if they cannot in exceptional circumstances be met). The Charter covers issues such as access to services, personal treatment of patients, the provision of information, registering with a doctor, hospital waiting times, care in hospitals, community services, ambulance waiting times, dental, optical and pharmaceutical services, and maternity services. Under the Charter, patients are guaranteed admission to a hospital within 18 months of being placed on a waiting list.

A new NHS Charter is expected to be introduced in 1999. Further information is available free of charge from the Health Information Service (tel: 0800-665544).

Health boards, NHS Trusts and GP practices may also have their own local charters setting out the standard of service they aim to provide.

COMPLAINTS

The Patient's Charter includes the right to have any complaint about the service provided by the NHS dealt with quickly, with a full written reply being provided by a relevant chief executive. There are two levels to the NHS complaints procedure: first, resolution of a complaint locally, following a direct approach to the relevant service provider; second, an independent review procedure if the complaint

---

AMBULANCE ACTIVITY
Year ending 31 March 1997

Health Board	Road Ambulance Service		Ambulance car service	
	Responses	*Total mileage*	*Patient journeys*	*Mileage*
Argyll and Clyde	225,727	1,599,498	16,112	218,903
Ayrshire and Arran	179,037	1,649,490	11,839	266,819
Borders	66,246	760,731	5,999	197,311
Dumfries and Galloway	71,313	1,053,711	5,420	273,841
Fife	174,454	1,347,668	23,686	422,619
Forth Valley	118,800	816,400	32,865	577,998
Grampian	193,614	1,854,597	22,222	283,498
Greater Glasgow	354,170	1,820,820	165,816	1,182,437
Highland	69,812	1,592,537	8,731	403,375
Lanarkshire	230,948	1,616,190	79,004	971,388
Lothian	296,804	1,907,680	55,300	663,926
Orkney	3,038	43,779	84	2,941
Shetland	8,197	60,361	—	—
Tayside	185,879	1,635,980	44,898	577,210
Western Isles	12,129	176,639	3,229	78,826
Scotland	2,190,168	17,936,081	475,205	6,121,092

is not resolved locally. As a final resort, patients may approach the Health Service Commissioner (see page 65) if they are dissatisfied with the response of the NHS to a complaint.

NHS TRIBUNALS

The National Health Service Tribunal (Scotland) (see page 62) considers representations that the continued inclusion of a doctor, dentist, optician or pharmacist on the list of a health authority or health board would be prejudicial to the efficiency of the service concerned.

ORGANIZATIONS

HEALTH BOARDS

The web site for the health boards is: http://www.show.scot.nhs.uk

ARGYLL AND CLYDE
Ross House, Hawkhead Road, Paisley PA2 7BN
Tel: 0141-842 7200; fax 0141-848 1414
Chairman, M. D. Jones
General Manager, N. McConachie

AYRSHIRE AND ARRAN
PO Box 13, Boswell House, 10 Arthur Street, Ayr KA7 1QJ
Tel: 01292-611040; fax 01292-885894
Chairman, Dr J. Morrow
General Manager, Mrs W. Hatton

BORDERS
Newstead, Melrose, Roxburghshire TD9 OSE
Tel: 01896-825500; fax 01896-823401
Chairman, D. A. C. Kilshaw, OBE
General Manager, Dr L. Burley

DUMFRIES AND GALLOWAY
Grierson House, The Crichton Hospital, Bankend Road, Dumfries DG1 4ZG
Tel: 01387-272700; fax 01387-252375
Chairman, J. Ross, CBE
General Manager, N. Campbell

FIFE
Springfield House, Cupar KY15 9UP
Tel: 01334-656200; fax 01334-652210
Chairman, Mrs C. Stenhouse
General Manager, M. Murray

FORTH VALLEY
33 Spittal Street, Stirling FK8 1DX
Tel: 01786-463031; fax 01786-451474
Chairman, E. Bell-Scott
General Manager, D. Hird

GRAMPIAN
Summerfield House, 2 Eday Road, Aberdeen AB15 6RE
Tel: 01224-663456; fax 01224-404014
Chairman, Dr C. MacLeod, CBE
General Manager, F. E. L. Hartnett, OBE

GREATER GLASGOW
Dalian House, PO Box 15329, 350 St Vincent Street, Glasgow G3 8YZ
Tel: 0141-201 4444; fax 0141-201 4601
Chairman, Prof. D. Hamblen
General Manager, C. J. Spry

HIGHLAND
Beechwood Park, Inverness IV2 3HG
Tel: 01463-717123; fax 01463-235189
Chairman, Mrs C. Thomson
General Manager (acting), E. Baigal

LANARKSHIRE
14 Beckford Street, Hamilton, Lanarkshire ML3 0TA
Tel: 01698-281313; fax 01698-423134
Chairman, I. Livingstone, CBE
General Manager, Prof. T. A. Divers

LOTHIAN
148 Pleasance, Edinburgh EH8 9RS
Tel: 0131-536 9000; fax 0131-536 9009
Chairman, Mrs M. Ford
General Manager, T. Jones

ORKNEY
Garden House, New Scapa Road, Kirkwall, Orkney KW15 1BQ
Tel: 01856-885400; fax 01856-885411
Chairman, I. Leslie
General Manager, Mrs J. Wellden

SHETLAND
Brevik House, South Road, Lerwick ZE1 0TG
Tel: 01595-696767; fax 01595-696727
Chairman, J. Telford
General Manager, B. J. Atherton

TAYSIDE
Gateway House, Luna Place, Dundee Technology Park, Dundee DD2 1TP
Tel: 01382-561818; fax 01382-424003
Chairman, Mrs F. Havenga
General Manager, T. Brett

WESTERN ISLES
37 South Beach Street, Stornoway, Isle of Lewis HS1 2BN
Tel: 01851-702997; fax 01851-706720
Chairman, A. Matheson
General Manager, M. Maclennan

HEALTH PROMOTION

HEALTH EDUCATION BOARD FOR SCOTLAND
Woodburn House, Canaan Lane, Edinburgh EH10 4SG
Tel: 0131-536 5500
Chairman, D. Campbell
Chief Executive, Prof. A. Tannahill

AMBULANCE

SCOTTISH AMBULANCE SERVICE
National Headquarters, Tipperlinn Road, Edinburgh EH10 5UU
Tel: 0131-446 7000

BLOOD TRANSFUSION SERVICE

SCOTTISH NATIONAL BLOOD TRANSFUSION SERVICE
21 Ellen's Glen Road, Edinburgh EH17 7QT
Tel: 0131-536 5700
National Director, A. McMillan-Douglas

PALLIATIVE CARE

SCOTTISH PARTNERSHIP AGENCY FOR PALLIATIVE AND CANCER CARE
1A Cambridge Street, Edinburgh EH1 2DY
Tel: 0131-229 0538
Director, Mrs M. Stevenson

NHS TRUSTS

ABERDEEN ROYAL HOSPITALS NHS TRUST
Foresterhill House, Ashgrove Road West, Aberdeen AB9 8AQ
Tel: 01224-681818

ANGUS NHS TRUST
Whitehills Hospital, Forfar, Angus DD8 3DY
Tel: 01307-464551

ARGYLL AND BUTE NHS TRUST
Aros, Lochgilphead, Argyll PA31 8LB
Tel: 01546-606600

AYRSHIRE AND ARRAN COMMUNITY HEALTH CARE NHS TRUST
1A Hunter's Avenue, Ayr KA8 9DW
Tel: 01292-281821

BORDERS COMMUNITY HEALTH SERVICES NHS TRUST
Huntlyburn House, Melrose, Roxburghshire TD6 9BP
Tel: 01896-662300

BORDERS GENERAL HOSPITAL NHS TRUST
Melrose, Roxburghshire TD6 9BS
Tel: 01896-754333

CAITHNESS AND SUTHERLAND NHS TRUST
Caithness General Hospital, Bankhead Road, Wick, Caithness KW1 5NS
Tel: 01955-605050

CENTRAL SCOTLAND HEALTHCARE NHS TRUST
Royal Scottish National Hospital, Old Denny Road, Larbert, Stirlingshire FK5 4SD
Tel: 01324-570700

DUMFRIES AND GALLOWAY ACUTE AND MATERNITY HOSPITALS NHS TRUST
Bankend Road, Dumfries DG1 4AP
Tel: 01387-246246

DUMFRIES AND GALLOWAY COMMUNITY HEALTH NHS TRUST
Crichton Hall, Crichton Royal Hospital, Bankend Road, Dumfries DG1 4TG
Tel: 01387-255301

DUNDEE HEALTHCARE NHS TRUST
Royal Dundee Liff Hospital, Dundee DD2 5NF
Tel: 01382-580441

DUNDEE TEACHING HOSPITALS NHS TRUST
Ninewells Hospital and Medical School, Dundee DD1 9SY
Tel: 01382-660111

EAST AND MIDLOTHIAN NHS TRUST
Edenhall Hospital, Pinkieburn, Musselburgh, Midlothian EH21 7TZ
Tel: 0131-536 8000

EDINBURGH HEALTHCARE NHS TRUST
Astley Ainslie Hospital, 133 Grange Loan, Edinburgh EH9 2HL
Tel: 0131-537 9525

EDINBURGH SICK CHILDREN'S NHS TRUST
Royal Hospital for Sick Children, Sciennes Road, Edinburgh EH9 1LF
Tel: 0131-536 0000

FALKIRK AND DISTRICT ROYAL INFIRMARY NHS TRUST
Major's Loan, Falkirk FK1 5QE
Tel: 01324-624000

FIFE HEALTHCARE NHS TRUST
Cameron House, Cameron Bridge, Leven, Fife KY8 5RG
Tel: 01592-712812

GLASGOW DENTAL HOSPITAL AND
SCHOOL NHS TRUST
378 Sauchiehall Street, Glasgow G2 3JZ
Tel: 0141-211 9600

GLASGOW ROYAL INFIRMARY UNIVERSITY
NHS TRUST
Glasgow Royal Infirmary, 84 Castle Street,
Glasgow G4 0SF
Tel: 0141-552 4000

GRAMPIAN HEALTHCARE NHS TRUST
Westholme, Woodend Hospital, Eday Road,
Aberdeen AB2 6LS
Tel: 01224-663131

GREATER GLASGOW COMMUNITY AND
MENTAL HEALTH SERVICES NHS TRUST
Gartnavel Royal Hospital, 1055 Great
Western Road, Glasgow G12 0XH
Tel: 0141-211 3600

HAIRMYRES AND STONEHOUSE HOSPITAL
NHS TRUST
Hairmyres Hospital, Eaglesham Road, East
Kilbride, South Lanarkshire G75 8RG
Tel: 01355-220292

HIGHLAND COMMUNITIES NHS TRUST
Royal Northern Infirmary, Inverness IV3 5SF
Tel: 01463-242860

INVERCLYDE ROYAL NHS TRUST
Larkfield Road, Greenock, Renfrewshire PA16
0XN
Tel: 01475-633777

KIRKCALDY ACUTE HOSPITALS NHS
TRUSTS
Hayfield House, Hayfield Road, Kirkcaldy,
Fife KY2 5AH
Tel: 01592-643355

LANARKSHIRE HEALTHCARE NHS TRUST
Strathclyde Hospital, Airbles Road,
Motherwell ML1 3BW
Tel: 01698-230500

LAW HOSPITAL NHS TRUST
Carluke ML8 5ER
Tel: 01698-361100

LOMOND HEALTHCARE NHS TRUST
Vale of Leven District Hospital, Main Street,
Alexandria, Dunbartonshire G83 0UA
Tel: 01389-754121

MONKLANDS AND BELLSHILL HOSPITALS
NHS TRUST
Monkscourt Avenue, Airdrie ML6 0JS
Tel: 01236-748748

MORAY HEALTH SERVICES
Maryhill House, 317 High Street, Elgin,
Morayshire IV30 1AJ
Tel: 01343-543131

NORTH AYRSHIRE AND ARRAN NHS TRUST
Crosshouse Hospital, Kilmarnock, Ayrshire
KA2 0BE
Tel: 01563-521133

PERTH AND KINROSS HEALTHCARE NHS
TRUST
Perth Royal Infirmary, Perth PH1 1NX
Tel: 01738-623311

QUEEN MARGARET HOSPITAL NHS TRUST
Whitefield Road, Dunfermline, Fife KY12 0SU
Tel: 01383-623623

RAIGMORE HOSPITAL NHS TRUST
Old Perth Road, Inverness IV2 3UJ
Tel: 01463-704000

RENFREWSHIRE HEALTHCARE NHS
TRUST
Dykebar Hospital, Grahamston Road, Paisley
PA2 7DE
Tel: 0141-884 5122

ROYAL ALEXANDRA HOSPITAL NHS TRUST
Corsebar Road, Paisley PA2 9PN
Tel: 0141-887 9111

ROYAL INFIRMARY OF EDINBURGH NHS
TRUST
1 Lauriston Place, Edinburgh EH3 9YW
Tel: 0131-536 1000

SCOTTISH AMBULANCE SERVICE NHS
TRUST
National Headquarters, Tipperlinn Road,
Edinburgh EH10 5UU
Tel: 0131-447 7711

SOUTH AYRSHIRE HOSPITALS NHS TRUST
Ayr Hospital, Dalmellington Road, Ayr KA6
6DX
Tel: 01292-610555

SOUTHERN GENERAL HOSPITAL NHS
TRUST
Management Office, 1345 Govan Road,
Glasgow G51 4TF
Tel: 0141-201 1100

STIRLING ROYAL INFIRMARY NHS TRUST
Livilands, Stirling FK8 2AU
Tel: 01786-434000

STOBHILL NHS TRUST
133 Balornock Road, Glasgow G21 3UW
Tel: 0141-201 3000

VICTORIA INFIRMARY NHS TRUST
Queens Park House, Langside Road, Glasgow
G42 9TY
Tel: 0141-201 6000

WEST GLASGOW HOSPITALS UNIVERSITY
NHS TRUST
Western Infirmary, Dumbarton Road,
Glasgow G11 6NT
Tel: 0141-211 2000

WEST LOTHIAN NHS TRUST
St John's Hospital at Howden, Howden Road
West, Livingston, West Lothian EH54 6PP
Tel: 01506-419666

WESTERN GENERAL HOSPITALS NHS
TRUST
Western General Hospital, Crewe Road,
Edinburgh EH4 2XU
Tel: 0131-537 1000

YORKHILL NHS TRUST
Royal Hospital for Sick Children, Dalnier
Street, Yorkhill, Glasgow G3 8SJ
Tel: 0141-201 4000

PERSONAL SOCIAL SERVICES

Social work services became a devolved responsibility on 1 July 1999. The children's services functions of the Social Work Services Group have passed to the Children and Young People Group of the Scottish Executive Education Department. The community care functions of the Social Work Services Group have passed to the Scottish Executive Health Department. (The Social Work Services Group within the Scottish Executive Justice Department retains only its criminal justice social work functions.)

Social work services for elderly people, disabled people, families and children, and those with mental disorders are administered by local authorities according to policies and standards set by the Scottish Executive. Each authority has a Director of Social Work (*see* Council Directory) and a Social Work Committee responsible for the social services functions placed upon them. Local authorities provide, enable and commission care after assessing the needs of their population. The private and voluntary sectors also play an important role in the delivery of social services.

The community care reforms introduced in 1993 were intended to enable vulnerable groups to live in the community rather than in residential homes wherever possible, and to offer them as independent a lifestyle as possible.

At 31 March 1997 in Scotland, there were 24,000 beds in residential care homes, 37,000 public-sector sheltered houses and 19,000 day care places. A total of 84,000 clients received home care.

Finance

The Personal Social Services programme is financed partly by central government, with decisions on expenditure allocations being made at local authority level.

TOTAL PUBLIC EXPENDITURE ON SOCIAL WORK 1995–6
£ million

	Current	Capital	Total
Central government*	46.7	1.3	48.0
Local authority†	1,060.9	32.2	1,093.1
Total	1,107.6	33.5	1,141.1

* Includes grants to former list 'D' schools and to voluntary bodies, and certain specific grants by central government to local authorities
† Includes an allocation of central administration costs
Source: Scottish Office, *Scottish Abstract of Statistics 1998* (Crown copyright)

NET REVENUE EXPENDITURE OF LOCAL AUTHORITIES ON SOCIAL WORK 1995–6
£million

Administration and casework	175.0
Residential care of children	102.7
Residential care of older people	153.0
Residential care of people with learning disabilities or mental health problems	42.4
Residential care of physically disabled people	10.7
Day care of children	31.2
Day centres for people with learning disabilities or mental health problems	52.4
Day centres for physically disabled people	11.6
Home help services	130.9
Children's panels	8.1
Other services	234.0
Loan charges	40.7
Total	952.1

Source: The Stationery Office, *Scottish Abstract of Statistics 1998* (Crown copyright)

Staff

STAFF OF LOCAL AUTHORITY SOCIAL WORK DEPARTMENTS 1997*

Central/strategic, fieldwork and special location staff	13,494
Home care staff	10,866
Day centre staff	3,876
Residential care staff	8,160
Secondment	74
Total staff	36,470

* Figures are provisional, and exclude the Scottish Borders
Source: The Stationery Office, *Scottish Abstract of Statistics 1998* (Crown copyright)

ELDERLY PEOPLE

Services for elderly people are designed to enable them to remain living in their own homes for as long as possible. Local authority services include advice, domestic help, meals in the home, alterations to the home to aid mobility, emergency alarm systems, day and/or night attendants, laundry services and the provision of day centres and recreational facilities. Charges may be made for these services. Respite care may also be provided in order to allow carers temporary relief from their responsibilities.

Local authorities and the private sector also provide 'sheltered housing' for elderly people, sometimes with resident wardens.

If an elderly person is admitted to a residential home, charges are made according to a means test; if the person cannot afford to pay, the costs are met by the local authority.

RESIDENTIAL CARE HOMES FOR OLDER PEOPLE 1997

	Local authority homes	Registered homes*	All homes
No. homes	246	418	664
No. beds	7,694	8,833	16,527
No. residents†	7,108	7,661	14,769
Ratio of residents/ full-time staff	1.2	1.2	1.2
Average home size	31	22	25

* Private and voluntary

† Includes holiday/respite residents

Source: SOHD, *Community Care, Scotland 1997* (Crown copyright)

DISABLED PEOPLE

The group of physically disabled people consists mainly of those who have a disability unrelated to normal ageing. Services for disabled people are designed to enable them to remain living in their own homes wherever possible. Local authority services include advice, adaptations to the home, meals in the home, help with personal care, occupational therapy, educational facilities and recreational facilities. Respite care may also be provided in order to allow carers temporary relief from their responsibilities.

Special housing may be available for disabled people who can live independently, and residential accommodation for those who cannot.

RESIDENTIAL CARE HOMES FOR PEOPLE WITH PHYSICAL DISABILITIES 1997

Number of homes	41
Number of beds	839
Number of residents (including holiday/respite residents)	726
Ratio of residents/full-time staff	0.7
Average home size	20

Source: SOHD, *Community Care, Scotland 1997* (Crown copyright)

FAMILIES AND CHILDREN

Local authorities are required to provide services aimed at safeguarding the welfare of children in need and, wherever possible, allowing them to be brought up by their families. Services include advice, counselling, help in the home and the provision of family

centres. Many authorities also provide short-term refuge accommodation for women and children.

Day Care

In allocating day-care places to children, local authorities give priority to children with special needs, whether in terms of their health, learning abilities or social needs. They also provide a registration and inspection service in relation to childminders, playgroups and private day nurseries in the local authority area.

A national child care strategy is being developed by the Government, under which day care and out-of-school child care facilities will be extended to match more closely the needs of working parents.

A survey in 1997 of 3,540 facilities providing daycare for children in Scotland found that there were about 91,000 term-time places and 49,000 places in school holiday time for children under eight. About 113,500 children attended the facilities, 38 per cent of them for all or part of each day Monday to Friday. Of the different facilities, 46 per cent were playgroups and 28 per cent were nurseries. The largest age group attending these was that of three- and four-year-olds. There were also playschemes, out-of-school care schemes, crèches and family centres. Over 24,000 adults (paid staff and volunteers) were involved in day care, of whom 93 per cent were women, 31 per cent were full-time workers, and 63 per cent were paid staff.

There were also 8,243 childminders registered with local authorities, looking after 34,983 children under eight.

Source: SWSG, *Social Work Daycare Services for Children in Scotland, November 1997* (Crown copyright)

Child Protection

Children considered to be at risk of physical injury, neglect or sexual abuse are made subject to a case conference and placed on the local authority's child protection register. Local authority social services staff, school nurses, health visitors and other agencies work together to prevent and detect cases of abuse. In Scotland in 1995–6 1,024 boys and 1,083 girls were reported as having been subject to case conferences. Of these, 15.0 per cent were judged to be at risk of neglect, 30.8 per cent of physical injury, 17.5 per cent of sexual abuse and 5.8 per cent of emotional abuse. More boys than girls suffered physical injury, while twice as many girls as boys were victims of sexual abuse.

Local Authority Care

The Children in Care (Scotland) Act 1995 governs the provision by local authorities of accommodation for children who have no parent or guardian or whose parents or guardians are unable or unwilling to care for them. A family proceedings court may also issue a care order in cases where a child is being neglected or abused, or is not attending school; the court must be satisfied that this would positively contribute to the well-being of the child.

Children who are being looked after by local authorities may live at home, with friends or relatives, in other community accommodation, with foster carers who receive payments to cover the expenses of caring for the child or children, or in residential care. Children's homes may be run by the local authority or by the private or voluntary sectors; all homes are subject to inspection procedures.

CHILDREN IN CARE/LOOKED AFTER*
As at 31 March

	1997		1998	
	No.	%	No.	%
Male	6,629	58	6,279	58
Female	4,728	42	4,512	42
Total	11,357	100	10,791	100

* Figures include estimates for those authorities that were unable to provide data

Source: Scottish Office, *Statistical Bulletin* (Crown copyright)

At 31 March 1998 a total of 10,791 children (an average of 9.4 children per 1,000 members of the population aged 0–17 years) was being looked after. About 51 per cent of these were living at home; 25 per cent were with foster carers, 17 per cent were in residential care and 7 per cent were living with friends or relatives or in other community accommodation (*Source*: Scottish Office, *Statistical Bulletin* (Crown copyright)).

The number of children being looked after varies considerably from authority to authority, depending on factors such as the size of the authority, the size and age structure of the local population, and the authority's policy and resources.

The implementation of the Children in Care (Scotland) Act 1995 extended the powers and responsibilities of local authorities to look after children who previously have left care at the age of 16. Also, a number of respite placements which were not hitherto considered as care now fall within the definition of being 'looked after'. Thus, although the number of children being looked

after has been falling steadily for some years, the number of older teenagers in care increased between 1997 and 1998. The largest proportion of children being looked after is in the age band 12–16 years (45.7 per cent in 1998). Boys outnumber girls in all age bands.

Adoption

Local authorities are required to provide an adoption service, either directly or via approved voluntary societies. The number of adoption applications in Scotland has fallen steadily over the last decade, to only a little over half as many applications in 1998 as in 1988. Applications in 1998 were taken out for 469 children, 211 boys and 257 girls. The largest age group of children for whom adoption applications are made is 5–11 years, with the average age of children for whom applications are made being just under seven years. Less than 10 per cent of applications are made for children less than one year old.

PEOPLE WITH LEARNING DISABILITIES

Services for people with learning disabilities (i.e. mental handicap) are designed to enable them to remain living in the community wherever possible. Local authority services include short-term care, support in the home, the provision of day care centres, and help with other activities outside the home. Residential care is provided for the severely or profoundly disabled, generally in small or group homes. In 1997 more than 75 per cent of homes had 10 beds or fewer. Over 20 per cent of the people admitted to this type of home in 1997 were aged 15–20, while only 6 per cent of residents were over 65.

PEOPLE WITH LEARNING DISABILITIES RESIDENT IN HOSPITALS AND HOMES AND ATTENDING DAY CENTRES
As at 31 March

	1996	1997
Hospitals, no. residents	3,218	n/a
Homes, no. residents	4,075	4,491
Daycare centres, persons on register	7,555	8,054

Source: Scottish Office Home Department, *Community Care, Scotland 1997* (Crown copyright)

PEOPLE WITH MENTAL HEALTH PROBLEMS

Under the Care Programme Approach, mentally ill people should be assessed by specialist services and receive a care plan, and a key worker should be appointed for each patient. Regular reviews of the patient's

progress should be conducted. Local
authorities provide help and advice to mentally
ill people and their families, and places in day
centres and social centres. Social workers can
apply for a mentally disturbed person to be
compulsorily detained in hospital. Where
appropriate, mentally ill people are provided
with accommodation in special hospitals or in
residential homes. These are generally small
homes, most commonly run by voluntary
organizations.

Mental Illness Specific Grants assist
projects addressing care for people with mental
health problems. In 1996–7, 371 such projects
were supported by grants.

In July 1998 the Government announced
that the system of care for mentally ill people
would be reorganized and the Mental Health
(Scotland) Act 1984 reviewed. The review
committee is to report in summer 2000.

PEOPLE WITH MENTAL HEALTH
PROBLEMS RESIDENT IN HOSPITALS AND
HOMES AND ATTENDING DAY CENTRES
As at 31 March

	1996	1997
Hospitals, no. residents	10,216	n/a
Homes, no. residents	1,146	1,192
Daycare centres, persons on register	1,350	1,695

Source: SOHD, *Community Care, Scotland 1997*
(Crown copyright)

RELIGION

About 24 per cent of the population of Scotland (about 1.2 million people) professes active membership of a religious faith. Of this number, the overwhelming majority (92.9 per cent) is Christian (in the Trinitarian sense); 65 per cent of Christians (725,494 people) adhere to the Church of Scotland and other Presbyterian churches, 22 per cent (249,180) to the Roman Catholic Church, just under 5 per cent (54,382) to the Scottish Episcopal Church, 2 per cent (23,732) to Orthodox churches, and 6 per cent (71,550) to other Christian churches, including Methodists, Baptists, Pentecostal churches, Congregational churches, assemblies of Brethren, the Religious Society of Friends (Quakers) and the Salvation Army. About 14 per cent of the adult population regularly attends a Christian church.

About 0.75 per cent of the population (37,271 people) is affiliated to non-Trinitarian churches, e.g. Jehovah's Witnesses, the Church of Jesus Christ of Latter-Day Saints (Mormons), the Church of Christ, Scientist and the Unitarian churches.

Just under 1 per cent of the population (47,971 people) are adherents of other faiths, including Buddhism, Hinduism, Islam, Judaism, Sikhism and a number of new religious movements. There are sizeable Islamic communities in Glasgow and Edinburgh, and a significant Jewish community, particularly in Glasgow. The Samye Ling Tibetan Buddhist Centre, based in Eskdalemuir, Dumfriesshire, is building a Buddhist retreat centre on Holy Island, a small island off the Isle of Arran.

Over the past decade adherence to religion has been falling overall, but a steady decline in membership of the Trinitarian Christian churches and Judaism has been offset by a growth in non-Trinitarian churches, Islam and other faiths. By the first years of the new century a projected 22 per cent of Scotland's population will be adherents of a religion, of whom 91 per cent will be members of Christian churches.

ADHERENTS TO RELIGIONS IN SCOTLAND

	1990	1995	2000 (projected estimate)
Christianity			
(Trinitarian)	1,255,268	1,125,092	1,032,013
Non-Trinitarian			
churches	34,704	37,271	42,258
Buddhism	1,370	1,950	2,270
Hinduism	3,550*	3,950*	4,275
Judaism	3,274	2,341†	1,700
Islam	21,000	24,600*	30,275
Sikhism	8,400*	12,000*	13,650
Other	3,092	3,888	3,967
Total	1,330,658	1,211,092	1,130,408

* Estimate

† Heads of households, male or female, affiliated to synagogues. The figures represent about one-third of the Jewish community

Source: Based on tables from *UK Christian Handbook Religious Trends No. 1 1998-9* (Christian Research/Paternoster Publishing, 1998); figures in text are for 1995

ADULT CHURCH ATTENDANCE IN SCOTLAND

	1990	1995	2000 (projected estimate)
Church of			
Scotland	236,200	216,300	196,200
Other			
Presbyterian	21,100	17,900	15,000
Baptist	19,900	18,300	16,900
Episcopal	16,100	16,600	17,100
Roman Catholic	283,600	248,900	233,300
Independent	31,700	35,100	37,000
Other churches	20,500	22,600	24,300
Total	629,100	575,700	539,800
% of adult population	15.2	13.8	13.3

Source: *UK Christian Handbook Religious Trends No. 1 1998-9*

Inter-Church and Inter-Faith Co-operation

The main umbrella body for the Christian churches in the UK is the Council of Churches for Britain and Ireland (formerly the British Council of Churches). Ecumenical bodies in Scotland are Action of Churches Together in Scotland (ACTS) and the Churches Agency for Inter-Faith Relations in Scotland. The Church of Scotland, the Methodist Church, the Religious Society of Friends (Quakers), the

Roman Catholic Church, the Salvation Army, the Scottish Episcopal Church and the United Reformed Church belong to both. ACTS also includes the Congregational Federation, the Scottish Congregational Church and the United Free Church; the Eastern Orthodox Church has associate membership. The Evangelical Alliance, representing evangelical Christians, has an office in Scotland.

The Scottish Inter-Faith Consultative Group is composed of Christians, Buddhists, Hindus, Jews, Muslims, Sikhs and representatives from other inter-faith groups. In late 1999 it may change its name to the Scottish Inter-Faith Council. Churches Together in Britain and Ireland also has a Commission on Inter-Faith Relations.

Several of the UK-wide inter-church and inter-faith bodies do not have offices in Scotland; in these cases the contact details for the UK office are given.

ACTION OF CHURCHES TOGETHER IN SCOTLAND
Scottish Churches House, Kirk Street, Dunblane, Perthshire FK15 0AJ
Tel: 01786-823588
General Secretary, Dr K. Franz

CHURCHES AGENCY FOR INTER-FAITH RELATIONS IN SCOTLAND
Flat 1/1, 326 West Princes Street, Glasgow G4 9HA
Secretary, Sr I. Smythe

COUNCIL OF CHRISTIANS AND JEWS
Drayton House, 30 Gordon Street, London WC1H 0AN
Tel: 0171-388 3322
Director, Sr M. Shepherd

CHURCHES TOGETHER IN BRITAIN AND IRELAND
Inter-Church House, 35–41 Lower Marsh, London SE1 7RL
Tel: 0171-620 4444
General Secretary, Dr D. Goodbourn

EVANGELICAL ALLIANCE
Challenge House, 29 Canal Street, Glasgow G4 0AD
Tel: 0141-332 8700
General Secretary, Revd D. Anderson

FREE CHURCHES' COUNCIL
27 Tavistock Square, London WC1H 9HH
Tel: 0171-387 8413
General Secretary, Revd G. H. Roper

INTER FAITH NETWORK FOR THE UNITED KINGDOM
5–7 Tavistock Place, London WC1H 9SN
Tel: 0171-388 0008
Director, B. Pearce

SCOTTISH INTER-FAITH CONSULTATIVE GROUP
Flat 1/1, 326 West Princes Street, Glasgow G4 9HA
Secretary, Sr I. Smythe

Christian Churches

see Churches section

Non-Christian Faiths

Several non-Christian religions with significant membership in Scotland do not have representative bodies specific to Scotland. In the following list, contact details for the UK body, or bodies, are given where no Scottish representative body has been identified.

BUDDHISM

THE BUDDHIST SOCIETY
58 Eccleston Square, London SW1V 1PH
Tel: 0171-834 5858
General Secretary, R. C. Maddox

SAMYE LING TIBETAN CENTRE
Eskdalemuir, Langholm, Dumfriesshire DG13 0QL
Tel: 01387-373232
Abbot: Lama Yeshe Losal

HINDUISM

ARYA PRATINIDHI SABHA (UK) AND ARYA SAMAJ LONDON
69A Argyle Road, London W13 0LY
Tel: 0181-991 1732
President, Prof. S. N. Bharadwaj

INTERNATIONAL SOCIETY FOR KRISHNA CONSCIOUSNESS (ISKCON)
Bhaktivedanta Manor, Dharam Marg, Hilfield Lane, Aldenham, Watford, Herts WD2 8EZ
Tel: 01923-857244
Governing Body Commissioner, Sivarama Swami

NATIONAL COUNCIL OF HINDU TEMPLES (UK)
Bhaktivedanta Manor, Dharam Marg, Hilfield Lane, Aldenham, Watford WD2 8EZ
Tel: 01923-856269
Secretary, V. K. Aery

SWAMINARAYAN HINDU MISSION
105–119 Brentfield Road, London NW10 8JB
Tel: 0181-965 2651
Chairman, Sadhu Atmaswarup Das

VISHWA HINDU PARISHAD (UK)
48 Wharfedale Gardens, Thornton Heath,
Surrey CR7 6LB
Tel: 0181-684 9716
General Secretary, K. Ruparelia

ISLAM

ISLAMIC COUNCIL OF SCOTLAND
30 Clyde Place, Glasgow G5 8AA
Director, B. Man

IMAMS AND MOSQUES COUNCIL
20–22 Creffield Road, London W5 3RP
Tel: 0181-992 6636
Director, Dr M. A. Z. Badawi

MUSLIM WORLD LEAGUE
46 Goodge Street, London W1P 1FJ
Tel: 0171-636 7568
Director, U. A. Baidulmaal

UNION OF MUSLIM ORGANIZATIONS OF
THE UK AND EIRE
109 Campden Hill Road, London W8 7TL
Tel: 0171-229 0538
General Secretary, Dr S. A. Pasha

JUDAISM

CHIEF RABBINATE
735 High Road, London N12 0US
Tel: 0181-343 6301
Chief Rabbi, Prof. Jonathan Sacks
Executive Director, Mrs S. Weinberg

BETH DIN (COURT OF THE CHIEF RABBI)
735 High Road, London N12 0US
Tel: 0181-343 6280
Registrar, vacant
Dayanim, Rabbi C. Ehrentreu; Rabbi
I. Binstock; Rabbi C. D. Kaplin; Rabbi M.
Gelley

BOARD OF DEPUTIES OF BRITISH JEWS
Commonwealth House, 1–19 New Oxford
Street, London WC1A 1NF
Tel: 0171-543 5400
Director-General, N. A. Nagler

ASSEMBLY OF MASORTI SYNAGOGUES
1097 Finchley Road, London NW11 0PU
Tel: 0181-201 8772
Director, H. Freedman

FEDERATION OF SYNAGOGUES
65 Watford Way, London NW4 3AQ
Tel: 0181-202 2263
Head of Administration, G. Coleman

REFORM SYNAGOGUES OF GREAT BRITAIN
The Sternberg Centre for Judaism, 80 East
End Road, London N3 2SY
Tel: 0181-349 4731
Chief Executive, Rabbi A. Bayfield

SPANISH AND PORTUGUESE JEWS'
CONGREGATION
2 Ashworth Road, London W9 1JY
Tel: 0171-289 2573
Chief Administrator and Secretary, H. Miller

UNION OF LIBERAL AND PROGRESSIVE
SYNAGOGUES
The Montagu Centre, 21 Maple Street,
London W1P 6DS
Tel: 0171-580 1663
Executive Director, Rabbi Dr C. H.
Middleburgh

UNION OF ORTHODOX HEBREW
CONGREGATIONS
140 Stamford Hill, London N16 6QT
Tel: 0181-802 6226

UNITED SYNAGOGUE HEAD OFFICE
735 High Road, London N12 0US
Tel: 0181-343 8989
Chief Executive, G. Willman

SIKHISM

SIKH MISSIONARY SOCIETY UK
10 Featherstone Road, Southall, Middx
UB2 5AA
Tel: 0181-574 1902
Hon. General Secretary, M. Singh

WORLD SIKH FOUNDATION
33 Wargrave Road, South Harrow, Middx
HA2 8LL
Tel: 0181-864 9228
Secretary, Mrs H. Bharara

THE CHRISTIAN CHURCHES

Christianity is believed to have reached the Roman province of Britain from Gaul in the third century or slightly earlier, but spread no further northwards than the limits of Roman rule, leaving the northern part of Britain to be evangelized by Celtic missionaries. The first Christian church in Scotland, at Whithorn, was established by St Ninian in AD 397. But it was with the arrival c.AD 563 of St Columba from Ireland on the island of Iona, and his creation there of an abbey and missionary centre, that Christianity in Scotland took firm root. It was slow to spread, however, despite the work of missionaries such as St Kentigern (also known as St Mungo), the patron saint of Glasgow. Iona remained the religious centre until the time of the Viking raids, in the early ninth century.

After the Synod of Whitby (AD 663) asserted the practices of the Roman Church over those of the Celtic, the Roman Church gradually became dominant throughout Scotland. In c.AD 850 the Pictish king Kenneth mac Alpin established a new religious centre at Dunkeld, but this too was destroyed by the Vikings and the religious centre shifted to St Andrews, where the cult of that saint was growing.

Malcolm III (1058–93) introduced a number of reforms in the Church, including the banning of Gaelic from use in church services. His wife Margaret encouraged monastic foundations and revived the monastery at Iona. In the reign of David I (1124–53), a full episcopal structure with nine bishoprics was established, with St Andrews as the leading see.

The Reformation

By the late 15th century the church was the largest and richest institution in the country, with revenues far exceeding those of the state. However, the widening gap between the higher clergy, who often combined religious and secular functions, and the underpaid parish priests provided fertile ground for dissent among the lower clergy when the new Reform doctrines of Luther and Calvin were introduced in the mid-16th century from the continent by John Knox, a disaffected priest.

The Reformers' ideas quickly became popular, particularly in the east and among the lesser nobility. In 1555 nobles who favoured the Protestant cause were organized, with the help of Knox, into the Lords of the Congregation; in 1557, these reforming nobles signed the 'First Bond', in which they declared their intention to overthrow the Roman church. The regent, Mary of Guise, outlawed Knox and his followers, provoking riots by Protestants and a brief war in 1559.

A Parliament (the 'Reformation Parliament') called on 1 August 1560 in the name of Queen Mary but without a royal presence, abolished the Latin Mass and rejected the jurisdiction of the Pope; the first assembly of the Church of Scotland ratified the Confession of Faith, drawn up by a committee including John Knox.

In 1578, the Second Book of Discipline provided for the establishment of the kirk session as the governing body for each church and set out the overall organization of the Kirk into presbyteries, provinces and a general assembly.

The Bishops' Wars

In 1592 Parliament passed an Act guaranteeing the liberties of the Kirk and its presbyterian government, although James VI and I and later Stewart monarchs made several attempts to restore episcopacy. Scottish fears that Charles I would reinstate Roman Catholicism led to the signing in 1638 of the National Covenant, which reasserted the right of the people to keep the reformed church. At the end of 1638 the General Assembly abolished the episcopacy and proscribed the use of the Book of Common Prayer. In the ensuing Bishops' Wars of 1639–40, an army of Covenanters took Durham and Newcastle before peace was restored in 1641. When the civil war broke out in 1644, the Scottish Covenanters sided with Cromwell's army, concluding the Solemn League and Covenant with the English Parliament on condition that England would adopt a presbyterian church.

The restoration of Charles II in 1660 brought a reinstatement of episcopacy and intolerance of presbyterianism. Covenanters were persecuted and the Covenant declared illegal. Several waves of protest and repression followed. James VII and II issued decrees in 1687–8 allowing Catholics and Quakers, and later Presbyterians, to hold meetings in private houses; the various Presbyterian factions reunited, fearing a return to Catholicism. A presbyterian church was restored in 1690 and secured by the Act of Settlement 1690 and the Act of Union 1707.

The 18th, 19th and early 20th centuries saw a series of divergent and convergent movements in the Kirk and the formation of successive splinter groups, which subsequently regrouped (see below, Presbyterian churches). Five smaller Presbyterian churches exist today.

MEMBERSHIP OF INSTITUTIONAL
CHURCHES IN SCOTLAND 1995

	Member-ship	Churches	Ministers/priests
Total membership of institutional churches	1,053,542	2,757	2,573
Presbyterian*	725,494	1,958	1,382
Roman Catholic (mass attendance)	249,180	464	936
Anglican	55,136	320	244
of which Scottish Episcopal	54,382	316	230
Orthodox	23,732	15	11

* Including Church of Scotland and other Presbyterian churches

MEMBERSHIP OF FREE CHURCHES IN
SCOTLAND 1995

	Member-ship	Churches	Ministers/priests
Total free church membership	71,550	1,087	593
Baptist	18,083	208	180
Independent[1]	27,572	470	146
of which Scottish Congregational	8,673	62	38
Brethren assemblies	12,826	323	50
Methodist	6,312	76	31
New Churches	3,460	40	29
Pentecostal[2]	6,681	112	89
Other[3]	9,442	200	269
of which Quakers	705	31	—
Lutherans	775	7	4
Salvation Army	5,187	112	178

1. Total of Brethren, Congregational and other independent churches

2. Total of mainstream Afro-Caribbean and Overseas Apostolic

3. Total of Central, Holiness, Lutheran and overseas nationals churches and denominations

Source: UK Christian Handbook Religious Trends No. 1
1998–9

THE CHURCH OF SCOTLAND

The Church of Scotland is the established (i.e. national) church of Scotland. It was established in 1567, and its contractual relation with the state is expressed in a series of statutes from that year onward, concluding with an Act of 1921 setting out the constitution of the new Church and one of 1925 handing over the state endowments to the Church.

The Church is Reformed and evangelical in doctrine, and presbyterian in constitution, i.e. based on a hierarchy of councils of ministers and elders and, since 1990, of members of a diaconate. At local level the kirk session consists of the parish minister and ruling elders. At district level the presbyteries, of which there are 47, consist of all the ministers in the district, one ruling elder from each congregation, and those members of the diaconate who qualify for membership. The General Assembly is the supreme authority, and is presided over by a Moderator chosen annually by the Assembly. The Sovereign, if not present in person, is represented by a Lord High Commissioner who is appointed each year by the Crown.

The Church of Scotland has about 700,000 members, 1,200 ministers and 1,600 churches. There are about 100 ministers and other personnel working overseas.

Lord High Commissioner (1999), The Lord Hogg of Cumbernauld
Moderator of the General Assembly (1999), The Rt. Revd J. B. Cairns
Principal Clerk, Revd F. A. J. Macdonald
Depute Clerk, Revd M. A. MacLean
Procurator, R. A. Dunlop, QC
Law Agent and Solicitor of the Church, Mrs J. S. Wilson
Parliamentary Agent, I. McCulloch (London)
General Treasurer, D. F. Ross

CHURCH OFFICE
121 George Street, Edinburgh EH2 4YN.
Tel: 0131-225 5722

PRESBYTERIES AND CLERKS
Edinburgh, Revd W. P. Graham
West Lothian, Revd D. Shaw
Lothian, J. D. McCulloch

Melrose and Peebles, Revd J. H. Brown
Duns, Revd A. C. D. Cartwright
Jedburgh, Revd A. D. Reid

Annandale and Eskdale, Revd C. B. Haston
Dumfries and Kirkcudbright, Revd G. M. A. Savage
Wigtown and Stranraer, Revd D. Dutton

Ayr, Revd J. Crichton

Irvine and Kilmarnock, Revd C. G. F. Brockie
Ardrossan, Revd D. Broster
Lanark, Revd I. D. Cunningham
Paisley, Revd D. Kay
Greenock, Revd D. Mill
Glasgow, Revd A. Cunningham
Hamilton, Revd J. H. Wilson
Dumbarton, Revd D. P. Munro

South Argyll, M. A. J. Gossip
Dunoon, Revd R. Samuel
Lorn and Mull, Revd W. Hogg

Falkirk, Revd D. E. McClements
Stirling, Revd B. W. Dunsmore

Dunfermline, Revd W. E. Farquhar
Kirkcaldy, Revd B. L. Tomlinson
St Andrews, Revd P. Meager

Dunkeld and Meigle, Revd A. B. Reid
Perth, Revd A. M. Millar
Dundee, Revd J. A. Roy
Angus, Revd M. I. G. Rooney

Aberdeen, Revd A. Douglas
Kincardine and Deeside, Revd J. W. S. Brown
Gordon, Revd I. U. Thomson
Buchan, Revd R. Neilson
Moray, Revd D. J. Ferguson

Abernethy, Revd J. A. I. MacEwan
Inverness, Revd A. S. Younger
Lochaber, Revd A. Ramsay

Ross, Revd R. M. MacKinnon
Sutherland, Revd J. L. Goskirk
Caithness, Revd M. G. Mappin
Lochcarron/Skye, Revd A. I. Macarthur
Uist, Revd M. Smith
Lewis, Revd T. S. Sinclair

Orkney (Finstown), Revd T. Hunt
Shetland (Lerwick), Revd N. R. Whyte
England (London), Revd W. A. Cairns

Europe (Geneva), Revd J. W. McLeod

The minimum stipend of a minister in the Church of Scotland in 1999 was £16,737.

THE SCOTTISH EPISCOPAL CHURCH

The Scottish Episcopal Church was founded after the Act of Settlement (1690) established the presbyterian nature of the Church of Scotland. The Scottish Episcopal Church is in full communion with the Church of England but is autonomous. The governing authority is the General Synod, an elected body of 180 members which meets once a year. The diocesan bishop who convenes and presides at meetings of the General Synod is called the Primus and is elected by his fellow bishops.

There are 51,353 members of the Scottish Episcopal Church, of whom 32,047 are communicants. There are seven bishops, 175 stipendiary clergy, and 320 churches and places of worship.

THE GENERAL SYNOD OF THE SCOTTISH EPISCOPAL CHURCH
21 Grosvenor Crescent, Edinburgh EH12 5EE
Tel: 0131-225 6357
Secretary-General, J. F. Stuart

PRIMUS OF THE SCOTTISH EPISCOPAL CHURCH
Most Revd Richard F. Holloway (Bishop of Edinburgh), *elected* 1992

DIOCESES

ABERDEEN AND ORKNEY
Bishop, Rt. Revd A. Bruce Cameron, *b.* 1941, *cons.* 1992, *elected* 1992
Clergy, 23

ARGYLL AND THE ISLES
Bishop, Rt. Revd Douglas M. Cameron, *b.* 1935, *cons.* 1993, *elected* 1992
Clergy, 8

BRECHIN
Bishop, Rt. Revd Neville Chamberlain, *b.* 1939, *cons.* 1997, *elected* 1997
Clergy, 16

EDINBURGH
Bishop, Rt. Revd Richard F. Holloway, *b.* 1933, *cons.* 1986, *elected* 1986
Clergy, 52

GLASGOW AND GALLOWAY
Bishop, Rt. Revd Idris Jones, *b.* 1943, *cons.* 1998, *elected* 1998
Clergy, 41

MORAY, ROSS AND CAITHNESS
Bishop, Rt. Revd John Crook, *b.* 1940, *Bishop-elect*
Clergy, 10

ST ANDREWS, DUNKELD AND DUNBLANE
Bishop, Rt. Revd Michael H. G. Henley, *b.* 1938, *cons.* 1995, *elected* 1995
Clergy, 25

The minimum stipend of a diocesan bishop of the Scottish Episcopal Church was £22,410 in 1999 (i.e. 1.5 x the minimum clergy stipend of £14,940).

THE ROMAN CATHOLIC CHURCH

The Roman Catholic Church is one world-wide Christian church, with an estimated 890.9 million adherents, acknowledging as its head the Bishop of Rome, known as the Pope (Father). The Pope is held to be the successor of St Peter and a direct line of succession is therefore claimed from the earliest Christian communities. The Pope exercises spiritual authority over the Church with the advice and assistance of the Sacred College of Cardinals, the supreme council of the Church. He is also advised about the concerns of the Church locally by his ambassadors, who liaise with the Bishops' Conference in each country.

The Roman Catholic Church universally and the Vatican City State are run by the Curia, which is made up of the Secretariat of State, the Sacred Council for the Public Affairs of the Church, and various congregations, secretariats and tribunals assisted by commissions and offices. The Vatican State has its own diplomatic service, with representatives known as nuncios and apostolic delegates.

The Bishops' Conference

The Bishops' Conference of Scotland is the permanently constituted assembly of the Bishops of Scotland. To promote its work, the Conference establishes various agencies which have an advisory function in relation to the Conference. The more important of these agencies are called Commissions and each one has a Bishop President who, with the other members of the Commissions, is appointed by the Conference.

The Roman Catholic Church in Scotland has around 250,000 members, two archbishops, six bishops, 936 priests and 464 churches.

SECRETARIAT OF THE BISHOPS'
CONFERENCE OF SCOTLAND
Candida Casa, 8 Corsehill Road, Ayr KA7 2ST
Tel: 01292-256750
President, HE Cardinal Archbishop Winning
General Secretary, Rt. Revd Maurice Taylor

ARCHDIOCESES

ST ANDREWS AND EDINBURGH
Archbishop, Most Revd Keith Patrick O'Brien,
  cons. 1985
Clergy, 192
Diocesan Curia, 113 Whitehouse Loan,
  Edinburgh EH9 1BD. Tel: 0131-452 8244

GLASGOW
Archbishop, HE Cardinal Thomas Winning,
  cons. 1971, *apptd* 1974
Clergy, 253
Diocesan Curia, 196 Clyde Street, Glasgow
  G1 4JY. Tel: 0141-226 5898

DIOCESES

ABERDEEN
Bishop, Rt. Revd Mario Conti, *cons.* 1977
Clergy, 58
Bishop's Residence, 3 Queen's Cross, Aberdeen
  AB2 6BR. Tel: 01224-319154

ARGYLL AND THE ISLES
Bishop, vacant
Clergy, 33
Diocesan Curia, St Columba's Cathedral,
  Esplanade, Oban PA34 5AB. Tel: 01631-
  571003

DUNKELD
Bishop, Rt. Revd Vincent Logan, *cons.* 1981
Clergy, 51
Diocesan Curia, 29 Roseangle, Dundee
  DD1 4LR. Tel: 01382-25453

GALLOWAY
Bishop, Rt. Revd Maurice Taylor, *cons.* 1981
Clergy, 66
Diocesan Curia, 8 Corsehill Road, Ayr
  KA7 2ST. Tel: 01292-266750

MOTHERWELL
Bishop, Rt. Revd Joseph Devine, *cons.* 1977,
  apptd 1983
Clergy, 168
Diocesan Curia, Coursington Road,
  Motherwell ML1 1PW. Tel: 01698-269114

PAISLEY
Bishop, Rt. Revd John A. Mone, *cons.* 1984,
  apptd 1988
Clergy, 86
Diocesan Curia, Cathedral House, 8 East
  Buchanan Street, Paisley, Renfrewshire
  PA1 1HS. Tel: 0141-889 3601

PRESBYTERIAN CHURCHES

THE FREE CHURCH OF SCOTLAND

The Free Church of Scotland was formed in 1843, when over 400 ministers withdrew from the Church of Scotland as a result of interference in the internal affairs of the church by the civil authorities. In 1900, all but 26 ministers joined with others to form the United Free Church (most of which rejoined the Church of Scotland in 1929). In 1904 the remaining 26 ministers were recognized by the House of Lords as continuing the Free Church of Scotland. This Church is also known as the 'Wee Frees'.

The Church maintains strict adherence to the Westminster Confession of Faith of 1648 and accepts the Bible as the sole rule of faith and conduct. Its General Assembly meets annually. It also has links with Reformed Churches overseas. The Free Church of Scotland has 6,000 members, 110 ministers and 140 churches. *General Treasurer*, I. D. Gill, The Mound, Edinburgh EH1 2LS. Tel: 0131-226 5286

UNITED FREE CHURCH OF SCOTLAND

The United Free Church of Scotland has existed in its present form since 1929, but has its origins in divisions in the Church of Scotland in the 18th century. The Secession Church broke away from the Church of Scotland in 1733, and the Relief Church in 1761. In 1847 the Secession and Relief Churches united, becoming the United Presbyterian Church of Scotland. In 1900 this church united with a majority of the Free Church of Scotland to become the United Free Church of Scotland. The majority of members rejoined the Church of Scotland in 1929, with the minority continuing as the United Free Church.

The Church accepts the Bible as the supreme standard of faith and conduct and adheres to the Westminster Confession of Faith. It is opposed to the state establishment of religion. The system of government is presbyterian. It has approximately 6,000 members, 41 ministers and 70 churches. *Moderator* (1999–2000), Revd A. D. Scrimgeour

General Secretary, Revd J. O. Fulton, 11 Newton Place, Glasgow G3 7PR. Tel: 0141-332 3435

THE FREE PRESBYTERIAN CHURCH OF SCOTLAND

The Free Presbyterian Church of Scotland was formed in 1893 by two ministers of the Free Church of Scotland who refused to accept a Declaratory Act passed by the Free Church General Assembly in 1892. The Free Presbyterian Church of Scotland is Calvinistic in doctrine and emphasizes observance of the Sabbath. It adheres strictly to the Westminster Confession of Faith.

The Church has about 3,000 members in Scotland and about 4,000 in overseas congregations. It has 20 ministers and 50 churches. *Moderator*, Revd G. G. Hutton, Free Presbyterian Manse, Broadford, Isle of Skye IV49 4AQ

Clerk of Synod, Revd J. MacLeod, 16 Matheson Road, Stornoway, Isle of Lewis HS1 2LA. Tel: 01851-702755

ASSOCIATED PRESBYTERIAN CHURCHES OF SCOTLAND

The Associated Presbyterian Churches came into being in 1989 as a result of a division within the Free Presbyterian Church of Scotland. Following two controversial disciplinary cases, the culmination of deepening differences within the Church, a presbytery was formed calling itself the Associated Presbyterian Churches (APC). The Associated Presbyterian Churches has about 1,000 members, 15 ministers and 20 churches. *Clerk of the Scottish Presbytery*, Revd Dr M. MacInnes, Drumalin, 16 Drummond Road, Inverness IV2 4NB. Tel: 01463-223983

REFORMED PRESBYTERIAN CHURCH OF SCOTLAND

The Reformed Presbyterian Church of Scotland has its origins in the Covenanter movement. After the 'Glorious Revolution' of 1688, a minority of Presbyterians in southern Scotland did not accept the religious settlement and remained outside the Church of Scotland. Known as 'Cameronians', they met in 'Societies' and formed the Reformed Presbyterian Church of Scotland in 1743. In 1872 the majority of the church joined the Free Church of Scotland.

The Church regards the Bible as its sole standard and adheres strictly to the Westminster Confession of Faith. The Church is presbyterian in structure, with the Synod the supreme court. At present there are four congregations and approximately 200 members and adherents. *Clerk of Synod (pro tem)*, Revd A. Sinclair Horne, 17 George IV Bridge, Edinburgh EH1 1EE. Tel. 0131-220 1450

OTHER CHURCHES

AFRO-WEST INDIAN UNITED COUNCIL OF CHURCHES
c/o New Testament Church of God, Arcadian Gardens, High Road, London N22 5AA
Tel: 0181-888 9427
Secretary, Bishop E. Brown

COUNCIL OF AFRICAN AND AFRO-CARIBBEAN CHURCHES UK
31 Norton House, Sidney Road, London SW9 0UJ
Tel: 0171-274 5589
Chairman, His Grace The Most Revd Father Olu A. Abiola

BAPTIST UNION OF SCOTLAND
14 Aytoun Road, Glasgow G41 5RT

EASTERN ORTHODOX CHURCH
(PATRIARCHATE OF CONSTANTINOPLE)
*Archbishop of Constantinople, New Rome and
Oecumenical Patriarch,* Bartholomew,
elected 1991
Representative in Great Britain, Archbishop
Gregorios of Thyateira and Great Britain,
5 Craven Hill, London W2 3EN. Tel: 0171-
723 4787

LUTHERAN CHURCH
Lutheran Council of Great Britain, 30 Thanet
Street, London WC1H 9QH
Tel: 0171-383 3081
General Secretary, Revd T. Bruch

METHODIST CHURCH
20 Inglewood Crescent, East Kilbride,
Glasgow G75 8QD

PENTECOSTAL CHURCHES
Assemblies of God in Great Britain and Ireland,
3 Cypress Grove, Denmore, Aberdeen
AB23 8LB
Elim Pentecostal Church, 146 Wishaw Road,
Waterloo, Wishaw, Lanarkshire ML2 8EN

THE RELIGIOUS SOCIETY OF FRIENDS
(QUAKERS)
Friends House, Euston Road, London
NW1 2BJ
Tel: 0171-663 1000

THE SALVATION ARMY
Territorial HQ, 101 Newington Causeway,
London SE1 6BN
Tel: 0171-332 0022
General, J. Gowans
UK Territorial Commander, A. Hughes

SCOTTISH CONGREGATIONAL CHURCH
PO Box 189, Glasgow G1 2BX
Tel: 0141-332 7667
President, Dr J. Merrilees
General Secretary, Revd J. Arthur

THE SEVENTH-DAY ADVENTIST CHURCH
Stanborough Park, Watford WD2 6JP
Tel: 01923-672251
President of the British Union Conference,
Pastor C. R. Perry

NON-TRINITARIAN CHURCHES

THE CHURCH OF CHRIST, SCIENTIST
2 Elysium Gate, 126 New Kings Road,
London SW6 4LZ
Tel: 0171-371 0600
District Manager for Great Britain and Ireland,
H. Joynes

THE CHURCH OF JESUS CHRIST OF
LATTER-DAY SAINTS
751 Warwick Road, Solihull, W. Midlands
B91 3DQ
Tel: 0121-712 1202
President of the Europe North Area, Elder S. J.
Condie

JEHOVAH'S WITNESSES
Watch Tower House, The Ridgeway, London
NW7 1RN
Tel: 0181-906 2211

GENERAL ASSEMBLY OF UNITARIAN AND
FREE CHRISTIAN CHURCHES
Essex Hall, 1–6 Essex Street, Strand, London
WC2R 3HY
Tel: 0171-240 2384
General Secretary, J. J. Teagle

DEFENCE

Defence is one of the powers reserved to Westminster and the Scottish Parliament has no jurisdiction over it. However, there are a number of important armed forces installations in Scotland. In particular, all the UK's nuclear weaponry is held at the Clyde naval base.

The following gives details of the main commands and forces in Scotland.

SCOTTISH COMMANDS

FLAG OFFICER SCOTLAND, NORTHERN ENGLAND AND NORTHERN IRELAND
HM Naval Base Clyde, Helensburgh, Dunbartonshire G84 8HL
Tel: 01436-674321
Flag Officer Scotland, Northern England and Northern Ireland, Rear-Adm. A. M. Gregory, OBE

GENERAL OFFICER COMMANDING SCOTLAND
Army HQ Scotland, Annandale Block, Craigiehall, South Queensferry, West Lothian EH30 9TN
Tel: 0131-336 1761
General Officer Commanding Scotland, Maj.-Gen. M. J. Strudwick, CBE
HQ 51 Highland Brigade, Highland House, 7 St Leonard's Bank, Perth PH2 8EB
HQ 52 Lowland Brigade, Edinburgh Castle, Edinburgh EH1 2YT

AIR OFFICER SCOTLAND AND NORTHERN IRELAND
RAF Leuchars, St Andrews, Fife KY16 0JX
Tel: 01334-839471
Air Officer Scotland and Northern Ireland, Air Cdre J. H. Haines, OBE

NAVAL BASE

HM NAVAL BASE CLYDE
Helensburgh, Dunbartonshire G84 8HL
Tel: 01436-674321

THE ARMY

ROYAL ARMOURED CORPS
The Royal Scots Dragoon Guards (Carabiniers and Greys)
Home HQ, The Castle, Edinburgh EH1 2YT
Tel: 0131-310 5100
Colonel-in-Chief, HM The Queen

INFANTRY

SCOTS GUARDS
Regimental HQ, Wellington Barracks, Birdcage Walk, London SW1E 6HQ
Tel: 0171-414 3324
Colonel-in-Chief, HM The Queen

SCOTTISH DIVISION
Divisional Offices, The Castle, Edinburgh EH1 2YT. Tel: 0131-310 5001
HQ Infantry, Imber Road, Warminster, Wilts BA12 0DJ. Tel: 01985-222674
Training Centre, Infantry Training Centre, Vimy Barracks, Catterick, N. Yorks DL9 4HH
Colonel Commandant, Maj.-Gen. M. J. Strudwick, CBE
Divisional Lieutenant-Colonel, Lt.-Col. G. A. Middlemiss

THE ROYAL SCOTS (THE ROYAL REGIMENT)
Regimental HQ, The Castle, Edinburgh EH1 2YT
Tel: 0131-310 5014
Colonel-in-Chief, HRH The Princess Royal, KG, GCVO

THE ROYAL HIGHLAND FUSILIERS (PRINCESS MARGARET'S OWN GLASGOW AND AYRSHIRE REGIMENT)
Regimental HQ, 518 Sauchiehall Street, Glasgow G2 3LW
Tel: 0141-332 0961/5639
Colonel-in-Chief, HRH The Princess Margaret, Countess of Snowdon, CI, GCVO

THE KING'S OWN SCOTTISH BORDERERS
Regimental HQ, The Barracks, Berwick-on-Tweed TD15 1DG
Tel: 01289-307426
Colonel-in-Chief, HRH Princess Alice, Duchess of Gloucester, GCB, CI, GCVO, GBE

THE BLACK WATCH (ROYAL HIGHLAND REGIMENT)
Regimental HQ, Balhousie Castle, Perth PH1 5HR
Tel: 01738-621281; 0131-310 8530
Colonel-in-Chief, HM Queen Elizabeth the Queen Mother

THE HIGHLANDERS (SEAFORTH,
GORDONS AND CAMERONS)
Regimental HQ, Cameron Barracks, Inverness
IV2 3XD. Tel: 01463-224380
Outstation, Viewfield Road, Aberdeen
AB15 7XH. Tel: 01224-318174
Colonel-in-Chief, HRH The Prince Philip,
Duke of Edinburgh, KG, KT, OM, GBE

THE ARGYLL AND SUTHERLAND
HIGHLANDERS (PRINCESS LOUISE'S)
Regimental HQ, The Castle, Stirling FK8 1EH
Tel: 01786-475165
Colonel-in-Chief, HM The Queen

ARMY PERSONNEL CENTRE
Kentigern House, 65 Brown Street, Glasgow
G2 8EX
Tel: 0141-248 7890
Chief Executive, Maj.-Gen. D. L. Burden,
CB, CBE

MAIN RAF BASES

RAF KINLOSS
Kinloss, Forres, Moray IV36 3UH
Tel: 01309-672161

RAF LEUCHARS
St Andrews, Fife KY16 0JX
Tel: 01334-839471

RAF LOSSIEMOUTH
Lossiemouth, Moray IV31 6SD
Tel: 01343-812121

RESERVE FORCES

ROYAL NAVY RESERVES
There are two Royal Naval Reserve units in
Scotland, with a total of 383 members at April
1999.

HMS DALRIADA
Navy Buildings, Eldon Street, Greenock
PA16 7SL
Tel: 01475-724481

HMS SCOTIA
c/o HMS *Caledonia*, Hilton Road, Rosyth,
Fife KY11 2XT
Tel: 01383-425794

TERRITORIAL ARMY
The post-Strategic Defence Review
establishment of the Territorial Army in
Scotland, including the Officers' Training
Corps, is 4,202, with effect from 1 July 1999.

There are TA/reservist centres in
Aberdeen, Arbroath, Cumbernauld, Cupar,
Dumbarton, Dundee, Dunfermline, Dunoon,
Elgin, Forfar, Glenrothes, Grangemouth,
Invergowrie, Inverness, Keith, Kirkcaldy,
Kirkwall, Lerwick, Leuchars, Perth,
Peterhead, St Andrews, Stirling, Stornoway
and Wick (Highlands), and Ayr, Bathgate,
Dumfries, East Kilbride, Edinburgh,
Galashiels, Glasgow, Irvine, Livingston,
Motherwell and Paisley (Lowlands).

HIGHLANDS TERRITORIAL AND
VOLUNTEER RESERVE ASSOCIATION
Seathwood, 365 Perth Road, Dundee DD2 1LX
Tel: 01382-668283
Secretary, Col. J. R. Hensman, OBE

LOWLANDS TERRITORIAL AND
VOLUNTEER RESERVE ASSOCIATION
Lowland House, 60 Avenuepark Street,
Glasgow G20 8LW
Tel: 0141-945 4951
Secretary, Col. R. S. B. Watson, OBE

ROYAL AUXILIARY AIR FORCE (RAuxAF)
There are three units of the RAuxAF in
Scotland, with a total of about 280 members at
April 1999.

NO. 2 (CITY OF EDINBURGH) MARITIME
HQ UNIT, RAuxAF
25 Learmonth Terrace, Edinburgh EH4 1NZ
Tel: 0131-332 2333

NO. 2622 (HIGHLAND) SQUADRON, RAuxAF
REGIMENT
RAF Lossiemouth, Moray IV31 6SD
Tel: 01343-812121

AIR TRANSPORTABLE SURGICAL
SQUADRON, RAuxAF
RAF Leuchars, St Andrews, Fife KY16 0JY
Tel: 01334-839471

THE SCOTTISH ECONOMY

As in any economy, total output produced in Scotland can be thought of as reflecting both the scale (or capacity) of the economy, and the rate of utilization of that capacity. For a given size of labour force, for example, Scottish output is likely to be lower when the unemployment rate is high since the labour force is unlikely to be fully utilized in these circumstances. The following article considers the scale of the Scottish economy as a whole; capacity utilization; the sectoral structure of the Scottish economy; and other salient features.

This is necessarily a brief overview; a recent review of the Scottish economy (Jeremy Peat and Stephen Boyle, *An Illustrated Guide to the Scottish Economy*, Duckworth, London, 1999) provides useful supplementary information and further discussion of many of the topics covered here. The principal source for statistical information presented here is the Office of National Statistics (ONS), as published by the Scottish Office in the *Scottish Economic Bulletin*, no. 54 (March 1997), no. 56 (March 1998) and no. 58 (March 1999). Trade figures are those of the Scottish Council Development and Industry. Figures on household spending and consumption come from the ONS Family Spending survey.

THE SCALE OF THE SCOTTISH ECONOMY

The most commonly employed indicator of an economy's scale is its gross domestic product (GDP), which measures the value of the goods and services produced in an economy over a particular period, usually a single year. Scotland's GDP in 1996 was £54,430 million (at 1996 prices) or 8.6 per cent of UK GDP. These data, however, exclude the oil and gas output from the UK Continental Shelf, which is treated as a separate region in the national accounts; if 80 per cent of this output were attributed to Scotland, estimated GDP would have been increased by over 20 per cent.

Other measures of scale include population and employment. Table 1 indicates that Scotland's shares of UK population and UK employment were 8.5 per cent and 8.7 per cent respectively in 1996. Scotland is therefore a comparatively small region of the UK, except where scale is measured in terms of land area. Scotland accounts for over 32 per cent of the UK's land area and has the lowest population density (average population per square km) of all eleven standard regions of the UK (and just

over a tenth of the density of the south-east of England).

TABLE 1. THE SCALE OF THE SCOTTISH REGION 1996

	UK	Scotland	as % of UK
Area (sq. km)	240,883	77,097	32.0
Population	58,801,500	5,128,000	8.7
Population density (person/sq. km)	240.7	66.4	27.6
Total employment	26,682,000	2,278,000	8.5
GDP (1996 prices)	£629,841	£54,430	8.6
GDP per head	£10,711	£10,614	99.1

Although it is not a measure of scale, GDP per head of population (*see* final row of Table 1) is the most commonly employed measure of the economic prosperity of regions and nations. Scottish GDP per head, at £10,614 in 1996, is 99 per cent of the UK average, and was third highest among standard regions (after south-east England and East Anglia). Although attribution of 80 per cent of the output of oil and gas would increase GDP per head significantly, the rankings of regions would be unaffected.

Until recently, data on GDP per head appeared to indicate a gradual convergence of Scotland to the UK average. However, the most recent estimates of GDP, which are based on the European System of Accounts 1995, have cast doubts on the validity of this view. These estimates suggest that Scottish GDP per head was in fact only 96.8 per cent of the UK level in 1996 and actually fell to only 95.5 per cent of UK GDP per head in 1997. This implied a fall to fifth position among the standard regions.

As can be inferred from Table 2 (*see* below), there is considerable variation in GDP per head among the sub-regions of Scotland, e.g. in 1995 in Grampian, GDP per head was 33 per cent higher than in Scotland as a whole, whereas in Highlands and Islands it was nearly 19 per cent below the Scottish average. The dominance of the Strathclyde region, accounting for 41.2 per cent of GDP, is apparent, whereas Lothian, the next most important region, accounts for just over 18 per cent of GDP.

TABLE 2. GDP AT FACTOR COST (CURRENT PRICES) FOR THE SCOTTISH REGIONS 1995

	£ m	£ per head	as % of Scotland
Borders	956	9,003	88.3
Central	2,538	9,265	90.8
Dumfries and Galloway	1,413	9,555	93.7
Fife	2,923	8,314	81.5
Grampian	7,228	13,566	133.0
Highlands and Islands	2,326	8,298	81.4
Lothian	9,677	12,656	124.1
Strathclyde	21,656	9,483	93.0
Tayside	3,802	9,611	94.2

Source: Office for National Statistics (ONS), published by the Scottish Office, 1998

TRADE

One important feature of the scale of an economy is that smaller economies tend to be more open to trade, with both exports and imports tending to be relatively more important. For the UK as a whole, the export to GDP ratio is around 30 per cent. The ratio for Scotland is more than double this, at 62 per cent. However, much of Scotland's trade consists of exports to the other regions of the UK, while exports to the rest of the world account for some 25 per cent of Scottish GDP. Manufacturing exports are estimated to account for some 75 per cent of total exports to the rest of the world, and 75 per cent of these were, in turn, attributable in 1996 to only three subsectors: office machinery, including computers (37.1 per cent); radio, television and communications (16.3 per cent); and whisky (12.4 per cent). Caution is required in interpreting these figures as contributions to the nation's balance of trade, however, since office machinery, for example, also imports a much larger proportion of its inputs than the whisky industry.

Scotland's main export markets outside the UK are the European Union (58.4 per cent in 1996) and North America (12.6 per cent).

PUBLIC EXPENDITURE

The scale of a regional economy, particularly in terms of its geographical size and population density, is important in understanding the level of public expenditure per head of population. In particular, where the population of a region is geographically dispersed, the provision of a given level of public services becomes more expensive, which partly explains the public sector deficit in Scotland.

The devolution debate has tended to focus attention on regional public finances in Scotland. Many elements of government revenues and some elements of government expenditure are not directly measured at the regional level and so have to be estimated, which has given rise to controversy. However, most commentators take the view that Scotland receives more than its population share of public expenditures while contributing roughly its population share to tax revenues. Accordingly, many believe that there is a public sector deficit in Scotland, with public sector expenditures exceeding revenues, even when the unemployment rate, and so expenditure on benefits, is low.

Public expenditure in Scotland is divided into three elements: identifiable (Scottish Office (now Scottish Executive/Scottish Parliament) spending plus social security); non-identifiable (mostly public goods such as defence, foreign affairs, etc.); and other spending (servicing of debt, etc.). Only the identifiable component can be reliably estimated, with Scotland's share of the other expenditures being determined in a formulaic way, usually using population shares. Total expenditure was estimated to be £31.4 billion in 1996–7, of which £24.7 billion was identifiable (Scottish Office, *Government Expenditure and Revenue in Scotland 1996/7*, Glasgow, 1998). This amounted to 10.1 per cent of UK government expenditure, well in excess of Scotland's population share of 8.7 per cent. This could be justified in terms of a greater need for public expenditure given the greater cost of providing comparable public services in Scotland. However, the last 'needs assessment' exercise was conducted in 1976 and suggested that Scottish identified expenditure should be 116 per cent of the corresponding English level, whereas it is currently 130 per cent. Since there is also some evidence that Scotland has become more affluent relative to the UK as a whole, there is pressure to reduce Scotland's share of expenditures. Indeed, this is implied by the Barnett Formula, which governs the allocation of expenditures to the Scottish 'block' (or assigned budget under devolution).

Total public sector revenues in 1996–7 were estimated to be £24.7 billion excluding oil and gas, amounting to 8.7 per cent of total UK revenues, precisely Scotland's population share. This implies a public sector deficit (an excess of expenditure over revenues) of £7.1 billion excluding oil and gas revenues. There is controversy surrounding Scotland's share of oil and gas revenues, though some recent research implies that £2.9 billion revenue from this source is appropriate, leaving a deficit of £3.8

billion after adjustment for privatization, or 5.8 per cent of GDP. If this is accurate, it is in excess of the Maastricht requirement of 3 per cent of GDP as indicating a sustainable fiscal deficit and suitability for membership of the single European currency. However, there are doubts about elements of the calculations as well as the rigour with which such criteria are applied.

CHANGES IN OUTPUT AND EMPLOYMENT OVER TIME

The scale of the Scottish economy at a particular point in time provides only a snapshot of performance. It is also important to understand the evolution of the economy over time. An economy's rate of growth is often measured in terms of its average percentage rate of change of GDP over time. Figure 1 plots these rates of growth for Scotland and the rest of the UK (RUK). Perhaps the most striking feature of the data is the volatility apparent in growth rates measured as rates of change of actual GDP. This reflects the tendency of actual output to vary in a cyclical manner, with the level of GDP falling in a recession and so generating negative growth rates. It is clear that the cycles in activity in Scotland and the rest of the UK are broadly in phase, although the last recession was exceptional in that the rest of the UK was more adversely affected than Scotland, a reversal of the historical pattern. It is also

clear that the trend rate of growth over the period is positive in both regions. In the rest of the UK, the simple average of growth rates over the period was 2.2 per cent, whereas for Scotland it was 1.4 per cent. While the difference may not seem substantial, if such a growth rate differential were to be sustained, the cumulative effect on levels of GDP would be dramatic. However, estimates of differential growth depend critically on the period over which they are measured. Over the last five years, for example, the average annual growth rate in Scotland was 1.6 per cent, greater than that in the rest of the UK (1.3 per cent), largely as a consequence of the differential impact of the last recession.

Until recently, Scottish GDP per head was thought to have caught up with that in the UK. This would be possible in a regional economy like Scotland, even with slower GDP growth, because in every decade of this century Scotland has lost population through net out-migration; in 1861 Scotland's share of UK population stood at 12.5 per cent but by 1994 it had fallen to 8.8 per cent. The factors governing regional and national growth remain little understood, though recently emphasis has been placed on public investment in infrastructure, investment in human resources (through education and training) and research and development activity, as well as population and physical capital growth.

Data on total employment from the Labour Force Survey are available from 1984.

FIGURE 1. RATES OF ECONOMIC GROWTH IN SCOTLAND AND THE REST OF THE UK 1970–95

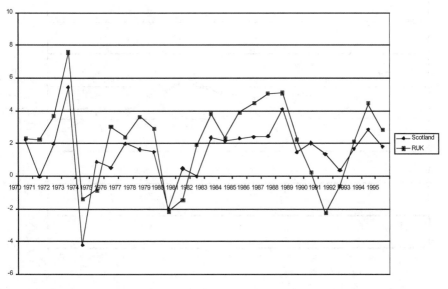

These indicate that employment grew by around 12 per cent in both Scotland and the UK over the period to 1998. Employment grew through most of the 1980s, peaking at around 2.3 million in 1992, before contracting substantially and then gradually recovering to the 1992 level. Growth in employees in employment was slightly less (10 per cent over the period), with growth in self-employment accounting for the remainder. Most of the growth in employment over the period, however, is accounted for by an expansion in part-time female employment (which rose by some 87,000 or 17 per cent over the period to 610,000 in 1998).

REGIONAL UTILIZATION OF RESOURCES

The most obvious measure of the regional utilization of resources is the regional unemployment rate, although at best this measures the utilization of the labour force. Traditionally, attention has focussed on an unemployment rate measured in terms of claimants of the relevant benefit, but the considerable changes to the benefits system over time have implications for the comparability of the data on the rate of unemployment which are independent of any change in labour utilization. Some of the difficulties of interpretation are overcome by adoption of the government's new 'headline' rate of unemployment, which is measured

through a household survey using the International Labour Organization (ILO) definition. Recent unemployment rates for Scotland and the UK are presented in Figure 2. Unemployment rates tend to fluctuate with the cycle in GDP; an increase in activity leads to an increase in employment, although typically with a lag, and this tends to push unemployment rates down. The unemployment rates peaked in the mid-1980s, and then fell until the beginning of the 1990s, when economic activity slowed and unemployment rose. From 1993 unemployment has tended to fall. In the UK context, it has often been argued that there exists a north-south divide, with northern regions such as Scotland typically experiencing lower growth and higher unemployment. The unemployment differentials did appear to be fairly stable until recently when the Scottish unemployment rate fell below that of the UK. However, the signs are that this variation in the historical pattern may prove to be a short-lived reflection of the especially severe impact of the last recession on the south.

Unemployment rates vary significantly among the 54 'travel to work' areas in Scotland (*see* Table 3). In April 1999, claimant counts (typically less than the corresponding ILO measure) varied from 1.6 per cent of the workforce in Banff to 12.0 per cent in Girvan. Unemployment rates are also systematically higher for men than for women. In the first

FIGURE 2. REGIONAL UNEMPLOYMENT RATES (ILO DEFINITION)

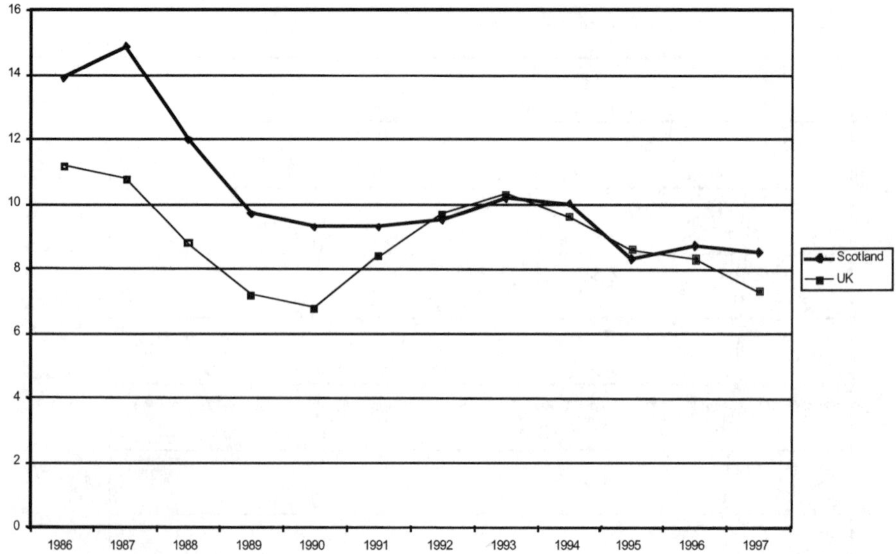

Source: ONS, *Labour Force Survey*

quarter of 1999, for example, the overall headline rate of unemployment (ILO) was 7.6 per cent (as against 6.3 per cent for the UK). However, the unemployment rate for men was 8.5 per cent, as against 6.4 per cent for women; and the differential is more substantial on the claimant count measure. The duration of unemployment spells has been tending to fall with the overall unemployment rate, but men also tend to suffer disproportionately from long spells of unemployment (on claimant basis).

TABLE 3. CLAIMANT COUNT BY TRAVEL TO WORK AREA (TTWA)

Count of claimants of unemployment-related benefit, i.e. jobseeker's allowance

TTWA	No. of claimants	Rates (%)
Aberdeen	4,969	2.3
Annan	502	4.5
Ayr	2,878	5.8
Badenoch	234	4.4
Banff	328	1.6
Berwickshire	380	5.9
Brechin and Montrose	949	5.4
Campbeltown	360	7.5
Crieff	293	4.2
Dingwall	845	5.9
Dufftown	208	4.2
Dumbarton	2,491	7.8
Dumfries	2,170	5.8
Dundee	7,400	7.4
Dunfermline	3,913	6.8
Dunoon and Rothesay	718	7.3
East Ayrshire	4,528	9.4
Edinburgh	15,683	3.7
Elgin and Forres	1,088	3.8
Falkirk	4.356	7.1
Forfar	853	4.6
Fraserburgh	340	2.5
Galashiels and Peebles	925	3.7
Girvan	371	12.0
Glasgow	43,099	6.8
Greenock	2,560	6.8
Hawick	570	5.9
Huntly	188	5.7
Inverness	1,970	3.9
Islay and Mull	248	7.4
Keith and Buckie	578	6.5
Kelso and Jedburgh	220	3.0
Kirkcaldy	6,456	8.4
Kirkcudbright	304	5.2
Lewis and Harris	855	8.9
Lochaber	418	4.3
Lochgilphead	140	3.1
Motherwell and Lanark	9,228	7.6
Newton Stewart	296	9.9
North Ayrshire	5,132	10.1
Oban	325	3.6
Orkney Islands	309	3.2
Perth	1,493	3.5
Peterhead	660	3.9
Pitlochry	84	2.3
Shetland Isles	363	2.4
Skye and Ullapool	555	7.3
St Andrews	778	4.4
Stirling	3,258	5.9
Stranraer	651	7.5
Sutherland	471	9.2
Thurso	369	5.6
Uists and Barra	210	8.3
Wick	436	8.7

Source: Benefits Agency administrative system

THE SECTORAL STRUCTURE OF THE SCOTTISH ECONOMY

Table 4 presents estimates of GDP by industry groups in 1996 and Figure 3 (see over) illustrates the percentage shares of total 1996 GDP attributable to broad industry groups. The traditional notion of Scotland's economy as being characterized by specialization in heavy industries, with shipbuilding as a key activity, was true of the first half of the century, but is outdated now when services account for over 63 per cent of output (68 per cent in the UK). In employment terms, services are even more dominant, accounting for three-quarters of total employment in Scotland.

TABLE 4. GDP BY INDUSTRY GROUPS

	Scotland		UK	
	£m	% of Scotland	£m	% of UK
Agriculture, etc.	1,642	3.0	11,790	1.9
Mining, quarrying	1,220	2.2	4,398	0.7
Manufacturing	13,103	22.2	137,006	21.8
Electricity, gas, etc.	1,828	3.4	13,606	2.2
Construction	3,282	6.0	33,746	5.4
Distribution, hotels, etc.	7,237	13.3	93,091	14.8
Transport, etc.	4,181	7.7	54,056	8.6
Financial and business services	10,780	19.8	164,282	26.1
Public administration, etc.	3,709	6.8	38,244	6.1
Education, health, etc.	8,250	15.2	81,876	13.0
Other services	2,160	4.0	24,713	3.9
Adjustment for financial services	–1,962	–3.6	–26,968	–4.3

Perhaps the most striking feature of Figure 3 is the broad similarity between the industrial structure of Scotland's economy and that of the UK as a whole. Both have come to be dominated by services, although there are some differences in detail. The most noticeable relative specialization in Scotland is in mining and quarrying, where Scotland

FIGURE 3. PERCENTAGES OF GDP BY INDUSTRY GROUP, SCOTLAND AND THE UK 1996

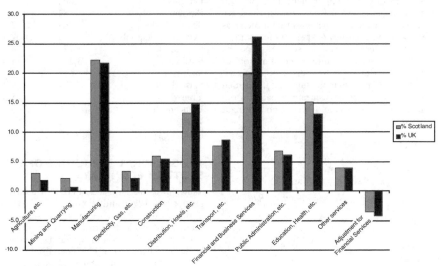

Source: ONS, *Regional Accounts*

accounts for nearly 28 per cent of UK GDP. Agriculture, hunting, forestry and fishing accounts for 13.9 per cent of the UK total, whereas Scotland as a whole contributes 8.6 per cent of UK GDP. There is also comparative specialization in electricity, gas, etc., which contributes 13.4 per cent of UK GDP. However, each of these sectors is small in terms of their percentage contribution to GDP in each region. Financial and business services is the most important contributor to UK GDP (26.1 per cent), but is second most important in Scotland (19.8 per cent of GDP). In Scotland the manufacturing sector is most important (22.2 per cent), but is only slightly more important relatively than in the UK as a whole (21.8 per cent). The rankings of the third and fourth most important sectors in the UK as a whole – distribution, hotels and catering, etc. (14.8 per cent) and education, social work and health services (13.0 per cent) – are again reversed for Scotland. Scotland has historically enjoyed a higher than average share of education and health expenditures, partly reflecting a perceived greater need. Transport, public administration and construction feature as the next most important sectors in terms of contribution to GDP, with Scotland relatively specialized in the latter two sectors. However, the differences in structure are comparatively slight, or concentrated in comparatively small sectors; the predominant impression is of the similarity of the industrial structures of Scotland and the UK.

A single year's data on industry groups output shares gives no indication of the extent of the restructuring that has occurred over time. The Scottish economy has undergone significant structural change over the last few decades. Figure 4 summarizes the structure of the Scottish economy in 1971. One of the most striking features of Figure 4, when contrasted with the current situation, is the decline of manufacturing from 30 per cent to 22 per cent between 1971 and 1996. Equally dramatic is the growth of financial industries over the same period, from 3.1 per cent to 13.9 per cent. The decline in manufacturing reflects the contraction in heavier industries like steel and shipbuilding, but conceals rapid growth in the electronics sector where substantial inward investment has stimulated the creation of 'Silicon Glen' (*see* below). The growth in the financial sector has been one of Scotland's recent success stories; the sector is international in scope, manages over £200 billion of funds, and is characterized by over 30 major financial institutions, many of which are household names (e.g. the Bank of Scotland, the Royal Bank of Scotland). The life and general insurance sector contains a number of world leaders, such as Standard Life. While some of the apparent shift to services may reflect a shedding of former 'in-house' services (which reduces measured output in manufacturing and increases it in services), there is no doubt that a substantial restructuring has occurred in the Scottish economy over the latter part of the century.

Less dramatic but nonetheless substantial changes have occurred in the outputs of other sectors. Thus agriculture's share has fallen from 5 per cent to 3 per cent and construction's from 8 per cent to 6 per cent.

FIGURE 4. THE SECTORAL COMPOSITION OF SCOTTISH GDP 1971

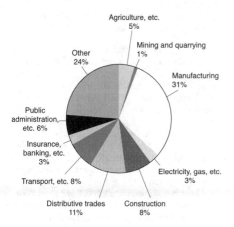

There has been little comment so far on the discovery and exploitation of North Sea oil, which now has a history spanning over two decades. The special treatment of North Sea oil production in the national accounts has been noted above, as has the fact that the attribution of a share of this to the Scottish economy could substantially increase Scottish GDP (though the precise share that can be deemed 'Scottish' remains controversial). However, offshore activity has generated much associated onshore activity. In 1994 some 21,000 people were employed directly by the oil and gas industry, but over 60,000 jobs were attributed to the sector in total, through jobs in supporting activities. Although low oil prices cast doubt on the likelihood of further development of the less accessible fields, the impact of this has been mitigated to some degree by technological change. The industry is expected to continue to make a significant contribution to the Scottish economy, although the revenues from oil and gas production are in decline.

Another omission from the discussion of structural changes so far is the tourism industry. This is because official statistics do not recognize the existence of a tourism 'industry' as such. Many industries are influenced by tourist expenditures, such as hotels and catering, but they are not exclusively devoted to satisfying tourist needs. Accordingly, the importance of tourism is estimated in a variety of ways, from data on the numbers of visits, average duration of visits and average daily tourist expenditures. Spending by tourists is estimated to be in excess of £2 billion per year and estimates of the employment impact range up to 75,000.

SECTORAL EMPLOYMENT PATTERNS

The sectoral pattern of employment, summarized in Table 5, tells a similar story of a shift to a service economy. The primary industries are here defined as: agriculture, hunting, forestry and fishing; mining and quarrying; and electricity, gas and water supply. Table 4 shows that they account for 3.5 per cent of Scottish employee jobs, and only 2.1 per cent of total UK employee jobs, so Scotland is more specialized in these industries than is the UK as a whole. The tertiary industries cover all services and dominate the Scottish economy, accounting for 74 per cent of employment, slightly less than their 76 per cent share in the UK. The major part of the production and construction industries make up the secondary sector. Scotland is slightly more specialized in these industries, with 22.1 per cent of its employment concentrated here, against just over 21.4 per cent for the UK as a whole.

TABLE 5. EMPLOYEE JOBS BY SEX AND BROAD INDUSTRY GROUP (DECEMBER 1998, NOT SEASONALLY ADJUSTED)

	Scotland	UK
Male		
Full-time	898,000	10,646,000
Part-time	114,000	1,570,000
Female		
Full-time	556,000	6,344,000
Part-time	462,000	5,448,000
Total	2,030,000	24,008,000
Primary	72,000	513,000
Secondary	448,000	5,211,000
Tertiary	1,510,000	18,284,000

Source: ONS

The longer-term picture is one of a significant contraction in the secondary sector, concentrated in Scotland's traditional heavy industries, combined with a substantial expansion in the tertiary sector. In 1970, for example, the production industries accounted for over 900,000 employees, or 44 per cent of total employees in employment in Scotland, with the tertiary sector accounting for 1,049,000 employees or just under 51 per cent of the total.

Table 5 also presents data on the sex composition of employee jobs in Scotland and the UK. In terms of numbers of employee jobs, the workforce in both regions is now fairly evenly divided between males and females; indeed, in Scotland slightly over half of employee jobs are now held by females. This reflects a sustained increase in female employment and a steady contraction in male employment; in 1970 female employment accounted for 38.4 per cent of total employment. However, some 45 per cent of female employment is part-time whereas only 11 per cent of male employment is part-time. If part-time employment is taken to be 'third time', then female full-time-equivalent employment is only 42 per cent of the total of such employment. The trends in female employment in part reflect changes in Scotland's industrial structure, in particular the shift to services from heavy manufacturing.

Table 6 provides a more detailed picture of the current sectoral composition of employment in Scotland. The largest concentration of employment is in the wholesale, retail trade and repairs sector, which accounts for 16.3 per cent of total employees in Scotland and 17.4 per cent in the UK as a whole. Manufacturing is the second biggest employer, with 15.5 per cent of employees in Scotland and 17.0 per cent in the UK. The third most important employer in Scotland is health and social work, with 13.1 per cent of employees, and the fourth is real estate, renting and business activities, with 11.1 per cent; the positions of these two sectors are reversed in the UK, accounting for 10.7 per cent and 14.2 per cent respectively of total employment there.

TABLE 6. EMPLOYEE JOBS BY INDUSTRY (DECEMBER 1998, NOT SEASONALLY ADJUSTED)

	Scotland	%	UK	%
Agriculture, hunting, forestry, fishing	32,000	1.6	296,000	1.2
Mining and quarrying	24,000	1.2	74,000	0.3
Manufacturing	315,000	15.5	4,077,000	17.0
Electricity, gas, water supply	16,000	0.8	143,000	0.6
Construction	133,000	6.5	1,133,000	4.7
Wholesale, retail trade, and repairs	332,000	16.3	4,174,000	17.4
Hotels and restaurants	113,000	5.6	1,300,000	5.4
Transport, etc.	110,000	5.4	1,416,000	5.9
Financial intermediation	89,000	4.4	1,029,000	4.3
Real estate, renting, business activities	225,000	11.1	3,405,000	14.2
Public administration, etc.	125,000	6.2	1,328,000	5.5
Education	152,000	7.5	1,931,000	8.0
Health and social work	266,000	13.1	2,571,000	10.7
Other services	99,000	4.9	1,128,000	4.7

The biggest difference in relative specialization occurs in mining and quarrying, wherein Scotland employs over 32 per cent of total UK employees, compared to its overall employment share of 8.5 per cent, although the sector accounts for only 1.2 per cent of total Scottish employment. The next biggest specializations in Scotland relative to the UK are in construction (11.7 per cent of total UK employment in this sector), electricity, gas and water supply (11.1 per cent), agriculture, hunting, forestry and fishing (10.8 per cent), and health and social work (10.3 per cent). The most under-represented sectors relative to the UK are real estate, renting and business activities (with 6.6 per cent of total UK employment in this sector); manufacturing (7.7 per cent), education (7.8 per cent) and wholesale, retail trade and repairs (7.9 per cent). The current position does not offer clear-cut support for the view that Scotland is over-represented in the contracting sectors and under-represented in the expanding sectors, although the data used here remain highly aggregated.

There are some marked differences in the relative importance of sectors as a source of employment and as a contributor to GDP. These reflect differences in labour productivity, which are considered below.

Historically, sectoral distribution was somewhat different, with Scotland specializing in heavy manufacturing. The precise changes are difficult to establish given the various changes in sectoral definitions and discontinuities in the data, but some orders of magnitude can be established; for example, in 1970 employment in manufacturing industries was 708,000, so its current level represents a fall of 55 per cent since 1970. In contrast, employment in services has risen by over 44 per cent since that date.

THE STRUCTURE OF SCOTTISH MANUFACTURING

The regional distribution of gross value added by manufacturing subsector is shown in Table 7. The last line shows the aggregate share of manufacturing gross value-added. Thus the rest of the UK produced 92.2 per cent of total UK manufacturing value-added in 1993, while Scotland had 7.8 per cent. Against this overall national share, Scotland was comparatively specialized in wood and wood products (13.5 per cent of total UK employment in this subsector); food products, beverages and tobacco (including whisky, 12.2 per cent); electrical and optical equipment (10.9 per cent). Scotland was comparatively under-represented in leather and leather products (3.4 per cent); manufactures not elsewhere specified (3.8 per cent); chemicals, etc. (4.7 per cent).

TABLE 7. SCOTTISH SHARE OF UK MANUFACTURING GROSS VALUE-ADDED AT FACTOR COST BY SECTOR IN 1993 (%)

	Scotland	RUK
Food products, beverages, tobacco	12.2	87.8
Textiles and textile products	12	88.0
Leather and leather products	3.4	96.6
Wood and wood products	13.5	86.5
Pulp, paper, publishing and print	7.5	92.5
Chemicals, chemical products	4.7	95.3
Rubber and plastic products	6.8	93.2
Other non-metallic mineral products	7.2	92.8
Metals and fabricated metal production	6.7	93.3
Machinery and equipment n.e.s.	8	92.0
Electrical and optical equipment	10.9	89.1
Transport equipment	4.8	95.2
Manufactures n.e.s.	3.8	96.2
Total	7.8	92.2

Further detail on the structure of manufacturing in Scotland is presented in Table 8, where total manufacturing has been subdivided into three subsectors: food, drink and tobacco; a modern sector; and a traditional sector. These latter two distinctions are subjective.

TABLE 8. DISTRIBUTION OF MANUFACTURING BY BROAD SECTOR IN 1993 (%)

	Scotland	UK
Food, drink and tobacco	21.4	14.0
Modern	67.0	75.6
Traditional	11.6	10.4
Total	100	100

Modern: Pulp, paper, publishing and print; chemicals, chemical products; rubber and plastic products; other non-metallic mineral products; metals and fabricated metal products; machinery and equipment n.e.s.; electrical and optical equipment; transport equipment

Traditional: Textiles and textile products; leather and leather products; wood and wood products; manufactures not elsewhere specified (n.e.s.)

A striking feature of this table is Scotland's relative dependence on the food, drink and tobacco subsector, and a slightly greater concentration in the more traditional manufacturing activities. Food, drink and tobacco primarily services the domestic economy. Although whisky is a notable exception to this, it accounts for only 20 per cent of the subsector's employment. Nevertheless, in recent years manufacturing in Scotland has been essentially a tale of two distinct subsectors: electronics, and the rest of manufacturing. Between the first quarters of 1990 and 1998 electronics grew by 200 per cent, compared to growth of about 29 per cent in the UK. Over the same period, manufacturing as a whole grew by some 26 per cent in Scotland but only by around 4 per cent in the UK as a whole. However, the manufacturing sector, excluding electronics, actually contracted by some 13 per cent in Scotland while remaining fairly constant in the UK as a whole; 'Silicon Glen' is the major success story of Scottish manufacturing.

FOREIGN OWNERSHIP

A further aspect of the structure of Scottish manufacturing is the extent of foreign ownership. This has been an increasingly important feature of the manufacturing sector, with the number of foreign-owned plants rising from 65 in 1950 to 357 in 1994, by which time foreign-owned plants accounted for over a quarter of manufacturing employment. This is in part a consequence of a regional policy that has sought to encourage inward investment. Inward investors tended to be concentrated in the fastest-growing 'high-tech' sectors such as electronics, producing computers and workstations or semiconductors. Foreign-owned components of manufacturing tend to have higher productivity, export a higher proportion of their output (though they also import a larger proportion of inputs) and pay higher wages. There is also some suggestion that they improve efficiency in supplier and customer firms.

ADDITIONAL FEATURES OF THE SCOTTISH ECONOMY

REGIONAL COMPETITIVENESS

The Department of Trade and Industry produces a regular review of regional competitiveness. Considerable emphasis is attached to this concept, which is defined as the ability of regions to generate high income and employment levels while remaining exposed to domestic and international competition. Some indicators, such as GDP per head and unemployment rates, are primarily regarded as the outcome of the competitiveness process. Other indicators, such as labour productivity and the rate of new firm formation, are reported as sources of differential competitiveness. Indicators such as average earnings have a less clear-cut status; lower earnings reduce costs and increase competitiveness, but higher earnings also make it easier to sustain higher income levels.

There are two features of regional competitiveness: price competitiveness and non-price competitiveness. Scotland's ability to compete on price depends on the cost of its inputs and the productivity of those inputs. Although attention should focus on all inputs, data on labour are more readily available than data on land and capital. In 1997 the average gross weekly earnings of male employees in Scotland amounted to £378 or about £19,000 per year. Real earnings increased for both males and females over the period from 1986, by some 17 per cent for males and 22 per cent for females. Real wages rose by more in Great Britain, however, rising by 22 per cent and 34 per cent respectively.

This does not necessarily mean that competitiveness declined in Scotland over the period, because increases in wage costs can be offset by increases in labour productivity.

However, though aggregate labour productivity (as reflected in GDP per head) was, until recently, thought to have converged on the national average, doubt has now been cast on this. Data for gross value-added per head (from the Scottish Production Database, maintained by the Scottish Executive) suggest that labour in the production industries as a whole is approximately 12 per cent more productive in Scotland than in England. There were variations in output per head across sectors, however, ranging from £23,876 in food to £111,560 in coke, oil and nuclear processing. These data are heavily influenced by, among other things, the capital intensity of the industry, which highlights the need for caution in interpreting productivity differentials.

Firms do not, however, compete on price alone, and rates of new firm formation, expenditures on research and development and innovation rates have all been postulated to contribute to regional competitiveness. On these criteria Scotland tends to perform poorly, with the south-east of England tending to dominate. Scotland is not favoured either by its 'peripherality'. Although single indices of peripherality are problematic, Scotland has been ranked as the second most peripheral economy of the standard regions of the UK; Northern Ireland is the only economy to fare worse in this respect.

FIGURE 5. PERCENTAGE DISTRIBUTION OF HOUSEHOLD EXPENDITURE IN SCOTLAND AND THE UK 1997–8

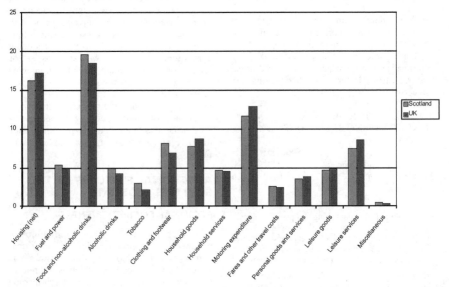

Source: ONS, *Family Spending*

HOUSEHOLD INCOMES AND CONSUMPTION EXPENDITURES

Average weekly household spending in Scotland in 1997–8 was £297.7, compared to £328.8 in the UK as a whole. On average over the last decade average household spending in Scotland has been around 90 per cent of that in the UK, though some caution is required given the comparatively small sample of households on which the data are based. It seems likely that this is due not to the supposed greater thrift of Scots but rather to their lower average household income. In 1995–6 the average gross weekly income of Scottish households was £338, only 88 per cent of the UK figure of £381.

Figure 5 summarizes the distribution of household expenditure for both Scotland and the UK in 1997–8. The spending patterns are broadly similar, though Scots tend to spend proportionately more on fuel, food, tobacco and alcohol, and transport. They spend less on housing, household goods and leisure activities. These reflect the differences in average household incomes, climate and spatial dispersion of the population, as well as differences in tastes.

In 1995–6, wages and salaries accounted for some 57 per cent of household incomes in Scotland (59 per cent in the UK), with social security payments the next most important source, contributing 27 per cent of the total in Scotland (26 per cent in the UK). Workers in Scotland receive lower average gross weekly earnings than those in the UK as a whole, and have experienced lower real wage growth. If all other things were equal, the lower wages would be good news for price competitiveness, but bad news for living standards and consumption demand. If the higher wages in the UK as a whole are compensated for by higher total factor productivity, then price competitiveness as well as incomes may be greater in the UK as a whole than in Scotland.

CURRENCY

The unit of currency is the pound sterling (£) of 100 pence. The decimal system was introduced on 15 February 1971.

Since 1 January 1999, trade within the European Union has been conducted in the single European currency, the euro; euro notes and coins will not enter circulation until 2002.

COIN

	Metal	Standard weight (g)	Standard diameter (cm)
Penny	bronze	3.564	2.032
Penny	copper-plated steel	3.564	2.032
2 pence	bronze	7.128	2.591
2 pence	copper-plated steel	7.128	2.591
5p	cupro-nickel	3.25	1.80
10p	cupro-nickel	6.5	2.45
20p	cupro-nickel	5.0	2.14
25p Crown	cupro-nickel	28.28	3.861
50p	cupro-nickel	13.5	3.0
* 50p	cupro-nickel	8.00	2.73
£1	nickel-brass	9.5	2.25
† £2	nickel-brass	15.98	2.84
£2	cupro-nickel, nickel-brass	12.00	2.84
£5 Crown	cupro-nickel	28.28	3.861

* New 50p coin introduced on 1 September 1997

† Commemorative coins; not intended for general circulation

Legal Tender

Gold (dated 1838 onwards, if not below least current weight)	to any amount
£5 (Crown since 1990)	to any amount
£2	to any amount
£1	to any amount
50p	up to £10
25p (Crown pre-1990)	up to £10
20p	up to £10
10p	up to £5
5p	up to £5
2p	up to 20p
1p	up to 20p

BANKNOTES

Bank of England notes are currently issued in denominations of £5, £10, £20 and £50 for the amount of the fiduciary note issue, and are legal tender in England and Wales. No £1 notes have been issued since 1984 and in 1998 the outstanding notes were written off.

The current E series of notes was introduced from June 1990. The predominant identifying feature of each note is the portrayal on the back of a prominent British historical figure. The figures portrayed in the current series are:

£5 June 1990–	George Stephenson
£10 April 1992–	Charles Dickens
£20 June 1991–June 1999	Michael Faraday
£20 June 1999–	Sir Edward Elgar
£50 April 1994–	Sir John Houblon

Although the Bank of England stopped issuing a £1 note in 1983, the Scottish £1 note continues to be issued.

Legal Tender

Bank of England banknotes which are no longer legal tender are payable when presented at the head office of the Bank of England in London.

Scottish banknotes are not legal tender but they are an authorized currency and enjoy a status comparable to that of Bank of England notes. They are generally accepted by banks irrespective of their place of issue.

Scottish Banknotes

The banks of issue in Scotland are the Bank of Scotland, the Clydesdale Bank and the Royal Bank of Scotland.

BANK OF SCOTLAND
The Mound, Edinburgh EH1 1YZ
Tel: 0131-442 7777
Denominations of notes issued: £5, £10, £20, £50, £100

CLYDESDALE BANK
30 St Vincent Place, Glasgow G1 2HL
Tel: 0141-248 7070
Denominations of notes issued: £5, £10, £20, £50, £100

ROYAL BANK OF SCOTLAND
PO Box 31, 42 St Andrew Square, Edinburgh EH2 2YE
Tel: 0131-556 8555
Denominations of notes issued: £1, £5, £10, £20, £100

Note Circulation in Scotland

in the four weeks ending 29 May 1999

	Circulation authorized by certificate	Average circulation	Average amount of Bank of England notes and coin held*
	£	£	£
Bank of Scotland	1,289,222	544,253,441	553,167,497
Clydesdale Bank	498,773	399,740,768	403,218,560
Royal Bank of Scotland	888,355	935,807,839	943,362,065

*Includes Bank of England notes deposited at the Bank of England which, by virtue of the Currency and Bank Note Act 1928, are to be treated as gold coin by the Bank

BANKING

Banking in the UK is regulated by the Banking Act 1987 as amended by the European Community's Second Banking Co-ordination Directive, which came into effect on 1 January 1993. The Banking Act 1987 established a single category of banks eligible to carry out banking business; these are known as authorized institutions. Authorization under the Act is granted by the Bank of England; it is an offence for anyone not on the Bank's list of authorized institutions to conduct deposit-taking business, unless they are exempted from the requirements of the Act (e.g. building societies).

The Government announced in 1997 that it will transfer responsibility for banking supervision to the Financial Services Authority. Once the necessary legislation has been passed (probably in 2000), the FSA will be responsible for the authorization and supervision of banks and the supervision of clearing and settlement systems.

The implementation of the Second Banking Co-ordination Directive permits banks incorporated in one EU member state to carry on certain banking activities in another member state without the need for authorization by that state. Consequently, the Bank of England no longer authorizes banks incorporated in other EU states with branches in the UK; the authorization of their home state supervisor is sufficient provided that certain notification requirements are met. As at end June 1999, a total of 594 institutions were authorized to carry out banking business in the UK, 335 authorized under the Banking Act 1987 and 259 recognized under the Second Banking Co-ordination Directive as European authorized institutions (EAIs).

In the British banking system, the main institutions are the Bank of England (the central bank), the retail banks, the merchant banks and the overseas banks. In its role as the central bank, the Bank of England (see page 53) acts as banker to the Government and as a note-issuing authority; it also oversees the efficient functioning of payment and settlement systems. In Scotland, the Bank of Scotland, the Royal Bank of Scotland and the Clydesdale Bank (see also pages 164–5) are also banks of issue.

Since May 1997, the Bank of England has had operational responsibility for monetary policy. At monthly meetings of its monetary policy committee the Bank sets the interest rate at which it will lend to the money markets.

OFFICIAL INTEREST RATES 1998–9

4 June 1998	7.50%
8 October 1998	7.25%
10 December 1998	6.25%
7 January 1999	6.00%
4 February 1999	5.50%
8 April 1999	5.25%
10 June 1999	5.00%

Retail Banks

The major retail banks are Abbey National, Alliance and Leicester, Bank of Scotland, Barclays, Clydesdale, Halifax, HSBC (formerly known as Midland), Lloyds/TSB, National Westminster, Northern Rock, Royal Bank of Scotland and the Woolwich. The Clydesdale Bank is also a major retail bank in Scotland.

Retail banks offer a wide variety of financial services to companies and individuals, including current and deposit accounts, loan and overdraft facilities, automated teller (cash dispenser) machines, cheque guarantee cards, credit cards and debit cards.

The Banking Ombudsman scheme provides independent and impartial arbitration in disputes between a bank and its customer.

Banking hours differ throughout the UK. Many banks now open longer hours and some at weekends, and hours vary from branch to branch. Current core opening hours in Scotland are Monday to Friday 9 a.m. to 5 p.m.

Payment Clearings

The Association for Payment Clearing Services (APACS) is an umbrella organization for payment clearings in the UK. It operates three clearing companies: BACS Ltd, the Cheque and Credit Clearing Company Ltd, and CHAPS Clearing Company Ltd.

ASSOCIATION FOR PAYMENT CLEARING SERVICES (APACS)
Mercury House, Triton Court, 14 Finsbury Square, London EC2A 1LQ
Tel: 0171-711 6200

BACS LTD
De Havilland Road, Edgware, Middx HA8 5QA
Bulk clearing of electronic debits and credits (e.g. direct debits and salary credits)

CHEQUE AND CREDIT CLEARING
COMPANY LTD
Mercury House, Triton Court, 14 Finsbury
Square, London EC2A 1LQ
Bulk clearing systems for inter-bank cheques
and paper credit items in Great Britain

CHAPS CLEARING COMPANY LTD
Mercury House, Triton Court, 14 Finsbury
Square, London EC2A 1LQ
Same-day clearing for high-value electronic
funds transfers throughout the UK in sterling
and globally in euros

MAJOR RETAIL BANKS: FINANCIAL RESULTS 1997

Bank Group	Profit before taxation £m	Profit after taxation £m	Total assets £m	Number of UK branches
Abbey National	1,520	1,105	177,800	793
Alliance and Leicester	455.2	317.9	27,579	316
Bank of Scotland	1,011.9	580.6	59,796	325
Barclays	1,918	1,380	219,494	1,950
Clydesdale	146.2	99.4	7,861	274
Halifax	1,705	1,171	145,000	814
HSBC*	1,522	1,043	104,846	1,700
Lloyds/TSB Group	3,015	2,133	167,997	2,700
NatWest Group	2,142	1,641	185,993	1,727
Northern Rock	202.6	136.6	18,157	107
Royal Bank of Scotland Group	1,001.0	637.0	79,676	664
Woolwich	495.9	331.3	33,239	406

* Formerly known as Midland Bank

THE ENERGY INDUSTRIES

The main primary sources of energy in Britain are oil, natural gas, coal, nuclear power and water power. The main secondary sources (i.e. sources derived from the primary sources) are electricity, coke and smokeless fuels, and petroleum products.

Policy and legislation on the generation and supply of electricity from coal, oil and gas, and nuclear fuels, remains a matter reserved to the UK Government after devolution. The Department of the Environment, Transport and the Regions is responsible for promoting energy efficiency.

INDIGENOUS PRODUCTION OF PRIMARY FUELS (UK)
Million tonnes of oil equivalent

	1997	1998p
Coal	31.5	27.0
Petroleum	140.4	145.2
Natural gas	86.2	90.3
Primary electricity		
Nuclear	22.99	23.28
Natural flow hydro	0.41	0.50
Total	281.9	286.2

p provisional

INLAND ENERGY CONSUMPTION BY PRIMARY FUEL (UK)
Million tonnes of oil equivalent, seasonally adjusted

	1997	1998p
Coal	42.9	43.1
Petroleum	77.0	76.7
Natural gas	88.7	92.2
Primary electricity	24.83	25.19
Nuclear	22.99	23.28
Natural flow hydro	0.42	0.50
Net imports	1.42	1.41
Total	233.5	237.2

p provisional

UK TRADE IN FUELS AND RELATED MATERIALS 1997p

	Quantity*	Value†
Imports		
Coal and other solid fuel	15.1	687
Crude petroleum	40.0	2,170
Petroleum products	17.8	1,414
Natural gas	0.4	43
Electricity	1.1	335
Total	74.5	4,648
Total (fob)‡	—	4,105
Exports		
Coal and other solid fuel	0.9	69
Crude petroleum	79.6	4,441
Petroleum products	37.1	2,886
Natural gas	1.5	76
Electricity	—	3
Total	119.0	7,475
Total (fob)‡	—	7,475

p provisional

* Million tonnes of oil equivalent

† £ million

‡ Adjusted to exclude estimated costs of insurance, freight, etc.

Source: Department of Trade and Industry, *Energy Trends*, May 1999 (Crown copyright)

OIL AND GAS

The United Kingdom Continental Shelf (UKCS) is treated as a separate region in official economic statistics. Calculation of Scottish oil and gas outputs and revenue deriving from the UKCS is difficult and controversial. Recent research from Aberdeen University suggests that there is considerable variation from year to year in the Scottish proportion of UK tax revenue from oil and gas, depending on a number of factors, including division of the North Sea, relative expense of developing the North Sea fields, and oil price fluctuations. According to this analysis, Scotland's share of UK oil and gas revenue was 80 per cent in 1996–7, but the drop in oil prices over the last two years has reduced this to an estimated 75 per cent for 1997 and 66 per cent for 1998 (calendar years). The following table shows the total value of UKCS oil and gas production and investment in 1997–8.

	1997 £m	1998p £m
Total income	18,955	16,950
Operating costs	4,150	4,190
Exploration expenditure	1,194	762
Gross trading profits*	13,832	11,289
Contribution to GDP	1.9%	1.5%
Capital investment	4,333	5,086
Contribution to industrial investment	18%	18%

p provisional

* Net of stock appreciation

OIL

Until the 1960s Britain imported almost all its oil supplies. In 1969 oil was discovered in the Arbroath field of the UKCS. The first oilfield to be brought into production was the Argyll field in 1975, and since the mid-1970s Britain has been a major producer of crude oil.

There are estimated to be reserves of 2,015 million tonnes of oil in the UKCS. Royalties are payable on fields approved before April 1982 and petroleum revenue tax is levied on fields approved between 1975 and March 1993.

Licences for exploration and production are granted to companies by the Department of Trade and Industry; the leading British oil companies are British Petroleum (BP) and Shell Transport and Trading. At the end of 1998, 1,021 offshore licences and 150 onshore licences had been awarded, and there were 121 offshore oilfields in production in the UK.

There are four oil terminals and two refineries in Scotland.

OIL COMING ASHORE AT SCOTTISH
TERMINALS 1997*
Million tonnes

Sullom Voe	31.7
Flotta, Orkney Islands	9.8
Forties Leeward	38.1
Nigg Bay, Cromarty Firth	0.4
Total	80.0

* Figures do not reflect total oil production in Scotland, because some oil produced is exported directly by tanker from offshore fields

CAPACITY OF SCOTTISH REFINERIES 1997
Million tonnes p.a.

Grangemouth	8.9
Dundee	0.7
Total	9.6

GAS

In 1965 gas was discovered in the North Sea off the South Yorkshire coast, in the West Sole field, which became the first gasfield in production in 1967.

By the end of 1998 there were 80 offshore gasfields producing natural gas and associated gases (mainly methane). There are estimated to be 1,795,000 million cubic metres of recoverable gas reserves in existing discoveries. Two new North Sea fields, Elgin-Franklin and Shearwater, are due to come into operation in 2000; their production will be piped to terminals at Bacton, Norfolk.

There are three gas terminals in Scotland, at St Fergus, Aberdeenshire.

GAS BROUGHT ASHORE AT SCOTTISH
TERMINALS 1998*
Million cubic m

Far North Liquids and Associated Gas System (FLAGS)	7,400
Frig, Fulmar and Miller Lines	21,300
Scottish Area Gas Evacuation (SAGE)	9,800
Total	38,500

* Figures do not reflect total Scottish gas production, because some gas produced is piped to terminals in England

Source: Department of Trade and Industry

Since 1986 the British gas industry, nationalized in 1949, has been progressively privatized. Competition was introduced into the industrial gas market from 1986, and supply of gas to the domestic market was opened to companies other than British Gas from April 1996 onwards. Gas companies can now also sell electricity to their customers. Similarly, electricity companies can also offer gas.

The Office of Gas and Electricity Markets is the regulatory body for the gas and electricity industries in Britain; for its office in Scotland, see page 64.

NATURAL GAS PRODUCTION AND SUPPLY
(UK)
GWh

	1997	1998p
Gross gas production	998,343	1,048,353
Exports	21,666	31,604
Imports	14,062	10,582
Gas available	927,790	956,076
Gas transmitted‡	911,798	948,401

p provisional

‡ Figures differ from gas available mainly because of stock changes

NATURAL GAS CONSUMPTION
GWh

	1997	1998p
Electricity generators	243,361	253,348
Iron and steel industry	20,725	22,754
Other industries	174,763	175,747
Domestic	341,347	360,266
Public administration, commerce and agriculture	112,347	118,860
Total	892,544	930,975

p provisional

Source: Department of Trade and Industry

ELECTRICITY

There are currently 27 electricity generating companies in Britain. The 12 regional electricity companies (RECs) formed under the Electricity Act 1989 currently have a monopoly on sales of 100 kW or less to consumers in their franchise areas; over this limit competition has been introduced. Competition was introduced into the domestic electricity market in 1998–9. Electricity companies can now also sell gas to their customers. Similarly, gas companies can also offer electricity. Generators sell the electricity they produce into an open commodity market (the Pool) from which buyers purchase.

In Scotland, three new companies were formed under the Electricity Act 1989: ScottishPower PLC and Scottish Hydro-Electric PLC (now Scottish and Southern Energy PLC), which are responsible for generation, transmission, distribution and supply; and Scottish Nuclear Ltd. ScottishPower and Scottish Hydro-Electric were floated on the stock market in 1991. Scottish Nuclear was incorporated into British Energy in 1995.

ScottishPower operates six power stations in Scotland. Scottish and Southern Energy operates a large power station at Peterhead, 56 hydro stations in Scotland, and a diesel backup station in Lerwick, Shetland; it also operates a number of power stations in England and Wales.

The Electricity Association is the electricity industry's main trade association, providing representational and professional services for the electricity companies. EA Technology Ltd provides distribution and utilization research, development and technology transfer. The Office of Gas and Electricity Markets (*see* page 64) is the regulatory body for the electricity industry.

ELECTRICITY PRODUCTION IN SCOTLAND 1998
GWh

	Electricity generated 1998	Amount exported to England	From renewable sources
Scottish Power	24,500	c.6,000	c.2%
Scottish and Southern Energy*	14,167	3,260	c.11%

* Scottish and Southern Energy figures are for 1997–8 financial year

NUCLEAR POWER

About half of Scotland's electricity is generated by nuclear power stations. British Energy PLC owns two Advanced Gas-Cooled Reactors (AGRs) at Torness and Hunterston B. British Nuclear Fuels Ltd (BNFL) owns the Magnox nuclear reactor at Chapelcross.

BNFL, which is in public ownership, provides reprocessing, waste management and effluent treatment services. The UK Atomic Energy Authority is responsible for the decommissioning of nuclear reactors and other nuclear facilities used in research and development. UK Nirex, which is owned by the nuclear generating companies and the Government, is responsible for the disposal of intermediate and some low-level nuclear waste. The Nuclear Installations Inspectorate of the Health and Safety Executive (*see* page 58) is the nuclear industry's regulator.

In 1998 the closure was announced of the nuclear reactor at Dounreay, which started up in 1956.

NUCLEAR POWER GENERATION 1997–8
Terawatt hours

Hunterston B	8.73
Torness	9.27
Total by British Energy	18.0
Chapelcross*	1.40

* 1998–9 figure

BNFL
BNFL Risley, Warrington, Cheshire WA3 6AS
Tel: 01925-832000
Chief Executive, J. Taylor

BRITISH ENERGY PLC
10 Lochside Place, Edinburgh EH12 9DF
Tel: 0131-527 2000
Chief Executive (acting), P. Hollins

SCOTTISH AND SOUTHERN ENERGY PLC
Dunkeld Road, Perth PH1 5WA
Tel: 01738-455040
Chief Executive, J. Forbes

SCOTTISHPOWER PLC
1 Atlantic Quay, Glasgow G2 8SP
Tel: 0141-248 8200
Chief Executive, I. Robinson

ELECTRICITY ASSOCIATION LTD
30 Millbank, London SW1P 4RD
Tel: 0171-963 5700
Chief Executive, P. E. G. Daubeney

EA TECHNOLOGY LTD
Capenhurst, Chester CH1 6ES
Tel: 0151-339 4181
Managing Director, Dr S. F. Exell

RENEWABLE ENERGY SOURCES

Renewable sources of energy principally include biofuels, hydro, wind, waste and solar.

The UK Government intends to achieve 10 per cent of the UK's electricity needs from renewables by 2010 and to meet the UK's international commitments to future reductions on greenhouse gases. Following the establishment of the Scottish Parliament, decisions on renewable sources of energy have been devolved.

The Scottish Renewables Obligation Orders (SROs) have been the Government's principal mechanism for developing renewable energy sources. They are similar to the Non-Fossil Fuel Obligation Renewables Orders in England and Wales. SRO Orders require ScottishPower and Scottish and Southern Energy to buy specified amounts of electricity from specified renewable sources; the first order was made in 1994 and the latest in March 1999.

Of the 109 projects awarded contracts so far (for about 340 MW), ten projects (27 MW capacity) have been commissioned. Six of these are wind schemes (combined capacity $c.21.5$ MW), two are hydro schemes (combined capacity $c.1.5$ MW), and two are waste-to-energy schemes (combined capacity $c.3.8$ MW). Four wind-farms are now completed. The latest SRO Order included, for the first time, three wave-power projects.

No specific mechanism to support the development of solar energy projects exists, but the Department of Trade and Industry currently funds initiatives and channels European grant funding. There are several small-scale (less than 1 MW) solar projects in operation in various places around Scotland.

THE WATER INDUSTRY

Overall responsibility for national water policy in Scotland rested with the Secretary of State for Scotland until July 1999, when responsibility was devolved to the Scottish Executive. Most aspects of water policy are currently administered through the Scottish Executive Rural Affairs Department.

Water supply and sewerage services were the responsibility of the local authorities and the Central Scotland Water Development Board until 1996. In April 1996 the provision of water and sewerage services became the responsibility of three public water authorities, covering the north, east and west of Scotland, under the terms of the Local Government etc. (Scotland) Act 1994.

The Act also provided for the Scottish Water and Sewerage Customers Council to be established to represent consumer interests. The Council is to be abolished under the provisions of the Water Industries Act 1999, whose provisions have been accepted by the Scottish Executive, and will be replaced in late 1999 by a Water Industry Commissioner, whose role is to promote customers' interests. The Commissioner will make longer-term recommendations about charging and efficiency to the Scottish Executive and will be advised by three water industry consultative committees, one for each water authority.

The Scottish Environment Protection Agency (*see* page 69) is responsible for promoting the cleanliness of rivers, lochs and coastal waters, and controlling pollution.

WATER RESOURCES 1997

	No.	Yield (Ml/day)
Reservoirs and lochs	287	3,018
Feeder intakes	27	—
River intakes	223	422
Bore-holes	35	77
Underground springs	103	46
Total	*676	3,562

* Including compensation reservoirs

WATER CONSUMPTION 1997

Total (Ml/day)	2,336.3
Potable	2,320.3
Unmetered	1,781.7
Metered	538.5
Non-potable†	16.0
Total (l/head/day)	468.6
Unmetered	357.4
Metered and non-potable†	109.9

† `Non-potable' supplied for industrial purposes. Metered supplies in general relate to commercial and industrial use and unmetered to domestic use

Source: The Scottish Office

Methods of Charging

The water authorities set charges for domestic and non-domestic water and sewerage provision through charges schemes which have to be approved by the Scottish Water and Sewerage Customers Council. The authorities are required to publish a summary of their charges schemes.

EAST OF SCOTLAND WATER AUTHORITY
Pentland Gait, 597 Calder Road, Edinburgh
EH11 4HJ
Tel: 0131-453 7500
Chief Executive, R. Rennet

NORTH OF SCOTLAND WATER AUTHORITY
Cairngorm House, Beechwood Park North, Inverness IV2 3ED
Tel: 01463-245400
Chief Executive, A. Findlay

WEST OF SCOTLAND WATER AUTHORITY
419 Balmore Road, Glasgow G22 6NU
Tel: 0141-355 5333
Chief Executive, E. Chambers

SCOTTISH WATER AND SEWERAGE CUSTOMERS COUNCIL
Ochil House, Springkerse Business Park, Stirling FK7 7XE
Tel: 01786-430200
The Council will be replaced by the Water Industry Commissioner at the same address
Director, Dr V. Nash

WATER UK
1 Queen Anne's Gate, London, SW1H 9BT
Tel: 0171-344 1844
Water UK is the trade association for almost all the water service companies in the UK, including the three Scottish water authorities.
Chief Executive, Ms P. Taylor

TRANSPORT

CIVIL AVIATION

UK airlines are operated entirely by the private sector. Scottish airports are served by several major British airlines, including British Airways, Air UK, Britannia Airways, British Midland, Monarch Airlines and EasyJet; by British Airways franchise Loganair (which operates several inter-island services) and franchised partner British Regional Airlines, and by other airlines such as Highland Airways, Gill-air and Business Air.

Among European airlines, SAS provides links to Scandinavia, KLM with the Netherlands and further afield, and RyanAir and Aer Lingus with Ireland. The Norwegian carrier Ugland Air provides oil industry charters from Sumburgh to Norwegian airports, and Wideroe, also Norwegian, operates scheduled flights in summer on the same route.

The Civil Aviation Authority is responsible for the economic regulation of UK airlines and the larger airports, and for the safety regulation of the UK civil aviation industry. Through its wholly-owned subsidiary company National Air Traffic Services Ltd, the CAA is also responsible for the provision of air traffic control services over Britain and its surrounding seas and at most major British airports.

Airports

Scotland's four largest airports, Aberdeen, Edinburgh, Glasgow and Prestwick, are owned and operated by the British Airports Authority (BAA plc). They have flights to destinations within Scotland, other parts of the UK and internationally.

Highlands and Islands Airports Ltd (HIAL) owns and operates ten Scottish airports and receives subsidies for providing links to remote areas of Scotland. Routes which are directly subsidized are:
Glasgow – Campbeltown – Tiree – Barra
Kirkwall – Papa Westray
Kirkwall – North Ronaldsay
Stornoway – Benbecula – Barra
Sumburgh – Fair Isle
HIAL's airports are Barra, Benbecula, Campbeltown, Inverness, Islay, Kirkwall, Stornoway, Sumburgh, Tiree, and Wick.

A number of airports and small airfields are controlled by local authorities, including Dundee, Orkney and Shetland. Orkney Islands Council has airfields at Eday, North Ronaldsay, Papa Westray, Sanday, Stronsay and Westray. Shetland Islands Council runs Tingwall airport at Lerwick, and gives assistance to airstrips on Foula, Out Skerries and Papa Stour, which are run by local airstrip trusts. Fetlar and Whalsay have airstrips for emergency use, with only occasional other services according to need. Baltasound airstrip on Unst, currently owned and operated by Shetland Islands Council, operates only for about three hours a day and is under review at the time of going to press. Fair Isle airfield is owned, like the whole island, by the National Trust for Scotland. Airports and airfields at Glenrothes, Cumbernauld and Perth (Scone) are privately owned. Scatsta in Shetland and Flotta in Orkney are also privately owned, principally serving the oil industry.

Airport operating hours at Barra are subject to tide variation, since aircraft land on and take off from the beach. Tiree's operating hours are also subject to the variations at Barra, as flights to and from Tiree are via Barra.

Operating hours vary seasonally at several smaller airports and airfields, including Campbeltown, Inverness, Islay and Wick.

BAA PLC
Scottish Airport Division, St Andrew's Drive, Glasgow Airport, Paisley KA9 4DG
Tel: 0141-887 1111; fax: 0141-887 1699

HIGHLANDS AND ISLANDS AIRPORTS LTD
Head Office, Inverness Airport, Inverness IV7 2JB
Tel: 01667-462445

Passenger Journeys

Over 14 million passenger journeys were made through Scottish airports in 1997, including terminal, transit, scheduled and charter passengers. The following list covers BAA, HIAL and local authority controlled airports.

AIR PASSENGERS 1997

Aberdeen (BAA)	2,662,960
Barra (HIAL)	9,045
Benbecula (HIAL)	36,519
Campbeltown (HIAL)	9,595
Dundee	10,583
Edinburgh (BAA)	4,588,507
Glasgow (BAA)	6,566,927
Inverness (HIAL)	340,742
Islay (HIAL)	21,282

Kirkwall (HIAL)	90,610
Lerwick (Tingwall)	4,029
Prestwick (BAA)	564,043
Stornoway (HIAL)	96,070
Sumburgh (HIAL)	305,740
Tiree (HIAL)	4,988
Unst	1,806
Wick (HIAL)	41,057

Source: Civil Aviation Authority

RAILWAYS

Responsibility for legislation on railways will not be devolved to the Scottish Parliament but remains with the UK Government.

Since 1994, responsibility for managing Britain's nationalized railway infrastructure has rested with Railtrack, which was floated on the Stock Exchange in 1996. Railtrack owns all operational track and land pertaining to the railway system, manages the track and charges for access to it, and is responsible for signalling and timetabling. It also owns the stations, and leases most of them out to the train operating companies. Infrastructure support functions are provided by private-sector companies. Railtrack invests in infrastructure principally using finance raised by track charges, and takes investment decisions in consultation with rail operators. It is also responsible for overall safety on the railways.

Railtrack does not operate train services. Since 1994 all passenger services have been franchised to 25 private-sector train-operators, via a competitive tendering process overseen by the Director of the Office of Passenger Rail Franchising. The Government continues to subsidize loss-making but socially necessary rail services. The Franchising Director is responsible for monitoring the performance of the franchisees and allocating and administering government subsidy payments.

The independent Rail Regulator is responsible for the licensing of new railway operators, approving access agreements, promoting the use and development of the network, preventing anti-competitive practices (in conjunction with the Director-General of Fair Trading) and protecting the interests of rail users.

The White Paper *New Deal for Transport*, published in July 1998, announced plans to establish a Strategic Rail Authority which will manage passenger railway franchising, take responsibility for increasing the use of the railways for freight transport, and lead strategic planning of passenger and freight rail services. The Railway Bill published in July 1999 will give effect to these plans once enacted.

Rail Users' Consultative Committees monitor the policies and performance of train and station operators in their area. They are statutory bodies and have a legal right to make recommendations for changes.

OFFICE OF THE RAIL REGULATOR (ORR)
1 Waterhouse Square, 138–142 Holborn,
London EC1N 2ST
Tel: 0171-282 2000
Rail Regulator, J. Swift, QC

RAILTRACK
Scottish Office, Level 2, Buchanan House, 58 Port Dundas Road, Glasgow G4 0LQ
Tel: 0141-335 2424

SCOTRAIL
Caledonian Chambers, 87 Union Street,
Glasgow G1 3TA
Tel: 0141-332 9811

RAIL USERS' CONSULTATIVE COMMITTEE
FOR SCOTLAND
5th Floor, Corunna House, 29 Cadogan Street,
Glasgow G2 7AB
Tel: 0141-221 7760

Services

Scotland is served by Great North Eastern Railway, Scotrail Railways and Virgin Trains operating companies. There are 335 stations in passenger service. Railtrack owns all of these with the exception of the station at Prestwick Airport, which is privately owned. In 1998 there were 48,895,771 passenger journeys within Scotland, and 51,185,284 originating in Scotland. The total ticket revenue for journeys beginning in Scotland was £162.7 million.

Railtrack publishes a national timetable which contains details of rail services operated over the Railtrack network, coastal shipping information and connections with Ireland, the Isle of Man, the Isle of Wight, the Channel Islands and some European destinations.

The national rail enquiries service offers telephone information about train times and fares for any part of the country:

NATIONAL RAIL ENQUIRIES
Tel: 0345-484950

EUROSTAR
Tel: 0345-303030

Glasgow Underground Railway

The Glasgow Underground railway system opened in 1897 and reopened following modernization in 1980. It has fifteen stations and 6.55 route miles of track. Strathclyde Passenger Transport is responsible for the

Underground. In 1998–9 there were 14.6 million passenger journeys, of which 7 million were with a season ticket. Total ticket revenue in 1997–8 was £8.26 million.

STRATHCLYDE PASSENGER TRANSPORT
Consort House, 12 West George Street, Glasgow G2 1HN
Tel: 0141-332 6811
Customer enquiries: tel. 0141-332 7133

Channel Tunnel Links

Passenger services operated by Eurostar (UK) Ltd run from Waterloo station in London and Ashford, Kent, via the Channel Tunnel to Paris, Brussels and Lille. Connecting services from Edinburgh via London began in 1997. The introduction of through services from Edinburgh, not stopping in London, is the subject of a government review which reported in late 1998 and of a subsequent process of investigation.

ROADS

Responsibility for Scotland's road network and for policy on bus transport now rests with the Scottish Parliament and Ministers, operating through the Scottish Executive Development Department. The highway authority for non-trunk roads is, in general, the unitary authority in whose area the roads lie.

The costs of construction, improvement and maintenance are met by central government. Total expenditure on building and maintaining trunk roads in Scotland was estimated at £170 million in 1997–8.

A review of roads policy in Scotland is currently in progress.

ROAD LENGTHS
as at April 1998

	miles	km
Total roads	32,999	55,266
Trunk roads (including motorways)	2,019	3,266
Motorways	212	344

MOTORWAYS

M8	Edinburgh to Newhouse, Baillieston to West Ferry Interchange
M9	Edinburgh to Dunblane
M73	Maryville to Mollinsburn
M74	Glasgow to Paddy's Rickle Bridge, Cleuchbrae to Gretna
M77	Ayr Road Route
M80	Stirling to Haggs/Glasgow (M8) to Stepps
M90	Inverkeithing to Perth
M876	Dennyloanhead (M80) to Kincardine Bridge

PRINCIPAL ROAD BRIDGES

Tay Road Bridge, over Firth of Tay – 2,245 m/7,365 ft
Forth Road Bridge, over Firth of Forth –1,987 m/6,156 ft
Erskine Bridge, over River Clyde – 1,321 m/4,336 ft
Kessock Bridge, over Kessock Narrows –1,052 m/3,453 ft
Skye Bridge, over Kyle of Lochalsh – 520 m/6,156 ft

ROAD PASSENGER SERVICES

There is an extensive network of bus and coach services in Scotland, particularly in rural areas. In 1997–8 there were 438 million passenger bus journeys in Scotland.

Until 1988 most road passenger transport services in Great Britain were provided by the public sector; the Scottish Bus Group was the largest operator in Scotland. Since the late 1980s almost all bus and coach services in Great Britain have been privatized; the privatization of the Scottish Bus Group was completed in 1991. However, local authorities can subsidize the provision of socially necessary services after competitive tendering.

One of the largest bus operators in Great Britain, Stagecoach Holdings, is based in Scotland, at Perth. National Express runs a national network of coach routes, mainly operating through franchises. There is also a large number of smaller private operators.

Information on local bus routes and timetables can be obtained from bus stations and tourist board offices; telephone numbers can be found in local telephone directories.

HIGHLAND SCOTTISH BUSES
Tel: 01463-233371

NATIONAL EXPRESS COACH SERVICES
Tel: 08705-808080/0990-808080

SCOTTISH CITYLINK EXPRESS COACH SERVICES
Tel: 08705-505050/0990-505050

STAGECOACH HOLDINGS
Tel: 01738-629339/442111 (administration)

Postbus Services

Since 1968 the Royal Mail has operated a postbus service in Scotland, providing passenger transport in rural areas of the country. There are currently 119 postbuses covering 128 routes throughout Scotland, including the Western Isles, Orkney and Shetland, as well as three routes in Northern Ireland and a similar network in England and Wales. Many of the services receive financial assistance from local councils. A wheelchair-accessible service in Midlothian was introduced in 1998.

The postbus service has its Scottish head office at the Royal Mail headquarters in Edinburgh but is largely administered from Inverness, from where timetables and other information are available.

ROYAL MAIL SCOTLAND AND NORTHERN IRELAND
HQ, 102 West Port, Edinburgh EH3 9HS

POST BUS SUPPORT
Royal Mail, 7 Strothers Lane, Inverness IV1 1AA
Tel: 01463-256228; customer services: 0345-740740
Fax: 01463-256392

DRIVING AND VEHICLE LICENCES

The Driver and Vehicle Licensing Agency (DVLA) (*see* page 56) is responsible for issuing driving licences, registering and licensing vehicles, and collecting excise duty in Great Britain. The Driving Standards Agency (*see* page 56) is responsible for carrying out driving tests and approving driving instructors.

A leaflet, *What You Need to Know About Driving Licences* (form D100), is available from post offices.

DRIVING LICENCE FEES
as at 1 April 1999

First provisional licence	£23.50
Changing a provisional to a full licence after passing a driving test	£8.50
Renewal of licence	£8.50
Renewal of licence including PCV or LGV entitlements	£28.50
Renewal after disqualification	£24.50
Renewal after drinking and driving disqualification	£33.50
Medical renewal	free
Medical renewal (over 70)	free
Duplicate licence	£13.50
Exchange licence	£13.50
Removing endorsements	£13.50
Replacement (change of name or address)	free

DRIVING TEST FEES
(weekday rate/evening and Saturday rate)
as at 1 April 1999

For cars	£36.75/£46
For motor cycles*	£45/£55
For lorries, buses	£73.50/£92
For invalid carriages	free
Written theory test	£15

* Before riding on public roads, learner motor cyclists and learner moped riders are required to have completed Compulsory Basic Training, provided by DSA-approved training bodies. Prices vary.

An extended driving test was introduced in 1992 for those convicted of dangerous driving. The fee is £73.50/£92 (car) or £90/£110 (motorcycle).

Motor Vehicle Licences

Registration and first licensing of vehicles is done through local Vehicle Registration Offices of the DVLA. Local facilities for relicensing are available at any post office which deals with vehicle licensing, or by postal application to the post offices shown on form V100, available at any post office. This form also provides guidance on registering and licensing vehicles.

Details of the present duties chargeable on motor vehicles are available at post offices and Vehicle Registration Offices.

VEHICLE EXCISE DUTY RATES
from 10 March 1999

	Twelve months £	Six months £
Motor Cars		
Light vans, cars, taxis, etc.		
Under 1100cc*	100.00	55.00
Over 1100cc*	155.00	85.25
Motor Cycles		
With or without sidecar, not over 150 cc	15.00	—
With or without sidecar, 150–250 cc	40.00	—
Others	60.00	33.00
Electric motorcycles (including tricycles)	15.00	—
Tricycles (not over 450 kg)		
Not over 150 cc	15.00	—
Others	60.00	33.00
Buses†		
Seating 9–16 persons	160.00 (155.00)	88.00 (85.25)
Seating 17–35 persons	210.00 (155.00)	115.50 (85.25)
Seating 36–60 persons	320.00 (155.00)	176.00 (85.25)

Seating over 60 persons	480.00	264.00
	(155.00)	(85.25)

* Rate from 1 June 1999

† Figures in parentheses refer to reduced pollution vehicles

MoT Testing

Cars, motor cycles, motor caravans, light goods and dual-purpose vehicles more than three years old must be covered by a current MoT test certificate, which must be renewed annually. The MoT testing scheme is administered by the Vehicle Inspectorate.

A fee is payable to MoT testing stations, which must be authorized to carry out tests. The maximum fees, which are prescribed by regulations, are:

For cars and light vans	£30.87
For solo motor cycles	£12.74
For motor cycle combinations	£21.28
For three-wheeled vehicles	£25.02
For non-public service vehicle buses	£38.08
For light goods vehicles 3,000–3,500 kg	£32.77

SHIPPING AND PORTS

Sea transport, both of passengers and freight, is important in Scotland, particularly between the many islands in the north and west and between the islands and the mainland. Major ferry operators include Stena Line (which runs a service between Stranraer and Belfast), P. & O. Scottish Ferries (serving Orkney and Shetland), and Caledonian MacBrayne (serving the Western Isles). P. & O. Scottish Ferries are also UK agents for Smyril, running services from Lerwick to Norway, Denmark, the Faröe Islands and Iceland. Shetland Islands Council operates an inter-island service in Shetland; inter-island services in Orkney are run by Orkney Ferries Ltd.

Ferry Services

Passenger ferry services within Scotland include the following:

From	To
Aberdeen (P&O)	Lerwick (Shetland)
Aberdeen (P&O)	Stromness
Ardrossan (CM)	Brodick (Arran)
Claonaig (Kintyre) (CM)	Lochranza (Arran)*
Colintraive (Argyll) (CM)	Rhubodach (Bute)
Colonsay (CM)	Port Askaig (Islay)*
Fionnphort (Mull) (CM)	Iona
Gourock (CM)	Dunoon (Cowal)
Gourock (CM)	Kilcreggan, Helensburgh
Kennacraig (CM)	Port Ellen (Islay), Port Askaig
Largs (CM)	Cumbrae Slip (Cumbrae)
Lochaline (Lochaber) (CM)	Fishnish (Mull)
Mallaig (CM)	Armadale (Skye)*
Mallaig (CM)	Castlebay
Mallaig (CM)	Lochboisdale (S. Uist)
Mallaig small isles service (CM)	Eigg, Muck, Rum, Canna
Oban (CM)	Castlebay (Barra)
Oban (CM)	Colonsay
Oban (CM)	Craignure (Mull)
Oban (CM)	Lismore
Oban (CM)	Tobermory (Mull), Coll, Tiree
Otternish (N. Uist) (CM)	Leverburgh (Harris)
Sconser (Skye) (CM)	Raasay
Scrabster (P&O)	Stromness (Orkney)
Tarbert (Kintyre) (CM)	Portavadie (Cowal)*
Tayinloan (CM)	Gigha
Tobermory (CM)	Kilchoan
Uig (Skye) (CM)	Tarbert (Harris)
Uig (CM)	Lochmaddy (N. Uist)
Ullapool (CM)	Stornoway (Lewis)
Wemyss Bay (CM)	Rothesay (Bute)

* Summer only

CM Caledonian MacBrayne service

P&O P. & O. Scottish Ferries service

FERRY OPERATORS

CALEDONIAN MACBRAYNE
Tel: 01475-650100 (general enquiries); 01475-650000 (car ferry reservations)
Fax: 01475-637607

HEBRIDEAN CRUISES
Services to Rum, Eigg, Muck and Canna
Tel: 01687-450224; fax: 01687-450224

ORKNEY FERRIES LTD
Tel: 01856-872044/811397

P. & O. SCOTTISH FERRIES
Offices, Aberdeen, Kirkwall, Lerwick, Stromness
Tel: see local telephone directories

SEACAT
Tel: 0990-523523

STENA LINE
Tel: 0990-707070 (passengers); 0845-0704000 (freight)

VIKING SEA TAXIS
Services to several small Shetland islands
Tel: 01595-692463/859431

Ports

There are 57 ports of significant size in Scotland. Ports are owned and operated by private companies (including shipping lines), local authorities or trusts. The telephone number given for each port is the number of the port rather than of the port authority; wherever possible, a 24-hour number has been given.

RUN BY THE LOCAL AUTHORITY

Buckie Harbour	01542-831700
Burghead	01343-830371
Campbeltown	01586-552552
Cockenzie Harbour	01620-827282
Dunbar	01620-827282
Dunoon Pier	01369-702652
Flotta	01856-884000
Gairloch	01445-712140
Gigha	01546-602233
Girvan	01292-612302
Kinlochbervie	01971-521235
Kirkwall	01856-873636
Kyle of Lochalsh	01599-534167
Lochinver Harbour	01571-844247
Macduff	01261-832236
Oban (North Pier)	01631-568892
Perth	01738-624056
Rothesay	01700-503842
Scalloway	01806-242551
Stromness	01856-873636
Sullom Voe	01806-242551
Uig	01470-542381

RUN BY TRUSTS

Aberdeen	01224-597000
Fraserburgh	01346-515858
Invergordon	01349-852308
Inverness	01463-715715
Lerwick	01595-692991
Mallaig	01687-462154
Montrose	01674-672302
Peterhead	01779-474281
Scrabster	01847-892779
Stornoway	01851-702688
Tarbert (East Loch Tarbert)	01880-820344
Ullapool	01854-612091
Wick	01955-602030

RUN BY CALEDONIAN MACBRAYNE LTD
(Tel: 01475-650100):

Brodick	01770-302166
Gourock	01475-650100
Kennacraig	01880-730253
Largs	01475-674134
Lochboisdale	01878-700288
Oban (Ferry Terminal)	01631-562285
Port Ellen	01496-302047

RUN BY CLYDEPORT PLC
(Tel: 0141-221 8733)

Ardrossan	0141-2218733
Glasgow	0141-2218733
Greenock	0141-2218733
Hunterston	0141-2218733

RUN BY FORTH PORTS PLC
(Tel: 0131-554 6473)

Braefoot Bay	0131-5544343
Burntisland	01592-873708
Dundee	01382-224121
Grangemouth	01324-777432
Granton	0131-5544343
Leith	0131-5544343
Methil	01333-426725

RUN BY OTHER OPERATORS

Ardrishaig (British Waterways)	01546-603210
Cairnryan (P.& O. European Ferries)	01581-200663
Stranraer (Stena Line)	01776-802121

Marine Safety

By 1 October 2002 all roll-on, roll-off ferries operating to and from the UK will be required to meet the new international safety standards on stability established by the Stockholm Agreement.

The Maritime and Coastguard Agency (see page 61) was established in 1998 by the merger of the Coastguard Agency and the Marine Safety Agency, and is an executive agency of the Department of the Environment, Transport and the Regions. Its aims are to develop, promote and enforce high standards of marine safety, to minimize loss of life amongst seafarers and coastal users, and to minimize pollution of the sea and coastline from ships.

HM Coastguard in Scotland (see page 61) is divided into two search and rescue regions, one covering the north and east of Scotland and the other covering the west of Scotland and Northern Ireland.

Locations hazardous to shipping in coastal waters are marked by lighthouses and other lights and buoys. The lighthouse authority for Scotland (and the Isle of Man) is the Northern Lighthouse Board (*see* pages 63–4). The Board maintains 84 lighthouses, 116 minor lights and many buoys. No Scottish lighthouses are now manned; the last to convert to automated operation was Fair Isle in 1998.

Harbour authorities are responsible for pilotage within their harbour areas; and the Ports Act 1991 provides for the transfer of lights and buoys to harbour authorities where these are used for mainly local navigation.

SHIPPING FORECAST AREAS

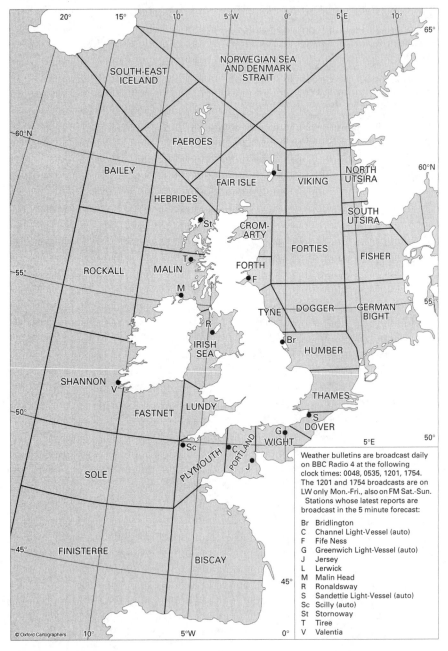

Weather bulletins are broadcast daily on BBC Radio 4 at the following clock times: 0048, 0535, 1201, 1754. The 1201 and 1754 broadcasts are on LW only Mon.-Fri., also on FM Sat.-Sun. Stations whose latest reports are broadcast in the 5 minute forecast:

Br Bridlington
C   Channel Light-Vessel (auto)
F   Fife Ness
G   Greenwich Light-Vessel (auto)
J   Jersey
L   Lerwick
M   Malin Head
R   Ronaldsway
S   Sandettie Light-Vessel (auto)
Sc Scilly (auto)
St Stornoway
T   Tiree
V   Valentia

FORECAST SERVICES

Localized forecasts can be obtained by telephone or fax by dialing the prefix code followed by (+) the appropriate area code given below.

Weathercall Service

Prefix codes:
For local seven-day forecast   tel. 09068-500 4+
For local same-day forecast   fax 09065-300 1+

Area numbers:
South-west Scotland	20
West and central Scotland	21
Edinburgh, Fife, Lothian, Borders	22
East and central Scotland	23
Grampian and east Highlands	24
North-west Scotland	25
Caithness, Orkney and Shetland	26

For national ten-day forecast tel. 09068-575575
fax 09065-200200
Weathercall helpdesk   tel. 0870-600 4242
MetFAX helpline   tel. 08700-750075
fax 08700-750076

Marinecall Service

Prefix codes:
For inshore conditions (up to 12 miles off the coast) for same and next day
tel. 09068-110010+
For data by fax   fax 09060-100+

Area codes:
Cape Wrath to Rattray Head, including Orkney	451
Rattray Head to Berwick-upon-Tweed	452
Berwick-upon-Tweed to Whitby	453
Colwyn Bay to Mull of Galloway	461
Mull of Galloway to Mull of Kintyre, including the North Channel and Firth of Clyde	462
Mull of Kintyre to Ardnamurchan Point	463
Ardnamurchan Point to Cape Wrath, including the Western Isles	464

For four-day offshore forecasts
fax 09060-100+

Area codes:
Rockall, Malin, Bailey, Hebrides and Faröes	468
Fair Isle, Viking, Cromarty, Forth, Forties and Fisher	469

For 24-hour shipping forecasts
tel. 09060-100441

Specialist Forecasting Services

The Met. Office provides a variety of national and local weather forecast services. Information about the full range can be obtained from its web site at http://www.met-office.gov.uk or the helpline 08700-750077.

AIRMET AVIATION FORECASTS
A specialized forecast for pilots, updated three times daily. Calls are charged at 50p a minute.
For Scottish region   tel. 09068-771342
fax 09060-700509

GRAMPIAN AND HIGHLAND ROADLINE
For weather conditions on roads in these areas:
Grampian   tel. 0336-401199
Highland   tel. 0336-401363

MOUNTAINCALL
(until April 2000)
Prefix code   0891-500+

Area codes:
West Highlands	441
East Highlands	442

SCOTTISH SKICALL
(until April 2000)
Prefix code   0891-500+

Area codes:
All resorts	777
Glencoe	771
The Lecht	772
Cairngorm	773
Glenshee	774
Nevis Range	775

SCOTTISH AVALANCHE SERVICE
For forecasts of avalanche risk in Scottish ski resorts   tel. 0800 096 0007

Charges

As at January 1999 (unless otherwise stated):
Calls prefixed by 09060	£1.00 a minute.
Calls prefixed by 09065	£1.50 a minute
Calls prefixed by 09068	60p a minute
Calls prefixed by 0336	50p a minute

THE MEDIA

Cross-Media Ownership

There are rules on cross-media ownership to prevent undue concentration of ownership. These were amended by the Broadcasting Act 1996. Radio companies are now permitted to own one AM, one FM and one other (AM or FM) service; ownership of the third licence is subject to a public interest test. Local newspapers with a circulation under 20 per cent in an area are also allowed to own one AM, one FM and one other service, and may control a regional Channel 3 television service subject to a public interest test. Local newspapers with a circulation between 20 and 50 per cent in an area may own one AM and one FM service, subject to a public interest test, but may not control a regional Channel 3 service. Those with a circulation over 50 per cent may own one radio service in the area (provided that more than one independent local radio service serves the area) subject to a public interest test.

Ownership controls on the number of television or radio licences have been removed; holdings are now restricted to 15 per cent of the total television audience or 15 per cent of the total points available in the radio points scheme. Ownership controls on cable operators have also been removed. National newspapers with less than 20 per cent of national circulation may apply to control any broadcasting licences, subject to a public interest test. National newspapers with more than 20 per cent of national circulation may not have more than a 20 per cent interest in a licence to provide a Channel 3 service, Channel 5 or national and local analogue radio services.

BROADCASTING

The British Broadcasting Corporation (see page 53) is responsible for public service broadcasting in the UK. Its constitution and finances are governed by royal charter and agreement. On 1 May 1996 a new royal charter came into force, establishing the framework for the BBC's activities until 2006.

The Independent Television Commission (see page 60) and the Radio Authority were set up under the terms of the Broadcasting Act 1990. The ITC is the regulator and licensing authority for all commercially-funded television services, including cable and satellite services. The Radio Authority is the regulator and licensing authority for all independent radio services.

Complaints

The Broadcasting Standards Commission was set up in April 1997 under the Broadcasting Act 1996 and was formed from the merger of the Broadcasting Complaints Commission and the Broadcasting Standards Council. The Commission considers and adjudicates upon complaints of unfair treatment or unwarranted infringement of privacy in all broadcast programmes and advertisements on television, radio, cable, satellite and digital services. It also monitors the portrayal of violence and sex, and matters of taste and decency. Its new code of practice came into force on 1 January 1998.

BROADCASTING STANDARDS COMMISSION
7 The Sanctuary, London SW1P 3JS
Tel: 0171-233 0544
Chairman, vacant
Director, S. Whittle

TELEVISION

All channels are broadcast in colour on 625 lines UHF from a network of transmitting stations. Transmissions are available to more than 99 per cent of the population.

The BBC broadcasts two UK-wide television services, BBC 1 and BBC 2; in Scotland these services are designated BBC Scotland on 1 and BBC Scotland on 2. News 24 is a 24-hour BBC television news service broadcast by cable during the day and on BBC 1 at night.

The ITV Network Centre is wholly owned by the ITV companies and undertakes the commissioning and scheduling of those television programmes which are shown across the ITV network. Through its sister organization, the ITV Association, it also provides a range of services to the ITV companies where a common approach is required.

The total number of receiving television licences in the UK at July 1999 was 22,274,792, of which 98.8 per cent were for colour televisions. Annual television licence fees are: monochrome £33.50; colour £101.00.

British Sky Broadcasting broadcasts 13 wholly owned channels and 10 joint venture channels, and distributes 33 multi-channels for third parties.

No overall statistics are available for subscriptions in the UK to satellite television services; British Sky Broadcasting had 7.75 million subscribers at March 1999 (7.2 million analogue and 551,000 digital), though an increasing number of these view through cable.

At April 1999 there were 4,239,881 homes connected to cable television.

Digital television multiplex licences have been awarded, including one to SDN Ltd which guarantees space for Gaelic programmes in Scotland.

BBC TELEVISION

BBC SCOTLAND
BBC Broadcasting House, Queen Margaret Drive, Glasgow G12 8DG
Tel: 0141-339 8844
BBC Broadcasting House, Beechgrove Terrace, Aberdeen AB9 2ZT
Tel: 01224-625233
BBC Broadcasting House, 5 Queen Street, Edinburgh EH2 1JF
Tel: 0131-225 3131

INDEPENDENT TELEVISION

INDEPENDENT TELEVISION NETWORK COMPANIES IN SCOTLAND

BORDER TELEVISION PLC
Area, the Borders
The Television Centre, Carlisle CA1 3NT
Tel: 01228-25101

GRAMPIAN TELEVISION PLC
Group, Scottish Media
Area, northern Scotland
Queen's Cross, Aberdeen AB15 2XJ
Tel: 01224-846846

SCOTTISH TELEVISION PLC
Group, Scottish Media
Area, central Scotland
Cowcaddens, Glasgow G2 3PR
Tel: 0141-300 3000

OTHER INDEPENDENT TELEVISION COMPANIES

CHANNEL 5 BROADCASTING LTD
22 Long Acre, London WC2E 9LY
Tel: 0171-550 5555

CHANNEL FOUR TELEVISION CORPORATION
227 West George Street, Glasgow G2 2ND
Tel: 0141-568 7100

GMTV LTD (BREAKFAST TELEVISION)
London Television Centre, Upper Ground, London SE1 9TT
Tel: 0171-827 7000

INDEPENDENT TELEVISION NEWS LTD
200 Gray's Inn Road, London WC1X 8XZ
Tel: 0171-833 3000

ITN SCOTTISH BUREAU
c/o STV, Cowcaddens, Glasgow G2 3PR
Tel: 0141-332 1093

TELETEXT LTD (SCOTTISH EDITOR)
c/o Newstel Information Ltd, Pentagon Centre, 36 Washington Street, Glasgow G3 8AZ
Tel: 0141-243 2716/0141-221 4457

DIRECT BROADCASTING BY SATELLITE TELEVISION

BRITISH SKY BROADCASTING LTD
Grant Way, Isleworth, Middx TW7 5QD
Tel: 0171-705 3000

RADIO

UK domestic radio services are broadcast across three wavebands: FM (or VHF), medium wave (also referred to as AM) and long wave (used by BBC Radio 4). In the UK the FM waveband extends in frequency from 87.5 MHz to 108 MHz and the medium wave band extends from 531 kHz to 1602 kHz. Some radios are still calibrated in wavelengths rather than frequency. To convert frequency to wavelength, divide 300,000 by the frequency in kHz.

The frequencies allocated for terrestrial digital radio in the UK are 217.5 to 230 MHz. It is necessary to have a radio set with a digital decoder in order to receive digital radio broadcasts.

BBC RADIO

BBC Radio broadcasts five network services to the UK, Isle of Man and the Channel Islands. There is also a tier of national regional services, including Scotland. The BBC World Service broadcasts over 1,000 hours of programmes a week in 44 languages including English.

BBC NETWORK SERVICES

BBC RADIO
Broadcasting House, Portland Place, London W1A 1AA
Tel: 0171-580 4468
Radio 1: *frequencies:* 97.6–99.8 FM
Radio 2: *frequencies:* 88–90.2 FM
Radio 3: *frequencies:* 90.2–92.4 FM
Radio 4: *frequencies:* 94.6–96.1 FM and 103.5–105 FM; 1449 AM, plus eight local fillers on AM; 5.55 a.m.–1.00 a.m. daily, with BBC World Service overnight
Radio 5 Live: *frequencies:* 693 AM and 909 AM, plus one local filler

BBC WORLD SERVICE
Bush House, Strand, London WC2B 4PH
Tel 0171-240 3456

BBC RADIO SCOTLAND

BBC SCOTLAND
Queen Margaret Drive, Glasgow G12 8DG
Tel: 0141-339 8844
BBC Broadcasting House, Beechgrove
   Terrace, Aberdeen AB9 2ZT
Tel: 01224-625233
BBC Broadcasting House, 5 Queen Street,
   Edinburgh EH2 1JF
Tel: 0131-225 3131
Frequencies: 810 AM plus two local fillers;
   92.4–94.7 FM
Local programmes on FM as above:
   Highlands; North-East; Borders; South-
   West (also 585 AM); Orkney; Shetland

RADIO HIGHLAND
7 Culduthel Road, Inverness IV2 4AD
Tel: 01463-720720
Frequency: 104.9 FM

RADIO NAN GAIDHEAL (GAELIC SERVICE)
Rosebank, Church Street, Stornoway, Isle of
Lewis HS1 2LS
Tel: 01851-705000
Area, Western Highlands and Islands, Moray
   Firth and central Scotland
Frequencies: 103.5–105 FM; 990 AM available
in Aberdeen

RADIO ORKNEY
Castle Street, Kirkwall, Orkney KW15 1DF
Tel: 01856-873939
Frequency: 93.7 FM

RADIO SHETLAND
Brentham House, Harbour Street, Lerwick,
Shetland ZE1 0LR
Tel: 01595-694747
Frequencies: 92–95 FM

RADIO SOLWAY
Elmbank, Lover's Walk, Dumfries DG1 1NZ
Tel: 01387-268008
Frequency: 94.7 FM

RADIO TWEED
Municipal Buildings, High Street, Selkirk TD7
4BU
Tel: 01750-21884
Frequency: 93.5 FM

INDEPENDENT RADIO

INDEPENDENT NATIONAL RADIO STATIONS

CLASSIC FM
Academic House, 24–28 Oval Road, London
NW1 7DQ
Tel: 0171-343 9000
Frequencies: 99.9–101.9 FM

TALK RADIO
76 Oxford Street, London W1N 0TR
Tel: 0171-636 1089
Frequencies: 1053/1089 AM

VIRGIN RADIO
1 Golden Square, London W1R 4DJ
Tel: 0171-434 1215
Frequencies: 1215/1197/1233/1242/1260 AM

INDEPENDENT REGIONAL LOCAL RADIO STATIONS

SCOT FM
Area, central Scotland
1 Albert Quay, Leith EH6 7DN
Tel: 0131-554 6677
Frequencies: 100.3/101.1 FM

INDEPENDENT LOCAL RADIO STATIONS

96.3 QFM
26 Lady Lane, Paisley PA1 2LG
Tel: 0141-887 9630
Frequency: 96.3 FM

ARGYLL FM
Unit 6, Old Quay, Campbeltown, Argyll
PA28 6ED
Tel: 01586-551800
Frequency: to be announced. Expected on air
   November 1999

BEAT 106
PO Box 25061, Glasgow G3 7WW
Frequencies: 105.7/106.1 FM

CENTRAL FM
201 High Street, Falkirk FK1 1DU
Tel: 01324-611164
Frequency: 103.1 FM

CLAN FM
PO Box 9083, Dalziel Workspace, Motherwell
ML1 1YU
Frequency: to be announced. Expected on air
   late 1999

CLYDE 1 (FM) AND 2 (AM)
Clydebank Business Park, Clydebank,
Glasgow G81 2RX
Tel: 0141-565 2200
Frequencies: 102.5 FM; 103.3 FM (Firth of
Clyde); 97.0 FM (Vale of Leven); 1152 AM

DISCOVERY 102
8 South Tay Street, Dundee DD1 1PA
Tel: 01382-901000
Frequency: 102.0 FM

FORTH AM AND FM
Forth House, Forth Street, Edinburgh
EH1 3LF
Tel: 0131-556 9255
Frequencies: 1548 AM, 97.3/97.6/102.2 FM

HEARTLAND FM
Atholl Curling Rink, Lower Oakfield,
Pitlochry, Perthshire PH16 5HQ
Tel: 01796-474040
Frequency: 97.5 FM

ISLES FM
PO Box 333, Stornoway, Isle of Lewis
HS1 2PU
Tel: 01851-703333
Frequency: 103.0 FM

KINGDOM FM
Haig House, Haig Business Park, Markinch,
Fife KY7 6AQ
Tel: 01592-753753
Frequencies: 95.2/96.1 FM

LOCHBROOM FM
Radio House, Mill Street, Ullapool, Wester
Ross IV26 2UN
Tel: 01854-613131
Frequency: 102.2 FM

MORAY FIRTH RADIO
Scorguie Place, Inverness IV3 6SF
Tel: 01463-224433
Frequencies: 97.4 FM, 1107 AM
Local opt-outs: 96.6 FM (MFR Speysound);
102.8 FM (MFR Keith Community
Radio); 96.7 FM (MFR Kinnaird Radio);
102.5 FM (MFR Caithness)

NECR (NORTH-EAST COMMUNITY RADIO)
Town House, Kintore, Inverurie,
Aberdeenshire AB51 0US
Tel: 01467-632909
Frequencies: 97.1 FM (Braemar); 102.1 FM
(Meldrum and Inverurie); 102.6 FM
(Kildrummy); 103.2 FM (Colpy)

NEVIS RADIO
Inverlochy, Fort William, Inverness-shire
PH33 6LU
Tel: 01397-700007
Frequencies: 96.6 FM (Fort William); 97.0 FM
(Glencoe); 102.3 FM (Skye); 102.4 FM
(Loch Leven)

NORTHSOUND ONE (FM) AND TWO (AM)
45 Kings Gate, Aberdeen AB15 4EL
Tel: 01224-337000
Frequencies: 1035 AM, 96.9/97.6/103.0 FM

OBAN FM
132 George Street, Oban, Argyll PA34 5NT
Tel: 01631-570057
Frequency: 103.3 FM

RADIO BORDERS
Tweedside Park, Galashiels TD1 3TD
Tel: 01896-759444
Frequencies: 96.8/97.5/103.1/103.4 FM

RADIO TAY AM AND TAY FM
6 North Isla Street, Dundee DD3 7JQ
Tel: 01382-200800
Frequencies: 1161 AM, 102.8 FM (Dundee);
1584 AM, 96.4 FM (Perth)

RNA FM
Arbroath Infirmary, Rosemount Road,
Arbroath, Angus DD11 2AT
Tel: 01241-879660
Frequency: 96.6 FM

SIBC
Market Street, Lerwick, Shetland ZE1 0JN
Tel: 01595-695299
Frequencies: 96.2/102.2 FM

SOUTH WEST SOUND
Campbell House, Bankend Road, Dumfries
DG1 4TH
Tel: 01387-250999
Frequencies: 96.5/97.0/103.0 FM

WAVES RADIO PETERHEAD
Unit 2, Blackhouse Industrial Estate,
Peterhead AB42 1BW
Tel: 01779-491012
Frequency: 101.2 FM

WEST SOUND AM AND WEST FM
Radio House, 54A Holmston Road, Ayr KA7
3BE
Tel: 01292-283662
Frequencies: 1035 AM, 96.7 FM (Ayr); 97.5
FM (Girvan)

THE PRESS

The press is subject to the laws on publication and the Press Complaints Commission (*see* below) was set up by the industry as a means of self-regulation. It is not state-subsidized and receives few tax concessions. The income of most newspapers and periodicals is derived largely from sales and from advertising; the press is the largest advertising medium in Britain.

Complaints

The Press Complaints Commission was founded by the newspaper and magazine industry in January 1991 to replace the Press Council (established in 1953). It is a voluntary, non-statutory body set up to operate the press's self-regulation system following the Calcutt report in 1990 on privacy and related matters, when the industry feared that a failure to regulate itself might lead to statutory regulation of the press. The Commission is funded by the industry through the Press Standards Board of Finance.

The Commission's objects are to consider, adjudicate, conciliate, and resolve complaints of unfair treatment by the press; and to ensure that the press maintains the highest professional standards with respect for generally recognized freedoms, including freedom of expression, the public's right to know, and the right of the press to operate free from improper pressure. The Commission judges newspaper and magazine conduct by a code of practice drafted by editors, agreed by the industry and ratified by the Commission.

Seven of the Commission's members are editors of national, regional and local newspapers and magazines, and nine, including the chairman, are drawn from other fields. One member has been appointed Privacy Commissioner with special powers to investigate complaints about invasion of privacy.

PRESS COMPLAINTS COMMISSION
1 Salisbury Square, London EC4Y 8AE
Tel: 0171-353 1248
Chairman, Lord Wakeham, PC
Director, G. Black

NEWSPAPERS

Newspapers are usually financially independent of any political party, though most adopt a political stance in their editorial comments, usually reflecting proprietorial influence. Ownership of the national and regional daily newspapers is concentrated in the hands of large corporations whose interests cover publishing and communications. The rules on cross-media ownership, as amended by the Broadcasting Act 1996, limit the extent to which newspaper organizations may become involved in broadcasting (*see* page 182).

Scotland has a number of daily and Sunday newspapers (including Scottish editions of some of the UK national newspapers), as well as local daily and weekly newspapers. The following list shows the main editorial offices of the major newspapers in Scotland, including the Scottish editorial offices of UK national newspapers.

NATIONAL DAILY NEWSPAPERS

DAILY STAR OF SCOTLAND
Park House, Park Circus Place, Glasgow
G3 6AN
Tel: 0141-352 2552

DAILY TELEGRAPH
5 Coates Crescent, Edinburgh EH3 7AL
Tel: 0131-225 3313

FINANCIAL TIMES
3rd Floor, 80 George Street, Edinburgh
EH2 2HN
Tel: 0131-220 1420

THE GUARDIAN
PO Box 25000, Glasgow G1 5YF
Tel: 0141-553 0875

THE HERALD
195 Albion Street, Glasgow G1 1QP
Tel: 0141-552 6255

THE INDEPENDENT
Correspondent in Scotland, J. O'Sullivan
Top Left Flat, 8 Cumberland Street,
Edinburgh EH3 6SA
Tel: 0131-557 4904

THE SCOTSMAN
20 North Bridge, Edinburgh EH1 1YT
Tel: 0131-243 3207

SCOTTISH DAILY MAIL
197 Albion Street, Glasgow G1 1QP
Tel: 0141-553 4600

SCOTTISH EXPRESS
Park House, Park Circus Place, Glasgow
G3 6AF
Tel: 0141-332 9600

SCOTTISH MIRROR
40 Anderston Quay, Glasgow G3 8DA
Tel: 0141-248 7000

THE SCOTTISH SUN
124 Portman Street, Glasgow G41 1EJ
Tel: 0141-420 5100

REGIONAL DAILY NEWSPAPERS

COURIER AND ADVERTISER
2 Albert Square, Dundee DD1 9QJ
Tel: 01382-223131

DAILY RECORD
40 Anderston Quay, Glasgow G3 8DA
Tel: 0141-248 7000

EDINBURGH EVENING NEWS
20 North Bridge, Edinburgh EH1 1YT
Tel: 0131-243 3558

EVENING EXPRESS
PO Box 43, Lang Stracht, Mastrick, Aberdeen
AB15 6DF
Tel: 01224-690222

EVENING TIMES
195 Albion Street, Glasgow G1 1QP
Tel: 0141-552 6255

GREENOCK TELEGRAPH
Pitreavie Business Park, Dunfermline
KY11 8QS
Tel: 01383-728201

PAISLEY DAILY EXPRESS
1 Woodside Terrace, Glasgow G3 7UY
Tel: 0141-353 3366

PRESS AND JOURNAL
PO Box 43, Lang Stracht, Mastrick, Aberdeen
AB15 6DF
Tel: 01224-690222

WEEKLY NEWSPAPERS

THE INDEPENDENT ON SUNDAY
Correspondent in Scotland, J. O'Sullivan
Top Left Flat, 8 Cumberland Street,
Edinburgh EH3 6SA
Tel: 0131-557 4904

MAIL ON SUNDAY IN SCOTLAND
197 Albion Street, Glasgow G1 1QP
Tel: 0141-553 4600

THE OBSERVER
11 Broughton Place, Edinburgh EH1 3RL
Tel: 0131-558 8110

SCOTLAND ON SUNDAY
20 North Bridge, Edinburgh EH1 1YT
Tel: 0131-243 3472

SCOTTISH SUNDAY EXPRESS
Park House, Park Circus Place, Glasgow
G3 6AF
Tel: 0141-332 9600

THE SUNDAY HERALD
195 Albion Street, Glasgow G1 1QP
Tel: 0141-552 6255

SUNDAY MAIL
40 Anderston Quay, Glasgow G3 8DA
Tel: 0141-248 7000

SUNDAY MIRROR
40 Anderston Quay, Glasgow G3 8DA
Tel: 0141-248 7000

SUNDAY POST
Courier Place, Dundee DD1 9QJ
Tel: 01382-223131

WEEKLY NEWS
Courier Place, Dundee DD1 9QJ
Tel: 01382-223131

BOOK PUBLISHERS

The following are members of the Scottish Publishers Association. The Association publishes the *Directory of Publishing in Scotland*.

SCOTTISH PUBLISHERS ASSOCIATION
Scottish Book Centre, 137 Dundee Street,
Edinburgh EH11 1BG
Tel: 0131-228 6866

FULL MEMBERS

ACAIR LTD
7 James Street, Stornoway, Isle of Lewis
HS1 2QN
Tel: 01851-703020

APPLETREE PRESS LTD
Old Potato Station, 14 Howard Street South,
Belfast BT7 1BA
Tel: 01232-243074

ARGYLL PUBLISHING
Glendaruel, Argyll PA22 3AE
Tel: 01369-820229

ASSOCIATION FOR SCOTTISH LITERARY
STUDIES
c/o Department of Scottish History,
University of Glasgow, 9 University Gardens,
Glasgow G12 8QH
Tel: 0141-330 5309

ATELIER BOOKS
6 Dundas Street, Edinburgh EH3 6HZ
Tel: 0131-557 4050

B. & W. PUBLISHING
29 Inverleith Row, Edinburgh EH3 5QH
Tel: 0131-552 5555

BARRINGTON STOKE LTD
10 Belford Terrace, Edinburgh EH4 3DQ
Tel: 0131-315 4933

BIRLINN LTD
Unit 8, Canongate Venture, 5 New Street,
Edinburgh EH8 8BH
Tel: 0131-556 6660

BROWN, SON & FERGUSON LTD
4–10 Darnley Street, Glasgow G41 2SD
Tel: 0141-429 1234

CANONGATE BOOKS
14 High Street, Edinburgh EH1 1TE
Tel: 0131-557 5111

CHURCHILL LIVINGSTONE
Robert Stevenson House, 1–3 Baxter's Place,
Edinburgh EH1 3AF
Tel: 0131-556 2424

EDINBURGH UNIVERSITY PRESS
22 George Square, Edinburgh EH8 9LF
Tel: 0131-650 4218

FLORIS BOOKS
15 Harrison Gardens, Edinburgh EH11 1SH
Tel: 0131-337 2372

THE GLASGOW ROYAL CONCERT HALL
2 Sauchiehall Street, Glasgow G2 3NY
Tel: 0141-332 6633

GLOWWORM AND THE AMAISING
PUBLISHING HOUSE
Unit 7, Greendykes Industrial Estate,
Greendykes Road, Broxburn, W. Lothian
EH52 6PG
Tel: 01506-857570

GOBLINSHEAD
130B Inveresk Road, Musselburgh,
Midlothian EH21 7AY
Tel: 0131-665 2894

GORDON WRIGHT PUBLISHING LTD
25 Mayfield Road, Edinburgh EH9 2NQ
Tel: 0131-667 1300

W. GREEN
21 Alva Street, Edinburgh EH2 4PS
Tel: 0131-225 4879

HARPERCOLLINS PUBLISHERS
Westerhill Road, Bishopbriggs, Glasgow
G64 2QT
Tel: 0141-772 3200

HEALTH EDUCATION BOARD FOR
SCOTLAND
Woodburn House, Canaan Lane, Edinburgh
EH10 4SG
Tel: 0131-536 5500

HOUSE OF LOCHAR
Isle of Colonsay, Argyll PA61 7YP
Tel: 01951-200232

JOHNSTONE MEDIA
55 Melville Street, Edinburgh EH3 7HL
Tel: 0131-220 5380

KEPPEL PUBLISHING
The Grey House, Kenbridge Road, New
Galloway, Kirkcudbrightshire DG7 3RP
Tel: 01644-420272

KINGFISHER PUBLICATIONS PLC
7 Hopetoun Crescent, Edinburgh EH7 4AY
Tel: 0131-556 5929

LOMOND BOOKS
36 West Shore Road, Granton, Edinburgh
EH5 1QD
Tel: 0131-551 2261

LUATH PRESS LTD
543/2 Castlehill, Edinburgh EH1 2ND
Tel: 0131-225 4326

MAINSTREAM PUBLISHING CO.
7 Albany Street, Edinburgh EH1 3UG
Tel: 0131-557 2959

MERCAT PRESS
at James Thin Ltd, 53-59 South Bridge,
Edinburgh EH1 1YS
Tel: 0131-622 8252

THE NATIONAL ARCHIVES OF SCOTLAND
(formerly the Scottish Record Office)
HM General Register House, Edinburgh
EH1 3YY
Tel: 0131-535 1314

NATIONAL GALLERIES OF SCOTLAND
Belford Road, Edinburgh EH4 3DR
Tel: 0131-556 8921

NATIONAL MUSEUMS OF SCOTLAND
PUBLISHING
Chambers Street, Edinburgh EH1 1JF
Tel: 0131-247 4186

NEIL WILSON PUBLISHING LTD
Suite 303A, The Pentagon Centre, 36
Washington Street, Glasgow G3 8AZ
Tel: 0141-221 1117

THE ORCADIAN LTD
PO Box 18, Hell's Half Acre, Hatston,
Kirkwall, Orkney KW15 1DW
Tel: 01856-879000

POLYGON
22 George Square, Edinburgh EH8 9LF
Tel: 0131-650 4214

THE RAMSAY HEAD PRESS
15 Gloucester Place, Edinburgh EH3 6EE
Tel: 0131-225 5646

RICHARD STENLAKE PUBLISHING
Ochiltree Sawmill, The Lade, Ochiltree,
Ayrshire KA18 2NX
Tel: 01290-423114

RUTLAND PRESS
15 Rutland Square, Edinburgh EH1 2BE
Tel: 0131-229 7545

ST ANDREW PRESS
121 George Street, Edinburgh EH2 4YN
Tel: 0131-225 5722

THE SALTIRE SOCIETY
9 Fountain Close, 22 High Street, Edinburgh
EH1 1TF
Tel: 0131-556 1836

SCOTTISH COUNCIL FOR RESEARCH IN
EDUCATION
15 St John Street, Edinburgh EH8 8JR
Tel: 0131-557 2944

SCOTTISH CULTURAL PRESS AND
SCOTTISH CHILDREN'S PRESS
Unit 14, Leith Walk Business Centre, 130
Leith Walk, Edinburgh EH6 5DT
Tel: 0131-555 5950

SCOTTISH NATURAL HERITAGE
Publications Section, Battleby, Redgorton,
Perth PH1 3EW
Tel: 01738-627921

SPORTSCOTLAND
Caledonia House, Redheughs Rigg, South
Gyle, Edinburgh EH12 9DQ
Tel: 0131-317 7200

SCOTTISH TEXT SOCIETY
27 George Street, Edinburgh EH8 9LD

THE SHETLAND TIMES LTD
Prince Alfred Street, Lerwick, Shetland
ZE1 0EP
Tel: 01595-695531

THISTLE PRESS
West Bank, Western Road, Insch,
Aberdeenshire AB52 6JR
Tel: 01464-821053

TUCKWELL PRESS LTD
The Mill House, Phantassie, East Linton, E.
Lothian EH40 3DG
Tel: 01620-860164

UNIT FOR THE STUDY OF GOVERNMENT
IN SCOTLAND
Chisholm House, 1 Surgeon Square, High
School Yards, Edinburgh EH1 1LZ
Tel: 0131-650 2456

WHITTLES PUBLISHING
Roseleigh House, Harbour Road,
Latheronwheel, Caithness KW5 6DW
Tel: 01593-741240

WILD GOOSE PUBLICATIONS
Unit 15, 6 Harmony Row, Govan, Glasgow
G51 3BA
Tel: 0141-440 0985

ASSOCIATE MEMBERS

CITIZENS ADVICE SCOTLAND
26 George Square, Edinburgh EH8 9LD
Tel: 0131-667 0156

THE GAELIC BOOKS COUNCIL
22 Mansfield Street, Glasgow G11 5QP
Tel: 0141-337 6211

RCAHMS
John Sinclair House, 16 Bernard Terrace,
Edinburgh EH8 9NX
Tel: 0131-662 1456

SCOTTISH BOOK TRUST
Scottish Book Centre, 137 Dundee Street,
Edinburgh EH11 1BG
Tel: 0131-229 3663

STRAIGHTLINE PUBLISHING LTD
29 Main Street, Bothwell, Glasgow G71 8RD
Tel: 01698-853000

WIGWAM DIGITAL LTD
51 Wren Court, Strathclyde Business Park,
Bellshill, Strathclyde ML4 3NQ
Tel: 01698-844160

ZIPO PUBLISHING LTD
4 Cowan Street, Hillhead, Glasgow G12 8PF
Tel: 0141-339 9729

LIBRARY MEMBERS

A. K. BELL LIBRARY
York Place, Perth PH2 8EP
Tel: 01738-444949

CLYDEBANK DISTRICT LIBRARIES
Clydebank Central Library, Dumbarton
Road, Clydebank G81 1XH
Tel: 0141-952 1416

EDINBURGH CITY LIBRARIES
Central Library, George IV Bridge,
Edinburgh EH1 1EG
Tel: 0131-225 5584

GLASGOW CITY LIBRARIES PUBLICATIONS
BOARD
The Mitchell Library, North Street, Glasgow
G3 7DN
Tel: 0141-287 2846

NATIONAL LIBRARY OF SCOTLAND
George IV Bridge, Edinburgh EH1 1EW
Tel: 0131-226 4531

SCOTTISH LIBRARY ASSOCIATION
Scottish Centre for Information and Library
Services, 1 John Street, Hamilton ML3 7EU
Tel: 01698-458888

SMALL PRESSES

AA ENTERPRISES
7 Mount Road, Berwick-upon-Tweed

BALNAIN BOOKS
c/o Seol, Unit 8, Canongate Venture, 5 New
Street, Edinburgh EH8 8BH
Tel: 0131-556 6660

BLACK ACE BOOKS
PO Box 6557, Forfar DD8 2YS
Tel: 01307-465096

CHAPMAN
4 Broughton Place, Edinburgh EH1 3RX
Tel: 0131-557 2207

DIONYSIA PRESS
20A Montgomery Street, Edinburgh EH7 5JS
Tel: 0131-478 2572

DUDU NSOMBA PUBLICATIONS
4 Gailes Park, Bothwell, Glasgow G71 8TS
Tel: 01698-854290

EPER
University of Edinburgh, 21 Hill Place,
Edinburgh EH8 9OP
Tel: 0131-650 6200

FORTH NATURALIST AND HISTORIAN
The University of Stirling, Stirling FK9 4LA
Tel: 01259-215091

THE GLENEIL PRESS
Whittingehame, Haddington, E. Lothian
EH41 4QA
Tel: 01620-860292

MERCHISTON PUBLISHING
PMPC Department, Napier University,
Craighouse Road, Edinburgh EH10 5LG
Tel: 0131-445 2227

THE NEW IONA PRESS
7 Drynie Terrace, Inverness IV2 4UP
Tel: 01463-242384

PARISH EDUCATION
18 Inverleith Terrace, Edinburgh EH3 5NS
Tel: 0131-332 0343

EU INFORMATION

Scotland's relations with the European Union (EU) remain a reserved power after devolution. However, since EU policies and legislation affect many of the matters for which the Scottish Parliament and Executive are responsible, the Parliament may choose to scrutinize EU proposals to ensure that Scotland's interests are taken into consideration.

Where national legislation is required to fulfil the UK's obligation to implement EC legislation, the Scottish Parliament and Executive may choose whether to implement EC obligations which cover devolved matters in Scotland, or to agree on compliance with the relevant GB or UK legislation. The Scottish Ministers will be actively involved in decision-making on EU matters.

The Scottish Executive has its own office in Brussels to represent Scotland's interests and complement the work of the UK Permanent Representative to the EU (UKREP). The office may also gather intelligence on behalf of the Scottish Executive and Parliament and act as a base for visits to Brussels by Scottish Ministers and officials of the Scottish Executive.

SCOTTISH EXECUTIVE EU OFFICE
Scotland House, 6 Rond Point Schuman,
B-1040 Brussels, Belgium
Tel: 00-322-282 8331

INFORMATION SOURCES

Information about the EU is available from a variety of sources at different levels. The European Commission is developing a decentralized information network which aims to meet both general and specialized needs. The following are available in Scotland:

EUROPEAN COMMISSION
REPRESENTATIVE OFFICE
9 Alva Street, Edinburgh EH2 4PH
Tel: 0131-225 2058; fax: 0131-226 4105

EUROPEAN PARLIAMENT INFORMATION
OFFICE
c/o European Commission Representative
Office

Euro Info Centres

The centres provide mainly information on the EU relevant to business (particularly small and medium-sized businesses), such as company law, relevant European legislation, taxation and public contracts. They can also offer an advisory service, for which a charge may be made.

GLASGOW
Franborough House, 123 Bothwell Street,
Glasgow G2 7JP
Tel: 0141-221 0999; fax 0141-221 6539
E-mail: euroinfocentre@scotent.co.uk

INVERNESS
20 Bridge Street, Inverness IV1 1QR
Tel: 01463-702560; fax: 01463-715600
E-mail: eic@sprite.co.uk

European Documentation Centres

Based in university libraries, the documentation centres hold reference collections of major official documents of the EU institutions, and other publications.

UNIVERSITY OF ABERDEEN
The Taylor Library, Dunbar Street, Aberdeen
AB24 3JB
Tel: 01224-273819; fax: 01224-273819
E-mail: e.a.mackie@abdn.ac.uk

UNIVERSITY OF DUNDEE
The Law Library, Perth Road, Dundee
DD1 4HN
Tel: 01382-344102; fax: 01482-228669
E-mail: a.duncan@dundee.ac.uk

UNIVERSITY OF EDINBURGH
The Europa Library, Old College, South
Bridge, Edinburgh EH8 9YL
Tel: 0131-650 2041; fax: 0131-650 6343
E-mail: kdt@festival.ed.ac.uk

UNIVERSITY OF GLASGOW
The Library, Hillhead Street, Glasgow G12
8QE
Tel: 0141-330 6722; fax: 0141-330 4952
E-mail: gxlr30@gla.ac.uk

European Reference Centres

The reference centres keep less comprehensive collections of publications.

EDINBURGH
National Library of Scotland, George IV
Bridge, Edinburgh EH1 1EW
Tel: 0131-226 4531; fax: 0131-220 6662

STIRLING
The Library, Stirling University, Stirling
FK9 4LA
Tel: 01786-467231; fax: 01786-466866
E-mail: j.w.allan@stir.ac.uk

Carrefour Centres

The Carrefour centres are based in rural areas. They provide information on EU policy concerning rural areas and rural issues, and promote awareness of rural development.

HIGHLANDS AND ISLANDS RURAL
CARREFOUR CENTRE
Business Information Source, 20 Bridge Street, Inverness IV1 1QR
Tel: 01463-715400; fax: 01463-715600
E-mail: bis.enquiries@bis.uk.com

Public Information Relay

These are information points at a number of public libraries where general reference documents about the EU are held and free information leaflets are available. At present there are public information relay points at about 34 local public libraries in Scotland, at least one in each local authority area.

European Resource Centres

The resource centres hold printed and electronic information on Europe for schools, and stocks of free publications on European affairs, the EU institutions, and the countries of the EU.

EURODESK SCOTLAND
Community Learning Scotland, Rosebery House, 9 Haymarket Terrace, Edinburgh
EH12 5EZ
Tel: 0131-313 2488; fax: 0131-313 6800
E-mail: eurodesk@cls.dircon.co.uk

Citizens First

Citizens First is a free telephone service providing public information on various aspects of European citizenship. Callers can order free guides and factsheets on living, working and travelling in the EU, study and training in another EU country; equal opportunities, the single market, and other subjects. The materials are published in all EU languages, including Gaelic.
Freephone: 0800-581591
Web: http://europa.eu.int/citizens

LOCAL ENTERPRISE COMPANIES

Local enterprise companies operate under the aegis of either Highlands and Islands Enterprise (HIE) (*see* page 59) or Scottish Enterprise (SE) (*see* pages 68–9). These two statutory bodies were set up in 1991 to further the development of the Scottish economy, working with the private and public sectors. Many of their functions are delegated to the local enterprise companies.

ARGYLL AND THE ISLANDS ENTERPRISE (HIE)
The Enterprise Centre, Kilmory Industrial Estate, Lochgilphead, Argyll PA31 8SH
Tel: 01546-602281/602563
Chief Executive, K. Abernethy

CAITHNESS AND SUTHERLAND ENTERPRISE (HIE)
Tollemache House, High Street, Thurso, Caithness KW14 8AZ
Tel: 01847-896115
Chief Executive, N. Money

DUMFRIES AND GALLOWAY ENTERPRISE COMPANY (SE)
Solway House, Dumfries Business Park, Dumfries DG1 3SJ
Tel: 01387-245000
Chief Executive, Ms I. Walker

DUNBARTONSHIRE ENTERPRISE (SE)
2nd Floor, Spectrum House, Clydebank Business Park, Clydebank, Glasgow G81 2DR
Tel: 0141-951 2121
Chief Executive, D. Anderson

ENTERPRISE AYRSHIRE (SE)
17-19 Hill Street, Kilmarnock KA3 1HA
Tel: 01563-526623
Chief Executive, Ms E. Connolly

FIFE ENTERPRISE LTD (SE)
Kingdom House, Saltire Centre, Glenrothes, Fife KY6 2AQ
Tel: 01592-623000
Chief Executive, R. MacKenzie

FORTH VALLEY ENTERPRISE (SE)
Laurel House, Laurelhill Business Park, Stirling FK7 9JQ
Tel: 01786-451919
Chief Executive, W. Morton

GLASGOW DEVELOPMENT AGENCY (SE)
Atrium Court, 50 Waterloo Street, Glasgow G2 6HQ
Tel: 0141-204 1111
Chief Executive, S. Gulliver

GRAMPIAN ENTERPRISE LTD (SE)
27 Albyn Place, Aberdeen AB10 1DB
Tel: 01224-575100
Chief Executive, E. Gillespie

INVERNESS AND NAIRN ENTERPRISE (HIE)
13B Harbour Road, Longman Industrial Estate, Inverness IV1 1SY
Tel: 01463-713504
Chief Executive, W. Sylvester

LANARKSHIRE DEVELOPMENT AGENCY (SE)
New Lanarkshire House, Dove Wynd, Strathclyde Business Park, Bellshill ML4 3AD
Tel: 01698-745454
Chief Executive, I. Carmichael

LOCHABER LTD (HIE)
St Mary's House, Gordon Square, Fort William PH33 6DY
Tel: 01397-704326
Chief Executive, Ms J. Wright

LOTHIAN AND EDINBURGH ENTERPRISE (SE)
Apex House, 99 Haymarket Terrace, Edinburgh EH12 5HD
Tel: 0131-313 4000
Chief Executive, D. Crichton

MORAY, BADENOCH AND STRATHSPEY ENTERPRISE (HIE/SE)
Unit 8, Elgin Business Centre, Maisondieu Road, Elgin, Morayshire IV30 1RH
Tel: 01343-550567
Chief Executive, R. Ruane

ORKNEY ENTERPRISE (HIE)
14 Queen Street, Kirkwall, Orkney KW15 1JE
Tel: 01856-874638
Chief Executive, K. Grant

RENFREWSHIRE ENTERPRISE (SE)
27 Causeyside Street, Paisley PA1 1UL
Tel: 0141-848 0101
Chief Executive, A. Cassidy

ROSS AND CROMARTY ENTERPRISE (HIE)
69–71 High Street, Invergordon, Ross and
Cromarty IV18 0AA
Tel: 01349-853666
Chief Executive, G. Cox

SCOTTISH BORDERS ENTERPRISE (SE)
Bridge Street, Galashiels TD1 1SW
Tel: 01896-758991
Chief Executive, D. P. Douglas

SCOTTISH ENTERPRISE TAYSIDE (SE)
45 North Lindsay Street, Dundee DD1 1HT
Tel: 01382-223100
Chief Executive, G. McKee

SHETLAND ENTERPRISE (HIE)
Toll Clock Shopping Centre, 26 North Road,
Lerwick, Shetland ZE1 0PE
Tel: 01595-693177
Chief Executive, D. Finch

SKYE AND LOCHALSH ENTERPRISE (HIE)
Kings House, The Green, Portree, Isle of
Skye IV51 9BS
Tel: 01478-612841
Chief Executive, R. Muir

WESTERN ISLES ENTERPRISE (HIE)
3 Harbour View, Cromwell Street Quay,
Stornoway, Isle of Lewis HS1 2DF
Tel: 01851-703625/703905
Chief Executive, D. MacAulay

PROFESSIONAL AND TRADE BODIES

The Certification Officer (*see* page 54) is responsible for receiving and scrutinizing annual returns from employers' associations. Many employers' associations are members of the Confederation of British Industry (CBI).

CONFEDERATION OF BRITISH INDUSTRY, SCOTLAND

Beresford House, 5 Claremont Terrace, Glasgow G3 7XT
Tel: 0141-332 8661

The Confederation of British Industry was founded in 1965 and is an independent non-party political body financed by industry and commerce. It exists primarily to ensure that the Government understands the intentions, needs and problems of British business. It is the recognized spokesman for the business viewpoint and is consulted as such by the Government.

The CBI represents, directly and indirectly, some 250,000 companies, large and small, from all sectors.

The governing body of the CBI is the 200-strong Council, which meets four times a year in London under the chairmanship of the President. It is assisted by 17 expert standing committees which advise on the main aspects of policy. There are 13 regional councils and offices, covering the administrative regions of England, Wales, Scotland and Northern Ireland. There is also an office in Brussels.
President, Sir Clive Thompson
Scottish Regional Director, I. McMillan

PROFESSIONAL AND TRADE BODIES

The following list includes the main professional institutions, employers' associations and trade associations in Scotland, and the Scottish offices of UK institutions.

ABERDEEN FISH CURERS AND
MERCHANTS ASSOCIATION
South Esplanade West, Aberdeen AB11 9FJ
Tel: 01224-897744
Managing Director, R. H. Milne

ACCOUNTANTS OF SCOTLAND,
INSTITUTE OF CHARTERED
27 Queen Street, Edinburgh EH2 1LA
Tel: 0131-225 5673
Chief Executive, P. W. Johnston

ACCOUNTANTS, ASSOCIATION OF
CHARTERED CERTIFIED
1 Woodside Place, Glasgow G3 7QF
Tel: 0141-309 4000
Head, ACCA Scotland, W. Cunningham

ACTUARIES IN SCOTLAND, FACULTY OF
18 Dublin Street, Edinburgh EH2 3PP
Tel: 0131-240 1300
Secretary, W. Mair

ADVANCED CONCRETE AND MASONRY,
CENTRE FOR
Department of CSEE, University of Paisley,
Paisley PA1 2BE
Tel: 0141-848 3267
Chief Executive, Prof. P. J. M. Bartos

ADVERTISING, INSTITUTE OF
PRACTITIONERS IN
c/o Feather Brooksbank, The Old Assembly
Hall, 37 Constitution Street, Edinburgh
EH6 7BY
Tel: 0131-555 2554
Chairman, G. Brooksbank

ADVOCATES, FACULTY OF
Advocates Library, Parliament House,
Edinburgh EH1 1RF
Tel: 0131-226 5071
Dean, G. N. H. Emslie, QC

ARBITRATORS (ARBITERS) SCOTTISH
BRANCH, CHARTERED INSTITUTES OF
Whittinghame House, 1099 Great Western
Road, Glasgow G12 0AA
Tel: 0141-334 7222
Hon. Secretary and Treasurer, B. L. Smith

ARCHITECTS IN SCOTLAND, ROYAL
INCORPORATION OF
15 Rutland Square, Edinburgh EH1 2BE
Tel: 0131-229 7545
Secretary, S. Tombs

ARTISTS, SOCIETY OF SCOTTISH
11A Leslie Place, Edinburgh EH4 1NF
Tel: 0131-332 2041
Secretary, Mrs S. Cornish

ASSESSORS' ASSOCIATION, SCOTTISH
Chesser House, 500 Gorgie Road, Edinburgh
EH11 3YJ
Tel: 0131-469 5589
Vice President, J. A. Cardwell

AUCTIONEERS AND APPRAISERS IN
SCOTLAND, INSTITUTE OF
The Rural Centre, West Mains, Ingliston,
Newbridge, Midlothian EH28 8NZ
Tel: 0131-472 4067
Secretary, W. Blair

BAKERS, SCOTTISH ASSOCIATION OF
MASTER
4 Torphichen Street, Edinburgh EH3 8JQ
Tel: 0131-229 1401
Chief Executive, I. Hay

BANKERS, COMMITTEE OF SCOTTISH
CLEARING
38 Drumsheugh Gardens, Edinburgh EH3 7SW
Tel: 0131-473 7770
Chairman, Sir George Mathewson, CBE, FRSE

BANKERS IN SCOTLAND, CHARTERED
INSTITUTE OF
Drumsheugh House, 38B Drumsheugh
Gardens, Edinburgh EH3 7SW
Tel: 0131-473 7777
Chief Executive, C. W. Munn

BEEF AND LAMB ASSOCIATION, SCOTTISH
QUALITY
The Rural Centre, West Mains, Ingliston,
Newbridge, Midlothian EH28 8NZ
Tel: 0131-472 4040
Chief Executive, B. Simpson

BOILER AND RADIATOR MANUFACTURERS
ASSOCIATION
Savoy Tower, 77 Renfrew Street, Glasgow
G2 3BZ
Tel: 0141-332 0826
Secretary, J. Carruthers

BOOKSELLERS ASSOCIATION
Milngavie Bookshop, 37 Douglas Street,
Milngavie, Glasgow G62 6PE
Tel: 0141-956 4752
Hon. Secretary, R. Lane

BOX AND PACKAGING ASSOCIATION,
BRITISH
64 High Street, Kirkintilloch, Glasgow
G66 1PR
Tel: 0141-777 7272
Secretary, T. Bullimore

BREWERS' ASSOCIATION OF SCOTLAND
6 St Colme Street, Edinburgh EH3 6AD
Tel: 0131-225 4681
Secretary, G. Miller

BUILDERS, FEDERATION OF MASTER
540 Gorgie Road, Edinburgh EH11 3AL
Tel: 0131-455 7997
Regional Director, Mrs M. Thomson

BUILDING CONTRACTORS ASSOCIATION,
SCOTTISH
4 Woodside Place, Glasgow G3 7QF
Tel: 0141-353 5050
Association Secretary, N. J. Smith

BUILDING EMPLOYERS' FEDERATION,
SCOTTISH
Carron Grange, Carrongrange Avenue,
Stenhousemuir FK5 3BQ
Tel: 01324-555550
Chief Executive, S. C. Patten, FRSA

BUILDING SOCIETIES
ASSOCIATION/COUNCIL OF MORTGAGE
LENDERS – COMMITTEE FOR SCOTLAND
Northern Rock PLC, 11 Castle Street,
Edinburgh EH2 3AH
Tel: 0131-226 3401
Chairman, R. B. Swanson

BUSINESS ENTERPRISE SCOTLAND
18 Forth Street, Edinburgh EH1 3LH
Tel: 0131-550 3839
Chief Executive, R. Miller

BUSINESS WOMEN'S FORUM
12 Kelvinside Gardens, Glasgow G20 6BB
Tel: 0141-946 5062
Chairperson, Ms C. McCloskey

CBS NETWORK
Society Place, West Calder, W. Lothian
EH55 8EA
Tel: 01506-871370
Company Secretary, J. Pearce

CHARITY FUNDRAISING MANAGERS,
INSTITUTE OF (ICFM SCOTLAND)
c/o Bank of Scotland, 12 Bankhead Crossway
South, Edinburgh EH11 4EN
Tel: 0131-453 6517
Development Officer, Ms A. Morrison

CHIROPRACTIC ASSOCIATION, SCOTTISH
St Boswells Chiropractic Clinic, 16 Jenny
Moores Road, St Boswells, Melrose TD6 0AL
Tel: 01835-823645
Secretary, Dr C. I. How

CHRISTMAS TREE GROWERS
ASSOCIATION, BRITISH
18 Cluny Place, Edinburgh EH10 4RL
Tel: 0131-447 0499
Secretary, R. M. Hay

CLAY INDUSTRIES, SCOTTISH EMPLOYERS'
COUNCIL FOR THE
c/o Caradale Brick, Etna Works, Lower
Bathville, Armadale, W. Lothian EH48 2LZ
Tel: 01501-730671
Managing Director, V. J. Burgoyne

COLLEGES, ASSOCIATION OF SCOTTISH
Argyll Court, Castle Business Park, Stirling
FK9 4TY
Tel: 01786-892100
Chief Officer, T. Kelly

COMMERCE AND ENTERPRISE,
EDINBURGH CHAMBER OF
Conference House, The Exchange, 152
Morrison Street, Edinburgh EH3 8EB
Tel: 0131-477 7000
Chief Executive, P. Stillwell

COMMERCE AND MANUFACTURES,
GLASGOW CHAMBER OF
30 George Square, Glasgow G2 1EQ
Tel: 0141-204 2121
Chief Executive, P. V. Burdon

COMMERCE, SCOTTISH CHAMBERS OF
Conference House, The Exchange, 152
Morrison Street, Edinburgh EH3 8EB
Tel: 0131-477 8025
Director, L. Gold

CONVEYANCING AND EXECUTRY
SERVICES BOARD, SCOTTISH
Room 426, Mulberry House, 16-22 Picardy
Place, Edinburgh EH1 3YT
Tel: 0131-556 1945
Secretary, R. H. Paterson

CROFTERS UNION, SCOTTISH
Old Mill, Broadford, Isle of Skye IV49 9AQ
Tel: 01471-822529
Director, R. Dutton

DAIRY ASSOCIATION, SCOTTISH
46 Underwood Road, Paisley PA3 5TL
Tel: 0141-848 0009
Company Secretary, K. Hunter

DANCE TEACHERS' ALLIANCE, SCOTTISH
101 Park Road, Glasgow G4 9JE
Tel: 0141-339 8944
President, Ms S. McDonald

DECORATORS FEDERATION, SCOTTISH
222 Queensferry Road, Edinburgh EH4 2BN
Tel: 0131-343 3300
Director, A. McKinney

DESIGNERS, CHARTERED SOCIETY OF
(SCOTTISH BRANCH)
Randal Design, 90 Mitchell Street, Glasgow
G1 3NQ
Tel: 0141-221 2142
President, L. Gibbon

DEVELOPMENT AND INDUSTRY,
SCOTTISH COUNCIL
23 Chester Street, Edinburgh EH3 7ET
Tel: 0131-225 7911
Chief Executive, A. Wilson

DIETITIANS SCOTLAND
Queen Margaret University College,
Clerwood Terrace, Edinburgh EH12 8TS
Tel: 0131-317 3523
Senior Lecturer, Dr F. Pender

DIRECT MARKETING ASSOCIATION (UK)
LTD
41 Comely Bank, Edinburgh EH4 1AF
Tel: 0131-315 4422
Manager, Scottish Office, J. Scobie

DISPOSABLE PRODUCTS ASSOCIATION,
BRITISH
64 High Street, Kirkintilloch, Glasgow
G66 1PR
Tel: 0141-777 7272
Secretary, T. Bullimore

DRILLING CONTRACTORS (NORTH SEA
CHAPTER), INTERNATIONAL ASSOCIATION
OF
Wood International Centre, Craigshaw Drive,
West Tullos, Aberdeen AB12 3AG
Tel: 01224-874800
Director of European Offshore Affairs, D. Krahn

ENERGY, INSTITUTE OF
Mercaston Campus, 10 Colinton Road,
Edinburgh EH10 5DT
Tel: 0131-455 2253
Chairman, J. Currie

ENGINEERING CONTRACTORS,
FEDERATION OF CIVIL
105 West George Street, Glasgow G2 1QL
Tel: 0141-221 3181
Chief Executive, P. T. Hughes, OBE

ENGINEERING, SCOTTISH
105 West George Street, Glasgow G2 1QL
Tel: 0141-221 3181
Chief Executive, P. T. Hughes, OBE

ENGINEERS AND SHIPBUILDERS IN
SCOTLAND, INSTITUTION OF
Clydeport Building, 16 Robertson Street,
Glasgow G2 8DS
Tel: 0141-248 3721
President, Sir Robert Easton, CBE

ENVIRONMENTAL HEALTH INSTITUTE OF
SCOTLAND, ROYAL
3 Manor Place, Edinburgh EH3 7DH
Tel: 0131-225 6999
Director of Professional Development, T. Bell

ENVIRONMENTAL MANAGEMENT,
INSTITUTE OF
63 Northumberland Street, Edinburgh
EH3 6JQ
Tel: 0131-558 8810
Director, A. Peckham

FARM VENISON, SCOTTISH
Balcormo Mains, Leven, Fife KY8 5QF
Tel: 01333-360229
Chairman, J. Gilmour

FARMERS' UNION OF SCOTLAND,
NATIONAL
The Rural Centre, West Mains, Ingliston,
Newbridge, Midlothian EH28 8LT
Tel: 0131-472 4000
Chief Executive, E. R. Brown

FINANCIAL ENTERPRISE, SCOTTISH
91 George Street, Edinburgh EH2 3ES
Tel: 0131-225 6990
Executive Director, R. Perman

FISHERMEN'S ASSOCIATION LTD,
SCOTTISH PELAGIC
1 Frithside Street, Fraserburgh,
Aberdeenshire AB43 9AR
Tel: 01346-510714
Chairman, A. West

FISHERMEN'S ORGANIZATION, SCOTTISH
Braehead, 601 Queensferry Road, Edinburgh
EH4 6EA
Tel: 0131-339 7972
Chief Executive, I. MacSween

FOOD SCIENCE AND TECHNOLOGY,
INSTITUTE OF
Glasgow Scientific Services, 64 Everard
Drive, Glasgow G21 1XG
Tel: 0141-562 2203
Secretary, Scottish Branch, Dr C. McDonald

FORESTERS, INSTITUTE OF CHARTERED
7A St Colme Street, Edinburgh EH3 6AA
Tel: 0131-225 2705
Executive Director, Ms M. W. Dick, FRSA

FOREST PRODUCTS ASSOCIATION,
UNITED KINGDOM
Office 14, John Player Building, Stirling
Enterprise Park, Springbank Road, Stirling
FK7 7RP
Tel: 01786-449029
Executive Director, D. J. Sulman

FORESTRY CONTRACTING ASSOCIATION
Dalfling, Blairdaff, Inverurie, Aberdeenshire
AB51 5LA
Tel: 01467-651368
Chief Executive, B. Hudson

FORESTRY INDUSTRY COUNCIL
5 Dublin Street, Edinburgh EH1 3PG
Tel: 0131-556 0186
Executive Director, P. Wilson

FORESTRY SOCIETY, ROYAL SCOTTISH
Hagg-on-Esk, Canonbie, Dumfriesshire
DG14 0BE
Tel: 013873-71518
Director, A. G. Little

FREIGHT TRANSPORT ASSOCIATION LTD
Hermes House, Melville Terrace, Stirling
FK8 2ND
Tel: 01786-457500
Director-General, D. C. Green

GENERAL PRACTITIONERS, ROYAL
COLLEGE OF
25 Queen Street, Edinburgh EH2 1JA
Tel: 0131-247 3680
Chairman, Dr C. Hunter

GOLFERS' ASSOCIATION, PROFESSIONAL
Glenbervie Golf Club, Stirling Road, Larbert,
Falkirk FK5 4SJ
Tel: 01324-562451
Scottish Region Secretary, P. Lloyd

GROCERS FEDERATION, SCOTTISH
222-224 Queensferry Road, Edinburgh
EH4 2BN
Tel: 0131-343 3300
Chief Executive, L. Dewar

HARRIS TWEED AUTHORITY
6 Garden Road, Stornoway, Isle of Lewis
HS1 2QJ
Tel: 01851-702269
Chief Executive and Secretary, I. A. Mackenzie

HEADTEACHERS' ASSOCIATION OF
SCOTLAND
Faculty of Education, University of
Strathclyde, Southbrae Drive, Glasgow
G13 1PP
Tel: 0141-950 3298
General Secretary, G. S. Ross

HEATING AND VENTILATING
CONTRACTORS ASSOCIATION
Bush House, Bush Estate, Midlothian
EH26 0SB
Tel: 0131-445 5580
Regional Officer, B. Dyer

HOSPITALITY ASSOCIATION, BRITISH
(SCOTTISH OFFICE)
Saltire Court, 20 Castle Terrace, Edinburgh
EH1 2EN
Tel: 0131-200 7484
Secretary, J. Loudon

HOUSE-BUILDERS ASSOCIATION,
SCOTTISH
Carron Grange, Carrongrange Avenue,
Stenhousemuir FK5 3BQ
Tel: 01324-555550
Director, S. C. Patten

HOUSING FEDERATIONS, SCOTTISH
ASSOCIATION OF
38 York Place, Edinburgh EH1 3HU
Tel: 0131-556 5777
Director, D. Orr

HOUSING IN SCOTLAND, CHARTERED
INSTITUTE OF
6 Palmerston Place, Edinburgh EH12 5AA
Tel: 0131-225 4544
Director, A. Ferguson

INDEXERS, SOCIETY OF (SCOTTISH
GROUP)
Bentfield, 3 Marine Terrace, Gullane, E.
Lothian EH31 2AY
Tel: 01620-842247
Scottish Group Organizer, Mrs A. McCarthy

INDUSTRIAL SOCIETY
4 West Regent Street, Glasgow G2 1RW
Tel: 0141-332 2827
Chief Executive, Ms S. Neville

INFORMATION SCIENTISTS, INSTITUTE
OF (SCOTTISH BRANCH)
39 Mansion House Road, Edinburgh EH9 2JD
Tel: 0131-667 9006
Chairman, Miss M. Kvebekk

LAW ACCOUNTANTS IN SCOTLAND,
SOCIETY OF
17 Golden Square, Aberdeen AB10 1NY
Tel: 01224-408408
General Secretary, Mrs C. A. Pike

LAW LIBRARIANS GROUP, SCOTTISH
c/o Shepherd and Wedderburn, Saltire Court,
20 Castle Terrace, Edinburgh EH1 2ET
Tel: 0131-228 9900
Librarian, Ms F. McLaren

LAW SOCIETY OF SCOTLAND
26 Drumsheugh Gardens, Edinburgh EH3 7YR
Tel: 0131-226 7411
Secretary, D. R. Mill

LEATHER PRODUCERS' ASSOCIATION,
SCOTTISH
c/o Anderson Fyfe, 90 St Vincent Street,
Glasgow G2 5UB
Tel: 0141-248 4381

LIBRARY AND INFORMATION COUNCIL,
SCOTTISH
1 John Street, Hamilton ML3 7EU
Tel: 01698-458888
Director, R. Craig

LIBRARY ASSOCIATION, SCOTTISH
1 John Street, Hamilton ML3 7EU
Tel: 01698-458888
Director, R. Craig

LOCAL AUTHORITIES, CONVENTION OF
SCOTTISH (COSLA)
Rosebery House, 9 Haymarket Terrace,
Edinburgh EH12 5XZ
Tel: 0131-474 9200
Public Relations Officer, Ms M. Ferrier

LOCAL AUTHORITY CHIEF EXECUTIVES
AND SENIOR MANAGERS, SOCIETY OF
c/o Angus Council, The Cross, Forfar, Angus
DD8 1BX
Tel: 01307-473020
Hon. Secretary, A. Watson

LOCAL GOVERNMENT INFORMATION
UNIT, SCOTTISH
Room 507, Baltic Chambers, 50 Wellington
Street, Glasgow G2 6HJ
Tel: 0141-226 4636
Director, P. Vestri

MALT DISTILLERS ASSOCIATION OF
SCOTLAND
1 North Street, Elgin IV30 1UA
Tel: 01343-544077
Secretary, Grigor and Young Solicitors

MANAGEMENT EDUCATION AND
TRAINING IN SCOTLAND, ASSOCIATION
FOR (AMETS)
c/o Cottrell Building, University of Stirling,
Stirling FK9 4LA
Tel: 01786-467364
Chairman, Prof. F. Pignatelli

MANAGERS IN GENERAL PRACTICE,
ASSOCIATION OF
Netherwyndings Mill, Stonehaven,
Kincardineshire AB39 3UU
Tel: 01569-764284
Membership Administrator, Mrs D. Thomson

MARINE INDUSTRIES FEDERATION,
BRITISH
Westgate, Toward, Dunoon, Argyll PA23 7VA
Tel: 01369-870251
President, D. Wilkie

MARINE TRADES ASSOCIATION, SCOTTISH
18–20 Queens Road, Aberdeen AB15 4ZT
Tel: 01224-645454
Chief Executive, R. McColl

MARKETING, CHARTERED INSTITUTE OF
29 St Vincent Place, Glasgow G1 2DT
Tel: 0141-221 7700
Director, Scotland, G. Holliman

MEDICAL ASSOCIATION, BRITISH
(SCOTTISH OFFICE)
3 Hill Place, Edinburgh EH8 9EQ
Tel: 0131-662 4820
Scottish Secretary, Dr B. T. Potter

MESSENGERS-AT-ARMS AND SHERIFF
OFFICERS, SOCIETY OF
21 Ainslie Place, Edinburgh EH3 6AJ
Tel: 0131-225 9110
Administrative Secretary, A. Hogg

METALS FEDERATION, BRITISH
114 West George Street, Glasgow G2 1QF
Tel: 0141-332 7484
Regional Marketing Partner, G. Ross

MINING INSTITUTE OF SCOTLAND
26 Durness Avenue, Bearsden, Glasgow
G61 2AL
Tel: 0141-942 7348
Branch Secretary, Dr D. O. Davies

MOTOR TRADE ASSOCIATION, SCOTTISH
3 Palmerston Place, Edinburgh EH12 5AF
Tel: 0131-225 3643
Director, A. Dow

MUSEUMS COUNCIL, SCOTTISH
County House, 20–22 Torphichen Street,
Edinburgh EH3 8JB
Tel: 0131-229 7465
Director, Ms J. Ryder

NEWSPAPER PUBLISHERS ASSOCIATION,
SCOTTISH
48 Palmerston Place, Edinburgh EH12 5DE
Tel: 0131-220 4353
Director, J. B. Raeburn

NEWSPAPER SOCIETY, SCOTTISH DAILY
48 Palmerston Place, Edinburgh EH12 5DE
Tel: 0131-220 4353
Director, J. B. Raeburn

NURSING IN SCOTLAND, INDEPENDENT
FEDERATION OF
Office 5, 18 Crowhill Road, Bishopbriggs
G64 1QY
Tel: 0141-772 9222
General Secretary, Ms I. F. O'Neill

NURSING, MIDWIFERY AND HEALTH
VISITING FOR SCOTLAND, NATIONAL
BOARD FOR
22 Queen Street, Edinburgh EH2 1NT
Tel: 0131-226 7371
Chief Executive, D. C. Benton

NURSING OF THE UNITED KINGDOM,
ROYAL COLLEGE OF
42 South Oswald Road, Edinburgh EH9 2HH
Tel: 0131-662 1010
Scottish Board Secretary, Ms J. Andrews

OFFSHORE CONTRACTORS' ASSOCIATION
12 Queens Road, Aberdeen AB15 4ZT
Tel: 01224-645450
Chief Executive, I. M. Bell

OFFSHORE OPERATORS ASSOCIATION LTD,
UK
9 Albyn Terrace, Aberdeen AB10 1YP
Tel: 01224-626652
Director-General, J. Wils

OPTOMETRISTS, SCOTTISH COMMITTEE
OF
7 Queens Buildings, Queensferry Road,
Rosyth, Fife KY11 2RA
Tel: 01383-419444
Secretary, D. S. Hutton

PAPER FEDERATION OF GREAT BRITAIN
5 Dublin Street, Edinburgh EH1 3PG
Tel: 0131-556 0122
District Secretary, H. W. Mill

PASSENGER TRANSPORT UK,
CONFEDERATION OF
41 Laigh Road, Newton Mearns, Glasgow
G77 5EX
Tel: 0141-577 6455
Regional Secretary, P. Thompson

PHARMACEUTICAL FEDERATION,
SCOTTISH
135 Wellington Street, Glasgow G2 2XD
Tel: 0141-221 1235
Secretary, F. E. J. McCrossin

PHARMACEUTICAL SOCIETY OF GREAT
BRITAIN, ROYAL
36 York Place, Edinburgh EH1 3HU
Tel: 0131-556 4386
Secretary, Dr S. Stevens

PHYSICIANS AND SURGEONS OF
GLASGOW, ROYAL COLLEGE OF
232–242 St Vincent Street, Glasgow G2 5RJ
Tel: 0141-221 6072
Hon. Secretary, Dr C. Semple

PHYSICIANS OF EDINBURGH, ROYAL
COLLEGE OF
9 Queen Street, Edinburgh EH2 1JQ
Tel: 0131-225 7324
Secretary, Dr A. C. Parker

PLUMBING EMPLOYERS' FEDERATION,
SCOTTISH AND NORTHERN IRELAND
2 Walker Street, Edinburgh EH3 7LB
Tel: 0131-225 2255
Director and Secretary, R. D. Burgon

POLYOLEFIN TEXTILES ASSOCIATION,
BRITISH
c/o Priestoun, Edzell, Angus DD9 7UD
Tel: 01356-648521
Secretary, R. H. B. Learoyd

PRINT EMPLOYERS FEDERATION,
SCOTTISH
48 Palmerston Place, Edinburgh EH12 5DE
Tel: 0131-220 4353
Director, J. B. Raeburn

PROCURATOR FISCALS' SOCIETY
Stuart House, 181 High Street, Linlithgow
EH49 7EN
Tel: 01506-844556
Procurator Officer, Ms L. Ruxton

PRODUCERS ALLIANCE FOR CINEMA AND
TELEVISION
249 West George Street, Glasgow G2 4QE
Tel: 0141-302 1720
Manager, Ms M. Scott

PROPERTY MANAGERS ASSOCIATION
SCOTLAND LTD
2 Blythswood Square, Glasgow G2 4AD
Tel: 0141-248 4672
Secretary, J. Millar

PUBLIC FINANCE AND ACCOUNTANCY,
CHARTERED INSTITUTE OF
CIPFA Scotland, 8 North West Circus Place,
Edinburgh EH3 6ST
Tel: 0131-220 4316
Director, I. P. Doig

PUBLIC RELATIONS CONSULTANTS
ASSOCIATION, SCOTTISH
c/o Barkers Scotland, 234 West George
Street, Glasgow G42 4QY
Tel: 0141-248 5030
Chairman, N. McGhee

PUBLISHERS' ASSOCIATION, SCOTTISH
Scottish Book Centre, 137 Dundee Street,
Edinburgh EH11 1BG
Tel: 0131-228 6866
Director, Ms L. Fannin

RETAIL CONSORTIUM, SCOTTISH
222–224 Queensferry Road, Edinburgh
EH4 2BN
Tel: 0131-332 6619
Director, P. Browne

RETAIL NEWSAGENTS, NATIONAL
FEDERATION OF
6A Weir Street, Falkirk FK1 1RA
Tel: 01324-625293
Chief Executive, R. Clarke

ROAD HAULAGE ASSOCIATION LTD
Roadway House, 17 Royal Terrace, Glasgow
G3 7NY
Tel: 0141-332 9201
Director-General, S. J. Norris

ROOFING CONTRACTORS LTD, NATIONAL
FEDERATION OF
PO Box 28011, Edinburgh EH16 6WN
Tel: 0131-467 1998
Secretary, A. McKinney

SALMON GROWERS ASSOCIATION, THE
SCOTTISH
Drummond House, Scott Street, Perth
PH1 5EJ
Tel: 01738-635420
Chief Executive, W. J. J. Crowe

SCOTCH WHISKY ASSOCIATION
20 Atholl Crescent, Edinburgh EH3 8HF
Tel: 0131-222 9200
Director-General, H. Morison

SELECT
Bush House, Bush Estate, Midlothian
EH26 0SB
Tel: 0131-445 5577
Managing Director, M. D. Goodwin, OBE

SHELLFISH GROWERS, ASSOCIATION OF
SCOTTISH
Mountview, Ardvasar, Isle of Skye IV45 8RU
Tel: 01471-844324
Chairman, D. McLeod

SIGN LANGUAGE INTERPRETERS,
SCOTTISH ASSOCIATION OF
54 Queen Street, Edinburgh EH2 3NS
Tel: 0131-225 9995
Director, Mrs D. Mair

SKIN, HIDE AND LEATHER TRADERS
ASSOCIATION LTD
Douglas House, Douglas Road, Melrose,
Roxburghshire TD6 9QT
Tel: 01896-822233
Secretary-General, A. D. Cox, MBE

SMALL BUSINESSES, FEDERATION OF
Scottish Office, 74 Berkeley Street, Glasgow
G3 7DS
Tel: 0141-221 0775
Scotland Parliamentary Officer, J. Downie

SOCIAL WORK, CENTRAL COUNCIL FOR
EDUCATION AND TRAINING IN
78–80 George Street, Edinburgh EH2 3BU
Tel: 0131-220 0093
Head, Ms G. Doherty

SOFTWARE FEDERATION, SCOTTISH
Innovation Centre, 1 Michaelson Square,
Kirkton Campus, Livingston EH54 7DP
Tel: 01506-472200
Chairman, R. Dunn

SPEED
14 and 19 Hardengreen Business Centre,
Dalhousie Road, Eskbank EH22 3NX
Tel: 0131-654 1500
Secretary, I. Rodgers

SURGEONS OF EDINBURGH, ROYAL
COLLEGE OF
Nicolson Street, Edinburgh EH8 9DW
Tel: 0131-527 1600
Secretary, Miss A. S. Campbell

SURVEYORS, ROYAL INSTITUTION OF
CHARTERED
9 Manor Place, Edinburgh EH3 7DN
Tel: 0131-225 7078
Director, Ms E. Masterman

TEACHERS, PROFESSIONAL ASSOCIATION
OF
4–6 Oak Lane, Edinburgh EH12 6XH
Tel: 0131-317 8282
Secretary for Scotland, R. J. S. Christie

TEACHING COUNCIL FOR SCOTLAND,
GENERAL
Clerwood House, 96 Clermiston Road,
Edinburgh EH12 6UT
Tel: 0131-314 6000
Registrar, D. I. M. Sutherland

TIMBER FRAME INDUSTRIES, SCOTTISH
CONSORTIUM OF
TRADA Offices, Office 30, Stirling Business
Centre, Well Green Place, Stirling FK8 2DZ
Tel: 01786-445075
Chairman, R. Mackelvie

TIMBER GROWERS ASSOCIATION LTD
5 Dublin Street Lane South, Edinburgh
EH1 3PX
Tel: 0131-538 7111
Executive Chairman, L. Yull

TIMBER TRADE ASSOCIATION, SCOTTISH
Office 14, John Player Building, Stirling
Enterprise Park, Springbank Road, Stirling
FK7 7RP
Tel: 01786-451623
Secretary, D. J. Sulman

TOWN PLANNING INSTITUTE, ROYAL
57 Melville Street, Edinburgh EH3 7HL
Tel: 0131-226 1959
Director, G. U'ren

TRANSPORT, CHARTERED INSTITUTE OF
22 Westbourne Drive, Bearsden, Glasgow
G61 4BH
Tel: 0141-332 2258
Chairman, Scottish Branch, S. Hindshaw

TROUT, SCOTTISH QUALITY
Craigs House, 82 Craigs Road, East Craigs,
Edinburgh EH12 8NJ
Tel: 0131-317 2503
Chief Executive, Ms M. Mitchell

VETERINARY ASSOCIATION, BRITISH
Scottish Branch, c/o Animal Health Office, 32
Reidhaven Street, Elgin IV30 1VE
Tel: 01343-543871
Hon. Secretary, F. Sless

WATER AND ENVIRONMENTAL
MANAGEMENT, CHARTERED
INSTITUTION OF
c/o Scottish Environment Protection Agency,
Erskine Court, Castle Business Park, Stirling
FK9 4TR
Tel: 01786-457700
Chief Executive, A. Paton

WATER OFFICERS, INSTITUTION OF
3 Provost Walk, Monifieth, Angus DD5 4SJ
Tel: 01382-563501
Scottish Area Secretary, L. Scobie

WIND ENERGY ASSOCIATION, BRITISH
(SCOTTISH BRANCH)
c/o Energy Unlimited, 5 Leighton Avenue,
Dunblane, Stirling FK15 0EB
Tel: 01786-825839
Chairman, R. Forrest

WOOD TECHNOLOGY, SCOTTISH
INSTITUTE FOR
University of Abertay Dundee, Bell Street,
Dundee DD1 1HG
Tel: 01382-308930
Technical Director, Dr D. Sinclair

WRIGHTS' AND BUILDERS' ASSOCIATION,
SCOTTISH MASTER
98 West George Street, Glasgow G2 1PJ
Tel: 0141-333 1679
General Secretary, J. F. Lindsay

TRADE UNIONS

The Certification Officer is responsible for certifying the independence of trade unions, receiving and scrutinizing annual returns from trade unions, dealing with complaints about trade union elections and ensuring compliance with statutory requirements governing political funds and union mergers. It is expected that in autumn 1999 the Certification Officer will become responsible for assisting individuals taking action against their trade union when they have not been afforded their statutory rights or when specific union rules have been breached; these duties were the responsibility of the Commissioner for the Rights of Trade Union Members, a post which is being abolished.

The Central Arbitration Committee arbitrates in industrial disputes between trade unions and employers, and determines disclosure of information complaints.

CERTIFICATION OFFICE FOR TRADE UNIONS AND EMPLOYERS' ASSOCIATIONS, SCOTLAND
58 Frederick Street, Edinburgh EH2 1LN
Tel: 0131-226 3224
Assistant Certification Officer for Scotland, J. L. J. Craig

THE CENTRAL ARBITRATION COMMITTEE
Brandon House, 180 Borough High Street, London SE1 1LW
Tel: 0171-210 3737/8
Chairman, Prof. Sir John Wood, CBE
Secretary, S. Gouldstone

SCOTTISH TRADES UNION CONGRESS
333 Woodlands Road, Glasgow G3 6NG
Tel: 0141-337 8100

The Congress was formed in 1897 and acts as a national centre for the trade union movement in Scotland. The STUC promotes the rights and welfare of those in work and helps the unemployed. It helps its member unions to promote membership in new areas and industries, and campaigns for rights at work for all employees, including part-time and temporary workers, whether union members or not. It makes representations to government and employers. The Annual Congress in April elects a 38-member General Council on the basis of six industrial sections.

In 1999 the STUC consisted of 46 unions with a membership of 629,360 and 34 directly affiliated Trade Councils.

Chairman, M. Smith
General Secretary, B. Speirs

UNIONS AFFILIATED TO THE SCOTTISH TRADES UNION CONGRESS
as at 1 July 1999

AMALGAMATED ENGINEERING AND ELECTRICAL UNION (AEEU)
145–165 West Regent Street, Glasgow G2 4RZ
Tel: 0141-248 7131
National Officer, D. Carrigan

ASSOCIATED SOCIETY OF LOCOMOTIVE ENGINEERS AND FIREMEN (ASLEF)
1 Coxton Place, Glasgow G33 4EW
Tel: 0141-774 7395
Scottish Secretary, P. O'Connor

ASSOCIATION OF FIRST DIVISION CIVIL SERVANTS
2 Caxton Street, London SW1H 0QH
Tel: 0171-343 1111
General Secretary, J. Baume

ASSOCIATION OF UNIVERSITY TEACHERS
6 Castle Street, Edinburgh EH2 3AT
Tel: 0131-226 6694
Regional Secretary, D. Bleiman

BRITISH ACTORS' EQUITY ASSOCIATION
114 Union Street, Glasgow G1 3QQ
Tel: 0141-248 2472
Scottish Secretary, L. Boswell

BRITISH AIR LINE PILOTS ASSOCIATION (BALPA)
81 New Road, Harlington, Hayes, Middx UB3 5BG
Tel: 0181-476 4000
General Secretary, C. Darke

BRITISH DIETETIC ASSOCIATION
Department of Dietetics, Raigmore Hospital, Old Perth Road, Inverness IV2 3UJ
Tel: 01463-764000
Scottish Officer, Mrs M. Butters

BRITISH ORTHOPTIC SOCIETY
Orthoptic Department, Perth Royal Infirmary, Taymount Terrace, Perth PH1 1NX
Tel: 01738-623311
Scottish Regional Representative, Mrs J. Stewart

Orthoptic Department, Royal Alexandra
Hospital, Corsebar Road, Paisley PA2 2PN
Tel: 0141-887 9111
Scottish Regional Representative, Mrs D. Russell

BROADCASTING, ENTERTAINMENT,
CINEMATOGRAPH AND THEATRE UNION
(BECTU)
114 Union Street, Glasgow G2 3QQ
Tel: 0141-248 9558
Scottish Field Officer, P. McManus

THE CHARTERED SOCIETY OF
PHYSIOTHERAPY
14 Bedford Row, London WC1R 4ED
Tel: 0171-306 6666
Chief Executive, P. Gray

COLLIERY OFFICIALS AND STAFF AREA
NUM
7 Eastercraig Gardens, Saline, Dunfermline
KY12 9TH
Tel: 01383-852526
Secretary, A. Kenney

COMMUNICATION WORKERS UNION
Dundee (E) Branch, Room 201, Telephone
Exchange, 8 Willisdon Street, Dundee DD1
1DB
Tel: 01382-223612/302385
Scottish Secretary, M. Keenan

Granthouse Inn, Duns, Berwickshire
TD11 3RW
Scottish Secretary (Duns), T. McGee

COMMUNITY AND DISTRICT NURSING
ASSOCIATION
Fountain House, 1–3 Woodside Crescent,
Glasgow G3 7UJ
Tel: 0141-333 0335
Professional Officer, Ms S. Russell

THE EDUCATIONAL INSTITUTE OF
SCOTLAND
46 Moray Place, Edinburgh EH3 6BH
Tel: 0131-225 6244
General Secretary, R. A. Smith

ENGINEERS' AND MANAGERS'
ASSOCIATION
30 New Street, Musselburgh, Midlothian
EH21 6JP
Tel: 0131-665 4487
National Officer, Ms A. Douglas

THE FIRE BRIGADES UNION
4th Floor, 52 St Enoch Square, Glasgow
G1 4AA
Tel: 0141-221 2309
Scottish Regional Secretary, T. Tierney

GMB
(formerly General, Municipal, Boilermakers
and Allied Trades Union)
Fountain House, 1–3 Woodside Crescent,
Glasgow G3 7UJ
Tel: 0141-332 8641
Regional Secretary, R. Parker

GRAPHICAL, PAPER AND MEDIA UNION
Graphical House, 222 Clyde Street, Glasgow
G1 4JT
Tel: 0141-221 7730
Scottish Branch Secretary, D. Munro

76 Constitution Street, Leith, Edinburgh
EH6 6RP
Tel: 0131-553 5880
East of Scotland Branch Secretary, G. Lamont

INDEPENDENT UNION OF HALIFAX STAFF
Simmons House, 46 Old Bath Road, Charvil,
Reading RG10 9QR
Tel: 0118-934 1808
General Secretary, G. Nichols

INSTITUTION OF PROFESSIONALS,
MANAGERS AND SPECIALISTS
18 Melville Terrace, Stirling FK8 2NQ
Tel: 01786-465999
National Officer, A. Denney

IRON AND STEEL TRADES
CONFEDERATION
20 Quarry Street, Hamilton ML3 7AR
Tel: 01698-422924
Divisional Officer, J. Brandon

MANUFACTURING, SCIENCE AND
FINANCE UNION (MSF)
1 Woodlands Terrace, Glasgow G3 6DD
Tel: 0141-331 1216
Regional Secretary, J. Wall

MUSICIANS' UNION
11 Sandyford Place, Sauchiehall Street,
Glasgow G3 7NB
Tel: 0141-248 3723
Scottish District Organizer, I. Smith

NASUWT (NATIONAL ASSOCIATION OF
SCHOOLMASTERS/UNION OF WOMEN
TEACHERS)
5th Floor, Stock Exchange House, 7 Nelson
Mandela Place, Glasgow G2 1AY
Tel: 0141-229 5790
Scotland Official, Ms C. Fox

NATIONAL ASSOCIATION OF COLLIERY
OVERMEN, DEPUTIES AND SHOTFIRERS
19 Cadzow Street, Hamilton ML3 6EE
Tel: 01698-284981
Scottish Area Secretary, R. Letham

NATIONAL LEAGUE OF THE BLIND AND DISABLED
36 Cardross Place, Dundee DD4 9RE
Tel: 01382-815624
Scottish Secretary, Mrs L. Stewart

NATIONAL UNION OF JOURNALISTS (NUJ)
114 Union Street, Glasgow G1 3QQ
Tel: 0141-248 6648
Scottish Organizer, P. Holleran

NATIONAL UNION OF KNITWEAR,
FOOTWEAR AND APPAREL TRADES
Orwell, 6 London Road, Kilmarnock KA3 7AD
Tel: 01563-527476
District Secretary, J. Steele

NATIONAL UNION OF MARINE, AVIATION
AND SHIPPING TRANSPORT OFFICERS
Oceanair House, 750-760 High Road,
London E11 3BB
Tel: 0181-989 6677
General Secretary, B. D. Orrell

NATIONAL UNION OF MINEWORKERS
(NUM)
30 New Street, Musselburgh, Midlothian
EH21 6JP
Tel: 0131-665 4111
Scottish Area Secretary, N. Wilson

NATIONAL UNION OF RAIL, MARITIME
AND TRANSPORT WORKERS (RMT)
180 Hope Street, Glasgow G2 2UE
Tel: 0141-332 1117
Divisional Organizer, P. McGarry

PUBLIC AND COMMERCIAL SERVICES
UNION (PCS)
6 Hillside Crescent, Edinburgh EH7 5AR
Tel: 0131-556 0407
Joint Scottish Officers, P. Kelly; M. McCann

SCOTTISH CARPET WORKERS' UNION
Viewfield Business Centre, 62 Viewfield
Road, Ayr KA8 8HH
Tel: 01292-261676
Secretary, R. Smillie

SCOTTISH FURTHER AND HIGHER
EDUCATION ASSOCIATION
Suite 2C, Ingram House, 227 Ingram Street,
Glasgow G1 1DA
Tel: 0141-221 0118
General Secretary, E. H. Smith

SCOTTISH PRISON OFFICERS'
ASSOCIATION
21 Calder Road, Edinburgh EH11 3PF
Tel: 0131-443 8105
General Secretary, D. Turner

SCOTTISH SECONDARY TEACHERS'
ASSOCIATION
15 Dundas Street, Edinburgh EH3 6QG
Tel: 0131-556 5919
General Secretary, D. H. Eaglesham

SOCIETY OF CHIROPODISTS AND
PODIATRISTS
53 Welbeck Street, London W1M 7HE
Tel: 0171-486 3381
Chief Executive, Ms H. B. De Lyon

THE SOCIETY OF RADIOGRAPHERS
6 Victoria Road, Brookfield, Johnstone,
Renfrewshire PA5 8TZ
Tel: 01505-382039
Scotland Officer, Ms E. Stow

SOCIETY OF TELECOM EXECUTIVES
22A Caroline Street, St Paul's Square,
Birmingham B3 1UE
Tel: 0121-236 2637
Scottish Secretary, Ms. S. Clowes

TRANSPORT AND GENERAL WORKERS'
UNION (TGWU)
290 Bath Street, Glasgow G2 4LD
Tel: 0141-332 7321
Scottish Secretary, J. Elsby

TRANSPORT SALARIED STAFFS'
ASSOCIATION
180 Hope Street, Glasgow G2 2UE
Tel: 0141-332 4698
Scottish Secretary, R.S. King

UNiFI
146 Argyle Street, Glasgow G2 8BL
Tel: 0141-221 6475/6
Deputy General Secretary, S. Boyle

UNION OF CONSTRUCTION, ALLIED
TRADES AND TECHNICIANS (UCATT)
6 Fitzroy Place, Glasgow G3 7RL
Tel: 0141-221 4893
Scottish Secretary, A. S. Ritchie

UNION OF SHOP, DISTRIBUTIVE AND
ALLIED WORKERS (USDAW)
Muirfield, 342 Albert Drive, Glasgow
G41 5PG
Tel: 0141-427 6561
Scottish Divisional Officer, F. Whitelaw

UNISON
Unison House, 14 West Campbell Street,
Glasgow G2 6RX
Tel: 0141-332 0006
Scottish Secretary, M. Smith

ARTS ORGANIZATIONS

The following list of arts organizations includes those organizations and institutions which are in receipt of revenue grants or three-year funding from the Scottish Arts Council (*see* page 68).

7:84 THEATRE COMPANY
333 Woodlands Road, Glasgow G3 6NG
Tel: 0141-334 6686

AN LANNTAIR
Town Hall, South Beach, Stornoway, Isle of Lewis
Tel: 01851-703307

AN TUIREANN
Arts Centre, Struan Road, Portree, Isle of Skye IV51 9EG
Tel: 01478-613306

ART.TM (HIGHLAND PRINTMAKERS WORKSHOP)
20 Bank Street, Inverness IV1 1QE
Tel: 01463-712240

ARTLINK (EDINBURGH AND THE LOTHIANS)
13A Spittal Street, Edinburgh EH3 9DY
Tel: 0131-229 3555

ART IN PARTNERSHIP
233 Cowgate, Edinburgh EH1 1NY
Tel: 0131-225 4463

ARVON AT MONIACK MHOR
Teavarran, Kiltarlity, Beauly, Inverness-shire IV4 7HT
Tel: 01463-741675

ASSEMBLY DIRECT
2nd Floor, 89 Giles Street, Edinburgh EH6 6BZ
Tel: 0131-553 4000

ASSOCIATION FOR SCOTTISH LITERARY STUDIES
Department of Scottish History, University of Glasgow, 9 University Gardens, Glasgow G12 8QH
Tel: 0141-330 5309

BOILERHOUSE THEATRE COMPANY
c/o Royal Lyceum Theatre, 30B Grindlay Street, Edinburgh EH3 9AX
Tel: 0131-221 1677

BORDERLINE THEATRE COMPANY
North Harbour Street, Ayr KA8 8AA
Tel: 01292-281010

BT SCOTTISH ENSEMBLE
2 Anchor Lane, Glasgow G1 2HW
Tel: 0141-221 2222

BYRE THEATRE
Abbey Street, St Andrews KY16 9LA
Tel: 01334-476288

CAPPELLA NOVA
172 Hyndland Road, Glasgow G12 9HZ
Tel: 0141-552 0634

CENTRE FOR CONTEMPORARY ARTS
350 Sauchiehall Street, Glasgow G3 3JD
Tel: 0141-332 0522

CITIZENS' THEATRE
Gorbals, Glasgow G5 9DS
Tel: 0141-429 5561

COLLECTIVE GALLERY
22–28 Cockburn Street, Edinburgh EH1 1NY
Tel: 0131-220 1260

COMMUNICADO THEATRE COMPANY
2 Hill Street, Edinburgh EH2 3JZ
Tel: 0131-624 4040

CRAWFORD ARTS CENTRE
93 North Street, St Andrews KY16 9AL
Tel: 01334-474610

CUMBERNAULD THEATRE
Kildrum, Cumbernauld G67 2BN
Tel: 01236-737235

DUMFRIES AND GALLOWAY ARTS ASSOCIATION
c/o Dumfries and Galloway City Council, 30 Edinburgh Road, Dumfries DG1 1JQ
Tel: 01387-260000

DUNDEE CONTEMPORARY ARTS
152 Nethergate, Dundee DD1 4DY
Tel: 01382-432000

DUNDEE REPERTORY THEATRE
Tay Square, Dundee DD1 1PB
Tel: 01382-227684

EDEN COURT THEATRE
Bishop's Road, Inverness IV3 5SA
Tel: 01463-234234

EDINBURGH BOOK FESTIVAL
Scottish Book Centre, 137 Dundee Street,
  Edinburgh EH11 1BG
Tel: 0131-228 5444

EDINBURGH CONTEMPORARY ARTS
TRUST
16 Clerwood Gardens, Edinburgh EH12 2PT
Tel: 0131-539 8877

EDINBURGH FESTIVAL FRINGE SOCIETY
The Fringe Office, 180 High Street,
  Edinburgh EH1 1QS
Tel: 0131-226 5257

EDINBURGH INTERNATIONAL FESTIVAL
SOCIETY
Edinburgh Festival Centre, Castlehill,
  Edinburgh EH1 1ND
Tel: 0131-473 2000

EDINBURGH PRINTMAKERS WORKSHOP
23 Union Street, Edinburgh EH1 3LR
Tel: 0131-557 2479

EDINBURGH SCULPTURE WORKSHOP
25 Hawthornvale, Edinburgh EH6 4JT
Tel: 0131-551 4490

ENTERPRISE MUSIC SCOTLAND
Westburn House, Westburn Park, Aberdeen
  AB2 5DE
Tel: 01224-574422

FÈISAN NAN GÀIDHEAL
Nicholson Buildings, Wentworth Street,
  Portree, Isle of Skye IV51 9EJ
Tel: 01478-613355

FRUITMARKET GALLERY
29 Market Street, Edinburgh EH1 1DF
Tel: 0131-225 2383

GAELIC BOOKS COUNCIL
22 Mansfield Street, Glasgow G11 5QP
Tel: 0141-337 6211

GLASGOW PRINT STUDIO
22 King Street, Glasgow G1 2HF
Tel: 0141-552 0704

HEBRIDES ENSEMBLE
11 Palmerston Place, Edinburgh EH12 5AF
Tel: 0131-225 2006

HI ARTS (HIGHLAND AND ISLANDS ARTS)
Bridge House, Bridge Street, Inverness
  IV1 1QR
Tel: 01463-234171

THE LEMON TREE
5 West North Street, Aberdeen AB2 3AT
Tel: 01224-642230

LYTH ARTS CENTRE
Lyth, nr Wick, Caithness KW1 4UD
Tel: 01955-641270

MACROBERT ARTS CENTRE
University of Stirling, Stirling FK9 4LA
Tel: 01786-467155

NATIONAL FEDERATION OF MUSIC
SOCIETIES SCOTLAND
63 Threestanes Road, Stratheven, Lanarkshire
  ML10 6EB
Tel: 01357-522138

NVA
62 Kelvingrove Street, Glasgow G3 7SA
Tel: 0141-353 3223

PARAGON ENSEMBLE SCOTLAND
20 Renfrew Street, Glasgow G2 3BW
Tel: 0141-322 9903

PEACOCK PRINTMAKERS
21 Castle Street, Aberdeen AB1 1AJ
Tel: 01224-639539

PERTH REPERTORY THEATRE
High Street, Perth PH1 5UW
Tel: 01783-472700

PIER ARTS CENTRE
Victoria Street, Stromness, Orkney KW16 3AA
Tel: 01856-850209

PITLOCHRY FESTIVAL THEATRE
Pitlochry PH16 5DR
Tel: 01796-472680

PORTFOLIO GALLERY
43 Candlemaker Row, Edinburgh EH1 3LR
Tel: 0131-220 1911

PROISEACT NAN EALAN/NATIONAL
GAELIC ARTS AGENCY
10 Shell Street, Stornoway HS1 2BS
Tel: 01851-704493

PROJECT ABILITY
Centre for Developmental Arts, 18 Albion
  Street, Glasgow G1 1LH
Tel: 0141-552 2822

PUPPET AND ANIMATION FESTIVAL
The Netherbow Arts Centre, 43–45 High
Street, Edinburgh EH1 1SR
Tel: 0131-557 5724

ROYAL LYCEUM THEATRE COMPANY
Grindlay Street, Edinburgh EH3 9AX
Tel: 0131-229 7404

ROYAL SCOTTISH NATIONAL ORCHESTRA
73 Claremont Street, Glasgow G3 7HA
Tel: 0141-226 3868

ST MAGNUS FESTIVAL
Stramdal, Nicolson Street, Kirkwall, Orkney
KW15 1BD
Tel: 01856-872952

SCOTTISH BALLET
261 West Princes Street, Glasgow G4 9EE
Tel: 0141-331 2931

SCOTTISH CHAMBER ORCHESTRA
4 Royal Terrace, Edinburgh EH7 5AB
Tel: 0131-557 6800

SCOTTISH DANCE THEATRE
Dundee Repertory Theatre, Tay Square,
Dundee DD1 1PB
Tel: 01382-342600

SCOTTISH INTERNATIONAL CHILDREN'S
FESTIVAL
45A George Street, Edinburgh EH2 2HT
Tel: 0131-225 8050

SCOTTISH MUSIC INFORMATION CENTRE
1 Bowmont Gardens, Glasgow G12 9LR
Tel: 0141-334 6393

SCOTTISH OPERA
39 Elmbank Crescent, Glasgow G2 4PT
Tel: 0141-248 4567

SCOTTISH POETRY LIBRARY
Tweeddale Court, 14 High Street, Edinburgh
EH1 1TE
Tel: 0131-557 2876

SCOTTISH PUBLISHERS ASSOCIATION
Scottish Book Centre, 137 Dundee Street,
Edinburgh EH11 1BG
Tel: 0131-228 6866

SCOTTISH SCULPTURE WORKSHOP
1 Main Street, Lumsden, Huntly,
Aberdeenshire AB54 4JN
Tel: 01464-861372

SCOTTISH STORYTELLING CENTRE
The Netherbow Arts Centre, 43–45 High
Street, Edinburgh EH1 1SR
Tel: 0131-556 9579

SCOTTISH YOUTH DANCE THEATRE
69 Dublin Street, Edinburgh EH3 6NS
Tel: 0131-556 8844

SHETLAND ARTS TRUST
Pitt Lane, Lerwick, Shetland ZE1 0DN
Tel: 01595-694001

STILLS GALLERY
23 Cockburn Street, Edinburgh EH1 1BP
Tel: 0131-622 6200

STREET LEVEL
26 King Street, Glasgow G1 5QP
Tel: 0141-552 2151

SUSPECT CULTURE
Strathclyde Arts Centre, 12 Washington
Street, Glasgow G3 8AZ
Tel: 0141-248 8052

TAG THEATRE COMPANY
18 Albion Street, Glasgow G1 1LH
Tel: 0141-552 4949

TALBOT RICE GALLERY
Old College, South Bridge, Edinburgh
EH8 9YL
Tel: 0131-650 2211

THEATRE WORKSHOP
34 Hamilton Place, Edinburgh EH3 5AX
Tel: 0131-226 5425

TOSG THEATRE COMPANY
Sàbhal Mor Ostaig, Sleat, Isle of Skye
IV44 8RQ
Tel: 01471-844443

TRADITIONAL MUSIC AND SONG
ASSOCIATION
95–97 St Leonard's Street, Edinburgh
EH8 9QY
Tel: 0131-667 5587

TRAMWAY
c/o Tramway Marketing, Cultural Leisure
Services, Glasgow City Council, 229
George Street, Glasgow G1 1QU
Tel: 0141-287 5429

TRANSMISSION GALLERY
28 King Street, Trongate, Glasgow G1 5QP
Tel: 0141-552 4813

TRAVERSE THEATRE
Cambridge Street, Edinburgh EH1 2ED
Tel: 0131-228 3223

TRAVELLING GALLERY
City Arts Centre, 2 Market Street, Edinburgh
EH1 1DE
Tel: 0131-529 3930

TRON THEATRE
63 Trongate, Glasgow G1 5HB
Tel: 0141-552 4267

WASPS
256 Alexandra Parade, Glasgow G31 3AJ
Tel: 0141-554 2499

SPORT AND PHYSICAL RECREATION ORGANIZATIONS

A wide variety of sports is played in Scotland, of which football (soccer and rugby) and golf are among the most popular. The Scottish Football Association (soccer) and the Scottish Football Union (rugby) were both founded in 1873. The first Open Golf Championship was held in 1860 in St Andrews, although the game itself has been played for several centuries. The ancient Scottish games of curling and shinty are still popular, and the Highlands offer good conditions for mountain and field sports. Highland games are held in many places across Scotland in the summer and combine traditional sporting activities such as tossing the caber and hammer throwing with Highland dancing, piping and other entertainments.

In 1994-6 about 60 per cent of the population participated in some form of sport.

SPORTS PARTICIPATION BY GENDER 1994–6
(percentages)

Sex	All sports	Selected sports*
Male	65	56
Female	55	43

SPORTS PARTICIPATION BY AGE 1994–6
(percentages)

Age	All sports	Selected sports
16–24	80	75
25–34	72	65
35–54	62	51
55+	39	24

* Excludes walking, dancing, snooker, billiards, pool
Source: Scottish Sports Council

Support for the development of sport and physical recreation is the responsibility of sportscotland (see below). Sportscotland is the advisory body to the Scottish Parliament and aims to increase participation in sport, particularly among young people, and to develop potential and increase Scottish sporting success at the highest levels. It is responsible for the Scottish national sports centres, which provide professionally coached training courses and a training base for several national squads.

SPORTSCOTLAND
(formerly the Scottish Sports Council)
Caledonia House, South Gyle, Edinburgh
EH12 9DQ
Tel: 0131-317 7200
Chief Executive, F. A. L. Alstead, CBE

SCOTTISH NATIONAL SPORTS CENTRES
Cumbrae, Millport, Isle of Cumbrae
KA28 0HQ
Tel: 01475-530757
Glenmore Lodge, Aviemore, Inverness-shire
PH22 1QU
Tel: 01479-861256
Inverclyde, Burnside Road, Largs, Ayrshire
KA30 8RW
Tel: 01475-674666

The following list includes the main organizations concerned with sports and physical recreation in Scotland.

AEROMODELLING

SCOTTISH AEROMODELLERS ASSOCATION
79 Provost Milne Grove, South Queensferry,
Edinburgh EH30 9PL
Tel: 0131-331 3322
Secretary, H. West

ANGLING

THE SALMON AND TROUT ASSOCIATION
(SCOTLAND)
PO Box 2005, Aberfeldy, Perthshire PH15 2YH
Tel: 01887-829239
Administrator, P. Fothringham

SCOTTISH ANGLERS NATIONAL
ASSOCIATION
Caledonia House, South Gyle, Edinburgh
EH12 9DQ
Tel: 0131-339 8808
Administrator, Mrs H. Bull

SCOTTISH FEDERATION FOR COARSE
ANGLING
8 Longbraes Gardens, Kirkcaldy, Fife
KY2 5YG
Tel: 01592-642242
Secretary, S. Clerkin

SCOTTISH FEDERATION OF SEA ANGLERS
Caledonia House, South Gyle, Edinburgh
EH12 9DQ
Tel: 0131-317 7192
Administrator, D. Wilkie

ARCHERY

SCOTTISH ARCHERY ASSOCIATION
4 Howard Street, Falkirk FK1 5JG
Tel: 01324-624363
Secretary, Miss M. C. Taylor

SCOTTISH FIELD ARCHERY ASSOCIATION
12 Antonine Grove, Bonnybridge,
  Stirlingshire FK4 2DW
Tel: 01324-819189
Liaison Officer, I. Oldershaw

ATHLETICS

SCOTTISH ATHLETICS FEDERATION
Caledonia House, South Gyle, Edinburgh
  EH12 9DQ
Tel: 0131-317 7320
General Manager, N. F. Park

THE THISTLE AWARDS SCHEME
Caledonia House, South Gyle, Edinburgh
  EH12 9DQ
Tel: 0131-317 7323
Administrator, Ms W. Dalziel

BADMINTON

SCOTTISH BADMINTON UNION
Cockburn Centre, 40 Bogmoor Place,
  Glasgow G51 4TQ
Tel: 0141-445 1218
Chief Executive, Miss A. Smillie

SCOTTISH SCHOOLS BADMINTON UNION
The Sheiling, Brownsburn Road, Airdrie
  ML6 9QG
Tel: 01236-760943
Secretary, H. Ainsley

BASKETBALL

SCOTTISH BASKETBALL ASSOCIATION
Caledonia House, South Gyle, Edinburgh
  EH12 9DQ
Tel: 0131-317 7260
Chief Executive Officer, Mrs S. F. E. Mason

SCOTTISH SCHOOLS BASKETBALL
ASSOCIATION
Caledonia House, South Gyle, Edinburgh
  EH12 9DQ
Tel: 0131-317 7260
Chairman, T. Hardie

BATON TWIRLING

SCOTTISH FEDERATION OF BATON
TWIRLING
55 Springkell Avenue, Maxwell Park, Glasgow
  G41 1DP
Secretary, D. Wood

BILLIARDS

SCOTTISH BILLIARDS AND SNOOKER
ASSOCIATION
PO Box 147, Dunfermline KY12 8ZB
Tel: 01383-625373
Secretary, A. T. Craig

BOWLS

SCOTTISH BOWLING ASSOCIATION
50 Wellington Street, Glasgow G2 6EF
Tel: 0141-221 8999
Secretary, R. Black

SCOTTISH INDOOR BOWLING
ASSOCIATION
41 Montfode Court, Ardrossan, Ayrshire
  KA22 7NJ
Tel: 01294-468372
Secretary, J. Barclay

SCOTTISH WOMEN'S BOWLING
ASSOCIATION
Kingston House, 3 Jamaica Street, Greenock
  PA15 1XX
Tel: 01475-724676
Secretary, Mrs E. Allan

SCOTTISH WOMEN'S INDOOR BOWLING
ASSOCIATION
39/7 Murray Burn Park, Edinburgh EH14 2PQ
Tel: 0131-453 2305
Hon. Secretary, Mrs M. Old

BOXING

SCOTTISH AMATEUR BOXING
ASSOCIATION
96 High Street, Lochee, Dundee DD2 3AY
Tel: 01382-508261
Executive Director, F. Hendry

CANOEING

SCOTTISH CANOE ASSOCIATION
Caledonia House, South Gyle, Edinburgh
  EH12 9DQ
Tel: 0131-317 7314
Administrators, Mrs M. Winter, Miss R. Todd

CAVING

GRAMPIAN SPELEOLOGICAL GROUP
8 Scone Gardens, Edinburgh EH8 7DQ
Tel: 0131-661 1123
Recorder, A. Jeffreys

CAMPING AND CARAVANNING

THE CAMPING AND CARAVANNING CLUB
20 The Oval, Clarkston, Glasgow G76 8LY
Tel: 0141-637 5740
Secretary, Mrs P. McIlraith

CRICKET

SCOTTISH CRICKET UNION
Caledonia House, South Gyle, Edinburgh
EH12 9DQ
Tel: 0131-317 7247
General Manager, A. Ritchie

CROQUET

SCOTTISH CROQUET ASSOCIATION
14 Greenbank Crescent, Edinburgh EH10 5SG
Tel: 0131-222 4185
Treasurer, T. Foster

CURLING

ROYAL CALEDONIAN CURLING CLUB
Cairnie House, Ingliston Showground,
   Newbridge, Midlothian EH28 2NB
Tel: 0131-333 3003
Secretary, W. J. Duthie Thomson

CYCLING

CTC SCOTLAND
10 Woodhall Terrace, Edinburgh EH14 5BR
Tel: 0131-453 3366
Secretary, P. Hawkins

SCOTTISH CYCLISTS UNION
The Velodrome, London Road, Edinburgh
EH7 6AD
Tel: 0131-652 0187
Executive Development Officer, J. Riach

DANCE AND KEEP FIT

THE BRITISH ASSOCIATION OF TEACHERS
OF DANCING
23 Marywood Square, Glasgow G41 2BP
Tel: 0141-423 4029
Secretary, Mrs K. Allan

FITNESS SCOTLAND
Caledonia House, South Gyle, Edinburgh
EH12 9DQ
Tel: 0131-317 7243
Manager, Ms J. Small

HEALTH AND BEAUTY EXERCISE
Ashgrove, 23 Carrick Road, Ayr KA7 2RD
Tel: 01292-262299
Organizer, Ms F. Gillanders

THE MEDAU SOCIETY OF GREAT BRITAIN
AND NORTHERN IRELAND
Sheiling of Blebo, Pittscottie, Fife KY15 5TX
Tel: 01334-828623
Scottish Representative, Ms R. Garton

ROYAL SCOTTISH COUNTRY DANCE
SOCIETY
12 Coates Crescent, Edinburgh EH3 7AF
Tel: 0131-225 3854
Secretary, Miss G. Parker

SCOTTISH DANCESPORT
93 Hillfoot Drive, Bearsden, Glasgow
   G61 3QG
Tel: 0141-563 2001
General Secretary/Administrator, Mrs M. Fraser

SCOTTISH OFFICIAL BOARD OF
HIGHLAND DANCING
32 Grange Loan, Edinburgh EH9 2NR
Tel: 0131-668 3965
Secretary, Miss M. Rowan

EQUESTRIANISM

SCOTTISH EQUESTRIAN ASSOCIATION
Boreland, Fearnan, Aberfeldy, Perthshire
   PH15 2PG
Tel: 01887-830606
Development Officer, I. M. Menzies

THE TREKKING AND RIDING SOCIETY OF
SCOTLAND
Boreland, Fearnan, Aberfeldy, Perthshire
   PH15 2PG
Tel: 01887-830274
Secretary, Mrs E. Menzies

FENCING

SCOTTISH FENCING
Cockburn Centre, 40 Bogmoor Place,
   Glasgow G51 4TQ
Tel: 0141-445 1602
Executive Administrator, C. Grahamslaw

FIELD SPORTS

SCOTTISH COUNTRYSIDE ALLIANCE
Redden, Kelso TD5 8HS
Tel: 01890-830333
Scottish Director, A. Murray

FOOTBALL

SCOTTISH AMATEUR FOOTBALL
ASSOCIATION
6 Park Gardens, Glasgow G3 7YF
Tel: 0141-333 0839
Secretary, H. Knapp

SCOTTISH FOOTBALL ASSOCIATION
6 Park Gardens, Glasgow G3 7YF
Tel: 0141-332 6372
Chief Executive, D. Taylor

SCOTTISH FOOTBALL LEAGUE
188 West Regent Street, Glasgow G2 4RY
Tel: 0141-248 3844
Secretary, P. Donald

SCOTTISH SCHOOLS FOOTBALL
ASSOCIATION
6 Park Gardens, Glasgow G3 7YF
Tel: 0141-353 3215
General Secretary, J. C. Watson

SCOTTISH WOMEN'S FOOTBALL
ASSOCIATION
4 Park Gardens, Glasgow G3 7YE
Tel: 0141-353 1162
Executive Administrator, Mrs M. McGonigle

GAMES (HIGHLAND AND BORDER)

SCOTTISH GAMES ASSOCIATION
24 Florence Place, Perth PH1 5BH
Tel: 01738-627782
Secretary, A. Rettie

GLIDING

SCOTTISH GLIDING ASSOCIATION
48 McIntosh Drive, Elgin, Moray IV30 6AW
Tel: 01343-547701
Secretary, R. M. Lambert

GOLF

THE GOLF FOUNDATION LTD
Foundation House, Hanbury Manor, Ware,
   Herts SG12 0UH
Tel: 01920-484044
Director, Miss L. Attwood

LADIES' GOLF UNION
The Scores, St Andrews, Fife KY16 9AT
Tel: 01334-475811
Secretary, Mrs J. Hall

ROYAL AND ANCIENT GOLF CLUB OF ST
ANDREWS
Golf Place, St Andrews, Fife KY16 9JD
Tel: 01334-472112
Secretary, P. Dawson

SCOTTISH GOLF UNION
Scottish National Golf Centre, Drumoig,
   Leuchars, St Andrews KY16 0DW
Tel: 01382-549500
Secretary, H. Grey

SCOTTISH LADIES GOLFING ASSOCIATION
Scottish National Golf Centre, Drumoig,
   Leuchars, St Andrews KY16 0DW
Tel: 01382-549502
Secretary, Mrs S. Simpson

SCOTTISH SCHOOLS GOLF ASSOCIATION
The Waid Academy, St Andrews Road,
   Anstruther, Fife KY10 3HD
Tel: 01333-592000
Secretary, Mrs D. Scott

GYMNASTICS

SCOTTISH GYMNASTICS
Withall Mill, Lanark Road, Edinburgh
   EH14 5DL
Tel: 0131-458 5657
President, Mrs L. Martin

HANDBALL

SCOTTISH HANDBALL ASSOCIATION
5 Skye Court, Ravenswood, Cumbernauld
   G67 1PA
Tel: 01236-730720
Secretary, Ms M. Menzies

HANG GLIDING

SCOTTISH HANG GLIDING AND
PARAGLIDING FEDERATION
16 Johnston Street, Menstrie,
   Clackmannanshire FK11 7DB
Tel: 01259-762055
Secretary, Mrs L. Wilson Wallace

HOCKEY

SCOTTISH HOCKEY UNION
34 Cramond Road North, Edinburgh EH4 6JD
Tel: 0131-312 8870
Chairman, P. Monaghan

SCOTTISH SCHOOLGIRLS AND YOUTH
HOCKEY ASSOCIATION
45 Echline, The Steadings, South
   Queensferry, Edinburgh EH30 9SW
Tel: 0131-331 2626
President, E. Connolly

SCOTTISH YOUTH HOCKEY BOARD
Marrald, Brabloch Crescent, Paisley PA3 4RG
Tel: 0141-887 9731
Chairman, G. Ralph

ICE HOCKEY

SCOTTISH ICE HOCKEY ASSOCIATION
Glenburn House, 21 Braeburn Drive, Currie,
Midlothian EH14 6AQ
Tel: 0131-449 3163
Secretary, Mrs A. Robertson

ICE SKATING

SCOTTISH ICE SKATING ASSOCIATION
c/o The Ice Sports Centre, Riversdale
Crescent, Edinburgh EH12 5XN
Tel: 0131-337 3976
Administrator, J. Macdonald

JUDO

SCOTTISH JUDO FEDERATION
Caledonia House, South Gyle, Edinburgh
EH12 9DQ
Tel: 0131-317 7270
Chief Executive, C. McIver

JU-JITSU

SCOTTISH JU-JITSU ASSOCIATION
3 Dens Street, Dundee DD4 6BU
Tel: 01382-458262
General Secretary, R. G. Ross

KARATE

SCOTTISH KARATE BOARD
2 Strathdee Road, Netherlee, Glasgow
G44 3TJ
Tel: 0141-633 1116
Secretary, J. A. Miller

LACROSSE

SCOTTISH LACROSSE ASSOCIATION
Scottish Lacrosse Administration Office, St
Leonards School, St Andrews KY16 9QU
Tel: 01334-472126
Secretary, Mrs J. Caithness

LAWN TENNIS

SCOTTISH LAWN TENNIS ASSOCIATION
Craiglockhart Tennis and Sports Centre, 177
Colinton Road, Edinburgh EH14 1BZ
Tel: 0131-444 1984
Secretary, Ms G. Grosset

MODERN PENTATHLON

SCOTTISH MODERN PENTATHLON
ASSOCIATION
16 Plewlands Terrace, Edinburgh EH10 5JZ
Chairman, R. Reekie

MOTOR SPORT

ROYAL SCOTTISH AUTOMOBILE CLUB
(MOTOR SPORT) LTD
11 Blythswood Square, Glasgow G2 4AG
Tel: 0141-204 4999
Secretary, J. C. Lord

SCOTTISH AUTO CYCLE UNION LTD
Block 2, Unit 6, Whiteside Industrial Estate,
Bathgate, W. Lothian EH48 2RX
Tel: 01506-630262
Secretary, G. Anderson

MOUNTAINEERING

MOUNTAIN BOTHIES ASSOCIATION
18 Castle View, Airth, Stirlingshire FK2 8GE
Tel: 01324-832700
General Secretary, Mrs L. Woods

MOUNTAIN RESCUE COMMITTEE OF
SCOTLAND
31 Craigfern Drive, Blanefield, Glasgow
G63 9DP
Tel: 01360-770431
Secretary, Dr R. Sharp

MOUNTAINEERING COUNCIL OF
SCOTLAND
4A St Catherine's Road, Perth PH1 5SE
Tel: 01738-638227
National Officer, K. Howett

SCOTTISH MOUNTAIN LEADER TRAINING
BOARD
Glenmore, Aviemore, Inverness-shire
PH22 1QU
Tel: 01479-861248
Secretary, A. Fyffe

MULTI-SPORT BODIES

SCOTTISH DISABILITY SPORT
Fife Institute of Physical and Recreational
Education, Viewfield Road, Glenrothes,
Fife KY6 2RB
Tel: 01592-415700
Administrator, Mrs M. MacPhee

NETBALL

NETBALL SCOTLAND
24 Ainslie Road, Hillington Business Park,
Hillington, Glasgow G52 4RU
Tel: 0141-570 4016
Administrator, D. McLaughlan

ORIENTEERING

SCOTTISH ORIENTEERING ASSOCIATION
10 Neuk Crescent, Houston, Johnstone
PA6 7DW
Tel: 01505-613094
Development Officer, D. Petrie

PARACHUTING

SCOTTISH SPORT PARACHUTE
ASSOCIATION
c/o Scottish Parachute Club, Strathallan
Airfield, nr Auchterarder, Perthshire
PH3 1LA
Tel: 01764-662572
Secretary, Ms A. Johnson

PETANQUE

SCOTTISH PETANQUE ASSOCIATION
16D Ballantine Place, Perth PH1 5RS
Tel: 01738-623982
Secretary, D. Adam

POLO

SCOTTISH POLO ASSOCIATION
The Grange, Cupar, Fife KY15 4QH
Tel: 01382-330234
Secretary, Capt. M. Fox-Pitt

SCOTTISH BICYCLE POLO ASSOCIATION
16 Edmiston Drive, Linwood, Paisley
PA3 3TD
Tel: 01505-328105
Secretary, A. McGee

POOL

SCOTTISH POOL ASSOCIATION
3 Strath Gardens, Dores, Inverness IV2 6TT
Tel: 01463-751282
Hon. General Secretary, N. A. Donald

ROWING

SCOTTISH AMATEUR ROWING
ASSOCIATION
71 Gillbrae Crescent, Georgetown, Dumfries
DG1 4DJ
Tel: 01387-264233
Secretary, G. West

SCOTTISH SCHOOLS ROWING COUNCIL
1 Kirkhill Gardens, Edinburgh EH16 5DF
Tel: 0131-667 5389
Secretary, R. H. C. Neil

RUGBY UNION

SCOTTISH RUGBY UNION
Murrayfield, Roseburn Street, Edinburgh
EH12 5PJ
Tel: 0131-346 5000
Chief Executive, W. Watson

SCOTTISH SCHOOLS RUGBY UNION
59 Lochinver Crescent, Dundee DD2 4TY
Tel: 01382-660907
Hon. Secretary, D. C. M. Stibbles

SCOTTISH WOMEN'S RUGBY UNION
Flat 3, 108 Comiston Road, Edinburgh
EH10 5QL
Tel: 0131-557 5663
Chairperson, Miss B. Wilson

SHINTY

THE CAMANACHD ASSOCIATION
Algarve, Badabrie, Banavie, Fort William,
Inverness-shire PH33 7LX
Tel: 01397-772772
Executive Officer, A. MacIntyre

SHOOTING

SCOTTISH ASSOCIATION FOR COUNTRY
SPORTS
River Lodge, Trochry, Dunkeld PH8 0DY
Tel: 01350-723259
Director, D. Cant

SCOTTISH AIR RIFLE AND PISTOL
ASSOCIATION
45 Glenartney Court, Glenrothes, Fife
KY7 6YF
Tel: 01592-743929
Secretary, E. B. Wallace

SCOTTISH CLAY TARGET ASSOCIATION
10 Balgibbon Drive, Callander, Perthshire
FK17 8EU
Tel: 01877-331323
Hon. Secretary, R. W. Forsyth

SCOTTISH PISTOL ASSOCIATION
Sandhole, Furnace, Inveraray, Argyll
PA32 8XU
Tel: 01499-500640
Joint Secretaries, Mrs M. McCarthy;
T. McCarthy

SCOTTISH SMALL-BORE RIFLE
ASSOCIATION
128 Easton Drive, Shield Hill, Falkirk
FK1 2DW
Tel: 01324-720440
Secretary, S. J. McIntosh, MBE

SCOTTISH TARGET SHOOTING
FEDERATION
1 Mortonhall Park Terrace, Edinburgh
EH17 8SU
Tel: 0131-664 9674
Hon. Secretary, C. R. Aitken

SKATEBOARDING

SKATEBOARD CONTACT/FEDERATION OF
SCOTTISH SKATEBOARDERS
16 Northwood Park, Livingston EH54 8BD
Tel: 01506-415308
Secretary, K. Omond

SKIING

ASSOCIATION OF SNOWSPORT SCHOOLS
IN UK
BASI, Glenmore, Aviemore, Inverness-shire
PH22 1QJ
Tel: 01479-861717
Hon. Secretary, R. Kinnaird

BRITISH ASSOCIATION OF SKI
INSTRUCTORS (BASI)
Glenmore, Aviemore, Inverness-shire
PH22 1QU
Tel: 01479-861717
Chief Executive, R. Kinnaird

BRITISH SKI AND SNOWBOARD
FEDERATION
258 Main Street, East Calder, Livingston, W.
Lothian EH53 0EE
Tel: 01506-884343
Operations Director, Ms F. McLean

SCOTTISH SCHOOLS SKI ASSOCIATION
Balwearie High School, Balwearie Gardens,
Kirkcaldy KY2 5LY
Tel: 01592-412262
Chairman, Mrs A. Frost

SNOWSPORT SCOTLAND
Caledonia House, South Gyle, Edinburgh
EH12 9DQ
Tel: 0131-317 7280
Development Manager, B. Crawford

SQUASH RACKETS

SCOTTISH SQUASH
Caledonia House, South Gyle, Edinburgh
EH12 9DQ
Tel: 0131-317 7343
Secretary, N. Brydon

SUB AQUA

BRITISH SUB AQUA CLUB (SCOTTISH
FEDERATION)
Veensgarth, Downies Village, Aberdeen
AB1 4QX
Secretary, Ms A. Farrow

SCOTTISH SUB AQUA CLUB
Cockburn Centre, 40 Bogmoor Place,
Glasgow G51 4TQ
Tel: 0141-425 1021
Administrative Secretary, Mrs A. Bannon

SURFING

SCOTTISH SURFING FEDERATION
13 Eton Terrace, Edinburgh EH4 1QD
Tel: 0131-332 8388
President, S. Christopherson

SWIMMING

SCOTTISH SWIMMING AWARDS OFFICE
44 Frederick Street, Edinburgh EH2 1EX
Tel: 0131-225 7271
Manager, Ms S. Bell

SCOTTISH AMATEUR SWIMMING
ASSOCIATION
Holmhills Farm, Greenlees Road,
Cambuslang, Glasgow G72 8DT
Tel: 0141-641 8818
Administration Manager, Miss G. Ross

SCOTTISH SCHOOLS SWIMMING
ASSOCIATION
55 Dalgety Gardens, Dalgety Bay,
Dunfermline KY11 9LF
Tel: 01383-825428
Hon. Secretary, Mrs C. Rees

THE SWIMMING TEACHERS ASSOCIATION
(SCOTTISH DIVISION)
Anchor House, Birch Street, Walsall WS2 8HZ
Tel: 01922-645097
Divisional Secretary, vacant

TABLE TENNIS

SCOTTISH TABLE TENNIS ASSOCIATION
Caledonia House, South Gyle, Edinburgh
EH12 9DQ
Tel: 0131-317 8077
Chairman, D. Clifford

TENPIN BOWLING

SCOTTISH TENPIN BOWLING
ASSOCIATION
6 Laightoun Drive, Condorrat, North
　Lanarkshire G67 4EX
Tel: 01236-732072
National Secretary, Mrs M. Killen

TRAMPOLINING

SCOTTISH TRAMPOLINE ASSOCIATION
(Part of Scottish Gymnastics from 1 January
2000)
90 Paradise Road, Kemnay, Aberdeenshire
　AB51 5ST
Tel: 01467-642045
Secretary, J. Morrison

TRIATHLON

SCOTTISH TRIATHLON ASSOCIATION
Glenearn Cottage, Edinburgh Road, Port
　Seton, E. Lothian EH32 0HQ
Tel: 01875-811344
Secretary, Ms J. Dunlop

TUG OF WAR

SCOTTISH TUG OF WAR ASSOCIATION
47 Finlay Avenue, East Calder, W. Lothian
　EH53 0RP
Tel: 01506-881650
Secretary, G. Gillespie

VOLLEYBALL

SCOTTISH VOLLEYBALL ASSOCIATION
48 The Pleasance, Edinburgh EH8 9TJ
Tel: 0131-556 4633
Director, N. S. Moody

WALKING

RAMBLERS' ASSOCIATION SCOTLAND
Kingfisher House, Auld Mart Business Park,
　Milnathort, Kinross KY13 9DA
Tel: 01577-861222
Director, D. Morris

WATER SKIING

SCOTTISH WATER SKI ASSOCIATION
Scottish Water Ski Centre, Townhill Country
　Park, Dunfermline KY12 0HT
Tel: 01383-620123
Chairman, D. Hope

WEIGHT-LIFTING

SCOTTISH AMATEUR WEIGHT-LIFTERS
ASSOCIATION
PO Box 26014, Newmilns, Ayrshire KA16 9YP
Tel: 01560-324376
Secretary, Ms L. Holland

WRESTLING

SCOTTISH AMATEUR WRESTLING
ASSOCIATION
Kelvin Hall, Argyle Street, Glasgow G3 8AW
Tel: 0141-334 3843
Secretary, A. Mitchell

YACHTING

ROYAL YACHTING ASSOCIATION,
SCOTLAND
Caledonia House, South Gyle, Edinburgh
　EH12 9DQ
Tel: 0131-317 7388
Hon. Secretary, S. Boyd

SOCIETIES AND INSTITUTIONS

Although this section is arranged in alphabetical order, organizations are usually listed by the key word in their title. The listing includes major charities, think tanks, special interest groups and recreational groups in Scotland, and the Scottish offices of UK organizations.

ACCIDENT PREVENTION COUNCIL, SCOTTISH
Slateford House, 53 Lanark Road, Edinburgh EH14 1TL
Tel: 0131-455 7457
Secretary, M. A. McDonnell

ADOPTION ADVICE SERVICE, SCOTTISH
16 Sandyford Place, Glasgow G3 7NB
Tel: 0141-339 0772
Joint Team Leaders, Mrs J. Atherton; Mrs R. McMillan

ADOPTION AND FOSTERING, BRITISH AGENCIES FOR
40 Shandwick Place, Edinburgh EH2 4RT
Tel: 0131-225 9285
Scottish Centre Manager, Ms B. Hudson

ADOPTION ASSOCIATION, SCOTTISH
2 Commercial Street, Leith, Edinburgh EH6 6JA
Tel: 0131-553 5060
Director, Ms A. Sutton

AGE CONCERN SCOTLAND
113 Rose Street, Edinburgh EH2 3DT
Tel: 0131-220 3345
Director, Ms M. O' Neill

AGRICULTURAL BENEVOLENT INSTITUTION, ROYAL SCOTTISH
Ingliston, Edinburgh EH28 8NB
Tel: 0131-333 1023
Director, I. C. Purves-Hume

ALCOHOL, SCOTTISH COUNCIL ON
2nd Floor, 166 Buchanan Street, Glasgow G1 2NH
Tel: 0141-333 9677
Chief Executive, Dr A. Foster

ALCOHOLICS ANONYMOUS
Scottish Service Office, Baltic Chambers, Glasgow G2 6HJ
Tel: 0141-226 2214

ALZHEIMER SCOTLAND – ACTION ON DEMENTIA
22 Drumsheugh Gardens, Edinburgh EH3 7RN
Tel: 0131-243 1453
Executive Director, J. Jackson

AMNESTY INTERNATIONAL UNITED KINGDOM
11 Jeffrey Street, Edinburgh EH1 1DR
Tel: 0131-557 2957
Scottish Fundraising Officer, G. Pope

AN COMUNN GAIDHEALACH
109 Church Street, Inverness IV1 1EY
Tel: 01463-231226
Chief Executive, D. J. MacSween

ANIMAL CONCERN
PO Box 3982, Glasgow G51 4WD
Tel: 0141-445 3570
Organizing Secretary, Dr M. Daly

ANTIQUARIES OF SCOTLAND, SOCIETY OF
Royal Museum of Scotland, Chambers Street, Edinburgh EH1 1JF
Tel: 0131-247 4115/4133
Director, Mrs F. Ashmore, FSA

APEX TRUST SCOTLAND
9 Great Stuart Street, Edinburgh EH3 7TP
Tel: 0131-220 0130
Director, Ms J. Freeman

ARBITRATION, SCOTTISH COUNCIL FOR
27 Melville Street, Edinburgh EH3 7GF
Tel: 0131-226 2552
Chief Executive, J. Arnott

ARCHAEOLOGY, COUNCIL FOR SCOTTISH
c/o National Museums of Scotland, Chambers Street, Edinburgh EH1 1JF
Tel: 0131-225 7534
Director, Dr S. Fraser

ARMY BENEVOLENT FUND
The Castle, Edinburgh EH1 2YT
Tel: 0131-310 5132
Scottish Director, Lt.-Col. I. Shepherd

ARTHRITIS CARE
68 Woodvale Avenue, Bearsden, Glasgow G61 2NZ
Tel: 0141-942 2322
Manager, Scotland, P. Wallace

ARTS AND BUSINESS (SCOTLAND)
13 Abercrombie Place, Edinburgh EH3 6LB
Tel: 0131-558 1277
Director, Ms A. Hogg

ASTHMA CAMPAIGN, NATIONAL
21 Coates Crescent, Edinburgh EH3 7AF
Tel: 0131-226 2544
Director, Scotland, Ms M. O'Donnell

AUTISTIC CHILDREN, SCOTTISH SOCIETY
FOR
Hilton House, Alloa Business Park, Whins
Road, Alloa FK10 3SA
Tel: 01259-720044
Appeals and Marketing Manager, Mrs H. Petrie

THE AUTOMOBILE ASSOCIATION LTD
Fanum House, Erskine Harbour, Erskine,
Renfrewshire PA8 6AT
Tel: 0141-848 8622
Head of Policy, Scotland, N. Greig

AYRSHIRE ARCHAEOLOGICAL AND
NATURAL HISTORY SOCIETY
10 Longlands Park, Ayr KA7 4RJ
Tel: 01292-441915
Hon. Secretary, Dr T. Mathews

AYRSHIRE CATTLE SOCIETY OF GREAT
BRITAIN AND IRELAND
1 Racecourse Road, Ayr KA7 2DE
Tel: 01292-267123
Chief Executive, S. J. Thomson

BAFTA SCOTLAND
249 West George Street, Glasgow G2 4QE
Tel: 0141-302 1770
Director, Ms A. Forsyth

BARNARDO'S
235 Corstorphine Road, Edinburgh EH12 7AR
Tel: 0131-334 9893
Director of Children's Services, Scotland,
H. R. Mackintosh

BIG ISSUE FOUNDATION SCOTLAND
29 College Street, Glasgow G1 1QH
Tel: 0141-559 5555
Chief Executive, Ms J. Cropper

BIRDS, *see* Scottish Society for the Protection
of Wild Birds

BIRTH CENTRE
40 Leamington Terrace, Edinburgh EH10 4JL
Tel: 0131-229 3667
Co-ordinators, Ms N. Edwards;
    Ms A. McLaughlin; Ms D. Purdue

BLIND, GUIDE DOGS FOR THE, *see* Guide
Dogs for the Blind Association

BLIND, SCOTTISH NATIONAL
FEDERATION FOR THE WELFARE OF THE
PO Box 500, Gillespie Crescent, Edinburgh
    EH10 4HZ
Tel: 0131-229 1456
Hon. Treasurer, J. B. M. Munro

BLOOD TRANSFUSION ASSOCIATION,
SCOTTISH NATIONAL
c/o Scottish National Blood Transfusion
    Service, Ellen's Glen Road,
    Edinburgh EH17 7QT
Secretary, W. Mack

BOOK TRUST, SCOTTISH
Scottish Book Centre, 137 Dundee Street,
    Edinburgh EH11 1BG
Tel: 0131-229 3663
Director, L. Fraser

BOTANICAL SOCIETY OF SCOTLAND
c/o Royal Botanic Garden, Inverleith Row,
    Edinburgh EH3 5LR
Tel: 0131-552 7171
Hon. General Secretary, R. Galt

BOYS' AND GIRLS' CLUBS OF SCOTLAND
88 Giles Street, Edinburgh EH6 6BZ
Tel: 0131-555 1729
Secretary, T. Leishman

BOYS' BRIGADE
Carronvale House, Carronvale Road, Larbert
    FK5 3LH
Tel: 01324-562008
Secretary for Scotland, I. McLaughlan

BOY SCOUTS ASSOCIATION, *see* Scout
Association

BRITISH LEGION SCOTLAND, ROYAL
New Haig House, Logie Green Road,
    Edinburgh EH7 4HR
Tel: 0131-557 2782
General Secretary, Maj.-Gen. J. D.
    MacDonald, CB, CBE

BRITISH RED CROSS
Alexandra House, 204 Bath Street, Glasgow
    G2 4HL
Tel: 0141-332 9591
Director, Scotland, D. Whyte

BURNS FEDERATION
Dick Institute, Elmbank Avenue, Kilmarnock
    KA1 3BU
Tel: 01563-572469
Chief Executive, Mrs S. Bell

BUSINESS FOR SCOTLAND
PO Box 23087, Edinburgh EH2 4YT
Tel: 0131-225 9134
Director, Ms S. Barber

BUSINESS IN THE ARTS SCOTLAND
39 Abercromby Place, Edinburgh EH3 6LB
Tel: 0131-558 1277
Director, Ms A. Hogg

BUSINESS IN THE COMMUNITY, SCOTTISH
30 Hanover Street, Edinburgh EH2 2DR
Tel: 0131-220 3001
Secretary, Ms J. McCulloch

CALEDONIAN HORTICULTURAL SOCIETY,
ROYAL
6 Kirkliston Road, South Queensferry
EH30 9LT
Tel: 0131-331 1011
Secretary, T. Mabbott

CAMPAIGN FOR NUCLEAR DISARMAMENT,
SCOTTISH
15 Barrland Street, Glasgow G41 1QH
Tel: 0141-423 1222
Administrator, J. Ainslie

CANCERBACUP
(formerly British Association of Cancer
United Patients (BACUP)
2/2, 30 Bell Street, Glasgow G1 1LG
Tel: 0141-553 1553
Manager, Ms J. Whelan

CANCER RELIEF, MACMILLAN
9 Castle Terrace, Edinburgh EH1 2DP
Tel: 0131-229 3276
Director, Scotland and Northern Ireland,
I. R. L. Gibson

CANCER RESEARCH CAMPAIGN
(SCOTLAND)
Thain House, 226 Queensferry Road,
Edinburgh EH4 2BP
Tel: 0131-343 1344
Regional Director, B. McKinlay

CANCER RESEARCH FUND, IMPERIAL
Wallace House, Maxwell Place, Stirling
FK8 1JU
Tel: 01786-446689
Scottish Fundraising Director, L. J. Brady

CAPABILITY SCOTLAND
22 Corstorphine Road, Edinburgh EH12 6HP
Tel: 0131-337 9876
Director, A. Dickson

CARE HOME OWNERS, SCOTTISH
ASSOCIATION OF
Ashlea House, Bracklinn Road, Callander,
Perthshire FK17 8EH
Tel: 01877-330325
Chairman, Dr C. M. Barron

CARERS NATIONAL ASSOCIATION
3rd Floor, 91 Mitchell Street, Glasgow
G1 3LN
Tel: 0141-221 9141
Scotland Manager, A. McGinley

CARNEGIE DUNFERMLINE TRUST
Abbey Park House, Dunfermline, Fife
KY12 7PB
Tel: 01383-723638
Secretary, W. C. Runciman

CARNEGIE HERO FUND TRUST
Abbey Park House, Dunfermline, Fife
KY12 7PB
Tel: 01383-723638
Secretary, W. C. Runciman

CARNEGIE UNITED KINGDOM TRUST
Comely Park House, Dunfermline, Fife
KY12 7EJ
Tel: 01383-721445
Secretary, C. J. Naylor, OBE

CATHOLIC INTERNATIONAL AID FUND,
SCOTTISH
19 Park Circus, Glasgow G3 5BE
Tel: 0141-354 5555
Executive Director, P. Chitnis

CHEST, HEART AND STROKE SCOTLAND
65 North Castle Street, Edinburgh EH2 3LT
Tel: 0131-225 6963
Chief Executive, D. Clark

CHILDBIRTH TRUST, NATIONAL
Stockbridge Health Centre, 1 India Place,
Edinburgh EH3 6EH
Tel: 0131-260 9201
Administrator, Ms K. McGlew

CHILD LAW CENTRE, SCOTTISH
4th Floor, Cranston House, 108 Argyle
Street, Glasgow G2 8BH
Tel: 0141-226 3434

CHILDLINE SCOTLAND
18 Albion Street, Glasgow G1 1LH
Tel: 0141-552 1123; helpline: 0800-1111
Director, Ms A. Houston

CHILDMINDING ASSOCIATION, SCOTTISH
Suite 3, 7 Melville Terrace, Stirling FK8 2ND
Tel: 01786-445377
Director, Mrs A. McNellan, MBE

CHILDREN 1ST (ROYAL SCOTTISH
SOCIETY FOR PREVENTION OF CRUELTY
TO CHILDREN)
Melville House, 41 Polwarth Terrace,
Edinburgh EH11 1NU
Tel: 0131-337 8539
Chief Executive, Ms M. McKay

CHILDREN IN SCOTLAND
Princes House, 5 Shandwick Place,
Edinburgh EH2 4RG
Tel: 0131-228 8484
Information Manager, Ms H. Walker

CHRISTIAN AID
41 George IV Bridge, Edinburgh EH1 1EL
Tel: 0131-220 1254
Scottish National Secretary, Revd J. Wylie

CHURCH HISTORY SOCIETY, SCOTTISH
Crown Manse, 39 Southside Road, Inverness
IV2 4XA
Tel: 01463-231140
Hon. Secretary, Revd Dr P. H. Donald

CHURCH OF SCOTLAND GUILD
121 George Street, Edinburgh EH2 4YN
Tel: 0131-225 5722
General Secretary, Mrs A. M. Twaddle

CITIZENS ADVICE SCOTLAND
26 George Square, Edinburgh EH8 9LD
Tel: 0131-667 0156
Chief Executive, Ms K. Lyle

CIVIC TRUST, SCOTTISH
The Tobacco Merchants House, 42 Miller
Street, Glasgow G1 1DT
Tel: 0141-221 1466
Director, J. N. P. Ford

COMMUNITY CARE FORUM, SCOTTISH
c/o 18–19 Claremont Crescent, Edinburgh
EH7 4QD
Tel: 0131-557 2711
National Development Officer, Mrs K. Jackson

COMMUNITY COUNCILS, ASSOCIATION OF
SCOTTISH
21 Grosvenor Street, Edinburgh EH12 5ED
Tel: 0131-225 4033
Chairman, J. Mackintosh

COMMUNITY SERVICE VOLUNTEERS
SCOTLAND
236 Clyde Street, Glasgow G1 4JH
Tel: 0141-204 1681
Chief Executive, Ms E. Hoodless

COMPLEMENTARY MEDICINE, SCOTTISH
COLLEGE OF
c/o The Complementary Medicine Centre, 11
Park Circus, Glasgow G3 6AX
Tel: 0141-332 4924
Clinic Director, B. Fleming

COMUNN NA GÀIDHLIG
5 Mitchell's Lane, Inverness IV2 3HQ
Tel: 01463-234138
Chief Executive, A. Campbell

CONSERVATION BUREAU, SCOTTISH
Historic Scotland, Longmore House,
Salisbury Place, Edinburgh EH9 1SH
Tel: 0131-668 8668
Manager, Dr C. E. Brown

COT DEATH TRUST, SCOTTISH
Royal Hospital for Sick Children, Yorkhill,
Glasgow G3 8SJ
Tel: 0141-357 3946
Executive Director, Mrs H. Brooke

COUPLE COUNSELLING SCOTLAND
40 North Castle Street, Edinburgh EH2 3BN
Tel: 0131-225 5006
Director, Mrs F. Love

CROFTERS UNION, SCOTTISH
Old Mill, Broadford, Isle of Skye IV49 9AQ
Tel: 01471-822529
Director, R. Dutton

CRUSAID SCOTLAND
24A Ainslie Place, Edinburgh EH3 6AJ
Tel: 0131-225 8918
Executive Director, W. D. Wilson

CRUSE BEREAVEMENT CARE
33-35 Boswall Parkway, Edinburgh EH5 2BR
Tel: 0131-551 1511
Chief Officer, Scotland, Mrs R. Hampton

CULTURAL STUDIES, CENTRE FOR
SCOTTISH
University of Strathclyde, Livingstone Tower,
26 Richmond Street, Glasgow G1 1XH
Tel: 0141-548 3518
Director, Dr K. G. Simpson

CYSTIC FIBROSIS TRUST
Princes House, 5 Shandwick Place,
Edinburgh EH2 4RG
Tel: 0131-211 1110
Regional Support Co-ordinator, Ms H.
Macfarlane

DARTS ASSOCIATION, SCOTTISH
213 Bonnyview Drive, West Heathryfold,
Aberdeen AB16 7EY
Tel: 01224-692535
General Secretary, L. A. Mutch

DAVID HUME INSTITUTE
21 George Square, Edinburgh EH8 9LD
Tel: 0131-650 4633
Director, Prof. B. Main

DEAF ASSOCIATION SCOTLAND, BRITISH
3rd Floor, Princes House, 5 Shandwick Place,
Edinburgh EH2 4RG
Tel: 0131-221 1137
Community Advocate Officer, E. Pulloch

DEAFNESS, SCOTTISH COUNCIL ON
Clerwood House, 96 Clermiston Road,
Edinburgh EH12 6UT
Tel: 0131-314 6075
Administrator, Mrs L. Sutherland

DEAF PEOPLE, HEARING DOGS FOR
29 Craighiehall Crescent, West Freelands,
Erskine, Renfrewshire PA8 7DD
Tel: 0141-812 6542
Scottish Representative, Mrs M. Arthur

DEAF PEOPLE, ROYAL NATIONAL
INSTITUTE FOR
9 Clairmont Gardens, Glasgow G3 7LW
Tel: 0141-332 0343 (voice); 0141-332 5023
(textphone)
Director, Scotland, Ms L. Lawson

DEER MANAGEMENT GROUPS,
ASSOCIATION OF
Dalhousie Estate Office, Brechin, Angus
DD9 6SG
Tel: 01356-624566
Secretary, R. M. J. Cooke

DEER SOCIETY, BRITISH (SCOTTISH
OFFICE)
Trian House, Comrie, Perthshire PH6 2HZ
Tel: 01764-670062
Scottish Secretary, H. Rose

DIABETIC ASSOCIATION, BRITISH
4th Floor, 34 West George Street, Glasgow
G2 1DA
Tel: 0141-332 2700
National Manager, Mrs D. Henry

DISABILITIES, SCOTTISH EMPLOYMENT
OPPORTUNITIES FOR PEOPLE WITH
5th Floor, Portcullis House, 21 India Street,
Glasgow G2 4PZ
Tel: 0141-226 4544
Regional Director, G. Bond

DISABILITY SCOTLAND
Princes House, 5 Shandwick Place,
Edinburgh EH2 4RG
Tel: 0131-229 8632
Director, R. Benson

DISTRICT SALMON FISHERY BOARDS,
ASSOCIATION OF
5A Lennox Street, Edinburgh EH4 1QB
Tel: 0131-343 2433
Director, A. Wallace

DOWN'S SYNDROME ASSOCIATION,
SCOTTISH
158–160 Balgreen Road, Edinburgh EH11 3AU
Tel: 0131-313 4225
Director, Ms K. Watchman

DRUGS FORUM, SCOTTISH
Shaftesbury House, 5 Waterloo Street,
Glasgow G2 6AY
Tel: 0141-221 1175
Information Officer, Ms I. Hendry

DUKE OF EDINBURGH'S AWARD
69 Dublin Street, Edinburgh EH3 6NS
Tel: 0131-556 9097
Secretary for Scotland, Miss J. Shepherd

DYSLEXIA ASSOCIATION, SCOTTISH
Unit 3, Stirling Business Centre, Wellgreen,
Stirling FK8 2DZ
Tel: 01786-446650
Chairman, Mrs J. Traill

DYSLEXIA INSTITUTE
74 Victoria Crescent Road, Dowanhill,
Glasgow G12 9JN
Tel: 0141-334 4549
Principal, Mrs E. MacKenzie

EARL HAIG FUND SCOTLAND
New Haig House, Logie Green Road,
Edinburgh EH7 4HR
Tel: 0131-557 2782
General Secretary, Maj.-Gen. J. D. MacDonald

EARLY MUSIC FORUM OF SCOTLAND
The Latch, Carlops, Penicuik, Midlothian
EH26 9NH
Tel: 01968-660530
Chairman, M. Campbell

ECCLESIASTICAL HISTORY SOCIETY
Department of History (Medieval), University
of Glasgow, Glasgow G12 8QQ
Tel: 0141-330 4087
Secretary, M. J. Kennedy

ENABLE (SCOTTISH SOCIETY FOR THE
MENTALLY HANDICAPPED)
7 Buchanan Street, Glasgow G1 3HL
Tel: 0141-226 4541
Director, N. Dunning

ENERGY AND ENVIRONMENT CENTRE,
SCOTTISH
School of Engineering, Napier University, 10
Colinton Road, Edinburgh EH10 5DT
Tel: 0131-455 2672
Director, T. W. Summers

ENGENDER
13 Gayfield Square, Edinburgh EH1 3NX
Tel: 0131-558 9596
Convenor, Ms S. Robertson

EPILEPSY ASSOCIATION OF SCOTLAND
48 Govan Road, Glasgow G51 1JL
Tel: 0141-427 4911
Head of Support Services, Mrs J. Cochrane

ERSKINE HOSPITAL
(formerly Princess Louise Scottish Hospital)
Bishopton, Renfrewshire PA7 5PU
Tel: 0141-812 1100
Chief Executive, Col. M. F. Gibson, OBE

EUROPEAN MOVEMENT
6 Hill Street, Edinburgh EH2 3JZ
Tel: 0131-220 0377
National Organizer, Ms B. MacLeod

EX-SERVICES MENTAL WELFARE SOCIETY
Hollybush House, Hollybush, by Ayr KA6 7EA
Tel: 01292-560214
Assistant Director, Scotland and Ireland,
Wg Cdr. D. Devine

FAIR ISLE BIRD OBSERVATORY TRUST
Fair Isle Bird Observatory, Fair Isle, Shetland
ZE2 9JU
Tel: 01595-760258
Administrator, H. Craig

FAMILY HISTORY SOCIETY
164 King Street, Aberdeen AB24 5BD
Tel: 01224-646323
Chairperson, Mrs G. Murton

FAMILY PLANNING ASSOCIATION
SCOTLAND
Unit 10, Firhill Business Centre, 76 Firhill
Road, Glasgow G20 7BA
Tel: 0141-576 5088
Director, Ms A. M. McKay

FÈISEAN NAN GÀIDHEAL
Nicholson Buildings, Wentworth Street,
Portree, Isle of Skye IV51 9EJ
Tel: 01478-613355
Director, A. Cormack

FINDHORN FOUNDATION
The Park, Findhorn, Forres, Moray IV36 3TZ
Tel: 01309-690311
Chiarmen, R. Alfred; Ms M. Hollander

FISHMONGERS' COMPANY
Fala Acre, Fala Village, Pathhead, Midlothian
EH37 5SY
Tel: 01875-833246
Salmon Fisheries Inspector for Scotland,
W. F. Beattie, MBE

FOSTER CARE ASSOCIATION, NATIONAL
2nd Floor, Ingram House, 227 Ingram Street,
Glasgow G1 1DA
Tel: 0141-204 1400
Administrator, Ms L. Curran

FRASER OF ALLANDER INSTITUTE FOR
RESEARCH ON THE SCOTTISH ECONOMY
University of Strathclyde, Curran Building,
100 Cathedral Street, Glasgow G4 0LN
Tel: 0141-548 3958
Director, Prof. B. Ashcroft

FRIENDS OF THE EARTH
72 Newhaven Road, Edinburgh EH6 5QG
Tel: 0131-554 9977
Scottish Director, K. Dunion, OBE

GAMBLERS ANONYMOUS
Helpline: 0141-630 1033

GAME CONSERVANCY
Scottish Headquarters, Couston, Newtyle,
Perthshire PH12 8UT
Tel: 01828-650543
Director, I. McCall

GARDENS SCHEME, SCOTLAND'S
31 Castle Terrace, Edinburgh EH1 2EL
Tel: 0131-229 1870
Director, R. S. St Clair-Ford

GENEALOGY SOCIETY, SCOTTISH
Library and Family History Centre,
15 Victoria Terrace, Edinburgh EH1 2JL
Tel: 0131-220 3677
Hon. Secretary, Miss J. P. S. Ferguson

GEOGRAPHICAL SOCIETY, ROYAL
SCOTTISH
Graham Hills Building, 40 George Street,
Glasgow G1 1QE
Tel: 0141-552 3330
Director, Dr D. M. Munro

GIFTED CHILDREN, NATIONAL
ASSOCIATION FOR
PO Box 2024, Glasgow G32 9YD
Tel: 0141-639 4797
Scottish Chairman, Dr A. Cunningham

GINGERBREAD SCOTLAND
1307 Argyll Street, Glasgow G3 8TL
Tel: 0141-576 7976

GIRLS' BRIGADE IN SCOTLAND
Boys' Brigade House, 168 Bath Street,
Glasgow G2 4TQ
Tel: 0141-332 1765
Brigade Secretary, Mrs A. Webster

GOVERNMENT IN SCOTLAND, UNIT FOR
THE STUDY OF
University of Edinburgh, Chisholm House,
High School Yards, Edinburgh EH1 1LZ
Tel: 0131-650 2456
Administrative Secretary, Mrs L. Adams

GUIDE ASSOCIATION SCOTLAND
16 Coates Crescent, Edinburgh EH3 7AH
Tel: 0131-226 4511
Executive Director, Miss S. Pitches

GUIDE DOGS FOR THE BLIND
ASSOCIATION
Princess Alexandra House, Dundee Road,
Forfar DD8 1JA
Tel: 01307-463531
Operations Manager (interim), D. Duncan

HARVEIAN SOCIETY OF EDINBURGH
Respiratory Medicine Unit, Department of
Medicine, The Royal Infirmary,
Edinburgh EH3 9YW
Tel: 0131-536 2351
Joint Secretaries, A. B. MacGregor;
Prof. N. J. Douglas

HAWICK ARCHAEOLOGICAL SOCIETY
Orrock House, Stirches Road, Hawick,
Roxburghshire TD9 7HF
Tel: 01450-375546
Hon. Secretary, I. W. Landles

HEAD TEACHERS IN SCOTLAND,
ASSOCIATION OF
Room B34, Northern College, Gardyne
Road, Dundee DD5 1NY
Tel: 01382-458802
General Secretary, J. C. Smith

HELP THE AGED
Heriot House, Heriothill Terrace, Edinburgh
EH7 4DY
Tel: 0131-556 4666
Scottish Executive, Ms E. Duncan

HIGHLAND CATTLE SOCIETY
59 Drumlanrig Street, Thornhill, Dumfries
DG3 5LY
Tel: 0901-880 8282
Secretary, A. H. G. Wilson

HOMOEOPATHY, SCOTTISH COLLEGE OF
17 Queens Crescent, Glasgow G4 9BL
Tel: 0141-332 3917
Principal, Ms M. Roy

HOUSE-BUILDING COUNCIL, NATIONAL
(NHBC)
42 Colinton Road, Edinburgh EH10 5BT
Tel: 0131-313 1001
Scottish Director, T. Kirk

HOUSING ASSOCIATION OMBUDSMAN FOR
SCOTLAND
2 Belford Road, Edinburgh EH4 3BL
Tel: 0131-220 0599
Ombudsman, J. Richards

HUMAN RIGHTS CENTRE, SCOTTISH
146 Holland Street, Glasgow G2 4NG
Tel: 0141-332 5960
Director, Prof. A. Miller

IMMIGRATION ADVISORY SERVICE
115 Bath Street, Glasgow G2 2SZ
Tel: 0141-248 2956

INVERNESS FIELD CLUB
6 Drumblair Crescent, Inverness IV2 4RG
Hon. Secretary, Miss I. McLean

JOHN MUIR TRUST
41 Commercial Street, Leith EH6 6JD
Tel: 0131-554 0114
Director, N. Hawkins

JUBILEE 2000 SCOTTISH COALITION
121 George Street, Edinburgh EH2 4TN
Tel: 0131-225 5722
Co-ordinator, Ms L. Hendry

KEEP SCOTLAND BEAUTIFUL
7 Melville Terrace, Stirling FK8 2ND
Tel: 01786-471333
Director, vacant

KENNEL CLUB, SCOTTISH
3 Brunswick Place, Edinburgh EH7 5HP
Tel: 0131-557 2877
Secretary-General, A. Sims

KING GEORGE'S FUND FOR SAILORS
HMS *Caledonia*, Rosyth, Fife KY11 2XH
Tel: 01383-419969
Area Organizer, Scotland, Cdr. A. C. Herdman

LANDOWNERS' FEDERATION, SCOTTISH
Stuart House, Eskmills Business Park,
    Musselburgh, Midlothian EH21 7PB
Tel: 0131-653 5400
Director, Dr M. S. Hankey

LAW AGENTS SOCIETY, SCOTTISH
11 Parliament Square, Edinburgh EH1 1RD
Tel: 0131-225 5051
Secretary, Mrs J. H. Webster, WS

LAW CENTRES, SCOTTISH ASSOCIATION
OF
c/o Paisley Law Centre, 65 George Street,
    Paisley PA1 2JY
Tel: 0141-561 7266
Secretary, Ms L. Welsh

LAW REPORTING, SCOTTISH COUNCIL OF
Law Society, 26 Drumsheugh Gardens,
    Edinburgh EH3 7YR
Tel: 0131-226 7411
Deputy Secretary, D. Cullen

LEONARD CHESHIRE SCOTLAND
236 Clyde Street, Glasgow G1 4JH
Tel: 0141-241 6180
Fundraising Manager, Scotland,
    Ms S. Robinson

LEUKAEMIA RESEARCH FUND
43 Westbourne Gardens, Glasgow G12 9XQ
Tel: 0141-339 0690
Secretary, Mrs C. Mulholland

LIFEBOATS, *see* Royal National Lifeboat
Institution

LIMBLESS EX-SERVICEMEN'S
ASSOCIATION, BRITISH
24 Dundas Street, Edinburgh EH3 6JN
Tel: 0131-538 6966
President, A. Delworth, MBE

LUNG FOUNDATION (SCOTLAND),
BRITISH
Royal College of Physicians and Surgeons,
    234–242 St Vincent Street, Glasgow
    G2 5RJ
Tel: 0141-204 4110
Manager, J. Brady

MARINE SCIENCE, SCOTTISH
ASSOCIATION FOR
PO Box 3, Oban, Argyll PA34 4AD
Tel: 01631-562244
Director, Dr G. B. Shimmield, FRSE

MASONS OF SCOTLAND, GRAND LODGE
OF ANTIENT FREE AND ACCEPTED
Freemasons' Hall, 96 George Street,
    Edinburgh EH2 3DH
Tel: 0131-225 5304
Grand Secretary, C. M. McGibbon

MENTAL HEALTH FOUNDATION
SCOTLAND
24 George Square, Glasgow G2 1EG
Tel: 0141-572 0125
Director (acting), T. Pickles

MENTAL HEALTH, SCOTTISH
ASSOCIATION FOR
Cumbrae House, 15 Carlton Court, Glasgow
    G5 9JP
Tel: 0141-568 7000
Chief Executive, Ms S. M. Barcus

MENTALLY HANDICAPPED, SCOTTISH
SOCIETY FOR THE, *see* ENABLE

MISSION TO DEEP SEA FISHERMEN, ROYAL
NATIONAL
Scottish Regional Office, Melita House,
    Station Road, Polmont,
    Stirlingshire FK2 0UD
Tel: 01324-716857
Director, Scotland, I. Baillie

MISSIONS TO SEAMEN
Containerbase, Gartsherrie Road, Coatbridge,
    Lanarkshire ML5 2DS
Tel: 01236-440132
Administration Manager for Scotland,
    Mrs L. C. Boyd

MOTOR NEURONE DISEASE ASSOCIATION,
SCOTTISH
76 Firhill Road, Glasgow G20 7BA
Tel: 0141-945 1077
Chief Executive, Ms A. MacFadyen

MULTIPLE SCLEROSIS SOCIETY
2A North Charlotte Street, Edinburgh
EH2 4HR
Tel: 0131-225 3600
Scottish General Secretary, T. J. Hope
Thomson

NATIONAL TRUST FOR SCOTLAND
5 Charlotte Square, Edinburgh EH2 4DU
Tel: 0131-226 5922
Director, T. Croft

NATIONAL UNION OF STUDENTS
SCOTLAND
29 Forth Street, Edinburgh EH1 3LE
Tel: 0131-556 6598
Director, Scotland, L. Jarnecki

NCH ACTION FOR CHILDREN SCOTLAND
17 Newton Place, Glasgow G3 7PY
Tel: 0141-332 4041
Director, Scotland, J. O'Hara

ONE PARENT FAMILIES SCOTLAND
13 Gayfield Square, Edinburgh EH1 3NX
Tel: 0131-556 3899
Director, Ms S. Robertson

ORNITHOLOGISTS' CLUB, SCOTTISH
21 Regent Terrace, Edinburgh EH7 5BT
Tel: 0131-556 6042
Secretary, Miss S. Laing

OUTWARD BOUND TRUST
Loch Eil Centre, Achdalieu, Corpach, Fort
William PH33 7NN
Tel: 01397-772866
General Manager, A. Shepherd

OXFAM IN SCOTLAND
5th Floor, Fleming House, 134 Renfrew
Street, Glasgow G3 6ST
Tel: 0141-331 2724
Head, Mrs M. Hearle

PARENT TEACHER COUNCIL, SCOTTISH
63–65 Shandwick Place, Edinburgh EH2 4SD
Tel: 0131-228 5320/1
Administrator, Ms I. Ferguson

PARKINSON'S DISEASE SOCIETY
(SCOTTISH RESOURCE)
10 Claremont Terrace, Glasgow G3 7XR
Tel: 0141-332 3343
Area Manager, Mrs S. Scott

PDSA (PEOPLE'S DISPENSARY FOR SICK
ANIMALS)
Community Activities Office, Veterinary
Centre, Muiry Fauld Drive,
Dollcross, Glasgow G31 5RT
Tel: 0141-778 9229
Community Activities Manager, Ms L.
Crawford

PERFORMING RIGHT SOCIETY LTD
3 Rothesay Place, Edinburgh EH3 7SL
Tel: 0131-226 5320
Team Manager, Ms A. Cooper

PHAB SCOTLAND
5A Warriston Road, Edinburgh EH3 5LQ
Tel: 0131-558 9912
Chief Executive, Miss F. Hird

PHILATELIC SOCIETY, SCOTTISH
19 Allan Park Drive, Edinburgh EH14 1LW
Tel: 0131-443 2636
Secretary, E. Mason

PHYSICAL EDUCATION, SCOTTISH
COUNCIL OF
Centre for Physical Education and Sports
Development, University of
Stirling, Stirling FK9 4LA
Tel: 01786-466906
Sports Development Assistant, R. Gowrie

PIPE BAND ASSOCIATION, ROYAL
SCOTTISH
45 Washington Street, Glasgow G3 8AZ
Tel: 0141-221 5414
Executive Officer, I. M. White

PIPERS' SOCIETY, ROYAL SCOTTISH
127 Rose Street Lane South, Edinburgh
EH2 4BB
Tel: 01620-842146
Secretary, Dr M. J. B. Lowe

POST OFFICE USERS' COUNCIL FOR
SCOTLAND
Room 306–7, 2 Greenside Lane, Edinburgh
EH1 3AH
Tel: 0131-244 5576
Scottish Secretary, R. L. L. King

POVERTY ALLIANCE
162 Buchanan Street, Glasgow G1 2LL
Tel: 0141-353 0440
Director, D. Killeen

PRESS ASSOCIATION
124 Portman Street, Kinning Park, Glasgow
G41 1EJ
Tel: 0141-429 0087
Editor, PA Scotland, R. Spencer

PREVENTION OF ACCIDENTS, ROYAL
SOCIETY FOR THE
Slateford House, 53 Lanark Road, Edinburgh
EH14 1TL
Tel: 0131-443 9442
Road Safety Manager, M. A. McDonnell

PRINCE'S SCOTTISH YOUTH BUSINESS
TRUST
6th Floor, Mercantile Chambers, 53 Bothwell
Street, Glasgow G2 6TS
Tel: 0141-248 4999
Director, D. W. Cooper

PRINCE'S TRUST
7th Floor, Fleming House, 134 Renfrew
Street, Glasgow G3 6ST
Tel: 0141-331 0211
Office Manager, Mrs Y. Murphy-Beggs

PRINCESS ROYAL TRUST FOR CARERS
Kirkstane House, 139 St Vincent Street,
Glasgow G2 5JF
Tel: 0141-221 5066
Chief Executive (acting), Ms V. Daybell

PROCURATORS IN GLASGOW, ROYAL
FACULTY OF
12 Nelson Mandela Place, Glasgow G2 1BT
Tel: 0141-331 0533
General Manager, I. C. Pearson

PROPERTY NETWORK, SCOTTISH
University of Paisley, Paisley PA1 2BE
Tel: 0141-561 7300
General Manager, Ms A. Neilson

PUBLIC POLICY, CENTRE FOR SCOTTISH
20 Forth Street, Edinburgh EH1 3LH
Tel: 0131-477 8219
Director, G. Hassan

PUBLIC TRANSPORT, SCOTTISH
ASSOCIATION FOR
5 St Vincent Place, Glasgow G1 2DH
Tel: 0141-639 3697
Secretary, A. Reid

QUARRIERS
(formerly Quarriers Homes)
Head Office, Quarriers Village, Bridge
of Weir, Renfrewshire PA11 3SX
Tel: 01505-612224
Director, G. E. Lee

QUEEN'S NURSING INSTITUTE
31 Castle Terrace, Edinburgh EH1 2EL
Tel: 0131-229 2333
Director, G. D. C. Preston

QUEEN VICTORIA SCHOOL
Dunblane, Perthshire FK15 0JY
Tel: 01786-822288
Headmaster, B. Raine

RECORD SOCIETY, SCOTTISH
Department of Scottish History, University of
Glasgow, Glasgow G12 8QH
Tel: 0141-339 8855 ext 5682
Hon. Secretary, J. Kirk, Ph.D.

REFUGEE COUNCIL, SCOTTISH
43 Broughton Street, Edinburgh EH1 3JU
Tel: 0131-557 8083/4
Manager/Policy Development Officer,
R. Albeson

REGISTRARS OF SCOTLAND, ASSOCIATION
OF
7 East Fergus Place, Kirkcaldy KY1 1XT
Tel: 01592-412121
Hon. Secretary, E. A. Kilgour

ROYAL ACADEMY OF ENGINEERING
c/o Department of Petroleum Engineering,
Herriot-Watt University, Riccarton,
Edinburgh EH14 4ES
Tel: 0131-451 3128
Scottish Convenor, Prof. B. Smart

ROYAL CELTIC SOCIETY
23 Rutland Street, Edinburgh EH1 2RN
Tel: 0131-228 6449
Secretary, J. G. Cameron, WS

ROYAL HIGHLAND AND AGRICULTURAL
SOCIETY OF SCOTLAND
Royal Highland Centre, Ingliston, Edinburgh
EH28 8NF
Tel: 0131-335 6200
Chief Executive, R. Jones

ROYAL MEDICAL SOCIETY
Students Centre, 5/5 Bristo Square,
Edinburgh EH8 9AL
Tel: 0131-650 2672
Senior President, P. Mills

ROYAL NATIONAL INSTITUTE FOR THE
BLIND SCOTLAND
Dunedin House, 25 Ravelston Terrace,
Edinburgh EH4 3TP
Tel: 0131-311 8500
Director, A. Murray

ROYAL NATIONAL LIFEBOAT
INSTITUTION SCOTLAND
Belleview House, Hopetoun Street,
Edinburgh EH7 4ND
Tel: 0131-557 9171
Organizing Secretary, Mrs M. Fitzgerald

ROYAL NAVAL AND ROYAL MARINE
ASSOCIATION
Heriot Hill House, 1 Broughton Road,
Edinburgh EH7 4EW
Tel: 0131-556 2973
Hon. Secretary, W. Tovey

ROYAL SCOTTISH ACADEMY
The Mound, Edinburgh EH2 2EL
Tel: 0131-225 6671
Administrative Secretary, B. Laidlaw

ROYAL SOCIETY OF EDINBURGH
22-24 George Street, Edinburgh EH2 2PQ
Tel: 0131-240 5000
Executive Secretary, Dr W. Duncan

ROYAL UNITED KINGDOM BENEFICENT
ASSOCIATION
PO Box 16058, Gargunnock, by Stirling
FK8 3YN
Tel: 01698-860446
Representative in Scotland, Mrs M. Graham

RURAL FORUM
Highland House, St Catherine's Road, Perth
PH1 5RY
Tel: 01738-634565

RURAL SCOTLAND, ASSOCIATION FOR
THE PROTECTION OF
3rd Floor, Gladstone's Land, 483
Lawnmarket, Edinburgh EH1 2NT
Tel: 0131-225 7012/3
Director, Mrs J. Geddes

SACRO
31 Palmerston Place, Edinburgh EH12 5AP
Tel: 0131-226 4222
Chief Executive, Ms S. Matheson

ST ANDREW ANIMAL FUND
Queensferry Chambers, 10 Queensferry
Street, Edinburgh EH2 4PG
Tel: 0131-225 2116
Secretary, L. Ward

ST ANDREW'S CHILDREN'S SOCIETY LTD
Gillis Centre, 113 Whitehouse Loan,
Edinburgh EH9 1BB
Tel: 0131-452 8248
Director, S. J. Small

ST MARGARET'S CHILDREN AND FAMILY
CARE SOCIETY
274 Bath Street, Glasgow G2 4JR
Tel: 0141-332 8371
Director, Mrs M. Campbell

SALTIRE SOCIETY
9 Fountain Close, 22 High Street, Edinburgh
EH1 1TF
Tel: 0131-556 1836
Administrator, Mrs K. Munro

SAMARITANS
Tel: 0345-909090

SAVE THE CHILDREN SCOTLAND
2nd Floor, Haymarket House,
8 Clifton Terrace, Edinburgh EH12 5DR
Tel: 0131-527 8200
Programme Director, Scotland, Mrs A. Davies

SCHIZOPHRENIA ASSOCIATION OF GREAT
BRITAIN
59 Barrington Drive, Glasgow G4 9ES
Tel: 0141-339 3705
Scottish Director, Mrs A. Good

SCHIZOPHRENIA FELLOWSHIP
(SCOTLAND), NATIONAL
Claremont House, 130 East Claremont
Street, Edinburgh EH7 4LB
Tel: 0131-557 8969
Chief Executive, Ms M. Weir

SCOTS LANGUAGE RESOURCE CENTRE
ASSOCIATION
A. K. Bell Library, 2–8 York Place, Perth
PH2 8EP
Tel: 01738-440199
Secretary, Ms L. Roe

SCOTS LANGUAGE SOCIETY
c/o Scots Language Resouce Centre, A. K.
Bell Library, 2–8 York Place, Perth
PH2 8EP
Tel: 01738-440199
Secretary, D. H. Brown

SCOTS LEID ASSOCIE
Edintore Cottage, Drummuir, Keith,
Banffshire AB55 5PJ
Tel: 01542-810396

SCOTS SPEAKERS' CURN
c/o 30 Barrington Drive, Glasgow G4 9DT
Secretary, L. C. Wilson

SCOTS TUNG
27 Stoneyhill Avenue, Musselburgh,
Midlothian EH21 6SB
Tel: 0131-665 5440
Secretary, R. Fairnie

SCOTTISH CHIEFS, STANDING COUNCIL OF
Hope Chambers, 52 Leith Walk, Edinburgh EH6 5HW
Tel: 0131-554 6321
General Secretary, G. A. Way of Plean

SCOTTISH HISTORY SOCIETY
Department of Scottish History, 17 Buccleuch Place, University of Edinburgh, Edinburgh EH8 9LN
Tel: 0131-650 4030
Hon. Secretary, Dr S. Boardman

SCOTTISH NATIONAL DICTIONARY ASSOCIATION
27 George Square, Edinburgh EH8 9LD
Tel: 0131-650 4149
Editorial Director, Ms I. Macleod

SCOTTISH NATIONAL INSTITUTION FOR THE WAR BLINDED
PO Box 500, Gillespie Crescent, Edinburgh EH10 4HZ
Tel: 0131-229 1456
Secretary, J. B. M. Munro

SCOTTISH NATIONAL WAR MEMORIAL
The Castle, Edinburgh EH1 2YT
Tel: 0131-226 7393
Secretary, Lt.-Col. H. D. R. Mackay

SCOTTISH SOCIETY FOR THE PREVENTION OF CRUELTY TO ANIMALS
Braehead Mains, 603 Queensferry Road, Edinburgh EH4 6EA
Tel: 0131-339 0222
Chief Executive, J. Morris, CBE

SCOTTISH SOCIETY FOR THE PROTECTION OF WILD BIRDS
Foremount House, Kilbarchan, Renfrewshire PA10 2EZ
Tel: 01505-702419
Secretary, Dr J. A. Gibson

SCOUT ASSOCIATION (SCOTTISH COUNCIL)
Fordell Firs, Hillend, Dunfermline, Fife KY11 5HQ
Tel: 01383-419073
Chief Executive, J. A. Duffy

SEA CADETS
Northern Area HQ, HMS *Caledonia*, Rosyth, Fife FK11 2XH
Tel: 01383-416300
Area Office Manager, A. E. Parr

SELF-CATERERS, ASSOCIATION OF SCOTLAND'S
Dalreoch, Dunning, Perth PH2 0QJ
Tel: 01764-684600
Secretary, Mrs W. W. Marshall

SHELTER SCOTLAND
4th Floor, Scotia Bank House, 6 South Charlotte Street, Edinburgh EH2 4AW
Tel: 0131-473 7170
Director, Ms E. Nicholson

SINGLE HOMELESS, SCOTTISH COUNCIL FOR
5th Floor, Wellgate House, 200 Cowgate, Edinburgh EH1 1NQ
Tel: 0131-226 4382
Director, R. Aldridge

SOCIAL WORKERS, BRITISH ASSOCIATION OF
28 North Bridge, Edinburgh EH1 1QG
Tel: 0131-225 4549
Scottish Secretary, Mrs R. Stark

SOLICITORS IN THE SUPREME COURT OF SCOTLAND, SOCIETY OF
SSC Library, Parliament House, 11 Parliament Square, Edinburgh EH1 1RF
Tel: 0131-225 6268
Secretary, I. L. S. Balfour

SPEAKERS CLUBS, ASSOCIATION OF
Ryvoan, 38 Smithfield Crescent, Blairgowrie PH10 6UD
Tel: 01250-875262
Contact, J. Gibb

SPINA BIFIDA ASSOCIATION, SCOTTISH
190 Queensferry Road, Edinburgh EH4 2BW
Tel: 0131-332 0743
Chief Executive, A. H. D. Wynd

SPORTS AID FOUNDATION
76 Constitution Street, Leith, Edinburgh EH6 6RP
Tel: 0131-555 4584

SPORTS MEDICINE AND SPORTS SCIENCE, SCOTTISH INSTITUTE OF
University of Strathclyde, Jordanhill Campus, 76 Southbrae Drive, Glasgow G13 1PP
Tel: 0141-950 3189
Manager, E. Samuel

SSAFA FORCES HELP
New Haig House, Logie Green Road, Edinburgh EH7 4HR
Tel: 0131-557 1697
Branch Secretary, Ms J. Spence

STEWART SOCIETY
2 York Place, Edinburgh EH1 3EP
Tel: 0131-557 6824
Hon. Secretary, Mrs M. Walker

SUE RYDER FOUNDATION (SCOTLAND)
General Office, Unit 23, Thistle Business
    Park, Broxburn, West Lothian EH52 5AS
Tel: 01506-852183
Regional Manager, R. McDonald

SUSTRANS SCOTLAND
3 Coates Place, Edinburgh EH3 7AA
Tel: 0131-623 7600
Administration Manager, Ms H. Maxfield

TARTANS SOCIETY, SCOTTISH
Hall of Records, Port-na-Craig Road,
    Pitlochry PH16 5ND
Tel: 01796-474079
Archivist, K. Lumsden

THISTLE FOUNDATION
Niddrie Mains Road, Edinburgh EH16 4EA
Tel: 0131-661 3366
Director, Ms J. Fisher

TURNING POINT SCOTLAND
121 West Street, Glasgow G5 8BA
Tel: 0141-418 0882
Chief Executive, Ms N. Maciver

UNICEF IN SCOTLAND
43 Aytoun Road, Glasgow G41 5HW
Tel: 0141-422 1662
Scottish Officer, Mrs A. Forrester

UNITED NATIONS ASSOCIATION
40 Grosvenor Lane, Glasgow G12 9AA
Tel: 0141-339 5408
National Officer, Ms F. Mildmay

VARIETY CLUB OF GREAT BRITAIN
437 Crow Road, Glasgow G11 7DZ
Tel: 0141-357 4411
Executive Secretary, Ms P. A. Jenkins

VICTIM SUPPORT SCOTLAND
15/23 Hardwell Close, Edinburgh EH8 9RX
Tel: 0131-668 4486
Director, Ms A. Paterson

VOLUNTARY ORGANIZATIONS, SCOTTISH
COUNCIL FOR
18–19 Claremont Crescent, Edinburgh
    EH7 4QD
Tel: 0131-556 3882
Director, M. Sime

WILDFOWL AND WETLANDS TRUST –
CAERLAVEROCK
Eastpark Farm, Caerlaverock, Dumfriesshire
    DG1 4RS
Tel: 01387-770200
Centre Manager, J. B. Doherty

WILDLIFE TRUST, SCOTTISH
Cramond House, Kirk Cramond, Cramond
    Glebe Road, Edinburgh EH4 6NS
Tel: 0131-312 7765
Chief Executive, S. Sankey

WOMEN'S AID, SCOTTISH
Norton Park, 57 Albion Road, Edinburgh
    EH7 5QY
Tel: 0131-475 2372
National Worker, Ms K. Arnot

WOMEN'S ROYAL VOLUNTARY SERVICE
44 Albany Street, Edinburgh EH1 3QR
Tel: 0131-558 8028
Administrator, Scotland, Mrs M. Alexander

WOMEN'S RURAL INSTITUTES, SCOTTISH
42 Heriot Row, Edinburgh EH3 6ES
Tel: 0131-225 1724
General Secretary, Mrs A. Peacock

WOODLAND TRUST SCOTLAND
Glenruthven Mill, Abbey Road, Auchterarder,
    Perthshire PH3 1DP
Tel: 01764-662554
Operations Director, Scotland, Ms A. Douglas

WRITERS TO HM SIGNET, SOCIETY OF
Signet Library, Parliament Square, Edinburgh
    EH1 1RF
Tel: 0131-220 3426
General Manager, J. R. C. Foster

WWF-SCOTLAND (WORLD WIDE FUND
FOR NATURE)
8 The Square, Aberfeldy, Perthshire
    PH15 2DD
Tel: 01887-820449
Head, WWF Scotland, S. Pepper

YOUNG MEN'S CHRISTIAN ASSOCIATION
James Love House, 11 Rutland Street,
    Edinburgh EH1 2AE
Tel: 0131-228 1464
National General Secretary, J. Knox

YOUNG WOMEN'S CHRISTIAN
ASSOCIATION OF GREAT BRITAIN
7 Randolph Crescent, Edinburgh EH3 7TH
Tel: 0131-225 7592
Scottish Director, Miss I. A. Carr

YOUTH CLUBS UK
Balfour House, 19 Bonnington Grove,
    Edinburgh EH6 4BL
Tel: 0131-554 2561
Chief Executive, Scotland, Ms C. Downie

YOUTH HOSTELS ASSOCIATION,
SCOTTISH
7 Glebe Crescent, Stirling FK8 2JA
Tel: 01786-891400
General Secretary, W. Forsyth

YOUTHLINK SCOTLAND
Central Hall, West Tollcross, Edinburgh
    EH3 9BP
Tel: 0131-229 0339
Chief Executive, G. Johnston

YOUTH THEATRE, SCOTTISH
6th Floor, Gordon Chambers, 90 Mitchell
    Street, Glasgow G1 3NQ
Tel: 0141-221 5127
General Manager, Ms C. Lappin

ZOOLOGICAL SOCIETY OF SCOTLAND,
ROYAL
Scottish National Zoological Park, Edinburgh
    Zoo, 134 Corstorphine Road,
    Edinburgh EH12 6TS
Tel: 0131-334 9171
Director, D. Waugh, PH.D.

THE LAND

AREA

as at 31 March 1981

	Scotland		United Kingdom	
	sq. miles	sq. km	sq. miles	sq. km
Land	29,767	77,097	93,006	240,883
Inland water*	653	1,692	1,242	3,218
Total	30,420	78,789	94,248	244,101

* Excluding tidal water

Source: The Stationery Office, *Annual Abstract of Statistics 1999* (Crown copyright)

USES OF LAND 1996

percentage of total area

	Scotland	UK
Agricultural land		
Crops and bare fallow	8	20
Grasses and rough grazing[1]	65	51
Other[2]	2	3
Forest and woodland[3]	15	10
Urban land not otherwise specified[4]	11	15

1. Includes grasses over and under five years old, and sole right and common grazing
2. Set-aside and other land on agricultural holdings. Excludes woodland on agricultural holdings
3. Forestry Commission data; covers both private and state-owned land. Includes woodland on agricultural holdings
4. Land used for urban and other purposes, e.g. transport and recreation, and for non-agricultural, semi-natural environments, e.g. grouse moors, sand dunes, inland waters

Source: The Stationery Office, *Digest of Environmental Statistics 20, 1998* (Crown copyright)

GEOGRAPHY

Scotland occupies the northern portion of the main island of Great Britain and includes the Inner and Outer Hebrides, and the Orkney, Shetland, and many other islands. It lies between 60° 51′ 30″ and 54° 38′ N. latitude and between 1° 45′ 32″ and 6° 14′ W. longitude, with England to the south, the Atlantic Ocean on the north and west, and the North Sea on the east.

The greatest length of the mainland (Cape Wrath to the Mull of Galloway) is 274 miles, and the greatest breadth (Buchan Ness to Applecross) is 154 miles. The customary measurement of the island of Great Britain is from the site of John o' Groats house, near Duncansby Head, Caithness, to Land's End, Cornwall, a total distance of 603 miles (965 km) in a straight line and approximately 900 miles (1,440 km) by road.

Relief

There are three natural orographic divisions of mainland Scotland. The southern uplands have their highest points in Merrick (2,764 ft/814 m), Rhinns of Kells (2,669 ft/814 m), and Cairnsmuir of Carsphairn (2,614 ft/796 m), in the west; and the Tweedsmuir Hills in the east (Broad Law 2,756 ft/830 m, Dollar Law 2,682 ft/817 m, Hartfell 2,651ft/808 m).

The central lowlands, formed by the valleys of the Clyde, Forth and Tay, divide the southern uplands from the northern Highlands, which extend almost from the extreme north of the mainland to the central lowlands, and are divided into a northern and a southern system by the Great Glen.

The Grampian Mountains, which entirely cover the southern Highland area, include in the west Ben Nevis (4,406 ft/1,343 m), the highest point in the British Isles, and in the east the Cairngorm Mountains (Ben Macdui 4,296 ft/1,309 m, Braeriach 4,248 ft/1,295 m, Cairn Gorm 4,084 ft/1,246 m). The north-western Highland area contains the mountains of Wester and Easter Ross (Carn Eighe 3,880 ft/1,183 m, Sgurr na Lapaich 3,775 ft/1,150 m).

Created, like the central lowlands, by a major geological fault, the Great Glen (60 miles/96 km long) runs between Inverness and Fort William, and contains Loch Ness, Loch Oich and Loch Lochy. These are linked to each other and to the north-east and south-west coasts of Scotland by the Caledonian Canal, the River Lochy and the long sea-loch Loch Linnhe, providing a navigable passage between the Moray Firth and the Inner Hebrides.

In 1891 Sir Hugh Munro compiled a list of the 284 mountains in Scotland over 3,000 feet (914 m) high. These mountains have become popularly known as the Munros. The 219 mountains between 2,500 feet (762 m) and 3,000 feet, with a drop of at least 500 feet (150 m) between each listed hill and an adjacent higher point, are known as Corbetts, after John Rookes Corbett, who listed them in 1930.

Hydrography

The western coast is fragmented by peninsulas and islands and deeply indented by sea-lochs (fjords), the longest of which is Loch Fyne (42 miles long) in Argyll. Although the east coast tends to be less fractured and lower, there are several great drowned inlets (firths), for instance the Firth of Forth, the Firth of Tay and the Moray Firth. The Firth of Clyde is the chief example of this feature in the west.

The lochs are the principal hydrographic feature. The largest in Scotland and in Britain is Loch Lomond (27.46 sq. miles/71.12 sq. km), in the Grampian valleys; the longest and deepest is Loch Ness (24 miles/38 km long and 800 ft/244 m deep), in the Great Glen. Loch Shin (20 miles/32 km long) and Loch Maree in the Highlands are the longest lochs in the north-west Highlands

The longest river is the Tay (117 miles/188 km), noted for its salmon. It flows into the North Sea, with Dundee on the estuary, which is spanned by the Tay Bridge (10,289 ft/3,137 m), opened in 1887, and the Tay Road Bridge (7,365 ft/2,245 m), opened in 1966. The present Tay rail bridge is the second to have been built; the original collapsed in 1879, only a year after completion, with the loss of 150 lives.

Other noted salmon rivers are the Dee (90 miles/144 km) which flows into the North Sea at Aberdeen, and the Spey (110 miles/172 km), the swiftest flowing river in the British Isles, which flows into the Moray Firth. The Tweed, which gave its name to the woollen cloth produced along its banks, marks in the lower stretches of its 96-mile (155 km) course the border between Scotland and England.

The most important river commercially is the Clyde (106 miles/171 m), formed by the junction of the Daer and Portrail water, which flows through the city of Glasgow to the Firth of Clyde. During its course it passes over the picturesque Falls of Clyde, Bonnington Linn (30 ft/9 m), Corra Linn (84 ft/26 m), Dundaff Linn (10 ft/3 m) and Stonebyres Linn (80 ft/24 m), above and below Lanark. The Forth (66 miles/106 km), upon which stands Edinburgh, is spanned by the Forth (Railway) Bridge (1890), which is 5,330 feet (1,625 m) long, and the Forth (Road) Bridge (1964), which has a total length of 6,156 feet (1,987 m) (over water) and a single span of 3,300 feet (1,006 m).

The highest waterfall in Scotland, and the British Isles, is Eas a'Chùal Aluinn with a total height of 658 feet (200 m), which falls from Glas Bheinn in Sutherland. The Falls of Glomach, on a head-stream of the Elchaig in Wester Ross, have a drop of 370 feet (113 m).

THE ISLANDS

ORKNEY

The Orkney Islands lie about six miles north of the mainland, separated from it by the Pentland Firth. Of the 90 islands and islets (holms and skerries) in the group, about one-third are inhabited.

The populations of the islands shown here at the 1991 census include those of smaller islands forming part of the same civil parish.

Mainland	15,128
Burray	363
Eday	166
Flotta and Fara	126
Graemsay and Hoy	477
North Ronaldsay	92
Papa Westray	85
Rousay	291
Sanday	533
Shapinsay	322
South Ronaldsay	943
Stronsay	382
Westray	704

The islands are rich in prehistoric and Scandinavian remains, the most notable being the Stone Age village of Skara Brae, the burial chamber of Maeshowe, the many brochs (towers) and the 12th-century St Magnus Cathedral. Scapa Flow, between Mainland and Hoy, was the war station of the British Grand Fleet from 1914 to 1919 and the scene of the scuttling of the surrendered German High Seas Fleet (21 June 1919).

Most of the islands are low-lying and fertile, and farming (principally beef cattle) is the main industry. Flotta, to the south of Scapa Flow, is the site of the oil terminal for the Piper, Claymore and Tartan fields in the North Sea.

The chief town is Kirkwall (population 6,881) on Mainland.

SHETLAND

The Shetland Islands lie about 50 miles north of the Orkneys, with Fair Isle about half-way between the two groups. Out Stack, off Muckle Flugga, one mile north of Unst, is the most northerly part of the British Isles (60° 51′ 30″ N. lat.).

There are over 100 islands, of which 16 are inhabited. Populations at the 1991 census were:

Mainland	17,596
Bressay	352
East Burra	72
Fair Isle	67
Fetlar	90
Housay	85
Muckle Roe	115
Trondra	117
Unst	1,055
West Burra	857
Whalsay	1,041
Yell	1,075

Shetland's many archaeological sites include Jarlshof, Mousa and Clickhimin, and its long connection with Scandinavia has resulted in a strong Norse influence on its place-names and dialect.

Industries include fishing, knitwear and farming. In addition to the fishing fleet there are fish processing factories, while the traditional handknitting of Fair Isle and Unst is supplemented now with machine-knitted garments. Farming is mainly crofting, with sheep being raised on the moorland and hills of the islands. Latterly the islands have become a centre of the North Sea oil industry, with pipelines from the Brent and Ninian fields running to the terminal at Sullom Voe, the largest of its kind in Europe. Lerwick is the main centre for supply services for offshore oil exploration and development.

The chief town is Lerwick (population 7,901) on Mainland.

THE HEBRIDES

Until the late 13th century the Hebrides included other Scottish islands in the Firth of Clyde, the peninsula of Kintyre (Argyll), the Isle of Man, and the (Irish) Isle of Rathlin. The origin of the name is stated to be the Greek *Eboudai*, latinized as *Hebudes* by Pliny, and corrupted to its present form. The Norwegian name *Sudreyjar* (Southern Islands) was latinized as *Sodorenses*, a name that survives in the Anglican bishopric of Sodor and Man.

There are over 500 islands and islets, of which about 100 are inhabited, though mountainous terrain and extensive peat bogs mean that only a fraction of the total area is under cultivation. Stone, Bronze and Iron Age settlement has left many remains, including those at Callanish on Lewis, and Norse colonization influenced language, customs and place-names. Occupations include farming (mostly crofting and stock-raising), fishing and the manufacture of tweeds and other woollens. Tourism is also important to the economy.

The Inner Hebrides

The Inner Hebrides lie off the west coast of Scotland and relatively close to the mainland. The largest and best-known is Skye (area 643 sq. miles/1,648 sq. km; population (1991 census) 8,868; chief town, Portree), which contains the Cuillin Hills (Sgurr Alasdair 3,257 ft/993 m), the Red Hills (Beinn na Caillich 2,403 ft/732 m), Bla Bheinn (3,046 ft/928 m) and The Storr (2,358 ft/ m). Skye is also famous as the refuge of the Young Pretender in 1746. Other islands in the Highland council area include Raasay (population 163), Rum, Eigg and Muck.

Further south the Inner Hebridean islands include:

Arran – population 4,474; containing Goat Fell (2,868 ft/874 m) and Caisteal Abhail (2,735 ft/834 m)

Coll and Tiree – population 940

Colonsay and Oronsay – population 106

Islay – area 235 sq. miles/602 sq.km; population 3,538

Jura – area 160 sq. miles/410 sq.km; population 196; with a range of hills culminating in the Paps of Jura (Beinn-an-Oir, 2,576 ft/784 m, and Beinn Chaolais, 2,477 ft/734 m)

Mull – area 367 sq. miles/941 sq. km; population 2,708; chief town Tobermory; containing Ben More (3,171 ft/966 m)

The Outer Hebrides

The Outer Hebrides, separated from the mainland by the Minch, now form the Eilean Siar/Western Isles council area. The populations of the main islands at the 1991 census were:

Lewis with Harris	21,737
Baleshare	55
Barra	1,244
Benbecula	1,803
Bernera	262
Berneray	141
Eriskay	179
Grimsay	215
North Uist	1,404
Scalpay	382
South Uist	2,106
Vatersay	72

The main islands are Lewis with Harris (area 770 sq. miles/1,974 sq. km), whose chief town, Stornoway, is the administrative headquarters.

THE ENVIRONMENT

Recent UK governments have increasingly seen environmental policy as part of a broader concept of sustainable development. This involves achieving environmental, economic and social objectives simultaneously, taking environmental impact into account in all areas of policy rather than considering environmental policy in isolation. Government policy and operations are subject to scrutiny by the parliamentary environmental audit committee.

The UK government is committed to sustainable development under the terms of the Rio Declaration, which was adopted at the 1992 UN Conference on Environment and Development (UNCED), and to meeting certain internationally agreed environmental targets with regard to the reduction of greenhouse gases, improving air and water quality, protecting the sea, increasing and protecting forest and woodland areas, achieving energy savings, reducing and recycling waste, reducing empty housing, etc. While these targets apply to Scotland as part of the UK, policy on sustainable development and the environment has been devolved to the Scottish Parliament and Executive.

The UK Government's sustainable development strategy, *A Better Quality of Life*, published on 17 May 1999, acknowledges that devolution gives the Scottish Parliament freedom to adopt a separate approach to sustainable development if it considers this necessary in order to reflect more closely Scottish circumstances and priorities. Thus it will be for the Scottish Parliament to decide how to participate in the overall UK programme.

In February 1999 the Scottish Office published *Down to Earth: A Scottish Perspective on Sustainable Development*, covering planning for sustainability, energy, sustainability in industry, waste, housing, transport, and other subjects. The Secretary of State for Scotland's Advisory Group on Sustainable Development (AGSD) in March 1999 published *Scotland the Sustainable?: Ten Action Points for the Scottish Parliament*. It recommended that the Scottish Parliament and Executive should set up a Sustainable Development Commission; set sustainability aims, objectives, targets and timescales; take a pro-active approach to the sustainability of construction and the built environment; strengthen the role of the planning system in delivering national and local sustainable development; and support

innovation in sustainable development. An action plan with a further ten recommendations for the Parliament and Executive was laid out in *Scotland the Sustainable?: The Learning Process*, published at the same time.

Local Agenda 21

As elsewhere in the world, local government and organizations seek to promote sustainable development through the Local Agenda 21 programme, under which local authorities draw up a sustainable development strategy for their area, to protect and enhance the local environment while meeting social needs and promoting economic success. The programme is managed by the Local Agenda 21 Steering Group, made up of representatives from the Local Government Association, the Convention of Scottish Local Authorities, the Association of Local Authorities of Northern Ireland, the TUC, the Advisory Committee on Business and the Environment, the World-Wide Fund for Nature, and other organizations.

Although local authorities are under no statutory obligation to take part in Local Agenda 21, most local authorities are engaged in or committed to the programme. In February 1999, the Scottish Office published *Changed Days: Local Agenda 21 in Scotland*, describing the progress and activities of each council under the initiative. For Local Agenda 21 officers and contacts at each council, *see* Council Directory.

The government website about sustainable development in Scotland is at http://www.sustainable.scotland.gov.uk.

ADVISORY COMMITTEE ON BUSINESS AND THE ENVIRONMENT
Floor 6/D9, Ashdown House, 123 Victoria
    Street, London SW1E 6DE
Tel: 0171-890 6624

CONVENTION OF SCOTTISH LOCAL
AUTHORITIES
see page 199

EDUCATION FOR SUSTAINABLE
DEVELOPMENT GROUP
Saltcoats, Gullane, East Lothian EH31 2AG
Tel./fax: 01620-843565

ENVIRONMENTAL TECHNOLOGY BEST PRACTICE PROGRAMME
Environment and Energy helpline: 0800-585794
Web: http://www.environment.detr.gov.uk/bpp/helpline.htm

GOVERNMENT PANEL ON SUSTAINABLE DEVELOPMENT
Zone 4/D9 Ashdown House, 123 Victoria Street, London SW1E 6DE
Tel: 0171-890 4962
Web: http://www.detr.gov.uk/environment

IMPROVEMENT AND DEVELOPMENT AGENCY (LOCAL AGENDA 21)
Layden House, 76-78 Turnmill Street, London EC1M 5QU
Tel: 0171-296 6599
Web: http://www.la21-uk.org.uk

SCOTTISH ENVIRONMENT PROTECTION AGENCY
see page 69

SUSTAINABLE DEVELOPMENT TEAM
Scottish Executive Rural Affairs Department, Victoria Quay, Edinburgh EH6 6QQ
Tel: 0131-244 0395; fax: 0131-244 0195
E-mail: sustainable@scotland.gov.uk

UK BIODIVERSITY GROUP
c/o Biodiversity Action Plan Secretariat, European Wildlife Division, Department of the Environment, Transport and the Regions, Room 902D, Tollgate House, Houlton Street, Bristol BS2 9DJ
Tel: 0117-987 8974
Web: http://www.jncc.gov.uk/ukbg

COUNTRYSIDE CONSERVATION

National Parks

Currently there are no National Parks in Scotland. The National Parks and Access to the Countryside Act 1949 dealt only with England and Wales and made no provision for Scotland. In 1998 the Government announced that it would consider the creation of National Parks in Scotland. Scottish Natural Heritage submitted proposals to the Government; it will be for the Scottish Parliament to legislate.

National Park status would enable the co-ordination of resources and development across a wide area that attracts large numbers of visitors. Scottish Natural Heritage has recommended that the first National Park should be Loch Lomond and the Trossachs, and the second the Cairngorms. It is hoped that subsequent designations will be made as the result of local demand.

National Scenic Areas

National Scenic Areas have a broadly equivalent status to the Areas of Outstanding Natural Beauty in England and Wales. Scottish Natural Heritage recognizes areas of national scenic significance. At mid 1999 there were 40 of these, covering a total area of 1,001,800 hectares (2,475,448 acres).

National Scenic Areas would continue to exist after the designation of National Parks. A review is pending to determine whether any areas should be added to or removed from the current list.

Development within National Scenic Areas is dealt with by the local planning authority, which is required to consult Scottish Natural Heritage concerning certain categories of development. Land management uses can also be modified in the interest of scenic conservation.

Assynt-Coigach (Highland), 90,200 ha/
    222,884 acres
Ben Nevis and Glen Coe (Highland/Argyll
    and Bute/Perth and Kinross), 101,600 ha/
    251,053 acres
Cairngorm Mountains (Highland/
    Aberdeenshire/Moray), 67,200 ha/
    166,051 acres
Cuillin Hills (Highland), 21,900 ha/54,115
    acres
Deeside and Lochnagar (Aberdeenshire/
    Angus), 40,000 ha/98,840 acres
Dornoch Firth (Highland), 7,500 ha/18,532
    acres
East Stewartry Coast (Dumfries and
    Galloway), 4,500 ha/11,119 acres

Eildon and Leaderfoot (Scottish Borders), 3,600 ha/8,896 acres

Fleet Valley (Dumfries and Galloway), 5,300 ha/13,096 acres

Glen Affric (Highland), 19,300 ha/47,690 acres

Glen Strathfarrar (Highland), 3,800 ha/9,390 acres

Hoy and West Mainland (Orkney Islands), 14,800 ha/36,571 acres

Jura (Argyll and Bute), 21,800 ha/53,868 acres

Kintail (Highland), 15,500 ha/38,300 acres

Knapdale (Argyll and Bute), 19,800 ha/48,926 acres

Knoydart (Highland), 39,500 ha/97,604 acres

Kyle of Tongue (Highland), 18,500 ha/45,713 acres

Kyles of Bute (Argyll and Bute), 4,400 ha/10,872 acres

Loch na Keal, Mull (Argyll and Bute), 12,700 ha/31,382 acres

Loch Lomond (Argyll and Bute/Stirling/West Dunbartonshire), 27,400 ha/67,705 acres

Loch Rannoch and Glen Lyon (Perth and Kinross/Stirling), 48,400 ha/119,596 acres

Loch Shiel (Highland), 13,400 ha/33,111 acres

Loch Tummel (Perth and Kinross), 9,200 ha/22,733 acres

Lynn of Lorn (Argyll and Bute), 4,800 ha/11,861 acres

Morar, Moidart and Ardnamurchan (Highland), 13,500 ha/33,358 acres

North-west Sutherland (Highland), 20,500 ha/50,655 acres

Nith Estuary (Dumfries and Galloway), 9,300 ha/22,980 acres

North Arran (North Ayrshire), 23,800 ha/58,810 acres

River Earn (Perth and Kinross), 3,000 ha/7,413 acres

River Tay (Perth and Kinross), 5,600 ha/13,838 acres

St Kilda (Western Isles), 900 ha/2,224 acres

Scarba, Lunga and the Garvellachs (Argyll and Bute), 1,900 ha/4,695 acres

Shetland (Shetland Islands), 11,600 ha/28,664 acres

Small Isles (Highland), 15,500 ha/38,300 acres

South Lewis, Harris and North Uist (Western Isles), 109,600 ha/270,822 acres

South Uist Machair (Western Isles), 6,100 ha/15,073 acres

The Trossachs (Stirling), 4,600 ha/11,367 acres

Trotternish (Highland), 5,000 ha/12,355 acres

Upper Tweeddale (Scottish Borders), 10,500 ha/25,945 acres

Wester Ross (Highland), 145,300 ha/359,036 acres

NATURE CONSERVATION AREAS

Sites of Special Scientific Interest

Site of Special Scientific Interest (SSSI) is a legal notification applied to land which Scottish Natural Heritage (SNH) identifies as being of special interest because of its flora, fauna, geological or physiographical features. In some cases, SSSIs are managed as nature reserves.

SNH must notify the designation of a SSSI to the local planning authority, every owner/occupier of the land, and the Scottish Executive. Forestry and agricultural departments and a number of other bodies are also informed of this notification.

Objections to the notification of a SSSI are dealt with by the appropriate regional board or the main board of SNH, depending on the nature of the objection. Unresolved objections on scientific grounds must be referred to the Advisory Committee for SSSI.

The protection of these sites depends on the co-operation of individual landowners and occupiers. Owner/occupiers must consult SNH and gain written consent before they can undertake certain listed activities on the site. Funds are available through management agreements and grants to assist owners and occupiers in conserving sites' interests. As a last resort a site can be purchased.

At 31 March 1999, there were in Scotland 1,448 SSSIs, with an area of 919,597 ha/2,272,324 acres.

National Nature Reserves

National Nature Reserves are defined in the National Parks and Access to the Countryside Act 1949 as land designated for the study and preservation of flora and fauna, or of geological or physiographical features.

Scottish Natural Heritage can designate as a National Nature Reserve land which is being managed as a nature reserve under an agreement with one of the statutory nature conservation agencies; land held and managed by SNH; or land held and managed as a nature reserve by another approved body. SNH can make by-laws to protect reserves from undesirable activities; these are subject to confirmation by the Scottish Executive.

At 31 March 1999, there were in Scotland 71 National Nature Reserves, with an area of 114,277 ha/282,378 acres.

Local Nature Reserves

Local Nature Reserves are defined in the National Parks and Access to the Countryside Act 1949 as land designated for the study and preservation of flora and fauna, or of geological or physiographical features. The Act gives local authorities the power to acquire, declare and manage local nature reserves in consultation with Scottish Natural Heritage. Conservation trusts can also own and manage non-statutory local nature reserves.

At 31 March 1999, there were in Scotland 29 Local Nature Reserves, with an area of 9,297 ha/22,973 acres.

Forest Nature Reserves

Forest Enterprise (an executive agency of the Forestry Commission) is responsible for the management of the Commission's forests. It has created 46 Forest Nature Reserves with the aim of protecting and conserving special forms of natural habitat, flora and fauna. There are about 300 SSSIs on the estates, some of which are also Nature Reserves.

Forest Nature Reserves extend in size from under 50 hectares (124 acres) to over 500 hectares (1,236 acres). Several of the largest are in Scotland, including the Black Wood of Rannoch, by Loch Rannoch; Culbin Forest, near Forres; Glen Affric, near Fort Augustus; Kylerhea, Isle of Skye; and Starr Forest, in Galloway Forest Park.

Forest Enterprise also manages 18 Caledonian Forest Reserves in Scotland. These reserves are intended to protect and expand 16,000 hectares of native oak and pine woods in the Scottish highlands.

Marine Nature Reserves

The Wildlife and Countryside Act 1981 gives the Scottish Executive power to designate Marine Nature Reserves, and Scottish Natural Heritage powers to select and manage them. Marine Nature Reserves provide protection for marine flora and fauna and for geological and physiographical features on land covered by tidal waters or parts of the sea in or adjacent to the UK. Reserves also provide opportunities for study and research. No statutory Marine Nature Reserves have been designated in Scotland to date.

WILDLIFE CONSERVATION

The Wildlife and Countryside Act 1981 gives legal protection to a wide range of wild animals and plants. Subject to parliamentary approval, the Secretary of State for the Environment, Transport and the Regions may vary the animals and plants given legal protection. The most recent variation of Schedules 5 and 8 came into effect in March and April 1998.

Under Section 9 and Schedule 5 of the Act it is illegal without a licence to kill, injure, take, possess or sell any of the listed animals (whether alive or dead) and to disturb its place of shelter and protection or to destroy that place.

Under Section 13 and Schedule 8 of the Act it is illegal without a licence to pick, uproot, sell or destroy any of the listed plants and, unless authorized, to uproot any wild plant.

The Act lays down a close season for wild birds (other than game birds) from 1 February to 31 August inclusive, each year. Exceptions to these dates are made for:

Capercaillie – 1 February to 30 September
Snipe – 1 February to 11 August
Wild Duck and *Wild Goose* (below high water mark) – 21 February to 31 August

Birds which may be killed or taken in Scotland outside the close season (except on Sundays and on Christmas Day) are the above-named, plus coot, certain wild duck (gadwall, goldeneye, mallard, pintail, pochard, shoveler, teal, tufted duck, wigeon), certain wild geese (Canada, greylag, pink-footed), moorhen, golden plover and woodcock.

Certain wild birds may be killed or taken subject to the conditions of a general licence at any time by authorized persons: crow, collared dove, gull (great and lesser black-backed or herring), jackdaw, jay, magpie, pigeon (feral or wood), rook, sparrow (house) and starling. Conditions usually apply where the birds pose a threat to agriculture, public health, air safety, other bird species, and to prevent the spread of disease.

All other British birds are fully protected by law throughout the year.

International Conventions

The UK is party to a number of international conventions protecting wildlife and its habitats, including:
- the Ramsar Convention on Wetlands of International Importance (ratified 1976)
- the Bonn Convention on the Conservation of Migratory Species of Wild Animals (ratified 1979)

- the Bern Convention on the Conservation of European Wildlife and Natural Habitats (ratified 1982)
- the Convention on Trade in Endangered Species of Wild Fauna and Flora (CITES) (ratified 1975)

It is also subject to the European Directive on the Conservation of Natural Habitats of Wild Fauna and Flora (1992), which became law in the UK in 1994, and the Council (EC) Directive on the Conservation of Wild Birds (1979). More information on protected species of animals and plants in Scotland may be obtained from Scottish Natural Heritage (*see* page 70).

CLOSE SEASONS
and Restrictions on Game

Shooting game or hares at night is prohibited, with certain exceptions. Although there are no legal restrictions, it is not customary to kill game on a Sunday or Christmas Day. If shooting is to take place on a Sunday, it should begin after noon.

All dates are inclusive.

GAME BIRDS

Black game (heathfowl) – 11 December to 19 August
Grouse (muirfowl) – 11 December to 11 August
Partridge – 2 February to 31 August
Pheasant – 2 February to 30 September
Ptarmigan – 11 December to 11 August

For the regulation of shooting wild birds other than game birds, e.g. capercaillie, woodcock, wild duck and geese, *see* page 240.

HUNTING AND GROUND GAME

There is no statutory close time for fox-hunting or rabbit-shooting, nor for hares. However, under the Hares Preservation Act 1892 the sale of hares (except imported ones) or leverets in Great Britain is prohibited from 1 March to 31 July inclusive. The recognized date for the opening of the fox-hunting season is 1 November, and it continues until the following April.

DEER

The statutory close seasons for deer are:

Fallow deer
Male	1 May–31 July
Female	16 February–20 October

Red deer
Male	21 October–30 June
Female	16 February–20 October

Roe deer
Male	21 October–31 March
Female	1 April–20 October

Sika deer
Male	21 October–30 June
Female	16 February–20 October

Red/Sika hybrids
Male	21 October–30 June
Female	16 February–20 October

ANGLING

Brown Trout

The statutory close time for fishing for brown trout is from 7 October to 14 March inclusive.

Salmon

The Scottish Parliament is responsible for the regulation of salmon fishing, through the Scottish Executive Rural Affairs Department. Local management is devolved to district salmon fishery boards. The annual close time for salmon fishing in each salmon fishery district is set by law. District salmon fishery boards may apply to change the annual close time for their district. Weekly close time for nets is 6 p.m. on Friday to 6 a.m. on Monday. Weekly close time for salmon angling is Sunday.

Details of regulations may be obtained from the Inspector of Salmon and Freshwater Fisheries.

INSPECTOR OF SALMON AND
FRESHWATER FISHERIES
Pentland House, 47 Robb's Loan, Edinburgh
EH14 1TY
Tel: 0131-244 6227; fax: 0131-244 6313

ASSOCIATION OF DISTRICT SALMON
FISHERY BOARDS
5A Lennox Street, Edinburgh EH4 1QB
Tel: 0131-343 2433
Director, A. Wallace

Sea Trout

The regulations on fishing for sea trout are the same as those on fishing for salmon.

Coarse Fishing

The Scottish Parliament is responsible for the regulation of coarse fishing, through the Scottish Executive Rural Affairs Department. Information may be obtained from the Inspector of Salmon and Freshwater Fisheries.

Licences

No licence is required to fish in Scotland. In the case of salmon fishing, a person must have the legal right to fish or written permission from a person having such right. To fish for freshwater fish, including trout, permission should be obtained from the riparian owner. Where a protection order is in force, it is an offence to fish for freshwater fish in inland waters without a permit.

THE PEOPLE

POPULATION

The first official census of population in Great Britain was taken in 1801 and a census has been taken every ten years since, except in 1941 when there was no census because of war. The next official census in the UK is due in April 2001.

CENSUS RESULTS (SCOTLAND) 1801–1991

	Total	Male	Female
1801	1,608,000	739,000	869,000
1811	1,806,000	826,000	980,000
1821	2,092,000	983,000	1,109,000
1831	2,364,000	1,114,000	1,250,000
1841	2,620,000	1,242,000	1,378,000
1851	2,889,000	1,376,000	1,513,000
1861	3,062,000	1,450,000	1,612,000
1871	3,360,000	1,603,000	1,757,000
1881	3,736,000	1,799,000	1,936,000
1891	4,026,000	1,943,000	2,083,000
1901	4,472,000	2,174,000	2,298,000
1911	4,761,000	2,309,000	2,452,000
1921	4,882,000	2,348,000	2,535,000
1931	4,843,000	2,326,000	2,517,000
1951	5,096,000	2,434,000	2,662,000
1961	5,179,000	2,483,000	2,697,000
1971	5,229,000	2,515,000	2,714,000
1981	5,131,000	2,466,000	2,664,000
1991	4,998,567	2,391,961	2,606,606

POPULATION BY AGE AND SEX 1997

The estimated population at 30 June 1997 was 5,122,500, which represented a decrease of 5,500 since 1996 but an overall increase of about 123,000 since the 1991 census. In 1997 the population of Scotland was 8.6 per cent of the total population of the UK (59,009,000).

Age	Total	Male	Female
0–14	955,859	489,247	466,612
15–29	1,042,991	530,872	512,119
30–44	1,162,155	579,365	582,790
45–59	924,214	453,024	471,190
60–74	698,361	316,967	381,394
75+	338,920	114,832	224,088
Total	5,122,500	2,484,307	2,638,193
% of total	100	48.5	51.5

Source: The Stationery Office, *Annual Report of the Registrar-General for Scotland 1997* (Crown copyright)

PROJECTED POPULATION 2001–21 (MID-YEAR)

Age	2001	2011	2021
0–14	924,000	837,000	801,000
15–29	975,000	959,000	877,000
30–44	1,195,000	1,008,000	905,000
45–59	967,000	1,100,000	1,085,000
60–74	695,000	778,000	902,000
75+	351,000	375,000	423,000
Total	5,107,000	5,057,000	4,993,000

Source: The Stationery Office, *Annual Report of the Registrar-General for Scotland 1997* (Crown copyright)

RESIDENT POPULATION BY ETHNIC GROUP (1991 CENSUS)

Ethnic group	Total	Male	Female
Caribbean	934	490	444
African	2,773	1,588	1,185
Other black	2,646	1,415	1,231
Indian	10,050	5,295	4,755
Pakistani	21,192	10,810	10,382
Bangladeshi	1,134	634	500
Chinese	10,476	5,482	4,994
Other Asian	4,604	2,162	2,442
Other	8,825	4,848	3,577
White	4,935,933	2,359,237	2,576,696
All ethnic groups	4,998,567	2,391,961	2,606,606

Source: General Register Office (Scotland) (Crown copyright)

AVERAGE POPULATION DENSITY

The average density of population at the 1991 census was 0.65 persons per hectare. For population density by council area, *see* Council Directory

BIRTHS

In 1997 there were 59,440 live births in Scotland. The birth rate (live births per 1,000 members of the population) was 11.6, a little below the rate of 12.3 for the UK as a whole. Of the total number of live births, 62.3 per cent were to married parents. While the birth rate overall has fallen since 1987, and especially since 1991, the proportion of births outside marriage has increased markedly, from 22.8 per cent to 37.6 per cent.

LIVE BIRTHS 1997

	Number	Percentage
All live births	59,440	100
To married parents	37,052	62.3
To unmarried parents		
Joint registration	18,163	30.5
Sole registration	4,225	7.1

LIVE BIRTHS OUTSIDE MARRIAGE 1997
By age of mother and type of registration

Age	Total	*Joint registration* %	*Sole registration* %
Under 20	4,529	70.8	29.2
20–24	6,884	80.4	19.6
25–29	5,710	84.8	15.2
30–34	3,643	87.5	12.5
35 and over	1,802	86.0	14.0
All ages	22,388	81.1	18.9

Source: The Stationery Office, *Annual Report of Registrar-General for Scotland 1997* (Crown copyright)

ABORTIONS

A total of 12,080 legal pregnancy terminations were performed in Scotland in 1997 (an increase of about 9 per cent since 1990), of which women aged between 20 and 34 accounted for over half. The number of girls under 16 undergoing abortions in 1997 was 289, 2.4 per cent of the total; but the percentage of under-16s undergoing abortions rose by 16 per cent between 1990 and 1997.

LEGAL ABORTIONS 1997p
By age of mother

Under 16	289
16–19	2,428
20–34	7,929
35–44	1,410
45 and over	24
Total	12,080

p provisional

Source: The Stationery Office, *Annual Abstract of Statistics 1999* (Crown copyright)

LIFE EXPECTANCY

LIFE TABLES 1994–6
(interim figures)

Age	Male	Female
0	72.1	77.6
5	67.7	73.2
10	62.7	68.2
15	57.8	63.2
20	53.1	58.3
25	48.3	53.4
30	43.6	48.6
35	38.9	43.7
40	34.2	38.9
45	29.6	34.2
50	25.2	29.6
55	21.0	25.2
60	17.2	21.0
65	13.7	17.2
70	10.8	13.7
75	8.3	10.6
80	6.2	7.9
85	4.6	5.7

Source: The Stationery Office, *Annual Abstract of Statistics 1999* (Crown copyright)

DEATHS

There were 59,494 deaths in 1997; the death rate was 11.6, slightly above the UK average. Infant mortality (deaths under one year of age) was 5.3 per 1,000 live births (UK average 5.8).

DEATHS AND DEATH RATES 1997p

	Deaths	Death rate*
Males	28,305	11.4
Females	31,189	11.8
Total	59,494	11.6

p provisional

* Deaths per 1,000 population

Sources: The Stationery Office, *Annual Abstract of Statistics 1999*; General Register Office for Scotland

MARRIAGE AND DIVORCE

At just under 30,000, the number of marriages in 1997 reflects a gradual but steady decline over the past decade. At the same time, the divorce rate (11 per thousand population members in 1997), has remained relatively stable.

Year	Marriages No.	Rate*	Divorces No.	Rate*
1987	35,813	14.0	12,133	10.2
1988	35,599	14.0	11,472	9.8
1989	35,326	13.9	11,659	10.0
1990	34,672	13.6	12,272	10.5
1991	33,762	13.2	12,399	10.6
1992	35,057	13.7	12,479	10.8
1993	33,366	13.0	12,787	11.1
1994	31,480	12.3	13,133	11.5
1995	30,663	11.9	12,249	10.8
1996	30,242	11.8	12,308	10.9
1997	29,811	11.6	12,222	11.0

* Per 1,000 members of population.

Source: The Stationery Office, *Annual Abstract of Statistics 1999* (Crown copyright)

LANGUAGES

The main language of Scotland is English. Gaelic is a recognized minority language and the various Scots dialects are widely spoken.

GAELIC

The Gaelic language was introduced into Scotland from Ireland in the fifth century or before, and was at its strongest from the ninth to the 12th centuries. Despite the steady advance of English from the Middle Ages onwards, Gaelic remained the main language in much of rural Scotland until the early 17th century. However, in 1616 James VI and I passed an Act proscribing Gaelic, and with the suppression of Highland culture following the Jacobite rising of 1745 and the depopulation of Gaelic-speaking areas by the Highland clearances in the 19th century, the language declined.

The movement for the revival of Gaelic grew in the late 19th and early 20th centuries. A clause was inserted in the Education Act 1918 allowing Gaelic to be taught in Gaelic-speaking areas, although it was not until 1958 that a local education authority (Inverness-shire) first adopted a bilingual policy, teaching Gaelic in primary schools in Gaelic-speaking areas.

At the time of the 1991 census, 1.4 per cent of the population of Scotland, mainly in the Highlands and the Western Isles, were able to speak Gaelic. This represents a fall of 0.2 per cent since the 1981 census. The percentage of Gaelic speakers was highest among people aged 65 and over (2.2 per cent), and lowest among people aged three to 15 (0.9 per cent). Geographically, by far the highest proportion of Gaelic speakers to total population occurred in the Western Isles area, where over 68 per cent of people speak Gaelic.

The following table shows the total number of persons aged three and over who speak Gaelic, by region and as a percentage of the total population, at the 1991 census.

Region	Total persons	% of population
Borders	103,881	0.5
Central	267,492	0.6
Dumfries and Galloway	147,805	0.4
Fife	341,199	0.5
Grampian	503,888	0.5
Highland	204,004	7.5
Lothian	726,010	0.6
Strathclyde	2,248,706	0.8
Tayside	383,848	0.7
Orkney Islands	19,612	0.5
Shetland Islands	22,522	0.5
Western Isles	29,600	68.4
Total	4,998,567	1.4

The following table shows Gaelic speakers as a percentage of the total population, by age group, at the 1981 and 1991 censuses.

Age	1981	1991
3–15	1.0	0.9
16–44	1.4	1.1
45–64	2.0	1.6
65+	2.7	2.2
Total	1.6	1.4

Source: General Register Office (Scotland), 1991 Census Monitor for Scotland (Crown copyright)

Promotion of Gaelic

In recent years, more official measures have been taken to promote the revival of Gaelic, and the Scottish Executive includes a junior minister for Gaelic.

Gaelic is taught as an academic subject at universities including Aberdeen, Edinburgh and Glasgow, at numerous colleges of education, and in some schools, principally in Gaelic-speaking areas. Sàbhal Mor Ostaig (see page 123) is the Gaelic-medium further and higher education college.

BBC programmes in Gaelic are broadcast throughout the country. BBC Scotland delivered 116 hours of Gaelic television programmes in 1997–8 and an average of 45 hours of Gaelic radio programmes per week. The Scottish and Grampian independent stations also broadcast regular Gaelic television programmes. The Gaelic-language radio station BBC Radio nan Gaidheal is now available to 90 per cent of the audience in Scotland. There are local community radio stations in Stornoway, Ullapool, Portree and Fort William.

In 1992 the Gaelic Television Committee/Comataidh Telebhisein Gàidhlig) (now the Gaelic Broadcasting Committee/Comataidh Craolaidh Gàidhlig) was established to fund up to 200 additional hours of Gaelic-medium television. The committee's remit was extended to radio programmes by the Broadcasting Act 1996. The fund's income was £9.05 million in 1998 and about £8.5 million in 1999.

A number of institutions for the promotion of the Gaelic language and culture exist. Comunn na Gàidhlig (see page 222) is the national development agency for Scottish Gaelic. It promotes the use of the Gaelic language, the continuance of Gaelic culture in education and the arts, and the integration of Gaelic into social and economic development, including the promotion of Gaelic businesses. An Comunn Gaidhealach (see page 219) promotes Gaelic culture through everyday use of the language and encourages the traditions of music, literature and folklore.

LOWLAND SCOTTISH

Several dialects, known collectively as Lowland Scots, Lallans or Doric, are widely spoken in the south, east and extreme north of the country. 'Scots' is the term commonly used in Scotland itself and in the European Charter for Minority and Regional Languages, which recognizes Scots as a minority language. In the last 20 years the term 'Doric' has come to be used locally in the north-east to refer exclusively to the group of dialects in that area.

Although the UK government ratified the European Charter in 1998, no official recognition or encouragement has yet been given to Scots. The General Register Office (Scotland) has estimated that 1.5 million, or 30 per cent of the population, are Scots speakers.

Promotion of Scots

Courses in Scots language and literature are taught at several universities, further and higher education colleges and community colleges. The Scots Language Resource Centre is the lead agency for the promotion of Scots and supports other bodies engaged in the promotion and study of Scots language and culture, including the Scottish National Dictionary Association, the Scots Language Society, the Scots Leid Associe, the Scots Speakers' Curn and Scots Tung (see Societies and Institutions).

CAPITAL CITY

EDINBURGH

Edinburgh is the capital of and seat of government in Scotland. The city is built on a group of hills and contains in Princes Street one of the most beautiful thoroughfares in the world. In 1995 UNESCO designated Edinburgh Old and New Towns a World Heritage Site. There are three universities: Edinburgh (1583), Heriot-Watt (1966), and Napier (1992). The Edinburgh International Festival, held in August each year, has become one of the world's principal festivals of the performing arts.

The principal buildings include: the Castle, which now houses the Stone of Scone and also contains St Margaret's Chapel (12th century), the oldest building in Edinburgh, and the Scottish National War Memorial (1923); the Palace of Holyroodhouse (begun 1501 by James IV, rebuilding completed 1679); Parliament House (1632–40), the present seat of the judicature; St Giles' Cathedral (15th century, but the site of a church since AD 854); St Mary's (Scottish Episcopal) Cathedral (Sir George Gilbert Scott); the General Register House (Robert Adam, 1774); the National and the Signet Libraries (founded 1682 and 1722); the National Gallery (1859); the Royal Scottish Academy; the National Portrait Gallery (1889); the Royal Museum of Scotland (1861); the New Royal Observatory (1896); St Cecilia's Hall (1762), the first purpose-built concert hall in Scotland; the Usher Hall; and the Edinburgh International Conference Centre, opened in 1995. The Museum of Scotland opened 1998. The new Scottish Parliament building is due to open in 2001.

Other places of interest include Arthur's Seat (a volcanic hill 823 ft/251 m high overlooking the city), Calton Hill, the Royal Botanic Garden Edinburgh, the Physic Garden (1676), and the Firth of Forth road bridge (1964) and rail bridge (1890).

OTHER PRINCIPAL CITIES

ABERDEEN

Aberdeen, 130 miles north-east of Edinburgh, received its charter as a royal burgh in 1179. Scotland's third largest city, Aberdeen is the second largest Scottish fishing port and the main centre for offshore oil exploration and production. It is also an ancient university town (Aberdeen University, founded 1495; Robert Gordon University, 1992) and a distinguished research centre. Other industries include engineering, food processing, textiles, paper manufacturing and chemicals.

Places of interest include: King's College (from 1500); St Machar's Cathedral (1370–1424); Brig o' Balgownie (1314–18), Duthie Park (1881) and Winter Gardens (1972); Hazlehead Park; the Kirk of St Nicholas (from 12th century); the Mercat Cross (1686); Marischal College (founded 1593, present building 1891), the second largest granite building in Europe, and Marischal Museum; Provost Skene's House (from 1545); the Art Gallery (1884); Robert Gordon's College (begun by William Adam, 1731) and Robert Gordon University; the Gordon Highlanders Museum; the Satrosphere Hands-On Discovery Centre, and the Aberdeen Maritime Museum, which incorporates Provost Ross's House (1593) and the former Trinity Church.

DUNDEE

Dundee, which received its charter as a royal burgh in 1327, is situated on the north bank of the Tay estuary. The city's port and dock installations are important to the offshore oil industry and the airport also provides servicing facilities. Principal industries include textiles, computers and other electronic industries, lasers, printing, tyre manufacture, food processing, carpets, engineering, clothing manufacture and tourism. There are two universities, Dundee (1967) and Abertay Dundee (1994).

The unique City Churches – three churches under one roof, together with the 15th-century St Mary's Tower – are the city's most prominent architectural feature. Dundee has two historic ships: the Dundee-built RRS *Discovery* (built 1901), which took Captain Scott to the Antarctic, lies alongside Discovery Quay, and the frigate *Unicorn* (built 1825), the only British-built wooden warship still afloat, is moored in Victoria Dock. Places of interest include Mills Public Observatory, the Tay road and rail bridges, the Dundee Museum and Art Gallery (1872), McManus Galleries, the new Contemporary Arts Centre, Barrack Street Museum, Claypotts Castle (a town house built 1569–88), Broughty Castle (1454), Caledon Shipyard (1874), and Verdant Works (Textile Heritage Centre).

GLASGOW

Glasgow, a royal burgh (1611), is Scotland's principal commercial and industrial centre. The city occupies the north and south banks of the river Clyde, formerly one of the chief commercial estuaries in the world. The main industries include engineering, electronics, finance, chemicals and printing. The city has also developed recently as a cultural, tourism and conference centre. It was designated European City of Culture in 1990 and City of Architecture and Design in 1999. There are two universities: Glasgow (1451) and Strathclyde (1964). The city was raised to an archdiocese in 1492.

Among the chief buildings are the 13th-century Gothic Cathedral, the only mainland Scottish cathedral to have survived the Reformation intact; the University (Sir George Gilbert Scott); the City Chambers; the Royal Exchange (1829); the Royal Concert Hall; St Mungo Museum of Religious Life and Art, Pollok House; the Hunterian Museum (1805); the People's Palace (1898); the New Glasgow School of Art (Charles Rennie Mackintosh, 1896); Glasgow Art Gallery and Museum, Kelvingrove (1893); the Gallery of Modern Art; the Burrell Collection museum and the Mitchell Library (1911). The city is home to the Scottish National Orchestra (founded 1950), Scottish Opera (founded 1962) and Scottish Ballet.

INVERNESS

Inverness, a royal burgh, is the largest town in the Highlands and their administrative centre. It is situated at the northern end of the Great Glen, where the River Ness flows into the Beauly Firth, now spanned by the Kessock Bridge across to the Black Isle. Originally built on the axis between the medieval castle and the Old High Church, the town now has a population of 50,000. Inverness Castle was occupied and then destroyed by the Jacobites in 1746 and in the 19th century replaced by a courthouse and prison. The battlefield at Culloden, where the Jacobites were finally defeated on 16 April 1746, lies to the east of the town.

Other important buildings include the late Victorian Town House (1882), the Highland Council Buildings (1876), the episcopal St Andrew's Cathedral (1869), and the modern Eden Court Theatre (1976). Industries include light engineering, biotechnology, electronics, service industries and tourism. Nearby is the oil platform construction yard at Ardersier.

PERTH

Perth is situated in north-central Scotland, on the right bank of the Tay. It became a burgh in 1106 and a royal burgh in 1210, and was one of the cities which fulfilled the function of Scottish capital until the mid-15th century, a number of Parliaments and Council meetings being held there in the medieval period. The Blackfriars monastery was a favoured residence of James I, who founded Charterhouse, the last monastery to be established in Scotland, in Perth in 1425.

Little now remains to indicate Perth's former position as one of the chief towns of medieval Scotland, the ancient monasteries and castles having fallen victim to floods and conflict. The main buildings are St John's Kirk (founded by David I *c*.1125; Perth was also known as St John's Town until the 16th century); Perth Bridge; the King James VI Hospital; the Old Academy; the Sheriff Court buildings; Huntingtower Castle (16th century); Scone Palace (built 1802–13 on the site of the medieval palace); and Balhousie Castle (present building, 1862).

The city lies between two large areas of open parkland and has a wealth of fine Georgian buildings. The principal industries are now tourism, agriculture, insurance, whisky and transport.

STIRLING

Stirling, a royal burgh since *c*.1124, lies on the River Forth in the centre of Scotland. It was one of the chief cities to serve as the Scottish capital between the 13th and the 16th centuries, and the castle was a royal residence from *c*.1226. Stirling was the site of the Parliament which took over the government from John Balliol in 1295, the birthplace of James IV and the site of the coronations of Mary and of James VI.

Stirling's strategic situation led to its being the site of several battles. English armies were defeated at the Battle of Stirling Bridge in 1297 by Scots led by William Wallace, and at Bannockburn in 1314 by forces led by Robert Bruce.

The local economy comprises mainly service industries with some manufacturing. The city houses the headquarters of Scottish Amicable, the Bank of Bermuda and Scottish Natural Heritage. Stirling is also an important tourist centre.

Places of interest include Stirling Castle; Argyll's Lodgings; the National Wallace Monument (1887); the Bannockburn Heritage Centre; Rob Roy Centre; Old Town Jail; Inchmahome Priory (1238); Cambuskenneth Abbey (1147); the Church of the Holy Rood (16th and 17th centuries); the Smith Art Gallery and Museum; and the Changing Room contemporary art gallery.

HISTORY

3rd millennium BC: Earliest evidence of human settlement in Scotland, by Middle Stone Age hunters and fishermen.

Early 2nd millennium BC: New Stone Age farmers began to cultivate crops and rear livestock; their settlements were on the west coast and in the north, and included Skara Brae and Maeshowe (Orkney).

c.1800 BC *onwards:* Settlement by the Early Bronze Age 'Beaker folk', so-called from the shape of their drinking vessels, in eastern Scotland.

c.700 BC *onwards:* Further settlement by tribes displaced from further south by new incursions from mainland Europe. This, and the development of Iron Age technology, increased competition and conflict between communities; brochs, duns and other defended settlements built.

1st and 2nd centuries AD: Roman invasions of southern Britain from AD 43 displaced southern tribes northwards. Julius Agricola, the Roman governor of Britain AD 77–84, advanced into Caledonia, culminating with a victory at Mons Graupius in the north-east, probably in AD 84; he was recalled to Rome shortly afterwards and his forward policy was not pursued. Hadrian set the northern boundary of the Roman empire in Britain and ordered the construction of a wall to defend it. Hadrian's Wall marked the frontier until the Roman troops withdrew from Britain in AD 407–10, except *c.*AD 144–190, when the frontier moved north to the Forth–Clyde isthmus and a turf wall, the Antonine Wall, was manned.

2nd to 9th centuries: Successive colonizations of different parts of Scotland by Picts, Scots, Britons, Angles and Vikings, and continual warfare between them. The Picts, believed to be a non-Indo-European race, occupied the area north of the Forth. The Scots, a Gaelic-speaking people of northern Ireland, colonized the area of Argyll and Bute (the kingdom of Dalriada) in the fifth century AD and then expanded eastwards and northwards. The Britons, speaking a Brythonic Celtic language, colonized Scotland from the south from the first century BC; they lost control of south-eastern Scotland (incorporated into the kingdom of Northumbria) to the Angles in the early seventh century but retained south-western Scotland and Cumbria. Viking raids from the late eighth century were followed by Norse settlement in the north and west from the mid-ninth century onwards.

397: First Christian church in Scotland established at Whithorn by St Ninian.

c.563: Arrival of St Columba (d. 597) on Iona from Ireland and establishment of a monastery there.

685: Northward incursions by Angles halted by Picts at battle of Nechtansmere, near Forfar.

c.736: King Aengus of the Picts captured Dunadd, royal centre of Dalriada, thus acquiring overlordship of the Scots. In 756, in league with the Northumbrians, he defeated the north Britons at Dumbarton.

c.794 onwards: Viking raids and Norse settlement in Argyll, Caithness and Sutherland, Orkney, Shetland, and the Western Isles. By 890 Orkney, Shetland, the Hebrides and Caithness had become part of the kingdom of Norway under Harald Fairhair and in 987 Earl Sigurd of Orkney annexed Sutherland, Ross and Moray.

843: Unification of the areas which now comprise Scotland began, when Kenneth mac Alpin, king of the Scots from *c.*834, became also king of the Picts, joining the two lands to form the kingdom of Alba (comprising Scotland north of a line between the Forth and Clyde rivers).

c.973/4: Lothian, the eastern part of the area between the Forth and the Tweed, ceded or leased to Kenneth II of Alba by Edgar of England.

1010: Malcolm II defeated a Norse army at Dufftown and further secured his northern border by marrying his daughter to the Earl of Orkney.

c.1018: Malcolm II's victory over a Northumbrian army at Carham restored Scottish possession of Lothian, lost earlier in his reign. At about this time Malcolm placed his grandson Duncan on the throne of the British kingdom of Strathclyde, bringing under Scots rule virtually all of what is now Scotland. The hybrid name 'Scotland' began to supplant the Gaelic name 'Alba'.

1040: Duncan I slain in battle by Macbeth, who ruled until 1057. Macbeth fell at the battle of Lumphanan to Malcolm III (Canmore), aided by Earl Siward of Northumbria and Edward the Confessor of England.

1098: Magnus III of Norway devastated the Western Isles; but an uprising in the mid 12th century drove the Norse from most of mainland Argyll. From then onwards the Norse possessions were gradually incorporated into the kingdom of Scotland.

Late 11th century onwards: Frequent conflict between Scotland and England over territory and the extent of England's political influence, and between the Scottish crown and rebellious Highland leaders, such as Somerled, who became Lord of the Isles in 1156.

Towns and burghs developed, encouraged by trade with the Normans, and by the court's increasing sophistication. David I granted the status of burgh, with special trading privileges, to numerous towns. By 1283 most of the towns in Scotland, except a few in the west Highlands and the Hebrides, had acquired the status of either royal or baronial burghs. Royal burghs were also centres of justice where the king's sheriffs held courts.

1237: Treaty of York, establishing Scotland's border with England.

1266: Treaty of Perth, by which Magnus IV of Norway ceded the Hebrides and the Isle of Man to Scotland.

1296–1328: Wars of Independence. The failure of the Scottish royal line with the death of Margaret of Norway in 1290 led to disputes over the throne which were resolved by the adjudication of Edward I of England. He awarded the throne to John Balliol in 1292, but Balliol's refusal to be a puppet king led to war.

A Parliament held in Stirling in 1295 overturned Balliol's government and appointed a ruling Council, which made an alliance with Philip IV of France against England. (The treaty became known as 'the Auld Alliance' and was the basis for Scottish military support for France in the following centuries.)

Balliol surrendered to Edward I in 1296 and Edward attempted to rule Scotland himself. Resistance was led by William Wallace, who defeated the English at Stirling Bridge (1297), and Robert Bruce, crowned in 1306, who held most of Scotland by 1311 and routed Edward II's army at Bannockburn (1314).

Edward did not renounce his claim to Scotland, however, and when Bruce rejected a papal truce in 1317, Pope John XXII excommunicated him and placed Scotland under interdict. The bishops' reply, passionately defending Scotland's independence, became known as the Declaration of Arbroath

England recognized Scotland's independence in the Treaty of Northampton in 1328, although this did not prevent subsequent clashes between the two countries.

1371 onwards: The early Stewart kings Robert II and Robert III were weak administrators, and rivalries between the barons resulted in lawlessness on which parliamentary attempts at legislation had little practical effect. In particular, the throne had little control of the Highlands or the Western Isles.

The Highlands and Lowlands were in many respects becoming two nations. Predating and underlying the basically Norman feudal system was the clan system, based on attachment to the land and loyalty to the clan chieftain, and this continued to exist in the Highlands in an undiluted form and to pose continual challenges to the king's power in the north and west.

1411: Outbreak of open warfare in the Highlands. Donald, Lord of the Isles, defeated at Harlaw near Inverurie by the Earl of Mar and a local army including burgesses of Aberdeen. Donald retreated, but with his local power intact.

1424: James I introduced a series of legislative reforms aimed at controlling the nobles, creating a fair and efficient judiciary, and raising national revenue. In 1426 Parliament abolished all laws other than the king's. James backed this up by force in 1428 by arresting and in some cases executing about 50 Highland chiefs.

1468–9: Orkney and Shetland ceded to Scotland as a pledge for the unpaid dowry of Margaret of Denmark, wife of James III, though Danish claims of suzerainty persisted, to be relinquished only in 1590 with the marriage of Anne of Denmark to James VI.

1493: After continual strife in the reign of James III, James IV annexed the lands and titles of John, Lord of the Isles, to the crown, and made a series of expeditions to the west between 1493 and 1498; subsequently he was faced with rebellion (1504–7) from John's son Donald Dubh. The integration of the west into the kingdom remained fragile, and James's granting of governorships to the Earls of Argyll and Huntly in 1500–1, bolstering the power of the Campbells and Gordons, was resented by other clans.

1511–3: James IV signed a treaty with France in 1511, in which Scotland pledged to make war on England if France did so. He was almost at once drawn into a war of little direct relevance to Scotland, supporting the French against the Holy League, of which England was a member. James and many of his nobles fell at Flodden (1513), a disastrous defeat for the Scots.

1544–50: Renewed hostilities with England. The 'Rough Wooing' was a campaign waged by Henry VIII on the Catholic, pro-French Scottish monarchy in retaliation for the breaking of a treaty by which Mary (later Queen of Scots) was to marry his son Edward. The whole of the south-east was ravaged and the great abbeys sacked.

1555–1560: The doctrines of Luther and Calvin, introduced into Scotland by John Knox, a disaffected priest, quickly became popular with the lower clergy and lower nobility. The outlawing of Knox and his followers in 1559 provoked riots by Protestants and a brief war. The 'Reformation Parliament', held on 1 August 1560 in the name of Queen Mary but without a royal presence, rejected the jurisdiction of the Pope. A Protestant majority in government was established, and forced Mary's abdication in 1567 (*see also* page 145).

1603: James VI of Scotland succeeded Elizabeth I on the throne of England (his mother, Mary Queen of Scots, was the great-granddaughter of Henry VII), his successors reigning as sovereigns of Great Britain.

1618: James VI and I attempted to bring the Church in Scotland into line with English practice in the Five Articles of Perth, passed by a General Assembly of the Church in August.

1638: The National Covenant overturned the Five Articles and reasserted the right of the people to keep the reformed church. The General Assembly abolished the episcopacy and proscribed the use of the Book of Common Prayer (*see also* page 145).

1666: The Pentland Rising, a popular revolt against the repression of Covenanters which followed the Restoration, and in particular the prohibition of conventicles (outdoor religious meetings), failed when a poorly armed force of a few thousand Covenanters was defeated by government troops at Rullion Green.

1688–9: After the abdication (by flight) in 1688 of James VII and II, the crown devolved upon William III (grandson of Charles I) and Mary II (elder daughter of James VII and II). In April 1689 the Convention of the Estates issued the Claim of Right and the Articles of Grievances, which asserted the independence of the Scottish parliament and Presbyterianism as the established Church. William and Mary were offered the Scottish crown on condition that they accepted these proposals.

From April 1689 Graham of Claverhouse roused the Highlands on behalf of James, but died after a military success at Killiecrankie in July.

1692: The clan chiefs who had opposed William were offered pardon if they took an oath of allegiance before 1 January 1692 and threatened with persecution if they did not. The clan of MacDonald of Glencoe missed the deadline by a few days, news that the chief had taken the oath was kept from the Privy Council, and a detachment of Campbell soldiers was sent to Glencoe and billeted with the MacDonalds with secret orders to destroy them; 38 people were killed. The violation of the tradition of hospitality and the Government's implication in the massacre turned Glencoe into a Jacobite rallying cause.

1707: Act of Union, joining Scotland and England politically under one Parliament in London.

1714: Queen Anne (younger daughter of James VII and II) succeeded by George I (great-grandson of James VI and I). In 1715, armed risings on behalf of James Stuart (the Old Pretender, son of James VII and II) led to the indecisive battle of Sheriffmuir, and the Jacobite movement died down until 1745.

1720s onwards: Introduction of new methods and technology by Scots landowners (including some heads of clans). Landowners became increasingly concerned with making profit from their lands, which often involved turning large areas over to cattle and sheep at the expense of small tenants; the depopulation of the Highlands began.

From 1723 to 1725 there were periodic protests by the Galloway Levellers, dispossessed tenants who had been evicted by lairds in Galloway in order to enclose pastures for fattening cattle.

1745–6: Charles Stuart (son of James Stuart, the Old Pretender) landed in Scotland and rallied supporters to the Jacobite cause. His forces defeated royalist troops at Prestonpans and advanced as far as Derby (1746). From Derby, the adherents of 'James VIII and III' (the title claimed for his father by Charles Stuart) fell back on the defensive and were finally crushed at Culloden on 16 April 1746.

1746–8: After the Jacobite rebellion, the clan system was suppressed by the Government to prevent further rebellion; the lands of those chiefs who had supported the Jacobite cause were confiscated (the forfeited estates were restored in 1784), and the bearing of weapons and the playing of the great pipes were outlawed. The wearing of Highland dress was also proscribed from 1746 to 1782, although it made a comeback, in a romanticized form, in the early 19th century.

1767: Building of Edinburgh New Town (designed by James Craig) began. Elsewhere, from the 1770s onward, a new model of village planning, stone-built and based on a central market square or high street, was applied by landowners, businessmen and government bodies in over a hundred villages, with the specific aim of economic development.

1770: An Act of Parliament created the Clyde Trust, authorizing plans to deepen the Clyde. This initiated a process of development which led to the building of the shipyards and docks in Glasgow in the 19th century.

Other technological and industrial developments around this time (e.g. the opening of the Carron Ironworks in 1759; James Watt's patenting of an improved steam engine in 1769; the introduction of large water-powered spinning mills from 1779) laid the basis for Scotland's industrial economy in the 19th and 20th centuries.

1785–1820: First period of Highland Clearances. As the majority of Highland estates were reorganized for sheep-farming, thousands of tenants were 'cleared' from land their families had farmed for generations with no security of tenure other than the unwritten contract of clan loyalty. Clearances took place across Sutherland in 1785–6, 1800, 1807, 1809, 1812–14 and 1819–20. Some evicted tenants emigrated to the Lowlands and overseas; others were moved forcibly to the coast where they were expected to work as fishermen.

1790: Opening of the Forth–Clyde Canal, Britain's first sea-to-sea canal. The 250 miles of military road-building by General Wade in the early 18th century had improved communications in the Highlands, and from 1802 onwards Thomas Telford, engineer to the Commission for Highland Roads and Bridges, oversaw the construction of nearly 1,000 miles of roads. The Caledonian Canal was built between 1804 and 1822.

1793: Beginning of war with France and formation of Highland regiments (e.g. Cameron Highlanders, Argyll Highlanders, Gordon Highlanders). Lairds recruited energetically in the Highlands, and the Scottish regiments played a significant part in the creation and defence of the British Empire, and in all Britain's wars of the 19th and 20th centuries.

1820: Following years of economic depression, exacerbated by rising grain prices after the Corn Laws of 1815, riots and a strike in the west culminated in a march from Glasgow to Falkirk and an attempt by a small band of radicals to seize the Carron ironworks. Both actions were crushed by government forces and the leaders executed or transported. The incidents became known as the 'Radical War'.

1830 onwards: New smelting processes enabled the development of the iron industry, and related industries, such as coal-mining, also flourished.

1840–54: Second wave of Highland Clearances, from Ross-shire and the Isles. Emigration was increased by severe famine in 1846–7.

1841: Govan shipyard founded by Robert Napier. Aided by a fast-growing local steel industry, by the 1870s and 1880s Scotland had become the world leader in shipbuilding, particularly with the introduction of steel-hulled steamships.

1850s onwards: Development of the herring fishing industry on the east coast. New net technology and later the use of steamboats increased catches, and the development of the railways enabled efficient transport of the processed fish.

1855: Foundation of the United Coal and Iron Miners' Association, Scotland's first effective labour organization.

1867: Franchise extended to all males. In 1869 women won the right to vote in municipal elections, but did not win the right to vote in parliamentary elections on the same terms as men until 1928.

1872: The Education (Scotland) Act brought burgh and parish schools under state control, though education was not provided free until 1892.

1882: Formation of the Highland Land Leagues. 'Battle of the Braes' in Skye, where crofters defied police and landlords in defence of their grazing rights. Continuing trouble with crofters forced the government to set up a Royal Commission, leading to the adoption of the Crofters' (Holdings) Act in 1886, which gave crofters security of tenure, fixed rents and other rights.

1885: Establishment of the Scottish Office at Whitehall, and the post of Secretary for Scotland.

1886: Scottish Home Rule Association founded.

1897: Formation of the Scottish Trades Union Congress. Organized labour was to achieve considerable strength during the Great War and was particularly militant during the inter-war period.

1910: Scottish National Committee set up to promote self-government, but the issue was shelved on the outbreak of the First World War; the Scottish Home Rule Association was refounded in 1918 and the Scots National League was formed in 1921.

1920s: Successive Home Rule Bills presented to Parliament in 1924, 1926, 1927 and 1928 failed.

1934: Founding of the Scottish National Party through a merger of the National Party of Scotland (formerly the Scots National League) and the Scottish Party (formed 1932).

Scottish literary renaissance in parallel with the growth of nationalism in politics, many Scottish writers of the 1930s (e.g. Hugh MacDiarmid, Lewis Spence, Eric Linklater, Compton Mackenzie, Neil Gunn, Edwin Muir, Naomi Mitchison, Lewis Grassic Gibbon) exploring Scotland's identity, often writing in Scots.

1959 onwards: Large oil and gas reserves discovered in North Sea. The first oil was pumped ashore in 1975.

1970s to 1990s: Decline of Scotland's industrial and manufacturing base; mines, shipyards, iron and steel works and factories closed down. The fishing industry also contracted severely.

Heavy industry replaced increasingly by energy supply (oil and gas, hydroelectric power), electronics, tourism and related industries, and whisky. Membership of the European Union benefited agriculture, urban regeneration and small-scale industry in the Highlands and Islands.

1976: Crofting Reform Act enabled crofters to buy their land.

1979: Referendum on the Scotland and Wales Act introduced by the Labour government to give devolution to Scotland and Wales. The referendum failed to reach the requisite 40 per cent of affirmative votes, partly because of a high level of abstention, and the Act was abandoned.

1996: Stone of Destiny returned to Scotland. The Stone was reputedly brought to Scotland from Ireland by the Dalriadic king Fergus in the sixth century and was a key part of the coronation ceremonies of Scottish kings. It was taken from Scone to Westminster Abbey by Edward I in 1296.

1997, 11 September: Referendum on the reinstatement of a separate Scottish Parliament; 74.3 per cent voted in favour of a Scottish Parliament and 63.5 per cent in favour of it having the power to adjust tax rates.

1999:
6 May: Scottish Parliament elections held.
12 May: Scottish Parliament met for the first time since 1709.
1 July: Official opening of Scottish Parliament by the Queen; power now formally devolved from Westminster to Edinburgh.

KINGS AND QUEENS OF SCOTS, 834 TO 1603

REIGN	
*c.*834–860	Kenneth mac Alpin, king of Scots, and also of Picts from 843; Kenneth I of Alba
860–63	Donald I
863–77	Constantine I
877–78	Aed
878–89	Giric
889–900	Donald II
900–43	Constantine II (abdicated)
944–54	Malcolm I
954–63	Indulf
963–67	Dubh (Duff)
967–71	Culain
971–95	Kenneth II
995–97	Constantine III
997	Kenneth III
997 –1005	Grig
1005–34	Malcolm II (*c.*954–1034)

THE HOUSE OF ATHOLL

1034–40	Duncan I
1040–57	Macbeth (*c.*1005–57)
1057–58	Lulach (*c.*1032–58)
1058–93	Malcolm III (Canmore) (*c.*1031–93)
1093–97	Donald III Ban (*c.*1033–1100) Deposed May 1094, restored November 1094
1094	Duncan II (*c.*1060–94)
1097–1107	Edgar (*c.*1074–1107)
1107–24	Alexander I (The Fierce) (*c.*1077–1124)
1124–53	David I (The Saint) (*c.*1085–1153)
1153–65	Malcolm IV (The Maiden) (*c.*1141–65)
1165–1214	William I (The Lion) (*c.*1142–1214)
1214–49	Alexander II (1198–1249)
1249–86	Alexander III (1241–86)
1286–90	Margaret (The Maid of Norway) (1283–90)

First Interregnum 1290–92
Throne disputed by 13 competitors. Crown awarded to John Balliol by adjudication of Edward I of England

THE HOUSE OF BALLIOL

1292–96	John (Balliol) (c.1250–1313)

Second Interregnum 1296–1306
Edward I of England declared John Balliol to have forfeited the throne for contumacy in 1296 and took the government of Scotland into his own hands

THE HOUSE OF BRUCE

1306–29	Robert I (Bruce) (1274–1329)
1329–71	David II (1324–71)

1332 Edward Balliol, son of John Balliol, crowned King of Scots September, expelled December

1333–36	Edward Balliol restored as King of Scots

THE HOUSE OF STEWART

1371–90	Robert II (Stewart) (1316–90)
1390–1406	Robert III (c.1337–1406)
1406–37	James I (1394–1437)
1437–60	James II (1430–60)
1460–88	James III (1452–88)
1488–1513	James IV (1473–1513)
1513–42	James V (1512–42)
1542–67	Mary (1542–87)
1567–1625	James VI (and I of England) (1566–1625) Succeeded 1603 to the English throne, so joining the English and Scottish crowns

THE HOUSE OF HANOVER

1714–27	George I (Elector of Hanover) (1660–1727)
1727–60	George II (1683–1760)
1760–1820	George III (1738–1820)

Regency 1811–20
Prince of Wales regent owing to the insanity of George III

1820–30	George IV (1762–1830)
1830–37	William IV (1765–1837)
1837–1901	Victoria (1819–1901)

THE HOUSE OF SAXE-COBURG AND GOTHA

1901–10	Edward VII (1841–1910)

THE HOUSE OF WINDSOR

1910–36	George V (1865–1936)
1936	Edward VIII (1894–1972)
1936–52	George VI (1895–1952)
1952–	Elizabeth II (1926–)

BRITISH KINGS AND QUEENS SINCE 1603

THE HOUSE OF STUART

REIGN

1603–25	James I (and VI of Scotland) (1566–1625)
1625–49	Charles I (1600–49)

Commonwealth declared 19 May 1649

1649–53	Government by a council of state
1653–58	Oliver Cromwell, Lord Protector
1658–59	Richard Cromwell, Lord Protector
1660–85	Charles II (1630–85)
1685–88	James II and VII (1633–1701)

Interregnum 11 December 1688 to 12 February 1689

1689–1702 and	William III (1650–1702)
1689–94	Mary II (1662–94)
1702–14	Anne (1665–1714)

HISTORIC BUILDINGS AND MONUMENTS

Under the Planning (Listed Buildings and Conservation Areas) (Scotland) Act 1997 and the Ancient Monuments and Archaeological Areas Act 1979, the Scottish Executive is responsible for listing buildings and scheduling monuments in Scotland on the advice of Historic Scotland (see page 59), the Historic Buildings Council for Scotland (see page 59) and the Ancient Monuments Board for Scotland (see page 52).

Listed buildings are classified into Grade A, Grade B and Grade C. The main purpose of listing is to ensure that care is taken in deciding the future of a building. No changes which affect the architectural or historic character of a listed building can be made without listed building consent (in addition to planning permission where relevant). It is a criminal offence to demolish a listed building, or alter it in such a way as to affect its character, without consent. There are currently about 44,462 listed buildings in Scotland.

All monuments proposed for scheduling are considered to be of national importance. Where buildings are both scheduled and listed, ancient monuments legislation takes precedence. The main purpose of scheduling a monument is to preserve it for the future and to protect it from damage, destruction or any unnecessary interference. Once a monument has been scheduled, scheduled monument consent is required before any works are carried out. The scope of the control is more extensive and more detailed than that applied to listed buildings, but certain minor works may be carried out without consent. It is a criminal offence to carry out unauthorized work to scheduled monuments. There are currently about 7,035 scheduled monuments in Scotland.

Opening to the Public

The following is a selection of the many historic buildings and monuments open to the public. The admission charges given are the standard charges for 1999–2000; many properties have concessionary rates for children, etc. Opening hours vary. Many properties are closed in winter and some are also closed in the mornings. Most properties are closed on Christmas Eve, Christmas Day, Boxing Day and New Year's Day, and many are closed on Good Friday. Information about a specific property should be checked by telephone.

*Closed in winter (usually October to March)
†Closed in winter, and in mornings in summer
HS Historic Scotland property
NTS National Trust for Scotland property

* *Abbotsford House*, Melrose, Borders. Tel: 01896-752043. Adm. £3.50. Sir Walter Scott's house

Aberdour Castle (HS), Aberdour, Burntisland, Fife. Tel: 01383-860519. Closed Sun. mornings, Thurs. afternoons, and Fri. in winter. Adm. £1.80. Fourteenth-century castle built by the Douglas family

* *Alloa Tower* (NTS), Alloa. Tel: 01259-211701. Closed mornings. Adm. £2.50. Remodelled medieval tower and dungeon

Antonine Wall (HS), between the Clyde and the Forth. Adm. free. Built about AD 142, consists of ditch, turf rampart and road, with forts every two miles

Arbroath Abbey (HS), Arbroath, Angus. Tel: 01241-878756. Adm. £1.80. Site of Declaration of Arbroath 1320

Argyll's Lodging (HS), Stirling. Tel: 01786-461146. Adm. £2.80. Fine example of a 17th-century town residence

Balmoral Castle, nr Braemar. Tel: 013397-42334. Open mid-April to end July. Adm. £4.00. Baronial-style castle built for Victoria and Albert. The Queen's private residence

* *Balvenie Castle* (HS), Dufftown, Keith, Banffshire. Tel: 01340-820121. Adm. £1.20. Thirteenth-century castle owned by the Comyns

* *Bishop's and Earl's Palaces* (HS), Kirkwall, Orkney. Tel: 01856-871918. Adm. £1.80. A 12th-century hall-house and an early 17th-century palace

Black House, Arnol (HS), Lewis, Western Isles. Tel: 01851-710395. Closed Sun.; also Fri. in winter. Adm. £2.00. Traditional Lewis thatched house

Blackness Castle (HS), nr Linlithgow, W. Lothian. Tel: 01506-834807. Closed Sun. mornings, Thurs. afternoons, and Fri. in winter. Adm. £1.80. Fourteenth-century castle

* *Blair Castle*, Blair Atholl. Tel: 01796-481207. Adm. £6.00. Mid 18th-century mansion with 13th-century tower; seat of the Dukes of Atholl

* *Bonawe Iron Furnace* (HS), Argyll and Bute. Tel: 01866-822432. Adm. £2.50. Charcoal-fuelled ironworks founded in 1753

Bothwell Castle (HS), Uddingston, Glasgow. Tel: 01698-816894. Closed Sun. mornings, Thurs. afternoons, and Fri. in winter. Adm.

£1.80. Largest 13th-century castle in Scotland

† *Bowhill*, Selkirk. Tel: 01750-22204. House open July only; grounds open April–June, Aug. except Fri., daily in July. Adm. £4.50; grounds only, £2.00. Seat of the Dukes of Buccleuch and Queensberry; fine collection of paintings, including portrait miniatures

* *Brodick Castle* (NTS), Isle of Arran. Tel: 01770-302202. Gardens open all year. Adm. £5.00; gardens and park only, £2.50. Site of the ancient seat of the Dukes of Hamilton

* *Brodie Castle* (NTS), Forres, Moray. Tel: 01309-641371. Grounds open all year. Adm. £4.40; grounds free. A 16th-century castle with later additions

Brough of Birsay (HS), Orkney. Adm. £1.00. Remains of Norse church and village on the tidal island of Birsay

Burns Cottage and Museum, Alloway, Ayrshire. Tel: 01292-441215. Adm. £2.80. Birthplace of Robert Burns

Caerlaverock Castle (HS), nr Dumfries. Tel: 01387-770244. Adm. £2.50. Fine early classical Renaissance building

Calanais Standing Stones (HS), Lewis, Western Isles. Tel: 01851-621422. Adm. £1.50. Standing stones in a cross-shaped setting, dating from 3000 BC

* *Carlyle's Birthplace* (NTS), Ecclefechan, Lockerbie, Dumfriesshire. Tel: 01576-300666. Adm. £2.00. Closed Tues.–Thurs. and mornings. Birthplace of Thomas Carlyle

Castle Campbell (HS), Dollar Glen, nr Stirling. Tel: 01259-742408. Closed Sun. mornings, Thurs. afternoons, and Fri. in winter. Adm. £2.50. Fifteenth-century castle with parapet walk

* *Castle Fraser* (NTS), Sauchen, Inverurie, Aberdeenshire. Tel: 01330-833463. Garden and grounds open all year. Adm. £4.40; garden and grounds only, £2.10. Castle built between 1575 and 1636

Cathertuns (Brown and White) (HS), nr Brechin. Adm. free. Two large Iron Age hill forts

* *Cawdor Castle*, Inverness. Tel: 01667-404615. Adm. £5.40; grounds only, £2.80. A 14th-century keep with 15th- and 17th-century additions

Clava Cairns (HS), Highland. Adm. free. Late Neolithic or early Bronze Age cairns

Corgarff Castle (HS), Strathdon, Aberdeenshire. Tel: 01975-651460. Closed weekdays in winter. Adm. £2.50. Former 16th-century tower house converted into barracks

Craigmillar Castle (HS), Edinburgh. Tel: 0131-661 4445. Closed Sun. mornings, Thurs. afternoons, and Fri. in winter. Adm. £1.80

* *Craignethan Castle* (HS), nr Lanark. Tel: 01555-860364. Adm. £1.80. Castle dating from the 16th century, with Britain's only stone vaulted artillery chamber

* *Crathes Castle* (NTS), nr Banchory. Tel: 01330-844525. Garden and grounds open all year. Adm. castle, garden and grounds, £5.00; each site, £2.10. A 16th-century baronial castle in woodland, fields and gardens

* *Crichton Castle* (HS), nr Pathhead, Midlothian. Tel: 01875-320017. Adm. £1.80. Castle with Italian-style faceted stonework facade

* *Crossraguel Abbey* (HS), nr Maybole, Ayrshire. Tel: 01655-883113. Adm. £1.80. Remains of 13th-century abbey

* *Culross Palace, Town House and Study* (NTS), Culross, Dunfermline. Tel: 01383-880359. Town House and Study closed mornings. Adm. £4.40. Refurbished 16th- and 17th-century buildings

* *Culzean Castle* (NTS), S. Ayrshire. Tel: 01655-760274. Country park open all year. Adm. £7.00; country park only, £3.50. An 18th-century Adam castle with oval staircase and circular saloon

Dirleton Castle (HS), Dirleton, North Berwick, E. Lothian. Tel: 01620-850330. Adm. £2.50. Twelfth-century castle with 16th-century gardens

Doune Castle (HS), Doune, Perthshire. Tel: 01786-841742. Closed Sun. mornings, Thurs. afternoons, and Fri. in winter. Adm. £2.30. Fourteenth-century castle built for the Regent Albany

† *Drum Castle* (NTS), Drumoak, by Banchory, Aberdeenshire. Tel: 01330-811204. Grounds open all year. Adm. £4.40; garden and grounds only, £2.10. Late 13th-century tower house

Dryburgh Abbey (HS), Scottish Borders. Tel: 01835-822381. Closed Sun. mornings in winter. Adm. £2.50. A 12th-century abbey containing tomb of Sir Walter Scott

Duff House (HS), Banff. Tel: 01261-818181. Closed Mon.–Wed. in winter. Adm. £3.00. Georgian mansion housing part of National Galleries of Scotland collection

Dumbarton Castle (HS), Dumbarton. Tel: 01389-732167. Closed Sun. mornings, Thurs. afternoons, and Fri. in winter. Adm. £1.80. Castle overlooking River Clyde

* *Dundonald Castle* (HS), Dundonald, Kilmarnock, Ayrshire. Tel: 01563-851489. Adm. £1.50. Castle built by the Stewart royal dynasty

Dundrennan Abbey (HS), nr Kirkcudbright. Tel: 01557-500262. Closed weekdays in winter. Adm. £1.50. Remote 12th-century abbey

Dunfermline Palace and Abbey (HS), Dunfermline, Fife. Tel: 01383-739026. Closed Sun. mornings, Thurs. afternoons, and Fri. in winter. Adm. £1.80. Remains of palace and Benedictine abbey

* *Dunrobin Castle*, Golspie, Sutherland. Tel: 01408-633177. Adm. £5.50. The most northerly of Scotland's great castles, seat of the Earls of Sutherland

Dunstaffnage Castle and Chapel (HS), nr Oban. Tel: 01631-562465. Closed Sun. mornings, Thurs. afternoons, and Fri. in winter. Adm. £1.80. Fine 13th-century castle, briefly the prison of Flora Macdonald

* *Dunvegan Castle*, Skye. Tel: 01470-521206. Adm. £5.20; gardens only, £3.70. A 13th-century castle with later additions; home of the chiefs of the Clan MacLeod; trips to seal colony

Edinburgh Castle (HS). Tel: 0131-225 9846. Adm. £6.50; war memorial free. Includes the Scottish National War Memorial, Scottish United Services Museum and historic apartments

Edzell Castle (HS), nr Brechin. Tel: 01356-648631. Closed Sun. mornings, Thurs. afternoons and Fri. in winter. Adm. £2.50. Medieval tower house; unique walled garden

* *Eilean Donan Castle*, Wester Ross. Tel: 01599-555202. Adm. £3.75. A 13th-century castle with Jacobite relics

* *Elcho Castle* (HS), nr Perth. Tel: 01738-639998. Adm. £1.80. Sixteenth-century fortified mansion

Elgin Cathedral (HS), Moray. Tel: 01343-547171. Closed Sun. mornings, Thurs. afternoons and Fri. in winter. Adm. £2.80. A 13th-century cathedral with fine chapterhouse

* *Falkland Palace* (NTS), Falkland, Cupar, Fife. Tel: 01337-857397. Adm. £5.00; garden only, £2.50. Country residence of the Stewart kings and queens, built between 1502 and 1541

* *Floors Castle*, Kelso. Tel: 01573-223333. Adm. £5.00. Largest inhabited castle in Scotland; seat of the Dukes of Roxburghe

Fort George (HS), Highland. Tel: 01667-462800. Closed Sunday mornings in winter. Adm. £3.00. An 18th-century fort

* *Fyvie Castle* (NTS), nr Turriff, Grampian. Tel: 01651-891266. Closed mornings May–June and September, grounds open all year. Adm. £4.40. Fifteenth-century castle with finest wheel stair in Scotland

* *Georgian House* (NTS), Edinburgh. Tel: 0131-226 3318. Closed Sun. mornings. Adm. £4.40. Fine example of 18th-century New Town architecture

* *Gladstone's Land* (NTS), Edinburgh. Tel: 0131-226 5856. Closed Sun. mornings. Adm. £3.20. Typical 17th-century Old Town tenement building with remarkable painted ceilings

* *Glamis Castle*, Angus. Tel: 01307-840393. Adm. £5.40; grounds only, £2.50. Seat of the Lyon family (later Earls of Strathmore and Kinghorne) since 1372

Glasgow Cathedral (HS). Tel: 0141-552 6891. Closed Sun. mornings. Adm. free. Medieval cathedral with elaborately vaulted crypt

Glenelg Broch (HS), Highland. Adm. free. Two broch towers with well-preserved structural features

Glenfinnan Monument (NTS), Glenfinnan, Highland. Tel: 01397-722250. Adm. free. Visitor centre (adm. £1.50) closed in winter. Monument erected by Alexander Macdonald of Glenaladale in 1815 in tribute to the clansmen who fought and died in the cause of Prince Charles Edward Stuart

† *Haddo House* (NTS), nr Tarves, Ellon, Aberdeenshire. Tel: 01651-851440. Garden and country park open all year. Adm. £4.40. Georgian mansion house, home to Earls of Gordon and Marquesses of Aberdeen

* *Hermitage Castle* (HS), nr Newcastleton, Roxburghshire. Tel: 01387-376222. Adm. £1.80. Fortress in the Scottish Borders

* *The Hill House* (NTS), Helensburgh. Tel: 01436-673900. Adm. £6.00. Designed by Charles Rennie Mackintosh

* *Hill of Tarvit Mansionhouse* (NTS), nr Cupar, Fife. Tel: 01334-653127. Mansionhouse closed mornings; grounds open all year. Adm. £3.90. Rebuilt in 1906, with collection of paintings, furniture and Chinese porcelain

* *Holmwood House* (NTS), Glasgow. Tel: 0141-637 2129. Closed mornings. Adm. £3.20. House designed by Alexander 'Greek' Thomson

* *Hopetoun House*, nr Edinburgh. Tel: 0131-331 2451. Adm. £5.00. House designed by Sir William Bruce, enlarged by William Adam

* *House of Dun* (NTS), nr Montrose. Tel: 01674-810264. Closed mornings; grounds open all year. Adm. £3.90. Georgian house with walled garden

* *House of the Binns* (NTS), nr Edinburgh. Tel: 01506-834255. Closed Fri.; parkland open daily. Adm. £3.90. Home of Dalyell family since 1612

Huntingtower Castle (HS), nr Perth. Tel: 01738-627231. Closed Sun. mornings, Thurs. afternoons, and Fri. in winter. Adm. £1.80. Castle with painted ceilings

Huntly Castle (HS). Tel: 01466-793191. Closed Sun. mornings, Thurs. afternoons and Fri. in winter. Adm. £2.50. Ruin of a 16th- and 17th-century house

* *Inchcolm Abbey* (HS), Firth of Forth. Tel: 01383-823332. Adm. £2.50. Abbey founded in 1192 on island in Firth of Forth

* *Inchmahome Priory* (HS), on an island in the Lake of Menteith. Tel: 01877-385294. Adm. £3.00. Thirteenth-century Augustinian priory

* *Inveraray Castle*, Argyll. Tel: 01499-302203. Adm. £3.60. Gothic-style 18th-century castle; seat of the Dukes of Argyll

Iona Abbey, Inner Hebrides. Tel: 01828-640411. Adm. £2.00. Monastery founded by St Columba in AD 563

Italian Chapel, Lamb Holm, Orkney. Tel: 01856-781268. Adm. free. Two Nissan huts painted in the style of an Italian chapel

* *Jarlshof* (HS), Shetland. Tel: 01950-460112. Adm. £2.50. Remains from Stone Age

Jedburgh Abbey (HS), Scottish Borders. Tel: 01835-863925. Adm. £3.00. Romanesque and early Gothic church founded c.1138

* *Kellie Castle* (NTS), nr Pittenweem, Anstruther. Tel: 01333-720271. Closed mornings; grounds open all year. Adm. £3.90. Restored 14th-century castle

Kelso Abbey (HS), Scottish Borders. Adm. free. Remains of great abbey church founded 1128

* *Kildrummy Castle* (HS), nr Alford, Aberdeenshire. Tel: 01975-571331. Adm. £1.80. Thirteenth-century castle, from where the 1715 Jacobite Rising was organized

Kinnaird Head Castle Lighthouse and Museum (HS), Fraserburgh, Aberdeenshire. Tel: 01346-511022. Adm. charge. Northern Lighthouse Company's first lighthouse, still in working order

Lauriston Castle, Edinburgh. Tel: 0131-336 1921. Closed Fri., and weekdays in winter. Adm. £4.50. A 1590s tower house set in 30 acres of parkland

* *Leith Hall* (NTS), nr Kennethmont, Huntly. Tel: 01464-831216. Closed mornings; grounds open all year. Adm. £4.40. Mansion house with semicircular stables, in 286-acre estate

Linlithgow Palace (HS). Tel: 01506-842896. Adm. £2.50. Ruin of royal palace in park setting. Birthplace of Mary, Queen of Scots

* *Lochleven Castle* (HS), on an island in Loch Leven. Tel: 01388-040483. Closed Sun. mornings, Thurs. afternoons, and Fri. in winter. Adm. £3.00. Scene of Mary, Queen of Scots' imprisonment.

Maes Howe (HS), Orkney. Tel: 01856-761606. Closed Sun. mornings, Thurs. afternoons and Fri. in winter. Adm. £2.50. Neolithic tomb

* *Meigle Sculptured Stones* (HS), Angus. Tel: 01828-640612. Adm. £1.80. Celtic Christian stones

Melrose Abbey (HS), Scottish Borders. Tel: 01896-822562. Adm. £3.00. Ruin of Cistercian abbey founded c.1136

* *Mount Stuart House*, Isle of Bute. Tel: 01700-503877. Closed Tues. and Thurs. Adm. £6.00. Spectacular Victorian Gothic house with stained glass and marble

Mousa Broch (HS), Shetland. Adm. free. Finest surviving Iron Age broch tower

Nether Largie Cairns (HS), Argyll and Bute. Adm. free. Bronze Age and Neolithic cairns

New Abbey Corn Mill (HS), nr Dumfries. Tel: 01387-850260. Closed Sun. mornings, Thurs. afternoons and Fri. in winter. Adm. £2.80. Water-powered mill

* *Newark Castle* (HS), Port Glasgow, Renfrewshire. Tel: 01475-741858. Adm. £1.80. Virtually intact 15th-century castle

Palace of Holyroodhouse, Edinburgh. Tel: 0131-556 7371. Closed when the Queen is in residence. Adm. £5.50. The Queen's official Scottish residence. Main part of the palace built 1671–9

* *Paxton House*, near Berwick upon Tweed, Borders. Tel: 01289-386291. Adm. £4.50. A Palladian country house built in 1758

* *Pitmedden Great Garden* (NTS), Pitmedden, Aberdeenshire. Tel: 01651-842352. Adm. £3.90. Formal 17th-century garden

Pollok House (NTS), Glasgow. Tel: 0141-649 7151. Adm. £3.20. Eighteenth-century house with collection of paintings, porcelain and furnishings, set in Pollok Country Park

Provost Skene's House, Aberdeen. Tel: 01224-641086. Adm. free. A 16th-century house with period room settings

Ring of Brogar (HS), Orkney. Adm. free. Neolithic circle of upright stones with an enclosing ditch

Rothesay Castle (HS), Isle of Bute. Tel: 01700-502691. Closed Sun. mornings, Thurs. afternoons, and Fri. in winter. Adm. £1.80. A 13th-century circular castle

Ruthwell Cross (HS), Dumfries and Galloway. Adm. free. Seventh-century Anglian cross

St Andrews Castle and Cathedral (HS), Fife. Tel: 01334-477196 (castle); 01334-472563 (cathedral). Adm. £2.50 (castle); £1.80 (cathedral); £3.50 (combined ticket). Ruins of 13th-century castle and remains of the largest cathedral in Scotland

* *Scone Palace*, Perth. Tel: 01738-552300. Adm. £5.40. House built 1802–13 on the site of a medieval palace

Scott Monument, Edinburgh. Tel: 0131-529 4068. Adm. £2.50. Monument affording fine views of the city

Skara Brae (HS), Orkney. Tel: 01856-841815. Adm. £3.20 (winter); £4.00 (summer, joint ticket with Skaill House). Stone-Age village with adjacent 17th-century house

* *Smailholm Tower* (HS), Scottish Borders. Tel: 01573-460365. Adm. £1.80. Well-preserved tower-house

Spynie Palace (HS), Elgin, Moray. Tel: 01343-546358. Closed weekdays in winter. Adm. £1.80. Residence of Bishops of Moray from 14th to 17th centuries.

Stirling Castle (HS). Tel: 01786-450000. Adm. £5.00. Great Hall and gatehouse of James IV, palace of James V, Chapel Royal remodelled by James VI

Sweetheart Abbey (HS), New Abbey Village, Dumfries. Tel: 01387-850397. Closed Sun. mornings, Thurs. afternoons, and Fri. in winter. Adm. £1.20. Remains of 13th/early 14th-century abbey; burial site of John Balliol's heart

Tantallon Castle (HS), E. Lothian. Tel: 01620-892727. Closed Sun. mornings, Thurs. afternoons and Fri. in winter. Adm. £2.50. Fortification with earthwork defences and a 14th-century curtain wall with towers

* *Threave Castle* (HS), Dumfries and Galloway. Tel: 0411-223101. Adm. £1.80, including ferry trip. Late 14th-century tower on an island; reached by boat, long walk to castle

Tolquhon Castle (HS), nr Aberdeen. Tel: 01651-851286. Closed weekdays in winter. Adm. £1.80. Mansion house with 15th-century tower

* *Traquair House*, Innerleithen, Peeblesshire. Tel: 01896-830323. Adm. £5.00. Scotland's oldest inhabited house

Urquhart Castle (HS), Loch Ness. Tel: 01456-450551. Adm. £3.80. Castle remains with well-preserved tower

Wallace Monument, Stirling. Tel: 01786-472140. Adm. £3.25. Exhibitions about Sir William Wallace and others, and a diorama showing the view from the top of the monument

* *Whithorn* (HS), nr Newton Stewart, Dumfries and Galloway. Tel: 01988-500700. Adm. charge. Site of first Christian church in Scotland

MUSEUMS AND GALLERIES

There are some 296 museums and galleries in Scotland, of which 288 are fully or provisionally registered with the Museums and Galleries Commission. Registration indicates that they have an appropriate constitution, are soundly financed, have satisfactory collection management standards and public services, and have access to professional curatorial advice. Museums should achieve full or provisional registration status in order to be eligible for grants from the Museums and Galleries Commission and from the Scottish Museums Council. Of the registered museums in Scotland, 136 are run by a local authority and 111 are independently run.

The national collections in Scotland are the National Galleries of Scotland and the National Museums of Scotland, which are funded by direct government grant-in-aid. An online art museum (http://www.24hourmuseum.org.uk) has also been awarded national collection status.

Local authority museums are funded by the local authority and may also receive grants from the Museums and Galleries Commission. Independent museums and galleries mainly rely on their own resources but are also eligible for grants from the Museums and Galleries Commission.

The Scottish Museums Council (*see* page 200) is one of ten area museum councils in the UK. It is an independent charity that receives an annual grant from the Scottish Executive, and gives advice and support to museums in Scotland. It may offer improvement grants and also assists with training and marketing.

Opening to the Public

The following is a selection of the museums and art galleries in Scotland. The admission charges given are the standard charges for 1999–2000, where a charge is made; many museums have concessionary rates for children, etc. Where no charge is shown, admission is free. Opening hours vary. Most museums are closed on Christmas Eve, Christmas Day, Boxing Day and New Year's Day; some are closed on Good Friday or the May Day Bank Holiday. Some smaller museums close at lunchtimes. Information about a specific museum or gallery should be checked by telephone.

* Local authority museum/gallery

ABERDEEN
* *Aberdeen Art Gallery*, Schoolhill. Tel: 01224-523700. Closed Sun. mornings. Art from the 18th to 20th century
* *Aberdeen Maritime Museum*, Shiprow. Tel: 01224-337700. Adm. £3.50. Maritime history, including shipbuilding and North Sea oil
* *Arts Centre Gallery*, King Street. Tel: 01224-635208. Exhibitions of contemporary art
Gordon Highlanders Museum, St Luke's, Viewfield Road. Tel: 01224-311200. Adm. £2.00
Marischal Museum, University of Aberdeen, Broad Street. Tel: 01224-274301. Foreign ethnography, local history and archaeology
* *Tolbooth Museum of Civic History*, Castle Street. Tel: 01224-621167. Adm. £2.50. The history of Aberdeen, housed in what was originally the city's prison

ALFORD
Grampian Transport Museum. Tel: 01975-562292. Adm. £3.50. Large collection of road transport vehicles

ANSTRUTHER
Scottish Fisheries Museum, St Ayles, Harbourhead. Tel: 01333-310628. Adm. £2.50. Marine aquarium, fishing boats, period interior and other fishing artefacts

ARBROATH
* *Arbroath Museum*, Ladyloan. Tel: 01241-875598. Local history museum

BLANTYRE
David Livingstone Centre, Station Road. Tel: 01698-823140. Adm. £2.95. Museum relating the life of David Livingstone

CREETOWN
Creetown Gem Rock Museum and Gallery, Chain Road. Tel: 01671-820357. Adm. £2.75. Minerals, crystals and gemstones from around the world

DUMFRIES
* *Burns House*, Burns Street. Tel: 01387-255297. The house where Robert Burns died
Robert Burns Centre, Mill Road. Tel: 01387-264808. Displays and exhibitions relating to Robert Burns and to Dumfries during his lifetime

* *Dumfries Museum and Camera Obscura*, The Observatory. Tel: 01387-253374. Adm. free to museum; £1.50 to Camera Obscura. Natural history, archaeology and folk collections

Shambellie House Museum of Costume, New Abbey. Tel: 01387-850375. Adm. £2.50. Costumes from the 1850s to the 1920s

DUNDEE

* *Broughty Castle Museum*, Broughty Ferry. Tel: 01382-436916. A former estuary fort housing a museum of local history, arms and armour, seashore life and whaling

Discovery Point, Riverside. Tel: 01382-201245. Adm. £5.00. Visitor centre telling the story of Scott's voyage to Antarctica; incorporates the *Discovery*

* *McManus Galleries*, Albert Square. Tel: 01382-432084. Local history museum and gallery showing temporary art exhibitions

EDINBURGH

Britannia, Leith docks. Tel: 0131-555 5566. Former royal yacht with royal barge and royal family picture gallery. Tickets must be pre-booked

* *City Art Centre*, Market Street. Tel: 0131-529 3993. Closed Sun. Late 19th- and 20th-century art and temporary exhibitions

* *Fruit Market Gallery*, Market Street. Tel: 0131-225 2383. Contemporary art gallery

* *Huntly House Museum*, Canongate. Tel: 0131-529 4143. Closed Sun. Local history, silver, glass and Scottish pottery

* *Museum of Childhood*, High Street. Tel: 0131-529 4142. Closed Sun. Toys, games, clothes and exhibits relating to the social history of childhood

Museum of Flight, East Fortune Airfield, nr North Berwick. Tel: 01620-880308. Adm. £3.00. Display of aircraft

Museum of Scotland, Chambers Street. Tel: 0131-247 4422. Closed Sun mornings. Adm. £3.00. Scottish history from prehistoric times to the present

National Gallery of Scotland, The Mound. Tel: 0131-624 6200. Closed Sun. mornings. Paintings, drawings and prints from the 16th to 20th century, and the national collection of Scottish art

* *The People's Story*, Canongate. Tel: 0131-529 4057. Closed Sun. Edinburgh life since the 18th century

Royal Museum of Scotland, Chambers Street. Tel: 0131-225 7534. Closed Sun. mornings. Adm. £3.00. Scottish and international collections from prehistoric times to the present

Royal Scots Regimental Museum, Edinburgh Castle. Tel: 0131-310 5016. Adm. free (Adm. to Edinburgh Castle (HS), £6.50)

Scottish Agricultural Museum, Ingliston. Tel: 0131-333 2674. Closed Sat. and Sun. in winter. History of agriculture in Scotland

Scottish National Gallery of Modern Art, Belford Road. Tel: 0131-624 6200. Closed Sun. mornings. Twentieth-century painting, sculpture and graphic art

Scottish National Portrait Gallery, Queen Street. Tel: 0131-624 6200. Closed Sun. mornings. Portraits of eminent people in Scottish history, and the national collection of photography

Scottish United Services Museum, Edinburgh Castle. Tel: 0131-225 7534. Adm. free (Adm. to Edinburgh Castle (HS), £6.50). Collections connected to the Scottish armed forces since the 17th century

* *The Writers' Museum*, Lawnmarket. Tel: 0131-529 4901. Closed Sun. Robert Louis Stevenson, Walter Scott and Robert Burns exhibits

FORT WILLIAM

West Highland Museum, Cameron Square. Tel: 01397-702169. Closed Sun. Adm. £2.00. Includes tartan collections and exhibits relating to 1745 uprising

FRASERBURGH

* *Museum of Scottish Lighthouses*, Kinnaird Head. Tel: 01346-511022. Adm. £2.75. Lighthouse artefacts, including the original Kinnaird Head lighthouse

GLASGOW

* *Burrell Collection*, Pollokshaws Road. Tel: 0141-649 7151. Paintings, textiles, furniture, ceramics, stained glass and silver from classical times to the 19th century

Collins Gallery, University of Strathclyde, Richmond Street. Tel: 0141-552 4400 ext. 2558. Touring exhibitions of contemporary work by Scottish artists

* *Gallery of Modern Art*, Queen Street. Tel: 0141-229 1996. Collection of contemporary Scottish and world art

* *Glasgow Art Gallery and Museum*, Kelvingrove. Tel: 0141-287 2699. Includes Old Masters, 19th-century French paintings and armour collection

Glasgow School of Art, Renfrew Street. Tel: 0141-353 4500. Exhibitions, mainly of contemporary art, in Rennie Mackintosh building

* *House for an Art Lover*, Bellahouston Park, Dumbreck Road. Tel: 0141-353 4770. Adm. £3.50. Based on Rennie Mackintosh designs

Hunterian Art Gallery, Hillhead Street. Tel: 0141-330 5431. Closed Sun. Rennie Mackintosh and Whistler collections; Old Masters, Scottish paintings and modern paintings, sculpture and prints

* *McLellan Galleries*, Sauchiehall Street. Tel: 0141-332 7521. Adm. charge. Temporary exhibitions

* *Museum of Transport*, Bunhouse Road. Tel: 0141-287 2720. Includes a reproduction of a 1938 Glasgow street, cars since the 1930s, trams and a Glasgow subway station

* *People's Palace Museum*, Glasgow Green. Tel: 0141-554 0223. History of Glasgow since 1175

* *Pollok House*, Pollokshaws Road. Tel: 0141-616 6410. Adm. £3.20. Palladian house containing the Stirling Maxwell art collection

* *Provand's Lordship*, Castle Street. Tel: 0141-553 2557. Closed until April 2000. Exhibition of period displays housed in medieval buildings

Royal Highland Fusiliers Museum, Sauchiehall Street. Tel: 0141-332 5639

* *St Mungo Museum of Religious Life and Art*, Castle Street. Tel: 0141-553 2557. Explores universal themes through objects of all the main world religions

* *Scotland Street School Museum of Education*, Scotland Street. Tel: 0141-429 1202. The history of education in Scotland, in a building designed by Rennie Mackintosh

GLENCOE
Glencoe and North Lorn Folk Museum, Glencoe. No telephone. Closed in winter. Adm. £1.00. Restored cottage with local and natural history exhibits

GREENOCK
* *McLean Museum and Art Gallery*, Kelly Street. Tel: 01475-715624. Local and natural history museum and temporary art exhibitions

INVERARAY
Inveraray Jail, Church Square. Tel: 01499-302381. Adm. £4.50. A 19th-century courthouse with two prisons

Inveraray Maritime Museum and *Arctic Penguin*, Maritime Heritage Centre, Inveraray Pier. Tel: 01499-302213. Adm. £3.00. Museum of Clyde ships and shipyards

INVERNESS
* *Inverness Museum and Art Gallery*, Castle Wynd. Tel: 01463-237114. The history of the Highlands

Queen's Own Highlanders Regimental Museum, Fort George, nr Inverness. Tel: 01463-224380. Adm. free (Adm. to Fort George (HS), £3.00)

IRVINE
Scottish Maritime Museum, Laird Forge, Gottries Road. Tel: 01294-278283. Adm. £2.00. Full-size ships, an exhibition gallery, an educational centre and a restored tenement flat

JOHN O'GROATS
Last House Museum. Tel: 01955-611250. Local history museum in a restored 18th-century house

KILMARTIN
Kilmartin House Museum. Tel: 01546-510278. Adm. £3.90. Landscape and archaeology of Argyll

KINGUSSIE
* *Highland Folk Museum*, Duke Street. Tel: 01540-661307. Adm. £3.00. Highland artefacts

KIRKCALDY
* *Kirkcaldy Museum and Art Gallery*, War Memorial Gardens. Tel: 01592-412860. Historical displays and collection of paintings including works by the Scottish Colourists and Camden Town group

KIRKWALL
* *Tankerness House Museum*, Broad Street. Tel: 01856-873191. Closed Sundays in winter. Two restored farmsteads

LERWICK
* *Shetland Museum*, Lower Hillhead. Tel: 01595-695057. Museum depicting all aspects of island life

LOCHMADDY
Taigh Chearsabhagh. Tel: 01876-500293. Adm. £1.00. Local history museum

MOTHERWELL
* *Motherwell Heritage Centre*, High Road. Tel: 01698-251000. Includes Technopolis, a multi-media local history exhibition

NEWTONGRANGE

Scottish Mining Museum, Lady Victoria Colliery. Tel: 0131-663 7519. Adm. £4.00. Museum of mining history

PAISLEY

* *Paisley Museum and Art Galleries*, High Street. Tel: 0141-889 3151. Local and natural history and a collection of Paisley shawls

PEEBLES

* *Tweeddale Museum and Art Gallery*, Chambers Institute, High Street. Tel: 01721-724820. Local history museum and contemporary art gallery

PERTH

Black Watch Regimental Museum, Balhousie Castle, Hay Street. Tel: 01738-621281 ext. 8530
* *Perth Museum and Art Gallery*, George Street. Tel: 01738-632488. Local history museum and art exhibitions

ST ANDREWS

British Golf Museum, Bruce Embankment. Tel: 01334-478880. Adm. £3.75. Museum of the history and development of golf
* *St Andrews Museum*, Kinburn Park, Double Dykes Road. Tel: 01334-412690. Local history and temporary exhibitions

STIRLING

Argyll and Sutherland Highlanders Museum, Stirling Castle. Tel: 01786-475165. Adm. free (Adm. to Stirling Castle (HS), £5.00)
Smith Art Gallery and Museum, Dumbarton Road. Tel: 01786-471917. Scottish paintings and artefacts

STORNOWAY

* *An Lanntair Gallery*, Town Hall, South Beach. Tel: 01851-703307. Contemporary art exhibitions

STRANRAER

* *Stranraer Museum*, George Street. Tel: 01776-705088. Exhibition on farming, archaeology and polar explorers

WANLOCKHEAD, VIA BIGGAR

Museum of Leadmining. Tel: 01659-74387. Adm. £3.95. The history of leadmining in Scotland

THE NATIONAL FLAGS

THE SCOTTISH FLAG

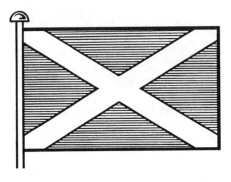

The flag of Scotland is known as the Saltire. It is a white diagonal cross on a blue field (saltire argent in a field azure) and symbolizes St Andrew, the patron saint of Scotland.

A traditional explanation for the adoption of the St Andrew's cross as the symbol of Scotland is that the Saltire appeared in the sky to the Pictish king Hungus as an omen of victory over the Anglo-Saxons at the battle of Aethelstaneford. The Saltire was adopted as a national symbol at about the same time as St Andrew was adopted as Scotland's patron saint, and by the mid 14th century it was being used on coins. From about that time also, it has been used as a symbol of the struggle for independence.

THE NATIONAL FLAG

The national flag of the United Kingdom is the Union Flag, generally known as the Union Jack.

The Union Flag is a combination of the cross of St George, patron saint of England, the cross of St Andrew, patron saint of Scotland, and a cross similar to that of St Patrick, patron saint of Ireland.

The Union Flag was first introduced in 1606 after the union of the kingdoms of England and Scotland under one sovereign. The cross of St Patrick was added in 1801 after the union of Great Britain and Ireland.

DAYS FOR FLYING FLAGS

It is the practice to fly the Union Flag daily on some customs houses. In all other cases, flags are flown on government buildings by command of The Queen.

Days for hoisting the Union Flag are notified to the Department for Culture, Media and Sport by The Queen's command and communicated by the department to other government departments. On the days appointed, the Union Flag is flown on government buildings in the UK from 8 a.m. to sunset.

Both the Union Flag and the Saltire are flown in Scotland. The Saltire is flown from government buildings alongside, but not superior to, the Union Flag on the flag-flying days, which are the same days as those announced by the Department for Culture, Media and Sport. On Europe Day only, the EU flag flies alongside the Union Flag and the Saltire.

The Queen's Accession	6 February
Birthday of The Duke of York	19 February
Birthday of The Earl of Wessex	10 March
Commonwealth Day (2000)	13 March
Birthday of The Queen	21 April
* Europe Day	9 May
Coronation Day	2 June
The Queen's Official Birthday (2000)	10 June
Birthday of The Duke of Edinburgh	10 June
Birthday of Queen Elizabeth the Queen Mother	4 August
Birthday of The Princess Royal	15 August
Birthday of The Princess Margaret	21 August
Remembrance Sunday (2000)	12 November
Birthday of The Prince Charles, Duke of Rothesay	14 November
The Queen's Wedding Day	20 November
St Andrew's Day	30 November

* The Union Flag should fly alongside the EU flag. On government buildings that have only one flagpole, the Union Flag should take precedence

FLAGS AT HALF-MAST

Flags are flown at half-mast (i.e. two-thirds up between the top and bottom of the flagstaff) on the following occasions:

(a) From the announcement of the death up to the funeral of the Sovereign, except on Proclamation Day, when flags are hoisted right up from 11 a.m. to sunset

(b) The funerals of members of the royal family, subject to special commands from The Queen in each case

(c) The funerals of foreign rulers, subject to special commands from The Queen in each case

(d) The funerals of prime ministers and ex-prime ministers of the UK, subject to special commands from The Queen in each case

(e) Other occasions by special command of The Queen

On occasions when days for flying flags coincide with days for flying flags at half-mast, the following rules are observed. Flags are flown:

(a) although a member of the royal family, or a near relative of the royal family, may be lying dead, unless special commands are received from The Queen to the contrary

(b) although it may be the day of the funeral of a foreign ruler

If the body of a very distinguished subject is lying at a government office, the flag may fly at half-mast on that office until the body has left (provided it is a day on which the flag would fly) and then the flag is to be hoisted right up. On all other government buildings the flag will fly as usual.

THE ROYAL STANDARD

The Royal Standard is hoisted only when the Queen is actually present in the building, and never when Her Majesty is passing in procession.

NATIONAL ANTHEM

The official national anthem throughout the UK is *God Save The Queen*.

At national events and international competitions (primarily sporting), Scottish songs are sometimes used, including *Scotland the Brave* at the Commonwealth Games and *Flower of Scotland* for international rugby matches.

In 1998 the *Herald* newspaper ran a competition for a new Scottish anthem and the winner, announced in January 1999, was William Jackson's *Land of Light*.

NATIONAL DAY

The national day is 30 November, the festival of St Andrew, the patron saint of Scotland.

St Andrew, one of the apostles and brother of Simon Peter, was born at Bethsaida on the Sea of Galilee and lived at Capernaum. He preached the gospel in Asia Minor and in Scythia along the shores of the Black Sea and became the patron saint of Russia. It is believed that he suffered crucifixion at Patras in Achaea, on a *crux decussata* (now known as St Andrew's Cross) and that his relics were removed from Patras to Constantinople and thence to Scotland, probably in the eighth century, since which time he has been the patron saint of Scotland. The church and settlement founded at the place where the relics were brought ashore became the town of St Andrews.

THE QUEEN'S HOUSEHOLD

Office: Buckingham Palace, London SW1A 1AA
Tel: 0171-930 4832
Web: http://www.royal.gov.uk

The Lord Chamberlain is the most senior member of The Queen's Household and under him come the heads of the six departments: the Private Secretary, the Keeper of the Privy Purse, the Comptroller of the Lord Chamberlain's Office, the Master of the Household, the Crown Equerry, and the Director of the Royal Collection. Positions in these departments are full-time salaried posts.

There are also a number of honorary or now largely ceremonial appointments which carry no remuneration or a small honorarium. In the following list, honorary appointments are indicated by an asterisk.

GREAT OFFICERS OF STATE

Lord Chamberlain, The Lord Camoys, GCVO, PC
* *Lord Steward,* The Viscount Ridley, KG, GCVO, TD
* *Master of the Horse,* The Lord Vestey

LADIES-IN-WAITING AND EQUERRIES

* *Mistress of the Robes,* The Duchess of Grafton, GCVO
* *Ladies of the Bedchamber,* The Countess of Airlie, DCVO; The Lady Farnham, CVO
Women of the Bedchamber, Hon. Mary Morrison, DCVO; Lady Susan Hussey, DCVO; Lady Dugdale, DCVO; The Lady Elton, CVO; Mrs Christian Adams (temp.)
Equerries, Lt.-Col. Sir Guy Acland, Bt., MVO; Sqn. Ldr. S. Brailsford

THE PRIVATE SECRETARY'S OFFICE

Private Secretary to The Queen, Sir Robin Janvrin, KCVO, CB
Deputy Private Secretary, vacant
Communications Secretary, S. Lewis

PRESS OFFICE
Press Secretary, G. Crawford, LVO
Deputy Press Secretary, Miss P. Russell-Smith

THE PRIVY PURSE AND TREASURER'S OFFICE

Keeper of the Privy Purse and Treasurer to The Queen, Sir Michael Peat, KCVO
Chief Accountant and Paymaster, I. McGregor
Personnel Officer, Miss P. Lloyd
Resident Factor, Balmoral, P. Ord, FRICS

THE LORD CHAMBERLAIN'S OFFICE

Comptroller, Lt.-Col. W. H. M. Ross, CVO, OBE
Assistant Comptroller, Lt.-Col. R. Cartwright
State Invitations Assistant, J. O. Hope

Marshal of the Diplomatic Corps, Vice-Adm. Sir James Weatherall, KBE
Vice-Marshal, P. Astley, LVO

MASTER OF THE HOUSEHOLD'S DEPARTMENT

Master of the Household, Maj.-Gen. Sir Simon Cooper, KCVO
Deputy Master of the Household, Lt.-Col. C. Richards
Superintendent, The Palace of Holyroodhouse, Lt.-Col. D. Anderson, OBE

ROYAL MEWS DEPARTMENT

Crown Equerry, Lt.-Col. S. Gilbart-Denham, CVO

THE ROYAL COLLECTION

Director of Royal Collection and Surveyor of The Queen's Works of Art, H. Roberts, CVO, FSA
Surveyor of The Queen's Pictures, C. Lloyd, LVO
Director of Media Affairs, R. Arbiter, LVO
Financial Director, M. Stevens

ROYAL COLLECTION ENTERPRISES LTD
Managing Director, M. E. K. Hewlett, LVO

THE QUEEN'S HOUSEHOLD IN SCOTLAND

* *Hereditary Lord High Constable of Scotland,* The Earl of Erroll
* *Hereditary Master of the Household in Scotland,* The Duke of Argyll
Lord Lyon King of Arms, Sir Malcolm Innes of Edingight, KCVO, WS
* *Hereditary Banner-Bearer for Scotland,* The Earl of Dundee
* *Hereditary Bearer of the National Flag of Scotland,* The Earl of Lauderdale
* *Hereditary Keeper of the Palace of Holyroodhouse,* The Duke of Hamilton and Brandon
* *Governor of Edinburgh Castle,* Maj.-Gen. M. J. Strudwick, CBE
* *Historiographer,* Prof. T. C. Smout, CBE, FBA, FRSE, FSA Scot.
* *Botanist,* Prof. D. Henderson, CBE, FRSE
* *Painter and Limner,* vacant
* *Sculptor in Ordinary,* Prof. Sir Eduardo Paolozzi, CBE, RA

* *Astronomer,* Prof. J. Brown, Ph.D., FRSE
* *Heralds and Pursuivants, see* page 55

ECCLESIASTICAL HOUSEHOLD

* *Dean of the Chapel Royal,* Very Revd J. Harkness, CB, OBE
* *Dean of the Order of the Thistle,* Very Revd G. I. Macmillan
* *Chaplains in Ordinary:* 10
Domestic Chaplain, Balmoral, Revd R. P. Sloan

MEDICAL HOUSEHOLD

* *Physicians in Scotland,* P. Brunt, OBE, MD, FRCP; A. Toft, CBE, FRCPE
* *Surgeons in Scotland,* J. Engeset, FRCS; I. Macintyre
Apothecary to the Household at Balmoral, D. J. A. Glass
Apothecary to the Household at the Palace of Holyroodhouse, Dr J. Cormack, MD, FRCPE, FRCGP

* ROYAL COMPANY OF ARCHERS (QUEEN'S BODYGUARD FOR SCOTLAND)

Captain-General and Gold Stick for Scotland, Maj. Sir Hew Hamilton-Dalrymple, Bt., KCVO
President of the Council and Silver Stick for Scotland, The Duke of Buccleuch and Queensberry, KT, VRD
Adjutant, Maj. the Hon. Sir Lachlan Maclean, Bt.
Secretary, Capt. J. D. B. Younger
Treasurer, J. M. Haldane of Gleneagles
*Members on the active list: c.*400

OTHER HONORARY APPOINTMENTS

Master of The Queen's Music, M. Williamson, CBE, AO
Poet Laureate (1999–2009), A. Motion

ROYAL SALUTES

Royal salutes are authorized at Edinburgh Castle and Stirling Castle, although in practice Edinburgh Castle is the only operating saluting station in Scotland.

A salute of 21 guns is fired on the following occasions:
(a) the anniversaries of the birth, accession and coronation of The Queen
(b) the anniversary of the birth of HM Queen Elizabeth the Queen Mother
(c) the anniversary of the birth of HRH Prince Philip, Duke of Edinburgh

A salute of 21 guns is fired in Edinburgh on the occasion of the opening of the General Assembly of the Church of Scotland.

A salute of 21 guns may also be fired in Edinburgh on the arrival of HM The Queen, HM Queen Elizabeth the Queen Mother, or a member of the royal family who is a Royal Highness on an official visit.

THE MOST ANCIENT AND MOST NOBLE ORDER OF THE THISTLE

Postnominal initials, KT (Knights); LT (Ladies)
Ribbon, Green
Motto, Nemo me impune lacessit (No one provokes me with impunity)

The Order of the Thistle is an exclusively Scottish order of knighthood. There is evidence of an order of chivalry in Scotland from at least the Middle Ages; James II created an order of knighthood in 1452, and James III (1460–88) may also have created an order and certainly used the thistle as the royal emblem. However, the present Order of the Thistle was founded by James VII and II in 1687, comprising the sovereign and eight knights. Following James's exile, the Order fell into abeyance until 1703 when it was revived by Queen Anne, who increased the number of knights to 12; since 1827 the maximum number of knights has been 16. Conferment of the Order also confers a knighthood on the recipient.

The Order's motto, *Nemo me impune lacessit*, is the motto of all Scottish regiments; it is usually translated into Scots as 'Wha daur meddle wi' me?'.

SOVEREIGN OF THE ORDER
The Queen

ROYAL KNIGHTS AND LADY
HM Queen Elizabeth the Queen Mother, 1937
HRH The Prince Philip, Duke of Edinburgh, 1952
HRH The Prince Charles, Duke of Rothesay, 1977

KNIGHTS BRETHREN AND LADIES
The Earl of Wemyss and March, 1966
Sir Donald Cameron of Lochiel, 1973
The Duke of Buccleuch and Queensberry, 1978
The Earl of Elgin and Kincardine, 1981
The Lord Thomson of Monifieth, 1981
The Lord MacLehose of Beoch, 1983
The Earl of Airlie, 1985
Capt. Sir Iain Tennant, 1986
The Viscount Younger of Leckie, 1995
The Viscount of Arbuthnott, 1996
The Earl of Crawford and Balcarres, 1996
Lady Marion Fraser, 1996
The Lord Macfarlane of Bearsden, 1996
The Lord Mackay of Clashfern, 1997

Chancellor, The Duke of Buccleuch and Queensberry, KT, VRD
Dean, The Very Revd G. I. Macmillan
Secretary and Lord Lyon King of Arms, Sir Malcolm Innes of Edingight, KCVO, WS
Usher of the Green Rod, Rear-Adm. C. H. Layman, CB, DSO, LVO
Chapel, The Thistle Chapel, St Giles's Cathedral, Edinburgh

PRECEDENCE IN SCOTLAND

The Sovereign
The Prince Philip, Duke of Edinburgh
The Lord High Commissioner to the General
Assembly of the Church of Scotland (while
the Assembly is sitting)
The Duke of Rothesay (eldest son of the
Sovereign)
The Sovereign's younger sons
The Sovereign's cousins
Lord-Lieutenants*
Lord Provosts of cities being *ex officio* Lord-
Lieutenants of those cities*
Sheriffs Principal*
Lord Chancellor of Great Britain
Moderator of the General Assembly of the
Church of Scotland
Keeper of the Great Seal (The First Minister)
Presiding Officer of the Scottish Parliament
Secretary of State for Scotland
Hereditary High Constable of Scotland
Hereditary Master of the Household
Dukes, according to their patent of creation:
(1) of England
(2) of Scotland
(3) of Great Britain
(4) of the United Kingdom
(5) those of Ireland created since the Union
between Great Britain and Ireland
Eldest sons of Dukes of the Blood Royal
Marquesses, according to their patent of
creation:
(1) of England
(2) of Scotland
(3) of Great Britain
(4) of the United Kingdom
(5) those of Ireland created since the Union
between Great Britain and Ireland
Dukes' eldest sons
Earls, according to their patent of creation:
(1) of England
(2) of Scotland
(3) of Great Britain
(4) of the United Kingdom
(5) those of Ireland created since the Union
between Great Britain and Ireland
Younger sons of Dukes of Blood Royal
Marquesses' eldest sons
Dukes' younger sons
Lord Justice-General
Lord Clerk Register
Lord Advocate
Advocate-General
Lord Justice-Clerk

---

* During term of office and within their own
counties/cities/sheriffdoms

Viscounts, according to their patent of
creation
(1) of England
(2) of Scotland
(3) of Great Britain
(4) of the United Kingdom
(5) those of Ireland created since the Union
between Great Britain and Ireland
Earls' eldest sons
Marquesses' younger sons
Lord-Barons, according to their patent of
creation:
(1) of England
(2) of Scotland
(3) of Great Britain
(4) of the United Kingdom
(5) those of Ireland created since the Union
between Great Britain and Ireland
Viscounts' eldest sons
Earls' younger sons
Lord-Barons' eldest sons
Knights of the Garter
Knights of the Thistle
Privy Counsellors
Senators of College of Justice (Lords of
Session)
Viscounts' younger sons
Lord-Barons' younger sons
Sons of Life Peers
Baronets
Knights Grand Cross of the Order of the
Bath
Knights Grand Commanders of the Order of
the Star of India
Knights Grand Cross of the Order of St
Michael and St George
Knights Grand Commanders of the Order of
the Indian Empire
Knights Grand Cross of the Royal Victorian
Order
Knights Commanders of the Order of the
Bath
Knights Commanders of the Order of the
Star of India
Knights Commanders of the Order of St
Michael and St George
Knights Commanders of the Order of the
Indian Empire
Knights Commanders of the Royal Victorian
Order
Solicitor-General for Scotland
Lyon King of Arms
Sheriffs Principal, except as shown above
Knights Bachelor
Sheriffs
Commanders of the Royal Victorian Order
Companions of the Order of the Bath

Companions of the Order of the Star of India
Companions of the Order of St Michael and
St George
Companions of the Order of the Indian
Empire
Lieutenants of the Royal Victorian Order
Companions of the Distinguished Service
Order
Eldest sons of younger sons of Peers
Baronets' eldest sons
Knights' eldest sons, in the same order as
their fathers
Members of the Royal Victorian Order
Baronets' younger sons
Knights' younger sons, in the same order as
their fathers
Queen's Counsel
Esquires
Gentlemen

FORMS OF ADDRESS

It is only possible to cover here the forms of address for peers, baronets and knights, their wife and children, Privy Counsellors, and holders of certain political, legal and civic posts; for chiefs of clans, *see* pages 274 and 275. Greater detail should be sought in one of the publications devoted to the subject.

Both formal and social forms of address are given where usage differs; nowadays, the social form is generally preferred to the formal, which increasingly is used only for official documents and on very formal occasions.

The form of address for a woman holding office is given if different from that of a man holding the same position, but only where a woman holds or has held that particular office, as new styles tend to be adopted only when circumstances require it.

F— represents forename
S— represents surname
D— represents a designation, e.g. a title (peer) or city (convenor)

BARON
see Lord of Parliament

BARON'S WIFE
see Lord of Parliament's wife

BARON'S CHILDREN
see Lord of Parliament's children

BARONESS IN OWN RIGHT
see Lady of Parliament in own right

BARONESS (WOMAN LIFE PEER)
Envelope, may be addressed in same way as for a Lord of Parliament's wife, or, if she prefers *(formal)*, The Right Hon. the Baroness D— ; *(social)*, The Baroness D—
Letter (formal), My Lady; *(social)*, Dear Lady D—
Spoken, Lady D—

BARONET
Envelope, Sir F— S—-, Bt.
Letter (formal), Dear Sir; *(social)*, Dear Sir F—
Spoken, Sir F—

BARONET'S WIFE
Envelope, Lady S—
Letter (formal), Dear Madam; *(social)*, Dear Lady S—
Spoken, Lady S—

CHAIRMAN OF SCOTTISH LAND COURT
As for Lords of Session

CONVENER OF COUNCIL
Envelope, The Convenor of D—
Letter, Dear Convener
Spoken, Convener

COUNTESS IN OWN RIGHT
As for an Earl's wife

COURTESY TITLES
The heir apparent to a Duke, Marquess or Earl uses the highest of his father's other titles as a courtesy title. The holder of a courtesy title is not styled The Most Hon. or The Right Hon., and in correspondence 'The' is omitted before the title. The heir apparent to a Scottish title may use the title 'Master' (*see* below).

DAME
Envelope, Dame F— S—, followed by appropriate post-nominal letters
Letter (formal), Dear Madam; *(social)*, Dear Dame F—
Spoken, Dame F—-

DUKE
Envelope (formal), His Grace the Duke of D—; *(social)*, The Duke of D—
Letter (formal), My Lord Duke; *(social)*, Dear Duke
Spoken (formal), Your Grace; *(social)*, Duke

DUKE'S WIFE
Envelope (formal), Her Grace the Duchess of D— ; *(social)*, The Duchess of D—
Letter (formal), Dear Madam; *(social)*, Dear Duchess
Spoken, Duchess

DUKE'S ELDEST SON
see Courtesy titles

DUKE'S YOUNGER SONS
Envelope, Lord F— S—
Letter (formal), My Lord; *(social)*, Dear Lord F—
Spoken (formal), My Lord; *(social)*, Lord F

DUKE'S DAUGHTER
Envelope, Lady F— S—
Letter (formal), Dear Madam; *(social)*, Dear Lady F—
Spoken, Lady F—

EARL
Envelope (formal), The Right Hon. the Earl (of) D— ; *(social)*, The Earl (of) D— *Letter (formal)*, My Lord; *(social)*, Dear Lord D— *Spoken (formal)*, My Lord; *(social)*, Lord D—

EARL'S WIFE
Envelope (formal), The Right Hon. the Countess (of) D— ; *(social)*, The Countess (of) D— *Letter (formal)*, Madam; *(social)*, Lady D— *Spoken (formal)*, Madam; *(social)*, Lady D—

EARL'S CHILDREN
Eldest son, see Courtesy titles
Younger sons, The Hon. F— S— (for forms of address, *see* Lord of Parliament's children)
Daughters, Lady F— S— (for forms of address, *see* Duke's daughter)

KNIGHT (BACHELOR)
Envelope, Sir F— S— *Letter (formal)*, Dear Sir; *(social)*, Dear Sir F— *Spoken*, Sir F—

KNIGHT (ORDERS OF CHIVALRY)
Envelope, Sir F— S—, followed by appropriate post-nominal letters. Otherwise as for Knight Bachelor

KNIGHT'S WIFE
As for Baronet's wife

LADY OF PARLIAMENT IN OWN RIGHT
As for Lord of Parliament's wife

LIFE PEER
As for Lord of Parliament/Baroness in own right

LIFE PEER'S WIFE
As for Lord of Parliament's wife

LIFE PEER'S CHILDREN
As for Lord of Parliament's children

LORD ADVOCATE
Usually admitted a member of the Privy Council on appointment.
Envelope, The Right (Rt.) Hon. the Lord Advocate, or The Right (Rt.) Hon. F— S— *Letter (formal)*, My Lord (if a peer), or Dear Sir; *(social)*, Dear Lord Advocate, or Dear Lord D— /Mr S— *Spoken*, Lord D— /Mr S—

LORD HIGH COMMISSIONER TO THE GENERAL ASSEMBLY
Envelope, His/Her Grace the Lord High Commissioner
Letter, Your Grace
Spoken, Your Grace

LORD JUSTICE-CLERK
Envelope, The Hon. the Lord Justice-Clerk; if a Privy Counsellor, The Right (Rt.) Hon. the Lord Justice-Clerk
Letter (formal), My Lord; *(social)*, Dear Lord Justice-Clerk
Spoken (formal), My Lord; *(social)*, Lord Justice-Clerk

LORD JUSTICE-GENERAL
Usually admitted a member of the Privy Council on appointment
Envelope, The Right (Rt.) Hon. the Lord Justice-General
Letter (formal), My Lord; *(social)*, Dear Lord Justice-General
Spoken (formal), My Lord; *(social)*, Lord Justice-General

LORD OF PARLIAMENT
Envelope (formal), The Right Hon. Lord D— ; *(social)*, The Lord D— *Letter (formal)*, My Lord; *(social)*, Dear Lord D— *Spoken*, Lord D—

LORD OF PARLIAMENT'S WIFE
Envelope (formal), The Right Hon. Lady D— ; *(social)*, The Lady D— *Letter (formal)*, My Lady; *(social)*, Dear Lady D— *Spoken*, Lady D—

LORD OF PARLIAMENT'S CHILDREN
Envelope, The Hon. F— S— *Letter*, Dear Mr/Miss/Mrs S— *Spoken*, Mr/Miss/Mrs S—

LORD/LADY OF SESSION
Envelope, The Hon. Lord/Lady D— ; if a Privy Counsellor, The Right (Rt.) Hon. Lord/Lady D— *Letter (formal)*, My Lord/Lady; *(social)*, Dear Lord/Lady D— *Spoken (formal)*, My Lord/Lady; *(social)*, Lord/Lady D—

LORD OF SESSION'S WIFE
As for the wife of a Lord of Parliament, except that there is no prefix before 'Lady'

LORD PROVOSTS – ABERDEEN AND DUNDEE
Envelope, The Lord Provost of Aberdeen/Dundee
Letter (formal), My Lord Provost; *(social),* Dear Lord Provost
Spoken, My Lord Provost

LORD PROVOSTS – EDINBURGH AND GLASGOW
Envelope, The Right (Rt.) Hon. the Lord Provost of Edinburgh/Glasgow; or (Edinburgh only) The Right (Rt.) Hon. F— S— , Lord Provost of Edinburgh
Letter (formal), My Lord Provost; *(social),* Dear Lord Provost
Spoken, My Lord Provost

LORD PROVOST'S WIFE/CONSORT
Envelope, The Lady Provost of D— (may be followed by her name)
Letter (formal), My Lady Provost; *(social),* Dear Lady Provost
Spoken, My Lady Provost/ Lady Provost

MARQUESS
Envelope (formal), The Most Hon. the Marquess of D— ; *(social),* The Marquess of D—
Letter (formal), My Lord; *(social),* Dear Lord D—
Spoken (formal), My Lord; *(social),* Lord D—

MARQUESS'S WIFE
Envelope (formal), The Most Hon. the Marchioness of D— ; *(social),* The Marchioness of D—
Letter (formal), Madam; *(social),* Dear Lady D—
Spoken, Lady D—

MARQUESS'S CHILDREN
Eldest son, see Courtesy titles
Younger sons, Lord F— S— (for forms of address, *see* Duke's younger sons)
Daughters, Lady F— S— (for forms of address, *see* Duke's daughter)

MARQUIS
see Marquess; 'Marquis' is sometimes used for titles predating the Union

MASTER
The title is used by the heir apparent to a Scottish peerage, though usually the heir apparent to a Duke, Marquess or Earl uses his courtesy title rather than 'Master'.
Envelope, The Master of D—
Letter (formal), Dear Sir; *(social),* Dear Master of D—
Spoken (formal), Master, or Sir; *(social),* Master, or Mr S—

MASTER'S WIFE
Addressed as for the wife of the appropriate peerage style, otherwise as Mrs S—

MEMBER OF SCOTTISH PARLIAMENT
Envelope, Mr/Miss/Mrs S— , MSP
Letter, Dear Mr/Miss/Mrs S—
Spoken, Mr/Miss/Mrs S—

MODERATOR OF THE GENERAL ASSEMBLY
Envelope, The Rt. Revd the Moderator of the General Assembly of the Church of Scotland
Letter (formal), Dear Moderator/Dear Sir; *(social),* Dear Dr/Mr S— /Dear Moderator
Spoken, Moderator
After their year in office, former Moderators are styled The Very Reverend

PRESIDING OFFICER
Style/title used before the Scottish Parliament elections, i.e. if a minister is a privy counsellor, he is styled Rt. Hon.
Envelope (ministerial business), addressed by his appointment; *(personal),* Sir F—/Mr/Miss/Mrs S— , The Presiding Officer
Letter, Dear Sir F—/Mr/Miss/Mrs S—
Spoken, addressed by his appointment or name

PRIVY COUNSELLOR
Envelope, The Right (or Rt.) Hon. F— S—
Letter, Dear Mr/Miss/Mrs S—
Spoken, Mr/Miss/Mrs S—
It is incorrect to use the letters PC after the name in conjunction with the prefix The Right Hon., unless the Privy Counsellor is a peer below the rank of Marquess and so is styled The Right Hon. because of his rank. In this case only, the post-nominal letters may be used in conjunction with the prefix The Right Hon.

PROVOST
Envelope, The Provost of D— , or F— S— , Esq., Provost of D— /Mrs F— S— , Provost of D—
Letter, Dear Provost
Spoken, Provost

SCOTTISH MINISTER
Style/title used before the Scottish Parliament elections, i.e. if a minister is a privy counsellor, he/she is styled Rt. Hon.
Envelope (ministerial business), minister addressed by his/her appointment; *(personal),* Mr/Miss/Mrs S— , followed by the minister's appointment
Letter, Dear Mr/Miss/Mrs S—
Spoken, addressed by his/herappointment or name

SHERIFF PRINCIPAL AND SHERIFF
Envelope, Sheriff F— S—
Letter, Dear Sheriff S—
Spoken (formal), My Lord/Lady (in court);
   (social), Sheriff S—

VISCOUNT
Envelope (formal), The Right Hon. the
   Viscount D— ; *(social)*, The Viscount
   D—
Letter (formal), My Lord; *(social)*, Dear Lord
   D—
Spoken, Lord D—

VISCOUNT'S WIFE
Envelope (formal), The Right Hon. the
   Viscountess D— ; *(social)*, The
   Viscountess D—
Letter (formal), Madam; *(social)*, Dear Lady
   D—
Spoken, Lady D—

VISCOUNT'S CHILDREN
As for Lord of Parliament's children

Chiefs of Clans and Names

As there are a number of different styles for
chiefs of clans and names, forms of address
vary widely. Male chiefs are styled by their
designation or estate rather than their
surname; 'Esquire' is not added. A female chief
is styled Madam or Mrs/Miss (according to her
preference) in addition to her estate. For a list
of examples, *see also* Chiefs of Clans and
Names, page 275.
Envelope, chief's designation
Letter (formal), Dear Chief (if writer is a
   member of the clan or name); Dear
   Sir/Madam; *(social)*, 'Dear' followed by
   chief's designation

CHIEF'S WIFE
As for her husband, with the addition of
'Mrs'.

CHIEF'S HEIR APPARENT
As for the chief, with the addition of
'younger' (yr), e.g.
F— S— of D—, yr
F— S— , yr. of D—

CHIEFS OF CLANS AND NAMES

The word 'clan', derived from the Gaelic 'clann', meaning children, originally referred to an extended family or tribe occupying a certain area of land. This was the early form of Gaelic society. As clan territories became established, 'clan' came to signify the people, including non-relatives, living on the lands owned by the chieftain and for whom the chieftain assumed a patriarchal responsibility, in return, particularly, for the loyalty of fighting men. Clan territory boundaries were broadly established by the 16th century. After the Jacobite rebellion in 1745–6, the clan system was suppressed by the Government to prevent further rebellion and gradually declined.

The title of chief is usually hereditary, passing to the nearest heir. However, a chief may nominate a successor, subject to the confirmation of the Lord Lyon King of Arms. If a title is dormant, the Lord Lyon can award it to a person bearing the clan name, although this decision may be revoked if a proven heir is found within 20 years.

The style 'of that Ilk' began to be used by some chiefs in the late 16th century. More recently, chiefs who do not have an estate have been recognized as 'of that Ilk.' Certain chiefs use the prefix 'The'. The duplication of surnames by chiefs (e.g. Macdonald of Macdonald) is a feature that became common after the Act of Union 1707.

Only chiefs of whole names or clans are included here, except certain special instances (marked *) who, though not chiefs of a whole name, were or are for some reason (e.g. the Macdonald forfeiture) independent. Under decision (*Campbell-Gray*, 1950) that a bearer of a 'double- or triple-barrelled' surname cannot be held chief of a part of such, several others cannot be included in the list at present.

STYLES

There are a number of different styles for chiefs of clans and names; the appropriate use depends on the title and designation of the person, and for exact guidance a specialist source should be consulted. The following examples show the more common styles:

F — represents forename
S — represents surname
D — represents designation

Examples:
The S—
The S— of D—
F— S— of D—
Sir F— S— of D—, Bt.
F— S— of that Ilk
Madam/Mrs/Miss S— of D— (according to preference)
Dame F— S— of D—, DBE
For forms of address, *see* page 274

CLAN CHIEFS

THE ROYAL HOUSE
HM The Queen

AGNEW
Sir Crispin Agnew of Lochnaw, Bt., QC
6 Palmerston Road, Edinburgh EH9 1TN

ANSTRUTHER
Sir Ralph Anstruther of that Ilk, Bt., GCVO, MC
Balcaskie, Pittenweem, Fife KY10 2RD

ARBUTHNOTT
The Viscount of Arbuthnott, KT, CBE, DSC
Arbuthnott House, Laurencekirk,
  Kincardineshire AB30 1PA

BARCLAY
Peter C. Barclay of Towie Barclay and of that
  Ilk
28A Gordon Place, London W8 4JE

BORTHWICK
The Lord Borthwick
Crookston, Heriot, Midlothian EH38 5YS

BOYD
The Lord Kilmarnock
194 Regent's Park Road, London NW1 8XP

BOYLE
The Earl of Glasgow
Kelburn, Fairlie, Ayrshire KA29 0BE

BRODIE
Ninian Brodie of Brodie
Brodie Castle, Forres, Morayshire IV36 0TE

BRUCE
The Earl of Elgin and Kincardine, KT
Broomhall, Dunfermline, Fife KY11 3DU

BUCHAN
David S. Buchan of Auchmacoy
Auchmacoy House, Ellon, Aberdeenshire

BURNETT
J. C. A. Burnett of Leys
Crathes Castle, Banchory, Kincardineshire

CAMERON
Sir Donald Cameron of Lochiel, KT, CVO, TD
Achnacarry, Spean Bridge, Inverness-shire

CAMPBELL
The Duke of Argyll
Inveraray, Argyll PA32 8XF

CARMICHAEL
Richard J. Carmichael of Carmichael
Carmichael, Thankerton, Biggar, Lanarkshire

CARNEGIE
The Duke of Fife
Elsick House, Stonehaven, Kincardineshire
   AB3 2NT

CATHCART
Maj.-Gen. The Earl Cathcart
Gately Hall, Dereham, Norfolk

CHARTERIS
The Earl of Wemyss and March, KT
Gosford House, Longniddry, East Lothian
   EH32 0PX

CLAN CHATTAN
M. K. Mackintosh of Clan Chattan
Maxwell Park, Gwelo, Zimbabwe

CHISHOLM
Hamish Chisholm of Chisholm *(The Chisholm)*
Elmpine, Beck Row, Bury St Edmunds, Suffolk

COCHRANE
The Earl of Dundonald
Lochnell Castle, Ledaig, Argyllshire

COLQUHOUN
Sir Ivar Colquhoun of Luss, Bt.
Camstraddan, Luss, Dunbartonshire G83 8NX

CRANSTOUN
David A. S. Cranstoun of that Ilk
Corehouse, Lanark

CRICHTON
vacant

CUMMING
Sir William Cumming of Altyre, Bt.
Altyre, Forres, Moray

DARROCH
Capt. Duncan Darroch of Gourock
The Red House, Branksome Park Road,
   Camberley, Surrey

DAVIDSON
Alister G. Davidson of Davidston
21 Winscombe Street, Takapuna, Auckland,
   New Zealand

DEWAR
Kenneth Dewar of that Ilk and Vogrie
The Dower House, Grayshott, nr Hindhead,
   Surrey

DRUMMOND
The Earl of Perth, PC
Stobhall, Perth PH2 6DR

DUNBAR
Sir James Dunbar of Mochrum, Bt.
211 Gardenville Drive, Yorktown, Virginia
   23693, USA

DUNDAS
David D. Dundas of Dundas
8 Derna Road, Kenwyn 7700, South Africa

DURIE
Andrew Durie of Durie
Finnich Malise, Croftamie, Stirlingshire G63
   0HA

ELIOTT
Mrs Margaret Eliott of Redheugh
Redheugh, Newcastleton, Roxburghshire

ERSKINE
The Earl of Mar and Kellie
Erskine House, Kirk Wynd, Clackmannan
   FK10 4JF

FARQUHARSON
Capt. A. Farquharson of Invercauld, MC
Invercauld, Braemar, Aberdeenshire AB35
   5TT

FERGUSSON
Sir Charles Fergusson of Kilkerran, Bt.
Kilkerran, Maybole, Ayrshire

FORBES
The Lord Forbes, KBE
Balforbes, Alford, Aberdeenshire AB33 8DR

FORSYTH
Alistair Forsyth of that Ilk
Ethie Castle, by Arbroath, Angus DD11 5SP

FRASER
The Lady Saltoun
Inverey House, Aberdeenshire AB35 5YB

FRASER (OF LOVAT)*
The Lord Lovat
Beaufort Lodge, Beauly, Inverness-shire IV4
   7AZ

GAYRE
R. Gayre of Gayre and Nigg
Minard Castle, Minard, Inverary, Argyll PA32
8YB

GORDON
The Marquess of Huntly
Aboyne Castle, Aberdeenshire AB34 5JP

GRAHAM
The Duke of Montrose
Buchanan Auld House, Drymen, Stirlingshire

GRANT
The Lord Strathspey
The House of Lords, London SW1A 0PW

GRIERSON
Sir Michael Grierson of Lag, Bt.
40c Palace Road, London SW2 3NJ

HAIG
The Earl Haig, OBE
Bemersyde, Melrose, Roxburghshire TD6 9DP

HALDANE
Martin Haldane of Gleneagles
Gleneagles, Auchterarder, Perthshire

HANNAY
Ramsey Hannay of Kirkdale and of that Ilk
Cardoness House, Gatehouse-of-Fleet,
 Kirkcudbrightshire

HAY
The Earl of Erroll
Woodbury Hall, Sandy, Beds

HENDERSON
John Henderson of Fordell
7 Owen Street, Toowoomba, Queensland,
 Australia

HUNTER
Pauline Hunter of Hunterston
Plovers Ridge, Lon Cecrist, Treaddur Bay,
 Holyhead, Gwynedd

IRVINE OF DRUM
David C. Irvine of Drum
20 Enville Road, Bowden, Altrincham,
 Cheshire WA14 2PQ

JARDINE
Sir Alexander Jardine of Applegirth, Bt.
Ash House, Thwaites, Millom, Cumbria LA18
 5HY

JOHNSTONE
The Earl of Annandale and Hartfell
Raehills, Lockerbie, Dumfriesshire

KEITH
The Earl of Kintore
The Stables, Keith Hall, Inverurie,
 Aberdeenshire AB51 0LD

KENNEDY
The Marquess of Ailsa
Cassillis House, Maybole, Ayrshire

KERR
The Marquess of Lothian, KCVO
Ferniehurst Castle, Jedburgh, Roxburghshire
 TN8 6NX

KINCAID
Mrs Heather V. Kincaid of Kincaid
4 Watling Street, Leintwardine, Craven Arms,
 Shropshire

LAMONT
Peter N. Lamont of that Ilk
St Patrick's College, Manly, NSW 2095,
 Australia

LEASK
Madam Leask of Leask
1 Vincent Road, Sheringham, Norfolk

LENNOX
Edward J. H. Lennox of that Ilk
Pools Farm, Downton on the Rock, Ludlow,
 Shropshire

LESLIE
The Earl of Rothes
Tanglewood, West Tytherley, Salisbury, Wilts
 SP5 1LX

LINDSAY
The Earl of Crawford and Balcarres, KT, PC
Balcarres, Colinsburgh, Fife

LOCKHART
Angus H. Lockhart of the Lee
Newholme, Dunsyre, Lanark

LUMSDEN
Gillem Lumsden of that Ilk and Blanerne
Stapely Howe, Hoe Benham, Newbury, Berks

MacALESTER
William St J. S. McAlester of Loup and
 Kennox
2 Avon Road East, Christchurch, Dorset

McBAIN
J. H. McBain of McBain
7025 North Finger Rock Place, Tucson,
 Arizona, USA

MACDONALD
The Lord Macdonald *(The Macdonald of Macdonald)*
Kinloch Lodge, Sleat, Isle of Skye

MACDONALD OF CLANRANALD*
Ranald A. Macdonald of Clanranald
Mornish House, Killin, Perthshire FK21 8TX

MACDONALD OF SLEAT (CLAN HUSTEAIN)*
Sir Ian Macdonald of Sleat, Bt.
Thorpe Hall, Rudston, Driffield, N. Humberside YO25 0JE

MacDONELL OF GLENGARRY*
Ranald MacDonell of Glengarry
Elonbank, Castle Street, Fortrose, Ross-shire IV10 8TH

MACDOUGALL
vacant

MacDOWALL
Fergus D. H. Macdowall of Garthland
9170 Ardmore Drive, North Saanich, British Columbia, Canada

MacGREGOR
Brig. Sir Gregor MacGregor of MacGregor, Bt.
Bannatyne, Newtyle, Blairgowrie, Perthshire PH12 8TR

MacINTYRE
James W. MacIntyre of Glenoe
15301 Pine Orchard Drive, Apartment 3H, Silver Spring, Maryland, USA

MACKAY
The Lord Reay
House of Lords, London SW1

MACKENZIE
The Earl of Cromartie
Castle Leod, Strathpeffer, Ross-shire IV14 9AA

MACKINNON
Madam Anne Mackinnon of Mackinnon
16 Purleigh Road, Bridgwater, Somerset

MACKINTOSH
The Mackintosh of Mackintosh
Moy Hall, Inverness IV13 7YQ

MacLACHLAN
vacant

MacLAREN
Donald MacLaren of MacLaren and Achleskine
Achleskine, Kirkton, Balquhidder, Lochearnhead

MACLEAN
The Hon. Sir Lachlan Maclean of Duart, Bt.
Arngask House, Glenfarg, Perthshire PH2 9QA

MacLENNAN
vacant

MacLEOD
John MacLeod of MacLeod
Dunvegan Castle, Isle of Skye

MacMILLAN
George MacMillan of MacMillan
Finlaystone, Langbank, Renfrewshire

MACNAB
J. C. Macnab of Macnab *(The Macnab)*
Leuchars Castle Farmhouse, Leuchars, Fife KY16 0EY

MACNAGHTEN
Sir Patrick Macnaghten of Macnaghten and Dundarave, Bt.
Dundarave, Bushmills, Co. Antrim

MACNEACAIL
Iain Macneacail of Macneacail and Scorrybreac
12 Fox Street, Ballina, NSW, Australia

MACNEIL OF BARRA
Ian R. Macneil of Barra *(The Macneil of Barra)*
95/6 Grange Loan, Edinburgh

MACPHERSON
The Hon. Sir William Macpherson of Cluny, TD
Newtown Castle, Blairgowrie, Perthshire

MacTAVISH
E. S. Dugald MacTavish of Dunardry

MacTHOMAS
Andrew P. C. MacThomas of Finegand
c/o Roslin Cottage, Pitmedden, Aberdeenshire AB41 7NY

MAITLAND
The Earl of Lauderdale
12 St Vincent Street, Edinburgh

MAKGILL
The Viscount of Oxfuird
Hill House, St Mary Bourne, Andover, Hants SP11 6BG

MALCOLM (MacCALLUM)
Robin N. L. Malcolm of Poltalloch
Duntrune Castle, Lochgilphead, Argyll

MAR
The Countess of Mar
St Michael's Farm, Great Witley, Worcs
WR6 6JB

MARJORIBANKS
Andrew Marjoribanks of that Ilk
10 Newark Street, Greenock

MATHESON
Maj. Sir Fergus Matheson of Matheson, Bt.
Old Rectory, Hedenham, Bungay, Suffolk
NR35 2LD

MENZIES
David R. Menzies of Menzies
Wester Auchnagallin Farmhouse, Braes of
    Castle Grant, Grantown on Spey PH26 3PL

MOFFAT
Madam Moffat of that Ilk
St Jasual, Bullocks Farm Lane, Wheeler End
    Common, High Wycombe

MONCREIFFE
vacant

MONTGOMERIE
The Earl of Eglinton and Winton
Balhomie, Cargill, Perth PH2 6DS

MORRISON
Dr Iain M. Morrison of Ruchdi
Magnolia Cottage, The Street, Walberton,
    Sussex

MUNRO
Hector W. Munro of Foulis
Foulis Castle, Evanton, Ross-shire IV16 9UX

MURRAY
The Duke of Atholl
Blair Castle, Blair Atholl, Perthshire

NESBITT (OR NISBET)
Robert Nesbitt of that Ilk
Upper Roundhurst Farm, Roundhurst,
    Haslemere, Surrey

NICOLSON
The Lord Carnock
90 Whitehall Court, London SW1A 2EL

OGILVY
The Earl of Airlie, KT, GCVO, PC
Cortachy Castle, Kirriemuir, Angus

RAMSAY
The Earl of Dalhousie, KT, GCVO, GBE, MC
Brechin Castle, Brechin, Angus DD7 6SH

RATTRAY
James S. Rattray of Rattray
Craighall, Rattray, Perthshire

ROBERTSON
Alexander G. H. Robertson of Struan *(Struan-
    Robertson)*
The Breach Farm, Goudhurst Road,
    Cranbrook, Kent

ROLLO
The Lord Rollo
Pitcairns, Dunning, Perthshire

ROSE
Miss Elizabeth Rose of Kilravock
Kilravock Castle, Croy, Inverness

ROSS
David C. Ross of that Ilk
Shandwick, Perth Road, Stanley, Perthshire

RUTHVEN
The Earl of Gowrie, PC
34 King Street, London WC2

SCOTT
The Duke of Buccleuch and Queensberry, KT,
    VRD
Bowhill, Selkirk

SCRYMGEOUR
The Earl of Dundee
Birkhill, Cupar, Fife

SEMPILL
The Lord Sempill
3 Vanburgh Place, Edinburgh EH6 8AE

SHAW
John Shaw of Tordarroch
Newhall, Balblair, by Conon Bridge,
    Ross-shire

SINCLAIR
The Earl of Caithness
137 Claxton Grove, London W6 8HB

SKENE
Danus Skene of Skene
Nether Pitlour, Strathmiglo, Fife

STIRLING
Fraser J. Stirling of Cader
44A Oakley Street, London SW3 5HA

STRANGE
Maj. Timothy Strange of Balcaskie
Little Holme, Porton Road, Amesbury, Wilts

SUTHERLAND
The Countess of Sutherland
House of Tongue, Brora, Sutherland

SWINTON
John Swinton of that Ilk
123 Superior Avenue SW, Calgary, Alberta,
    Canada

TROTTER
Alexander Trotter of Mortonhall
Charterhall, Duns, Berwickshire

URQUHART
Kenneth T. Urquhart of Urquhart
507 Jefferson Park Avenue, Jefferson, New
    Orleans, Louisiana 70121, USA

WALLACE
Ian F. Wallace of that Ilk
5 Lennox Street, Edinburgh EH4 1QB

WEDDERBURN OF THAT ILK
The Master of Dundee
Birkhill, Cupar, Fife

WEMYSS
David Wemyss of that Ilk
Invermay, Forteviot, Perthshire

LEGAL NOTES

These notes outline certain aspects of the law in Scotland as they might affect the average person. They focus principally on those aspects of Scots law which differ from the equivalent law in England and Wales. They are intended only as a broad guideline and are by no means definitive. The information is believed to be correct at the time of going to press, but the law is constantly changing, so expert advice should always be taken. In some cases, sources of further information are given in these notes.

Timely consultation with a solicitor is always advisable. Anyone in Scotland who does not have a solicitor can contact the Citizens' Advice Bureau (addresses in the telephone directory or at any post office or town hall) or the Law Society of Scotland (26 Drumsheugh Gardens, Edinburgh EH3 7YR) for assistance in finding one.

The legal aid and legal advice and assistance schemes exist to make the help of a lawyer available to those who would not otherwise be able to afford one. Entitlement depends upon an individual's means (see pages 286–7), but a solicitor or Citizens' Advice Bureau will be able to advise about this.

ADOPTION OF CHILDREN

The adoption of children is mainly governed by the Adoption (Scotland) Act 1978 (as amended by the Children (Scotland) Act 1995).

Anyone over 21 who is domiciled in the United Kingdom, the Channel Islands or the Isle of Man or has been habitually resident in any of those places throughout the year immediately preceding the date of an application, whether married, single, widowed or divorced, can apply to adopt a child.

The only organizations allowed to arrange adoptions are the adoption agencies provided by local authorities (these agencies are known collectively as the Scottish Adoption Service) or voluntary agencies approved as an adoption society.

Once an adoption has been arranged, a court order is necessary to make it legal. Petitions for adoption are made to the Sheriff Court or the Court of Session.

Each of the child's natural parents (or guardians) must consent to the adoption, unless the court dispenses with the consent or the natural parent does not have parental responsibilities or parental rights. Once adopted, the child, for all practical purposes, has the same legal status as a child born to the adoptive parents and the natural parents cease to have any rights or responsibilities where the child is concerned. As a general rule, the adopted child ceases to have any rights to the estates of his/her natural parents.

Registration and Certificates

All adoptions in Scotland are registered by the General Register Office for Scotland (see page 51). Certificates from the registers can be obtained in a similar way to birth certificates (see page 282).

Further information on qualification to adopt a child, adoption procedures, and tracing natural parents or children who have been adopted can be obtained from:

BRITISH AGENCIES FOR ADOPTION AND FOSTERING (BAAF)
Scottish Centre, 40 Shandwick Place, Edinburgh EH2 4RT
Tel: 0131-225 9285

SCOTTISH ADOPTION ADVICE SERVICE
16 Sandyford Place, Glasgow G3 7NB
Tel: 0141-339 0772

BIRTHS (REGISTRATION)

The birth of a child must be registered within 21 days at the registration office of either the district in which the baby was born or the district in which the mother was resident at the time of the birth.

If the child is born, either in or out of Scotland, on a ship, aircraft or land vehicle that ends its journey at any place in Scotland, the child, in most cases, will be registered as if born in that place.

Responsibility for registering the birth rests with the parents, except where the father of the child is not married to the mother and has not been married to her since the child's conception, in which case the mother is responsible for registration. Responsibility rests firstly with the parents, but if they fail particulars may be given to the registrar by:
– a relative of either parent
– the occupier of the house in which the baby was born
– a person present at the birth
– a person having charge of the child
Failure to register the birth within 21 days without reasonable cause may lead to a court decree being granted by a sheriff.

Further information is available from local registrars, whose addresses and telephone numbers can be found in local telephone directories.

CERTIFICATES OF BIRTHS, DEATHS OR MARRIAGES

Certificates of births, deaths or marriages that have taken place in Scotland since 1855 can be obtained from the General Register Office for Scotland or from the appropriate local registrar. The General Register Office for Scotland also keeps the Register of Divorces (including decrees of declaration of nullity of marriage), and holds parish registers dating from before 1855.

Fees for certificates (from 1 April 1999) are:

Certificates (full or abbreviated) of birth, death, marriage or adoption, £8.00
E-mail application in course of Internet search, £10.00

Particular search for each period of five years or part thereof in the statutory registers, whether specified entry is traced or not:
Personal application, £3.00
Postal application, £5.00
E-mail application, £7.00

Particular search for each period of five years or part thereof in the parochial registers, whether specified entry is traced or not:
Personal application, £5.00
Postal application, £5.00
E-mail application, £7.00

General search in the parochial registers and indexes to the statutory registers, per day or part thereof:
Full day (i.e. 9 a.m. to 4.30 p.m.) search with payment being made not less than 14 days in advance, £13.00
Full day search in any other case, £17.00
Afternoon (i.e. 1 p.m. to 4.30 p.m.) search, £10.00
One week search, £65.00

Further information can be obtained from:

THE GENERAL REGISTER OFFICE FOR SCOTLAND
New Register House, Edinburgh EH1 3YT
Tel: 0131-334 0380; fax: 0131-314 4400

CONSUMER LAW

UK legislation governing the sale and supply of goods applies to Scotland as follows:
– the Sale of Goods Act 1979 applies with some modifications and has been amended by the Sale and Supply of Goods Act 1994

– the Supply of Goods (Implied Terms) Act 1973 applies
– the Supply of Goods and Services Act 1982 does not extend to Scotland but some of its provisions were introduced by the Sale and Supply of Goods Act 1994
– only Parts II and III of the Unfair Contract Terms Act 1977 apply
– the Trade Descriptions Act 1968 applies with minor modifications
– the Consumer Credit Act 1974 applies

DEATHS

When a death occurs, if the death was expected, the doctor who attended the deceased during their final illness should be contacted. If the death is sudden and unexpected, the family doctor (if known) and police should be contacted immediately.

If the cause of death is quite clear the doctor will either:
– issue a certificate of cause of death needed by the registrar, provided that there are no unusual circumstances. If the body is to be cremated, the doctor will arrange for the signature of the second doctor needed to complete the cremation certificate; or
– if the doctor is uncertain as to the cause of death he will report the death to the local procurator fiscal who will make enquiries.

A fatal accident inquiry will be held before a sheriff where the death has resulted from an accident during the course of the employment of the person who has died, or where the person who has died was in legal custody, or where the Lord Advocate deems it in the public interest that an inquiry be held.

A death may be registered in any registration district in which the deceased was ordinarily resident immediately before his/her death or, if different, in the registration district in which the death took place. The death must normally be registered within eight days. If the death has been referred to the local procurator fiscal it cannot be registered until the registrar has received authority from the procurator fiscal to do so. Failure to register a death may lead to a court decree being granted by a sheriff. Whereas in most circumstances in England and Wales a certificate for burial or cremation must be obtained from the registrar before the burial or cremation can take place, in Scotland a body may be buried (but normally not cremated) before the death is registered.

Further information can be obtained from the General Register Office for Scotland (*see* above for contact details).

DIVORCE AND RELATED MATTERS

There are two main types of matrimonial action: those seeking the annulment of a marriage, and those seeking a judicial separation or divorce.

An action for 'declarator of nullity' can be brought only in the Court of Session.

An action for judicial separation or divorce may be raised in the Court of Session. It may also be raised in the Sheriff Court if either party was resident in the sheriffdom for 40 days immediately before the date of the action or for 40 days ending not more than 40 days before the date of the action. The fee for starting a divorce petition in the Sheriff Court is £74.

NULLITY OF MARRIAGE

A marriage is void (i.e. invalid) from the beginning if:
- the parties were within the prohibited degrees of consanguinity, affinity or adoption
- the parties were not male and female
- either of the parties was already married
- either of the parties was under the age of 16
- either of the parties did not truly consent to marry, e.g. in consequence of mental illness, intoxication, force or fear, or in a sham marriage where the intention was to avoid deportation
- the formalities of the marriage were defective, e.g. each of the parties did not submit a notice of intention to marry (a marriage notice) to the district registrar for the registration district in which the marriage was to be solemnized

A marriage may be voidable (i.e. a decree of nullity may be obtained but in the meantime the marriage remains valid) if either party was unable to consummate the marriage.

Where a spouse is capable of sexual intercourse but refuses to consummate the marriage, this is not a ground of nullity in Scots law, though it could be a ground for divorce.

When a marriage is void, it generally has no legal effect at all, and there is therefore no specific need to seek a declarator of nullity in the Court of Session (although it may be wise to do so, e.g. if one of the parties wishes to marry again). Nevertheless, a child conceived during a valid marriage is presumed to be the child of the 'husband'. A child's mother has parental responsibilities and parental rights in relation to the child whether or not she is or has been married to his father. A child's father has such responsibilities and rights in relation to the child only if married to the mother at the time of the child's conception or subsequently. A father is regarded as having been married to the mother at any time when he was a party to a purported marriage with her which was:
- voidable; or
- void but believed by them in good faith at that time to be valid.

When a marriage has been annulled, both parties are free to marry again.

DIVORCE

Divorce dissolves the marriage and leaves both parties at liberty to marry again. The sole ground for divorce is the irretrievable breakdown of the marriage; this must be proved on one or more of the following grounds:
- the defender has committed adultery; however the pursuer cannot rely on an act of adultery by the other party if, after discovery of the act of adultery, he or she has continued or resumed living together with the defender at any time after the end of a period of three months on which cohabitation has been continued or resumed
- the defender has behaved in such a way that the pursuer cannot reasonably be expected to continue living with him/her
- desertion, which is established by the defender having left the pursuer for a period of two years immediately preceding the action. Irretrievable breakdown is not established if, after the two year desertion period has expired, the parties resume living together at any time after the end of three months from the date when they first resume living together
- the defender and the pursuer have lived separately for two years immediately before the raising of the action and the defender consents to the decree
- the defender and the pursuer have lived separately for five years immediately before the raising of the action

Where a divorce action has been raised, it may be sisted or put on hold for a variety of reasons, including, though rarely, enabling the parties to seek to effect a reconciliation if the court feels that there may be a reasonable prospect of such reconciliation. If the parties do cohabit during such postponement, no account is taken of the cohabitation if the action later proceeds.

A simplified procedure for 'do-it-yourself' divorce was introduced in 1983 for certain divorces. If the action is based on two or five years' separation and will not be opposed, and if there are no children under 16, no financial claims and there is no sign that the applicant's spouse is unable to manage his or her affairs because of mental illness or handicap, the applicant can write directly to the local sheriff court or to the Court of Session for the appropriate forms to enable him or her to proceed. The fee is £57, unless the applicant receives income support, family credit or legal advice and assistance, in which case there is no fee.

The extract decree will be made available fourteen days after the divorce has been granted. The extract decree dissolves or annuls the marriage.

Further information can be obtained from any sheriff court, solicitor or Citizens' Advice Bureau, the Lord Advocate's Office (*see* page 61), or the following:

THE COURT OF SESSION
Parliament House, Parliament Square,
Edinburgh EH1 1RQ
Tel: 0131-225 2595

EMPLOYMENT LAW

PAY AND CONDITIONS

Responsibility for employment legislation rests with the UK Parliament and the legislation applies to all parts of Great Britain, with the exception of some separate anti-discrimination legislation for Northern Ireland.

The Employment Rights Act 1996 consolidates the statutory provisions relating to employees' rights. It covers matters such as pay and conditions (including authorized deductions from pay, trade union membership, disputes, and the rights of part-time employees) and termination of employment (including redundancy and unfair dismissal). The Working Time Regulations 1998 and the National Minimum Wage Act 1998 now supplement the 1996 Act. Procedure at Employment Tribunals is governed by separate Scottish regulations.

A number of laws protect employees from discrimination in employment on the grounds of sex, race or disability:
– The Equal Pay Act 1970 (as amended)
– The Sex Discrimination Act 1975 (as amended by the Sex Discrimination Act 1986)
– The Race Relations Act 1976
– The Disability Discrimination Act 1995
The Equal Opportunities Commission and the Commission for Racial Equality have the function of eliminating such discriminations in the workplace and can provide further information and assistance.

EQUAL OPPORTUNITIES COMMISSION
Stock Exchange House, 7 Nelson Mandela Place, Glasgow G2 1QW
Tel: 0141-248 5833; fax: 0141-248 5834

COMMISSION FOR RACIAL EQUALITY
45 Hanover Street, Edinburgh EH2 2PJ
Tel: 0131-226 5186; fax: 0131-226 5243

HOUSE PURCHASE

A contract for the sale of a house in Scotland rarely takes the form of a single document. The purchaser's solicitor issues a formal written offer to purchase. This is usually issued once a survey of the property has been carried out, but can more unusually be issued 'subject to survey'. The seller's solicitor will issue a qualified acceptance of the offer. This is then adjusted between the solicitors until a final concluding letter is issued. At this point the contract is formed and both parties are contractually bound. The letters passing between the solicitors are known as 'missives'.

Some conditions contained within the missives may require the seller to provide information so that the purchaser may be satisfied that the property is unaffected by any statutory notices for repairs or by any planning proposals. Property enquiry reports are obtained by the seller's solicitor from either the local authority or private companies who provide this information. These reports disclose whether the property is adversely affected, if it is served by public water and sewage services and whether the roads adjoining the property are maintained by the local authority.

The purchaser will also examine the title deeds for the property to make sure that there are no flaws in the title to be granted to the purchaser. Searches in the appropriate property register are made. A search is also carried out against both the purchaser and the seller to ensure there is no reason why either party cannot proceed with the transaction.

On the day of settlement the purchaser's solicitor will pass the purchase price to the seller's solicitor who in turn passes over the disposition, title deeds, an obligation to deliver a clear search brought down to disclose the recording of the purchaser's title and keys. The disposition is the deed which transfers ownership of the property from the seller to the purchaser. This deed has to be registered in the appropriate property register in order for the purchaser to have a right to the property – either the Register of Sasines or the newer Land Register which is being phased in by county to replace the old Register of Sasines.

ILLEGITIMACY AND LEGITIMATION

Under the Legitimation (Scotland) Act 1968, which came into operation on 8 June 1968, an illegitimate person automatically becomes legitimate when his/her parents marry, even where one of the parents was married to a third person at the time of the birth.

Illegitimate and legitimate people are given, for all practical purposes, equal status under the Law Reform (Parent and Child) Scotland Act 1986.

The Children (Scotland) Act 1995 gives the mother parental responsibility for her child when she is not married to the child's father. The father has no automatic parental rights when unmarried to the mother, but can acquire parental responsibility by applying to the court. The father of any child, regardless of parental rights, has a duty to aliment that child until he/she is 18 or has completed full-time education, whichever date is later. The Child Support Agency are entitled to make an assessment if this is not done, and the mother of the child can apply to the Child Support Agency for this to be done.

JURY SERVICE

A person charged with any serious crime is tried before a jury. Jury trials in Scottish civil cases in the Court of Session are becoming more common. In Scotland there are 12 members of a jury in a civil case in the Court of Session (the civil jury trial is confined to the Court of Session and a restricted number of actions) and 15 in a criminal trial. Jurors are expected to sit for the duration of the trial.

Every parliamentary or local government elector between the ages of 18 and 65 who has lived in the UK, the Channel Islands or the Isle of Man for any period of at least five years since reaching the age of 13 is qualified to serve on a jury in Scotland, unless ineligible or disqualified.

Those disqualified from jury service include:

- those who have at any time been sentenced by a court in the UK, the Channel Islands and the Isle of Man to a term of imprisonment or custody of five years or more
- those who have within the previous ten years served any part of a sentence of three months or more of imprisonment or detention

Members of the judiciary are ineligible for ten years after ceasing to hold their post, and others concerned with the administration of justice become eligible again only five years after ceasing to hold office. Members and officers of the Houses of Parliament, full time serving members of the armed forces, registered and practising members of the medical, dental, nursing, veterinary and pharmaceutical professions, ministers of religion, persons in holy orders and those who have served on a jury in the previous five years are excusable as of right.

The maximum fine for a person serving on a jury knowing himself/herself to be ineligible is £1,000. The maximum fine for failing to attend without good cause is also £1,000.

Further information can obtained from:

THE CLERK OF JUSTICIARY
High Court of Justiciary, Parliament House, Parliament Square, Edinburgh EH1 1RQ
Tel: 0131-225 2595

LANDLORD AND TENANT

When a property is rented to a tenant, the rights and responsibilities of the landlord and the tenant are determined largely by the tenancy agreement but also the general law of Scotland. The main provisions are mentioned below, but it is advisable to contact the Citizens' Advice Bureau or the local authority housing department for detailed information.

Assured and short assured tenancies exist for lettings after 2 January 1989; the relevant legislation is the Housing (Scotland) Act 1988. If a tenancy was granted on or after 2 January 1989, the tenant may have an assured tenancy giving that tenant greater rights. The tenant could, for example, stay in possession of the dwelling for as long as the tenant observed the terms of the tenancy. The landlord cannot obtain possession from such a tenant unless the landlord can establish a specific ground for possession (the grounds are set out in the 1988 Act) and obtains a court order. The rent payable continues throughout the period of the lease unless the rent has been fixed by the Rent Assessment Committee of the local authority. The Committee also has powers to determine other terms of the lease.

The 1988 Act also introduced short assured tenancies, which are tenancies of not less than six months where a notice has been served to the effect that the tenancy is a short assured tenancy. A landlord in a short assured tenancy has all the rights of a landlord in an ordinary assured tenancy to recover possession and also the right to regain possession on timeously giving notice to quit to the tenant, whether or not the tenant has observed the terms of the tenancy.

Most tenancies created before 2 January 1989 were regulated tenancies and the Rent

(Scotland) Act 1984 still applies where these exist. The Act defines, among other things, the circumstances in which a landlord can increase the rent when improvements are made to the property. The provisions of the 1984 Act do not apply to tenancies where the landlord is the Crown, a local authority, the development corporation of a new town or a housing corporation.

The Housing (Scotland) Act 1987 and its provisions relate to local authority responsibilities for housing, the right to buy, and local authority secured tenancies.

Tenancies in agricultural properties are governed by the Agricultural Holdings (Scotland) Act 1991.

Business premises in Scotland are not controlled by statute to the same extent as in England and Wales, although the Shops (Scotland) Act 1949 gives some security to tenants of shops. Tenants of shops can apply to the sheriff for a renewal of tenancy if threatened with eviction. This application may be dismissed on various grounds, including where the landlord has offered to sell the property to the tenant at an agreed price or, in the absence of agreement as to price, at a price fixed by a single arbiter appointed by the parties or the sheriff. The Act extends to properties where the Crown or government departments are the landlords or the tenants.

Under the Leases Act 1449 the landlord's successors (either purchasers or creditors) are bound by the agreement made with any tenants so long as the following conditions are met:
- the lease, if for more than one year, must be in writing
- there must be a rent
- there must be a term of expiry, and
- the tenant must have entered into possession

Many leases contain references to term and quarter days. The statutory dates of these are listed on page 11.

LEGAL AID

Under the Legal Aid (Scotland) Act 1986 and subsequent Regulations, people on low or moderate incomes may qualify for help with the costs of legal advice or representation. The scheme is administered by the Scottish Legal Aid Board.

There are three types of legal aid: civil legal aid, legal advice and assistance, and criminal legal aid.

CIVIL LEGAL AID

Applications for legal aid are made through a solicitor; the Citizens' Advice Bureau will have addresses for local solicitors.

Civil legal aid is available for proceedings in the following:
- the House of Lords
- the Court of Session
- the Lands Valuation Appeal Court
- the Scottish Land Court
- sheriff courts
- the Lands Tribunal for Scotland
- the Employment Appeal Tribunals
- the Restrictive Practices Court

Eligibility for civil legal aid is assessed and a civil legal aid certificate granted provided that:
- the applicant qualifies financially, and
- the applicant has reasonable grounds for taking or defending the action, and
- it is reasonable to grant legal aid in the circumstances of the case (for example, civil legal aid will not be granted where it appears that the applicant will gain only trivial advantage from the proceedings).

The financial criteria for eligibility are:
- a person is eligible if disposable income is £8,751 or less and disposable capital is £8,560 or less
- if disposable income is between £2,680 and £8,751, contributions are payable
- if disposable capital exceeds £3,000, contributions are payable

Emergency legal aid cover may be granted before a full application has been made and a means test has been carried out. In such cases means testing is carried out later and the applicant is required to meet the cost of any aid received which exceeded their entitlement.

A statutory charge is made if a person is awarded money or property in a case for which they have received legal aid.

LEGAL ADVICE AND ASSISTANCE

The legal advice and assistance scheme covers the costs of getting advice and help from a solicitor and, in some cases, representation in court under the 'assistance by way of representation' scheme (see below).

A person is eligible:
- if disposable income does not exceed £178 a week. If disposable income is between £75 and £178 a week, contributions are payable
- if disposable capital does not exceed £1,000 (£1,335 if the person has one dependant, £1,535 if two dependants, with an additional £100 for every other dependant). There are no contributions from capital

If a person is eligible, an initial amount of authorized expenditure can be incurred without the prior authority of the Scottish Legal Aid Board. The initial limit is £80 in most cases, but a higher initial limit of £150 applies in some circumstances, for example where a civil matter is only likely to be resolved in court, legal aid will be available to the client and the initial work is reasonable. Any increase in authorized expenditure must first be applied for from and granted by the Scottish Legal Aid Board.

Legal advice and assistance covers, for example, giving advice, writing letters, making an application for civil/criminal legal aid and seeking the advice of an advocate. Advice and assistance does not, in general, cover appearance before a court or tribunal other than advice by way of representation.

Assistance by way of representation is available in certain cases such as certain less serious criminal cases, some mental health proceedings and civil proceedings for fine default or breach of a court order.

CRIMINAL LEGAL AID

The procedure for application for criminal legal aid depends on the circumstances of each case. In solemn cases (more serious cases, such as homicide) heard before a jury, a person is automatically entitled to criminal legal aid until they are given bail or placed in custody. Thereafter, it is for the court to decide whether to grant legal aid. The court will do this if the person accused cannot meet the expenses of the case without 'undue hardship' on him or his dependants. In summary (less serious) cases the procedure depends on whether the person is in custody:

– anyone taken into custody has the right to free legal aid from the duty solicitor up to and including the first court appearance. Thereafter, if the person has decided to plead guilty, the duty solicitor will continue to act for him/her until the case is finished. If the person pleads not guilty to any charge, they must apply to the Scottish Legal Aid Board so that their solicitor can prepare their defence and represent them at the trial. The duty solicitor may be willing to act for the accused, or they can choose their own solicitor.

– if the person is not in custody and wishes to plead guilty, they are not entitled to criminal legal aid but may be entitled to legal advice and assistance, including assistance by way of representation. The court will not assign the person a solicitor, and they must therefore choose their own if they wish one.

– if the person is not in custody and wishes to plead not guilty, they can apply for criminal legal aid. This must be done within 14 days of the first court appearance at which they

made the plea. Again, the person must choose their own solicitor.

The Scottish Legal Aid Board will grant criminal legal aid if satisfied that the applicant or their family would suffer undue hardship if they had to pay for their own defence and that it is in the interests of justice to grant legal aid (the Board will consider, for example, whether there are difficult legal points to be decided, whether the applicant's job or liberty is at risk, and whether the applicant has a realistic defence).

If criminal legal aid is awarded, no contribution from the person will be required.

Further information may be obtained from:

SCOTTISH LEGAL AID BOARD
44 Drumsheugh Gardens, Edinburgh EH3 7SW
Tel: 0131-226 7061; fax: 0131-220 4878

MARRIAGE

REGULAR MARRIAGES

A regular marriage is one which is celebrated by a minister of religion or authorized registrar or other celebrant. Each of the parties must complete a marriage notice form and return it to the district registrar for the area in which they are to be married, irrespective of where they live, at least 15 days before the ceremony is due to take place. The district registrar must then enter the date of receipt and certain details in a marriage book kept for this purpose, and must also enter the names of the parties and the proposed date of the marriage in a list which is displayed in a conspicuous place at the registration office. This entry remains displayed until the date of the marriage has passed. All persons wishing to enter into a regular marriage in Scotland must follow the same preliminary procedure regardless of whether they intend to have a civil or a religious ceremony.

A marriage schedule, which is prepared by the registrar, will be issued to one or both of the parties in person up to seven days before a religious marriage; for a civil marriage the schedule will be available at the ceremony. The schedule must be handed to the celebrant before the ceremony starts; it must be signed immediately after the wedding and the marriage must be registered within three days.

Civil (as opposed to religious) marriage ceremonies are normally conducted by the district registrar in his office. However, if one of the parties cannot attend the registrar's office because of serious illness or serious bodily injury, the registrar may, on application by either party, solemnize the marriage anywhere in his registration district if delay of the wedding is undesirable.

In the case of a religious marriage, the authority to conduct a marriage is deemed to be vested in the authorized celebrant (a minister, priest or other such religious person) conducting the ceremony rather than the building in which it takes place; open-air religious ceremonies are therefore permissible in Scotland.

MARRIAGE BY COHABITATION WITH HABIT AND REPUTE

If two people live together constantly as husband and wife and are generally held to be such by the neighbourhood and among their friends and relations, there may arise a presumption from which marriage can be inferred. Before such a marriage can be registered, however, a decree of declarator of marriage must be obtained from the Court of Session.

CIVIL FEES

The basic statutory fee (from 1 April 1999) is £77, comprising a £12 per person fee for a statutory notice of intention to marry, a £45 fee for solemnization of the marriage in a register office, and an £8.00 fee for a copy of the marriage certificate.

Further information can be obtained from the General Register Office for Scotland (*see* page 51).

TOWN AND COUNTRY PLANNING

The principal legislation governing the development of land and buildings is the Town and Country Planning (Scotland) Act 1997. The uses of buildings are classified by the Town and Country Planning (Use Classes) (Scotland) Order 1997. It is advisable in all cases to contact the planning department of the local authority to check whether planning or other permission is needed.

VOTERS' QUALIFICATIONS

All persons registered in the electoral registers (which are compiled on a local basis) and over the age of 18 are entitled to vote at Scottish Parliament, UK Parliament, European Parliament and local government elections. To qualify for registration, a person must be:
- resident in the relevant constituency or ward on 10 October in the year before the electoral register comes into effect
- over 18 years old or will attain the age of 18 during the 12 months following the

publication of the annual register on 16 February
- a UK, European Union, Commonwealth or Republic of Ireland citizen

Peers registered in Scotland are entitled to vote in Scottish Parliament, European Parliament and local government elections.

Overseas electors (namely British citizens not resident in the UK on the qualifying date for the electoral register but who were registered as parliamentary electors at some point in the preceding 20 years) are only entitled to vote in UK Parliament and European Parliament elections. Similar provisions apply to enable those who were too young to be registered during the previous 20 years to register provided a parent or guardian was registered.

Peers and European Union citizens are not eligible to vote in UK Parliament elections.

Voters must be entered on an electoral register, which runs from 16 February each year to the following 15 February. Supplementary lists of electors are published throughout the duration of the register.

Further information can be obtained from the local authority's electoral registration officer (details in local telephone directories).

WILLS AND INTESTACY

WILLS

In Scotland any person over 12 and of sound mind can make a will. The person making the will can only freely dispose of what is known as the 'dead's part' of the estate because:
- the spouse has the right to inherit one-third of the moveable estate if there are children or other descendants, and one-half of it if there are not
- children are entitled to one-third of the moveable estate if there is a surviving spouse, and one-half of it if there is not

The remaining portion is the dead's part, and legacies and bequests are payable from this. Debts are payable out of the whole estate before any division.

From August 1995, wills no longer needed to be 'holographed' and it is now only necessary to have one witness. The person making the will still needs to sign each page. It is better that the will is not witnessed by a beneficiary although the attestation would still be sound and the beneficiary would not have to relinquish the gift.

Subsequent marriage does not revoke a will but the birth of a child who is not provided for may do so. A will may be revoked by a subsequent will, either expressly or by implication, but in so far as the two can be read together both have effect. If a subsequent will is revoked, the earlier will is revived.

Wills may be registered in the sheriff court books of the Sheriffdom in which the deceased lived or in the Books of Council and Session at the Registers of Scotland. If the will has been registered in the Books of Council and Session, the original will can be inspected and a copy obtained for a small fee. On the other hand, if the will has been registered in the sheriff court books, the original will have been returned to the ingiver; however, copies may still be obtained for a small fee from the photographed copy kept in the register.

Confirmation

Confirmation (the Scottish equivalent of English probate) is obtained in the sheriff court of the sheriffdom in which the deceased was resident at the time of death. Executors are either 'nominate' (named by the deceased in the will) or 'dative' (appointed by the court in cases where no executor is named in a will or in cases of intestacy). Applicants for confirmation must first provide an inventory of the deceased's estate and a schedule of debts, with an affidavit. In estates under £17,000 gross, confirmation can be obtained under a simplified procedure at reduced fees. The local sheriff clerk's office can provide assistance.

Further information can be obtained from:

REGISTERS OF SCOTLAND
Meadowbank House, 153 London Road,
Edinburgh, EH8 7AU
Tel: 0131-659 6111

INTESTACY

Intestacy occurs when someone dies without leaving a will or leaves a will which is invalid or which does not take effect for some reason. In such cases the person's estate (property, possessions, other assets following the payment of debts) passes to certain members of the family.

Under the Succession (Scotland) Act 1964, no distinction is made between 'moveable' and 'heritable' property in intestacy cases.

A surviving spouse is entitled to 'prior rights'. This means that, with effect from 1 April 1999, the spouse has the right to inherit:
– the matrimonial home up to a value of
  £130,000, or one matrimonial home if there
  is more than one, or, in certain
  circumstances, the value of the matrimonial
  home

– the furnishings and contents of that home, up
  to the value of £22,000
– £35,000 if the deceased left children or other
  descendants, or £58,000 if not
These figures are increased from time to time by regulations.

Once prior rights have been satisfied, what remains of the estate is generally divided between the surviving spouse and children (legitimate and illegitimate) according to 'legal' rights. Legal rights are:

Jus relicti(ae) – the right of a surviving spouse to one-half of the net moveable estate, after satisfaction of prior rights, if there are no surviving children; if there are surviving children, the spouse is entitled to one-third of the net moveable estate;

Legitim – the right of surviving children to one-half of the net moveable estate if there is no surviving spouse; if there is a surviving spouse, the children are entitled to one-third of the net moveable estate after the satisfaction of prior rights.

Where there are no surviving spouse or children, half of the estate is taken by the parents and half by the brothers and sisters. Failing that, the lines of succession, in general, are:
– to descendants
– if no descendants, then to collaterals (i.e.
  brothers and sisters) and parents
– surviving spouse
– if no collaterals or parents or spouse, then to
  ascendants collaterals (i.e. aunts and uncles),
  and so on in an ascending scale
If all lines of succession fail, then the estate passes to the Crown.

Relatives of the whole blood are preferred to relatives of the half blood. The right of representation, i.e. the right of the issue of a person who would have succeeded if he/she had survived the intestate, also applies.

ASTRONOMICAL DATA

JANUARY 2000

Sunrise and Sunset (GMT)

	Edinburgh 3°11′ 55°56′		Glasgow 4°14′ 55°52′		Inverness 4°12′ 57°28′	
	h m	h m	h m	h m	h m	h m
1	8 44	15 49	8 47	15 53	8 58	15 42
2	8 43	15 50	8 47	15 54	8 58	15 43
3	8 43	15 51	8 47	15 56	8 58	15 45
4	8 43	15 52	8 47	15 57	8 57	15 46
5	8 42	15 54	8 46	15 58	8 57	15 47
6	8 42	15 55	8 46	16 00	8 56	15 49
7	8 41	15 57	8 45	16 01	8 55	15 51
8	8 41	15 58	8 44	16 03	8 55	15 52
9	8 40	16 00	8 44	16 04	8 54	15 54
10	8 39	16 01	8 43	16 06	8 53	15 56
11	8 38	16 03	8 42	16 08	8 52	15 57
12	8 37	16 05	8 41	16 09	8 51	15 59
13	8 36	16 06	8 40	16 11	8 50	16 01
14	8 35	16 08	8 39	16 13	8 49	16 03
15	8 34	16 10	8 38	16 15	8 48	16 05
16	8 33	16 12	8 37	16 16	8 46	16 07
17	8 32	16 14	8 36	16 18	8 45	16 09
18	8 31	16 16	8 35	16 20	8 44	16 11
19	8 30	16 18	8 33	16 22	8 42	16 13
20	8 28	16 20	8 32	16 24	8 41	16 15
21	8 27	16 22	8 31	16 26	8 39	16 17
22	8 25	16 24	8 29	16 28	8 38	16 19
23	8 24	16 26	8 28	16 30	8 36	16 22
24	8 22	16 28	8 26	16 32	8 34	16 24
25	8 21	16 30	8 25	16 34	8 33	16 26
26	8 19	16 32	8 23	16 36	8 31	16 28
27	8 18	16 34	8 21	16 38	8 29	16 30
28	8 16	16 36	8 20	16 40	8 27	16 33
29	8 14	16 38	8 18	16 43	8 25	16 35
30	8 12	16 40	8 16	16 45	8 23	16 37
31	8 10	16 42	8 14	16 47	8 21	16 40

FEBRUARY 2000

Sunrise and Sunset (GMT)

	Edinburgh 3°11′ 55°56′		Glasgow 4°14′ 55°52′		Inverness 4°12′ 57°28′	
	h m	h m	h m	h m	h m	h m
1	8 09	16 45	8 13	16 49	8 19	16 42
2	8 07	16 47	8 11	16 51	8 17	16 44
3	8 05	16 49	8 09	16 53	8 15	16 47
4	8 03	16 51	8 07	16 56	8 13	16 49
5	8 01	16 53	8 05	16 58	8 11	16 51
6	7 59	16 55	8 03	17 00	8 09	16 54
7	7 57	16 58	8 01	17 02	8 07	16 56
8	7 55	17 00	7 59	17 04	8 05	16 58
9	7 53	17 02	7 57	17 06	8 02	17 01
10	7 51	17 04	7 54	17 09	8 00	17 03
11	7 48	17 06	7 52	17 11	7 58	17 05
12	7 46	17 09	7 50	17 13	7 55	17 08
13	7 44	17 11	7 48	17 15	7 53	17 10
14	7 42	17 13	7 46	17 17	7 51	17 12
15	7 39	17 15	7 43	17 20	7 48	17 15
16	7 37	17 17	7 41	17 22	7 46	17 17
17	7 35	17 20	7 39	17 24	7 43	17 19
18	7 33	17 22	7 37	17 26	7 41	17 22
19	7 30	17 24	7 34	17 28	7 38	17 24
20	7 28	17 26	7 32	17 30	7 36	17 26
21	7 26	17 28	7 30	17 33	7 33	17 29
22	7 23	17 30	7 27	17 35	7 31	17 31
23	7 21	17 33	7 25	17 37	7 28	17 33
24	7 18	17 35	7 22	17 39	7 26	17 36
25	7 16	17 37	7 20	17 41	7 23	17 38
26	7 13	17 39	7 17	17 43	7 20	17 40
27	7 11	17 41	7 15	17 45	7 18	17 42
28	7 08	17 43	7 13	17 48	7 15	17 45
29	7 06	17 45	7 10	17 50	7 13	17 47

Duration of Twilight at 56° N. (in minutes)

January	1st	11th	21st	31st
Civil	47	45	43	41
Nautical	96	93	90	87
Astronomical	141	138	134	130

February	1st	11th	21st	31st
Civil	41	39	38	38
Nautical	86	83	81	81
Astronomical	130	126	125	124

Moon Phases

January	d	h	m
New Moon	6	18	14
First Quarter	14	13	34
Full Moon	21	04	40
Last Quarter	28	07	57

February	d	h	m
New Moon	5	13	03
First Quarter	12	23	21
Full Moon	19	16	27
Last Quarter	27	03	53

MARCH 2000

Sunrise and Sunset (GMT)

	Edinburgh 3°11' 55°56'		Glasgow 4°14' 55°52'		Inverness 4°12' 57°28'	
	h m	h m	h m	h m	h m	h m
1	7 03	17 48	7 08	17 52	7 10	17 49
2	7 01	17 50	7 05	17 54	7 07	17 52
3	6 58	17 52	7 03	17 56	7 05	17 54
4	6 56	17 54	7 00	17 58	7 02	17 56
5	6 53	17 56	6 57	18 00	6 59	17 58
6	6 51	17 58	6 55	18 02	6 57	18 01
7	6 48	18 00	6 52	18 04	6 54	18 03
8	6 46	18 02	6 50	18 07	6 51	18 05
9	6 43	18 04	6 47	18 09	6 48	18 07
10	6 41	18 06	6 45	18 11	6 46	18 09
11	6 38	18 09	6 42	18 13	6 43	18 12
12	6 35	18 11	6 39	18 15	6 40	18 14
13	6 33	18 13	6 37	18 17	6 38	18 16
14	6 30	18 15	6 34	18 19	6 35	18 18
15	6 27	18 17	6 32	18 21	6 32	18 20
16	6 25	18 19	6 29	18 23	6 29	18 23
17	6 22	18 21	6 26	18 25	6 26	18 25
18	6 20	18 23	6 24	18 27	6 24	18 27
19	6 17	18 25	6 21	18 29	6 21	18 29
20	6 14	18 27	6 19	18 31	6 18	18 31
21	6 12	18 29	6 16	18 33	6 15	18 34
22	6 09	18 31	6 13	18 35	6 13	18 36
23	6 06	18 33	6 11	18 37	6 10	18 38
24	6 04	18 35	6 08	18 39	6 07	18 40
25	6 01	18 37	6 05	18 41	6 04	18 42
26	5 59	18 39	6 03	18 43	6 02	18 44
27	5 56	18 41	6 00	18 45	5 59	18 47
28	5 53	18 43	5 58	18 47	5 56	18 49
29	5 51	18 45	5 55	18 49	5 53	18 51
30	5 48	18 47	5 52	18 52	5 50	18 53
31	5 45	18 49	5 50	18 54	5 48	18 55

APRIL 2000

Sunrise and Sunset (GMT)

	Edinburgh 3°11' 55°56'		Glasgow 4°14' 55°52'		Inverness 4°12' 57°28'	
	h m	h m	h m	h m	h m	h m
1	5 43	18 51	5 47	18 56	5 45	18 58
2	5 40	18 53	5 44	18 58	5 42	19 00
3	5 38	18 55	5 42	19 00	5 39	19 02
4	5 35	18 58	5 39	19 02	5 37	19 04
5	5 32	19 00	5 37	19 04	5 34	19 06
6	5 30	19 02	5 34	19 06	5 31	19 08
7	5 27	19 04	5 32	19 08	5 28	19 11
8	5 25	19 06	5 29	19 10	5 26	19 13
9	5 22	19 08	5 26	19 12	5 23	19 15
10	5 19	19 10	5 24	19 14	5 20	19 17
11	5 17	19 12	5 21	19 16	5 18	19 19
12	5 14	19 14	5 19	19 18	5 15	19 21
13	5 12	19 16	5 16	19 20	5 12	19 24
14	5 09	19 18	5 14	19 22	5 10	19 26
15	5 07	19 20	5 11	19 24	5 07	19 28
16	5 04	19 22	5 09	19 26	5 04	19 30
17	5 02	19 24	5 06	19 28	5 02	19 32
18	4 59	19 26	5 04	19 30	4 59	19 35
19	4 57	19 28	5 01	19 32	4 56	19 37
20	4 54	19 30	4 59	19 34	4 54	19 39
21	4 52	19 32	4 56	19 36	4 51	19 41
22	4 50	19 34	4 54	19 38	4 49	19 43
23	4 47	19 36	4 52	19 40	4 46	19 46
24	4 45	19 38	4 49	19 42	4 43	19 48
25	4 42	19 40	4 47	19 44	4 41	19 50
26	4 40	19 42	4 44	19 46	4 38	19 52
27	4 38	19 44	4 42	19 48	4 36	19 54
28	4 35	19 46	4 40	19 50	4 33	19 56
29	4 33	19 48	4 38	19 52	4 31	19 59
30	4 31	19 50	4 35	19 54	4 29	20 01

Duration of Twilight at 56° N. (in minutes)

March	1st	11th	21st	31st
Civil	38	37	37	38
Nautical	81	80	82	84
Astronomical	124	125	129	136

Duration of Twilight at 56° N. (in minutes)

April	1st	11th	21st	31st
Civil	38	40	42	44
Nautical	85	90	96	105
Astronomical	137	148	167	200

Moon Phases

March	d	h	m
New Moon	6	05	17
First Quarter	13	06	59
Full Moon	20	04	44
Last Quarter	28	00	21

Moon Phases

April	d	h	m
New Moon	4	18	12
First Quarter	11	13	30
Full Moon	18	17	41
Last Quarter	26	19	30

MAY 2000

Sunrise and Sunset (GMT)

	Edinburgh 3°11′ 55°56′		Glasgow 4°14′ 55°52′		Inverness 4°12′ 57°28′	
	h m	h m	h m	h m	h m	h m
1	4 29	19 52	4 33	19 56	4 26	20 03
2	4 26	19 54	4 31	19 58	4 24	20 05
3	4 24	19 56	4 29	20 00	4 21	20 07
4	4 22	19 58	4 26	20 02	4 19	20 09
5	4 20	20 00	4 24	20 04	4 17	20 12
6	4 18	20 02	4 22	20 06	4 14	20 14
7	4 16	20 04	4 20	20 08	4 12	20 16
8	4 13	20 06	4 18	20 10	4 10	20 18
9	4 11	20 08	4 16	20 12	4 08	20 20
10	4 09	20 10	4 14	20 14	4 06	20 22
11	4 07	20 12	4 12	20 16	4 03	20 24
12	4 05	20 14	4 10	20 18	4 01	20 26
13	4 04	20 16	4 08	20 20	3 59	20 28
14	4 02	20 18	4 06	20 22	3 57	20 30
15	4 00	20 20	4 04	20 23	3 55	20 32
16	3 58	20 21	4 03	20 25	3 53	20 34
17	3 56	20 23	4 01	20 27	3 51	20 36
18	3 54	20 25	3 59	20 29	3 49	20 38
19	3 53	20 27	3 57	20 31	3 48	20 40
20	3 51	20 29	3 56	20 32	3 46	20 42
21	3 50	20 30	3 54	20 34	3 44	20 44
22	3 48	20 32	3 53	20 36	3 42	20 46
23	3 46	20 34	3 51	20 37	3 41	20 48
24	3 45	20 35	3 50	20 39	3 39	20 50
25	3 44	20 37	3 48	20 41	3 37	20 51
26	3 42	20 38	3 47	20 42	3 36	20 53
27	3 41	20 40	3 45	20 44	3 34	20 55
28	3 40	20 41	3 44	20 45	3 33	20 56
29	3 38	20 43	3 43	20 47	3 32	20 58
30	3 37	20 44	3 42	20 48	3 30	20 59
31	3 36	20 46	3 41	20 50	3 29	21 01

JUNE 2000

Sunrise and Sunset (GMT)

	Edinburgh 3°11′ 55°56′		Glasgow 4°14′ 55°52′		Inverness 4°12′ 57°28′	
	h m	h m	h m	h m	h m	h m
1	3 35	20 47	3 40	20 51	3 28	21 02
2	3 34	20 48	3 39	20 52	3 27	21 04
3	3 33	20 50	3 38	20 53	3 26	21 05
4	3 32	20 51	3 37	20 55	3 25	21 07
5	3 31	20 52	3 36	20 56	3 24	21 08
6	3 30	20 53	3 35	20 57	3 23	21 09
7	3 30	20 54	3 34	20 58	3 22	21 10
8	3 29	20 55	3 34	21 00	3 21	21 11
9	3 28	20 56	3 33	21 00	3 20	21 12
10	3 28	20 57	3 33	21 01	3 20	21 13
11	3 27	20 58	3 32	21 02	3 19	21 14
12	3 27	20 59	3 32	21 02	3 19	21 15
13	3 27	20 59	3 31	21 03	3 18	21 16
14	3 26	21 00	3 31	21 04	3 18	21 16
15	3 26	21 01	3 31	21 04	3 18	21 17
16	3 26	21 01	3 31	21 05	3 18	21 18
17	3 26	21 02	3 31	21 05	3 18	21 18
18	3 26	21 02	3 31	21 06	3 18	21 19
19	3 26	21 02	3 31	21 06	3 18	21 19
20	3 26	21 03	3 31	21 06	3 18	21 19
21	3 26	21 03	3 31	21 07	3 18	21 19
22	3 27	21 03	3 31	21 07	3 18	21 19
23	3 27	21 03	3 32	21 07	3 18	21 19
24	3 27	21 03	3 32	21 07	3 19	21 19
25	3 28	21 03	3 33	21 07	3 19	21 19
26	3 28	21 03	3 33	21 06	3 20	21 19
27	3 29	21 02	3 34	21 06	3 21	21 19
28	3 30	21 02	3 34	21 06	3 21	21 19
29	3 30	21 02	3 35	21 06	3 22	21 18
30	3 31	21 01	3 36	21 05	3 23	21 18

Duration of Twilight at 56° N. (in minutes)

May	1st	11th	21st	31st
Civil	45	49	53	57
Nautical	106	121	143	TAN
Astronomical	209	TAN	TAN	TAN

Duration of Twilight at 56° N. (in minutes)

June	1st	11th	21st	31st
Civil	58	61	63	62
Nautical	TAN	TAN	TAN	TAN
Astronomical	TAN	TAN	TAN	TAN

Moon Phases

May	d	h	m
New Moon	4	04	12
First Quarter	10	20	00
Full Moon	18	07	34
Last Quarter	26	11	55

Moon Phases

June	d	h	m
New Moon	2	12	14
First Quarter	9	03	29
Full Moon	16	22	27
Last Quarter	25	01	00

TAN Twilight all night

JULY 2000

Sunrise and Sunset (GMT)

	Edinburgh 3°11′ 55°56′		Glasgow 4°14′ 55°52′		Inverness 4°12′ 57°28′	
	h m	h m	h m	h m	h m	h m
1	3 32	21 01	3 36	21 05	3 24	21 17
2	3 33	21 00	3 37	21 04	3 25	21 17
3	3 34	21 00	3 38	21 04	3 26	21 16
4	3 35	20 59	3 39	21 03	3 27	21 15
5	3 36	20 59	3 40	21 02	3 28	21 14
6	3 37	20 58	3 41	21 01	3 29	21 13
7	3 38	20 57	3 42	21 01	3 30	21 12
8	3 39	20 56	3 44	21 00	3 31	21 11
9	3 40	20 55	3 45	20 59	3 33	21 10
10	3 41	20 54	3 46	20 58	3 34	21 09
11	3 43	20 53	3 47	20 57	3 36	21 08
12	3 44	20 52	3 49	20 56	3 37	21 07
13	3 45	20 51	3 50	20 54	3 39	21 05
14	3 47	20 49	3 52	20 53	3 40	21 04
15	3 48	20 48	3 53	20 52	3 42	21 03
16	3 50	20 47	3 54	20 51	3 43	21 01
17	3 51	20 45	3 56	20 49	3 45	21 00
18	3 53	20 44	3 58	20 48	3 47	20 58
19	3 55	20 42	3 59	20 46	3 49	20 56
20	3 56	20 41	4 01	20 45	3 50	20 55
21	3 58	20 39	4 02	20 43	3 52	20 53
22	3 59	20 38	4 04	20 42	3 54	20 51
23	4 01	20 36	4 06	20 40	3 56	20 49
24	4 03	20 34	4 07	20 38	3 58	20 48
25	4 05	20 33	4 09	20 36	4 00	20 46
26	4 06	20 31	4 11	20 35	4 01	20 44
27	4 08	20 29	4 13	20 33	4 03	20 42
28	4 10	20 27	4 15	20 31	4 05	20 40
29	4 12	20 25	4 16	20 29	4 07	20 38
30	4 14	20 23	4 18	20 27	4 09	20 36
31	4 16	20 21	4 20	20 25	4 11	20 33

Duration of Twilight at 56° N. (in minutes)

July	1st	11th	21st	31st
Civil	61	58	53	49
Nautical	TAN	TAN	144	122
Astronomical	TAN	TAN	TAN	TAN

Moon Phases

July	d	h	m
New Moon	1	19	20
First Quarter	8	12	53
Full Moon	16	13	55
Last Quarter	24	11	02
New Moon	31	02	25

AUGUST 2000

Sunrise and Sunset (GMT)

	Edinburgh 3°11′ 55°56′		Glasgow 4°14′ 55°52′		Inverness 4°12′ 57°28′	
	h m	h m	h m	h m	h m	h m
1	4 17	20 19	4 22	20 23	4 13	20 31
2	4 19	20 17	4 24	20 21	4 15	20 29
3	4 21	20 15	4 26	20 19	4 17	20 27
4	4 23	20 13	4 28	20 17	4 20	20 25
5	4 25	20 11	4 29	20 15	4 22	20 22
6	4 27	20 09	4 31	20 13	4 24	20 20
7	4 29	20 07	4 33	20 11	4 26	20 18
8	4 31	20 05	4 35	20 09	4 28	20 15
9	4 33	20 02	4 37	20 06	4 30	20 13
10	4 35	20 00	4 39	20 04	4 32	20 11
11	4 36	19 58	4 41	20 02	4 34	20 08
12	4 38	19 56	4 43	20 00	4 36	20 06
13	4 40	19 53	4 45	19 57	4 38	20 03
14	4 42	19 51	4 47	19 55	4 40	20 01
15	4 44	19 49	4 49	19 53	4 43	19 58
16	4 46	19 46	4 51	19 50	4 45	19 56
17	4 48	19 44	4 53	19 48	4 47	19 53
18	4 50	19 41	4 55	19 45	4 49	19 51
19	4 52	19 39	4 56	19 43	4 51	19 48
20	4 54	19 37	4 58	19 41	4 53	19 46
21	4 56	19 34	5 00	19 38	4 55	19 43
22	4 58	19 32	5 02	19 36	4 57	19 40
23	5 00	19 29	5 04	19 33	4 59	19 38
24	5 02	19 27	5 06	19 31	5 01	19 35
25	5 04	19 24	5 08	19 28	5 04	19 32
26	5 06	19 22	5 10	19 26	5 06	19 30
27	5 08	19 19	5 12	19 23	5 08	19 27
28	5 10	19 17	5 14	19 21	5 10	19 24
29	5 12	19 14	5 16	19 18	5 12	19 22
30	5 14	19 12	5 18	19 16	5 14	19 19
31	5 16	19 09	5 20	19 13	5 16	19 16

Duration of Twilight at 56° N. (in minutes)

August	1st	11th	21st	31st
Civil	48	45	42	40
Nautical	120	106	96	89
Astronomical	TAN	205	166	147

Moon Phases

August	d	h	m
First Quarter	7	01	02
Full Moon	15	05	13
Last Quarter	22	18	51
New Moon	29	10	19

SEPTEMBER 2000

Sunrise and Sunset (GMT)

	Edinburgh 3°11′ 55°56′		Glasgow 4°14′ 55°52′		Inverness 4°12′ 57°28′	
	h m	h m	h m	h m	h m	h m
1	5 18	19 06	5 22	19 10	5 18	19 14
2	5 19	19 04	5 24	19 08	5 20	19 11
3	5 21	19 01	5 26	19 05	5 22	19 08
4	5 23	18 59	5 28	19 03	5 25	19 05
5	5 25	18 56	5 30	19 00	5 27	19 03
6	5 27	18 53	5 32	18 57	5 29	19 00
7	5 29	18 51	5 34	18 55	5 31	18 57
8	5 31	18 48	5 35	18 52	5 33	18 54
9	5 33	18 46	5 37	18 50	5 35	18 52
10	5 35	18 43	5 39	18 47	5 37	18 49
11	5 37	18 40	5 41	18 44	5 39	18 46
12	5 39	18 38	5 43	18 42	5 41	18 43
13	5 41	18 35	5 45	18 39	5 43	18 41
14	5 43	18 32	5 47	18 36	5 45	18 38
15	5 45	18 30	5 49	18 34	5 48	18 35
16	5 47	18 27	5 51	18 31	5 50	18 32
17	5 49	18 24	5 53	18 28	5 52	18 29
18	5 51	18 22	5 55	18 26	5 54	18 27
19	5 52	18 19	5 57	18 23	5 56	18 24
20	5 54	18 16	5 59	18 21	5 58	18 21
21	5 56	18 14	6 01	18 18	6 00	18 18
22	5 58	18 11	6 03	18 15	6 02	18 15
23	6 00	18 08	6 05	18 13	6 04	18 13
24	6 02	18 06	6 06	18 10	6 06	18 10
25	6 04	18 03	6 08	18 07	6 08	18 07
26	6 06	18 01	6 10	18 05	6 11	18 04
27	6 08	17 58	6 12	18 02	6 13	18 01
28	6 10	17 55	6 14	17 59	6 15	17 59
29	6 12	17 53	6 16	17 57	6 17	17 56
30	6 14	17 50	6 18	17 54	6 19	17 53

Duration of Twilight at 56° N. (in minutes)

September	1st	11th	21st	31st
Civil	39	38	37	37
Nautical	89	84	82	80
Astronomical	146	135	129	126

Moon Phases

September	d	h	m
First Quarter	5	16	27
Full Moon	13	19	37
Last Quarter	21	01	28
New Moon	27	19	53

OCTOBER 2000

Sunrise and Sunset (GMT)

	Edinburgh 3°11′ 55°56′		Glasgow 4°14′ 55°52′		Inverness 4°12′ 57°28′	
	h m	h m	h m	h m	h m	h m
1	6 16	17 47	6 20	17 52	6 21	17 50
2	6 18	17 45	6 22	17 49	6 23	17 48
3	6 20	17 42	6 24	17 46	6 25	17 45
4	6 22	17 40	6 26	17 44	6 27	17 42
5	6 24	17 37	6 28	17 41	6 30	17 39
6	6 26	17 34	6 30	17 39	6 32	17 37
7	6 28	17 32	6 32	17 36	6 34	17 34
8	6 30	17 29	6 34	17 33	6 36	17 31
9	6 32	17 27	6 36	17 31	6 38	17 29
10	6 34	17 24	6 38	17 28	6 40	17 26
11	6 36	17 22	6 40	17 26	6 43	17 23
12	6 38	17 19	6 42	17 23	6 45	17 21
13	6 40	17 17	6 44	17 21	6 47	17 18
14	6 42	17 14	6 46	17 18	6 49	17 15
15	6 44	17 12	6 48	17 16	6 51	17 13
16	6 46	17 09	6 50	17 13	6 54	17 10
17	6 48	17 07	6 53	17 11	6 56	17 07
18	6 50	17 04	6 55	17 08	6 58	17 05
19	6 53	17 02	6 57	17 06	7 00	17 02
20	6 55	16 59	6 59	17 04	7 02	17 00
21	6 57	16 57	7 01	17 01	7 05	16 57
22	6 59	16 55	7 03	16 59	7 07	16 55
23	7 01	16 52	7 05	16 57	7 09	16 52
24	7 03	16 50	7 07	16 54	7 11	16 50
25	7 05	16 47	7 09	16 52	7 14	16 47
26	7 07	16 45	7 11	16 50	7 16	16 45
27	7 09	16 43	7 13	16 47	7 18	16 42
28	7 12	16 41	7 16	16 45	7 20	16 40
29	7 14	16 38	7 18	16 43	7 23	16 37
30	7 16	16 36	7 20	16 41	7 25	16 35
31	7 18	16 34	7 22	16 38	7 27	16 33

Duration of Twilight at 56° N. (in minutes)

October	1st	11th	21st	31st
Civil	37	37	38	40
Nautical	80	80	81	83
Astronomical	125	124	124	126

Moon Phases

October	d	h	m
First Quarter	5	10	59
Full Moon	13	08	53
Last Quarter	20	07	59
New Moon	27	07	58

NOVEMBER 2000

Sunrise and Sunset (GMT)

	Edinburgh 3°11′ 55°56′		Glasgow 4°14′ 55°52′		Inverness 4°12′ 57°28′	
	h m	h m	h m	h m	h m	h m
1	7 20	16 32	7 24	16 36	7 29	16 30
2	7 22	16 30	7 26	16 34	7 32	16 28
3	7 24	16 28	7 28	16 32	7 34	16 26
4	7 26	16 25	7 30	16 30	7 36	16 24
5	7 28	16 23	7 32	16 28	7 39	16 21
6	7 31	16 21	7 35	16 26	7 41	16 19
7	7 33	16 19	7 37	16 24	7 43	16 17
8	7 35	16 17	7 39	16 22	7 45	16 15
9	7 37	16 16	7 41	16 20	7 48	16 13
10	7 39	16 14	7 43	16 18	7 50	16 11
11	7 41	16 12	7 45	16 16	7 52	16 09
12	7 43	16 10	7 47	16 14	7 54	16 07
13	7 45	16 08	7 49	16 13	7 57	16 05
14	7 47	16 06	7 51	16 11	7 59	16 03
15	7 49	16 05	7 53	16 09	8 01	16 01
16	7 52	16 03	7 55	16 08	8 03	15 59
17	7 54	16 01	7 57	16 06	8 05	15 58
18	7 56	16 00	7 59	16 04	8 08	15 56
19	7 58	15 58	8 01	16 03	8 10	15 54
20	7 59	15 57	8 03	16 01	8 12	15 53
21	8 01	15 55	8 05	16 00	8 14	15 51
22	8 03	15 54	8 07	15 58	8 16	15 49
23	8 05	15 53	8 09	15 57	8 18	15 48
24	8 07	15 51	8 11	15 56	8 20	15 46
25	8 09	15 50	8 13	15 55	8 22	15 45
26	8 11	15 49	8 15	15 53	8 24	15 44
27	8 13	15 48	8 17	15 52	8 26	15 43
28	8 15	15 47	8 18	15 51	8 28	15 41
29	8 16	15 46	8 20	15 50	8 30	15 40
30	8 18	15 45	8 22	15 49	8 32	15 39

DECEMBER 2000

Sunrise and Sunset (GMT)

	Edinburgh 3°11′ 55°56′		Glasgow 4°14′ 55°52′		Inverness 4°12′ 57°28′	
	h m	h m	h m	h m	h m	h m
1	8 20	15 44	8 23	15 48	8 33	15 38
2	8 21	15 43	8 25	15 48	8 35	15 37
3	8 23	15 42	8 27	15 47	8 37	15 36
4	8 24	15 41	8 28	15 46	8 38	15 35
5	8 26	15 41	8 30	15 45	8 40	15 35
6	8 27	15 40	8 31	15 45	8 42	15 34
7	8 29	15 40	8 32	15 44	8 43	15 33
8	8 30	15 39	8 34	15 44	8 45	15 33
9	8 31	15 39	8 35	15 44	8 46	15 32
10	8 32	15 39	8 36	15 43	8 47	15 32
11	8 34	15 38	8 37	15 43	8 48	15 32
12	8 35	15 38	8 39	15 43	8 50	15 32
13	8 36	15 38	8 40	15 43	8 51	15 31
14	8 37	15 38	8 41	15 43	8 52	15 31
15	8 38	15 38	8 42	15 43	8 53	15 31
16	8 39	15 38	8 42	15 43	8 54	15 31
17	8 39	15 38	8 43	15 43	8 55	15 32
18	8 40	15 39	8 44	15 43	8 55	15 32
19	8 41	15 39	8 45	15 44	8 56	15 32
20	8 42	15 39	8 45	15 44	8 57	15 32
21	8 42	15 40	8 46	15 45	8 57	15 33
22	8 43	15 40	8 46	15 45	8 58	15 33
23	8 43	15 41	8 47	15 46	8 58	15 34
24	8 43	15 42	8 47	15 46	8 58	15 35
25	8 44	15 42	8 47	15 47	8 59	15 36
26	8 44	15 43	8 48	15 48	8 59	15 36
27	8 44	15 44	8 48	15 49	8 59	15 37
28	8 44	15 45	8 48	15 50	8 59	15 38
29	8 44	15 46	8 48	15 51	8 59	15 39
30	8 44	15 47	8 48	15 52	8 59	15 40
31	8 44	15 48	8 47	15 53	8 58	15 42

Duration of Twilight at 56° N. (in minutes)

November	1st	11th	21st	31st
Civil	40	41	43	45
Nautical	84	87	90	93
Astronomical	127	130	134	137

Duration of Twilight at 56° N. (in minutes)

December	1st	11th	21st	31st
Civil	45	47	47	47
Nautical	93	96	97	96
Astronomical	138	141	142	141

Moon Phases

November	d	h	m
First Quarter	4	07	27
Full Moon	11	21	15
Last Quarter	18	15	24
New Moon	25	23	11

Moon Phases

December	d	h	m
First Quarter	4	03	55
Full Moon	11	09	03
Last Quarter	18	00	41
New Moon	25	17	22

TIDAL DATA

Constants

The constant tidal difference may be used in conjunction with the time of high water at a standard port shown in the predictions data (pages 297–302) to find the time of high water at any of the ports or places listed below.

These tidal differences are very approximate and should be used only as a guide to the time of high water at the places below. More precise local data should be obtained for navigational and other nautical purposes.

All data allow high water time to be found in Greenwich Mean Time; this applies also to data for the months when British Summer Time is in operation and the hour's time difference should be allowed for.

Predictions

The data on pages 297–302 are daily predictions of the time and height of high water at Greenock and Leith. The time of the data is Greenwich Mean Time; this applies also to data for the months when British Summer Time is in operation and the hour's time difference should be allowed for. The datum of predictions for each port shows the difference of height, in metres from Ordnance data (Newlyn).

The tidal information for Greenock and Leith is reproduced with the permission of the UK Hydrographic Office and the Controller of HMSO. Crown copyright reserved.

Example

To find the time of high water at Stranraer at 2 January 2000:

Appropriate time of high water at Greenock	
Afternoon tide 2 January	2026 hrs
Tidal difference	- 0020 hrs
High water at Stranraer	2006 hrs

The columns headed 'Springs' and 'Neaps' show the height, in metres, of the tide above datum for mean high water springs and mean high water neaps respectively.

Port	Diff.		Springs	Neaps
		h m		
Aberdeen	Leith	- 1 19	4.3	3.4
Ardrossan	Greenock	- 0 15	3.2	2.6
Ayr	Greenock	- 0 25	3.0	2.5
Glasgow	Greenock	+ 0 26	4.7	4.0
Lerwick	Leith	- 3 48	2.2	1.6
Oban	Greenock	+ 5 43	4.0	2.9
Rosyth	Leith	+ 0 09	5.8	4.7
Scrabster	Leith	- 6 06	5.0	4.0
Stranraer	Greenock	- 0 20	3.0	2.4
Stromness	Leith	- 5 26	3.6	2.7
Ullapool	Leith	- 7 40	5.2	3.9
Wick	Leith	- 3 26	3.5	2.8

JANUARY 2000   *High water* GMT

		GREENOCK Datum of predictions 1.62m below				LEITH Datum of predictions 2.90m below			
		hr	ht m	hr	ht m	hr	ht m	hr	ht m
1	Saturday	08 41	3.0	20 26	3.1	10 47	4.5	23 15	4.7
2	Sunday	09 46	3.1	21 45	3.1	11 48	4.6	———	—
3	Monday	10 37	3.2	22 42	3.1	00 14	4.8	12 42	4.8
4	Tuesday	11 21	3.3	23 29	3.2	01 05	4.9	13 26	4.9
5	Wednesday	———	—	12 01	3.4	01 49	5.0	14 03	5.1
6	Thursday	00 09	3.2	12 38	3.5	02 27	5.1	14 37	5.2
7	Friday	00 45	3.2	13 10	3.5	03 02	5.1	15 09	5.2
8	Saturday	01 18	3.2	13 40	3.5	03 36	5.2	15 41	5.3
9	Sunday	01 52	3.2	14 11	3.5	04 10	5.2	16 15	5.3
10	Monday	02 29	3.2	14 45	3.5	04 46	5.2	16 50	5.2
11	Tuesday	03 08	3.2	15 21	3.5	05 23	5.1	17 27	5.2
12	Wednesday	03 49	3.2	16 00	3.4	06 04	5.0	18 07	5.1
13	Thursday	04 31	3.1	16 42	3.3	06 48	4.9	18 51	5.0
14	Friday	05 17	3.0	17 29	3.2	07 38	4.8	19 43	4.9
15	Saturday	06 07	3.0	18 26	3.1	08 37	4.7	20 46	4.8
16	Sunday	07 06	2.9	19 38	3.0	09 45	4.7	22 00	4.8
17	Monday	08 22	3.0	21 07	3.0	10 53	4.8	23 13	5.0
18	Tuesday	09 44	3.1	22 21	3.2	11 57	5.0	———	—
19	Wednesday	10 47	3.3	23 21	3.3	00 19	5.2	12 55	5.3
20	Thursday	11 39	3.5	———	—	01 18	5.5	13 46	5.6
21	Friday	00 16	3.4	12 28	3.7	02 11	5.7	14 34	5.7
22	Saturday	01 09	3.5	13 14	3.8	03 00	5.8	15 21	5.8
23	Sunday	01 59	3.5	13 58	3.9	03 49	5.8	16 08	5.8
24	Monday	02 46	3.5	14 41	3.9	04 37	5.7	16 56	5.7
25	Tuesday	03 29	3.4	15 23	3.9	05 24	5.5	17 45	5.5
26	Wednesday	04 10	3.4	16 04	3.8	06 13	5.2	18 35	5.3
27	Thursday	04 51	3.3	16 46	3.6	07 02	4.9	19 28	5.0
28	Friday	05 34	3.1	17 31	3.4	07 54	4.6	20 25	4.7
29	Saturday	06 21	3.0	18 19	3.2	08 49	4.4	21 24	4.5
30	Sunday	07 15	2.9	19 14	3.0	09 48	4.3	22 28	4.4
31	Monday	08 37	2.9	20 27	2.8	10 54	4.3	23 37	4.4

FEBRUARY 2000   *High water* GMT

		GREENOCK				LEITH			
1	Tuesday	10 03	3.0	22 13	2.9	———	—	12 03	4.5
2	Wednesday	10 56	3.1	23 10	2.9	00 40	4.6	13 00	4.7
3	Thursday	11 40	3.3	23 53	3.0	01 29	4.8	13 43	4.9
4	Friday	———	—	12 18	3.3	02 09	5.0	14 20	5.1
5	Saturday	00 30	3.0	12 52	3.4	02 44	5.1	14 53	5.2
6	Sunday	01 03	3.1	13 21	3.4	03 17	5.2	15 25	5.3
7	Monday	01 36	3.1	13 52	3.4	03 50	5.3	15 57	5.4
8	Tuesday	02 10	3.1	14 26	3.5	04 24	5.3	16 30	5.4
9	Wednesday	02 46	3.2	15 02	3.5	05 00	5.3	17 05	5.4
10	Thursday	03 23	3.2	15 39	3.4	05 38	5.2	17 43	5.3
11	Friday	04 01	3.2	16 18	3.4	06 20	5.0	18 26	5.2
12	Saturday	04 41	3.1	17 00	3.2	07 06	4.9	19 14	5.0
13	Sunday	05 26	3.0	17 50	3.1	08 01	4.7	20 14	4.8
14	Monday	06 19	2.9	18 55	2.9	09 09	4.6	21 32	4.7
15	Tuesday	07 30	2.8	20 42	2.8	10 26	4.6	22 56	4.8
16	Wednesday	09 19	2.9	22 14	3.0	11 39	4.8	———	—
17	Thursday	10 33	3.1	23 17	3.1	00 10	5.0	12 42	5.1
18	Friday	11 27	3.4	———	—	01 12	5.3	13 35	5.4
19	Saturday	00 11	3.3	12 16	3.6	02 03	5.5	14 22	5.7
20	Sunday	01 01	3.3	13 01	3.7	02 49	5.7	15 07	5.8
21	Monday	01 47	3.4	13 44	3.8	03 33	5.7	15 50	5.8
22	Tuesday	02 28	3.4	14 24	3.8	04 16	5.6	16 34	5.8
23	Wednesday	03 04	3.4	15 03	3.8	04 58	5.4	17 18	5.6
24	Thursday	03 39	3.4	15 40	3.7	05 40	5.2	18 01	5.3
25	Friday	04 14	3.3	16 17	3.6	06 22	4.9	18 47	5.0
26	Saturday	04 51	3.2	16 56	3.4	07 05	4.6	19 37	4.6
27	Sunday	05 32	3.0	17 39	3.1	07 55	4.4	20 34	4.3
28	Monday	06 20	2.9	18 29	2.9	08 53	4.2	21 38	4.2
29	Tuesday	07 20	2.7	19 30	2.7	09 58	4.1	22 51	4.2

MARCH 2000 *High water* GMT

		GREENOCK Datum of predictions 1.62m below				LEITH Datum of predictions 2.90m below			
		hr	ht m	hr	ht m	hr	ht m	hr	ht m
1	Wednesday	09 07	2.7	21 06	2.6	11 13	4.2	——	—
2	Thursday	10 28	2.9	22 47	2.8	00 08	4.3	12 27	4.5
3	Friday	11 15	3.1	23 32	2.9	01 04	4.6	13 17	4.7
4	Saturday	11 53	3.2	——	—	01 45	4.9	13 55	5.0
5	Sunday	00 09	3.0	12 26	3.3	02 20	5.1	14 29	5.2
6	Monday	00 43	3.0	12 57	3.3	02 53	5.3	15 01	5.4
7	Tuesday	01 14	3.1	13 29	3.4	03 26	5.4	15 33	5.5
8	Wednesday	01 47	3.1	14 04	3.4	04 00	5.5	16 07	5.6
9	Thursday	02 21	3.2	14 41	3.5	04 35	5.5	16 43	5.6
10	Friday	02 56	3.3	15 19	3.5	05 14	5.4	17 23	5.5
11	Saturday	03 32	3.3	15 57	3.4	05 55	5.2	18 07	5.3
12	Sunday	04 11	3.2	16 39	3.2	06 41	5.0	18 57	5.1
13	Monday	04 54	3.1	17 28	3.0	07 35	4.7	19 59	4.8
14	Tuesday	05 47	2.9	18 33	2.8	08 45	4.5	21 21	4.6
15	Wednesday	06 56	2.8	20 42	2.7	10 08	4.5	22 49	4.7
16	Thursday	09 02	2.8	22 13	2.9	11 26	4.7	——	—
17	Friday	10 19	3.1	23 11	3.1	00 05	4.9	12 31	5.0
18	Saturday	11 12	3.3	——	—	01 05	5.2	13 23	5.3
19	Sunday	00 01	3.2	12 00	3.5	01 52	5.4	14 08	5.6
20	Monday	00 46	3.3	12 43	3.6	02 34	5.5	14 49	5.7
21	Tuesday	01 28	3.3	13 25	3.6	03 13	5.6	15 30	5.7
22	Wednesday	02 03	3.3	14 03	3.7	03 52	5.5	16 11	5.7
23	Thursday	02 35	3.3	14 39	3.6	04 30	5.3	16 51	5.5
24	Friday	03 06	3.3	15 14	3.6	05 07	5.1	17 31	5.2
25	Saturday	03 38	3.3	15 49	3.5	05 44	4.9	18 12	4.9
26	Sunday	04 13	3.2	16 26	3.3	06 24	4.7	18 58	4.6
27	Monday	04 51	3.1	17 08	3.0	07 09	4.5	19 52	4.3
28	Tuesday	05 37	2.9	17 58	2.8	08 05	4.2	20 54	4.1
29	Wednesday	06 34	2.7	18 58	2.6	09 10	4.1	22 02	4.1
30	Thursday	07 47	2.6	20 13	2.6	10 22	4.1	23 18	4.2
31	Friday	09 40	2.7	22 04	2.7	11 38	4.3	——	—

APRIL 2000 *High water* GMT

1	Saturday	10 37	2.9	22 58	2.8	00 24	4.5	12 38	4.6
2	Sunday	11 16	3.1	23 37	3.0	01 10	4.9	13 21	4.9
3	Monday	11 51	3.2	——	—	01 47	5.1	13 57	5.2
4	Tuesday	00 12	3.0	12 26	3.3	02 23	5.4	14 32	5.4
5	Wednesday	00 47	3.1	13 03	3.3	02 57	5.5	15 06	5.6
6	Thursday	01 21	3.2	13 42	3.4	03 33	5.6	15 43	5.7
7	Friday	01 56	3.3	14 21	3.5	04 11	5.6	16 23	5.7
8	Saturday	02 32	3.4	15 01	3.5	04 51	5.5	17 06	5.6
9	Sunday	03 09	3.4	15 42	3.4	05 34	5.3	17 53	5.4
10	Monday	03 48	3.3	16 26	3.2	06 22	5.0	18 47	5.1
11	Tuesday	04 33	3.2	17 20	2.9	07 18	4.8	19 54	4.8
12	Wednesday	05 27	3.0	18 38	2.7	08 33	4.6	21 18	4.6
13	Thursday	06 41	2.8	20 45	2.7	09 56	4.5	22 41	4.7
14	Friday	08 45	2.9	22 01	2.9	11 11	4.7	23 53	4.9
15	Saturday	09 59	3.1	22 55	3.1	——	—	12 14	5.0
16	Sunday	10 52	3.3	23 42	3.2	00 51	5.1	13 06	5.3
17	Monday	11 38	3.4	——	—	01 36	5.3	13 49	5.5
18	Tuesday	00 24	3.2	12 21	3.4	02 15	5.4	14 30	5.6
19	Wednesday	01 02	3.3	13 01	3.4	02 51	5.4	15 09	5.6
20	Thursday	01 35	3.3	13 38	3.4	03 27	5.4	15 48	5.5
21	Friday	02 06	3.3	14 13	3.4	04 02	5.3	16 26	5.3
22	Saturday	02 36	3.3	14 48	3.4	04 37	5.1	17 04	5.1
23	Sunday	03 07	3.3	15 23	3.3	05 12	5.0	17 44	4.9
24	Monday	03 41	3.3	16 01	3.2	05 50	4.8	18 27	4.6
25	Tuesday	04 17	3.1	16 43	3.0	06 33	4.6	19 17	4.4
26	Wednesday	05 01	2.9	17 33	2.8	07 24	4.4	20 13	4.2
27	Thursday	05 56	2.7	18 33	2.7	08 26	4.2	21 17	4.2
28	Friday	07 03	2.6	19 40	2.6	09 35	4.2	22 24	4.3
29	Saturday	08 22	2.7	20 58	2.7	10 45	4.3	23 30	4.5
30	Sunday	09 38	2.8	22 08	2.8	11 47	4.6	——	—

MAY 2000   *High water*   GMT

		GREENOCK Datum of predictions 1.62m below				LEITH Datum of predictions 2.90m below			
		hr	ht m	hr	ht m	hr	ht m	hr	ht m
1	Monday	10 29	3.0	22 57	3.0	00 24	4.8	12 38	4.9
2	Tuesday	11 12	3.1	23 38	3.1	01 09	5.1	13 20	5.2
3	Wednesday	11 53	3.3	——	—	01 49	5.4	14 00	5.5
4	Thursday	00 17	3.2	12 37	3.3	02 28	5.6	14 39	5.7
5	Friday	00 56	3.3	13 20	3.4	03 07	5.7	15 21	5.8
6	Saturday	01 34	3.4	14 04	3.4	03 48	5.7	16 05	5.8
7	Sunday	02 13	3.5	14 48	3.4	04 31	5.6	16 52	5.7
8	Monday	02 52	3.5	15 34	3.3	05 17	5.4	17 44	5.4
9	Tuesday	03 34	3.5	16 25	3.1	06 08	5.2	18 41	5.1
10	Wednesday	04 21	3.3	17 28	2.9	07 08	4.9	19 50	4.9
11	Thursday	05 18	3.1	18 52	2.8	08 23	4.7	21 08	4.7
12	Friday	06 34	3.0	20 26	2.8	09 39	4.7	22 22	4.7
13	Saturday	08 16	3.0	21 35	2.9	10 49	4.8	23 31	4.8
14	Sunday	09 31	3.1	22 29	3.0	11 50	5.0	——	—
15	Monday	10 26	3.2	23 15	3.1	00 28	5.0	12 43	5.2
16	Tuesday	11 13	3.3	23 56	3.2	01 14	5.1	13 29	5.3
17	Wednesday	11 56	3.3	——	—	01 53	5.2	14 10	5.3
18	Thursday	00 34	3.2	12 36	3.3	02 29	5.2	14 49	5.3
19	Friday	01 08	3.2	13 13	3.2	03 04	5.3	15 27	5.3
20	Saturday	01 40	3.3	13 48	3.2	03 37	5.2	16 04	5.2
21	Sunday	02 10	3.3	14 23	3.2	04 10	5.1	16 41	5.0
22	Monday	02 42	3.3	15 00	3.1	04 45	5.0	17 20	4.9
23	Tuesday	03 15	3.3	15 39	3.0	05 22	4.9	18 01	4.7
24	Wednesday	03 50	3.2	16 22	2.9	06 04	4.7	18 46	4.5
25	Thursday	04 31	3.0	17 12	2.8	06 50	4.5	19 37	4.4
26	Friday	05 21	2.9	18 08	2.7	07 44	4.4	20 34	4.3
27	Saturday	06 23	2.7	19 07	2.7	08 47	4.4	21 36	4.4
28	Sunday	07 31	2.7	20 10	2.7	09 53	4.4	22 39	4.6
29	Monday	08 42	2.8	21 17	2.8	10 56	4.6	23 38	4.8
30	Tuesday	09 44	3.0	22 16	2.9	11 53	4.9	——	—
31	Wednesday	10 37	3.1	23 06	3.1	00 30	5.1	12 43	5.2

JUNE 2000   *High water*   GMT

		hr	ht m	hr	ht m	hr	ht m	hr	ht m
1	Thursday	11 25	3.2	23 51	3.2	01 17	5.4	13 30	5.5
2	Friday	——	—	12 13	3.3	02 00	5.6	14 16	5.7
3	Saturday	00 34	3.4	13 03	3.4	02 44	5.7	15 03	5.8
4	Sunday	01 17	3.5	13 52	3.4	03 28	5.7	15 51	5.8
5	Monday	02 00	3.6	14 42	3.3	04 14	5.7	16 41	5.7
6	Tuesday	02 42	3.6	15 33	3.3	05 03	5.5	17 35	5.5
7	Wednesday	03 27	3.6	16 28	3.1	05 57	5.3	18 33	5.3
8	Thursday	04 15	3.4	17 30	3.0	06 58	5.1	19 38	5.0
9	Friday	05 11	3.3	18 37	2.9	08 07	4.9	20 46	4.8
10	Saturday	06 16	3.1	19 49	2.9	09 15	4.9	21 53	4.7
11	Sunday	07 34	3.0	20 57	2.9	10 19	4.8	22 57	4.7
12	Monday	08 53	3.0	21 55	3.0	11 21	4.9	23 57	4.8
13	Tuesday	09 55	3.1	22 44	3.0	——	—	12 17	5.0
14	Wednesday	10 47	3.1	23 28	3.1	00 47	4.9	13 07	5.0
15	Thursday	11 32	3.1	——	—	01 31	5.0	13 51	5.1
16	Friday	00 08	3.2	12 13	3.1	02 09	5.1	14 32	5.1
17	Saturday	00 45	3.2	12 51	3.0	02 44	5.1	15 09	5.1
18	Sunday	01 18	3.3	13 27	3.0	03 17	5.2	15 45	5.1
19	Monday	01 50	3.3	14 02	3.0	03 49	5.1	16 21	5.0
20	Tuesday	02 20	3.3	14 39	3.0	04 24	5.1	16 57	5.0
21	Wednesday	02 53	3.3	15 19	3.0	05 00	5.0	17 36	4.9
22	Thursday	03 28	3.2	16 02	2.9	05 39	4.9	18 17	4.7
23	Friday	04 07	3.1	16 48	2.9	06 21	4.8	19 03	4.6
24	Saturday	04 51	3.0	17 37	2.8	07 07	4.7	19 53	4.5
25	Sunday	05 43	2.9	18 30	2.8	08 00	4.6	20 51	4.5
26	Monday	06 44	2.8	19 25	2.8	09 01	4.6	21 53	4.6
27	Tuesday	07 53	2.8	20 29	2.8	10 07	4.7	22 55	4.8
28	Wednesday	09 05	2.9	21 37	2.9	11 11	4.9	23 54	5.0
29	Thursday	10 08	3.1	22 37	3.1	——	—	12 11	5.1
30	Friday	11 04	3.2	23 29	3.2	00 48	5.3	13 07	5.4

JULY 2000 · *High water* GMT

		GREENOCK hr	ht m	hr	ht m	LEITH hr	ht m	hr	ht m
		GREENOCK Datum of predictions 1.62m below				LEITH Datum of predictions 2.90m below			
1	Saturday	11 57	3.3	—	—	01 38	5.5	13 59	5.6
2	Sunday	00 18	3.4	12 51	3.3	02 25	5.7	14 49	5.8
3	Monday	01 04	3.5	13 45	3.3	03 12	5.8	15 39	5.9
4	Tuesday	01 50	3.6	14 38	3.3	04 00	5.8	16 30	5.8
5	Wednesday	02 34	3.7	15 29	3.3	04 50	5.7	17 22	5.6
6	Thursday	03 19	3.7	16 20	3.2	05 42	5.6	18 16	5.4
7	Friday	04 05	3.6	17 11	3.1	06 39	5.3	19 13	5.1
8	Saturday	04 53	3.5	18 03	3.0	07 40	5.1	20 13	4.8
9	Sunday	05 47	3.3	18 57	2.9	08 42	4.9	21 14	4.6
10	Monday	06 45	3.1	20 00	2.9	09 43	4.8	22 15	4.5
11	Tuesday	07 56	3.0	21 11	2.9	10 45	4.7	23 17	4.5
12	Wednesday	09 18	2.9	22 12	2.9	11 48	4.7	—	—
13	Thursday	10 23	2.9	23 02	3.1	00 17	4.7	12 45	4.8
14	Friday	11 13	3.0	23 45	3.2	01 08	4.8	13 34	4.9
15	Saturday	11 56	3.0	—	—	01 50	5.0	14 16	5.0
16	Sunday	00 25	3.2	12 35	2.9	02 26	5.1	14 53	5.0
17	Monday	01 01	3.3	13 11	2.9	03 00	5.1	15 27	5.1
18	Tuesday	01 32	3.3	13 45	2.9	03 32	5.2	16 00	5.1
19	Wednesday	02 01	3.3	14 20	3.0	04 05	5.2	16 35	5.1
20	Thursday	02 33	3.3	14 58	3.0	04 39	5.2	17 11	5.0
21	Friday	03 07	3.3	15 38	3.0	05 15	5.1	17 49	5.0
22	Saturday	03 44	3.2	16 18	3.0	05 53	5.0	18 31	4.9
23	Sunday	04 23	3.1	17 01	2.9	06 34	4.9	19 16	4.7
24	Monday	05 08	3.0	17 48	2.9	07 20	4.8	20 09	4.7
25	Tuesday	06 00	2.9	18 39	2.8	08 16	4.7	21 10	4.6
26	Wednesday	07 06	2.8	19 41	2.8	09 24	4.7	22 18	4.7
27	Thursday	08 29	2.8	21 00	2.9	10 39	4.8	23 25	4.9
28	Friday	09 49	3.0	22 15	3.0	11 49	5.0	—	—
29	Saturday	10 53	3.1	23 13	3.2	00 26	5.1	12 52	5.3
30	Sunday	11 50	3.2	—	—	01 21	5.4	13 47	5.6
31	Monday	00 04	3.4	12 45	3.3	02 10	5.7	14 37	5.8

AUGUST 2000 · *High water* GMT

		GREENOCK hr	ht m	hr	ht m	LEITH hr	ht m	hr	ht m
1	Tuesday	00 52	3.6	13 38	3.3	02 57	5.8	15 26	5.9
2	Wednesday	01 38	3.7	14 28	3.4	03 44	5.9	16 14	5.8
3	Thursday	02 22	3.8	15 14	3.3	04 32	5.9	17 02	5.7
4	Friday	03 05	3.8	15 57	3.3	05 21	5.7	17 51	5.4
5	Saturday	03 46	3.7	16 38	3.2	06 12	5.5	18 41	5.1
6	Sunday	04 28	3.6	17 19	3.1	07 05	5.2	19 33	4.8
7	Monday	05 12	3.4	18 03	3.0	08 03	4.9	20 29	4.5
8	Tuesday	06 00	3.1	18 53	2.9	09 03	4.6	21 27	4.4
9	Wednesday	06 55	2.9	19 58	2.8	10 06	4.5	22 31	4.4
10	Thursday	08 08	2.7	21 35	2.9	11 14	4.4	23 40	4.5
11	Friday	10 02	2.8	22 37	3.0	—	—	12 22	4.5
12	Saturday	10 59	2.9	23 24	3.2	00 42	4.7	13 15	4.7
13	Sunday	11 43	2.9	—	—	01 29	4.9	13 58	4.9
14	Monday	00 05	3.2	12 22	3.0	02 07	5.1	14 33	5.1
15	Tuesday	00 41	3.3	12 56	3.0	02 40	5.2	15 05	5.2
16	Wednesday	01 12	3.3	13 27	3.0	03 12	5.3	15 37	5.3
17	Thursday	01 40	3.3	13 59	3.0	03 43	5.4	16 10	5.3
18	Friday	02 10	3.3	14 33	3.1	04 15	5.4	16 45	5.3
19	Saturday	02 44	3.3	15 09	3.1	04 49	5.4	17 21	5.2
20	Sunday	03 20	3.3	15 46	3.1	05 26	5.3	18 01	5.1
21	Monday	03 57	3.3	16 24	3.1	06 06	5.2	18 44	4.9
22	Tuesday	04 37	3.2	17 06	3.0	06 52	5.0	19 34	4.8
23	Wednesday	05 24	3.0	17 55	2.9	07 46	4.8	20 35	4.6
24	Thursday	06 26	2.8	18 56	2.8	08 56	4.7	21 49	4.6
25	Friday	08 02	2.7	20 27	2.8	10 19	4.7	23 04	4.8
26	Saturday	09 43	2.9	22 00	3.0	11 37	4.9	—	—
27	Sunday	10 51	3.1	23 00	3.3	00 11	5.1	12 44	5.3
28	Monday	11 46	3.3	23 51	3.5	01 08	5.4	13 37	5.6
29	Tuesday	—	—	12 37	3.3	01 56	5.7	14 25	5.8
30	Wednesday	00 38	3.6	13 25	3.4	02 41	5.9	15 09	5.9
31	Thursday	01 23	3.7	14 10	3.4	03 25	6.0	15 53	5.8

SEPTEMBER 2000   *High water*   GMT

		GREENOCK Datum of predictions 1.62m below				LEITH Datum of predictions 2.90m below			
		hr	ht m	hr	ht m	hr	ht m	hr	ht m
1	Friday	02 04	3.8	14 49	3.4	04 10	5.9	16 37	5.6
2	Saturday	02 44	3.8	15 25	3.4	04 55	5.8	17 20	5.4
3	Sunday	03 22	3.8	16 00	3.4	05 41	5.5	18 05	5.1
4	Monday	03 59	3.6	16 36	3.3	06 30	5.1	18 51	4.8
5	Tuesday	04 38	3.4	17 16	3.2	07 22	4.8	19 41	4.5
6	Wednesday	05 21	3.1	18 02	3.0	08 20	4.5	20 39	4.4
7	Thursday	06 11	2.9	18 58	2.9	09 24	4.3	21 44	4.3
8	Friday	07 15	2.7	20 26	2.8	10 36	4.2	22 56	4.3
9	Saturday	09 38	2.7	22 09	3.0	11 53	4.4	—	—
10	Sunday	10 41	2.9	22 59	3.2	00 09	4.6	12 51	4.7
11	Monday	11 23	3.0	23 39	3.3	01 02	4.8	13 33	4.9
12	Tuesday	—	—	12 00	3.1	01 41	5.1	14 07	5.1
13	Wednesday	00 15	3.3	12 33	3.1	02 14	5.3	14 39	5.3
14	Thursday	00 45	3.3	13 03	3.1	02 46	5.4	15 10	5.4
15	Friday	01 14	3.4	13 32	3.2	03 17	5.5	15 43	5.5
16	Saturday	01 46	3.4	14 05	3.3	03 49	5.6	16 17	5.5
17	Sunday	02 21	3.4	14 39	3.3	04 24	5.6	16 54	5.4
18	Monday	02 57	3.4	15 14	3.3	05 01	5.5	17 33	5.3
19	Tuesday	03 34	3.4	15 51	3.3	05 44	5.3	18 17	5.1
20	Wednesday	04 13	3.2	16 32	3.2	06 32	5.1	19 07	4.9
21	Thursday	04 59	3.0	17 21	3.1	07 29	4.9	20 10	4.7
22	Friday	06 02	2.8	18 24	2.9	08 43	4.7	21 30	4.6
23	Saturday	07 59	2.7	20 06	2.9	10 11	4.7	22 50	4.8
24	Sunday	09 46	2.9	21 46	3.1	11 31	5.0	23 58	5.1
25	Monday	10 47	3.2	22 45	3.4	—	—	12 34	5.3
26	Tuesday	11 36	3.3	23 34	3.6	00 53	5.4	13 25	5.6
27	Wednesday	—	—	12 22	3.4	01 39	5.7	14 08	5.7
28	Thursday	00 19	3.7	13 05	3.5	02 22	5.9	14 49	5.8
29	Friday	01 02	3.8	13 44	3.5	03 04	6.0	15 29	5.7
30	Saturday	01 42	3.8	14 18	3.5	03 46	5.9	16 09	5.6

OCTOBER 2000   *High water*   GMT

1	Sunday	02 19	3.8	14 50	3.5	04 29	5.7	16 49	5.4
2	Monday	02 55	3.7	15 23	3.5	05 12	5.4	17 29	5.1
3	Tuesday	03 31	3.6	15 58	3.4	05 57	5.1	18 10	4.9
4	Wednesday	04 08	3.4	16 36	3.3	06 45	4.7	18 57	4.6
5	Thursday	04 49	3.2	17 21	3.1	07 40	4.4	19 53	4.4
6	Friday	05 39	2.9	18 16	3.0	08 42	4.2	20 58	4.3
7	Saturday	06 42	2.7	19 25	2.9	09 51	4.2	22 09	4.3
8	Sunday	08 07	2.7	21 21	2.9	11 07	4.3	23 23	4.5
9	Monday	10 07	2.9	22 23	3.1	—	—	12 12	4.6
10	Tuesday	10 52	3.1	23 05	3.3	00 22	4.8	12 57	4.9
11	Wednesday	11 29	3.2	23 39	3.4	01 05	5.0	13 33	5.2
12	Thursday	—	—	12 02	3.3	01 41	5.3	14 07	5.4
13	Friday	00 11	3.4	12 33	3.3	02 14	5.5	14 40	5.6
14	Saturday	00 45	3.4	13 04	3.4	02 47	5.6	15 14	5.6
15	Sunday	01 21	3.5	13 37	3.5	03 22	5.7	15 50	5.7
16	Monday	01 59	3.5	14 13	3.5	04 00	5.7	16 28	5.6
17	Tuesday	02 37	3.5	14 49	3.6	04 42	5.6	17 09	5.4
18	Wednesday	03 16	3.4	15 27	3.5	05 27	5.4	17 55	5.2
19	Thursday	03 58	3.3	16 09	3.4	06 19	5.2	18 47	4.9
20	Friday	04 48	3.1	16 59	3.3	07 19	4.9	19 54	4.7
21	Saturday	06 00	2.8	18 06	3.1	08 38	4.7	21 18	4.7
22	Sunday	08 08	2.8	19 53	3.1	10 04	4.8	22 36	4.9
23	Monday	09 36	3.0	21 26	3.2	11 19	5.0	23 41	5.2
24	Tuesday	10 31	3.3	22 24	3.5	—	—	12 20	5.3
25	Wednesday	11 18	3.4	23 13	3.6	00 35	5.4	13 09	5.5
26	Thursday	12 00	3.5	23 57	3.7	01 21	5.7	13 50	5.6
27	Friday	—	—	12 39	3.5	02 03	5.8	14 28	5.6
28	Saturday	00 39	3.7	13 15	3.6	02 43	5.8	15 05	5.6
29	Sunday	01 18	3.7	13 48	3.6	03 24	5.7	15 43	5.5
30	Monday	01 54	3.7	14 20	3.6	04 06	5.5	16 19	5.4
31	Tuesday	02 30	3.6	14 53	3.6	04 46	5.3	16 56	5.2

NOVEMBER 2000 *High water* GMT

		GREENOCK Datum of predictions 1.62m below				LEITH Datum of predictions 2.90m below			
		hr	ht m	hr	ht m	hr	ht m	hr	ht m
1	Wednesday	03 05	3.5	15 27	3.6	05 28	5.0	17 34	5.0
2	Thursday	03 43	3.4	16 04	3.5	06 13	4.7	18 18	4.7
3	Friday	04 24	3.2	16 46	3.3	07 03	4.5	19 10	4.5
4	Saturday	05 14	3.0	17 38	3.1	08 00	4.3	20 12	4.4
5	Sunday	06 15	2.9	18 41	3.0	09 03	4.2	21 20	4.3
6	Monday	07 26	2.8	19 58	3.0	10 09	4.3	22 28	4.5
7	Tuesday	08 52	2.9	21 22	3.1	11 14	4.6	23 30	4.7
8	Wednesday	10 03	3.1	22 16	3.2	—	—	12 08	4.9
9	Thursday	10 48	3.2	22 58	3.3	00 20	5.0	12 53	5.2
10	Friday	11 26	3.3	23 37	3.4	01 03	5.2	13 32	5.4
11	Saturday	—	—	12 01	3.4	01 41	5.5	14 10	5.6
12	Sunday	00 17	3.5	12 37	3.5	02 19	5.7	14 47	5.7
13	Monday	00 58	3.5	13 14	3.6	02 59	5.8	15 26	5.7
14	Tuesday	01 41	3.6	13 52	3.7	03 41	5.8	16 06	5.7
15	Wednesday	02 23	3.5	14 31	3.8	04 27	5.7	16 50	5.5
16	Thursday	03 07	3.5	15 11	3.7	05 16	5.6	17 39	5.3
17	Friday	03 54	3.3	15 56	3.6	06 10	5.3	18 34	5.1
18	Saturday	04 52	3.1	16 49	3.4	07 13	5.0	19 43	4.9
19	Sunday	06 11	3.0	17 56	3.3	08 29	4.8	21 03	4.8
20	Monday	07 50	3.0	19 26	3.2	09 46	4.8	22 15	5.0
21	Tuesday	09 08	3.1	20 55	3.3	10 57	4.9	23 18	5.1
22	Wednesday	10 05	3.3	21 57	3.4	11 57	5.1	—	—
23	Thursday	10 52	3.4	22 49	3.5	00 13	5.3	12 48	5.2
24	Friday	11 34	3.5	23 34	3.6	01 02	5.5	13 30	5.4
25	Saturday	—	—	12 13	3.5	01 45	5.5	14 08	5.4
26	Sunday	00 16	3.5	12 49	3.6	02 27	5.5	14 45	5.4
27	Monday	00 56	3.5	13 23	3.6	03 07	5.5	15 20	5.4
28	Tuesday	01 32	3.5	13 55	3.6	03 47	5.3	15 55	5.3
29	Wednesday	02 08	3.4	14 29	3.7	04 25	5.2	16 29	5.2
30	Thursday	02 44	3.4	15 03	3.6	05 04	5.0	17 06	5.1

DECEMBER 2000 *High water* GMT

1	Friday	03 22	3.3	15 38	3.5	05 45	4.8	17 46	4.9
2	Saturday	04 04	3.2	16 18	3.4	06 30	4.6	18 33	4.7
3	Sunday	04 52	3.1	17 04	3.2	07 19	4.5	19 26	4.5
4	Monday	05 46	3.0	17 59	3.1	08 15	4.4	20 28	4.5
5	Tuesday	06 46	2.9	19 02	3.0	09 15	4.4	21 33	4.5
6	Wednesday	07 51	2.9	20 11	3.0	10 17	4.5	22 35	4.6
7	Thursday	08 59	3.0	21 20	3.1	11 16	4.8	23 32	4.9
8	Friday	10 00	3.1	22 17	3.2	—	—	12 10	5.0
9	Saturday	10 49	3.3	23 06	3.4	00 23	5.1	12 58	5.3
10	Sunday	11 32	3.4	23 53	3.5	01 11	5.4	13 41	5.5
11	Monday	—	—	12 14	3.6	01 56	5.6	14 23	5.7
12	Tuesday	00 40	3.5	12 56	3.7	02 41	5.8	15 06	5.7
13	Wednesday	01 28	3.5	13 38	3.8	03 27	5.9	15 50	5.8
14	Thursday	02 16	3.5	14 20	3.9	04 15	5.8	16 36	5.7
15	Friday	03 05	3.4	15 04	3.8	05 06	5.7	17 26	5.5
16	Saturday	03 56	3.3	15 50	3.8	06 00	5.4	18 22	5.3
17	Sunday	04 53	3.2	16 42	3.6	07 00	5.2	19 27	5.1
18	Monday	05 58	3.1	17 41	3.5	08 08	4.9	20 38	5.0
19	Tuesday	07 10	3.1	18 49	3.3	09 17	4.8	21 45	5.0
20	Wednesday	08 25	3.1	20 09	3.3	10 24	4.8	22 49	5.0
21	Thursday	09 29	3.2	21 24	3.3	11 27	4.8	23 49	5.0
22	Friday	10 22	3.3	22 24	3.3	—	—	12 23	4.9
23	Saturday	11 08	3.4	23 14	3.3	00 43	5.1	13 11	5.1
24	Sunday	11 49	3.5	23 58	3.3	01 31	5.2	13 52	5.2
25	Monday	—	—	12 28	3.5	02 14	5.2	14 29	5.2
26	Tuesday	00 39	3.3	13 04	3.6	02 54	5.2	15 04	5.3
27	Wednesday	01 16	3.3	13 38	3.6	03 32	5.2	15 37	5.3
28	Thursday	01 51	3.2	14 10	3.6	04 07	5.1	16 10	5.2
29	Friday	02 27	3.2	14 43	3.6	04 43	5.0	16 45	5.2
30	Saturday	03 04	3.2	15 17	3.5	05 20	4.9	17 22	5.0
31	Sunday	03 43	3.2	15 54	3.4	06 00	4.8	18 02	4.9

INDEX

terminals in Scotland 169
Gas and Electricity Markets (Scotland), Office of 64
GDP, by sector 159
changes in 155
statistics 154
UK as a whole 155
Genealogy Society, Scottish 224
General Assembly of Unitarian and Free Christian Churches 150
General Teaching Council for Scotland 121
Geographical Society, Royal Scottish 225
Geography 233-4
Gifted Children, National Association for 225
Gingerbread Scotland 225
Girls' Brigade in Scotland 225
Glasgow, airport 173
Archbishop (RC) 148
Archdiocese (1492) 248
Council 100
Education Authority 119
Lord Provost, forms of address 273
MPs 42
MSPs 30, 33
Presbytery 147
Underground Railway 174
Universities 191, 248
Glasgow Development Agency 193
Glasgow and Galloway, Bishop (SEC) 147
Glasgow Print Studio 208
Glencoe, Massacre 251
Gliding 214
Golf 214
Gordon, MP 43
MSP 30
Presbytery 147
Government of Scotland, See also Scottish Executive
pre-devolution 14
Government in Scotland, Unit for the Study of 189, 225
Graduate Teacher Training Registry 121
Grampian, police 81
Grampian Enterprise 193
Grampian and Highland Roadline 181
Grampian Mountains 233
Great Glen 233
Green Party (Scottish) 47
Greenock, Presbytery 147
Greenock and Inverclyde, MP 43
MSP 30
Greenock Telegraph 187
Guardian, The 186
Guide Association Scotland 225
Guide Dogs for the Blind Association 225
Gymnastics 214

H
Hamilton, MPs 43
MSPs 31

Presbytery 147
Handball 214
Hang gliding 214
Harveian Society of Edinburgh 225
Hawick Archaeological Society 225
Health, Common Services Agency 50
education 135
Medical Practices Committee 70
Medical Workforce, Scottish Advisory Committee on 67
NHS. See National Health Service (NHS)
Parliamentary Commissioner for Administration and Health Service 65
Public Health Policy Unit 50
Scottish Hospital Endowments Research Trust 69
targets 127
Health Appointments Advisory Committee 58
Health Boards 129
directory 134
Health Education 125, 135
Health Department 50, 129
Health Information Service 133
Health and Safety Executive (HSE), Nuclear Installations Inspectorate 170
Scotland Office 58
Hebrides, archaeological remains 235
areas 235
Norse influence 235
origin of name 235
populations 235-6
Hebrides Ensemble 208
Help the Aged 225
Herald, The 186
Heritage Lottery Fund (Scotland) (National Lottery Fund awards) 58
Herring fishing 252
HI Arts (Highland and Islands Arts) 208
Highland, Council 101
Education Authority 119
radio 184
Highland and Border Games 214
Highland Cattle Society 225
Highland dress, proscription 251
Highland Land Leagues 252
Highland regiments 252
Highland and Scottish Buses 175
Highlands, Clearances 252
depopulation 252
Highlands and Islands, MSPs 33
Rural Carrefour Centre (EU information) 191
Highlands and Islands Airports Ltd (HIAL) 173
Highlands and Islands Enterprise 59, 193
Hill Farming Advisory Committee for Scotland 59
Hinduism, organizations in UK 143
Historic Buildings Council for Scotland 255
Historic buildings and monuments, opening times 255-9